COMMUNITY EDUCATION AND TECHNICAL
ASSISTANCE CENTER

University of Colorado Health
Sciences Center
4200 E. 9th Ave., Box C 234
Denver, Colorado 80262
(303) 394-8251

Educating Young Handicapped Children

A Developmental Approach

S. Gray Garwood
Tulane University

and

Paul Alberto
Georgia State University

Rebecca F. DuBose
Peabody College

Betty A. and James M. Hare
Temple University

James Kauffman
University of Virginia

Thomas L. Kodera
Tulane University

M. Beth Langley
Peabody College

David A. Page
Nazareth College

Aspen Systems Corporation
Germantown, Maryland
London, England
1979

Library of Congress Cataloging in Publication Data

Garwood, S. Gray.
Educating young handicapped children.

Includes index.

1. Handicapped children—Education.
2. Developmental psychology.   II. Title.
LC4015.G34   371.9   79-13200
ISBN 0-89443-099-8

Library of Congress Catalog Card Number: 79-13200
ISBN: 0-89443-099-8

Printed in the United States of America

2 3 4 5

This book is dedicated to
Mr. and Mrs. Walter Renken, Sr.
*Without their help
and encouragement
this book would not be.*

Table of Contents

Preface

This book represents our belief that the intense interest in early childhood special education, which is reflected in PL 94-142, will necessitate a meld between programs that educate young children and programs that educate young handicapped children. Specifically, it seems most likely that professionals who work with young handicapped children will do so comparatively. That is, attempts to intervene in and facilitate the development of young handicapped children will probably be based strongly on knowledge of how normal or general development progresses. Also, it is not unfeasible that demands for a less restrictive environment for optimum development will lead to provision of public educational services for *all* preschool-aged children. If this happens, then certainly all professionals working with children will need to base their intervention efforts on developmental milestones in all areas of growth, especially the physical, cognitive, and social domains.

These three growth domains serve as markers in this book to isolate material significant to an eventual comprehensive view of the young child. Part I offers a special perspective. Part II discusses normal physical development and congenital and other conditions that result in physical and multiple handicaps as well as ways of working with physically handicapped preschool children. Part III focuses on cognitive development as well as on handicapping conditions that affect overall cognitive promise: sensory handicaps, learning disorders, and mental retardation. Finally, Part IV discusses social development, factors that affect it, and emotional disorders in early childhood. In each part, the special contributions by leading special educators focus specifically on ways of working with handicapped children. Reference material in the appendices helps select specific assessment and curriculum materials pertinent to early childhood. In addition, the appendices contain suggested forms to assist in preparing individualized educational programs as well as general guidelines for assessing developmental progress in young children.

I hope this book helps you help young children grow.

S. Gray Garwood
Tulane University
New Orleans, Louisiana

Part I

Early Childhood Special Education

Chapter 1

Special Education and Child Development: A New Perspective

S. Gray Garwood

PURPOSE OF THIS BOOK

The roots of American psychology lie in education. While some psychologists and some educators would prefer not to see such a statement in print, it is, nonetheless, true. Because of its interest in studying the learning process, psychology was naturally partnered with education. But this was for many an uneasy relationship. Psychology was seeking to establish itself as a science, resting on empirically collected data, theory, rigor, and control, and these aims were, for many, incompatible with education. Education, in the early part of this century, was considered neither a science nor an art, and, therefore, was not deemed an appropriate bedfellow for psychology, and the two disciplines separated. Psychology, relocated in liberal arts colleges, called itself a natural or a social science, depending on what it could get away with at the time. Since those times, much has happened to both disciplines: both have developed subfields such as regular education, special education, and administration in education, and developmental, social, and comparative in psychology.

In recent times the two fields have begun to form a new alliance. Psychology has moved into educational psychology, school psychology, counseling psychology, guidance, etc.; education has again become a natural laboratory for studying child behavior. Both fields have benefited from this renewed mutual interest.

One very obvious outgrowth of this renewed cooperation between psychology and education is occurring in the specialty areas of developmental psychology and early childhood, especially early-childhood special education. Early-childhood special education, itself a new subfield within education, is concerned with providing meaningful and appropriate educational experiences to preschool children who, by virtue of some handicapping condition, are not likely to benefit from regular preschool educational experiences. To insure the maximum educational benefit for such children, early-childhood special education has enlisted the support of developmental psychology. Together, these subfields are developing

3

effective ways to facilitate the development of young handicapped or exceptional children. Developmental psychology's key role is to provide information about how development occurs, which factors facilitate developmental progress, and which interfere. In turn, early-childhood special educators take this information and use it to structure learning environments to insure that preschool exceptional children have the best possible chance of developing their full potential.

Thus, this volume seeks to help students and practitioners in early-childhood special education and developmental psychology acquire this essential background information about the nature and course of development. Unlike other texts, however, this work seeks also to combine an explanation of normal developmental progress with atypical developmental information, thus helping the reader more readily incorporate important developmental concepts into significant educational practice.

THE DEVELOPMENTAL PERSPECTIVE

Developmental psychology is a special perspective within psychology concerned with studying human development from conception to death. Specifically, developmental psychologists are concerned with understanding the development of the physical and psychological processes that enable individuals to continuously adapt to the world as they progress through life. Recently, this concern has extended to increasing our knowledge of those factors external to the individual but which affect the rate and nature of developmental processes.

The mechanisms or processes used to explain developmental phenomena are tied to theoretical conceptions regarding the nature of development, and there is a long-standing debate within the field over which of two general views is the more appropriate and efficient. Understanding these views is important because they serve as the filtering device for the conception, interpretation, and application of most developmental research.

The Unity-of-Science Position

Adherents of this viewpoint regard developmental psychology as just one of many subfields of science, along with other areas of psychology (e.g., social, physiological) and other scientific specialties (e.g., biology, chemistry). Its task, like the task of the other sciences, is to reduce behavioral variables to their most elementary components in order to fit them into a natural science model. Accordingly, complex behavior is thought to be best understood by reducing it to those common elements that constitute all behavior.

In developmental psychology those supporting this general view have usually followed a stimulus-response approach to explaining behavior. According to this view, developmental differences result from differences in the number of stimulus-response associations in a person's behavior repertoire. Thus, seven-year-olds are regarded as more "developed" or mature than four-year-olds because they have amassed a larger number of behaviors and are consequently able to respond to more stimulus events.

Principles have been formulated to explain how behaviors arise and become associated. These principles cover both the initial antecedent conditions which determine development and the consequent secondary determinants which reinforce and shape response patterns to stimulus events. According to the unity-of-science position, learning principles such as Pavlov's classical conditioning or Skinner's operant learning paradigm apply to both humans and to nonhumans at all ages. Consequently, there is psychological continuity in development. More mature forms of behavior are theoretically believed to involve the same components as less mature forms of the same behaviors. Thus, the same principles should be able to explain varying levels of behavioral complexity. Another implication of the unity-of-science approach is that since the antecedent (stimulus) and consequent (reinforcement) determinants are environmental factors, development is basically a passive process by which the child mechanically responds to environmental stimulation and reinforcement. Consequently, the child is viewed as passive and not a determining factor in development.

The Organismic Position

Adherents of this approach believe development reflects both differentiation and integration. In the first instance, development is viewed as a continuous process of change, from a diffuse whole to more specific and refined parts, i.e., the differentiation of body tissue into specific body parts or the change over time in children from reliance on global to more specific social-interaction skills. Integration is the complementary process by which specific systems of functioning are developed from isolated physical or psychological structures. For example, the child's respiratory system is an integration of the diaphragm, the lungs, muscles, etc. Likewise, the child's developing personality is an integrated system of diverse psychological structures which allows others to understand the child and predict the child's behavior. Within this model the child's behavioral processes are seen as becoming increasingly more complex over time through differentiation and as reaching a more mature form through integration.

Characteristic of the organismic approach is the belief that successive levels of organization emerge as a child develops from an immature to a more mature state. Accordingly, within each level of organization (or stage) new behavioral forms appear. These behaviors, since they represent an integration of previous behaviors and not an additive effect, cannot be reduced to lower levels of organization. Thus, adherents of the organismic position tend to see development as marked by discrete stages, each successive stage qualitatively different from the previous stage.

Unity-of-science theorists have looked at external environmental variables (stimuli and reinforcements) as explanations of development. Organismic theorists, by contrast, usually adopt an interaction perspective, viewing all development as a product of genetic factors (individual predispositions) plus environmental factors (stimuli and reinforcements), all interacting in a multiplicative fashion to shape complex developmental phenomena. This interaction, then, is responsible for new and qualitatively different behaviors at each developmental period or stage.

Both theoretical conceptions of development have provided important insights into understanding human development. The unity-of-science position has made significant contributions to psychology by fostering experimental and theoretical rigor and by increasing knowledge of the socialization process and of the role of social learning and reinforcement in altering behavior. Ultimately, in education, this knowledge has become useful in the structuring of behavior modification techniques for developing self-help skills and behavior controls, task-analysis procedures, programmed instruction, and language or communication skills, to name but a few. Further, the organismic position has made significant contributions to psychological knowledge and to applied educational practices. These contributions include recognition of the critical role the child plays in the learning process, of the importance of environmental stimulation and early intervention to enhance learning, and of the importance of communication to learning.

Perhaps the most influential contribution of the organismic position has been its emphasis on the influence of individual-environment interaction and the effect of this interaction on development. This emphasis has led to a resurgence of involvement between educational practitioners and developmental researchers, as illustrated by the involvement of developmental psychologists and educational practitioners in such varied projects as infant-stimulation programs (i.e., the Brookline (Mass.) Early Education Project), preschool enrichment programs (i.e., George Peabody's Demonstration and Research Center for Early Education), cognitive skills training (i.e., Dave Wikert's cognitively oriented curriculum), and numerous others.

HISTORICAL OVERVIEW OF SPECIAL EDUCATION

Just as general education attempts to provide appropriate instruction to children within the normal range of social and intellectual functioning, *special education* seeks to insure that special children, children who are exceptional in some way, receive instruction appropriate to their capabilities and needs. But this has not always been the case. It is only recently that special educational services have become available on a widespread and sufficiently broad basis to encompass the needs of *all* exceptional children.

Before the eighteenth century, individuals with handicaps were regarded with hostility, fear, and superstition. They were somehow "cursed," and were not thought to be deserving of the rights due other human beings. The handicapping conditions recognized at the time were usually gross physical, mental, or sensory conditions that were very apparent to others. General education had not developed sufficiently for other handicapping conditions (mild retardation, emotional disorders, learning disorders, giftedness, etc.), to be recognized as exceptional. The typical handicapped individual, indeed, was one who might look something like the one-eyed hunchback of Notre Dame.

By the nineteenth century, developments in science and in philosophical appraisals of man's nature began to change views of the handicapped. John Locke, who regarded man's mind as a blank slate (tabula rasa) at birth, argued that man learned through sensory experience; that knowledge came from experience and not from God. Charles Darwin's *Origins of Species* also attacked the notion of divine creation and further helped to change thinking about man's origins. Another significant event was the attempt by Itard to train the Wild Boy of Aveyron. Itard, a consulting physician to the National Institute for Deaf-mutes, in Paris, was familiar with Locke's views, and when the Wild Boy was brought to the Institute for care, Itard asked permission to work with the boy, whom he named Victor.

Victor had apparently been abandoned as a small child and grew up as an animal: he could not speak, he selected food only by smell, and he displayed no affection or care for other humans. He walked with a swaying animal-like gait, frequently had convulsions, and would bite and scratch others if threatened. Itard started Victor on a sensory training program, and by 1801, Victor had developed the ability to eat and sleep normally, to keep himself clean, and had become sensitive to touch, taste, and smell. He showed affection for, and dependence on, his governess. And he had learned some crude symbolic skills like arranging letters to spell out the word "milk," or to produce monosyllabic sounds to indicate his desire for some item.

Five years later, in 1806, Victor had learned even more. Now he could distinguish gross sound differences, such as the difference between a drum and a bell. He could respond to differences in the tones of the human voice, and could distinguish colors and letters. But Victor still could not "think" as we know it, and, with puberty, many of these training gains were lost as he again became unmanageable. The training program was terminated, but despite this negative ending, Itard's work had shown one very significant thing: it was possible, through education and training, to help severely retarded individuals to develop self-help skills. This same message was also made clear in the United States by the work of one special teacher, Anne Sullivan, who worked with one special child, Helen Keller. Miss Keller, with the help of her teacher, was able to break through her blindness and deafness to become an important symbol for the value of special education.

It was not until the twentieth century, however, that special education became an organized and recognized profession. There were several organizations responsible for specific handicapping conditions (like the Convention of American Instructors of the Deaf, the American Association of Instructors of the Blind, and the American Association on Mental Deficiency), but there was little communication among them and their numbers were too small to have any great national impact. It can be said that Alexander Graham Bell, inventor of the telephone, was responsible for organizing special education. Bell, actively involved in training the deaf, twice petitioned the National Education Association (NEA) to create a new multidisciplinary division (a ''Department for the Education of Classes Requiring Special Methods of Instruction'') within NEA to deal with the educational needs of the handicapped. The NEA responded to Bell's petition, in 1897, but, unfortunately, named the new division the ''Department of Education of the Deaf, Blind, and the Feebleminded,'' after the three major handicapping conditions involved. Later, however, this department became known as the Department of Special Education.

With the organization of special education forces within the NEA, public schools began to hold classes for handicapped children, and, by 1911, there were special education classes in 99 American cities. World War I and the Great Depression interfered with this growth, however, and these classes decreased in number until after World War II. The War's effect on education in general was phenomenal, but on special education it was of paramount importance. Two factors were especially significant. The first resulted from the intelligence testing movement. During the war, nearly 1 million men were rejected for military service on the basis of some degree of mental incompetency. Yet many of these men were sufficiently competent to return home and *visibly* lead productive and useful lives. This helped to reduce some of the stigma associated with mental handicaps. But it was the war's aftermath that literally helped the handicapped to come out of their closets. Among the returning veterans were many thousands who were physically damaged, intellectually impaired, or emotionally disturbed who required both social rehabilitation programs and research programs to develop effective treatment. The handicapped now constituted a visible minority, and attitudes towards them began to change. Parents of handicapped children, no longer ashamed, began to organize pressure groups, like the United Cerebral Palsy Association, to demand access to educational resources, other than institutionalization, for handicapped children. Special education professional groups, like the Council for Exceptional Children, joined the parents and both groups were aided by the historic Supreme Court decision in *Brown v. Board of Education of Topeka* (1954). In this decision the Court ruled that state laws that permitted or required segregated public schools were in violation of the Fourteenth Amendment's ''equal protection under the law'' clause. The special-education pressure groups recognized that what applied to one minority group would also apply to another minority group, and thus were able to exert sufficient legal and social pressure to bring about the changes in federal law regarding the education of all handicapped children and youth. These important court cases and federal laws are summarized in Figures 1-1 and 1-2 below.

SPECIAL EDUCATION TODAY: The Effects of Public Law 94-142

Special education, as a profession, is just moving into its own, primarily because of federal legislative support. At the same time, handicapped children are today finally being accorded their rights as citizens, essentially as a result of Public Law 94-142 (referred to as the "Bill of Rights" for exceptional children), effective September, 1978.

Figure 1-1 Significant Court Decisions Affecting Special Education

Hobson v. Nathan (1967): The court ruled that schools could not assign children to special education classes on the basis of culturally discriminatory standardized test data.

Mills v. Board of Education of the District of Columbia (1971): The court ruled that all children previously excluded from public schools must have equal opportunity for a public education, regardless of the degree of severity of their handicap.

Pennsylvania Association for Retarded Children (now Citizens) v. the Commonwealth of Pennsylvania (1971): The court ruled that all mentally retarded children have a right to an education at public expense. This decision also included the parents' right to due process before the child's status in school could be altered in any way.

Lori Case v. State of California (1973): The court ruled against separating handicapped children into self-contained classrooms when it was possible to educate them in the same classrooms that "normal" children attended.

Figure 1-2 Significant Federal Legislation Affecting Special Education

PL 83-531 (1957):	The Cooperative Research Act provided the first research support for examining handicapping conditions.
PL 85-926 (1958):	Authorized training grants to colleges and universities to train special education leadership personnel. Also authorized payment of funds to states for teacher training in mental retardation.
PL 88-164 (1963):	Expanded handicapped categories to include not only mental retardation but also hard of hearing, deaf, speech impaired, visually impaired, seriously emotionally disturbed, crippled, or other health-impaired children needing special education as a result of their impairment.
PL 89-750 (1966):	Amended the Elementary and Secondary Education Act of 1965 to add Title VI, which authorized funds to initiate, improve, and expand programs for the handicapped; also created the Bureau of Education for the Handicapped and the National Advisory Committee on Handicapped Children.
PL 90-170 (1967):	Authorized programs in physical education and recreation for the handicapped and the training of leadership personnel, supervisors and researchers.
PL 90-576 (1968):	Authorized agencies other than colleges and universities or states to apply for grants.
PL 91-230 (1970):	Authorized funds for learning disabilities, and reinforced the federal government's role in educating handicapped children.
PL 94-142 (1975):	The Education of All Handicapped Children's Act. This legislation will be discussed in detail below.

Twenty-five years ago only about 40 colleges and universities reported that they offered course work in mental retardation; of these, only 15 offered doctoral training in special education. In fact, in 1953, only 4 doctorates and 130 master's degrees were awarded (Burke, 1976), indicating that, in spite of special education's long history, it had few professionals, either teachers or researchers. But this rather bleak picture was changed by the massive financial support which resulted in the federal legislation listed above. In 1960, nearly $1 million was funded for federally assisted special education programs. Four years later, that figure had risen to $13 million, and by 1976, over $40 million had been allocated to special education programs (Burke, 1976). Since much of these funds was channeled into training programs, the number of people.employed in special education has risen dramatically. Today, approximately one-quarter of a million people work in this field in some capacity. Under PL 94-142, this figure will double to meet the needs of exceptional children identified under this new law, as well as already identified children (Harvey, 1976).

PL 94-142

This law came into being because existing federal legislation was inadequate to the needs of all exceptional children. In 1975, despite nearly 20 years of federal support, almost 2 million handicapped children were being excluded from receiving a public education. In addition, many of the estimated 8 million exceptional children already receiving some form of special education service were not receiving "appropriate" educational services, and many were being placed in inappropriate educational settings because their handicaps were going undetected (Abeson and Zettel, 1977). Clearly, a greater effort was needed; Congress responded and President Gerald Ford signed PL 94-142 into law on November 29, 1975. Under this law, Congress spelled out national policy regarding the education of the handicapped:

> It is the purpose of this Act to assure that all handicapped children have available to them, within the time periods specified, a free appropriate public education emphasizing special education and related services designed to meet their unique needs (PL 94-142, 1975, Section 3, c.).

Thus, beginning in September, 1978, all handicapped children aged 3 to 18 became entitled to receive a free public education. And in 1980, this age range will be extended to cover the years 3 to 21. (These ages will hold unless they conflict with state law or court decision within a particular state.)

As mentioned earlier, this law has been called the handicapped child's Bill of Rights, for reasons outlined below. Under the law, each exceptional child has a right to:

- *education:* no longer can handicapped children be regarded as too severely handicapped to benefit from some form of education at public expense. Furthermore, handicapped children are now eligible to participate in *all* programs provided by public schools for nonhandicapped children.
- *nondiscriminatory evaluation:* testing and evaluation materials and procedures must be selected so as not to be culturally discriminatory; they are to be in the child's native language or mode or communication; and no one test can be the basis for a decision regarding the placement or a change in status of a child.
- *appropriate education:* each handicapped child must be provided with a written *individualized education program* or plan (IEP), which states what educational services will be provided to the child, and why. It must be agreed upon by parents or legal guardians, and school systems are legally responsible for providing the services described in each IEP. Furthermore, IEPs must be updated periodically, usually no less than once a year.
- *due process:* this is to insure that the child's legal rights are made available to the child. Due process requires written notice before any change in the child's status occurs, an opportunity for the child's parents or legal guardians to complain and to obtain an independent evaluation of the child, access to all relevant records, to a hearing, and to an appeal.
- *placement in the "least restrictive environment":* handicapped children must now be placed in an educational environment which is least restrictive of the child's development. They can no longer be placed only in self-contained classrooms, away from normal educational surroundings.

These are significant rights; their fulfillment will require dramatic changes in both regular and special education facilities, practices, and personnel needs and training. Special education, more than other "types" of education, is in a unique position relative to psychology, for much of its unique content has developed along with educational psychology, school psychology, and child or developmental psychology. Such cooperative efforts will become even more important now that appropriate educational services must be provided on the basis of individualized needs to younger exceptional children. Thus, it seems reasonable that preschool special education and developmental psychology will have a common base and a natural alliance.

WHO ARE EXCEPTIONAL CHILDREN?

Generally speaking, handicapped children have been traditionally categorized, on the basis of their major disability, into eight groups. But, as the previous sentence indicates, handicapped children may suffer from more than one handicapping condition, so that some may consider "multiple handicapping conditions'' as a separate handicapping category. These categories are briefly described below. (A more complete treatment of most of these exceptionalities will follow in later chapters.)

- *Emotionally Disturbed Children:* Children who exhibit learned behaviors which are consistently maladaptive or inappropriate. (See Chapter 15)

- *Learning-Disabled Children:* Children who exhibit a disorder in one or more of the basic psychological processes involved in understanding or in using spoken and/or written language. (See Chapter 9)

- *Mentally Retarded Children:* Children who exhibit subaverage general intellectual functioning which originates during the developmental period and which is associated with impaired adaptive behavior. (See Chapter 10)

- *Visually Handicapped Children:* Children who either have partial sight or who are blind. (See Chapter 11)

- *Hearing-Impaired Children:* Children who are hard of hearing or are deaf. (See Chapter 12)

- *Children with Speech Disorders:* Children whose speech deviates so much from that of others that it calls attention to itself, interferes with communication, and/or causes maladaptive behavior. (See Chapter 8)

- *Physically Handicapped Children:* Children who are crippled as a result of neurological, orthopedic, or chronic health disorders. (See Chapters 4 and 5)

- *Gifted Children:* Children who exhibit outstanding ability or attainment; often defined by an IQ of more than 120 points.

These separate categories of exceptionality have not come about because the behaviors which indicate the presence of one type of handicap are, in many cases, sufficiently different from the behaviors indicating another handicapping condition. In fact, accurate diagnosis of some handicapping conditions is still a major problem in special education. Instead, separate categories of exceptionality were created because of federal legislation. Public Law 85-926 authorized funds for mental retardation; later, PL 88-164 created several additional categories, and, finally, PL 91-230 added the category of learning disabilities. These and similar

---

Table 1-1 Percent of U.S. Children With Varying Handicapping Conditions, 1976*

Speech Impaired		3.50
Learning Disabled		3.00
Mentally Retarded		3.00
Emotionally Disturbed		2.00
Orthopedic/Health Impaired		0.50
Hearing Impaired		0.60
Visually Impaired		0.10
Multiply Handicapped		0.06
Total	Approximately	12.0

*Based on U.S. Government Statistics, 1977

Source: Bureau of Education for the Handicapped, 1977.

---

laws set up separate administrative budgets and procedures, thus solidifying the categorical approach to dealing with handicapped children. PL 94-142 attempts to reduce this reliance on categories of exceptionality. Several optional methods for dealing with handicapping conditions have been proposed from time to time to avoid the problems of separation into discrete groups. One approach has been to cluster children into only five groups according to the type of deviation. Kirk (1972) has proposed the following groups:

1. *communication disorders,* including learning disabilities and speech handicaps;
2. *mental deviations,* including gifted and the retarded;
3. *sensory handicaps,* including auditory and visual handicaps;
4. *neurological and orthopedic conditions,* including children with brain and/or physical handicaps;
5. *behavior disorders.*

Herb Quay (1973) proposed a classification system based on only three categories: process dysfunctions, experience defects, and experience deficits. *Process dysfunctions* would include children whose handicaps relate to sensory, motor, or neurological problems occurring *within* the child. Children who suffer from behavior disorders due to some form of environmental trauma would be placed in the *experience defects* group. *Experience deficits* include children who are handicapped because of insufficient experience or inadequate training.

One problem with these categorical approaches is their tendency to cause confusion. The varying labels (learning disabled, emotionally disturbed, educable mentally retarded, etc.) tend to imply that handicapped or exceptional children require different educational settings and instructional approaches. While this has some truth, it is certainly less true with preschool children's exceptionalities since categorical classification is less clear. Therefore, recent efforts to cluster exceptionalities by degree of severity, regardless of etiology, make good sense for early-childhood special education.

This recent effort describes handicapping conditions as mild, moderate, and severe. Under such a taxonomy, children with mild retardation, behavioral disturbance, or sensory loss, for example, can be dealt with in the same educational environment, which also includes children without handicaps. All such children could benefit from the same or similar instructional techniques, modified according to each child's needs. This is a noncategorical approach to preschool special education, and it holds for those children with moderate to severe disabilities. This is illustrated below.

Disability	Degree of Disability		
	Mild	Moderate	Severe
Mental Retardation	EMR	TMR	SMR
Behavior Disorder	Transitory	Phobic	Autism
Hearing Impairment	41-55 Decibel	56-70 Decibel	71 Decibel

According to this scheme, mildly handicapped children can be included in regular educational settings (mainstreamed). Children with moderate exceptionality can probably benefit more from separate classrooms within the same public school as children in the mild category. Severely handicapped children probably would require special strategies employed in institution-like settings.

Early Childhood Special Education: Why the Need?

Rough estimates indicate that about 1 million children below age 6 are handicapped in some way. These figures are only approximate because this age group has not received much attention prior to PL 94-142, when the age range was lowered to include 3-to-5-year-olds. Many of these handicapped children are to be found among the poor, where inadequate health care and diet conditions prevail. According to the Census Bureau, one in seven children were living in poverty conditions in 1973. Therefore, one good reason to intervene early is to attempt to locate the children from such environments who are "at risk" for handicapping conditions. DeWeerd (1976) reports that in a representative sample of 1,436 families with children between 6 months and 11 years, medical researchers found that among all socioeconomic levels children below age 3 could be described as follows:

- 26% had iron-deficiency anemia
- 26% had uncorrected or inadequately corrected visual disorders
- 18% had partial hearing losses
- 13% had ear infections which could lead to hearing losses

If such children can be found and exposed to early remediation, their need for special education services can be reduced. Both Karnes (1973) and Haring (1976) offer evidence that programs which provide early stimulation and which meet the educational needs of young children (such as those mentioned above) can reduce the number of children who will need long-term special services. In addition, developmental psychologists have identified early childhood as a critical period for much learning. If the child is exposed to appropriate learning experiences beginning in infancy and continuing through early childhood years, these critical learning periods can be maximized to the child's and society's benefit (Horowitz and Paden, 1973). Early-childhood special education may therefore be regarded not only as a remedial developmental effort but also as an important preventive measure to insure against the need for long-term remedial assistance.

DEVELOPING HUMAN COMPETENCIES: The Alliance Between Special Education and Developmental Psychology

The natural alliance between special education and developmental psychology mentioned earlier is a result of their unique complementarity. Developmental psychologists are interested in understanding the development of behavioral sequences, but are generally not applied practitioners per se. Special educators are applied researchers and practitioners whose concern is with helping handicapped children attain their potential. To this end, they develop instructional or educational strategies based on their understanding of normal developmental processes. So, in a sense, special educators translate research findings about the nature of normal developmental processes into particular ways of decreasing the delayed development of handicapped children. Not only is this a valuable service to the handicapped but also it provides the basis for an important link among theory, research, and practice. By applying psychological findings, special educators help further our knowledge of man's nature by providing the necessary feedback loop between research findings and applied practices.

For this feedback loop to be fully effective, psychologists and educators must have a common conception about the goal of the developmental process. Such conception is provided by the recently expressed concern over the development of human competencies. *Competence* has been identified as the ultimate direction of human growth: we all seek to become competent, fully functioning humans. The notion of competence includes three essential components (Ainsworth & Bell, 1973; Anderson & Messick, 1974; Connolly & Bruner, 1973):

1. Competence is reflected by man's *ability to select and use information* from the environment in developing appropriate strategies for action;
2. Competence is indicated by our *ability to initiate the behavioral activities* necessary to carry out these plans;
3. Competence describes the *ability to learn from one's successes and failures* by developing new strategies for action.

Thus, competence describes the development of the individual's overall effectiveness in dealing with the world. To become competent, the child must develop appropriate:

- cognitive skills for processing information about the world;
- behavior to satisfy needs, desires, and goals;
- emotional attitudes to guide behavior; and
- awareness of self and of others within the framework of a complex social network.

Given the general guidelines listed above, McDavid and Garwood (1978) have described a model for the development of human competencies which includes the development of a number of important ''survival'' skills. These survival components of the human competency model include:

1. physical-motor skills: to allow the child to manipulate efficiently and interact with the environment;
2. cognitive or intellectual skills: to enable the child to interpret and use information accessible through the senses;
3. social and interpersonal skills: to facilitate the child's effective interaction with other people and provide an accurate understanding of the world and its people;
4. feelings or attitudes related to oneself: to allow for an accurate conception of one's abilities and one's position in the world.

Specific examples of each of the four categories of human competencies are outlined in Table 1-2.

Table 1-2 A Model for the Development of Human Competencies

ATTRIBUTE OR COMPETENCE	EXAMPLE

Physical Development

• Large muscle motor skills	"I can run and I can skip rope."
• Small muscle motor skills	"I can button my coat and cut paper with my scissors."
• Perceptual-motor skills	"I can pick all the blue beads out of a box of mixed beads."
• Efficient coordination of behavioral responses	"I can walk a balance beam by putting one foot in front of the other and by using my arms for balance."

Cognitive or Intellectual Development

• Curiosity and exploration	"I like to go different places and try different things."
• Control of attention and selective perception	"I can pay attention to the teacher even when others are talking."
• Perceptual skills of discrimination, detecting a pattern, etc.	"I can find hidden figures in a picture puzzle."
• Language and communication skills	"I know the alphabet, I can read, and I can write."
• Cognitive categorization: concept formation	"I know the difference between a baseball and a softball."
• Memory and information retrieval skills	"I can do my multiplication tables up to the 4's."
• Critical thinking: analysis	"If the sun is in front of me and it is afternoon, I must be walking west."
• Creative thinking: synthesis	"I can draw a square and then make it into a car or a boat."
• Problem-solving: deductive application	"If I want to build a tree-house, I need nails, wood, a hammer, and a saw."
• Flexibility in information-processing strategies	"Since it didn't work that way, I'll try it this way to make it work."
• Qualitative & relational concepts (logical operations)	"$5 + 3 = 4 + 4$"

Table 1-2 *Continued*

Social and Interpersonal Skills and Societal Orientation

• Sensitivity in social relationships	"I know how my brother felt when he broke his favorite toy."
• Positive effect in interpersonal relationships	"I feel happy because I think you care for me."
• Appreciation of social roles	"He acts that way because he is the group leader today."
• Regulation of antisocial behavior	"I won't steal anything because I might get into trouble."
• Prosocial morality (altruism)	"I can't eat all of these cookies so I'll share with my friends."
• Acculturation: general reserve of information and knowledge	"I know what time it is; I can name the days of the week, the months of the year, and all the seasons."
• Facility in using resources for learning (resource seeking)	"I know how to work the tape-recorder and the record-player and how to use the dictionary."
• Positive attitudes toward education, school, and learning	"I like to learn about math and people and animals."
• Enjoyment of humor, play, and fantasy	"I like to play make-believe and make up funny stories."

Attitudes Toward Self

• A consolidated sense of identity, differentiating oneself from the rest of the world	"I am Pat, and no one else is exactly like me."
• A concept of the self as an agent to initiate and control	"If I work at it, I can do lots of things."
• Realistic appraisal of the self with realistic positive self-regard	"I can ride a skate-board as well as any one I know."
• Awareness and recognition of feelings	"Sometimes I get scared and I'm always glad when my parents come home."
• Motivation to seek competence . . . not only for the consequences, but also for success for its own sake	"I like to work puzzles; it makes me feel good to know I can do it by myself."

Source: Adapted from J.W. McDavid and S.G. Garwood's *Understanding Children.* Boston: D.C. Heath, 1978. Reprinted with permission of the publisher.

The examples of competent behavior given in Table 1-2 reflect cultural norms that provide a sense of direction for desired outcomes of education and indicate the kinds of skills needed for achieving competence in our society. In addition, this model points up the skills needed by anyone who plans to work with children, exceptional or otherwise. These skills include the ability to:

1. analyze the developmental processes associated with any growth area;
2. evaluate the status of a child at any point along the developmental continuum in order to know how far the child needs to go to become more competent; and
3. separate the required behaviors in any competency area into segments which handicapped children can confront and master.

Developing competence, then, involves understanding, analyzing, and evaluating handicapped children, as well as the application of specific skills of judgment and action. It is hoped this volume will help develop these very important skills for understanding and aiding exceptional children develop.

REFERENCES AND SUGGESTED READINGS

Abeson, A. & Zettel, J. The end of the quiet revolution: The Education for All Handicapped Children Act of 1975. *Exceptional Children,* 1977, *44,* 114-130.

Ainsworth, M. & Bell, S. Mother-infant interaction and the development of competence. In K. Connolly & J. Bruner (Eds.), *The growth of competence.* New York: Academic Press, 1973.

Anderson, S. & Messick, S. Social competency in young children. *Developmental Psychology,* 1974, *10,* 282-293.

Bruner, J.S. *The relevance of education.* New York: Norton, 1971.

Bureau of the Census. *Current population reports, consumer income: Characteristics of population below poverty level, 1974.* Series P60, No. 102.

Burke, P.J. Personnel preparation: Historical perspective. *Exceptional Children,* 1976, *43,* 144-147.

Connolly, K. & Bruner, J. (Eds.). *The growth of competence.* New York: Academic Press, 1973.

Erickson, M.T. *Child psychopathology: Assessment, etiology, and treatment.* Englewood Cliffs: Prentice-Hall, 1978.

Geer, W.C. The CEC tree and its roots. *Exceptional Children,* 1977, *44,* 82-89.

Haring, N.G. (Ed.). *Behavior of exceptional children.* Columbus, Ohio: Charles E. Merrill, 1974.

Haring, N.G., & Schufelbusch, R. *Teaching special children.* New York: McGraw-Hill, 1976.

Haring, N.G. Assessment and diagnosis of severely handicapping conditions. In M.A. Thomas (Ed.), *Hey, don't forget about me.* Reston, Va.: Council for Exceptional Children, 1976.

Harvey, J. Future trends in personnel preparation. *Exceptional Children, 1976, 43,* 148-150.

Hewett, F. *Education of exceptional learners.* Boston: Allyn and Bacon, 1974.

Horowitz, F.D., & Paden, L.Y. The effectiveness of environmental intervention programs. In B.M. Caldwell and H.N. Riccuiti (Eds.), *Review of child development and social policy.* Chicago: University of Chicago Press, 1973.

Karnes, M. Implications of research with disadvantaged children for early intervention with the handicapped. In J.B. Jordan & R.F. Dailey (Eds.) *Not all little wagons are red: The exceptional child's early years.* Reston, Va.: Council for Exceptional Children, 1973.

Kirk, S.A. *Educating exceptional children* (2nd ed.). Boston: Houghton-Mifflin, 1972.

Lerner, R.M. *Concepts and theories of human development.* Reading, Mass.: Addison-Wesley, 1976.

McDavid, J.W., & Garwood, S.G. *Understanding children.* Lexington, Mass.: D.C. Heath, 1978.

Melcher, J.W. Law, litigation, and handicapped children. *Exceptional Children,* 1976, *43,* 126-131.

Quay, H. Special education: Assumptions, techniques, and evaluative criteria. *Exceptional Children,* 1973, *40,* 165-170.

Part II

Physical Development

Chapter 2

Physical Development: The Young Child's Growing Body

S. Gray Garwood

INTRODUCTION

Physical development includes development of the body and related organs and systems such as the nervous and skeletal-muscular (motor) systems or the sense organs and limbs. Understanding the processes related to physical development is important to an understanding of normal and atypical development, because appropriate physical development is the key to intellectual, personal, and social development. For example, sensory organs allow us to take in information about the world. The motor system permits contact with the world. Neurological equipment guides our responses to this world; its efficiency and integrity determine our ability to profit intellectually from these interactions with the world. Thus, a child's body is not only the mechanism through which interactions with the physical and social world occur, but also represents an important symbol of the child's personality, because it provides the basis for comparison of self with others. For these reasons, a child's physical growth cannot be separated from that child's overall development.

The developmental process begins when male and female germ cells combine to form a fertilized egg. Too small for the naked eye to observe, this egg immediately begins a growth process that culminates in a human characterized by a host of complex behaviors: talking, walking, thinking, loving, evaluating, and so forth. Associated with this growth process are two factors critical in shaping development. The child inherits a unique biological makeup, and from the point of conception on the child exists in a dynamic environment. This biological component contributes the *nature* factor — a genetic plan for the development of body structures. The second, the *nurture* factor, refers to environmental events which facilitate or retard the normal course of development.

Because biologically determined behaviors cannot be considered outside an environmental context, it makes little sense to debate which of these two factors is the more critical to development. Most people concerned with human development accept this natural limitation on the scientific study of growth, and have come to regard human behavior as a dynamic system which includes both biological and environmental determinants in mutual interaction.

BIOLOGICAL CONTRIBUTIONS TO DEVELOPMENT

Historical Notes

Genetics is the study of biological inheritance and of environmental factors influencing this inheritance. Charles Darwin (1809 - 1882) is responsible for initiating scientific interest in genetics when he questioned the biblical interpretation of man's origins in his *Origins of Species* (1859). Darwin's investigations had convinced him that, given the hostile nature of the environment, only those members of a species with the best adaptive characteristics were likely to survive to reproduce. Terming this process *natural selection,* Darwin argued that these survival traits were initially random structural changes occurring "accidentally," then passed on within a species because the change facilitated survival.

Gregor Mendel (1822 - 1884), a Moravian monk and amateur mathematician and biologist who had read Darwin's book, grew and carefully observed more than 22 varieties of the garden pea, a self-pollinating plant. He reported these observations in 1865, at a scientific meeting, but his attempts to connect mathematical ratios with plant offspring were generally ignored. Nearly 35 years later his findings were rediscovered and subsequently have come to provide the basis for our modern views of genetics. Mendel's findings are summarized below.

1. Heritable characteristics are transmitted by factors (later called genes).
2. Mature organisms have two of each type of factor.
3. When these factors mix, one will be dominant and one will be recessive.
4. In reproductive cells, these factors divide to give each new reproductive cell only one of each pair of factors.
5. Random mating of male and female reproductive cells results in the large numbers of individual variations within a species.

Reproduction

Sexually mature males and females produce reproductive cells called *gametes*. Females produce their gametes *(ova)* in the ovary glands; males produce gametes *(spermatozoa)* in the testicles. During sexual intercourse, spermatozoa are released by the male and move into the female's Fallopian tubes. If the female has recently released an ovum, and this ovum is penetrated by a male gamete, fertilization occurs, a *zygote* is formed, and cell division begins.

The fertilized egg or *zygote* is a cellular body containing 23 pairs of *chromosomes,* a chemical substance containing genes. Half of the chromosomes in each pair are contributed by the mother and half by the father, resulting in a unique combination of chromosomes that accounts for individual variation. Each of these 23 pairs of chromosomes contains genetic information related to development of the body's physical structures. Cellular material continues to multiply into new cells by *mitosis,* a process by which chromosome material doubles when the two members of each pair split lengthwise, separate and move to opposite ends of the cell. The cell then pinches in at the middle and splits into two cells, each containing 23 pairs of chromosomes. The resulting two daughter cells then split into four cells, the four cells divide into sixteen cells, and eventually through this mitotic process, human structures develop.

Reproductive cells or gametes cannot divide by the mitotic process because too many chromosome pairs would result. Instead, gametes divide by a reproduction process termed *meiosis.* When male or female gametes are formed they also contain 23 pairs of chromosomes. As these gametes mature, one of each pair moves toward the opposite cell wall, culminating in 23 chromosomes lined up along one wall and a matching number lined up along the other cell wall. The cell then splits down the middle (think of it as splitting vertically whereas in mitosis the cell splits horizontally), creating two cells, each with only 23 chromosomes. Both male and female gametes divide by this meiotic process, and when a male gamete fertilizes a female gamete, the resulting fertilized egg contains a full complement of 46 chromosomes.

Chromosomes are chemical substances containing varying amounts of DNA (deoxyribonucleic acid) and RNA (ribonucleic acid). Each chromosome also contains thousands of genes, most of which are composed of DNA — the basis for hereditary transmission. The DNA molecule consists of chemical substances contained in two spirals wound around each other. These chemical substances cause the two spirals to unwind and separate. Each old spiral then acts as a template for the construction of a new companion spiral and, as new cells are formed, each new molecule contains one old and one new spiral. Thus, each new cell contains the individual's genetic code. (See Figure 2-1.) Cell division is guided by RNA, which carries the genetic blueprint from DNA to different body structures. In this manner, blue eyes, curly hair, arms, teeth, and so forth, are formed.

Gene pairs, half of which are from the mother and half from the father, are called *alleles.* Alleles contain instructions for creating general structures like fingers as well as for creating specific variations like double-jointed fingers. If a person has an identical allele pair for a particular gene, he or she is *homozygous* for that gene. If the gene pair members are unlike, the person is *heterozygous* for that gene. These differences are illustrated in this example: Some individuals taste a particular chemical substance as bitter; the allele accounting for this is noted as a *T, T* pair. To others, this substance is tasteless; these individuals possess a *t, t* pair. Within each of the two different pairs the alleles are identical so both groups are homozygous for their respective pairings and both have the same respective *genotype* (inherited characteristic). Individuals with a *T, t* pairing are heterozygous for this allele, but they also taste the substance as bitter, just as the *T, T* individuals do. The behavior of these two groups is identical: They have the same *phenotype* (outward appearance of similarity) but are genotypically different.

In the above example, the *T* allele is dominant over the *t* allele and masks any effect the *t* allele would have. Thus, alleles which mask the effects of other alleles result in genetic dominance over the recessive alleles they cover up. Recessive genetic traits emerge only when both parents contribute, as in the *t, t* pair. Paired recessive genes result in such characteristics as light eye color, very short fingers, curly hair, sickle cell amemia, and chemically induced mental retardation. A two-generation example illustrating dominant and recessive inheritance of eye color is shown on page 29.

Offspring sex is determined by one of the 23 pairs of chromosomes. In males, this chromosome pair is structured differently from all others. One of the pair is a large chromosome with many genes, called the *X* chromosome. The other half is small, contains only a few genes, and is called the *Y* chromosome. Female sex chromosomes contain two *X* chromosomes. When male gametes split during meiosis, the reproductive cells which result have one *X* and one *Y* chromosome,

Figure 2-1 DNA — The transmission of genetic information

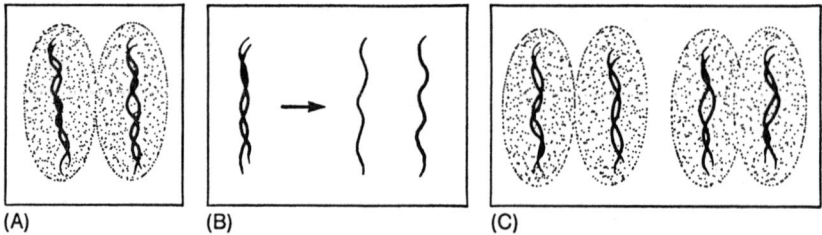

(A)   (B)   (C)

(A) A chromosome pair within a cell, which contains genetic information inherited from the parents. This information, consisting of chemical substances called deoxyribonucleic acid (DNA) arranged in the spiral forms, is located in each chromosome.

(B) DNA creates duplicate spirals in new cells by unwinding to collect and organize new materials so they match the existing spiral, and then rewinding the existing spiral with the newly created duplicate.

(C) The original cell multiplies into two and the DNA spirals rewind themselves. This process of cell division creates new but identical chromosome pairs containing the individual's genetic code.

f i r s t **g e n e r a t i o n**

Homozygous Individual:

Brown genotype

(Brown, Brown)

Heterozygous Individual:

Brown phenotype

(Brown, blue)

Mate and produce four
children; their possible
eye color combinations are:

Child 1:

Brown eyes

(Brown, Brown)

Child 2:

Brown eyes

(Brown, Brown)

Child 3:

Brown eyes

(Brown, Brown)

Child 4:

Brown eyes

(Brown, Brown)

s e c o n d **g e n e r a t i o n**

Upon maturity, Child 3 mates

with a Homozygous blue-eyed

spouse; their offsprings'

possible eye-color combinations

are:

Child 1:

Brown eyes

(Brown, blue)

Child 2:

Brown eyes

(Brown, blue)

Child 3:

Blue eyes

(blue, blue)

Child 4:

Blue eyes

(blue, blue)

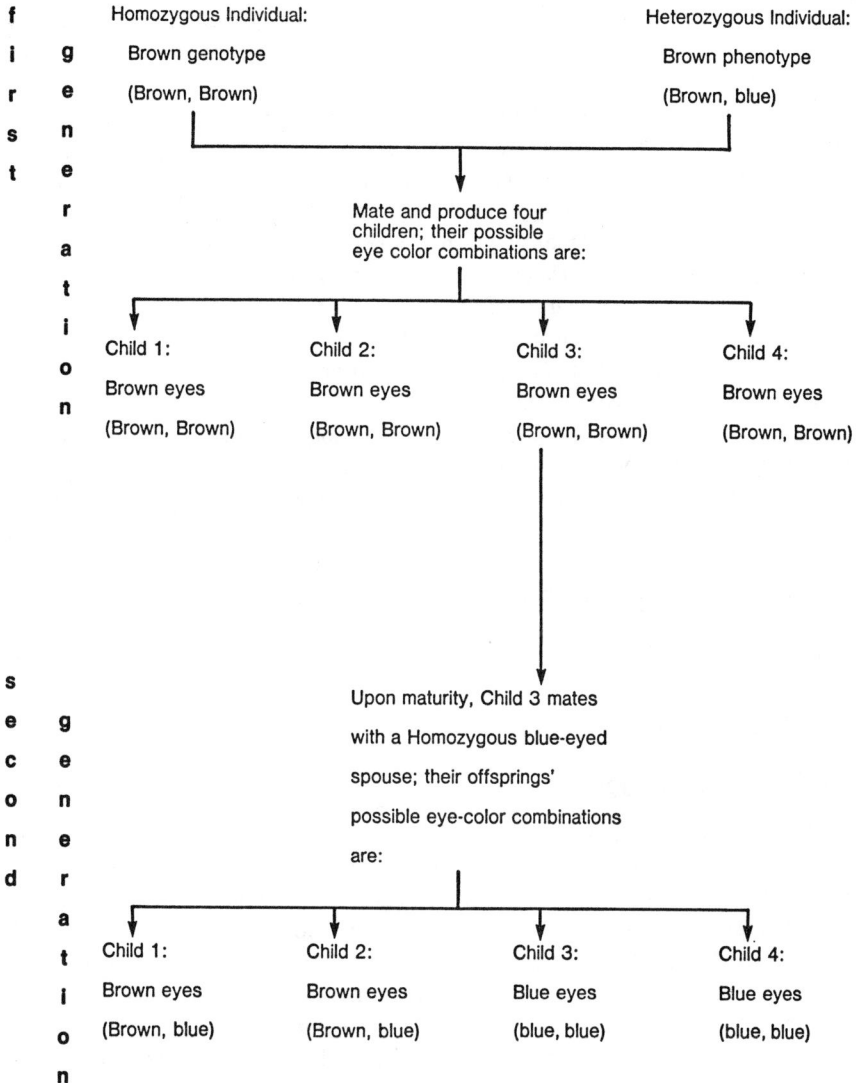

*The capital letter B in Brown indicates a dominant trait; the lower-case b in blue indicates a
recessive trait.

respectively. If the male gamete with the X chromosome fertilizes a female gamete, the offspring will be female (X,X); if the male gamete that contains the Y chromosome fertilizes an ovum, the resulting offspring will be male (X,Y). In this way, sex-linked characteristics are transmitted since they are carried on the sex chromosome.

Monozygotic or identical twins result when one ovum is fertilized by one spermatozoon. When the first mitotic cell division occurs, instead of remaining together as one mass, the new cells separate and two individuals begin to form. Since these individuals develop from the same zygote, they have the same genetic history. Dizygotic or fraternal twins are not really twins at all; they simply share the same uterus. Two ova are produced and fertilized by two spermatozoa at the same time; the offspring can be of either sex or can occur in combination. Both individuals have a different assortment of genes but share an identical uterine environment. Multiple births of more than two occur in the same manner.

Now that scientists understand how genes interact, it is possible to make predictions about a person's phenotypes and genotypes, and genetic counseling has lately become available to prospective parents. This service can provide information to couples about genetic trait combinations that result in early death or abnormalcy. As an example, consider *infantile amaurotic idiocy,* a condition inherited as a recessive trait, and which results in mental retardation, blindness, and early death. Through genetic counseling, prospective parents could make more realistic decisions about bearing children who might suffer from such a disorder.

EMBRYONIC DEVELOPMENT

The Period of the Zygote

The first seven to ten days after fertilization is called the period of the *zygote.* During this time the fertilized egg (zygote) develops into the embryo as follows: First, cleavage, or mitotic cell division, begins as the zygote travels down the Fallopian tube towards the uterus. By the third day enough cells have been formed so that a solid mass, the *morula,* is evident. The morula enters the uterine cavity about the fourth day after fertilization, and uterine fluids collect between its cells, forcing it to separate into two parts: an outer layer, the *trophoblast,* and an inner cell mass, the *embryoblast.* The trophoblast eventually develops into the *amnion,* a membranous sac surrounding the embryo and providing it protection from stress, and the *placenta,* a spongy network of blood vessels and tissues, which is the agent of nourishment for the embryo and the mechanism by which waste materials are removed from the embryo. The amnion is attached to the wall of the uterus through the placenta and the umbilical cord, a rope-like tissue mass which provides the developing embryo with oxygen from the mother's blood. The inner cell mass or embryoblast develops into the embryo, beginning with the differentiation of endodermic, ectodermic, and mesodermic tissues and the appearance of the embryonic disc, a thin plate-like mass of tissues. This occurs about the eighth day. By day ten, the embryo, with its membrane, is fully embedded in the upper portion of the uterus.

The Embryo

After the initial period of development described above, the developing organism is called an *embryo,* and the *embryonic period* lasts until about the beginning of the third month of pregnancy. This time period is critical in the development of physical structures, especially the fourth through the seventh weeks, when about 95 percent of the embryo's body parts appear. Any interference during this critical period could result in death or abnormal development. The list below summarizes the embryonic development occurring during the first three months (the first trimester).

Day	Characteristics of Development
1	Fertilization occurs and cell division (mitosis) begins
3-6	Zygote (morula) passes through the Fallopian tubes and enters the uterine cavity; the attachment process begins
7	Trophoblast and embryoblast have formed from morula; endodermic tissue appears
8	Ectodermic tissue appears; embryonic disc is formed
10	Zygote is completely embedded in uterus; period of the zygote ends
11	Placental circulation begins
16	Mesodermic tissue appears
18	The neural plate, the primitive central nervous system, appears
19	The brain is forming; the thyroid gland begins to develop
21	The heart tubes begin to fuse to form the primitive heart
22	Primitive heart begins to beat
26	Arm buds appear
27	Leg buds appear
30	Eye and nose structures form
31	The mouth begins to form
32	Hand structures appear
34	Foot structures appear
38	The upper lip is formed
40	The palate is developing
48	The beginnings of all essential internal and external physical structures have occurred; the embryo is about 30 mm. in length.

The process of tissue differentiation, which begins about the second week after fertilization, is characterized by the emergence of three primary germ layers: ectoderm, endoderm, and mesoderm. The organs derived from these various tissues are listed below.

Endoderm	Ectoderm	Mesoderm
Contributes to:	Contributes to:	Contributes to:
• liver	• skin	• skull
• pancreas	• hair	• muscles and connective tissue
• bladder	• nails	• dentine
• trachea	• mammary glands	• skin
• bronchi	• anterior pituitary gland	• blood and blood vessels
• lungs	• tooth enamel	• spleen
• pharynx	• inner ear	• adrenal cortex
• middle ear	• eye lens	• kidneys
• tonsils	• central and peripheral nervous system tissue	• reproductive organs
• parathyroids	• adrenal gland	
• urethra	• retina	
	• pineal body	
	• sweat glands	

How these primary tissues give rise to the body's very specialized organs and tissues was discovered by Hans Spemann (1869 - 1941). From research conducted in the 1920s and 1930s, Spemann reported that *epigenesis* (differentiation of a formless mass into different body parts) occurred through the actions of primary and secondary organizers which induce tissue differentiation of adjacent tissue. A primary organizer induces nearby tissue to differentiate and the differentiated tissue then acts as a secondary organizer on other adjacent and nondifferentiated tissue. Induction, however, is reciprocal, not a one-way process. As an induced tissue begins to differentiate it can act as an inducer on the original inducing tissue. Thus, primary and secondary organizers form an interaction system which leads to body tissue and organ development. Some of these important body structures and systems are described below.

The Cardiovascular System

Embryonic development is very rapid; it requires nourishment and oxygen as well as a method for disposing of wastes. For these reasons the cardiovascular system, composed of the heart and blood vessels, becomes functional first. Early in the third week, blood vessels and a primitive heart begin to form and by the end of that week the two are linked into a functional but primitive cardiovascular system. The primitive heart contains only two chambers at first but, between the fourth and fifth weeks, it takes on its adult appearance by developing four chambers: two upper *(atria)* and two lower *(ventricles)*.

The embryo's initial blood supply comes from the mother via the placenta, but by the second month, self-production of blood begins — first in the liver, then in the spleen, in bone marrow, and in lymph nodes. At birth, important circulatory changes take place, caused by the cessation of fetal blood circulation through the placenta and the onset of lung functioning.

The Urogenital System

The body's reproductive and elimination systems are closely associated. Parts of one system overlap and function as parts of the other system. The urinary system begins to develop during the fourth week and includes the:

- kidneys   a filter which collects body fluid wastes in the form of urine
- ureter   tubes carrying urine away from the kidneys
- bladder   the body's storage tank for urine
- urethra   the urine-eliminating canal connecting the bladder with the outside
- adrenal gland   a hormone-producing body

The reproductive system includes internal reproductive organs, genital ducts, and male or female external genitalia. Genetic sex is determined at fertilization but sexual differentiation does not begin until about the seventh week. Prior to that time both sexes have similar genital systems and thus all human embryos are potentially physically bisexual.

The Respiratory System

The respiratory system begins to emerge during the fourth week when a primitive pharynx develops, followed by the larynx, trachea, and the esophagus. Beginning with the fifth week, lung buds appear and begin to differentiate into the bronchi, the lungs, the pleural cavities, and the pleura, a membrane which surrounds the lungs. By 26 weeks, the lungs are normally sufficiently developed to permit survival if prematurely born. Around this time, *surfactant*, a chemical substance which covers the surface of the air cells lining the lungs prior to birth, is produced. At birth the lungs are about half-filled with fluids, which must be rapidly replaced with air. In this process, the birth cry (air being rapidly forced over the vocal cords) occurs.

33

The Digestive System

The primitive digestive system, consisting of three parts, begins to emerge during the fourth week. Included are:

- the *foregut*   contributes to development of the pharynx and the lower respiratory system, the esophagus, stomach, duodenum, liver, and pancreas
- the *midgut*   contributes to development of the duodenum, jejunum, ileum, cecum, appendix, and the colon
- the *hindgut*   contributes to the development of the colon, the rectum, and the upper portion of the anal canal

During the fifth week, embryonic development is so rapid that the abdomen becomes overcrowded. To avoid this overcrowded condition, the midgut moves into the umbilical cord and remains there until about the tenth week, when it moves back into the abdomen.

Branchial Apparatus

This apparatus consists of branchial arches, clefts (grooves), and muscles which form the face, tongue, palate, pharynx, and the neck. The arches appear as ridges on the site of the future head and neck, and are separated by grooves, or clefts. During the fourth week, face, ear, and neck structures begin to emerge. The roof of the mouth or palate begins to develop during the next week.

Skeletal and Muscular Systems

Mesodermic tissue begins to form into the body's skeletal and muscular systems during the fourth week. Arm, and then leg buds, also appear at this time. During the fifth week, extensive head growth occurs due to rapid growth of the brain. The elbow and wrists become visible, and primitive fingers begin to emerge. By the sixth week, the head has become visibly larger than the body's trunk, and primitive fingers and toes begin to develop. Thus, by the end of the first two months the embryo begins to look human. The head is now round, a neck exists, eyelids have emerged, and the limbs are well-developed, with well-differentiated fingers and toes.

The Nervous System and Sensory Organs

This system consists of many thousands of nerve cells elaborately interlaced and connecting all parts of the body. The nervous system consists of two parts: the central nervous system (CNS), or the brain and the spinal cord, and the peripheral nervous system, which includes neural pathways running throughout the body.

Figure 2-2 A diagram of brain areas and interconnections.

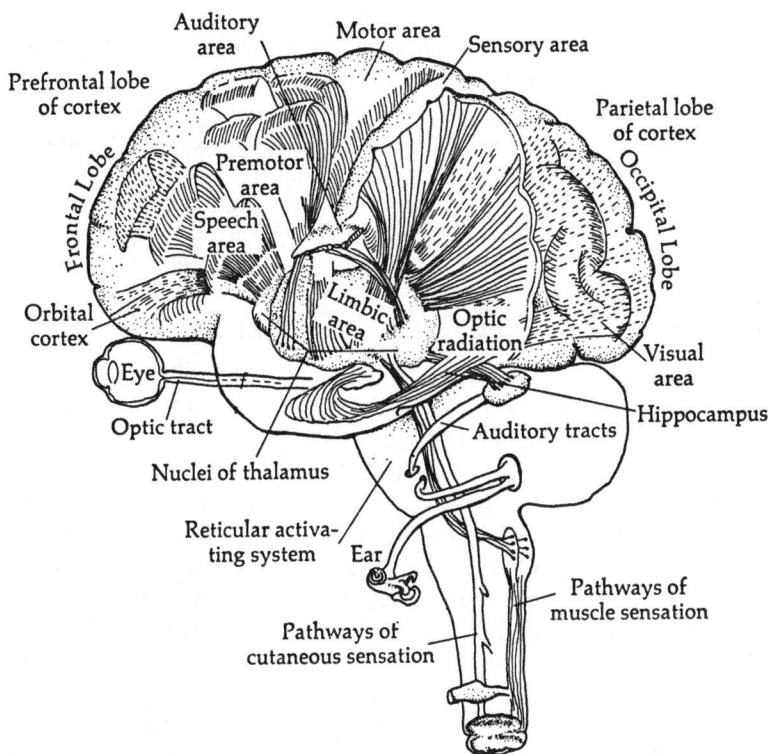

Auditory area
Motor area
Sensory area
Prefrontal lobe of cortex
Parietal lobe of cortex
Frontal Lobe
Occipital Lobe
Premotor area
Speech area
Limbic area
Optic radiation
Orbital cortex
Eye
Visual area
Optic tract
Auditory tracts
Hippocampus
Nuclei of thalamus
Reticular activating system
Ear
Pathways of muscle sensation
Pathways of cutaneous sensation

The nervous system regulates and coordinates body activities using three types of nerve cells or neurons: sensory, motor, and association. *Sensory* neurons transmit information from the body's sensory organs (eyes, ears, nose, mouth, and skin) and enable us to detect environmental stimuli through these organs. *Motor* neurons enable us to respond actively to environmental stimuli through impulses conveyed to the muscles. *Association* neurons connect sensory stimuli and motor actions through the central nervous system.

The CNS, which includes brain and spinal cord, is the center for integrating impulses traveling from higher to lower levels in the nervous system (voluntary behavior), and is also the site for reflex or nonvoluntary behavior (such as breathing, sneezing, eye-blinking). Several important areas of the brain, which facilitate coordination of voluntary and nonvoluntary processes, are outlined below. (See also Figure 2-2.)

Area	Function
• cerebrum	an association center (the signals for most actions originate here); receives sensory stimuli and translates, by motor neurons, into appropriate responses
• cerebellum	sorts out motor impulses and sends them to muscles at the appropriate time
• thalamus	acts as a relay center for incoming sensory impulses; regulates body temperature, appetite, water balance, carbohydrate and fat metabolism, blood pressure, emotional state, and sleep
• medulla	connects the spinal cord to the brain; contains nerve centers controlling many involuntary physiological processes like breathing, heart rate, blood vessel contraction/dilation, vomiting, etc.
• pons	connects the left and right hemispheres

The spinal cord connects and integrates sensory and motor neurons and thus allows for the production of purposeful and appropriate responses.

The nervous system begins to form during the third week when ectodermic tissue forms the neural plate, from which the neural tube and the neural crest are formed. The neural tube then differentiates into the central nervous system during the fourth week, and the neural crest begins to differentiate into the peripheral nervous system. The end of the neural tube that would be nearest the head develops into the brain and consists of the hindbrain, the midbrain, and the forebrain. The hindbrain differentiates into the lower portion of the brain stem, the medulla oblongata, the pons, and the cerebellum. The midbrain remains basically as it is and becomes the adult midbrain. The forebrain develops into the cerebrum, the largest part of the brain, which consists of two hemispheres. The surface layer of the two hemispheres contains five layers of neuron cell bodies and is called the cerebral cortex. The forebrain also gives rise to the hypothalamus, the thalamus, the epithalamus, and the pineal gland. In addition, part of the tissue forming the pituitary gland originates here; the remainder comes from the primitive mouth cavity.

The opposite end of the neural tube forms the spinal cord. The wall of this tube is composed of thick tissue, which forms all neurons and related nerve tissue of the spinal cord. Myelination of the spinal cord and CNS nerve fibers, which begins in midfetal life and continues for several years after birth, is the process by which the nerve fibers are coated with a fat-like substance called the *myelin sheath*. This sheath forms around portions of the nerve structures thus enabling impulses to be transmitted more efficiently.

Development of the eyes and ears begins in the fourth week. Eye development is first evident when a pair of optic grooves appears in the neural fold. As these grooves develop, optic vesicles form, connect with the forebrain, and become the optic stalks. At the same time the lens, retina, iris, and cornea are forming. Between the third and sixth week, eye development is in a critical period and eye formation can be seriously affected by environmental assault. The ears also begin to form during the fourth week: the inner ear develops from ectoderm tissue, the middle ear from the cartilages of the first two branchial arches, and the external ear out of the first branchial arch.

By the end of the embryonic period, the developing embryo has experienced phenomenal growth relative to its beginning status as a fertilized zygote. It is now about one inch long, and has well-formed arms, legs, fingers and toes; a human face with eyes, ears, a nose, and a mouth; a beating heart; and a responsive nervous system.

FETAL DEVELOPMENT

In the fetal period — (the next period of prenatal (prior to birth) development) — which extends from about the beginning of the second trimester to birth, the developing organism is called a *fetus*. During this period the remaining body parts appear and embryonic development is refined. The fetal trunk lengthens until normal body proportions are reached, and internal organs increase in their efficiency. These changes are outlined below.

Fetal Development

Week	Characteristic
12	fetus is about 3 inches long, weighs about three-quarters of an ounce; looks human in appearance; muscles are developing and spontaneous movements occur; external genitalia begin to appear; finger and toenails begin to form; eyelids begin to form
16	fetus is about 4 and ½'' in length; eyelid blinking begins; the mouth is capable of opening; hair begins to appear on head and body; hands are now capable of grasping
20	fetus is about 10 inches long and weighs about 8-9 ounces; sweat glands emerge; skin takes on adult form
24	eyes of fetus are now open; taste buds appear on tongue; capable of making crying sound, and of inhaling and exhaling
28	fetus can survive outside the womb if born prematurely
38	birth normally occurs

During the fetal period, spontaneous movements begin and continue to increase until birth. Kicking movements decrease but body squirming and head movement increase. By the fifth month the fetus has developed all the neurologically based reflexes necessary for survivial in the womb, while, at the same time, it is refining those reflexes that will be needed for survival outside the womb (urinating, swallowing, digestion reflexes, etc.). Finally, by about the seventh month, the fetus has developed to the point where life outside the womb is possible.

BIRTH

Birth occurs about 270 days after conception. As this time nears, the amount of calcium in the mother's pelvic joints decreases. enabling the mother's pelvis to open as widely as possible to facilitate the birth process. At the same time, the mother is developing larger and more flexible muscles around the uterus and vagina, to enable her to expel the fetus from her womb with the least discomfort. The fetus also prepares for birth by turning down in the womb so as to be born head first. When this turning down does not occur, the fetus is born buttocks first — a breech delivery. Although awkward, such a delivery is not necessarily abnormal. This shift in fetal position signals onset of labor. The process by which the fetus is expelled from the womb, labor, can begin as early as a few hours after the fetal shift has occurred, or as late as several weeks.

At birth, the condition of the neonate (newborn) is evaluated by attending physicians and delivery room nurses. One standardized system, in wide use today and developed by Apgar and Beck (1973), evaluates the general health status of the neonate 60 seconds after birth and again 5 minutes later. The Apgar Scales, which also seek to identify potential birth defects, include ratings for:

- Appearance, or skin color   if entire body is blue, rate 0
  if body is pink but arms and legs are bluish, rate 1
  if entire body is pink, rate 2

- Heart Rate (pulse)   no pulse, rate 0
  pulse rate less than 100, rate 1
  pulse rate over 100, rate 2

- Grimace (crying when   no response, rate 0
  slapped on feet)   slight cry or grimace, rate 1
  vigorous crying, rate 2

- Muscle Activity   limp and motionless, rate 0
  some arm and leg movement, rate 1
  active overall body motions, rate 2

- Breathing   no respiration, rate 0
  slow, irregular breathing, rate 1
  strong efforts to breathe, rate 2

Most normal babies score between 7 and 10, with higher scores indicating an active and vigorous baby. Scores below 4 usually suggest a baby in critical condition.

PHYSICAL DEVELOPMENT AFTER BIRTH

Body Development

When first emerging from the womb, the fetus weighs between 2.5 and 4 kilograms and is about 50 centimeters long. Sensory and neurological systems are relatively complete at birth, but muscular systems and body are very immature when compared to their final adult characteristics. With use and exercise, the muscles quickly strengthen and grow larger. Not only does body size increase, but relative proportions change drastically between birth and adolescence. Between ages one to five, body growth occurs most rapidly, most of it in the first three years, then levels off until puberty, when the adolescent growth spurt occurs.

Physical growth rate in the child is conditioned by many factors. Some of these are listed below.

1. *Genetics* — rate of growth tends to run in families, faster in some than in others;
2. *Race* — some racial groups (for example, blacks) tend to grow more rapidly than others — especially in terms of skeletal bone structure;
3. *Nutrition* — undernourishment can directly slow growth rate;
4. *Disease* — illness and infection may not only affect specific parts of the body in particular ways, but tend also to slow the overall rate of bodily growth.

Because several of these factors are related to atypical physical development, they will be discussed in more detail in the next chapter.

The general metabolism of bodily function gradually changes with age. Endurance and resistance to fatigue increase, and cyclical variations from sleep to wakefulness slow progressively. The young infant experiences peaks of activity and requires frequent feeding and rest to recover. The toddler eats less often but still needs a snack between meals. Although sleeping or resting less frequently, the toddler still needs a morning quiet time and an afternoon nap. Planning for day care and school programs must take these facts into account, since insufficient sleep and rest or hunger tend to have a much more disruptive effect on children than on adults.

Development of the Central Nervous System

The infant's brain and nervous system are not complete at birth. Although brain size is approaching its adult form, functioning is still limited, and rapid nervous system changes occur during the first few years of life. Most fully developed at birth is the midbrain, which controls such activities as sleeping and waking, elimination, and attention, and is the seat of reflex activity essential to survival.

These reflexes include the

1. *rooting reflex:* turning the head in response to stimulation near the mouth, which facilitates locating the nipple
2. *sucking reflex:* automatic sucking movements in response to lip stimulation
3. *swallowing reflex*

The midbrain area also governs primitive muscular reflexes like the Moro, the Babinski, and the grasp described later in this chapter.

The central nervous system associates and processes all incoming stimuli (sensory neurons) and all outgoing responses (motor neurons). Neural pathways, which travel from the brain down the spinal cord and spread out throughout the body, respond to external or internal stimuli, like changes in the environment or internal indications of need, by sending very rapid messages back to the central nervous system. Here the information is interpreted, an appropriate response selected, then relayed back to the body along the same pathways and the chosen response pattern is carried out. This response may involve simply moving to a warmer part of the room if one is cold or finding something to eat when hungry. The response pattern could also be withdrawing the hand from hot water or something as complex and integrated as touching auto brakes, changing steering patterns, watching oncoming traffic, and throwing up the arm to hold back a child from possible injury—all in a split second.

Without efficient processing of sensory stimuli the body reaction would be chaotic, in the presence of a multiplicity of nerves throughout the body. The saving element is a protective coating (myelin sheaths) developed around individual nerves, acting as insulation and increasing the efficiency with which messages are transmitted throughout the nervous system.

The nervous system contains literally billions of nerve cells or neurons arranged systematically throughout the body, linking together to form nerves. Each neuron is an elongated cell body containing hair-like extensions called *dendrites.* Neurons do not touch each other; no solid neural pathways exist. Instead, there is a small gap, a *synapse,* between each neuron. Information is transmitted along neural pathways by essentially electrochemical means. Stimulation of a part of the nervous system produces electrical activity, caused by changes in the positive and negative charges associated with interior and exterior parts of the nerve; this activity causes the impulse to ''sweep'' across the nerve fiber towards the synaptic gap. Here, a conducter or carrier chemical, called *Acetylcholine* (ACh), is produced to more or less ''squirt'' this impulse across the synaptic gap between the two neurons, allowing the continued transmission of the impulse. When the impulse reaches the synaptic gap of a second neuron, ACh again ''squirts'' it across to a third neuron, and so forth, until the message reaches the brain or muscles, a process requiring only a few milliseconds for completion. A second chemical substance, *Cholineoterase* (ChE), "cleans up" after each transmission across each synapse by neutralizing the ACh remaining around the synapse once the message impulse has passed. The neural pathway is now clear, permitting later transmissions of other impulses carrying other information.

Voluntary and Reflexive Behavior

Infants normally possess certain neuromuscular capacities for reflexive and nonreflexive behavior which prepare them for survival after birth. At first, these voluntary and nonreflexive activities are typically very diffuse and disorganized, while reflexive (automatic and involuntary) behaviors are more specific and focused. Some of these reflexive behaviors which facilitate survival are listed below.

Eyes: eyes close in response to light or air puffs; the pupils dilate and contract in response to light

Respiratory and Gastrointestinal: salivation; swallowing; sneezing; coughing; gagging; yawning

Abdominal and Pelvic: vomiting; hiccoughing; urinating; defecating

Three specific primitive reflexes which undergo significant developmental change as part of the normal developmental sequence are particularly important because they have diagnostic value for normal development:

1. *Plantar Reflex:* when the outer edge of the sole of the foot is touched, the big toe bends. In young infants this reflex includes the fanning out of the other toes as well and is labeled the *Babinski Reflex*. With age, this reflex becomes more difficult to elicit—an index of the infant's increasing shift from midbrain to cortical control over motor behavior.

2. *Grasp Reflex:* The grasp or *palmar* reflex is developmentally similar to the Babinski. When the infant's palm is stimulated the four fingers close into the palm. Gradually in the first six months of life this reflexive behavior gives way to voluntary behavior, indicating appropriate neurological development.

3. *Moro Reflex:* evoked by intense stimuli, such as pounding the table on which the infant is lying. When this happens, the infant will swing both arms out away from the body and up over the head and then bring them back. Like the other, this reflex tends to disappear after about the first four months of life, and is used as an index of appropriate neurological development.

Early Sensory Development

Technically, all sense organs are ready for use at normal birth, but since the uterine environment provides little opportunity for their use and exercise, they are not fully functional at birth.

Vision

The infant's eyes are open at birth, and the pupillary reflex (which controls the amount of light admitted to the sensory retinal surface within the eye) is intact. Since pigmentation is lacking, newborns are almost always blue- or grey-eyed (brown pigmentation appears later in those genetically destined to have dark eyes), but this lack is not thought to alter ocular sensory capacity. The ability to focus both eyes may take several days, so that coordinated focus is usually irregular and inconsistent for many weeks. Visual tracking (coordinated eye activity in following a moving object) is usually more a function of neuromuscular practice than of structural inadequacy and is usually not possible until about the second week or so. Thus, despite its instability the infant's visual system is ready to use at birth.

Hearing

Although the auditory system is apparently completely developed at birth, the auditory canals normally contain some amniotic fluid, and clearance of this obstruction to hearing may take several hours or longer.

Touch and other senses

Although the newborn responds to touch and vibration, these senses are generally not as well developed as the others, like smell and taste, but follow the developmental pattern described for vision and hearing. That is, all the sensory systems appear to be fully developed at birth and become more efficient with experience.

Motor Development

From birth, infants are capable of active interaction with their environment. Much of this activity is not just random motor activity (some of these non-random behaviors are shown in Table 2-1, p.43). The cortex, considerably underdeveloped at birth, takes control of motor activity as it develops, and substitutes deliberate and controlled responses for the earlier reflexive or uncontrolled responses. Partial development of the brain's motor area at birth permits some control of hands, arms, and upper trunk area. Motor development of the lower trunk region is slower, however, and the child doesn't develop complete control of leg movements until the second year.

This developmental lag defines the sequence of development of the infant's

---

Table 2-1 Behavioral Responses Available to Newborns and Young Infants

Visual Responses

- coordinate eye movements
- make compensatory movements
- visually pursue objects
- fixate on an object
- vary pupil size in response to light
- open and close eyelids

Facial Responses

- open and close mouth
- compress or purse lips in response to stimulation
- automatically suck objects
- yawn, grimace, or smile

Oral Responses

- cry
- cough
- sneeze
- swallow
- coo

Head Movements

- balance head in response to shifts in body position
- turn head to the left or right in response to stimulation near mouth (rooting reflex)
- move head up or down

Arm, Hand, and Leg Movements

- close hand (grasping reflex)
- rub face
- flex arms and legs
- extend arms and legs
- kick
- "step" when held upright with feet touching a surface

---

interaction with the world. The earliest interactions with the environment occur through the senses, then through turning the head, lifting the trunk, grasping, and eventually by crawling and then walking. Developing motor behavior is thus characterized by two concurrent patterns: *cephalocaudel* (development proceeds from the head to the tail region) and *proximodistal* (development proceeds from the body's inner regions to its extremities). Following this pattern, upper trunk muscles develop before lower trunk muscles and the body's large inner muscles develop before the fine muscles in the hands and feet. Therefore, children usually develop skills involving large muscles earlier than they do skills based on small or fine muscle activity, i.e., climbing and running develop before writing or cutting with scissors.

This is only a brief listing of some of the infant's available motor behavior. As can be seen, the infant is capable of a good bit more at birth than just sucking, crying, and randomly waving arms and legs.

During the first five years, children develop mastery of a number of essential psychomotor skills. Using large muscles in the upper trunk, they develop the ability to crawl, to sit up, and to pull to the standing position. When walking ability develops, it is quickly extended to include walking forward and then backwards, up steps and then down steps, running, hopping, and skipping. As control over these gross muscle activities develops, children also begin to demonstrate more control over activities involving small muscles (fine motor activities). Below is an illustrative list of increasingly more sophisticated motor behaviors and general norms for their appearance.

Behavior	Approximate Age at Onset (in months)
Walking	
Sits alone for 1 minute	8
Crawls	9
Stands by holding on	10
Creeps	11
Stands alone	15
Walks Alone	16
Walks backwards	18—21
Eating	
Eats with a spoon	15—36
Drinks from a cup	18
Pours from a pitcher	36

Writing

Makes crude scribbles	24
Makes horizontal and vertical lines	36—48
Forms recognizable letters	60—72

Playing with Blocks

Makes simple structures (rows & towers)	24—36
Makes complex structures (bridges & enclosures)	36—48
Uses in dramatic play to represent objects	48—60
Reproduces actual objects	60—72

Playing Motor Games

Kicks ball forward	22
Throws ball overhand	23
Catches bounced ball	48—52
Pedals tricycle	24—32
Climbing	36

The Development of Prehension

Prehension refers to controlled visually directed reaching, not just to grasping activity, and its development is important because of the control it gives the infant over the environment. The emergence of visually directed reaching indicates the beginnings of the infant's attempts to coordinate visual and motor systems, i.e., eye-hand coordination. Two scientists, Jean Piaget (1952) and Burton White (1971) have investigated the emergence of visually directed reaching, and their findings may be summarized as follows:

Months	Behaviors
1—2	objects being sucked aren't being grasped by hand; the hand is an object to be sucked; the infant doesn't look at what is being grasped
2—3	eyes follow hand's motions but the hand doesn't try to grasp what the eyes see; this is a "swiping" behavior
3—4	the hand grasps the object being sucked; the grasped object is brought to the mouth to be sucked
4—5	the hand reaches and grasps the seen object
5—6	true visually directed reaching occurs: the infant reaches for an object and examines it before bringing it to the mouth to be sucked

Table 2-2 The Endocrine System

Endocrine	Location	Hormone	Function	Developmental Changes
Pituitary	head	growth activating hormone, and stimulating hormones for thyroid, adrenals, and ovaries	master gland, with thymus acts to regulate growth; with thyroid acts to regulate metabolism; with ovaries acts to regulate female ovulation	active throughout life span
Thyroid	throat	thyroxine	regulates general metabolic rate	active throughout life span, but possibly more active in middle years
Parathyroid	throat	parathormone parathyroxine	regulates metabolism of specific chemicals affecting muscle tone, fatigue, and bone growth	active throughout life span; possibly more active in middle years
Adrenal	back	adrenaline, epinephrine, norepinephrine	assists with stress and demands for activity	active throughout life span

Adrenal cortex	back	corticosteroids	regulates salts in body fluids; promotes healing and relief of pain	active throughout life span
Pancreas	abdomen	insulin	regulates sugar metabolism in body tissues and storage of sugar in blood	active throughout life span; some deterioration in old age
Gonads	groin	androsterone, testosterone	regulate secondary sex characteristics (beard, hair etc.) and sexual arousal	inactive in childhood, active in mature years, and decline in activity in old age.
Ovaries (female)	abdomen	estrogen	regulate secondary sex characteristics (breasts, etc.) and sexual arousal	inactive in childhood, active in mature years, and decline in activity after middle age.
Thymus	chest	(not specifically identified)	regulates growth rate and immunity mechanisms	active in childhood, declines and disappears after puberty
Pineal	head	not specifically identified	not clearly identified	not clearly identified

Endocrine Development

The *endocrine* (ductless glands) system is a series of glands responsible for producing chemical substances called *hormones,* which regulate and integrate body functions. Development of these glands occurs early and plays an important role in body development. The production of glandular substances varies with stage of development. For example, the thymus and the pituitary are glands which help regulate growth rate, and the size and the activity of these two glands vary with age. The gonads (primary sex glands) are relatively inactive in childhood, more active in young adulthood, and again less active in the middle and late years. Some of the major functions of the endocrine system and their developmental changes are listed in Table 2-2.

Diet, Nutrition, and Medical Care

In the United States, we rarely see dramatically undernourished infants or children. But more moderate forms of malnutrition do occur within our population, not merely because of poverty, but often through careless planning, personal family tastes, superstitions, and habits. Infants and small children may suffer a shortage of iron, which can lead to anemia, or iodine, which can cause thyroid problems. Protein deficiencies are associated with sensory, perceptual, and mental lethargy (when mild) and with dwarfing and immobility (when severe). Parasitic infections, like pinworms, are more common than many people think and their effects can be similar to protein deficiencies.

While nature typically performs very well to insure the survival and development of fetus and infant, there is still much that can be done to assist nature. Public health, welfare services to families, and home economics extension services can contribute significantly to better diet and health care. Among the economically disadvantaged such provisions are seriously inadequate or totally lacking. The greatest tragedy occurs in those conditions which could be easily remedied if diagnosed early and given proper attention, but which become partially or totally irreversible at later stages. Middle-class children, especially in urban areas, typically have the benefit of good diets and consistent medical attention, so birth defects are much rarer among them as compared to the rate of birth defects among children of minority groups and the poor. Within these populations, inadequate diet and health conditions often go unrecognized until the child enters school—or even later—when it is frequently too late for total remediation. Middle-class teachers, believing that such conditions are detected prior to starting school, frequently regard the behavioral manifestations of such problems (inattentiveness, disobedience, distractibleness, and shyness) as social-adjustment problems rather than as medical ones. Thus, early and consistent diagnostic medical attention for all infants can significantly contribute towards physical, cognitive, and social growth and development.

REFERENCES AND SUGGESTED READINGS

Apgar, V., & Beck, J. *Is my baby allright?* New York: Trident Press, 1973.

Balinsky, B. I. *An introduction to embryology* (4th ed.). Philadelphia: W. B. Saunders, 1975.

Brasel, J. Cellular changes in intrauterine malnutrition. In M. Winick (Ed.), *Nutrition and fetal development*. New York: Wiley, 1974.

Brazelton, J. B. *Neonatal behavioral assessment scale.* Philadelphia: Lippincott, 1973.

Cratty, B. J. *Perceptual and motor development in infants and children.* Los Angeles: Macmillan, 1970.

Cohen, D. J., Dribble E., Grawe, J. M., & Polkin, W. Separating identical from fraternal twins. *Archives of General Psychiatry*, 1973, *29*, 465-469.

Eichorn, D. Physiological development. In P. Mussen (Ed.), *Carmichael's manual of child psychology*. New York: Wiley, 1970.

Fuller, J. L., & Thompson, W. R. *Behavior genetics.* New York: Wiley, 1960.

Gardner, E. J. *Principles of genetics* (4th ed.). New York: Wiley, 1972.

Gottlieb, G. Conceptions of prenatal development: Behavioral embryology. *Psychological Review*, 1976, *83*, 215-234.

Hetherington, E. M. (Ed.). *Review of child development research* (Vol. 5). Chicago: University of Chicago Press, 1976.

Horowitz, F. D. (Ed.) *Review of child development research* (Vol. 4). Chicago: University of Chicago Press, 1975.

Horowitz, N. H. The gene. *Scientific American*, 1956, *195*, 78-90.

Ledsma, S. & Fitzgerald, H. E. *A physical exercise and massage program for infants reared in groups* (Technical Report #5). Institute for Family and Child Study, Michigan State University, East Lansing, Mich, 1972.

Levy, J. *The baby exercise book.* New York: Pantheon, 1975.

Loehlin, J. C., Lindzey, G., & Spuhler, J. N. *Race differences in intelligence. San Francisco: W: H. Freeman, 1975 (See especially Chapter 8.)*

McClearn, G. E. Genetic influences on behavior and development. In P. Mussen (Ed.), *Carmichael's manual of child psychology*. New York: Wiley, 1970.

McDavid, J. W., & Garwood, S. G. *Understanding children.* Lexington, Mass.: D. C. Heath, 1978.

McLaughlin, C. J. *The black parents' handbook.* New York: Harcourt-Brace, Jovanovich, 1976.

Meredith, H. V. Somatic changes during human prenatal life. *Child Development*, 1975, *46*, 603-610.

Moore, K. L. *Before we are born: Basic embryology and birth defects.* Philadelphia: W. B. Saunders, 1974.

Nilsson, L. *How was I born?* New York: Delacorte Press, 1975.

Piaget, J. *The origins of intelligence in children.* New York: International Universities Press, 1952.

Stern, C. *Principles of human genetics* (3rd ed.). San Francisco: W. H. Freeman, 1973.

Tanner, J. M. Physical growth. In P. Mussen (Ed.), *Carmichael's manual of child psychology*. New York: Wiley, 1970.

Warren, N. Malnutrition and mental development. *Psychological Bulletin*, 1973, *80*, 324-328.

White, B. *Human infants: Experience and psychological development.* Englewood Cliffs: Prentice-Hall, 1971.

White, B. *The first three years of life.* Englewood Cliffs: Prentice-Hall, 1976.

Winick, M. (Ed.). *Nutrition and fetal development.* New York: Wiley, 1974.

Chapter 3

Physical and Physiological Bases of Handicaps

S. Gray Garwood

CONGENITAL MALFORMATIONS

Physical growth is under the control of the individual's genetic blueprint, which guides and controls both the rate and the nature of physical development. Associated with the maturational aspects of growth, however, are a host of environmental events or factors which are capable of altering nature's intent. Under optimal conditions, genetic and environmental factors interact to provide for normal conception, prenatal development, and birth. But there are times when conditions are not optimal, either as a result of a genetic accident or from environmental interactions which are hostile to normal development. When either of these abnormalities occurs, the basis for one or more handicapping conditions exists. Most handicapping conditions then are the result of *congenital malformations,* a term that refers to physical malformations present at birth. They may be large or small, inside the body or on its surface, cause about 15 percent of newborn deaths, and are the major source of severe illness and death during childhood. This chapter will describe many of these congenital conditions, as well as some of the diseases and injuries which can occur postnatally but which also give rise to handicaps in children.

We can identify two major causes of congenital malformations: one is genetic, the other is some type of environmental intervention into the course of normal development. Genetically caused malformations result from chromosomal abnormalities.

Chromosomal Abnormalities

You will recall from the previous chapter that genes provide information about how different cells will be combined to create neural tissue, hair texture, eye color, the correct number of limbs, and so forth. Chromosomes, which contain this genetic information, are arranged in pairs called *autosomes*. Man normally has 22 pairs of autosomes plus the sex chromosome, making a total of 23 pairs or 46 chromosomes. Normal development and tissue growth occur when the 22 autosomal pairs divide by mitosis. Remember that in this process the 46 chromosomes split into 96 and, when the cell divides into 2 daughter cells, each then has the normal complement of 46 chromosomes. But sometimes the mitotic process is flawed and chromosomal abnormalities stemming from numerical errors result.

While the 22 autosomes divide by the mitotic process, the sex or 23rd chromosome pair divide by meiosis. In this process the 46 male (XY) or female (XX) chromosomes are split into 23 at the top of the cell and 23 at the bottom. When the cell divides at the middle the resulting gametes have only half the normal number. This is neccssary so that when fertilization occurs the zygote will have a full complement of 46 chromosomes, half from each parent, and no more.

Numerical Abnormalities

Changes in the normal diploid number of chromosomes (46) may result in fewer than the normal number, a condition called *hypodiploidy* (usually 45), or more than the normal number, *hyperdiploidy* (usually 47 to 49). This indicates that some chromosomal pairs have more or less than the usual paired arrangement. When the affected chromosomal pair has only one of the pair, it is a *monosomy;* when it has more than the usual number, it is usually a *trisomy* (3) or a mosaic arrangement *(multisomy).*

Monosomies which occur from improper mitotic division are rare in living persons since an embryo without the normal supply of autosomes will usually not live. However, a monosomy can result from improper meiotic cell division and the resulting female can survive. This rare condition (3 out of 10,000 female births) is called *Turner's syndrome* (X,O), and the female has a characteristic short webbed neck, short fingers, low-set ears, a triangular mouth, and little sexual differentiation, especially after puberty occurs. Usually such a child is also mentally retarded.

Trisomies are more frequent and can occur in autosomes and in the sex chromosome. *Kleinfelter's syndrome* originates from a sex chromosome trisomy (XXY), a pattern resulting in a male with female characteristics, both of body shape and in glandular development. Usually these children are also mentally retarded as well as sterile. Autosome trisomies include a variety of syndromes with *Down's syndrome* the most frequent. Other sex chromosome trisomies are described in Table 3-1.

Down's syndrome, a trisomy of the 21st chromosomal pair, is believed to result from two different sources. One type results when, during the meiotic process, the female's 21st chromosomal pair doesn't split, resulting in a female gamete with 2 number 21s. When this gamete is fertilized, the zygote has 47 chromosomes, with 3 on pair number 21. This is Down's syndrome which results from *nondysjunction.*

An abnormal fusing of chromosome pairs (usually between pairs 15 and 21 and 21 and 22) results not in an abnormal number of chromosomes but an abnormal amount of chromosomal material. This is called the *translocation* type of mongolism or Down's. Regardless of the source of the defect, the child has a roundish head and almond-shaped eyes, creating an Oriental or Mongol appearance, and usually considerable mental retardation. (In rare cases, a child may have all the external appearance of mongolism but be of normal intelligence. This serves to illustrate the importance of not diagnosing strictly by external appearance.) Other autosome trisomies are described in Table 3-1.

Structural Abnormalities

Deviations from the normal amount of chromosomal material present in chromosomal pairs will result in structural abnormalities. One type of chromosomal structural defect involves the faulty or defective arrangement of chromosomal material within the normal 23 pairs. Part of the necessary chromosomal material may have been accidentally deleted in the cell-division process. Several such structural defects have been identified, including partial deletion of a portion of the 18th chromosomal pair. When this happens the child will suffer from severe mental retardation, microcephaly (abnormally small head), and other gross congenital anomalies. Another such defect is the *cri du chat* syndrome which occurs when part of chromosomal pair number 5 is incomplete. The child will be severely mentally retarded, and, in about half the cases, will sound like a cat mewing due to abnormal larynx development. Cri du chat syndrome is also characterized by a small brain (oligophrenia) and progressive degeneration and loss of cells and body tissues, congenital heart disease, and other gross anomalies.

About 10 to 15 percent of congenital abnormalities are caused by genetic mutations and result in such conditions as *achondroplasia* (short limbs, large head, and abdominal protrusion) or *polydactyly* (extra, often incompletely formed fingers or toes).

Using recently developed technology, scientists are now able to determine early in pregnancy the normalcy or abnormality of chromosomal structures in unborn children. With use of biopsy techniques, a sample of amniotic fluid is extracted and analyzed, allowing chromosome pairs to be identified. If abnormalities are found, parents may then decide if abortion is warranted.

Environmentally Caused Malformations

Teratogens are noxious or harmful environmental agents which can interfere with normal growth processes, especially if such interference occurs at a critical developmental period. We generally recognize three such critical periods for physical growth and development. First, the two weeks after the zygote is fertilized, when environmental disturbances can prevent the zygote from implanting

Table 3-1 Chromosomal Abnormalities

Sex Chromosome Trisomies

Chromosome Arrangement	Sex	Risk Factor	Characteristics
47, XXX	Female Phenotype	1:1000	• Normal in appearance, fertile, may be retarded
47, XXY	Male	1:500	• *Klinefelter's syndrome;* small testes, hyalinization of seminiferous tubules, aspermatogenesis, may be retarded
47, XYY	Male	1:1000	• Normal in appearance, often tall, may have personality disorder

Autosome Trisomies

Down's Syndrome*		1:600	• Mental retardation, flat nasal bridge, slant to eyelids, protruding tongue, simian crease in palm, congenital heart defects
E Syndrome (Pairs 17-18)		1:3300	• Mental retardation, growth retardation, prominent skull (back), short sternum, ventricular septal defect, micrognathia, low-set malformed ears, flexed fingers
D Syndrome (Pairs 13-15)		1:5500	• Mental deficiency, sloping forehead, malformed ears, microphthalamous bilateral cleft lip and/or palate, polydactyly, rocker-heels, short-lived

*Represent 10-15% of institutionalized mental defectives.

itself in the uterine wall, and can also cause early death and abortion. The second, and *most* critical period, ranges from about day 13 to 60 days after conception, a time when all body tissue and organs are developing, each with a different critical point. (Table 3-2 illustrates this for separate body structures.) The third is the fetal period when environmental interference can result in physiological defects, minor morphological abnormalities, and functional disturbances of the central nervous system.

Several of the teratogenic agents capable of altering the normal course of development and the effects of these agents on the developing organism are outlined below.

Androgenic Agents	synthetic progestins used to prevent abortion; have produced masculinization of female fetuses
Antibiotics	Tetracycline therapy during 2nd and 3rd trimesters may cause minor tooth defects and discoloration; pencillin is considered harmless
Antitumor Agents	tumor-inhibiting chemicals like *Aminopterin* or *Methotrexate* can induce major congenital malformations, especially of CNS
Thyroid Drugs	*potassium iodides* and *radioactive iodines* may cause congenital goiters *propylthiouracil* interferes with thyroxin formation in the fetus and may cause goiter
Thalidomide	an estimated 7000 infants malformed by this drug; effects ranged from total absence of limbs *(amelia)* through intermediate stages of development to *micromelia* (short limbs); may cause malformation of other structures
LSD and Marijuana	conflicting views about both; LSD may be teratogenic early in pregnancy; there are reports of limb malformation and abnormalities of the CNS; limb malformations have also been reported following use of LSD and marijuana

Infectious agents (a virus or a parasite) can also alter the normal sequence of development, depending on time of exposure. Several of these structure-altering infections are summarized below.

Rubella is infectious German measles. Fifteen to 20 percent of infants born to women who have had rubella during the first trimester are congenitally malformed, usually with eye, heart, and ear disorders.

Table 3-2 Critical Periods in Embryonic and Fetal Development

Developing Structures	Weeks during Which Major Damage Can Occur:	Weeks during Which Minor Damage Can Occur:
CNS	3 - 5½	5½ - 38
Heart	3½ - 6½	6½ - 8
Arms	4½ - 7	8
Eyes	4½ - 8½	8½ - 38
Legs	4½ - 7	8
Teeth	6½ - 8	8 - 16
Palate	6½ - 12	12 - 16
External Genitalia	7½ - 15	15 - 38
Ear	4 - 13	

Syphilis may be transmitted from an infected mother to the unborn child, but normally only in the latter half of pregnancy. This disease can kill the fetus; if the fetus survives, it may be weak, deformed, and mentally retarded. Its effects are most serious after the fourth month of pregnancy, so early treatment is necessary.

Cytomegalovirus is a viral infection, which, if contracted during the 2nd to 3rd trimesters, causes brain abnormalities *(microcephaly)* and eye abnormalities *(micropthalmia).*

Toxoplasma gondii is an intercellular parasite contracted from eating raw meat or poorly cooked meat, or by contact with infected animals. The parasite can cross the placental membrane and infect the fetus, causing destructive changes in brain and eye tissue, which results in microcephaly, microphthalmia, and hydrocephaly.

Erythroblastosis Fetalis is a disease resulting from genetically determined differences between the blood of the mother and that of the unborn child. If the embryo inherits a protein substance called the *Rh factor* from the father, and the mother lacks this substance, serious consequences can occur to the embryo if any of its blood accidentally mixes with the mother's blood. This is usually prevented by the placenta's filtration process, which allows for selective interchange of most plasma substances between the mother and the embryo. Since blood corpuscles are too large to pass directly through the membrane from either side, then, unless the placenta is torn, no problem exists for the *Rh positive* embryo that is carried by an *Rh negative* mother. But if the placental lining is torn and blood corpuscles containing the Rh positive factor from the embryo seep into the mother's bloodstream, then treatment for an infection ensues. The mother's body will generate antibodies to fight off this infection, and these antibodies are capable of passing through the placenta and entering the embryo's bloodstream. Here the mother's antibodies are capable of destroying large numbers of the embryo's oxygen-supplying red blood cells, and, if cell number is greatly reduced, death can occur. Less serious consequences include severe anemia, jaundice, and mental retardation.

In addition to teratogens and infections, fetal and embryonic development can be hampered by:

- *Irradiation:* X-ray treatment of pregnant mothers during the embryo's susceptible development period can cause microcephaly, mental retardation, and skeletal malformation. There is no evidence that diagnostic X-rays cause such abnormalities but caution is advised, especially during the first trimester.
- *Alcohol: Fetal alcohol syndrome,* a condition resulting from excessive alcohol consumption by the mother during pregnancy. Fetal-alcohol-syndrome infants are born with physical and mental disorders.
- *Diets:* Vitamins, minerals, proteins, and other essentials are transmitted through the placenta to the fetus. Inadequate diet may cause spontaneous abortions, premature births, stillbirths, physical deformities, and, perhaps, intellectual impairment.
- *Maternal Smoking:* There is evidence of a relationship between the amount of maternal use of tobacco and fetal heart defects and prematurity.
- *Maternal Emotional State:* Emotional changes in the mother which cause the increase in certain body chemicals (e.g., adrenalin) appear also to influence fetal development. Mothers who are irritable, anxious, and emotional during the later stages of pregnancy are more likely to produce infants that are hyperactive, irritable, and prone to sleeping and eating problems.
- *Maternal Age:* The years 20 to 35 seem to be the best years for child-bearing. Mothers below or above this age range have a disproportionate number of mortalities and a higher percentage of mentally retarded children.

EFFECTS OF CONGENITAL MALFORMATION ON DEVELOPING ORGANISM

The Cardiovascular System

The complexity of the cardiovascular system makes congenital malformations relatively common (0.7 percent of all live births). Three such malformations are *patent foramen ovale, patent ductus arteriosus,* and *ventricular septal defects* (VSD). The first condition results when the foramen ovale (opening between left and right atrium) fails to close. The second condition—the most common cardiac malformation associated with maternal rubella infection—occurs when the opening between the aorta and the ductus arteriosus fails to close as it should (usually by the 2nd week after birth). This condition occurs two to three times more frequently in females than in males. The last malformation is the most frequently reported cardiac defect and is a result of inadequate tissue growth and fusion that prevents improper closure of the dividing wall between the two ventricle cavities.

The Urogenital System

Congenital malformations of the urogenital system are also relatively common, at least in respect to the system's eliminative aspects. Kidney and ureter abnormalities occur in 3 to 4 percent of the population, and include duplication of the upper urinary tract, absence of one kidney, and abnormally positioned kidney(s). Reproductive abnormalities are less common but do occur. Gonadal sex (development of ovaries or testes) is controlled by the Y chromosome: if a Y is present, testes will develop and male hormones are produced to stimulate development of the male genital system; if there is no Y chromosome, internal and external female genitalia develop. Cases of true hermaphrodites are extremely rare: when it occurs both ovarian and testicular tissue are present, and the individual may appear as male or female but will have ambiguous external genitalia. More common are errors in sex determination known as *male* or *female pseudohermaphroditism* and *testicular feminization*. Male pseudohermaphrodites have a 46, XY chromosome constitution; external and internal genitalia are intersexual, most likely from insufficient necessary hormones or because the structures were formed after the critical period for their development. Female pseudohermaphrodites have a 46, XX chromosome makeup and most frequently have masculinized external genitalia but no ovarian abnormality. This condition probably results from excessive androgen production by fetal adrenal glands. Testicular feminization is very rare and the individual appears as a normal female but has testes and XY sex chromosomes.

Skeletal and Muscular Systems

Most skeletal and muscular malformations are genetically induced, but a number result from genetic and environmental interaction. Some examples include *Acrania* (partial or total absence of the cranium) and *Spina Bifida Occulta* (lack of closure of the vertebrae in the spinal column; this is common and frequently not obvious since the skin may cover the malformation). Major limb malformations are rare, but the drug thalidomide was responsible for major limb malformations in about 7,000 infants born between 1957 and 1962. Minor limb malformations are relatively common and include such conditions as polydactyly (extra fingers or toes), syndactyly (fusion of fingers or toes), and clubfoot *(Talipes Equinovarus),* which occurs about twice as many times in males.

Branchial Apparatus

Congenital malformation originates usually during the change of branchial apparatus into adult structures. Perhaps the most common are *cleft lip* and *cleft palate.* Cleft lip is a malformation of the upper lip, occurring about once in every 950 births, with or without cleft palate. Cleft palate occurs once in 2,500 births, also with or without cleft lip. Clefts are either genetically or environmentally induced and result from faulty tissue fusion.

The Digestive System

Congenital malformations include common conditions like *Pyloric Stenosis,* a narrowing of the opening between the stomach and the duodenum, which occurs once in every 700 male births and once in every 1,000 female births. Others include intestinal and anal malformations.

The Respiratory System

Major congenital malformations of the lower respiratory system are rare. Most common is *Tracheoesophageal Fistula,* an abnormal passage most frequently connecting the trachea and the upper portion of the esophagus, and occurring about once in 2,500 births. In this condition, as soon as an infant is fed, choking occurs, caused by the food's passage into the respiratory tract. In *hyaline membrane disease,* a newborn respiratory disorder, a major factor is absence of surfactant, causing formation of a thin membrane inside the lung which interferes with breathing.

The Nervous System

Congenital malformations of the CNS are common, mostly caused by defective closure of the neural tubes during the third and fourth weeks. Such defects may affect the nervous system or may include surrounding tissues, like bone or muscle tissues. Spina bifida occulta (described earlier) and spina bifida cystria are two examples. This latter condition is a severe type of spina bifida involving an external protrusion of the spinal cord through a defective vertebra. Spina bifida cystria, depending on the extent of the malformation, may involve partial or complete skeletal muscle paralysis.

Sensory Organs

Most congenital eye abnormalities are rare but two fairly common ones are cataracts and glaucoma, both resulting from maternal rubella infection. Inherited recessive genes are the most common cause of congenital deafness and rubella virus infection is a major environmental factor contributing to deafness.

METABOLIC DISORDERS

In 1934, Folling related the presence of phenylketones in the urine with mental retardation. This discovery gave credence to Garrod's (1909) early statement that inborn metabolic errors could be responsible for structural and/or behavioral deficits. We now know that more than 3 percent of all mental defectives possess some biochemical abnormality presumed to be associated with the causes of retardation, and believed to result from errors of carbohydrate, fat, and protein metabolism.

Metabolism involves the physical and chemical changes within the body, and covers both material changes (changing the nature of a substance) and energy changes (transformations of foods into energy). There are two basic aspects to metabolism: *anabolism* and *catabolism*. In anabolism, metabolic changes occur through a building-up process; in catabolism, through a breaking-down process. Thus, catabolic processes break foods into simpler substances which are then anabolized for use in building or maintaining body tissues or normal functioning.

The major components involved are carbohydrates, fats, and proteins. Carbohydrates are chemical elements found in the form of sugars and starches. Fats, or *lipids,* are chemical elements which break down into acid and alcohol substances to aid in body development and continued functioning. Proteins are chemical substances which produce amino acids, the body's building blocks, essential for tissue growth and repair. All these components are essential for normal development, and, with the endocrine glands, comprise the body's chemical system.

Metabolic disorders are usually classified as carbohydrate, fat, or amino-acid protein metabolic disorders.

Carbohydrate Disorders

Carbohydrate is the brain's major energy source, and thus carbohydrate abnormalities affect nervous system development. The following conditions illustrate this effect:

Disorder	Characterized by
Hypoglycemia (low blood-sugar levels)	mental retardation; seizures; respiratory problems; low blood-sugar levels; low birth weight TREATABLE.
Hyperglycemia (high blood-sugar levels)	mental retardation; diabetic coma TREATABLE.
Glycogen-storage diseases	abnormal accumulations of glycogen in body organs; absence of enzyme needed for carbohydrate metabolism. Types I & III are TREATABLE; Type II infants usually die before one year
Galactosemia	inability to digest milk; jaundice; retardation, if untreated; TREATABLE by removing milk from diet

These carbohydrate disorders can all lead to varying degrees of mental retardation, if undetected. However, if detected, nearly all are treatable. Therefore, early detection of such disorders is critical.

Protein (Amino Acid) Metabolism Disorders

These disorders are not believed to be related to a specific synthesis deficit of brain protein. Instead, on the basis of current knowledge, three categories are described: (1) *overflow aminoacidurias,* in which an amino acid overflows into the urine as a result of abnormal concentration of that amino acid in the blood; (2) *no-threshold aminoacidurias,* characterized by enzyme deficiencies without abnormal concentrations in the blood; (3) transport aminoacidurias, which result from faulty mechanisms for reabsorbing amino acids into the kidneys. These three types are listed below:

Overflow Aminoacidurias

Phenylketonuria	Maple-syrup urine disease
Tyrosinosis	Hypervalinemia
Isovaleric acidemia	Histidinemia
Hyperlysinemia	Oasthouse urine disease
Citrulinemia	Hyper-B-alaninemia
Hydroxprolinemia	Carnosinemia
Hyperprolinemia	Hypersarcosinemia

No-threshold Aminoacidurias

Homocystinuria	Cystathioninuria
Argininosuccinic acidurias	

Transport Aminoacidurias

Hartnup disease	Methionine malabsorption
Joseph's syndrome	

Phenylketonuria or PKU is a disorder which illustrates how overflow aminoacidurias occur. Phenylalanine hydroxylase is an enzyme (a chemical substance produced by the body to act in a catalytic manner on other parts of the body) which is involved in changing phenylalanine to tyrosine. PKU results when this transformation does not occur because of faulty enzyme action. When this error happens, phenylalanine accumulates in the blood and overflows in the urine. If undetected, PKU can cause mental retardation and associated disorders. PKU can be prevented if medical treatment is begun within the first 6 months.

Homocystinuria, a no-threshold disorder, includes mild to severe mental retardation, seizures, sparse hair, some spasticity, and abnormal lenses. The cause is believed to be a defective enzyme usually found in the brain and liver tissue. This disorder can be detected at birth by urine analysis. If found, a therapeutic diet can alleviate the problems associated with this deficiency.

Hartnup disease, an example of the transport disorder, results when certain chemical agents fail to be transported to the stomach and kidneys. It is characterized by mental retardation as well as by skin rash, spastic behavior, and tumors. Hartnup disease is treatable by nicotinic acid which results in improved skin condition and a cessation of most of the motor neurological disorders.

Fat Disorders

Just as carbohydrates are the brain's major energy source, fats (lipids) are its major chemical component. Many diseases have been recently identified as being associated with an accumulation of lipids. Some of these diseases, all of which can result in mental retardation, are briefly described below.

Amaurotic family idiocy (Tay-Sachs disease):

This defect begins during the first year and is related to an enzymatic defect in the metabolism of certain lipids involved in brain development. The term "amaurotic" refers to progressive degeneration, and, in Tay-Sachs disease (about 80 percent of infants with this disease are Jewish), brain deterioration is so rapid that the infant usually dies before age 2. Similar forms of this disease, which differ in age of onset, include *Jansky-Bielschowsky* disease (late infancy), *Vogt-Spielmeyer* disease (juvenile years), and *Kufs* disease (adult years).

Niemann-Pick Disease.

Similar to Tay-Sachs, this occurs in infancy, also mostly among Jewish children. The symptoms (which include jaundice, diarrhea, and eventual mental and physical deterioration) appear about half-way through the first year, though variations of this disease can occur late in life. Death occurs usually between 12 and 20 years.

Other lipid disorders are:

Gaucher's Disease	abnormal CNS development; in infancy, death occurs by age 2; no adequate treatment
Sulfatide Lipidosis	after 1-1½ years, mental deterioration sets in; absence of deep tendon reflexes is characteristic; no adequate treatment
Hurler's Syndrome	characterized by short stature; skeletal deformities; deafness; heart trouble; and mental retardation

The Hurler Group   similar to Hurler's but without mental and motor retardation; deterioration does sometimes occur between 2nd-4th year; occurs only in males

Sanfilippo Syndrome   mild early retardation, followed by rapid deterioration between 2nd and 4th years

ENDOCRINE DISORDERS

Cretinism or congenital hypothyroidism results from a lack of, or malformation of, the thyroid gland. Generally an afflicted child is lethargic, has thick facial features (eyes, lips, tongue), is often constipated, has respiratory problems, eats poorly, and cries with a low-pitched sound. Children may also acquire hypothyroidism after birth: these also become lethargic and placid, are constipated, are unable to tolerate cold, and possess slow deep-tendon reflexes. Early therapy (before 6 months of age) will enable a number of these children to develop low normal intelligence.

POSTNATAL HANDICAPPING CONDITIONS

A number of handicapping conditions, not present at birth, develop later. These include various physical dysfunctions such as blindness, heart trouble, and brain damage. Some of the most critical conditions are discussed below.

Physical Injury at Birth

Physical injuries at birth, such as bone damage, bleeding, or bruising, have implications for the child's development. This is especially true for bleeding, since excessive bleeding, affecting the infant's supply of oxygen, can be seriously harmful to the newborn. Oxygen supply is carried by the blood, and, if the infant's brain is without blood for even a few minutes (3-4), mild to severe brain damage may result. *Anoxic deprivation* is the term used to describe this condition.

Blindness

Severe (20/200 after correction) to total loss of vision is usually considered blindness from an educational standpoint. Blindness has a number of causes, the chief one being prenatal damage. Others include infectious diseases (meningitis or Rubella), trauma, and poisoning (retrolental fibroplasia). Unreliable reporting methods and classification difficulties preclude exact figures, but a conservative estimate of the incidence of blindness indicates that about 0.3 of every 1000 school-aged children are completely without sight and about 2 out of every 1000 are partially sighted. Blind children usually score slightly lower on IQ tests than do sighted children. This difference might be attributed to some related neurological defect, but, more likely, the parents of such children tend to overprotection, thus limiting their environmental interactions, and contributing to retarded cognitive development in the child.

Deafness

When hearing impairment renders the auditory system useless for communication, the resulting condition is deafness. Generally, about 3 percent of children under age 5 have hearing problems, and about 7 percent between ages 5 and 19. The causes of deafness vary. As mentioned earlier, prenatal exposure to rubella is one; others include meningitis and the tendency of deaf individuals to intermarry and perpetuate hereditary deafness. In about half the cases of deafness, however, the cause is unknown.

A hearing impairment can severely limit a child's exposure to environmental experiences, as well as communication with others, thus rendering development of normal speech very difficult. For many deaf children, special schooling is required.

Heart Trouble

The two major categories of childhood heart disease are the infectious and the congenital disorders. *Rheumatic fever,* the largest infectious disease contributing to childhood heart trouble, can strike many body tissues at the same time, like joints, skin, the brain, or the heart. Scarred tissue, left in the heart by rheumatic fever, can interfere with normal functioning and thus can produce permanent heart disease.

Children in the second category usually give evidence of some cardiac system abnormality at birth. One such disorder is referred to as *Patent ductus.* Some very rapid adjustments—closing off certain blood carrying lines and opening others—must occur immediately after birth to assure full function of the infant's oxygen-carrying system. One of these lines (the *ductus arteriosus*) may take too long in closing or may never close fully, resulting in a leaky, inefficient system for introducing fresh oxygen into the blood. When this happens, these babies are called ''blue babies'' because of their bluish appearance (especially around the lips) which is associated with their oxygen deficiency. In medical terminology, the condition is called ''patent ductus,'' which means ''open tube.'' The consequences of this disorder vary with duration and severity. If the condition persists without correcting itself, surgical procedures (even with very young children) can alleviate the problem.

Muscular Dystrophy

Characterized by progressive deterioration of muscle tissue, this disease is thought to be a hereditary disorder, probably involving a biochemical defect.

Whatever its cause, muscular dystrophy is neurologically based. Motor neuron cell bodies degenerate, causing atrophy (weakening) of the nerves connecting the motor system to muscle tissue, with resultant muscle paralysis. The affected child gradually becomes weaker and weaker until death ensues, usually due to a respiratory disorder.

Cerebral Palsy

Cerebral palsy results from damage to the brain's motor control system, is generally characterized by paralysis, weakness, and poor coordination, and may be accompanied by hearing and vision problems and mental retardation. The causes of cerebral palsy are complex and include the following: (1) birth injury (including anoxia and hemorrhage); (2) congenital cerebral defect, (3) postnatal head injury, (4) infection, and (5) unidentified or other causes. The percentage of occurrence within these five categories is about 55, 23, 5, 4 and 13, respectively.

About 3 out of each 1,000 children born in the United States will be affected by cerebral palsy, and in one-third of these children the disorder will be so severe as to offer little room for improvement. The degree of severity is reflected in the paralytic involvement. If only one limb is affected, it is referred to as *monoplegia*. If half the body is involved (dividing vertically), the condition is referred to as *hemiplegia*. When three limbs are impaired (which is rare) the condition is known as *triplegia*. When four limbs are paralyzed, the individual is a *quadriplegic*. Usually this degree of severity continuum also describes the degree of brain damage involved as well as the degree to which other defects, including mental retardation, are involved.

The classification system for cerebral palsy is generally based on the neurological source of the disorder. These subcategories and their frequency of occurrence are listed below:

1. *spasticity:* hyperactive reflexes, exaggerated stretch movements, 45 percent

2. *athetosis:* slow, involuntary, wormlike movements; uncontrollable and purposeless movements, 23 percent

3. *rigidity:* muscles are tense and resist passive motion, 11 percent

4. *ataxia:* disturbed balance and equilibrium, 11 percent

5. *other or mixed:* 10 percent

Epilepsy

Epilepsy is a convulsive disorder caused by excessive neuronal discharge within the brain, characterized by seizures. Seizures range from massive convulsions and loss of consciousness *(grand mal)* to very brief losses of consciousness with almost no outward signs of behavioral disturbance *(petit mal)*. A third type of epilepsy, *sensory* epilepsy, occurs after prolonged exposure to sensory stimuli such as reading or watching television.

A petit mal version of this disorder occurs most frequently in early childhood, and probably the high degree of incidence is related to brain damage occurring at, or prior to, birth. What causes epilepsy is still unknown but we do know that some individuals are inclined towards epileptic seizures as a result of infections, injuries, or metabolic disorders affecting the brain. This early childhood form of epilepsy, characterized by minor motor seizures (twitching), usually begins either between 3 and 6 months of age or after age 2, mostly between 3 and 5 years. Infants with this form of epilepsy may have as many as 100 attacks per day, usually in the early morning hours, always of very brief duration, and generally associated with some degree of mental retardation.

Minimal Brain Dysfunction (MBD)

This condition manifests behavioral signs of some brain dysfunction, but without corresponding direct neurological evidence of cerebral disorder. In epilepsy, for example, scar tissue and centers of dead neural cells are almost always evident. In all of the clearly defined neurological disorders, specific abnormal patterns of electrical activity in the brain (called "hard" signs) are observable. But in MBD, there are usually no hard signs, despite the fact that outward behavioral, or "soft" signs, indicate some degree of cerebral dysfunction. Among these soft signs of brain dysfunction are:

1. Abnormal motor functions usually indicated by high levels of activity *(hyperkinesis)* and impaired coordination: The hyperactive child is a restless and active infant, who walks and stands early, and is meddlesome as a toddler. In school, these children don't adjust well, irritate teachers, and have difficulty in learning. In addition, they have short attention spans, are easily distractible, and are verbally overactive.

2. Perceptual-cognitive abnormalities associated with distractibility and short attention spans: These children are not alert to visual detail, have very brief memory for what they have seen, are poor listeners, do not comprehend instructions readily, and are seen often as disobedient because of failure to carry out instructions.

3. Poor impulse control and low tolerance for frustration: These children, usually impulsive, show little ability to delay gratification of needs or desires, and consequently often display aggressive and destructive behavior. They appear to be poor planners; seldom think far ahead; are often reckless and act with little regard for their or other's safety, wear everything out

rapidly, appear stubborn, selfish, bossy, disobedient, and negativistic. Yet just as readily, this same impulsivity may reveal their needs for love and affection in the form of extraordinary dependence and attention-seeking.

4. Abnormal emotionality: In some children, rapid mood changes are characteristic. Either such children lack the capacity to experience and display emotions of all sorts, or this insensitivity is merely a consequence of extremely rapid shifts of attention and mood.

This syndrome is more prevalent in boys than in girls; girls are more likely to show signs of well-defined neurological disorder accompanying behavioral disorders, but boys often only show soft signs of behavioral disorders. Why these sex differences occur is not clearly known, but there is a likelihood that early oxygen deprivation (anoxia) may be one cause of MBD. Males show more signs of slight anoxia at birth (bluish color, lethargy, lack of appetite, inactivity) than do females. Several established physiological differences imply that males are more vulnerable to interference with oxygen distribution to neural tissue: they are larger and heavier at birth; are muscularly more active, requiring more oxygen; have larger heads (although less dense brain tissue) at birth; and typically have smaller carotid arteries which are the main source of blood to the brain.

The treatment of MBD is difficult because its physiological base is obscure, and the pattern of behavioral disorders can easily be confused with other conditions. Hyperactivity, for example, is not restricted to the MBD child; it may be the outcome of the child's response to tension, anxiety, stress, or overstimulation. Certain drugs have been effective with the hyperactive MBD child. These drugs (amphetamines) normally elevate sensory and motor activity levels; with MBD children, however, the drug apparently has a tranquilizing effect. Ritalin, the most common of these drugs, requires frequent administration and may produce side effects which can arrest the child's growth rate somewhat and pose some risk of retarding growth altogether. In addition, it produces a very unstable and erratic sense of body awareness that can interfere with stabilization of self-concept. A new drug called *Cylert* appears to be free of these undesirable effects.

Infections

Encephalitis is an inflammation of the brain tissue caused by a virus transmitted through the bloodstream. The many types of viral encephalitis almost all have symptoms which include headache, fever, lethargy, vomiting, seizures, and alterations of consciousness. Physically, these diseases result in neck stiffening, increased intracranial pressure, reflexive contraction and pain in the hamstring muscles when attempting to extend the leg, and signs associated with upper motor neuron disease. Several more severe forms of encephalitis are outlined below.

Eastern equine encephalitis (east of Appalachian Mountains) and Western equine encephalitis (west of the Appalachian Mountains)	transmitted by mosquitoes; can result in paralysis, and emotional, language, visual, and intellectual disturbances as well as seizures
Japanese encephalitis	transmitted by mosquitoes; can (though rarely does) result in paralysis, intellectual retardation, and personality changes
Poliomyelitis	caused by 3 different viruses; usually affects children; results in motor, but not sensory paralysis; has been greatly reduced by preventive vaccines
Subacute sclerosing encephalitis	characterized by early mood, personality and intellectual regression; seizures increase and the child becomes progressively demented; death follows

Meningitis, a bacterial infection, occurs mostly in children below age 5. It is caused by only a few types of bacteria, of which *Hemophilus influenzae* is the most common one in infancy and childhood. Found in respiratory infections leading to influenza and to influenzal meningitis, this bacterium produces the symptoms of lethargy, fever, meningeal signs, and seizures. Children who recover fully can be left with such conditions as spastic motor behavior, paralysis, deafness, intellectual and motor retardation, and hydrocephaly (water on the brain).

Poisons

Many chemical agents in the home are toxic or poisonous to children, and can affect central nervous system functioning. These toxins may be classified as drugs, household poisons, and agricultural chemicals. Several of the more important ones are listed below.

Drugs
    analgesics, like aspirin
    antihistamines
    anticonvulsants
    amphetamines
    corticosteroids
    sedatives
    tranquilizers

<u>Household Toxins</u>

   carbon tetrachloride
   tricheoroethylene
   methyl alcohol
   ethyl alcohol
   gasoline
   kerosene
   toluene (airplane glue)
   naphthalene (moth balls)
   lead-based paint
   home permanent neutralizing fluid
   carbon monoxide

<u>Agricultural Chemicals</u>

   pesticides, like DDT

Prematurity

The effects of "prematurity" on later growth and development of the child have been examined for many years. Normally, the time from conception to birth is 38 weeks. Although earlier delivery may occur normally, it more likely will occur in connection with disease or injury. It is difficult to distinguish the effects of normal early birth from the effects of early birth caused by some unusual event or condition. Research studies of physical and psychosocial development of premature infants have yielded different conclusions in each case. Studies of physical growth show that premature infants are smaller, weaker, and less well-adapted to life outside the uterus, but that these limitations usually disappear within the first year of life. After early childhood, prematurely born individuals are not recognizably different from others. There is scattered evidence, however, that many of the psychosocial effects of prematurity (greater anxiety and insecurity, excessive fear, social withdrawal) persist somewhat longer, perhaps even throughout childhood. But this observation must be intercepted by recognizing that a mother of a premature infant interacts differently with the child. Often believing her baby is delicate and vulnerable, and requiring extra care and attention, she is likely to become overprotective and foster the development of these psychosocial differences.

The concept of prematurity is now being seriously questioned. The World Health Organization (WHO) has recommended its abandonment, proposing instead to identify two kinds of unusual birth conditions:

1. *Low-birth-weight infants* (those weighing less than an agreed-upon birth weight; this low-birth-weight condition could result either from a short

gestation period or such factors as restricted prenatal nutrition, genetics, etc.)

2. *Short-gestation-period infants* (those of specifically known abbreviated prenatal gestation, regardless of physical size or weight at birth)

ATYPICAL PHYSICAL DEVELOPMENT

Children born with or developing a physical disorder such as those described in this chapter will obviously not develop in a "normal" manner, because the disorder alters their available modes of interaction with others. Atypical physical development is a collective label, describing a variety of physical handicapping conditions like blindness, deafness, cerebral palsy, muscular dystrophy, etc. These conditions all affect development, so consideration of atypical physical development is important because of the need to understand the vital relationships which occur between and among physical, social, and cognitive aspects of human development. Because we use our senses and our bodies in interacting with our world, both to take in and process knowledge and to learn efficient behavior for dealing with the physical and social world, any interference with normal development will have a subsequent effect on cognitive (Part IV) and social (Part V) development. And if we are really to help children with handicaps, we must understand how the nature of the disability can best be used to help the child develop.

REFERENCES AND SUGGESTED READING

Arey, L. B. *Developmental anatomy.* Philadelphia: W. B. Saunders, 1965.

Barnes, A. Prevention of congenital anomalies from the point-of-view of the obstetrician. In *Congenital malformations: Papers and discussions at the second international conference on congenital malformations.* New York: International Medical Congress, 1964.

Bickel, H., Hudson, F. P., & Woolf, L. I. (Eds.). *Phenylketonuria and other inborn errors of amino acid metabolism.* Stuttgart, Germany: Verlag, 1971.

Braine, M., Heimer, C. B., Heimer, B. B., Wortis, H., and Freedman, A. M. Factors associated with impairment of the early development of prematures. *Monographs of the Society for Research in Child Development,* 1966, *31,* (No. 106).

Carr, D. H. Cytogenetics of abortion. In K. Benirschke (Ed.), *Comparative aspects of reproduction failure.* New York: Springer-Verlag, 1967.

Corner, G. W. Congenital malformations: The problem and the task. In *Congenital malformations: Papers and discussions presented at the first international conference on congenital malformations.* Philadelphia: Lippincott, 1961.

Cruickshank, W. M. (Ed.). *Cerebral palsy: A developmental disability,* (3rd rev. ed.). Syracuse, N.Y.: Syracuse University Press, 1976.

Cruickshank, W. M., & Hallahan, D. P. (Eds.). *Perceptual and learning disabilities in children* (Vol. 1). Syracuse, N.Y.: Syracuse University Press, 1975.

Emery, A. E. H. *Heredity, disease, and man: Genetics in medicine.* Berkeley: University of California Press, 1968.

Gardner, R. A. *MBD: The family book about Minimal Brain Dysfunction.* New York: Aronson, Inc., 1973.

Garrod, A. E. *Inborn errors of metabolism.* London: Oxford University Press, 1909.

Gross, M. D., & Wilson, W. C. *Minimal brain dysfunction.* New York: Brunner-Mazel, 1974.

Harris, M. (Ed.). *Early diagnosis of human genetic defects* (HEW Publication No. (NIH) 72-25, 1971).

Herring, R. M., Philips, J., Goodman, H. O., & King, J. S. Enzymes in Down's Syndrome. *Lancet,* 1967, *1,* 1157.

Hurst, L. A. Etiology of mental disorders: Genetics. In B. Wolman (Ed.), *Manual of child psychopathology.* New York: McGraw-Hill, 1972.

Hutt, M. L., & Gibby, R. G. *The mentally retarded child* (3rd ed.). Boston: Allyn and Bacon, 1976.

Inhorn, S. L. Chromosomal studies of spontaneous human abortions. In D. H. M. Woollam (Ed.), *Advances in teratology* (Vol. 2). London: Logos Press, Academic Press, 1967.

Johnson, V. M., & Werner, R. A. *A step-by-step learning guide for retarded infants and children.* Syracuse, N.Y.: Syracuse University Press, 1975.

Koch, R., & de la Cruz, R. (Eds.). *Down's Syndrome (Mongolism): Research, prevention, and management.* New York: Brunner-Mazel, 1975.

Knudsen, A. G. *Genetics and disease.* New York: McGraw-Hill, 1965.

McClearn, G. E. Genetic influences on behavior and development. In P. Mussen (Ed.), *Carmichael's manual of child psychology.* New York: Wiley, 1970.

McDavid, J. W., and Garwood, S. G. *Understanding children.* Lexington, Mass.: D. C. Heath, 1978.

Marx, J. L. Drugs during pregnancy: Do they affect the unborn child? *Science,* 1973, *180* (4082), 174.

Meredith, H. V. Somatic changes during human prenatal life. *Child Development,* 1975, *46,* 603-610.

Moore, K. L. *Before we are born: Basic embryology and birth defects.* Philadelphia: W. B. Saunders, 1974.

Neel, J. V. Some genetic aspects of congenital defects. In M. Fishbein (Ed.), *Congenital malformations.* Philadelphia: Lippincott, 1961.

Powledge, T. M. Amniocentesis: Checking on babies not yet born. *New York Times,* April 4, 1976, p. 16.

Reed, E. Genetic anomalies in development. In F. Horowitz (Ed.), *Review of child development research* (Vol. 4). Chicago: The University of Chicago Press, 1975.

Sameroff, A. J., & Chandler, M. J. Reproductive risk and the continuum of caretaking casualty. In F. Horowitz (Ed.), *Review of child development research* (Vol. 4). Chicago: The University of Chicago Press, 1975.

Saxin, L., & Rapola, J. *Congenital defects.* New York: Holt, Rinehart and Winston, 1969.

Turpin, R., & Lejeune, J. *Human afflictions and chromosomal aberrations.* Oxford: Pergamon, 1969.

Wender, P. H. *Minimal brain dysfunction in children.* New York: Wiley, 1971.

Wolman, B. *Manual of child psychopathology.* New York: McGraw-Hill, 1972.

Chapter 4

Working With Young Physically-Impaired Children: Part A—The Nature of Physical Handicaps

M. Beth Langley

Physical or motor activity in young children is important for developmental progress. It helps in integrating and coordinating early experiences, facilitates perceptual, visual-motor, language, and social-emotional behaviors (Rosenbloom, 1977), and, thus, is a critical prerequisite and an important corollary to the acquisition of competency. Caldwell (1973, p. 7) poignantly illustrates the important role of physical activity in development: "If he (the child) has any kind of motor dysfunction he cannot get up and move to find something better, or at least, cannot move himself to a situation where the environment might make a better match with his own current developmental state."

DEFINITION AND CLASSIFICATION

In this chapter, physically handicapping conditions describe orthopedically-and health-impaired children. (Sensory handicaps are discussed later.) Orthopedically and health-impaired children have traditionally received the same instruction as a result of the medical origin of their impairments. PL 94-142 (p. 42478) has defined this classification of children:

> Orthopedically impaired means severe orthopedic impairment which adversely affects a child's educational performance. The term includes impairments caused by congenital anomaly, impairments caused by disease, and impairments from other causes such as fractures, or burns that can cause contractures. Other health impaired means limited strength, vitality or alertness due to chronic or acute health problems such as a heart condition, epilepsy, tuberculosis, rheumatic fever, nephritis, asthma, sickle cell anemia, hemophilia, lead poisoning, leukemia, or diabetes, which adversely affects a child's educational performance.

An estimated 5 in 1,000 school-aged children are orthopedically handicapped, totaling approximately 328,000 children, 28 percent of whom in 1975 were receiving no special educational services (Hallahan & Kauffman, 1978; Goldstein, 1978). Safford and Arbitman (1975) reported that 1 in 14 children are born with some form of birth defect. Disability, handicap, and impairment are frequently used interchangeably, although what may be a disability for one child may represent a handicap for another, depending on psychological state and, as the child grows older, the desired occupational goals and directions. While the difference may not be as apparent in the young child, the predisposition for one term over another is formed as the child leans to adjust to an impairment during preschool years. Impairment simply refers to the structural loss or defect, which, in some children, may be in some degree artificially restored (Love & Walthall, 1977). Disability implies the impairment's impact on daily activities and the resulting lack of, or limitation in, abilities. When a child is unable to adjust and allows the defect to inhibit maximal function, the impairment becomes a handicap.

How limited the child is physically to act upon his environment determines whether his impairment is considered mild, moderate, or severe. Love and Walthall (1977) have provided guidelines:

MILD: can ambulate (with or without prosthetics or orthoses), use arms, and communicate well enough for own needs

MODERATE: handicapped in locomotion, self-help, and communication, but not totally disabled; will require some special help

SEVERE: incapacitated and usually confined to a wheelchair; complete rehabilitation may not be possible.

Safford and Arbitman (1975, p. 6) postulated a more educationally relevant definition: "An orthopedic or neurological impairment is one incurred prenatally, at birth, or during infancy (and early childhood) and requires medical and educational intervention during the childhood years and often into adulthood." An additional educationally relevant definition has been provided by Hallahan and Kauffman (1978, pp. 378-379): "Physically handicapped children are defined as those whose nonsensory physical limitations or health problems interfere with their school attendance or learning to such an extent that special services, training, equipment or facilities are required."

THE DEVELOPMENTAL PROCESS

An age-old controversy has been: does a child "move to learn" or does he "learn to move?" The confusion is evidenced when one views the effects of a severe physical impairment on a child's learning during the sensory-motor period of cognitive development. In this stage, the normal child learns to integrate sensory information for adaptive behaviors, recognize that the world is a permanent place, and acquire goal-directed behaviors. Cognitive abilities in physically impaired children are often delayed as a result of their having passed the teachable moment in various stages of development. When the mind is most ready to learn specific skills, physical impairment inhibits optimum timing of the match between physical and mental readiness for skill acquisition. Uzgiris and Hunt (1975) have developed a Piagetian framework of six primary domains which allows one to see the progression of individual cognitive skills within the first 24 months of life as well as the influence of physical impairments upon the timing of learning skills critical for adaptive behavior.

The first domain, visual pursuit and permanence of objects, begins with looking and leads to the discovery that an object is present even when not in view and progresses through pursuit of slowly moving objects, lingering of glance at a point of disappearance of an object, acquisition of a partially hidden object and of an object hidden under one or two screens. Donlon (1966) has estimated that 50 percent of cerebral-palsied children have some form of visual impairment. Vertical gaze and the ability visually to cross the midline is frequently impaired in children who retain early reflex patterns. This prevents tracking objects to their place of disappearance and anticipating their path of travel. This child may not understand that once an object leaves his visual field it is still present somewhere in space. The child who has no use of upper limbs may not have the opportunity to receive visual feedback to check a mental image of the object's location if the child cannot physically remove or displace the barrier obstructing the object. Even at this point, the physically-handicapped child's teachable moment has been arrested and the effects are seen in delayed integration of visual with motor schemes for tracking and later for memory skills.

Development of means for achieving desired environmental events is initiated as the child engages in handwatching behaviors. With this domain, the child begins reaching and grasping when the hand and object are in view simultaneously, culminating in the ability to manipulate a string to obtain a toy. The effects of an asymmetrical tonic neck reflex are seen in the cerebral-palsied child's inabilitiy to grasp or pull objects to his midline. The child with upper unilateral or bilateral amputation will have no means of reaching or grasping, or, thus, of pulling objects to him at this early age. Neither child will have the opportunity to realize the use of intermediate means for achieving a desired result. When the teachable moment occurs for integrating seeing with reaching and grasping to use a tool, and for problem solving, neither child's body will be ready to assimilate these schemas.

The development of schemas in relation to objects, or object concept, emerges with the child's coordinating seeing, hearing, and sucking with grasping to suck the thumb, to bring hands and objects before the eyes, to shake and bang rattles, and to explore objects orally, visually, and auditorially. The infant then becomes interested in showing objects and finding them as they are named. In this stage, the child begins to discover the attributes that make up specific objects and learns to discriminate and associate characteristics necessary for classification. Already having passed the optimum time for developing behaviors dependent upon vision and movement, the cerebral-palsied and the amputee child are delayed even further in recognition and exploration of objects. The spina bifida child may not be able to venture out in his environment to explore and manipulate, and may be exposed to a limited range of experiences. The athetoid cerebral-palsied child often exhibits a high-frequency hearing loss, may have difficulty perceiving labels for objects, and may experience a language delay as a result of both a lack of experiential opportunities and reduced auditory capacity.

Evolving from the same set of behaviors as means-ends relationships, causality grows out of the child's desire to retain pleasurable stimuli. Initially, the child keeps an object in motion by kicking, shaking, and striking actions and later attempts to reactivate the toy by repeating the previously successful motor behaviors. The child then recognizes other people's potential to imitate actions, and, eventually, looks for the causes of action of mechanical toys. Severely physically-limited children may be unable to reach, kick, or in other ways manipulate the environment and, as a result, cannot cause a change in the surroundings, such as moving the mobile, shaking a rattle, or kicking a musical toy, They then lack the experience and opportunities to realize their abilities as an initiator of events. A cerebral-palsied child who lacks coordination of oral musculature will have difficulty employing words as causal agents. The verbal ability to direct others to cause a desirable event or to meet a physical need will not be realized until some adaptive means is designed that is appropriate for his developmental level. The teachable moment is passed for understanding concepts essential to later problem-solving through discovery as well as for using communication to effect a desired result.

The fifth domain, construction of objects in space, emerges with the child's coordination of looking and listening behaviors. The infant seeks to orient visually to sound sources, to search for dropped toys, and to attack or circumvent barriers to retrieving hidden objects. As the child moves in space and explores objects, he begins to realize that an object is the same regardless of its position in space. The child identifies his bottle even when the bottle is seen upside-down. Later, the child integrates his perceptions of different movements and objects and begins to experiment with combining two or more objects to release cubes into cans, stir spoons in cups, or to bang sticks on pans. The child learns to balance one object on top of another and to realize how much space must be taken up before blocks spill over when filling a box with them. The cerebral-palsied child may have retained reflexes that prevent turning toward sound sources or from tracking a ball that rolled under a chair as well as from moving to obtain these objects. A limb-deficient child will experience problems in understanding body relationships and in forming correct concepts of body and self. The child must first learn how to relate body to external stimuli before learning to play simultaneously with two objects. The ataxic cerebral-palsied child and the myelomeningocele child, both of whom are affected by impaired visual-perceptual abilities, will have difficulty forming intact three-dimensional images as well as perceiving an object as the same when viewed from different spatial perspectives.

Development of gestural and verbal skills progresses through a series of stages. Interest in sound and vocal mechanism motivates refining verbal imitations first through approximations and then through direct imitations of words in the receptive repertoire. Similar progression is seen in the acquisition of gestural imitations. First developed are simple gross motor imitations the infant can already perform. Imitations of gestures the infant can see its body perform are followed by ones which it cannot see the body enact and are the last to be acquired in the developmental sequence of imitation skills.

The effects of passing the teachable moment for acquiring imitation skills are reflected in the cerebral-palsied child's delayed acquisition of communication skills and postural control. Natural childhood games such as pat-a-cake and peek-a-boo rarely emerge in the child retaining the asymmetrical tonic neck reflex. Attempts to bring hands to the midline are met with resistance or extraneous abnormal movements. This child may never experience the appropriate kinesthetic or proprioceptive feedback that facilitates unconsciously executed imitative patterns critical to motor planning and independent self-care skills.

Piaget has defined the period of time between two and seven years of age as the preoperational stage during which the child discovers attributes, classifies, and, in general, learns to organize perceptions into logical sequences. The primary characteristic that represents the difference in the child's thinking in this stage is the ability to manipulate symbols to represent ideas (Phillips, 1969). By two years of age, the cognitive processes that dominated the sensory-motor period have been integrated and expanded to allow for a greater variety of problem-solving and reasoning skills. Classroom emphasis should focus on teaching the child how to discriminate critical variables to formulate similarities and differences, to focus on spatial and quantitative relationships, and to recall and analyze missing elements. Table 1 suggests tasks in all developmental areas appropriate for three-, four-, and five-year-olds.

The Piagetian cognitive developmental, as well as the Montessori, approaches propose structuring the environment in such a way that the child learns from explorations and manipulations of materials. Classrooms for children with neurological and orthopedic impairments should be stimulating but controlled. Cruickshank et al. (1961) offer numerous excellent suggestions for teaching perceptual, visual-motor, and number concepts to brain-injured children.

Berko (1966) and Marks (1974) have enumerated specific learning problems

Table 4-1 Developmental Tasks for 3-, 4-, and 5-Year-Olds

3 TO 3½ YEARS

COGNITIVE-ADAPTIVE

Spatial Relationships:
Copies a circle
Imitates straight cross
Copies four-block train with chimney
Imitates 3-cube pyramid
Nests four cups through visual comparison
Matches several nesting barrels that screw together
Completes Seguin formboard through trial and error
Puts together picture of man cut into 2 pieces at waist
Performs with Montessori cylinders

Visual-Motor Integration:
Cuts across a strip of paper
Screws together nesting kegs
Builds tower of 10-12 cubes

Quantitative Reasoning:
Begins to understand 1-1 correspondence
Counts serially to 5
Gives two blocks out of ten

Memory:
Remembers one color of six presented
Recognizes missing picture of three
Repeats two to three digits
Sorts two colors into opaque containers without matching

Association:
Sorts four colors without matching colored bowls
Matches objects to pictures that are not identical matches of the objects
Matches two-variable forms (color and shape)
Categorizes pictures of common objects

COMMUNICATION

Receptive:

Identifies five primary colors

Vocabulary consists of more than 1000 words

Comprehends wh- questions

Comprehends *no* used to indicate non-existence in syntactical forms

Comprehends verbs + ing ending

Expressive:

Labels five primary colors

90% of verbal responses intelligible

Repeats six to seven syllable sentences

Sentence length from four to five words

Deals with non-present situations verbally

Begins to use complex sentences

Uses plurals, past tense, personal pronouns, and prepositions *in, on, under* in syntactical structures

SOCIALIZATION

Personal-Social:

Likes to conform

Likes to give, share experiences and toys

Loves new words

Likes to make new friends

Cooperative play takes place of parallel

Afraid of dark, animals, policemen

Helps set the table and helps with other household tasks

Social-Self:

May wake self up and ask to toilet

Flushes toilet

Pushes feet into shoes: not right feet

Pulls on long pants independently

Undresses rapidly and well:·unbuttons

Dresses independently except for fastenings and heavy outer clothing

Laces holes but not in the correct sequence

Buttons by pulling button from opposite side when pushed by adult

Eats independently with only occasional help

Pours efficiently from a pitcher into a stable glass

Table 4-1 *Continued*

3½ TO 4 YEARS

COGNITIVE-ADAPTIVE

Spatial Relationships:
Imitates a 3-cube oblique bridge
Completes a 10-hole formboard
Assembles 10 nesting cups through trial and error
Puts together two halves of simple picture
Draws a man by forming a circle with appendages
Matches cut-out geometrical forms
Imitates a square: corners rounded
Copies a straight cross
Understands long and short

Quantitative Reasoning:
Matches quantity of blocks or small objects: 3, 4, 5,
Counts serially to 10
Sorts three sizes of objects

Inductive Reasoning:
Selects cubes matching a pattern
Alternates two colors when given a pattern to complete

Memory:
Remembers 1 picture from 15
Remembers two colored blocks from 6 (3 pairs)
Remembers at least one nursery rhyme

Discrimination:
Matches cut-out geometrical forms
Sorts some Decroly pictures
Completes simple Lotto games

Association:
Finds from a group another animal the same as a model depicted on another page
Groups miniature objects by general characteristics
Comprehends same-different concept

COMMUNICATION

Receptive:
Follows 2-stage commands
Points out animals, objects, foods from a large group of other pictures

Expressive:
Complex sentence structures used more frequently
Wh- questions and interrogative reversals dominate syntactical structures
Answers simple questions with three or more words

Receptive:

Recognizes time (day opposed to night) in pictures

Recognizes all major colors

Comprehends demonstrative nouns: *this, that, these*

Comprehends adjective + est suffix (fattest)

Comprehends negative *not* (not jumping)

SOCIALIZATION

Personal-Social:

Tensional outlets exaggerated

Demanding of adults

Jealous of attention paid to others

Enjoys playing with other children

Sings songs learned from listening to other children

Engages in dramatic play

Social-Self:

Wipes self with assistance

Manipulates medium-sized buttons

Fastens snaps

Washes and dries hands independently

Bathes self with supervision: assistance required to clean thoroughly

Applies toothpaste to brush

Brushes hair independently

Spreads soft foods on bread with knife

Serves self from container

Wipes mouth with napkin when reminded

Table 4-1 *Continued*

4 TO 5 YEARS

COGNITIVE-ADAPTIVE

Spatial Relationships:
Copies a square
Imitates 6-cube pyramid
Completes puzzles cut into several pieces
Makes two reversals with Pintner-Paterson manikin
Solves Seguin formboard by visual comparison
Matches simple parquetry patterns
Sequentially orders ten lengths of paper varying in size from large to small

Quantitative Reasoning:
Identifies number concepts
two and three (3 blocks from 10)
Comprehends 1-1 correspondence with differing variables:
(blocks on top of dots)

Sequential Memory:
Remembers two-step paper fold
Reproduces simple sequential tapping patterns
Repeats four digits
Recites a poem from memory

Discrimination:
Matches domino patterns
Tries to cut simple shapes
Matches letter and number cards
Sorts all Decroly patterns
Completes several Lotto cards simultaneously

Association:
Shifts categories when sorting shapes of different colors when cued (by shape first, then by color)

COMMUNICATION

Receptive:

Identifies opposite concepts; brother is a boy, sister is a ——; father is a man, mother is a ——.

Comprehends senses: what do we do with our eyes, ears?

Discriminates appropriate picture in response to "Show me which one has the longest ears, gives us milk."

Identifies which of two pictures is prettier or uglier

Comprehends prepositions: *at side of, in front of, between*

Comprehends noun + er suffix (painter)

Comprehends adjective + er suffix (smaller)

Comprehends simple imperative sentences

Comprehends noun phrase with two adjective modifiers (big red house)

Tends to reenact in body posture and gestures what is told in story

Expressive:

Manually demonstrates functional sequence of objects

Answers questions requiring analogy and comparison: ("Why do we have houses, why do we have books?")

Retells fairy tale in logical sequence

83

Table 4-1 *Continued*

SOCIALIZATION

Personal-Social:
Enjoys being defiant of parental demands
Enjoys bathroom and elimination words
Initiates action and stays with it without adult control
Goes around neighborhood independently
Prefers children of own sex but no hesitation about playing with the opposite sex
Enjoys playing in a group
Shares possessions
Accepts responsibility

Social-Self:
Knows name, address, and telephone number
Toilets self independently
Distinguishes front from back of clothing
Independently puts on button shirt
Turns shirt right side out
Buttons small buttons
Laces shoes but doesn't yet tie them
Engages zipper
Buckles
Washes face independently
Puts toys away, cleans up room
Hangs up coat

5 TO 6 YEARS

COGNITIVE-ADAPTIVE

Spatial Relationships:
Copies a triangle
Prints capital letters
Colors a circle, staying within lines
Copies 6-cube stairs
Copies a checked block pattern from its one-dimensional model
Completes puzzle of man divided into 6 parts
Puts together 2 halves of a rectangle cut diagonally
Copies a model of a square made with pegs
Completes Seguin formboard rapidly without errors
Projects size of object regardless of its physical appearance
Knows right or left on self but not on others

Quantitative Reasoning:
States 5 pennies worth more than nickel
Counts 10 objects
Matches one to one to a line of 6 blocks

Sequential Memory:
Imitates 2-stop triangular fold
Accomplishes a 4-step fold
Rote counts to 30

Memory:
Remembers domino patterns in order to select the same one after removal of a model

Inductive Reasoning:
Alternates 2 blocks of one color with a block of another color to complete a sequential pattern

Discrimination:
Creates words with letters to match a model word

Association:
Matches and sorts with paper and pencil, marking the one that does not belong

Table 4-1 *Continued*

COMMUNICATION

Receptive:
Follows 3-stage command
Comprehends quantitative adjectives:
pair, few, many
Comprehends verb-number agreement:
(is versus are)

Expressive:
Language essentially complete in structure and form
Correct usage of all parts of speech
100% production and use of all consonants
Corrects own errors in learning to pronounce new words
Reads by way of pictures
Relates fanciful tales in own words
Names penny, nickel, dime
Answers questions directly
Defines words in terms of use
Lacks the power of explicit reasoning

SOCIALIZATION

Personal-Social:

Tries only things which he feels he can accomplish

Self-centered: own action and pleasure take precedence over everything else

Differentiates self-concept by putting himself in opposition to mother: other times showers her with notes and presents he has made

Enjoys going places with father

Content to stay near home

Afraid of bodily harm; dogs, the dark, that mother will not return

Play involves make-believe

Dresses up in adult clothing

Shows an interest in sports requiring participation of several children

Prefers children of own age and best friends are of the same sex

Plays simple table games

Social-Self:

Selects own clothing

Ties laces independently

Draws own bath water

Bathes self with supervision

Uses table knife for cutting

Makes simple sandwiches

Gets own cereal

Handles self well at table

Assists in making bed

Empties trashcans and ashtrays

Sweeps with supervision

Wipes silverware and dishes

Folds simple articles: T-shirts, socks, towels

Makes simple purchases (gum, candy, bread)

Waters plants

Brushes teeth independently — handles toothpaste and applies on brush characteristic of children with neurological dysfunctioning, many of which are also applicable to children with musculoskeletal disorders. Problems of attention are foremost among learning difficulties. Hyperactivity refers to the child's inability to organize the environment and leaves the child unable to limit his movements. Distractibility tendencies arise from the child's hyperirritability of attention that prevents selective focusing on one stimulus out of many. Children with drifting attention spans find it difficult to maintain focus on critical variables. A child may begin sorting on the basis of shape and then appear to forget what to do and randomly sort the remaining shapes.

Children with inefficient muscular or skeletal systems experience problems in learning to automatize actions and to perform unconsciously a series of related actions. Their physical abilities may be so restricted that they must concentrate on each movement, thus eliciting a continually high anxiety level. Having to plan each move consciously, the child is susceptible to pressure and emotional lability, may exhibit outbursts of temper or laugh and cry inappropriately when the learning context becomes too tense. Perseveration is not uncommon: the child continues to respond with a previously successful behavior when that response is no longer appropriate. For example, he may continue attempts to nest cans when colored blocks should be sorted into them. The most outstanding learning characteristic that inhibits abstract reasoning is inability to shift thought processes. Once the child has decided an item is different because it is a different color, he cannot shift thought processes to a new concept using the same stimuli to decide that the items are different because of their quantity. After the child has sorted shapes on the basis of color, there is difficulty reorganizing attributes to sort by shape.

Perceptual difficulties are paramount among cerebral-palsied and spina-bifida children. Figure-ground discrimination, part-whole relationships, and missing-element tasks for such children are extremely difficult to solve. Errors in discrimination and visual closure abilities are frequent. Berko (1966) reported that cerebral-palsied children made ten times the errors of a normal child on a formboard task. Shurtleff (1966) found that children between the ages of 3 to 18 months, deprived of an upright posture, confused the letters d with b and 3 with E and evidenced other disorders of spatial organization.

Children with physical impairments may range from above average in intelligence to severe retardation depending upon the handicapping condition and the extent of brain injury. Approximately 75 percent of cerebral-palsied children are retarded to some extent. Young, Nulsen, Martin, and Thomas (1973) reported that only 50 percent of hydrocephalic children with spina-bifida obtain intelligence quotients above 80. Retardation is more prevalent in these groups as a result of the neurological etiology of their handicaps. Children with severe limb deficiencies and extremely fragile conditions such as osteogenesis imperfecta may function as retarded only as secondary to their primary impairments since many of these children are institutionalized at a very early age.

ORTHOPEDIC AND HEALTH IMPAIRMENTS

Three major categories of orthopedic and health impairments are described below. *Neurological impairments* include the major manifestations involving the brain and the spinal column. Among the *musculoskeletal disorders* are handicapping conditions resulting from birth defects and trauma to the muscles and skeleton. *Chronic health impairments* encompass a variety of conditions that focus on metabolic and genetic origins, and burns.

Neurological Disorders

Cerebral Palsy

Little's Disease or cerebral palsy is a condition resulting from a lesion to an immature brain either *in utero* or in early childhood. This nonprogressive condition renders the child incapable of coordinating his muscle actions and unable to maintain normal postures and balance in performing normal movements and motor skills. Johnson and Magrab (1976, p. 29) have defined a reflex as a "specific automatic patterned motor response which is induced by a particular stimulus and does not involve voluntary or conscious control." In a normal child, primitive reflexes are synthesized, elaborated, and reintegrated into more mature motor patterns. In the cerebral-palsied child, these reflexes remain static and constant, completely dominating his motor-skill development.

Prevalence figures estimate 7 of every 100,000 to 1.5 of every 1,000 children born manifest cerebral palsy and that about .15 percent of the child population is cerebral palsied (Hallahan & Kauffman, 1978). Among the more prevalent causes of cerebral palsy are anoxia (loss of oxygen), which accounts for one-third to one-half of all cerebral-palsied children; prematurity; hemorrhaging; Rh incompatibility; toxins and trauma. Any of these etiologies may occur prenatally, paranatally, or postnatally.

Cerebral-palsied and other physically-impaired children are classified into various functional levels depending on the number and type of limb involvements. This classification system is outlined below:

Diplegia:	all four limbs are involved but the lower limbs are the more severely impaired
Quadriplegia:	all four limbs are involved but the upper limbs are more severely impaired
Hemiplegia:	only one side of the body is involved (left arm and left leg)
Paraplegia:	only the lower limbs are involved
Monoplegia:	only one limb is involved

Pure forms of cerebral palsy are rare as the majority of children with this condition have a variety of mixed forms depending on the extent and locale of the brain lesion. The three major forms of cerebral palsy are spasticity, athetosis, and ataxia.

Approximately half of cerebral-palsied children are spastic and retain too much muscle tone (hypertonic). The damage to the brain is in the cerebrum, which controls voluntary, willed movement. A major cause of this form of cerebral palsy is damage to the brain cells as a result of cerebral hemorrhaging. Of the three major types of cerebral palsy, spastic children most often exhibit tonic neck reflexes. Visually, a high percentage of these children display strabismus and hemianopsia, in which they lack half the visual field in one or both eyes. Spastic children may have difficulty adjusting to changes in posture and righting themselves in space. Initiation of movement requires excessive effort and movements are uncontrollable; frequently, reactions are seen in limbs other than the one that is voluntarily being moved (referred to as associated movement). Rotation around the body axis is often lacking and flexion is difficult to achieve. Retention of the asymmetrical tonic neck reflex may cause one side of the body to grow shorter than the other and the child may develop scoliosis. Retraction of head, neck, and shoulders is a characteristic posture of spastic children. These children encounter problems with intentional reaching and grasping and often have tightly fisted hands. Restricted range of motion and hypertonic muscles frequently inhibit ability to support weight on arms and hands. The lower extremities are usually the more involved. Internal rotation, adduction, plantar flexion of toes, and scissoring of the legs at the knees frequently characterizes their gait. Walking on the toes is not uncommon.

Athetoid cerebral palsy results from injury (anoxia, lack of oxygen to the brain cells, is a primary cause) to the basal ganglia, the part of the brain responsible for channeling the amount and rate of impulses traveling from the brain to the muscles. Twenty-five percent of cerebral-palsied children are classified as athetoid and manifest fluctuating muscle tone. Athetoid children are often referred to as "floppy" children because they are often hypotonic, having too little muscle tone. Slow, writhing movements characterize their posture. Visually, athetoid children often exhibit nystagmus and encounter difficulty in achieving a vertical gaze. As athetoid children with a history of Rh incompatibility often manifest a high-frequency hearing loss, the teacher and parent should be alert to hearing problems.

Flexion and adduction patterns characterize hip postures. Because of hip adduction, better sitting balance is achieved on the floor than on chairs. Facial grimacing and drooling are common. Usually, a very weak grasp and excessive movement of fingers and hands predominate. The upper limbs are primarily the more involved. Figure 4-1 contrasts the different postures often associated with spastic and athetoid children as portrayed by Finnie (1975).

Comprising approximately 15 to 20 percent of the remaining forms of cerebral palsy, ataxia results from damage to the cerebellum, the area of the brain controlling balance and posture. The primary identifying characteristic of the ataxic child

Figure 4-1 Postural Characteristics of Spastic and Athetoid Children

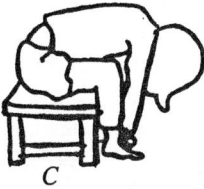

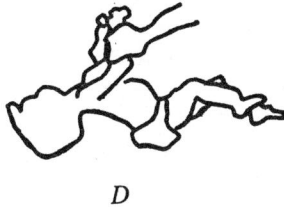

(A) Problems of an athetoid child with spasticity when he tries to sit
(B) Typical standing position of a spastic child
(C) Floppy child sitting, unable to raise his head and straighten his back
(D) Athetoid child being assisted to sit up from a lying position

Source: From *Handling the Young Cerebral-Palsied Child at Home,* second edition, by Nancie R. Finnie. Copyright © 1974 by Nancie R. Finnie, F.C.S.P. Additions for U.S. edition copyright © 1975 by E. P. Dutton & Co., Inc.

is the gait, and, because balance is unstable, the ataxic child exhibits a high lurching step. The sense of spatial relationships, especially awareness of body position in space, is often distorted. These children fall frequently and may not even be aware they are falling; in adulthood, they often are mistakenly thought intoxicated. Ataxic children tend to overreach since they have difficulty judging distance. They cannot focus on close visual stimuli for long periods without becoming nauseated.

Mephensin, Thorazin, Valium, or Dantrolene may be administered to facilitate muscle relaxation; side effects from these medications include loss of appetite, lethargy, anxiousness, withdrawal, abdominal cramps, and excessive crying. These signs should alert the teacher and parents to a need for re-evalution of prescribed medication.

Epilepsy

This is a convulsive disorder caused by an excess firing of electrical discharges in the brain cells and is manifested in seizures, loss of control over specific muscles in the body. Present in 4,000,000 individuals, epilepsy occurs in 30 percent of the population before the age of 4 and 1 out of every 50 children. While any form of brain damage is a potential cause of seizure disorders, the exact origin of the imbalance of electrical discharges is unknown. Abnormal brain wave activity, indicative of epilepsy, can be detected and identified by an electroencephalogram (EEG). Three major forms of epileptic seizures include (1) grand mal, (2) petit mal, and (3) psychomotor.

Typical patterns of a grand mal seizure include loss of consciousness and postural control, and muscle rigidity (tonic phase) which progresses to jerking reactions often accompanied by suspended breathing, loss of bowel and bladder control, and a frothing of saliva. Lasting from 1 to 10 minutes, a grand mal seizure is often preceded by an aura, a warning sign that a seizure is forthcoming. Auras may take the form of an unusual taste, smell, or sound, dizziness, weakness, sensation of fear, numbness or tingling, unusual color sensation, or headache. After regaining consciousness, a child will be confused and drowsy and will need to sleep several hours. The Epilepsy Foundation of America recommends the following if a grand mal seizure occurs in school:

1. Remain calm. Students will assume the same emotional reaction as their teacher. The seizure itself is painless to the child.

2. Do not try to restrain the child. Nothing can be done to stop a seizure once it has begun. It must run its course.

3. Clear the area around the child so that no injury from hard objects occurs. Try not to interfere with movements in any way.

4. Do not force anything between the teeth. If mouth is already open, a soft object like a handkerchief may be placed between the side teeth.
5. It generally is not necessary to call a doctor unless the attack is immediately followed by another major seizure or if the seizure lasts more than ten minutes.
6. When the seizure is over, let the child rest.
7. The child's parents and physician should be informed of the seizure.
8. Turn the incident into a learning experience for the entire class. Explain what a seizure is, that it is not contagious, and that it is nothing to be afraid of. Teach the class understanding toward the child, not pity, so that classmates will continue to accept the child as "one of the gang."

A child having a petit mal seizure may appear to be daydreaming and evidence a twitching of the eyelids or minimal head or extremity movements. No warning precedes these "little" seizures; the child maintains postural control, and while he loses contact with what is happening in the classroom for 5 to 30 seconds, the child may not even be aware of having a seizure. The petit mal seizure is the most common form among children 4 to 10 years of age and may recur many times during the day, interrupting attention span, memory, and thought processes in general. Petit mal seizures can be detected by observing repeated occurrences of two or more of the following signs: (1) head dropping; (2) daydreaming, lack of attentiveness; (3) slight jerky movements of arms or shoulders; (4) eyes rolling upward or twitching; (5) chewing or swallowing movements; (6) rhythmic movements of the head; and (7) purposeless body movements or sounds. The teacher should report observations to both parents and the school nurse.

Kinetic and myoclonic seizures are variant forms of petit mal seizures, in which the child experiences sudden loss of muscle tone and falling and sudden involuntary muscular contractions of the limbs and trunk, respectively. The child does not lose consciousness, and the seizures are brief but frequent. A child performing unusual but apparently purposeful motor behaviors inappropriate for the situation at hand may be exhibiting a psychomotor seizure. Lip smacking, constant chewing, repetitive arm and hand movements, and disrobing attempts are characteristic of such an episode and are frequently mistaken for hysterical or psychotic symptoms. Confusion and dizziness may occur and the child will actively resist help during the seizure, which may last from one minute to several hours. After the seizure, the child probably will not recall the incident and will want to sleep.

Dilantin, Phenobarbitol, Zarontin, Mysoline, and Tridone can control 80 percent of seizure activity, but often produce side effects such as hypertrophy (swelling) of the gums, nausea, dizziness, and a decreased state of arousal. Lack of sleep and poor diet can contribute to eliciting a seizure in an epileptic child, as can blinking lights and vestibular motion.

Status-epilepticus is a seizure condition in which the child progresses from one grand mal to another without regaining consciousness. Parents and medical assistance should be sought immediately.

Spina Bifida

This defect is characterized by an opening in the spinal column due to the lack of fusion of vertebrae during development and may occur at any point along the spinal cord between the head and lower end of the spine. Spina bifida occulta can be detected by palpating the lower back near the lower lumbar region; a tuft of hair covering a dimpled area may be the only overt sign. In spina bifida cystica, the surface of the child's back reveals an underlying formation of cysts, while a protruding mass of tissue is seen above the skin surface. There are two forms: meningocele and myelomeningocele. In the former, the coverings of the spinal column extend through the unfused vertebral arches, into a tumorlike sac. In myelomeningocele, the spinal cord and its nerve roots protrude through the vertebrae into a saclike mass of tissues. Cerebrospinal fluid is usually found in both sacs, and some form of paralysis results because of nerve damage, occurring below the site of the defect. One child per 300-400 births is born with spina bifida, one of the most common birth defects resulting in a physical impairment (Hallahan and Kauffman, 1978) (see Figure 4-2).

Surgically, the lesion is closed by direct excision of the protruding sac or dissection to separate and preserve as much neural tissue as possible. The skin may be closed directly or require secondary plastic surgery, depending on lesion size. Some surgeons decompress the sac to remove fluid before excision to allow the remaining contents to settle level with the skin (Wilson, 1965).

Children not selected for surgery are treated with antibiotics and dressings over the lesion. The myelomeningocele is washed, dressed, and protected from pressure each day. Meticulous care of the skin in the perineal area is essential to prevent skin infection. If weakness or paralysis is present in the legs, active or passive exercises are carried out. The child must be taught early to avoid extreme heat and cold. Frequent tissue breakdowns result from the sensory and neurological deficits. Treatment for tissue decomposition involves washing the lesion with a non-irritant soap three times a day, rinsing with clear water, and sprinkling granulated sugar over the wound. When the sugar has been on the wound for 20 minutes, it is rinsed away with clear water and the wound is covered with Maalox, which stays on until the next treatment period. The wound is kept uncovered until healed; treatment with heat lamps is also recommended (Wilson, 1965).

Clinical features of myelomeningocele include flaccid paralysis, muscle wasting and weakness, decreased or absent tendon reflexes and proprioceptive sensation, bowel and bladder incontinence, and hydrocephalus. Secondary and associated features of myelomeningocele are retarded physical, mental, or emotional

Figure 4-2 Myelodysplasia

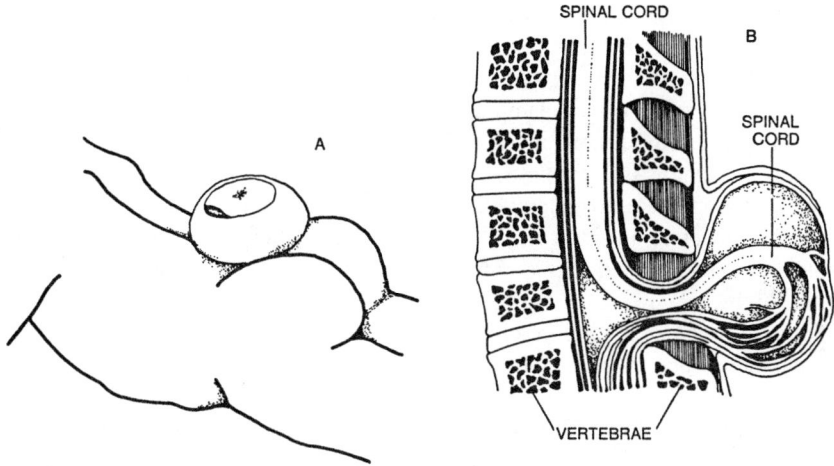

(A) the swelling of meningomyelocele as it presents at birth.
(B) a cross-section shows that portions of the usually defective spinal cord are contained within the meningomyelocele sac.

Source: Beverly R. Myers in *Medical problems in the classroom,* R. H. Haslam and P. J. Valletutti (eds.) Copyright © 1975 by University Park Press. Reprinted with permission.

development; dislocated hips; scoliosis, equinovarus; cleft lip and palate, soft tissue contractures; and eventual skeletal deformity due to unopposed muscle action, gravity, and posture.

Incontinence is an inability to control emptying of urine from the bladder or waste products from the intestines. Incontinence associated with myelomeningocele usually results from damage to the spinal cord that affects the second, third, and fourth sacral nerves and interferes with voluntary control of the sphincter muscles. Disturbance of the genitourinary system occurs with a high degree of incidence in myelomeningocele populations as the innervation to nerves serving this region is only partially present if it exists at all. Neurogenic vesicle dysfunction is perhaps the most common neurological deficit associated with myelomeningocele because of the low level of innervation to the bladder (Wilson, 1965). Although surgical procedures are frequently carried out to correct this deficiency, the system is kept intact as long as possible to develop a healthy body image and determine the child's capacity for effective utilization of reflex activity of the bladder or expression of urine by means of abdominal straining. The main objectives in caring for the genitourinary tract are prevention of drainage problems and prevention and management of infection. Major maintenance procedures are expression of the urine by the Crede or Valsava methods and treatment by chemotherapy, which includes administration of such drugs as lipo-gantrisin, Furadantin, and triple sulfa.

To afford children dry periods during the day when they enter school, procedures are performed which clamp off the urethra by pressure against the pelvic bone. These techniques, which may be handled by parent or teacher, include inserting a tampon into the introitus of the vagina in females and applying a harness-type apparatus to males which acts as a clamp by folding the penis between the ischia bones at an acute angle (Wilson, 1965). Many of these children are catheterized so that their urine empties into collection pouches strapped to the upper thigh.

Surgical procedures for correcting the genitourinary deficiency have included ileo cutaneous ureterostomies in which a transurethral resection of the bladder neck is performed in females (Nash, 1970), and formation of an intestinal loop (ileal-loop) in both sexes. This is the major procedure for urinary diversion and is accomplished by implanting the ureters into an isolated segment of the ileum or sigmoid colon. Pekarovic, Robinson, Lister, and Zachary (1968) found construction of an ileal-loop prevented further dilatation of the upper renal tract and made the patients more socially acceptable. Complications of the stoma occur in 43 percent of the cases, and include stenosis, prolapse, epithelial dysplasia of the mucosa, and internal and external bleeding of the structure. Children with ileal-loops often suffer ill effects from reabsorption from the loop, resulting in hyperchloraemic acidosis. Long-term hazards associated with adhesions around the transperitoneal reconstruction are also prevalent. These children must be made independent in caring for their own urinary needs and appliances, and teachers made cognizant of the importance of extreme cleanliness around the perineal area.

Extreme caution must be exerted when lifting myelomeningocele children. Support should be offered to the mid-back area and under the upper region of the thighs so that the child's hips are flexed and legs extended. Daily observations of physical status should include noting development of contractures, tissue breakdown, spinal changes, and any loss of sensation.

Hydrocephalus

Eighty percent of children with myelomeningoceles also manifest hydrocephalus, an imbalance between production of cerebrospinal fluid (CSF) and its absorption by the cortex and circulatory system. In small infants, this imbalance results in an enlargement of the ventricles with progressive cranial distension (Allen, 1964). The Arnold Chiari malformation, the most common cause of hydrocephalus in children having a myelomeningocele, produces an obstruction of CSF flow. This congenital anomaly of the hindbrain is characterized by elongation of the brain stem and cerebellum into the cervical portion of the spinal cord (Gold, et al., 1964). Sites at which obstructions usually occur are the foramen of Monroe, the third ventricle, aqueduct of Sylvius, foramina of Luschka and of Magendie, and most frequently involve a tumor of some type. Characteristics accompanying the development of hydrocephalus are a greatly enlarged head, thinned scalp, prominent scalp veins, upward retraction of the eyelids, inverted-triangular appearance of the face, strabismus due to sixth nerve paralysis, and spastic paraplegia. In more severe cases, neurologic deficiencies may include failure to evolve grasp and prehensile actions; inability to sit, stand, or walk; and generalized spasticity. When hydrocephalus appears in older children whose scalps are less pliable, attacks of nausea and vomiting with intermittent head pain occur. Episodes of neck retraction and extensor rigidity of the limbs often are present and papilledema may be found. With the reduction in the level of consciousness, lethargy and loss of recently acquired motor achievements, drowsiness, and confusion are evident (Allen, 1964).

Procedures to alleviate the excess fluid buildup involve insertion of a shunt to drain the fluid from the brain ventricles into either the abdominal (ventriculoperitoneal) or chest (ventriculoatrial) cavities via the jugular vein in the neck. These shunts assist in circulation of the fluid throughout the circulatory system and are most often constructed from silicone tubing. As the child grows older, the shunts must be changed to accommodate physical growth, necessitating frequent operations. A complication associated with shunts is their entanglement with brain tissue, causing a blockage of the shunt that prevents the circulation of the cerebrospinal fluid. Among the signs of a blocked shunt are vomiting, seizuring, loss of consciousness, drowsiness, headaches, and visual problems (see Figure 4-3).

Programs for children with the combined conditions of myelomeningocele and hydrocephalus must be developmental in nature with special emphasis placed on the children achieving self-sufficiency in their toileting and other self-care needs. Activities that train children in visual, perceptual, and eye-hand coordination skills should be stressed along with programs for developing a healthy body image. An essential area to be developed is that of meaningful comprehension and expression of language. When the teacher is aware not only of the child's physical disabilities but of how they influence the child's learning, she may then begin to plan for a curriculum that meets the child's developmental needs.

Musculoskeletal Conditions

Muscular Dystrophy

Prevalent in 4 of every 100,000 children, muscular dystrophy refers to a group of diseases that lead to progressive weakening of skeletal muscles. Among the dystrophies the most common childhood form is Duchenne, which, as are other forms, is inherited from the mother through sex-linked recessive transmission. A critical sign of this disease, which primarily affects males, is an elevated level of a muscle enzyme, creatine phosphokinase, in the blood stream (Harris & Cherry, 1974; Bleck, 1975).

Usually not apparent at birth, signs of muscular dystrophy become evident by three years of age when the child appears to be clumsy. Undiagnosed children who enter kindergarten may mistakenly be thought to exhibit learning disabilities or to be lazy. Prominent among early characteristics are a waddling gait due to weakness of the pelvic girdle muscles, tiptoeing, frequent falling, and difficulty in running, climbing stairs, and rising from the floor or low chairs (Brink, 1975). As

---

Figure 4-3 Ventriculoatrial Shunt

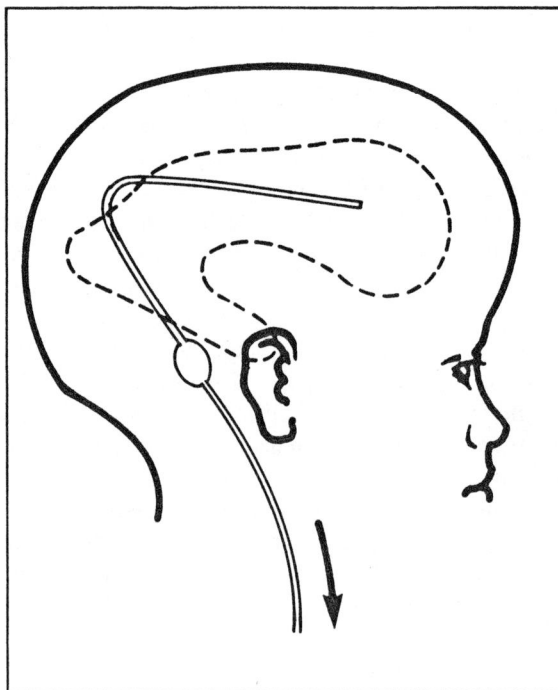

This is one method to relieve hydrocephalus. Place a tube in the ventricle and lead it out into the atrium of the heart so that the fluid is drained.

Source: Eugene E. Bleck in *Physically handicapped children: A medical atlas for teachers.* E.E. Bleck and D.A. Nagel (Eds.) Copyright © 1975 by Grune and Stratton. Reprinted with permission.

---

muscle fibers degenerate, deposits of fatty tissue cause the calf muscles to enlarge—a condition called pseudohypertrophy, because of the false appearance of increased muscle development. The child soon develops lower lumbar lordosis, in which posture is characterized by a protuberant abdomen resulting from deterioration of the muscles in the foot, the front thigh, hip, and abdomen. As muscles of the lower extremities weaken, the child develops the most characteristic sign of muscular dystrophy, Gower's sign, when the child rises by "walking up" his lower limbs with his hands. Edgington (1976, p. 41) described this maneuver in the following steps:

1. first rolls over on the stomach
2. lifts bottom in the air
3. pushes up to hands and knees
4. extends knees
5. proceeds to walk the hands up the legs so as to get to an upright position (see Figure 4-4)

Following the weakening of the lower extremity muscles, those of the shoulders and elbows deteriorate. The child has difficulty raising the arms above the head, lifting heavy objects, and stands with stooped shoulders. Fractures of the extremities are common from loss of bone calcium (osteoporosis) because of lack of muscle activity (Brink, 1975). With the weakened musculature, scoliosis contractures develop. Harris and Cherry (1974, p. 5) delineated the levels of performance that correspond with the severity of muscular weakness:

1. walks and climbs stairs without assistance
2. walks and climbs stairs with aid of a railing
3. walks independently and climbs stairs slowly with aid of a railing
4. walks independently and rises from a chair unassisted but cannot climb stairs
5. walks independently in bilateral knee-ankle orthoses
7. walks with orthoses and assistance of one person
8. stands in orthoses but unable to walk even with assistance
9. wheelchair bound

Most patients are confined to wheelchairs by age 10, although maintenance of ambulation is a primary goal and encouraged as long as possible; even during periods of illness, the child should ambulate frequently to prevent contractures and to maintain muscle tone and strength. Various motion activities are performed daily to sustain good joint position for functional weight bearing. Splinting at night and having the child lie prone with feet extending over the mattress edge inhibit flexion contractures. Aluminum and plastic orthoses can alleviate scoliosis and prevent contractures. Hydraulic lifts may be necessary as the child becomes more incapacitated. Harris and Cherry (1974) specified as the three primary purposes of

Figure 4-4 Gower's Sign

The characteristic pattern of ''climbing up the legs'' due to pelvic weakness may be observed when the child with muscular dystrophy changes from a prone to an erect position.

Source: Joyce D. Brink in *Medical problems in the classroom: An educator's guide.* R.M. Peterson and J. O. Cleveland (Eds.) Copyright © 1975 by Charles C. Thomas. Reprinted with permission.

surgery the release of contractures, the rebalancing of foot masculature, and the maintenance of ambulation.

Educationally, these children should be engaged in comprehensive programs with special emphasis on counseling and development of hobbies and other outside interests. Rehabilitation programs cannot arrest progression of the disease but can give the child self-confidence, independence, and social responsibility (Brink, 1975).

Death occurs between ages of 15 and 25, most often from cardiac or respiratory muscular involvement.

Osteogenesis Imperfecta

This brittle bone disease derives its name from the primary characteristic of its manifestation: fragile and repeatedly fractured bones. Unlike normal bone structure, the collagen fibers are loosely woven and the bones are deficient in protein and bone salts. The bones become weak and the extremities break easily, often healing in a deformed, shortened, and bowed position. The bones of the trunk may also be involved and the chest assumes a bee-hive shape with protrusions of the breastbone. Because the sclera of the eyes is also formed from collagen fibers, the eyes present a characteristic blue coloration of the sclera. Triangular in shape, the face also exhibits a flat broad forehead and poor development of teeth. The skin may be thin and almost translucent and there may be some form of hearing loss as a result of malformed inner and exterior bone structure of the ears.

Surgery is the most effective means of retarding the breakage. The procedure involves removing the entire bone shaft, cutting it into segments and then rethreading them onto a steel rod positioned between the ends of the long bones (Bleck, 1975). Depending on the extent of bone flexibility, "OI" children may be braced and can be ambulatory. Most often these children are in wheelchairs and teachers should exert extreme caution in handling them. Lifting should be similar to that described for the myelomeningocele child with support under the buttocks and behind the back of the child. Because of limited body surface these children perspire heavily and should wear cool, loose clothing during the summer. The condition stabilizes as the child grows older and training should emphasize academics and preparation for attendance in a school program with normal children.

Legg-Calve Perthes Disease

A common hip disorder seen among children between 3 and 10 years of age, this disease is most frequently noticeable at 4-5 years of age and affects four times as many boys as girls. The etiology of Legg-Calve Perthes is a disruption in the blood supply to and destruction of the growth center of the hip end of the thigh bone (Nagel, 1975). Throughout a 2-year process, the growth center fragments and degenerates and then rejuvenates. The onset may be gradual or sudden and is characterized by complaint of intermittent pain in the knee, thigh, or hip joint; limitation of motion; a limp in the involved leg; and loss of internal rotation of the hip.

Primary treatment consists of braces and casts that allow weight bearing in an abducted posture and protection of the hip joint while repair is in progress. In the classroom, care should be taken to prevent bumping, stumbling over, or injuring the leg. Swimming is a highly recommended rehabilitative activity.

Juvenile Rheumatoid Arthritis

A form of arthritis prevalent in children, juvenile rheumatoid arthritis (JRA) affects approximately 3 of every 100,000 children a year (Myers, 1975). Miller (1975) suggests that a disorder of the body's immunologic system is a contributing factor in this disease which becomes apparent between the ages of 1 and 4, and half of all children affected show symptoms before the age of 5 (Jacobs & Downey, 1974).

Clinical manifestations include high fevers, rash, general malaise and fatigue, and swollen joints, most frequently the wrists, ankles, knees, neck, elbows, fingers, and shoulders. Involvement of the jaw, producing pain and leading to a receding chin, is not uncommon. Irritability, loss of appetite, and anemia result from chronic pain associated with the swollen joints, particularly early in the day and after long periods of immobility. To lessen the pain, these children tend to flex all joints and sit rigidly. They tend to be small for their age, lose range of motion, and may develop contractures. Inflammation of the iris (uveitis) is frequently associated with JRA and without early detection and treatment may lead to blindness.

Medications include aspirin, gold salts, and cortisone to reduce the fever and relieve the swelling. Teachers and parents should be alert to the possibility of salicylate toxicity from the large dosages of aspirin. Other side effects may include high-tone hearing losses, hyperventilation, drowsiness, and gastrointestinal upset (Miller, 1975; Myers, 1975). Physical therapy techniques include full range of motion exercises and activities to maintain and increase joint mobility and muscle strength. The child should be encouraged to move frequently throughout the day to prevent stiffening and during play and naptime to lie face down with legs extended to inhibit flexion contractures (Jacobs & Downey, 1974).

Spinal Deformities

When the back of a normally developing child is viewed as the child assumes a standing position, the spine appears as a straight column. Any disturbance to the trunk muscles and nerves that results in a weakness of the trunk, lack of muscle support, asymmetrical muscle pull, or congenitally abnormally fused or partially formed vertebra may result in spinal deformities (Garrett, 1975). Kyphosis, lordosis, and scoliosis are frequently associated with other chronic health and crippling conditions such as asthma, myelomeningocele, cerebral palsy, and muscular dystrophy. Kyphosis is seen as a pronounced outward curvature, usually in the upper thoracic region of the spine and often referred to as humpback, while the term swayback is applied to lordosis, an inward curvature of the spine most frequently seen in the lower lumbar area. The most common and severe of the three major spinal deformities is scoliosis, an s-shaped lateral deviation of the spine, the cause of which is primarily ideopathic. Katz (1974) found that 5.6 percent of the general population exhibited scoliosis. Imperative in treatment of scoliosis is early detection. The first sign of scoliosis may be observed by asking the child to bend forward at a 90-degree angle. If the child has developed a deviation, one side of the rib cage will appear higher than the other and often one hip will be noticeably higher than the other. Silberstein (1975) indicated that treatment depended on the extent and location of the curve and the age of the child. No treatment is prescribed for a curvature of less than 20°, while a curvature of 20-50° requires the use of the Milwaukee brace for approximately a year in conjunction with exercise. This brace extends from the child's neck to the hips and is padded to counteract the spinal curvature. Surgery is indicated when the curvature exceeds 45-50° and consists of fusing the vertebrae so that they are in vertical alignment. While there is usually no pain associated with this condition, without correction it will progress as long as the spine continues to grow, eventually interfering with normal respiratory and cardiac functions.

Hip Dysplasia

When the head of the femur is pulled out of its normal alignment in the pelvis, a hip dislocation exists. Etiology of hip dislocation includes hormonal irregularities affecting the fetal pelvic ligaments, intrauterine and extrauterine environmental factors (Katz & Challenor, 1974), and accident trauma. Dislocation may be unilateral or bilateral and is often associated with cerebral palsy and myelomeningocele conditions.

Clinical manifestations include the Barlow sign in which a jerk may be felt when the child's hips are flexed at a 90° angle and adducted with pressure applied from the outside of the hips toward their sockets, asymmetrical skin creases, and apparent shortness of the involved leg. Palpation reveals one of the greater hip muscles to be higher than the other. Overt signs indicating hip displacement are seen in a waddling gait or a limp as the child walks, increased lumbar lordosis when standing, and complaints of pain in the hip joint. Diagnosis can be difficult and is most often made with radiographic changes. The most frequent course of treatment for a unilateral dislocation during the preschool period is a 6- to 8-week period of immobilization, sometimes with a body cast, depending on the degree of the dislocations, followed by two to three months of restricted activity and physical therapy (Silberstein, 1975).

Talipes equinovarus

This impairment, often referred to as a clubfoot, occurs in one to three per 1,000 live births. The primary clinical manifestation is an internally rotated foot whose heel points posteriorly and lateral portion of the foot touches the surface. A genetically predisposed condition, talipes equinovarus is frequently associated with myelomeningocele, hydrocephalus, and dwarfism. Corrective techniques include plaster casts, wrapping, and manipulation. Splints are often attached to the child's shoes and nightsplints may need to be worn until age five. Shoes with outersoled wedges maintain the corrected position of the foot. Surgery may be indicated in more severe cases. Once the foot position has been stablized, the child may engage in any form of physical activity.

The Limb-Deficient Child

Limb deficiencies in children may be of congenital or traumatic origin. While the effects of drugs such as thalidomide have contributed significantly to the congenital absence of limbs and metabolic disorders have also been suggested as probable causes, the origins of this disability are usually unknown. Shephard (1974) reported that the malformation occurs at the time when the limb buds are forming in the 4th to 8th gestational week.

Traumatic causes of limb deficiencies include exposure to extremes in temperature, lack of circulation, vascular diseases, thrombi or emboli (blood clots), malignant tumors, and injury due to accidents.

Classification of limb deficiencies depends upon the location of the absence and degree of limb present. Amelia refers to the total absence of the limb. Phocomelia and meromelia are interchangeable terms used to refer to partial absence of limbs.

Two basic types of partial limb deficiencies are terminal, in which all skeletal elements distal to the proximal limit of the deficiency are absent, viz., an entire arm may be absent, although the shoulder may be intact (Angliss, 1974). Intercalary deficiencies refer to the presence of the proximal and distal portion of the limb while the middle element is lacking. The limb will be reduced in size and the hand or foot will be near the trunk region (Safford and Arbitman, 1975).

Some delay in acquisition of motor skills, of course, will result from lack of a limb. The upper-limb deficient child will have difficulty with postural control and equilibrium reactions necessary first for sitting and later walking. Sitting balance and trunk control will be delayed in the child without lower extremities. Children lacking distal upper extremities can learn to manipulate and explore objects with their feet, lips, and tongue. The physical therapist will prescribe activities that will promote the lengthening of soft tissues that surround joints responsible for excessive range of motion.

Because of limited body surface, limb-deficient children perspire heavily, and, especially during the summer months, parents and teachers must be alert to excessive heat and the moisture that will collect on the child's clothing. Asymmetry or deformities may distort body image and self-concept. Fear of falling and rejection by others are not uncommon reactions in these children.

Decubitus ulcers, a breakdown in the soft tissues and skin over bony protuberances, may form at the ends of the stumps when a prosthesis does not fit properly or when the stump sock is not smooth or clean. These ulcers are difficult to heal and require continual monitoring and medication as well as dry heat and fresh air.

Chronic Health Conditions

Cystic Fibrosis

The most common fatal hereditary childhood disease, cystic fibrosis results in generalized dysfunction of the exocrine glands. Incidence ranges from 1 in 800 to 1 in 3,000. The disease is characterized by a widespread presence of abnormally thick viscid mucus in the respiratory and intestinal tracts. A thick gluey mucus is secreted and collects in the air passages, causing continuous respiratory infections, particularly pneumonia. Cysts as well as mucus are found in the pancreas and disrupt the production of digestive enzymes that metabolize food, specifically proteins, carbohydrates, and fats.

Clinical manifestations include the characteristic salty perspiration which is the primary diagnostic feature, chronic coughs, a voracious appetite, fatigue, frequent bulky and odorous stools, and a failure to gain weight adequately. The "sweat test" confirms the diagnosis of cystic fibrosis, as this child is born with a disorder in the reabsorption of salt and the first sign is usually the salty taste of the child's skin. Harvey (1975) described the appearance of the child with cystic fibrosis to include a large barrel-shaped chest, a protruding, distended abdomen, and thin extremities.

Major treatment involves postural drainage, in which the child is placed in various positions and vibrated vigorously over the chest regions to dislodge and propel the mucus and sleeps in mist tents to loosen the mucus. Controlling the child's diet and salt intake are also important.

The child should be encouraged to cough and allowed to leave the room often for bowel movements. Metabolism defects will necessitate larger amounts of food intake. Close supervision is needed to prevent excessive physical output, and emotional support to both the child and family is critical.

Asthma

Among the most common chronic childhood diseases, asthma manifests as a difficulty in breathing, greater upon exhalation, due to narrowed bronchial tubes which interfere with the normal flow of air in and out of the lungs. Prevalent among 1.5 million children, asthma accounts for 20 percent of days lost from school.

Children with asthma have an overabundance of antibodies to substances (antigens) to which they are allergic. Contact of antibody and antigen produces an explosion and release of chemicals from body cells that create reactions known as allergy (Harvey, 1975). Ingestants and inhalants are the two types of antigens producing asthma. Ingestants which are common antigens in early childhood include milk, eggs, nuts, chocolate, wheat, and citrus fruits. Many children are also allergic to various types of drugs. Among inhalant offenders are grass, tree and weed pollens, house dust, molds, wool, feather, kapok, and animal fur.

Mascia (1974) described three stages of asthma: (1) the oppression phase characterized by a tightening of the chest accompanied by difficulty in drawing air into the lungs, (2) wheezing, in which the child experiences an urgent need for air, often referred to as air hunger, and (3) the attack stage which follows an acute onset lasting from a few hours to a few days. Intractable asthma is the term applied to the attack when it is prolonged over a period of time.

Before an asthma attack, the child exhibits a clear running nose and a characteristic hacking dry cough followed by wheezing. During an attack the child will sit with his shoulders hunched forward to facilitate air intake (Harvey, 1975). Breathing will be very audible and a blue tinge may appear on lips and fingertips. The child will develop a large, rounded barrel-shapped chest, the rib cage elevated, the thorax distended. Elevation of the shoulders and development of pronounced kyphosis along with asymmetrical bone structure of the thorax are not uncommon (Mascia, 1974).

Physical therapy goals encompass breathing exercises, inhalation therapy, and physical training. The child is taught how to relax, to improve his posture, diaphragmatic and lower costal breathing, and coughing and drainage techniques.

The child's room should be free of smoke, sprays, and dust. Wooden or linoleum flooring is preferable to rugs and feather pillows; wool blankets should be replaced by synthetic materials. Stuffed animals, heavy drapery, and stuffed furniture should be avoided. Heating and air-conditioning vents and filters should be cleansed regularly. Electrostatic filters and humidifiers are helpful in maintaining a favorable room climate. Exposure to dampness and extreme heat and cold should be prevented as much as possible.

Drugs to relax the muscles of the bronchial tubes during an asthma attack may be administered orally, rectally, or through aerosol containers. Cortisone is prescribed in particularly severe attacks, and Aarane or Intal may be prescribed on a regular basis (Harvey, 1975). In the classroom the child should be allowed to rest and encouraged to breathe easily during the onset of an attack. Harvey (1975) recommends having the child drink warm water to inhibit mild attacks.

Hemophilia

This is a hereditary disorder in which the blood clots slowly or not at all. Affecting only males and transmitted by mothers, hemophilia occurs when the child has a deficiency of a protein factor responsible for the coagulation of the blood. In this disorder, platelets do not produce the chemical that initiates contraction of blood vessels and release of enzymes which aid in clotting.

Easy bruising and prolonged bleeding from minor cuts are noted within the first few years of life. The most debilitating aspect of hemophilia is frequent and recurrent bleeding into major weightbearing joints and into tissues causing destruction of the smooth white cartilage, thickening of the joint lining (Leavitt, 1975), tenderness, swelling, and permanent loss of joint mobility.

Burns

Approximately 2,000 children die each year from burns and 20 percent of burn victims are children under five (Cosman, 1974; Love & Walthall, 1977). Treatment of the burned child is a long drawn-out process, with numerous psychological and psychosocial implications. Major concerns are loss of body fluids and prevention of infection. Later treatment focuses on debridement of the dead tissue (first under anaesthesia, then with hydrotherapy) and on psychological and physiological rehabilitation. Problems associated with the burns are the development of joint contractures around the burned areas and decubitus ulcers from the lack of movement. The use of circular electronic beds aids in prevention of ulcers. The assessment of the burned areas is based on the Rule of Five's (Cosman, 1974). According to the Rule of Five's, each arm is 10 percent, each leg is 15 percent, posterior trunk is 20 percent as is the anterior trunk, and the head is 15 percent. The neck and perineal regions comprise the remaining percentage. Aggressiveness and emotional disturbances are frequently attempts to cope with the intense pain burned children experience, particularly during continued changings of dressings. Love and Walthall (1977) suggested that the characteristic behavior patterns of the burned child result from trauma and emotional threat, hormonal and metabolic imbalance, and infection. Gross scarring, nightmares, body-image disturbances from disfigurement, and social regression and withdrawal are issues that must be dealt with by sensitive, patient, and understanding teachers, medical personnel, and parents.

REFERENCES AND SUGGESTED READINGS

References for Chapter 4 have been included with references given at the end of Chapter 5.

Working With Young Physically-Impaired Children: Part B—Educational Programming

M. Beth Langley

EDUCATIONAL PROGRAMMING ASPECTS

Personnel

More than with any other type of handicapping condition, personnel working with the physically-impaired child must truly function as a multidisciplinary team if the child is to realize maximum potential.

A critical team member of any school serving a population of physically-handicapped children is the physical therapist (P.T.), who administers the various forms of physical therapy prescribed by the physician. Primarily concerned with the child's muscle tone, posture, range of motion, and locomotion abilities, the physical therapist also trains teachers and aides in transfer activities, proper positioning techniques, and principles of handling the child so as to facilitate maximum motor-skill development. Scarnati (1976) stressed the importance of the physical therapist in the preschool setting for both early physical intervention for the child and training for the parents. The physical therapist develops home programs to be implemented by the parents, whom he instructs in therapeutic techniques and their rationale.

Equally valuable to the multidisciplinary team in the preschool is the occupational therapist (O.T.). Often difficult to distinguish from the P.T., the occupational therapist's role is to facilitate arm, head, hand, and mouth movements based on evaluation of the child's functional developmental level. The occupational therapist's tools include toys, play, and activities of daily living (ADL) (typical activities: development of hand dominance; feeding programs; facilitation of reach, grasp, and release with a prosthesis; improvement in writing skills; and increase in range of motion in the upper extremities—Anderson, Greer, and McFadden, 1976).

The speech therapist working in the preschool with orthopedically and health-impaired children will coordinate her efforts with those of the physical and the occupational therapists in developing feeding and positioning techniques that will best facilitate prespeech behaviors and vocalizations. Two other major responsibilities of the speech therapist are design and adaptation of communication systems and development of language programs.

The teacher's role as a member of the multidisciplinary team is to provide adaptive instructional material and to individualize instructional approaches. In a preschool setting, the teacher serves as the environmental engineer by setting the conditions and arranging the environment in such a way as to encourage children to learn how to learn, express ideas, and participate in social and emotional experiences that will develop adaptive and independent-living behaviors.

Involving parents and primary caregivers in the child's preschool learning experiences promotes assumption of responsibility for continuing the educational process in the home. Unlike their physically-intact peers who abandon crayons, books, and paste at the end of the day, children whose physical impairments necessitate adaptive and specialized equipment cannot leave behind walkers, prostheses, braces, and adapted feeding and writing equipment. Communication boards, urinary devices, artificial limbs, and cuffs to hold spoons and crayons must become an integral part of the child's life in order for the child to function as independently as possible. Parents need support and instruction from school personnel to enable them to aid their child in accepting and using such appliances throughout waking hours.

These key people must integrate their efforts to allow the physically-impaired child to attain maximum physical and social-emotional independence and to achieve a positive self-concept during preschool years.

Environmental Aids to Development

Prostheses

A prosthesis, or artificial limb, acts as a substitute for a missing body part and encourages the child to maintain residual function in the deficient limb. Children are fitted with prostheses as early as possible to facilitate acceptance of the equipment, promote bilateral activities, incorporate the artificial limb into their body image, and improve balance and posture (Challenor & Katz, 1973). Additionally, use of a prosthesis prevents atrophy of muscles surrounding the residual limb. Artificial limbs are designed for cosmetic and functional purposes. Fitting of prostheses should coincide with developmental landmarks to facilitate all possible normal and sequential motor-skills development. The upper-limb deficient child will be fitted with prostheses when he has sitting balance, usually around 6 to 8 months when he is ready to stand (Shephard, 1974). Prosthetic devices are designed to match the child's central nervous system maturation and will become more complex as the child develops more control over his movements and as cognitive processes allow more complex motor-planning abilities. The severely retarded child will only rarely be fitted with functional prostheses as his level of thinking skills may prevent efficient use. Angliss (1974) reports that because the limbs are more sensitive to sensory feedback and prostheses are often heavy and restrict or reduce speed of movement, many children prefer to function independently of their prosthesis. The physical and the occupational therapists will work jointly to teach the child to use his feet for eating, dressing, and pre-academic skills. Maximum independence, both with and without prosthetic devices, is an ultimate goal for these children. Rolling activities prepare the upper-limb deficient child for assuming a sitting posture. Teaching him to stand is done through a sequential progression of movements. Facilitation of muscle strength and endurance as well as of equilibrium reactions and appropriate falling techniques are included among other physical-management goals of these children. More specific procedures and techniques are offered by Challenor and Katz (1974), Shephard (1974), and Angliss (1974).

Should the child experience trouble with or damage to the prosthetic limb while at school, the teacher should take no action other than alerting the prosthetist (the individual responsible for its construction) and the child's parents.

Adaptive Equipment, Orthotics, and Wheelchairs

Any piece of equipment designed to enable the child to perform with more independence can be considered adaptive equipment. More typically, such assistive devices include a variety of modifications of common objects used in daily living activities. Adaptive equipment facilitates components of movement in a developmental sequence, increases the child's range of motion, normalizes tone, decreases the tendency toward pathological reflexes, allows the child to function maximally with minimal pathology, eliminates the need for one-to-one assistance, and minimizes abnormal-looking postures. Disadvantages include immediate identification of the child's impairments; sensitivity about appearance; and limitation of opportunities for sensory feedback, free exploration of space, and physical contact with other children.

Equipment most often found in preschool settings are standing tables, cage balls, bolsters, wedges, floor sitters, and prone boards (see Figure 5-1). More specific equipment is discussed in the curriculum section. Commercial companies produce such adaptive equipment, but classroom teachers can work together with the P.T., O.T., school carpenters, and parents to design and construct the same materials. The advantages of school-personnel construction are that adaptations can be tailor-made for a specific child, are usually more creative, and can be constructed for nominal fees—usually, only the cost of the materials. Guidelines for making adaptive equipment are suggested by Bergman (1974), Finnie (1975), and Copeland, Ford and Solon (1976).

Braces, or orthotics, serve many functions for physically-impaired children but

Figure 5-1 Adaptive equipment

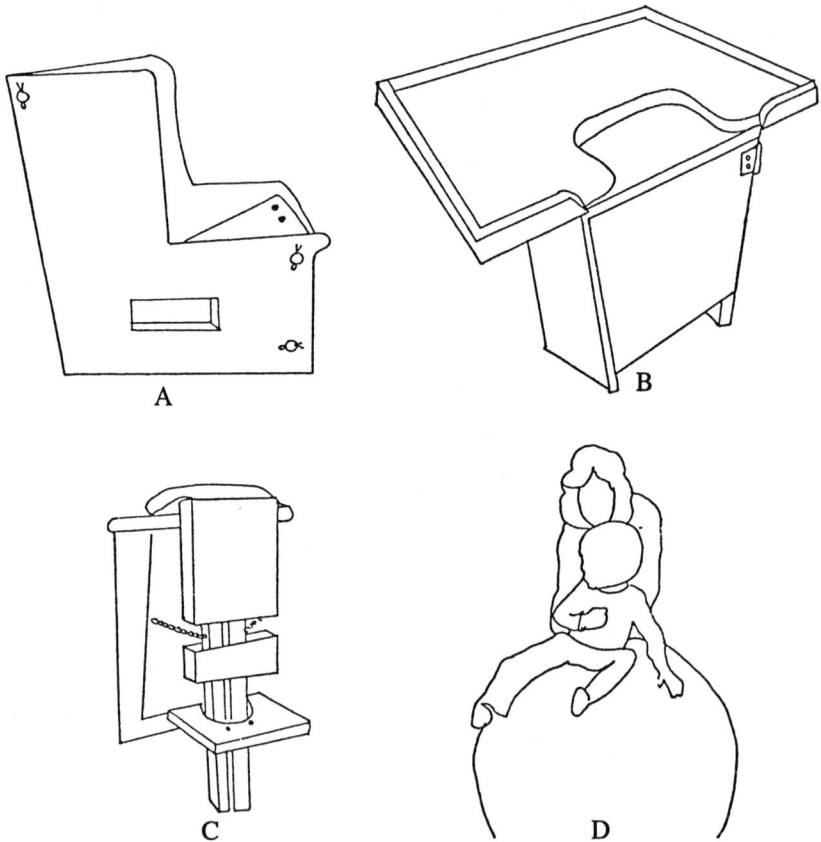

(A) Flexion box (B) Standing Table (C) Prone board (D) Cage ball

Source: Developmental physical management for the multi-disabled child. B. Buttram and G. Brown. University, Alabama: University of Alabama. Reprinted with permission.

primarily aid or substitute for weak muscles. Challenor (1974) named these purposes of bracing: (1) stabilization of joints for weight bearing, (2) prevention of contractures, (3) alignment and control of the body, (4) immobilization of painful joints, (5) positioning of proximal limbs for functional hand use, and (6) facilitation of desired movements for functional use and training.

Traditionally, braces were constructed from heavy metal; today, a majority of braces are designed from a lightweight polypropylene plastic and attached to the child with velcro fastenings. These braces are neither as heavy nor as hot as the metal ones, require less maintenance, involve less attention to the child as they can be worn under clothing, and encourage the child's independence in dressing as there are minimal or no buckles or locks to be fastened.

Depending on the child's need and size, wheelchairs come in a variety of designs, materials, and dimensions and with infinite adaptive equipment. Basically, there are two types of chairs (see Figure 5-2): for positioning and for locomotion. Relaxation chairs may be simple or complex and position the child for feeding and eye-hand activities as well as for encouraging normal motor postures. The Hogg Chair is characteristic of a chair used primarily to transport children who are nonambulatory or need supported sitting. A lightweight chair constructed from aluminum and plastic webbing strips, the Hogg Chair can fit under a table and in the trunk of a car. Its use is most appropriate for young children who are not ready

Figure 5-2 Two types of wheelchairs

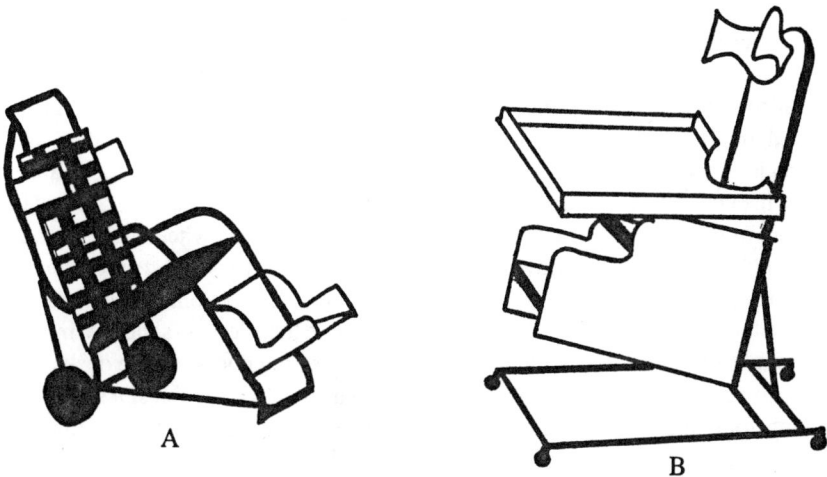

(A) Hogg chair (B) Relaxation chair

to propel themselves by maneuvering the wheels of a regular wheelchair. The preschool child most frequently uses either a "tiny-tot" wheelchair or a "growing child" wheelchair (Gordon, 1969).

Barrier-Free Architecture

Preschool and nursery school classes for a majority of physically impaired children have existed primarily in hospital and rehabilitation center settings. Now that education focuses on serving disabled children in the least restrictive environment, a move is on to integrate orthopedically- and health-impaired children into daycare and preschool centers with normal children. Preparation to receive this special population must necessarily encompass alleviating not only attitudinal, but also architectural, barriers. Bookbinder (1977) stressed that, regardless of the educational plan, no instructional service for a handicapped child can be effective if it is housed where the child is separated from other children by an invisible barrier of curiosity and fear.

Safford and Arbitman (1975) suggested that the emotional reaction of a youngster to an impaired child may be a response to a wheelchair, braces, or prosthetic limb, rather than to the child himself. To allay these responses, Meeting Street School developed simulated exercises to enable normal children to identify with the impaired child (Bookbinder, 1977).

Perhaps an easier issue to remedy is that of designing barrier-free architectural structures. Architectural barriers make children dependent, limit opportunities for experience, and lower self-esteem. For an active and curious child, an architectural barrier may be extremely frustrating. Buses with hydraulic lifts and devices for locking chairs into place will be required to transport wheelchair children. Specialized car seats, seat belts, or bean bag chairs and transfer boards may be required on regular buses transporting children who lack trunk stability and independent sitting balance. Reserved parking spaces for disabled people are a must in the community to allow easy access to business locales. Control buttons in elevators must be positioned within easy reach of a child in a wheelchair. Ramps with handrails and wide, shallow steps make ascension of curbs and steps easier for children dependent on wheelchairs, walkers, and braces. Electronically controlled doors or doors that open inwardly are more negotiable than double-action swinging doors, and toilet cubicles should have outwardly opening doors. While desks and tables should be high enough to accommodate a wheelchair, mirrors, sinks, toilets, drinking fountains, telephones, and light switches should all be low enough to facilitate independence in wheelchair children. Floor surfaces should be void of thick-pile carpet and made of a nonskid material. Table 5-1 gives measurements offered by Birch and Johnstone (1975) and Gutman and Gutman (1968); more extensive guidelines can be found in Love and Walthall (1977).

Table 5-1 Suggested Measurements for a Barrier-Free Design

Fixture	From Floor	Width	Depth
1. Toilet seat	20"		
2. Toilet cubicle		36 "	66 "
3. Table surfaces	30"		
4. Sinks	30"		
5. Cafeteria-serving trays	32"	34 "	
6. Handrails from wall	33"	1½"	1¼"
7. Mirrors	36"		
. Drinking fountains	36"		
9. Door handles	42"		
10. Elevator-control buttons	42"		
11. Light switches	42"		
12. Telephone dial	48"		
13. Door		3 ft.	

Curricular Considerations

Designing Educational Programs

Classroom design for physically handicapped children is not entirely atypical. Other than incorporation of special equipment and barrier-free architecture, desks should be spaced widely enough to allow passage of a wheelchair. Gordon (1969) reported the design of a unique circular table tailored to allow various sized wheelchairs and to decrease the possibility of objects falling or being knocked from the table surface. The value of sand and water tables for creative expressions has been noted by many (Safford & Arbitman, 1975, and Gordon, 1969).

An "ongoing curriculum" is an educational intervention process to integrate motor, cognitive, language, self-care, and social-skill development into a continuing program for children functioning on a sensory-motor preschool level. The concept implies that, while each child is engaged in activities promoting skill development in each of the five curriculum areas, the activities are not necessarily carried out independently. Head control, a motor activity, may be practiced as the child actively learns to recognize shapes and colors, a cognitive activity, as he is positioned over a wedge to facilitate midline manipulation of shape-sorting boxes

---

Table 5-2 Ongoing Curriculum

8:00 — 8:30   Arrival

Undressing

Toileting

Skin Check
   a. cuts, bruises, scrapes
   b. swollen or red areas around braces or prostheses
   c. chapped skin
   d. braces or prosthesis adjusted
   e. toes positioned correctly
   f. fingernails smooth and short

Positioning

8:30 — 8:45   Morning orientation to peers, teacher, self-awareness time

8:45 — 10:00   Curriculum activities: rotation through individual learning stations

   a. fine motor

   b. gross motor

   c. cognitive
      1. memory
      2. reasoning
      3. association
      4. discrimination
      5. quantitative reasoning
      6. spatial and seriation

   d. self care
      1. dressing
      2. grooming

   e. social
      1. self-concept
      2. body image
      3. interaction patterns

   f. language
      1. imitation
      2. reception
      3. expression formation

10:00 — 10:45	Snack	
		a. feeding
		b. socialization
		c. language
		d. fine motor
	Toileting	
	Positioning	
10:45 — 11:30	Continuation of rotation through instructional domains	
11:30 — 12:30	Lunch	
		a. feeding
		b. language
		c. socialization
		d. fine motor
12:30 — 1:00	Toileting	
	Positioning	
	Rest	
1:00 — 1:30	Group time for music and art	
		a. socialization development
		b. large-and-small-muscle coordination
		c. language development
		d. cognitive development
1:30 — 2:00	Preparation for end of day	
		a. dressing
		b. positioning

---

such as those produced by Fisher-Price and Tupperware. Grasping and hand-to-mouth skills, fine motor activities, may be integrated with self-feeding. The classroom can be sectioned into areas representing each curricular aspect so that the child can begin to anticipate and associate the corresponding activities. The teacher constantly must be aware of the child's physical comfort and needs, including positioning and toileting. A daily schedule that reflects the routine of an "ongoing curriculum" is presented in Table 5-2.

This strategy permits the child to continue in an activity even when the teacher is conducting an instructional program with another child. Thus, while one child may be positioned in the motor area in a flexion box to facilitate hip flexion and counteract extension patterns, the teacher may be working with another child in the language area. Each child is rotated through the various areas and repositioned until the child has performed tasks individualized to its needs in all areas.

Passive stretching of muscles and encouragement to continue ambulatory games as long as possible is emphasized with the muscular-dystrophied child. Even in the late ambulatory stage of the disease the child should stand and walk daily for a minimum of three hours to maintain joint alignment and prevent atrophy from disuse of the muscles (Harris and Cherry, 1974).

To counteract developing kyphosis in the asthmatic child, stretching exercises are suggested. The physical therapist or parent pulls back the elbows while stabilizing the trunk to stretch the pectoral muscles while the child clasps the hands behind the head. Other recommended exercises include lateral bending to maintain flexibility of the ribs, partial sit-ups, and leg raising to strengthen abdominal muscles and facilitate expiration (Mascia, 1974). Blowing and breathing exercises are valuable for both muscular-dystrophied and asthmatic children. Such exercises can be developed into gamelike activities consisting of blowing up balloons until they pop, blowing ping pong balls back and forth to other children or in a race, and blowing to activate the pinwheels.

Before any physical education program is begun for a physically-impaired child, the preschool teacher should be aware of several cautions (Cratty, 1973). Among these are that any exercise or activity program must first be prescribed or approved by the child's physician; after a comprehensive evaluation, some physical activities may be contraindicated for a physically-involved child, and that such children more quickly experience fatigue than do their normal peers. Invaluable sources for developmental activities appropriate for the younger nonambulatory child are offered by Cliff, Gray, and Nymann (1974), Cratty (1973), Finnie (1975), Johnson (1978), Kline (1977), and Levy (1977). Practical suggestions for teachers in a preschool setting can also be found in the *Guide to Early Developmental Training* (1977). Cratty (1969, 1972, and 1973) has developed numerous physical activities for the preacademic and physically-impaired child which stimulate mental and social as well as physical development. Other activities have been designed for older physically-impaired children by Pomeroy (1964) and Wheeler (1969). Use of light-weight, easy-to-propel balls, such as Nerf balls, Whiffle, and beach balls, encourage participation. These balls also travel at slower speeds than other balls and are not frightening upon contact. Skill Development Equipment Company produces uniquely designed, colorful, foam-constructed motor equipment ideal for physically-impaired children. Fred Sammons Company and Preston Company also manufacture specialized motor-development equipment.

Motor-Development Programming

Basic to all life-skill activities, the initiation of communication, the formation of concepts, and development of independence and a healthy self-concept is the ability to move. Limitations on movement affect all developmental skills. By preschool age, the child is fully mobile and can engage in group running, jumping, and climbing as well as solitary play such as riding tricycles and swinging. Through active participation, the preschool child learns to share turns and playthings and the linguistic concepts of possession, pronouns, and prepositions.

Independence is displayed as the child locates the bathroom, washes his hands, drinks at the water fountain, and serves himself at snack time. The interrelationship of physical skills and development becomes even more pronounced when the impairments limit play opportunities and independent, self-care skills. Rosenbloom (1977) implied that even as young as six months, infants deprived of an upright position developed perceptual disabilities. Maximizing the physically handicapped child's physical potential through developmental movements is critical to normalization.

Neurological maturation is the seat of normal physical development. The acquisition of normal motor milestones is dependent upon integration of basic reflex and postural mechanisms into higher-level movement patterns. In cerebral palsy, the injury to the brain inhibits neurological maturation by retention of primitive reflex patterns. Although the literature describes numerous reflexes, the seven most influential reflexes inhibiting acquisition of motoric milestones are: tonic labyrinthine, neck-righting, asymmetrical tonic neck, symmetrical tonic neck, grasp, positive supporting reflex, and the Moro reflex. If certain postural reactions are not developed, the child will not expand the early motor behaviors into more complex ones, which include the optical and labyrinthine righting reactions, the parachute reaction, the Landau reaction, and the body-righting reaction (Bobath, 1967). The effects of these reflexes and reactions on normal motor development are illustrated in Table 5-3.

Appropriate positioning techniques and range-of-motion activities, moving a joint through its entire range of movement, are critical to facilitation of an upright posture, appropriate sitting postures, locomotion, and inhibition of primitive reflex patterns. Adaptive equipment is frequently employed for positioning purposes. Sidelyers inhibit flexion patterns and promote body symmetry and midline skills. Wedges and bolsters inhibit flexion and facilitate extension patterns, head control, and manipulative skills. In addition, these two pieces of equipment prevent shoulder restriction and encourage weight bearing on forearms, reduce muscle tone and reaching against gravity. Large cage balls and vestibular boards are excellent for developing equilibrium and righting as well as protection reactions and body extension. Floor sitters enable the child without sitting balance to join his peers in group activities and to assume long-leg sitting. Flexion boxes, which aid in achieving hip and trunk flexion and in bringing the child's shoulders forward and using the hands together in the midline, are important equipment for the child with extension patterns or weak muscle tone. Prone boards and standing tables allow an upright posture and weight-bearing positions that strengthen lower-extremity muscles and free the child's hands for manipulative activities. Both pieces of adaptive equipment are frequently used with spina bifida children to improve circulation, bowel, bladder, and respiratory functions, and to facilitate body symmetry. Range-of-motion activities are performed by the physical therapist or the child's mother under direction of the physical therapist for the purpose of

---

Table 5-3 Differences in Developmental Milestones of C.P. Children as Compared to Normal Children

Skill	Normal Child	Cerebral-Palsied Child
Head up from prone	1-3 months	12 months
Reaches	3-5 months	14 months
Sits	6-8 months	20 months
Crawls	8 months	26 months
Single words	12 months	27 months
Stands	13 months	27 months
Walks alone	18 months	33 months

---

maintaining joint flexibility and preventing the development of contractures, the fixation of joints in abnormal postures. Excellent diagrams of range of motion activities are depicted in *Mothers can Help* (Cliff, Gray, and Nyman, 1974). Although cerebral-palsied children develop motor skills within the normal sequential framework, acquisition of basic milestones is delayed considerably. Denhoff (1955, p. 61) delineated the delays seen in a majority of cerebral-palsied children. These differences are presented in Table 5-3.

Children with spina bifida and hydrocephalus frequently exhibit delayed head and trunk control. Site of the lesion determines whether spina bifida children are confined to a wheelchair; above the twelfth thoracic level, the child will require a wheelchair for all ambulation; between the twelfth and fourth lumbar level, the child will be able to walk with the assistance of crutches and braces or a walker within his home and school environments. When the site of the lesion lies between the fourth lumbar and the second sacral level, the child may travel in his community aided by braces and a walker or crutches (Bleck, 1975).

Shepard (1974) suggests the use of prone boards, rollator walkers, and scooter boards with spina bifida children. Most of these children wear long leg braces with pelvic bands for hip stability, and achieve independent ambulation by rolling or crawling. They should be encouraged to perform the following activities to develop balance, arm strength, and weight transfers:

- child in a sitting position pushes down on hands to lift body from the surface
- child is held at high thighs and walked on hands and "wheelbarrowed"
- child stands with hands on a wall on which have been taped colored markers, moves one hand at a time to touch various colored markers (learns to balance by transferring weight with trunk to facilitate standing and walking)

- child stands facing you with hands on your shoulders as you kneel, encourage child to try to push you over
- child stands with hands against a large cage ball while you move it forward, backward, and sideways.

Physical management of these children should focus on maintenance of a stable, straight back; stability and alignment of the lower extremities in weight bearing; plantigrade feet; and mobility of hips (Shepard, 1974).

Rosenbloom (1977) found significantly depressed fine-motor abilities in children with spina bifida. He attributed the delay to primary use of their hands for supporting themselves with crutches rather than engaging in manipulative activities usually performed by preschool children.

In addition to training in falling, rolling, and standing, much emphasis is focused on training the child in using prostheses. Initially, the prosthesis is worn simply to build up the child's tolerance. Instruction is based on the child's motoric development, not on chronological age. The prosthesis should become a part of the child's body image, while maintaining residual muscle function in the involved limb. At two-and-a-half to three years, the upper-limb deficient child is taught how to hold silverware and to bring it to the mouth. Practice is performed during teaparties in which playdough is substituted for food. Later training is provided in fasteners, dressing, and toileting. At five years of age, the child should be expected to be independent in most activities of daily living (Angliss, 1974). In the preschool setting, the bilateral upper-amputee without prostheses should be allowed to use the feet during play as well as in art activities whenever necessary.

Communication Development Programming

Learning to communicate and to express ideas with peers may be experienced for the first time in the preschool setting for a child whose physical condition may have required spending most of infancy at home with adults. While the child's ability to use language effectively will depend largely on cognitive abilities, severely physically-involved children evidence aberrant trends in language development.

Cerebral-palsied children experience the most severe communication disability. Mecham (1966) reported that 70-80 percent of cerebral-palsied children have some speech involvement. Face, mouth, and diaphragm muscles responsible for speech production are affected by the injury to the brain as are the larger muscles controlling limbs and trunk. The oral musculature may be either hypotonic or hypertonic, depending upon the form of palsy. Neurological involvement prevents most cerebral-palsied children from coordinating their muscles for efficient, intelligible speech and they are said to be dysarthric. Another group—apraxic—cannot volitionally initiate speech sounds on demand even though they may nonintentionally produce natural childhood vocalizations and specific sounds during play.

Although athetoid children exhibit the most severe speech problems, all three major forms of cerebral palsy manifest similar communication patterns. Mecham (1966, p. 33) specified the following articulatory characteristics seen in cerebral-palsied children:

1. tongue-tip sounds, such as /d/, /t/, and /l/ are the most difficult to produce
2. production of sounds in the initial position was the easiest to produce; those in the final position were usually omitted
3. significantly more omissions of sounds occur than distortions or substitutions
4. sounds are articulated in the easiest manner possible and little effort is expended on refining the sound if it can be understood by others

While dysarthria is prominent among spastics and athetoids, ataxic children display neuromuscular speech problems primarily because of disordered feedback mechanisms resulting from disorientation in position and direction (Mecham, 1966).

Reverse breathing and rib flaring patterns make it difficult, if not impossible, for the cerebral-palsied child to sustain vocalization of phonemes. Voice quality is often characterized by hoarseness or muscles may be so spastic that the child is aphonic except for sounds that involuntarily escape through the vocal folds with exerted effort.

Research by Irwin (1952) concluded that consonant-vowel maturation is delayed approximately three years before the age of five-and-a-half. Acquisition of single words by cerebral-palsied children has ranged from 15 to 27 months (Byrne, 1959, Denhoff, 1955). Lags in the combination of two and three words have also been noted. A population studied by Byrne (1959) began using 2-word sentences at 36 months while Denhoff (1955) reported that the average onset of 2-word sentences in a population he investigated was 37 months. The same group of children studied by Byrne did not use 3-word sentences until 78 months. Myers (1965) and Dunsdon (1952) found significant delays in vocabulary verbal recall and verbal reasoning abilities. Generally, spastic children demonstrate better automatic language skills while athetoid children exhibit greater facility in representational language skills. Children with neuromuscular speech impairments many times find communication very frustrating because of the listener's impatience. Too often people merely nod when they don't understand or try to talk for the child. Children become resentful and frequently discouraged. Language development and sentence structure may, on the surface, appear to be delayed because many children soon discover that, if their verbal requests are to be met, they must communicate with as few words as possible to retain the listener's attention.

Hydrocephalic and spina bifida children also display unique but characteristic language patterns. They converse readily with whoever will listen and, although they talk fluently, their language reflects disorganized thought processes and weakness in conceptualization. Swisher and Pinsker (1971), Laurence (1971), and Parsons (1968) all reported on the prevalence of the ''Chatter-box'' syndrome or the ''Cocktail party'' syndrome characteristic of hydrocephalic children. Their speech is often delayed until two-and-a-half years of age, after which the output increases rapidly. The general consensus is they are hyperverbal, enjoy imitating, learning, and using new words, but their speech lacks content and their words are illogical. Parsons (1972) found these children read fluently but without comprehension, learn poems and songs easily, and do well on intelligence test items in which they recall simple sentences or a series of digits. When compared with normal peers on a word-phrase recall test, hydrocephalic children evidenced no significant difference in short-term memory abilities (Parsons, 1969).

Spain (1972) and Parsons (1968) found that hydrocephalic children demonstrated well-developed rules of syntax and morphology, but their ability to use language meaningfully was not as well developed. When based only on verbal output, the intellectual potential of hydrocephalics is often overestimated. They do well repeating stories from memory but cannot explain them; perform well on picture-vocabulary items, but fail on verbal tasks requiring reasoning and comprehension. The average scores of hydrocephalic children on the Illinois Test of Psycholinguistic Abilities are lower than those of normal peers. Younger children, in particular, demonstrate impaired abilities on auditory association and auditory-reception subtests.

A third group who exhibit language disabilities are children with total amelia or phocomelia. Because their opportunities to develop concepts are limited, these children are often restricted to the home and to their own life space. Their communicative utterances focus on having needs or desires attended to rather than on inquiring about their world, seeking new information, or sharing ideas in conversation. Vocabulary is deficient in prepositions, adverbs, and adjectives, and primarily comprised of first person pronouns, nouns, and verbs. One blind, total amelia child whom this writer has recently evaluated associated her mother's utterance of ''I'll be back in a minute'' with her mother's absence. When she desired to be left alone, this child requested, ''I want you to be back in a minute,'' meaning she wanted the person with her to leave. When asked, ''What do you brush your hair with?'' she replied, ''I brush my hair with mother,'' demonstrating confusion over the referent ''What.'' The concepts of same and different were not within this preschooler's linguistic repertoire since she had no means, tactual or visual, by which to compare and contrast objects.

To enable nonverbal children (or children who may be able to verbalize but whose speech is unintelligible) to communicate, conversation or communication boards can be designed for an individual child's needs. A communication board may be constructed of posterboard, plywood, and/or plexiglass, and contains pictures, words, symbols representing ideas, or letters and numbers to which the child points to convey his thoughts. Pointing can be accomplished with the child's finger, head, mouthstick, or even toes. Other forms of communication boards may consist of notebooks or cards kept in the pocket. One preschooler designed her own "communication board" by having this writer cut out frequently needed representational pictures and pasting them on colored circles. The circles were laminated and hole-punched in order to be strung on a necklace. Initially this child rejected a typical communication board but was motivated by the necklace to progress to a more conventional form of communication. Other children in this writer's classroom preferred a board on which were positioned magnetized inch cubes portraying pictures. To express responses or initiate requests and immediate needs, the children pushed the block representing their idea into a designated taped area on the board. The "response area" was positioned according to each child's range-of-motion abilities. While most communication boards are attached to the child's wheelchair, they can be positioned elsewhere for the ambulatory child. Bigge (1976), McDonald & Shultz (1973), and Vanderheiden & Grilley (1976) all offer excellent designs of various types of nonverbal communication devices. Usually communication boards are designed and constructed by the child's parents, teachers, and speech or occupational therapist, but many commercially produced communication machines are available from companies such as *Adaptive Therapeutic Company, Zygo Industries,* and *Voicetex.* Vicker (1974) and McDonald (1976) have provided valuable guidelines for developing a communication board:

1. It must be designed to match the child's cognitive and receptive language skills.
2. The child must be able to attend to visual and verbal symbols and have some means of storing and retrieving them.
3. The child must consistently be able to indicate responses so that any listener can interpret them.
4. The child's ambulatory, visual, and postural abilities must be evaluated to determine the type, size, and position of the board that will be most functional for the child.
5. The content of the board must reflect the child's needs in varying environments. Always a must is some way for the child to indicate "yes" and "no," feelings, and social amenities.
6. The board must be continually monitored and evaluated so that it can be modified with the child's expanding and changing needs.
7. There must be some motivation for the child to want to communicate.

Figure 5-3 Two examples of communication boards

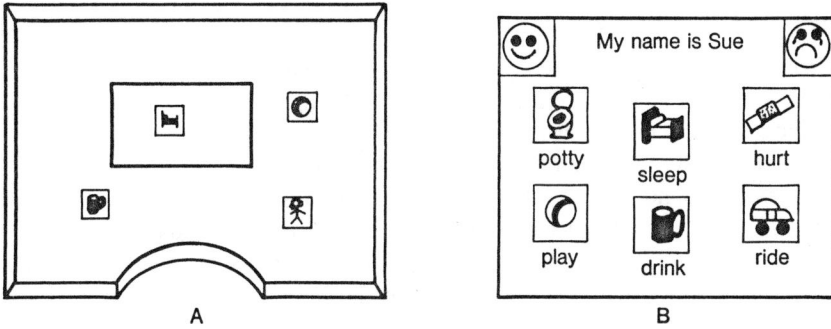

(A) A magnetized board on which the child responds by pushing the block representing his need into the rectangular space. (B) A direct selection board on which the child responds by pointing to the picture representing his need or message.

An alternative form of nonverbal communication system advocated for cerebral-palsied and other nonverbal children has been Bliss Symbols, developed in Ontario and based on approximately 100 idio- and pictographic symbols that can become quite abstract, requiring integrative cognitive functions. According to Vicker (1974), visual-perceptual difficulties are so pronounced in cerebral-palsied children that this plus the abstraction level of Bliss Symbols and their altered syntactic pattern must be considered before selecting this communication system for a child. For further information on Bliss Symbols, refer to a text edited by Vanderheiden and Grilley (1976).

An excellent language program for developing organized, functional syntactic generation is a system based on the Fitzgerald Key for the deaf. Designed by Fokes (1977), the *Fokes Sentence Builder* provides visual cues for structuring language into seven different categories. Another language-development program beneficial to brain-injured children is Lee's *Interactive Language Development System* (Lee, Koenigskencht, & Mulhern, 1975). Particularly useful in a preschool setting in which children work in groups, this program provides specific lessons designed to facilitate spontaneous use of indefinite and personal pronouns, primary and secondary verb forms, negatives, conjunctions, wh- questions, and interrogative reversals. McDonald and Chance (1964) have outlined detailed practical suggestions for preverbal skills that parents may carry out in the home with their cerebral-palsied preschooler. Crickmay (1966) and Mysak (1959) have described a series of reflex inhibiting postures and techniques designed to encourage speech production. Young (1962) developed motokinesthetic procedures for teaching children where and how to position their articulators for generating speech sounds.

Cognitive Programming

Within the cognitive realm, special material adaptations may include fastening handles or spools on puzzle pieces, attaching velcro or magnets to blocks for easier manipulation, and numerous modifications of writing implements from magnetic wrist cuffs to velcro and leather bands that hold paint brushes, pencils, and spoons for the child with no grasping ability. Multisensory, textured letters and numbers, and raised-line writing paper can be fastened on clipboards or secured to tables with masking tape. Pencils and crayons can be fastened to the child's chair or table with a long piece of string for retrieval, when the child drops the crayon. Spring-handled scissors make cutting less frustrating for the child with an uncoordinated or weak grasp. Cardboard or plastic templates of shapes, numbers, letters, animals, and even the child's name can be used to train discrimination and visual-motor integration skills. By taping the templates over a tagboard, the child lacking fine-motor movements to draw letters and shapes can successfully execute them through gross motor movements of his arm with a crayon. Once completely colored in, the templates can be removed to reveal numbers, child's name, or animal and transportation figures. Headbands can be adapted to hold paint brushes, crayons, and pointers. Styrofoam letters and numbers permit the child with headbands to hold up letters along with peers by piercing the styrofoam with the tip of the pointer. Similarly, sorting colors or shapes can be accomplished with cardboard figures, a magnet, paperclips, and a muffin tin. The magnet is attached to a special headstick and the paperclips to the figures. By tapping the colored discs with the headstick, the child can secure and then release them into the appropriate compartment by scraping the discs against the sides of the muffin tin. Such adaptations may be applied to any material.

Materials from *Developmental Learning Materials* and *Teaching Resources* are excellent for training part-whole associations, figure-ground relationships, missing element concepts, and visual and auditory discrimination and association skills. Zedler (1955) developed an innovative and exciting multisensory procedure for teaching brain-injured children letter identification, auditory discrimination, and sound-symbol associations in preparation for reading and writing. Cruickshank et al. (1961) created a wealth of methods for developing perceptual and quantitative abilities in this group. Robinault (1973) and Barry (1961) have designed equipment and procedures to facilitate perceptual, fine-motor, and language acquisition by multiply handicapped and aphasic children. Teaching procedures, adaptations of materials, and presentation of concepts and activities to preschool cerebral-palsied children have been extensively discussed by Hauessermann (1969).

Comprehensive service-delivery programs for preschool physically-involved children have been designed by Bigge and O'Donnell (1976); Connor, Williamson, and Siepp (1978); Davis and Langley (Note 1); Gordon (1969); Myer Children's Rehabilitation Institute; and Safford and Arbitman (1975). Harris Hillman School for the Multiply Handicapped in the Metropolitan School System of Nashville, Tennessee, is one of the country's most unique and comprehensive educational service-delivery institutions housing preschool physically involved children. Harris Hillman's architecture was designed for this special population, and school personnel have fully developed the concept of transdisciplinary teams to generate unique and innovative teaching procedures.

Body-Image and Self-Care Programming

Bigge and O'Donnell (1976) stressed the importance of inculcating self-care skills in early childhood to promote independence in adulthood. Nursery school or kindergarten is ideal for encouraging self-sufficiency within physical limitations. Teachers should not be overzealous in assisting the child with self-care needs when all that is needed is a tactual prompt at the elbow or a gesture to secure a cup or clothing article while the child performs the primary manipulative task. By talking with the occupational therapist, the teacher learns how much assistance the child needs and to encourage the child to practice techniques he has learned in occupational therapy sessions.

By preschool age, children should be able to rest crutches or walkers against sinks while they wash their hands, empty urine-collection bags, or use portable urinals with minimal assistance and manipulate zippers, braces, and cutlery with moderate help. Some children may need more time for eating, toileting, and dressing and should be allowed to begin preparation for such skills earlier than their peers so as to perform them independently as soon as possible. When helping the child with dressing skills, the teacher should remember that clothing should be removed first from the nonimpaired (lead) limb and first put on the involved limb. Loose-fitting clothes with front openings, elastic waists, and velcro attachments facilitate independence in dressing. Special dressing techniques designed for physically-impaired children have been presented in *Dressing Techniques for the Cerebral Palsied Child* (1954). Finnie (1975) has written detailed instructions for parents in dressing procedures for young cerebral-palsied children.

Some children will need adaptive equipment for feeding. Cups with sides partially cut out, with double handles or spout lids, aid children who are beginning to develop independent drinking behaviors. Spoon handles can be built up through use of plastic Clorox bottle handles, bicycle grip handles, or special washable foam material. Universal cuffs can easily be constructed from velcro and washcloths. Cake pans can be used for dishes when children are learning to scoop as the higher sides assist in the scooping actions, or special plate guards can be purchased. Dycem℗ matting is nonslip material that prevents plates and glasses from sliding. Bathtub stickers can serve the same purpose and are less expensive. Feeding techniques for the physically impaired have been described by Finnie (1975), Matheny and Ruby (1963), and Mueller (1972). *Adaptive Therapeutics Systems, Inc.* has designed a self-feeding system that can be completely operated by mouth.

Making the child more self-sufficient can be accomplished with special adaptations applied to light switches and door handles. Soap can be suspended from the faucet and encased in inexpensive netting to secure it while the child lathers the hands. These adaptive aids may be purchased from Fred Sammons *Be-OK Self-Help Aids*.

A healthy body image contributes significantly to success with self-care skills. Using impaired limbs as assists is critical if the limbs are to be incorporated into the child's body image. Often giving an impaired limb a nickname (Sam for boys, Samella for girls, etc.) motivates the child to employ it without attracting undue attention to the impairment. Self-concept and body-image games, especially songs created by Hap Palmer and Ella Jenkins, develop awareness of body parts in a social situation. Stimulating body parts with different textured materials, vibrators, and soft brushes can heighten a child's awareness of his body. Body puzzles such as those produced by *Developmental Learning Materials, Sesame Street, Instructo, Constructive Playthings,* and *Childcraft* are excellent for teaching body-image concepts. *Teaching Resources* manufactures a body-image puzzle that can be put together in numerous ways to depict various movements and the head is reversible to depict either a happy or sad face. Helping the child draw a self-portrait while looking in the mirror is excellent for developing a self-concept as well as reinforcing spatial and linguistic concepts. Creative talents and mental imagery can be evoked as the children turn tempera-painted handprints into turkeys and footprints into flowers with the print serving as the body of the flower.

Opportunities for fostering autonomy, self-expression, representational-play behaviors, and socialization skills are at their optimum during the preschool years. As children engage in play activities with other children, they begin to learn that not only are they separate entities with powers and limitations but that they must conform to certain social demands and adhere to peer-group expectations to win approval and effectively assert opinions and rights. Safford and Arbitman (1975) proposed several objectives that early educational experiences should address in the area of social-emotional development. Outstanding is encouraging the child to realize who he is and what he can and cannot do. A major responsibility entails helping the child develop a healthy self-concept. Disfigurements impede acquisition of the ability to feel good about one's self. A realistic and yet accepting attitude regarding the appearance of their bodies is essential to formation of positive peer relationships. Figure 5-4 is a very accurate self-portrait by an osteogenesis imperfecta child, outgoing, well accepted and liked by her peers.

Figure 5-4 A self-portrait drawn by a 12-year-old child with osteogenesis imperfecta

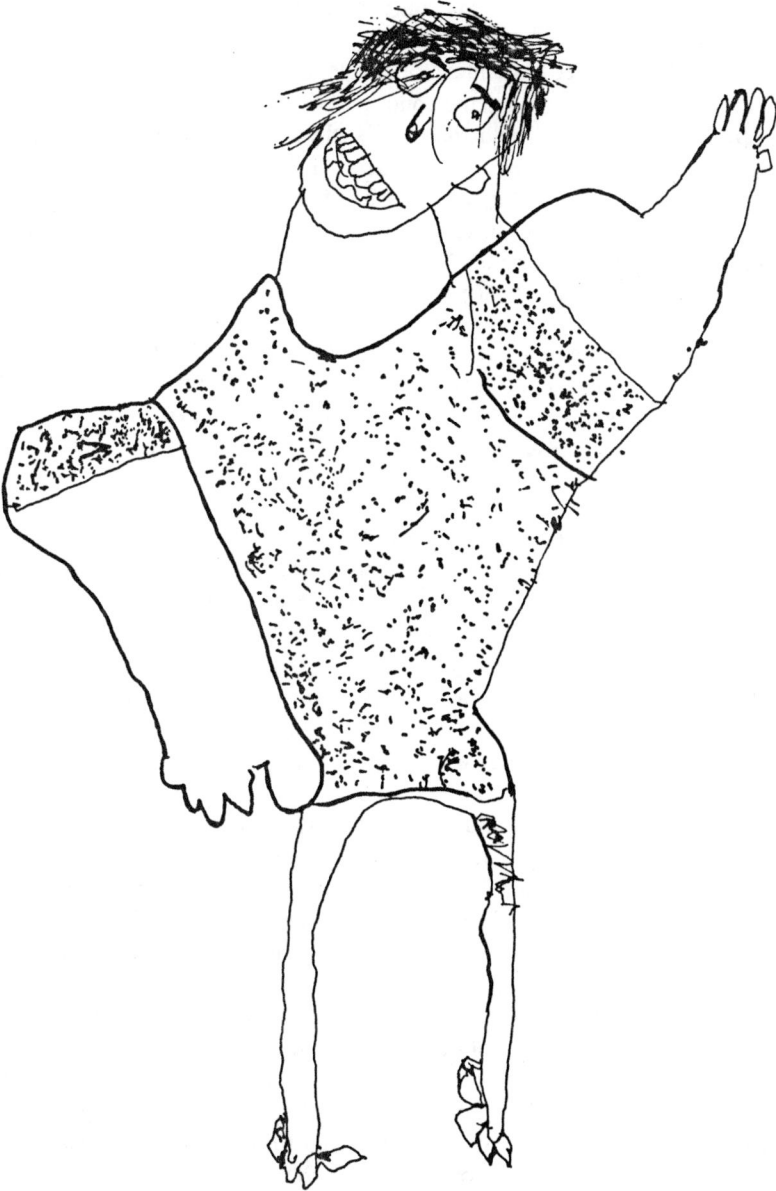

Major tasks during the preschool years (Safford and Arbitman, 1975) are channeling the child's aggressiveness and giving assistance to develop internal regulatory impulses, to acquire facility in communication, to see similarities and differences between himself and others, and to acquire an understanding and acceptance of human diversity.

The physically-impaired child must, of course, learn to cope with the handicap and with others' attitudes toward the condition. Connor, Williamson, and Siepp (1978, p. 267) explained, "both the child's physical limitations and the psychological limitations imposed by the parents and by the child's own fragile self-concept may affect his ability to establish self as an independently functioning human being." Emotional disturbances are understandable when one considers the effects a physical impairment impinges upon the socialization process as described by Battle (1974, p. 130):

> . . . part of coping involves acceptance of his functional limitations, his state of dependency, constant frustration in attempting tasks and in communicating and occasional physical discomforts from procedures, treatment, immobility, and changes as a result of growth and development.

No one personality style is characteristic of physically-impaired children. Emotional and psychological reaction to impairment will depend on age, age at the onset of disability, maturity and type of impairment and degree of disfigurement. Adjustment to the disability will be influenced by family and school attitudes (Myers, 1975). The child learns early that he or she is different and cannot do many things that peers accomplish with ease. Other children show fear—afraid they will "catch" what the child has, leaving the physically-handicapped one passive and isolated. A child may learn to use a handicap to manipulate the environment and becomes used to being attended to by others. A common circumstance encountered in classrooms where the child may be the only handicapped youngster is the tendency for peers to mother and attend to the child's every need.

The parent-child relationship is disturbed from the very beginning, parents not only learning to adjust emotionally and accept their impaired child, but coping with associated problems. Parents commonly feel guilt, denial, rejection, anxiety, disbelief, hostility, helplessness, and resentment. Long periods of hospitalization immediately after birth interfere with mother-infant attachment behaviors. The child requires continuing physical dependency. Numerous periods of separation for medical procedures, painful treatment, and hospitalizations cause children to withdraw from intimate social contacts. Connor, Williamson, and Siepp (1978) describe tendencies of parents to shield the child from experiences because of potentially hurtful encounters, to overlook what the child can do, to overprotect and fail to stimulate the child to function independently.

Overprotection, when providing extraordinary medical and therapeutic programs, is a natural response for parents. Mothers spend so much time transporting and lifting the child, while fulfilling their other career, home, and family responsibilities, that it is not surprising that such a high divorce rate exists among parents of handicapped children!

Several authors have commented on the behaviors that contribute to a teacher's effectiveness in working with the physically-handicapped. Safford and Arbitman (1975) insisted that psychological acceptance of the child's impairment was a precondition for effective coping, realistic planning, and serving the child's best interests. Lubin (1975) advises teachers of physically-impaired children to acknowledge their own feelings pertaining to stereotyping children and to try to identify with how the child perceives the world. The preschool setting will be for most physically-handicapped children their first experiences with peers, and teachers should attempt to arrange a secure and comforting atmosphere. Teachers should encourage parents to let children know when they leave and when they will return to develop the child's sense of trust and security. Sensitivity to the child's emotional and social concerns will enable the teacher to design a setting permitting the child to make independent choices and engage in interpersonal activities. Teachers must familiarize themselves with the child's physical limitations in order to encourage as much independence as possible. Consistency in demands and expectations is equally important as an understanding and stimulating environment. Ross (in Bigge and O'Donnell, 1976, p. 85) offered several suggestions that facilitate successful experiences in home and school environments:

1. accept the disability

2. set and maintain expectations for performance and accomplishment

3. support and encourage the child's attempts at independence

4. provide a variety of experiences in the child's area of strength

5. provide appropriate discipline

Helping children accept and understand their handicapped peers can be achieved through programs designed to develop social, affective behaviors. Two outstanding programs are *Developing Understanding of Self and Others* and the *Peabody Early Experiences Kit,* both published by American Guidance Service. Among the numerous children's books that have addressed the issues of the handicapped child, *Howie Helps Himself* (Fassler & Lasker, 1975) and *Don't Feel Sorry for Paul* (Wolf, 1974) focus on physically-handicapped children, cerebral-palsied and limb-deficient, respectively. *A Hospital Story: An Open Family Book for Parents and Children Together* (Stein, 1974) is an excellent source full of natural pictures of a child progressing through various phases of surgery. Reading this book prior to a peer's entrance into the hospital may alleviate the child's fears as well as peers' concern over the separation. Gross motor equipment such as the Sociobowl manufactured by Skill Development Equipment, a plastic wading pool, and snack time are excellent facilitators of social interaction. Jointly fingerpainting a large mural, engaging in a game of picture dominoes, and playing catch with soft balls are other activities that require little fine motor control and in which cooperative efforts are necessary for completing a task. These are but a few of the ways to encourage interactive play among physically-limited preschoolers.

Both parents and children will need support and encouragement as they progress in their acceptance of and adjustment to the orthopedic or health impairment. The preschool environment should offer stability and understanding while simultaneously providing opportunities for developing self-awareness and independence.

Assessment

Curriculum planning, regardless of the type of physical impairment, must be based on current assessment of the child's cognitive, linguistic, motoric, and social-personal development. Section 12 la. 532 of the Public Law 94-142 ensures handicapped children of their right to receive assessment procedures designed to evaluate their maximum potential and to consider the specific handicapping condition. Dworkin (1977, p. 39) quoted PL 94-142 Rules and Regulations to clarify the term evaluation:

> to determine whether a child is handicapped and the nature and extent of the special education and related services that the child needs. The term means procedures used selectively with an individual child and does not include basic tests administered to or procedures used with all children in a school, grade, or class.

While no instrument has been standardized on a physically-handicapped population, Table 5-4 displays instruments that most appropriately meet the assessment needs of handicapped children. More specific critique and analysis of these assessment tools and administration techniques have been outlined elsewhere by Langley (1977). Knowledge of assessment tools available for physically-handicapped children will assist the teacher in cooperatively planning with the school psychologist or psychometrist a judicious selection of a variety of tools that will yield accurate results upon which to develop an individual child's curriculum.

Table 5-4 Assessment Tools Appropriate for Physically Handicapped Children

TEST INSTRUMENT	AGE OR DEVELOP- MENTAL LEVEL	DEVELOP- MENTAL AREA	DESCRIPTION
Denver Developmental Screening Test LADOCA Project and Publisher Foundation, Inc. E. 51st Avenue & Lincoln St. Denver, Colorado 80216	Birth-6 years	Screening	An individually administered screening inventory designed to identify children's developmental delays. Measures four aspects of functioning: adaptive, fine and gross motor, language, and personal social development.
Developmental Profile Psychological Development Publications PO Box 3198 Aspen, Colorado 81611	Birth-11 years	Screening	An inventory of skills designed to screen child's development in five key areas of physical age, self-help age, social age, academic age, and communication age. Provides an individual profile depicting developmental age levels.
Haeussermann's Developmental Potential for Preschool Children Grune and Stratton 111 Fifth Avenue New York, New York 10003	2-6 years	Screening	Provides tasks for screening of functional vision and visual perceptual skills as they relate to cognitive development. Materials are common objects and can be manipulated by the child.

Table 5-4 *Continued*

TEST INSTRUMENT	AGE OR DEVELOPMENTAL LEVEL	DEVELOPMENTAL AREA	DESCRIPTION
Abstraction Test for C.P. Children In Irwin, O. C. & Hammill, D. Abstraction test for use with cerebral palsied children. *Cerebral Palsy Review*, 1964, 25, 3-9.	6-16 years	Cognitive Development	Evaluates abilities of cerebral-palsied children to perform mental processes of abstraction and categorization. Stimuli are presented auditorily and the child can respond verbally or by eye pointing.
Behavioral Characteristics Progression Chart VORT Corporation PO Box 11132 Palo Alto, California 94306		All developmental areas	Sequential chart of various developmental domains including orientation and mobility strands. Other areas covered are speech and language, fingerspelling, signing, and articulation. Dressing, grooming, ambulation by wheelchair, and other transportation strands are covered by this chart.
Columbia Mental Maturity Scale The Psychological Corporation 757 Third Avenue New York, New York 10017	3-9 years	Cognitive Development	Individual intelligence test requiring no verbal and a minimum of motor responses. The child responds by pointing to the picture that does not belong to a series of drawings on a 6'' × 19'' card. Child must have the concept of same and different.

Instrument	Age	Areas	Description
Detroit Test of Learning Aptitude Bobbs-Merrill Co., Inc. 4300 W. 62nd Street Indianapolis, Indiana 46206	3-17 years	Cognitive Development	A series of subtests which allow the examiner to assess the child's visual, auditory, and cognitive thought processes in order to pinpoint specific learning deficits.
Koontz Child Development Program Psychological Services 12031 Wilshire Blvd. Los Angeles, California 90025	1-48 months	All developmental areas	A behavior rating scale administered by parents, teachers, or therapists during a child's normal activity. Establishes level of functioning in gross skills. Text presents developmental activities appropriate for use with hearing and visually-impaired children.
Lexington Developmental Scale UCP of Bluegrass, Inc. Child Development Center of U.C.P.B. PO Box 8003 465 Springhill Drive Lexington, Kentucky 40503	Birth-6 years	Cognitive, Language, Motor, Personal-Social	Series of teacher-administered scales divided into two groupings: infant scales that assess motor, language, personal-social, cognitive, and emotional areas. The second series assesses children from 2-6 years in areas of gross and fine motor, perceptual motor, receptive and expressive language, classification, personal-social, cognitive and emotional areas.

Table 5-4 *Continued*

TEST INSTRUMENT	AGE OR DEVELOPMENTAL LEVEL	DEVELOPMENTAL AREA	DESCRIPTION
Mental Imagery Test In Robbins, S. An objective test for young cerebral-palsied children, *Cerebral Palsy Journal*, 1965, 26, 14-16.	3-6 years	Cognitive Development	Relative test of vividness of verbal imagery. Comprised of three subtests: (1) visual and auditory imagery; (2) auditory imagery alone; (3) auditory, kinesthetic, and tactile imagery.
Motor Free Visual Perception Test Academic Therapy 1539 Fourth Street San Rafael, California 94901	5-7 years	Visual Perception	This instrument requires only a pointing response to assess figure-ground, discrimination, visual closure, and form constancy.
Ordinal Scales of Psychological Development In Uzgiris, I. C. & Hunt, J. McV. *Assessment in Infancy: Ordinal Scales of psychological development.* Urbana, Ill.: University of Illinois Press, 1975.	Birth-24 months	Cognitive Development	Series of six ordinal scales based on Piagetian observations of sensory-motor schemas. Concerned with the hierarchical interrelationship of achievements at different levels. Six scales include visual pursuit and the permanence of objects, the development of means for obtaining desired environmental events, development of operational causality, construction of objects in space, and verbal and gestural imitation. Also assessed is the development of schemas for relating to objects.

Pictorial Test of Intelligence Houghton-Mifflin 666 Miami Circle, N.E. Atlanta, Georgia 30324	3-8 years	Cognitive Development	Instrument used in assessing general intellectual level. In order to respond the child need only be able to hear simple verbal instructions and to respond to visual stimuli. Subtests cover areas of picture vocabulary, form discrimination, information and comprehension, similarities in size and number, and immediate recall.
Articulation test for C. P. Children In Irwin, O.C. A manual for articulation testing for use with children with cerebral palsy. *Cerebral Palsy Review*, 1963, *24*, 13-16.	3-16 years	Language Development	Consists of five short parts: four short consonant tests and one vowel test. Intended to measure phonetic articulation. Uses verbal stimuli and requires the children to respond by imitation.
Basic Concept Inventory Follett Publishing Department D. M. 1010 W. Washington Blvd. Chicago, Illinois 60607	Kindergarten-second grade	Concepts Vocabulary	Consists of 10 very simply drawn pictures used to assess the child's knowledge of pronouns; present, past and future tenses; prepositions; and adjectives as well as his understanding of subject and predicate. Assesses not only language concepts, but also auditory discrimination, sequencing and expressive language.

Table 5-4 *Continued*

TEST INSTRUMENT	AGE OR DEVELOP-MENTAL LEVEL	DEVELOP-MENTAL AREA	DESCRIPTION
BOEHM and Tactile Test of Basic Concepts The Psychological Corporation 757 Third Avenue New York, New York 10017 and American Printing House for the Blind 1839 Frankfort Avenue Louisville, Kentucky	Kindergarten-second grade	Concepts Vocabulary	Assesses beginning school children's knowledge of frequently used basic concepts essential to success in an academic setting. Consists of 50 items concerning space, time, and quantity. Recently adapted for totally blind children.
Carrow Test of Auditory Comprehension Learning Concepts 2501 W. Lamar Austin, Texas 78705	3-7 years	Language Development	Receptive test of language comprehension that assesses the child's knowledge of nouns; verbs; adverbs; inflectional and derivational adjectives; noun-verb agreement; present, past, and future tenses; simple imperative; complex, conditional, and compound sentences. Format is a flip-type book with three pictures on a page.

Environmental Pre-Language Battery Charles E. Merrill Publishing Co. 1300 Alum Drive Columbus, Ohio 43216	12-18 months	Language Development	Designed for use by parents, paraprofessionals, and teachers for the assessment of the child's verbal and gestural imitation abilities and expressions of one- and emerging two-word construction.
Environmental Language Inventory Charles E. Merrill Publishing Co. 1300 Alum Drive Columbus, Ohio 43216	One and two word utterances	Language Development	Intensive assessment of the child's application of semantic grammatical rules in two- and three-word utterances. The child's expressive language is assessed in imitation, conversation, and play as he is provided with contextual and nonlinguistic cues.
GATE: Gestural Approach to Thought and Expression Beth Langley, M.A. Child Study Center Peabody College for Teachers Nashville, TN 37203	Birth-3 years	Language Development	A nonverbal scale designed to assess the manual and gestural communicative attempt of multihandicapped children and the prerequisite skills for signing.
Preschool Language Scale Charles Merrill Publishing Co. 1300 Alum Creek Drive Columbus, Ohio 43216	18-84 months	Language Development	Designed to isolate areas of strengths and weaknesses with regard to language facility. Consists of auditory comprehension and verbal ability scales as well as an articulation screening section.

Table 5-4 *Continued*

TEST INSTRUMENT	AGE OR DEVELOP-MENTAL LEVEL	DEVELOP-MENTAL AREA	DESCRIPTION
Receptive-Expressive-Emergent Language Scale Anhinga Press 550 Park Avenue East Tallahassee, Florida	Birth-3 years	Language Development	Primarily an interview scale, the REEL assesses the child's comprehension and expression of early language skills. The scale reveals any differences that may exist between the infant's C.A. and his combined receptive-expressive communication age.
Sequenced Inventory of Communication Development University of Washington Press Seattle, Washington 98105	4-48 months	Language Development	Comprehensive scale of receptive and expressive language development. The SICD surveys awareness, discrimination, understanding, imitation, responsiveness, and spontaneous language production. An articulation scale is also provided. This test is completely adaptable to totally blind children.
Children Move to Learn Communication Skill Builders 815 East Broadway PO Box 42050-G Tuscon, Arizona 85733	Head control through walking	Motor Development	Provides guidelines for observing head control, reaching, and grasping, trunk control, sitting, early mobility, and walking skills . . . a developmental program.

140

Instrument	Area	Scale/Age	Description
Cerebral Palsy Assessment Chart In Seman, S. et al. The cerebral palsy assessment chart. *Physical Therapy*, 1965, *45*, 463-469.	Motor Development	Postural reactions through ambulation	Chart from which the cerebral-palsied child's postural control may be assessed for the purpose of rehabilitative planning. The level which should next be emphasized is indicated in the scale.
Comprehensive Developmental Evaluation Chart El Paso Rehabilitation Center 2630 Richmond El Paso, Texas 79930	Motor Development	Birth-3 years	Assesses reflexes, gross-motor, manipulation, feeding, language, and cognitive social skills. Manual provides clear instructions for administration.
Evaluation of Ambulation in C.P. In Reimers, J. A. Scoring system for evaluation of ambulation in cerebral-palsied patients. *Developmental Medicine and Child Neurology*, 1972, *14*, 332-335.	Motor Development	Criterion Referenced	Graded system of assessing the gait and posture of cerebral-palsied children.

Table 5-4 *Continued*

TEST INSTRUMENT	AGE OR DEVELOPMENTAL LEVEL	DEVELOPMENTAL AREA	DESCRIPTION
Evaluation of Spastic Child In Wright, T. & Nicholson, J. Physiotherapy for the spastic child: An evaluation. *Developmental Medicine and Neurology*, 1973, *15*, 146-153.	Criterion Referenced	Motor Development	Tool for assessing tone, equilibrium, and motor-skill acquisition in cerebral-palsied children.
Graphic Method of Evaluation of Motor Development in Infants In Zdanska-Brincken, M. & Wolanski, N. A graphic method for the evaluation of motor development in infants. *Developmental Medicine and Neurology*, 1969, *11*, 228-241.	One month-ambulation	Motor Development	Graphic charts are set up as percentile grids. Assesses head and trunk movements sitting, standing, and walking. The child is compared with norms for normal children.

Instrument / Reference	Age Range	Domain	Description
Milani-Comparetti Developmental Chart In Milani-Comparetti, A. & Gidoni, E.A. Routine developmental examination in normal and retarded children. *Developmental Medicine and Child Neurology*, 1967, *9*, 631-638.	Birth 24 months	Motor Development	Graphic display that assesses the development and integration of reflex patterns as they mature into more complex motor skills of sitting, head control, rolling, creeping, standing, and walking.
Motor Development Test In Wolf, J. M. *The results of treatment in cerebral palsy.* Springfield, Ill.: Charles C. Thomas, 1969.	Infancy- 6 years	Motor Development	Separate scales are provided for the assessment of the upper extremities, for posture, and for locomotion. All activities are behavioral observations of the child's motor actions. The child is assessed in prone, supine, sitting, and standing position.
Stanford Function Developmental Assessment In Bleck, E.E. & Nagel, D.A.: *Physically Handicapped children: A medical atlas for teachers.* New York: Grune and Stratton, 1975.	Birth-10 years	Motor Development	This very detailed sequential scale offers behavioral tasks for evaluating both fine and gross motor skills. Gross motor skills include strength and coordination, locomotion, balance, eye-foot coordination and visual motor — upper limbs. Fine motor skills include reach, carry, and bilateral coordination, prehension, thumb-finger manipulation, grasp, placement, release, and eye-hand coordination, and graphics.

Table 5-4 *Continued*

TEST INSTRUMENT	AGE OR DEVELOP-MENTAL LEVEL	DEVELOP-MENTAL AREA	DESCRIPTION
Eating Assessment Tool In Schmidt, P. Feeding assessment and therapy for the neurologically impaired. *American Association for Education of the Severely and Profoundly Handicapped,* 1976.	Criterion referenced	Self-care Development	Feeding scale that may be used by various health professionals to assess gross motor eye-hand coordination, oral skills, and the environment as they relate to normal and abnormal feeding patterns.
Belthazar Scales of Adaptive Behavior Research Press Company 2612 North Mattis Avenue Champaign, Illinois 61820	Severely Handicapped	Social Development	Comprehensive checklist comprised of scales focusing on eating, dressing, and toileting. Included is a toileting questionnaire record sheet.
Lakeland Village Adaptive Behavior Grid Lakeland Village Medical Lake, Washington 99022	3 months-16 years	Social Self-care Development	Allows the evaluator to derive developmental levels for areas such as eating, dressing, toileting, grooming, mobility, recreation, socialization and behavior control, all of which are task analyzed.

REFERENCES AND SUGGESTED READINGS

Abercrombie, M. L. J. Some notes on spatial disability, movement, intelligence quotient and attentiveness. *Developmental Medicine and Child Neurology,* 1968, *10,* 206.

Allen, N. Developmental and degenerative diseases of the brain. In T. W. Farmer (Ed.), *Pediatric neurology.* New York: Harper and Row, Hoeber Medical Division, 1964.

Anderson, R. M., Greer, J. G., & McFadden, S. M. Occupational therapy for the schools. In R. M. Anderson & J. G. Greer (Eds.), *Educating the severely and profoundly retarded.* Baltimore: University Park Press, 1976.

Angliss, V. E. Habilitation of upper limb deficient children. *American Journal of Occupational Therapy,* 1974, *28* (7), 407-414.

Barry, H. The young aphasic child: Evaluation and training. Washington, D. C.: Alexander Graham Bell Association for the Deaf, Inc., 1961.

Battle, C. U. Disruptions in the socialization of a young, severely handicapped child. *Rehabilitation Literature,* 1974, *35* (5), 130-140.

Bergman, A. *Selected equipment for pediatric rehabilitation.* Valhalla, N. Y.: Blythedale Children's Hospital, 1974.

Berko, M. J. Psychological and linguistic implications of brain damage in children. In M. Mecham, F. G. Berko, M. F. Berko, & J. Palmer (Eds.), *Communication training in childhood brain damage.* Springfield, Ill.: Charles C. Thomas, 1966.

Bigge, J. L., & O'Donnell, P. A. *Teaching individuals with physical and multiple disabilities.* Columbus, Ohio: Charles E. Merrill, 1976.

Birch, J. W., & Johnstone, B. K. *Designing schools and schooling for the handicapped.* Springfield, Ill.: Charles C. Thomas, 1975.

Bleck, E. E. Muscular dystrophy: Duchenne type. In E. E. Bleck & N. A. Nagel (Eds.), *Physically handicapped children: A medical atlas for teachers.* New York: Grune and Stratton, 1975.

Bobath, B. The very early treatment of cerebral palsy. *Developmental Medicine and Child Neurology.* 1967, *9,* 373-390.

Bookbinder, S. What every child needs to know. *Exceptional Parent,* 1977, *7* (4).

Brink, J. D. Muscular dystrophy. In R. M. Peterson & J. O. Cleveland (Eds.), *Medical problems in the classroom: An educator's guide.* Springfield, Ill.: Charles C. Thomas, 1975.

Byrne, M. C. Speech and language development of athetoid and spastic children. *Journal of Speech and Hearing Disorders,* 1959, *24,* 231-240.

Caldwell, B. M. The importance of beginning early. In M. B. Karnes, J. B. Jordan, & R. F. Dailey (Eds.), *Not all little wagons are red.* Reston, Va.: Council for Exceptional Children, 1973.

Cashdan, A. The role of movement in language learning. In P. Wolf & R. McKieth (Eds.), *Planning for better living: Clinics in developmental medicine* (No. 33). London: Spastics International Medical Publications, 1969.

Challenor, Y. B., & Katz, J. F. Limb deficiency in infancy and childhood. In J. A. Downey & L. N. Low (Eds.), *The child with disabling illness: Principles of rehabilitation.* Philadelphia: W. B. Saunders, 1974.

Cliff, S., Gray, J., & Nymann, C. *Mothers can help: A therapist's guide for formulating a developmental text for parents of special children.* El Paso: The El Paso Rehabilitation Center, 1974.

Connors, F. P., Williamson, G. G., & Siepp, J. M. *Program guide for infants and toddlers with neuromotor and other developmental disabilities.* New York: Teachers' College Press, 1978.

Copeland, M., Ford, L., & Solon, N. *Occupational therapy for cerebral palsied children.* Baltimore: University Park Press, 1976.

Cosman, B. The burned child. In J. A. Downey & N. L. Low (Eds.) *The child with disabling illness: Principles of rehabilitation.* Philadelphia: W. B. Saunders, 1974.

Cratty, B. J. *Development through action: The physically handicapped, the retarded child.* Anaheim, Calif.: Skill Development Equipment Company, 1973.

Cratty, B. J. *Developmental games for the physically handicapped child.* Palo Alto, Calif.: Peek Publications, 1969.

Cratty, B. J., & Breen, J. *Educational games for the physically handicapped.* Denver: Love Publishing Company, 1972.

Cratty, B. J. *205 Activities for physical development.* Freeport, New York: Educational Activities, Inc., 1973.

Crickmay, M. C. *Speech therapy and the Bobath approach to cerebral palsy.* Springfield, Ill.: Charles C. Thomas, 1966.

Cruickshank, W., Bentzen, F. A., Ratzenburg, F. H., & Tannhauser, M. T. *A teaching method for brain injured and hyperactive children: A demonstration pilot study.* New York: Syracuse University, 1961.

Denhoff, E. Cerebral palsy: Medical aspects. In W. M. Cruickshank (Ed.), *Cerebral palsy: Its individual and community problems,* (1st ed.). New York: Syracuse University Press, 1955.

Donlon, E. T. Implications of visual disorders for cerebral palsy children. In W. M. Cruickshank (Ed.), *Cerebral palsy: Its individual and community problems,* (2nd ed.). New York: Syracuse University Press, 1966.

Dressing techniques for the cerebral palsied child. *American Journal of Occupational Therapy,* 1954, *VIII* (1) & (2), 8-10, 37-38, 48-52.

Dunsdon, M. *The educability of cerebral palsied children.* London: Newnes Educational Publishing Co., Ltd., 1952.

Dworkin, N. E. Public Law 94:142—A focus on assessment. *Diagnostique,* 1977, *No. 2,* 38-44.

Edgington, D. *The physically handicapped child in your classroom: A handbook for teachers.* Springfield, Ill.: Charles C. Thomas, 1976.

Education of handicapped children: Implementation of Part B of the Education of the Handicapped Act. *Federal Register,* 1977, *42* (163), 42474-42518.

Fassler, J., & Lasker, J. *Howie helps himself.* New York: Albert Whitman and Co., 1975.

Finnie, N. Handling the young cerebral palsied child at home. New York: E. P. Dutton and Company, 1975.

Fokes, J. *The Fokes Sentence Builder.* Boston: Teaching Resources, 1977.

Garrett, A. L. Orthopedic diseases. In R. M. Peterson, & J. O. Cleveland (Eds.), *Medical problems in the classroom: An educator's guide.* Springfield, Ill.: Charles C. Thomas, 1975.

Gold, A. P., Hammil, J. F., & Carter, S. Cerebrovascular diseases. In Farmer, T. W. (Ed.), *Pediatric neurology.* New York: Harper and Row, Hoeber Medical Division, 1964.

Goldstein, H. *Readings in physically handicapped education.* Guilford, Conn.: Special Learning Corporation, 1978.

Gordon, R. The design of a preschool "Learning laboratory" in a rehabilitation center. *Rehabilitation Monograph XXXIX.* New York: Institute of Rehabilitation Medicine, New York University Medical Center, 1969.

Gutman, E. M., & Gutman, C. R. *Wheelchair to independence.* Springfield, Ill.: Charles C. Thomas, 1968.

Haeussermann, E. Evaluating the developmental level of cerebral palsy preschool children. In J. M. Wolf & R. M. Anderson (Eds.), *The multiply handicapped child*. Springfield, Ill.: Charles C. Thomas, 1969.

Hallahan, D., & Kauffman, J. *Exceptional children: An introduction to special education*. Englewood Cliffs: Prentice-Hall, 1978.

Harris, S. E., & Cherry, D. B. Childhood progressive muscular dystrophy and the role of the physical therapist. *Physical Therapy*, 1974, *54*, 4-12.

Harvey, B. Cystic Fibrosis. In E. E. Bleck & D. A. Nagel (Eds.), *Physically handicapped children: A medical atlas for teachers*. New York: Grune and Stratton, 1975.

Held, R. Plasticity in sensory motor systems. *Scientific American*, 1965, *213* (5), 84.

Irwin, O. C. Speech development in the young child: Some factors related to the speech development of the infant child. *Journal of Speech and Hearing Disorders*, 1952, *17*, 269-279.

Jacobs, J. C., & Downey, J. A. Juvenile rheumatoid arthritis. In J. A. Downey & N. L. Low (Eds.), *The child with disabling illness: Principles of rehabilitation*. Philadelphia: W. B. Saunders, 1974.

Johnson, J. L. Programming for early motor responses within the classroom. *American Association for the Education of the Severely/Profoundly Handicapped Review*. 1978, *3*, 4-14.

Johnson, R. B., & Magrab, P. B. *Developmental disorders: Assessment treatment and education*. Baltimore: University Park Press, 1976.

Katz, J. F. Scoliosis. In J. A. Downey and N. L. Low (Eds.), *The child with a disabling illness: Principles of rehabilitation*. Philadelphia: W. B. Saunders, 1974.

Katz, J. F., & Challenor, Y. B. Childhood orthopedic syndromes. In J. A. Downey & N. L. Low (Eds.), *The child with disabling illness: Principles of rehabilitation*. Philadelphia: W. B. Saunders, 1974.

Kline, J. *Children move to learn: A guide to planning gross motor activities*. Tucson, Ariz.: Communication Skill Builders, 1977.

Langley, B. Functional assessment of the brain damaged physically handicapped child: Cognitive communication and motor variables. *Diagnostique*, 1977, *2*, (2), 31-37.

Laurence, E. R. Spina Bifida children in school: Preliminary report. *Developmental Medicine and Child Neurology*. 1971 (Supplement 25), 44-46.

Leavitt, T. J. Hemophilia. In E. E. Bleck and D. A. Nagel (Eds.), *Physically handicapped children: A medical atlas for teachers*. New York: Grune and Stratton, 1975.

Lee, L. L., Koenigskencht, R., & Mulhern, S. *Interactive language development teaching: A clinical presentation of grammatical structure*. Evanston, Ill.: Northwestern University Press, 1975.

Levy, J. *The baby exercise book*. New York: Pantheon, 1977.

Love, H. D., & Walthall, J. E. *A handbook of medical, educational, and psychological information for teachers of physically handicapped children*. Springfield, Ill.: Charles C. Thomas, 1977.

Lubin, G. I. Emotional implications. In R. M. Peterson & J. O. Cleveland (Eds.), *Medical problems in the classroom: An educator's guide*. Springfield, Ill.: Charles C. Thomas, 1975.

Mascia, A. V. Rehabilitation of the child with chronic asthma. In J. A. Downey & N. L. Low (Eds.), *The child with disabling illness: Principles of rehabilitation*. Philadelphia: W. B. Saunders, 1974.

Marks, N. C. *Cerebral palsied and learning disabled children: A handbook/guide to treatment rehabilitation and education*. Springfield, Ill.: Charles C. Thomas, 1974.

Matheny, M. M., & Ruby, D. O. A guide for feeding the cerebral palsied child. *Cerebral Palsy Review*, 1963, *24*, 14-16.

McDonald, E. T. Design and application of communication boards. In G. C. Vanderheiden & K.

Grilley (Eds.), *Nonvocal communication techniques and aids for the severely physically handicapped*. Baltimore: University Park Press, 1976.

McDonald, E. T., & Shultz, A. R. Communication boards for cerebral palsied children. *Journal of Speech and Hearing Disorders*, 1973, *XXXVIII* (1), 73-88.

Mecham, M. J. Appraisal of speech and hearing problems. In M. J. Mecham, M. J. Berko, F. G. Berko, & M. F. Palmer (Eds.), *Communication training in childhood brain damage*. Springfield, Ill.: Charles C. Thomas, 1966.

Miller, J. J. Juvenile rheumatoid arthritis. In E. E. Bleck & D. A. Nagel (Eds.), *Physically handicapped children: A medical atlas for teachers*. New York: Grune and Stratton, 1975.

Mueller, H. A. Facilitating feeding and prespeech. In P. H. Pearson & C. E. Williams (Eds.), *Physical therapy services in the developmental disabilities*. Springfield, Ill.: Charles C. Thomas, 1972.

Myers, B. A. Child with chronic illness. In R. H. A. Haslam & P. J. Valletutti (Eds.), *Medical problems in the classroom: The teacher's role in diagnosis and management*. Baltimore: University Park Press, 1975.

Mysak, E. Significance of neurophysiological orientation to cerebral palsy rehabilitation. *Journal of Speech and Hearing Disorders*, 1959, *24*. 221-230.

Nagel, D. A. Temporary orthopedic disabilities in children. In E. E. Bleck & D. A. Nagel (Eds.), *Physically handicapped children: A medical atlas for children*. New York: Grune and Stratton, 1975.

Nash, D. F. E. The impact of total care with special reference to myelo-dysplasia. *Developmental Medicine and Child Neurology*, 1970 (Supplement 22), 1-11.

Parsons, J. G. An investigation into the verbal facility of hydrocephalic children. *Developmental Medicine and Child Neurology*, 1968 (Supplement 16), 108-109.

Parsons, J. G. Assessment of aptitude in young people of school-leaving age handicapped by hydrocephalus or spina bifida ceptica. *Developmental Medicine and Child Neurology*, 1972, *27*, 101-108.

Parsons, J. G. Short-term verbal memory in hydrocephalic children. *Developmental Medicine and Child Neurology*, 1969 (Supplement 20), 75-77.

Pekarovic, E., Robinson, A., Lister, J., & Zachary, R. B. Pressure variations in intestinal loops used for urinary diversion. *Developmental Medicine and Child Neurology*, 1968 (Supplement 16), 87-92.

Phillips, J. L. *The origins of intellect: Piaget's theory*. San Francisco: W. H. Freeman, 1969.

Pomeroy, J. *Recreation for the physically handicapped*. New York: MacMillan, 1964.

Robinault, I P. *Functional aids for the multiply handicapped*. New York: Harper and Row, 1973.

Rosenbloom, L. The consequences of impaired movement—a hypothesis and review. In K. S. Holt (Ed.), *Movement and child development*. Philadelphia: Lippincott, 1977.

Ross, A. O. *The exceptional child in the family*. New York: Grune and Stratton, 1964. Cited in J. L. Bigge & P. A. O'Donnell. *Teaching individuals with physical & multiple disabilities*. Columbus, Ohio: Charles E. Merrill, 1976.

Safford, P.L., & Arbitman, D. C. *Developmental intervention with young physically handicapped children*. Springfield, Ill.: Charles C. Thomas, 1975.

Scarnati, R. A. The role of the physical therapist in special education. In R. M. Anderson & J. G. Greer (Eds.), *Educating the severely and profoundly retarded*. Baltimore: University Park Press, 1976.

Shepard, R. B. *Physiotherapy in pediatrics*. London: William Heinemann Books, 1974.

Shurtleff, D. T. Timing of learning in meningomyelocele patients. *Journal of American Physical Therapy Association*, 1966, *46*, 136-148.

Silberstein, C. E. Orthopedic problems in the classroom. In R. H. A. Haslam & P. J. Valletutti (Eds.),

Medical problems in the classroom: The teacher's role in diagnosis and management. Baltimore: University Park Press, 1975.

Spain, B. Verbal and performance ability in pre-school spina bifida. *Developmental Medicine and Child Neurology,* 1972 (Supplement 27), 155.

Stein, S. B. *A hospital story: An open family book for parents and children together.* New York: Walker and Company, 1974.

Swisher, L. P., & Pinsker, E. J. The language characteristics of hyperverbal, hydrocephalic children. *Developmental Medicine and Child Neurology,* 1971, *13,* 746-755.

Uzgiris, I. C., & Hunt, J. McV. *Assessment in infancy: Ordinal scales of psychological development.* Urbana Ill.: University of Illinois Press, 1975.

Vanderheiden, G. C., & Grilley, K. (Eds.), *Nonvocal communication techniques and aids for the severely physically handicapped.* Baltimore: University Park Press, 1975.

Vicker, B. A. *University hospital nonoral communication system project.* Ames, Iowa: University of Iowa, 1974.

Wabash Center for the Mentally Retarded. *Guide to early developmental training.* Boston: Allyn and Bacon, 1977.

Wheeler, R. H., & Hooley, A. M. *Physical education for the handicapped.* Philadelphia: Lea & Febiger, 1969.

Willson, M. A. Multidisciplinary problems of myelomeningocele and hydrocephalus. *Journal of the American Physical Therapy Association,* 1965, *45* (12), 1139-1146.

Wolf, B. *Don't feel sorry for Paul.* Philadelphia: Lippincott, 1974.

Wyke, B. The neurological basis of movement: A developmental review. In K. S. Holt (Ed.), *Movement and child development: Clinics in developmental medicine* (No. 55). Philadelphia: Lippincott, 1977.

Young, E. The moto-kinesthetic method as applied to the cerebral palsied. *Cerebral Palsy Review,* 1962, *23,* 7-8.

Young, H. F., Nulsen, F. E., Martin, H. W., & Thomas, P. The relationship of intelligence and the cerebral mantel in treated infantile hydrocephalus. *Pediatrics,* 1973, *52,* 38-44.

Zedler, E. Y. *Listening for speech sounds.* New York: Harper and Row, 1955.

Reference Note

Davis, J., & Langley, M. B. *A guide to developing a classroom curriculum for visually impaired multihandicapped infants.* Grant No. 300-75-307. U.S. Office of Education, Department of Health, Education, and Welfare. Nashville, Tenn.: George Peabody College, 1978.

Part III

Cognitive Development

Chapter 6

The Acquisition of Cognitive Competence

Thomas L. Kodera and S. Gray Garwood

THE NATURE OF COGNITION

Young children, continuously attempting to identify and interpret significant aspects of their experience, constantly demonstrate a variety of complex and interrelated cognitive behaviors. Thus, cognitive behaviors are associated with comprehending, remembering, and making sense out of one's experiences.

In spite of our ability to specify the components of cognition, it is difficult to define cognition precisely. In part, this derives from the involvement of cognition in nearly all behavioral processes. Few behaviors are purely cognitive, just as few are purely social or emotional. For example, *social cognition*—knowledge about social customs and styles of interpersonal relationships—significantly influences responses in social settings. As Flavell aptly states, "We only have a single head, after all, and it is firmly attached to the rest of the body" (1977, p. 3).

Some consensus about the cognitive components of behavior can be achieved by examining the functions served by cognitive behaviors. Behaviors contributing to any or all of these functions can be regarded as cognitive. These assumptions include:

Making Sense of Experience

Acts of cognition are thought to represent an individual's attempts to make sense of experience. This "sense" is accomplished whenever some subjective relationship is recognized between prior and present experiences, providing structure for interpreting present and future experiences. Experience, therefore, must be broken down into meaningful and manipulable units of information. This is frequently described as a creative or constructive process (Neisser, 1967), since experience is not clearly marked as either "this is where one behavior ends and the next begins" or "this is important and everything else you sense is irrelevant." Each individual constructs these markers, interprets the meaning of these units of information within the framework of existing knowledge, and represents and retains this information in some form, retrievable for later use.

Problem Solving

Rarely do individuals directly apply previously attained information to respond appropriately to the challenges presented by their environments. This is especially true of young children who, because of limited exposure, are likely to interpret or communicate their experiences inadequately or unconventionally. Thus, many situations constitute problems that must be resolved to promote effective interactions with objects, words, symbols, ideas, or people. The behavioral processes applied to problem solving—thought, reasoning, evaluation, transformation or reinterpretation of information, creativity, etc.—have all traditionally been labeled cognitive processes.

Establishing Executive Control

Application of cognitive activity for making sense of experience and solving problems requires behaviors which allow the individual to maintain control. These processes identify and mobilize strategies for coordinating cognitive behaviors to achieve a desired outcome. For example, memory for a recent experience is very brief unless the individual makes an effort to retain it. One way is actively rehearsing, as by conscious repetition, what was sensed—a cognitive-control process aimed at expanding the limits of short-term memory. (Memory strategies will be described more fully in the following chapter.)

Developing Mastery

The cognitive nature of many behaviors must often be interpreted within a developmental context. Many behaviors superficially show little involvement of the cognitive activities described above. Nonetheless, they may be significant precursors of later cognitive competencies, providing the basis for refining and mastering newly emerging cognitive skills. Infant behaviors, like exploration, play, and imitation, may thus be regarded as cognitively relevant if not cognitive *per se,* since they contribute measurably to later representational thought.

Summary: What is cognition?

"Cognition," includes a complexly interrelated system of behaviors, within which some cognitive behaviors identify, interpret, organize, retain, retrieve, and apply information units about experience with objects, words, ideas, and people. Other cognitive behaviors apply cognitive competencies appropriate to solving problems and thereby attain present and future goals. Still other behaviors are cognitively-relevant as they promote development and mastery of further cognitive competencies.

LEARNING: The Acquisition of Cognitive Competence

Thus far we have discussed identifying some of the component behaviors of cognition. Despite general agreement regarding these behaviors, a basic theoretical distinction in explaining how these behaviors are acquired separates professionals into two groups. Chapter one discussed differences between those who adhere to a unity-of-science view and an organismic view. Unity-of-science adherents accept a mechanistic view of man: man's behaviors are acquired by initial trial and error. Consequences which follow a random behavior provide the individual with feedback, which determines, largely, whether this particular response will be used again. Accordingly, man's behavior is shaped by environmental consequences of man's activity. Complex behavior represents only high levels of stimulus-response organization, and problem-solving activity depends on the individual's store of cognitive units (in this case S-R bonds) and the number and kind of reinforced relationships between these cognitive units.

According to the organismic view of man, cognitive activity (problem-solving behavior) originates within the individual as the result of a desire or need to understand the world.

Both points of view are here discussed. Neither completely explains all of human behavior. However, both can be effectively integrated into efficient educational strategies for teaching young children.

Cognition Viewed as a Product: Traditional Learning Approaches

Learning is generally defined as any relatively permanent change in behavior due to experience, a view that focuses on learning as a product. Hence, traditional measures of learning (intelligence tests) have focused on its quantitative aspects: the more learning products you have acquired the more "learned" you are. Within this framework, two types of learning mechanisms are postulated: signal learning and response learning.

Signal Learning

In *signal learning,* frequently called classical conditioning, previously unrelated events become associated because one event signals or predicts another important event; the two events are called stimuli. Any environmental event can be a stimulus if it is perceivable and is potentially informative. Of the stimuli associated in signal learning, one stimulus must have the property of reliably eliciting a specific response, called an *unconditional response.* For example, when we contact a source of great heat, the heat we feel is the stimulus that elicits the reflex of withdrawing the hand (an unconditioned response). This stimulus is given the special label *unconditional stimulus,* since no conditions other than the experience of the unconditional stimulus are required to produce the reflex response, or unconditional response. In most circumstances, any additional stimulus that consistently occurs immediately preceding the unconditional stimulus and is contingently related can be a *signal* of the unconditional event. Signals are often called *conditional stimuli* as their meaning and effectiveness depend upon an association with an unconditional event. The behavioral consequence of this association between a signal and an unconditional stimulus is that the signal now evokes a response (a *conditional response*) similar to that elicited by the unconditional stimulus. When an unconditional stimulus is unpleasant, we can avoid its unpleasant consequences by responding to the signal. When we discover stimuli that are signals of important environmental events, we become able to anticipate these events. These stimuli may then attract our attention, warning us of impending dangers or unpleasantness as well as preparing us to enjoy forthcoming pleasant experiences.

As with all learning, signal learning is possible only when potential signals and unconditional stimuli are contingently related. Before a stimulus can become a signal, it must be clear that the unconditional stimulus occurs only if it has been preceded by the potential signal and never in its absence. But what if sometimes the unconditional stimulus fails to occur following the signal? One likely result would be the attempt to identify other stimuli which indicate when the unconditional stimulus will follow the signal and when it will not. This would inevitably modify our original association between the signal and the unconditional stimulus. A combination of stimuli would be learned as a signal for the unconditional stimulus. If compound signals like this could not be discovered, extinction (weakening) of the association is likely to occur. When unconditional stimuli fail to follow signals consistently, signals less reliably evoke a response similar to that elicited by the unconditional stimulus. In this way, stimuli may lose their signal value just as they would if they were no longer contingently related to the unconditional stimulus.

In everyday experience, we frequently must identify compound stimuli as signals of important unconditional stimuli. Does this mean that we, as parents or educators, should provide many potential signals to promote signal learning? The answer is both no and yes. We can arrange contingent relationships between many stimuli and an unconditional stimulus, but only one stimulus tends to become a signal. This occurs for two reasons. First, we seek as signals that stimulus or compound stimulus that is most predictive of the unconditional stimulus. Once we have discovered a predictive signal for an unconditional stimulus, all other stimuli that we may subsequently encounter, even when equally predictive, are redundant. Since redundant stimuli provide no new information, they will not be associated with the unconditional stimulus. Second, we seek the simplest signal that predicts the unconditional stimulus. When many equally predictive stimuli are presented simultaneously, we need to learn only one of the stimuli as a signal for the unconditional stimulus. A single stimulus is the simplest possible signal; the other stimuli are redundant and can be ignored. When multiple stimuli redundantly occur, the signal is usually that stimulus which is most noticeable to the learner. Unfortunately, this generalization is difficult to apply since is is difficult to predict what a learner will notice.

In some cases redundant stimuli can make signal learning easier. When many potential signals are presented, the learner is more likely to recognize at least one of them as a signal. When it is most important that *some* signal be associated with the unconditional stimulus, signal learning can be promoted by redundancy. But when it is important that a specific stimulus become a signal, redundant stimuli would interfere with the desired learning. For this reason, we must be cautious that learning environments contain no irrelevant stimuli that provide the same information as the stimuli we wish the child to learn as signals. This problem is particularly pertinent when a learner is developmentally disabled. A child whose cognitive abilities are limited may tend to look for stimuli peripheral to the learning task rather than rely on his cognitive resources to solve a problem. If the child can note a signal in the teacher's face, for example, that indicates the correct response, the child may never learn independently to solve the problem. If the child consistently relied on these signals, the possible educational gains would be quite limited.

Response Learning

Response learning is an association between a response and its impact on the world around us. This class of learning products has been the focus of researchers in the areas of operant conditioning and instrumental learning. By discovering the important consequences that consistently follow specific responses, individuals form an association between a response and its consequence that reflects a cause and effect relationship. A response is observed to cause important environmental events and thus becomes meaningful. The meaning of a response is defined in terms of the specific consequences it produces. If, for example, young children find that by grimacing in a particular way they receive attention from another person, that grimace becomes a means for gaining attention.

The consequence of a response influences both the specific information represented in the association between the response and its consequence and the likelihood that the response will be used for obtaining this consequence. Response consequences are of two general classes: (1) *reinforcing events* or *reinforcers,* which we tend to seek because they are desirable, pleasant, or informative; and (2) *punishing events* or *punishers,* which we try to avoid because they are undesirable, unpleasant, or noninformative. Reinforcing and punishing events have readily observable effects on our behavior. Responses associated with reinforcing events become more probable and are likely to be repeated. Responses associated with punishing events become less probable and are less likely to be repeated.

The reinforcing or punishing nature of a response consequence is a cognitive evaluation, made within the context of the changes that responses produce in our experiences. Pleasant events that cease upon our response, for example, may be just as punishing response consequences as are unpleasant events produced by our responses. Similarly, unpleasant events that cease upon our response, may be just as rewarding or reinforcing as are pleasant events produced by our responses. For this reason, we must make further distinctions within the classes of reinforcing and punishing events.

Within the class of reinforcing events, we may distinguish between positive and negative reinforcers. *Positive reinforcers* are response consequences that occur whenever responses *produce* desirable, pleasant or informative events. *Negative reinforcers* occur whenever responses *avoid* or *end* undesirable, unpleasant, or noninformative events. Within the class of punishing events we may distinguish between positive and negative punishers. *Positive punishers* are response consequences that occur whenever responses *produce* undesirable, unpleasant, or noninformative events. *Negative punishers* occur whenever responses *end or cause the omission of* desirable, pleasant, or informative events. The adjectives "positive" and "negative," when applied to the classes of reinforcing or punishing events, are descriptive of how ongoing experience is affected by a particular response. Positive reinforcers and punishers are alike in the sense that a new event is introduced to our experience as a result of the response. However, this new event represents a change for the better in positive reinforcement and a change for the worse in positive punishment. Negative reinforcers and punishers are alike in the sense that some ongoing experience is interrupted or ended by a response. In negative reinforcement, however, this interruption also represents a change for the better. In negative punishment, this interruption deprives us of desirable, pleasant, or informative events and thus represents a change for the worse.

Discovery by children that responses are reinforced or punished either positively or negatively also provides information about the consequences of withholding a response. In general, when we discover that positively-reinforcing events are contingent upon a response, we can anticipate that withholding that response will lead to negative punishment. Since withholding a response is itself a response, the consequence is deprivation of an anticipated reinforcing event. When positively-punished responses are withheld, the consequence is very reinforcing since withholding a punished response avoids receiving the punishing event. When responses that are negatively reinforced or negatively punished are withheld, the consequence is a continuation of conditions as they exist.

Promoting Response Learning

If we accept the popular view of Dewey, Piaget, and Bruner that cognitive advances are generally action- or response-based and that experience is the best teacher, it follows that a primary goal of educators should be to promote effective response learning. Response learning occurs best in environments carefully arranged to provide clear and consistent consequences for appropriate responses.

These consequences must be specifically determined for each child to provide the greatest incentive to acquire and refine the response. At the same time, if the response is to become truly meaningful to the child, the response consequence should follow naturally from the response. A response that earns a piece of candy may be trivialized by this consequence unless a more natural consequence, such as receiving attention or praise, is also received. Because the way response consequences are selected and arranged can determine or undermine effective response learning, the characteristics of reinforcing and punishing events will be more intensively explored in the following paragraphs.

Despite our parallel treatment earlier of reinforcing and punishing events, punishment is not as effective as reinforcement for promoting stable response learning. In fact, despite the outcries among educators for discipline in the classroom, punishment is quite ineffective as even a behavioral-control technique. Why is this so? In part, it stems from the human tendency to be active and responsive. Cognitive advancement derives more from response production than response inhibition. Even when a response is consistently punished it is often valuable and adaptive to produce the previously punished response as a test. This test allows us to see if the consequences of a response have changed.

For children of preschool age or younger, punishment is particularly ineffective. It may be very difficult for them to identify the contexts in which particular responses are punished, since in other circumstances the same response may be correct or appropriate. Compounding this difficulty is the fact that before about age seven inhibiting or withholding responses is much more difficult than producing responses. The higher-level areas of the brain necessary for response inhibition are not well developed. Nor can children use words like "no" or "do not" to control their behavior. Rather, they seem to overlook these words, interpreting the verbal command as an instruction to perform a response.

Punishing events also produce side effects that interfere with response learning. Whenever punishment is delivered by a human agent, we learn either to avoid, or to direct our hostilities at, that agent. Thus, we are not associating the response with punishment but associating the punishment with the punishing agent. There is also a tendency to overuse punishment, which greatly diminishes the effectiveness of any punishment. Punishment also becomes less punishing if we simultaneously receive some reinforcement for the same response; for example, we can learn to tolerate the punishment when we discover that we gain much attention from the teacher and are able to make her day miserable.

Fortunately, reinforcing events are very effective in promoting response learning. The difficulty comes in selecting appropriate reinforcing events as response consequences. Reinforcing events are effective because they provide: (1) motivation for attempting a response, (2) a specific incentive for continuing to respond and attempt to learn, (3) a goal, purpose, or aim for the response, and (4) information about the effectiveness of our response or feedback. A motivation to attempt a response is a product both of the learning atmosphere and the individual's prior experience with reinforcing events. Children more readily respond (and learn) when they are in comfortable environments with supportive adults who encourage correct responses.

Prior experience with reinforcing events has a generalized effect on motivation to learn. White (1959) and Harter (1978) define a motivation for effectance or competence as an important human characteristic. We respond in order to perfect response skills and to control our environments and our experiences more effectively. This motivation for effectance is greatly influenced by prior reinforcement experience. When responses produce positive consequences we not only learn what specific responses produce specific consequences, but we also learn the more generalized notion that responses indeed have a consequence. This expectancy promotes learning that new response. From this we become more competent and our effectance or competence motivation becomes even stronger. Of course, if we experience frequent failure, our effectance motivation diminishes, and we may instead acquire a generalized motivation to avoid responding in learning situations.

The incentive function of reinforcing events is frequently overemphasized in educational practice. As a result, many individuals criticize the use of reinforcements when designing learning environments. Typical arguments are that learning should be its own reward and that there should be no need for some external incentives for learning. Note, however, that this does not deny the importance of the incentive function of reinforcing events; rather, it suggests that the incentive should derive from the task itself. Many learning tasks intrinsically provide enough challenge to keep a child responding and learning. Such tasks, providing a natural puzzle for a child, clearly should be the goal of most educational programs.

Many children, however, are unable to derive the intrinsic pleasure inherent in many learning tasks. It is frequently necessary to provide some sort of external incentive to maintain their interest in learning. In these cases, the teacher may award chocolates one by one to a child, or lavish the child with attention and praise, or allow special privileges. If incentives work, we should use them; the goal is to promote learning. But we must be concerned about the naturalness of these external incentives as consequences for the response, since unnatural consequences for responses tend to trivialize the meaning of that response. Even when using external incentives, especially material rewards, the child must be helped to discover the intrinsic incentives and pleasures that can be derived from the task itself. We must also be cautious that external incentives do not interfere with or distract from the learning task.

The incentive function of reinforcing events is probably less important than the feedback or informative function that reinforcing events serve. Often children learn more efficiently when simply informed of the correctness or incorrectness of responses. Feedback from their responses gives children knowledge of results.

This is a natural consequence and tends not to interfere with the learning task or distract the child. However, feedback is most effective with individuals who can derive some of the intrinsic incentives contained within a learning task.

As noted above, reinforcing events also provide a goal, purpose, or aim toward which a response to be learned can be directed. Because reinforcing events occur immediately following the response determined to be correct, they help the child identify and isolate the response to be learned. Most responses require coordinated movements of many muscles; these movements must be identified. Also, since behavior is ongoing and dynamic, what constitutes a response unit must be isolated; that is, the beginning and end points of the specific response need to be defined. Reinforcers and, for that matter, punishers tend to break up the flow of behavior so that these response units can be isolated more easily. They clearly indicate the end point of a response unit. The beginning point of the response must be abstracted by the child from subsequent experience.

All response consequences that are reinforcing to a child show these properties, but not all response consequences are reinforcing. We must, therefore, assume they are not learning an association between the response and the response consequence. We cannot assume all children will learn new responses when praise or candy are used as reinforcers, nor can we assume that if at one time candy is reinforcing it will always be so. Individual differences as to what events are perceived as reinforcing are great.

Since many factors influence the effectiveness of reinforcement, only an empirical test can define those response consequences that are reinforcing and that will promote response learning. We know that reinforcing events tend to make responses more probable and occur more frequently. Therefore, after the fact we can identify a response consequence as reinforcing if it has increased the probability or frequency of the to-be-learned response. If there has been no change in the frequency or probability of that behavior as, for example, when a child makes no improvement in the accuracy of responses, then it is very likely the response consequence is not reinforcing. If the probability of that response decreases and the response becomes less frequent, we must assume that the response consequence is punishing. Although very useful for diagnosing problems in the learning environment, this empirical test does not provide a guide for selecting reinforcers in advance.

At this stage, the best guide for selecting response consequences to promote response learning is observation of the individual child. We need general information about the child's likes and dislikes, preferences, interests, and special sensitivities. A child may be very responsive to a little bit of praise now and then for making appropriate responses; we may, therefore, hypothesize that this is an effective reinforcer and try it to see if it promotes response learning. The empirical test will provide the answer rather quickly.

Premack (1965), in identifying potential reinforcing events, stated that any activity that occurs relatively more frequently than another activity can be a reinforcer for the less frequent activity. If, in the course of a day, we observe that a child chooses to spend more time in art activities, or playground activities, or even arithmetic, than they do in reading, we can increase the probability of reading by making the opportunity to do arithmetic problems contingent upon doing a specified amount of reading first. We can often use the Premack principle to identify reinforcing events we might never imagine would be reinforcing. We have seen young retarded children avidly learning color concepts in order to earn the privilege of washing a window or polishing a shoe. As children become more skilled in certain academic areas, their interests in these activities increases, making these activities potential reinforcing events for new activities to be learned.

As we become skilled at observing children's preferences or experiences and activities, we become better able to identify potential reinforcing events. We can thus define the hierarchy of response consequences to which an individual child is already responsive, and then apply these consequences to foster subsequent response learning. But it is also possible to create reinforcing events, which then more closely represent what we customarily consider to be the natural consequences of responding.

How are new reinforcing events created? Learning researchers have identified a number of *primary reinforcers,* among which are food when we are hungry, water or liquids when we are thirsty, heat when we are cold, etc. All are like unconditional stimuli (as described in signal learning) in the sense that they are of major importance in meeting biological needs. Also included are events or experiences that meet acquired psychological needs, such as the presence of a caretaker for an infant, affection or assistance to a dependent child, or approval, praise, or informative feedback to a competent and independent child. These reinforcing events are called primary since they directly fulfill biological or psychological needs. *Created reinforcers* (often called secondary reinforcers, deriving their powers from some association with the primary reinforcer) may be thought of as signals for primary reinforcers. In our discussion of signal learning, we indicated that signals come to be responded to as if they were unconditioned stimuli. Responses similar to those evoked by the unconditional stimulus event come to be controlled by the signal. Since primary reinforcers provide strong incentives for response learning, signals associated with primary reinforcers also become powerful incentives for response learning. Tokens, like gold stars or points awarded for correct responding, are one example of created reinforcers. Neither gold stars nor points are intrinsically meaningful; they are not primary reinforcers because they do not directly meet biological or psychological needs. But they can become reinforcing because they are signals or perhaps symbols readily applied to represent approval for what the child has done or to provide feedback about the correctness or accuracy of response. In practice, these tokens can acquire reinforcing powers when accompanied by the reinforcing event we want them to signal. This requires that we praise or compliment for performance at the same time that we present this token.

With frequent pairing of events, tokens alone can become sufficient reinforcement to promote learning. However, just as signals undergo extinction when unconditional stimuli are removed for a long period, secondary reinforcers also lose their reinforcing power unless occasionally re-paired with the primary reinforcing event. In our token example, this would mean that we must still continue to give attention and approval or praise along with the presentation of the token, but this needn't be as frequent as before. It is also through creating reinforcing events that children learn to derive the intrinsic incentives contained within a learning task. Initially, children may attempt reading because they derive some primary reinforcement; when reading, they may discover that the teacher gives them attention and approval. But reading may be negatively reinforced, since it avoids the teacher's anger when children are not reading. At this time primary reinforcers function mainly to induce the child to read. If the primary reinforcers for reading are consistently applied and the child actively engages in that response, all of the events associated with reading can become secondary reinforcers as they signal to the child the means to obtain the teacher's approval and attention. Reading materials then become interesting because they are associated with the very desirable primary reinforcer.

When reading, children also become more competent. Motivation for competence is a powerful psychological need among children, and thus they are stimulated to perfect their reading skills. These newly emerging skills expose the child to the natural benefits gained from reading. They may find that by reading they can avoid having to ask embarrassing questions of other people, work more independently, or facilitate learning new skills. Reading can thereby become intrinsically reinforcing, since the child can now identify the advantages of the response. In other words, an activity that was initially engaged in as a means to an end, now can become an end in itself.

Another class of created reinforcers is illustrated by self-criticism and self-evaluation. Praise or criticism becomes for children a model for self-evaluation and self-criticism. ("That was a good job" or "You're trying very hard" or "This is wrong.") When they begin making these same comments to themselves and find that it corresponds with the teacher's evaluation, these self-evaluations become secondary reinforcers also. After a point, external evaluations no longer become important, as children acquire sufficient abilities to determine the appropriateness or inappropriateness of their own response.

Creating new secondary reinforcing events depends at some point on primary reinforcers, which are particularly important when the basic concern is getting a child interested in attempting a new response and maintaining that interest until able to discover secondary benefits. Particularly with low-functioning children, we may need to emphasize very basic primary reinforcements like material rewards to interest the child in a very important learning task. In these cases, we must be very confident that the end justifies the means. Primary reinforcers are very effective and can easily become manipulative. Incentives must also reflect the most mature type of reinforcement that the child is responsive to. If the child responds well to occasional praise, it would be absurd to introduce food as an incentive. If a child is responding to intrinsic incentives, the addition of external incentives (particularly food or frequent praise) may divert the response to these external incentives. Regardless of the type of reinforcing event used in learning programs, we should also set up the conditions required to create new secondary reinforcers.

Reinforcing events are also affected by frequency of use or occurrence. This is most easily illustrated when candy or some form of food is used as an external incentive for learning. After a point, satiation sets in when the same reinforcing events are used repeatedly. As appetite diminishes, so too does the reinforcing value of candy or food decrease. Also, a child may be so inundated with praise that another pat on the back has no effect on behavior. Perhaps the best way around the problem of satiation is to provide a variety of reinforcing events as consequences for responses. Another approach is to allow a period of time before using the same reinforcing events for the same tasks. This might mean breaking down the lessons to be learned into small units spread throughout the day.

Skinner (1953) found that intermittent reinforcement, meaning that reinforcing events are not provided following every correct response, maintained learning activities at a very high level. Intermittent reinforcements are always delivered contingent upon a response, but every response need not be reinforced. When children are first exposed to a new response, this approach tends to prolong the learning time, most likely because more frequent information is needed to identify and isolate the necessary response. Once the basic response has been identified, intermittent reinforcement will maintain the child's attempts at perfecting the response skill and applying that response skill in subsequent learning situations. Intermittent reinforcement also increases resistance to extinction.

When an individual is deprived of a specific reinforcing event, its effectiveness as a reinforcer is increased. It makes sense that children who are hungry will work very hard and learn more readily when food is a reinforcing event. Children deprived of human affection and attention may also strive very hard in an environment that provides attention and affection for learning appropriate or correct responses.

Getting Responses to Occur

To promote response learning, it is often necessary to teach a child a new response. If the outcome of this response were clearly significant to the child, we would rely on children's inherent tendency (due to competence or effectance motivation) to modify, reorganize, refine, and perfect their present responses to produce the appropriate responses. This form of "discovery learning," which may be very beneficial in the long run, can be facilitated, however.

One approach, called *shaping,* involves reinforcement of those responses that successively approximate the appropriate target response. Initially, responses only remotely similar to the target are reinforced. As these become more probable, closer approximations of the target responses are sought before presenting reinforcements.

A more direct approach to getting responses to occur is called by various names: *prompting, guiding,* or *"putting through."* With this approach, new responses are acquired with the assistance of a teacher who physically guides the child through the appropriate response. For example, if the child is to learn to move a lever or turn a wheel, the teacher may place the child's hands on the apparatus and direct them through the correct sequence. As the child acquires greater control of the response, the teacher then may abbreviate this direction, applying only occasional prompts.

Another direct approach is *blocking.* Here, the learning task is structured to prevent the occurrence of inappropriate responses; the child's "incorrect" response is interrupted by some intervention of the teacher.

An advantage of the direct approaches is the relatively error-free learning, avoiding the emotional and motivational consequences of failure. More importantly, they reduce the likelihood of learning incompatible, competing responses that interfere with association of the appropriate response with its consequences.

Response Chains: Many complex behavioral skills require coordination of various responses. Such response chains represent a higher-level version of response learning. The essential difference between response chains and response learning is that the consequences of response chains are produced only upon successful completion of a relatively fixed *sequence* of responses; isolated response segments do not produce the same consequences. A response chain is vividly illustrated by tying a shoe, which requires coordination of many responses in appropriate sequence.

Learning of response chains progresses in an interesting manner. Young children frequently encounter circumstances where a simple response they have mastered proves ineffective in producing a desired consequence or attaining a desired goal. In such circumstances, they may need to perform an additional response to achieve the terminal response to reach their goal. With experience, they can learn to coordinate these two simple responses in sequence whenever required. Increasingly greater chains of responses would be built up in a similar manner. In general, it appears that response chains are built up from end to beginning rather than the reverse.

This is particularly important when attempting to promote the learning of response chains. Most effective as a strategy is to identify the terminal response in the chain and to work progressively forward in the sequence, thus permitting the child to recognize the consequences of the response sequence. Each new response added to the sequence is then immediately followed by an already-mastered response sequence, which ultimately produces the desired consequences.

Discrimination Learning: Discrimination learning results when the consequences of responses predictably vary, depending upon the contexts within which these responses occur. Discrimination learning could therefore be described as the product of signal learning imposed on response learning. A complex form of discrimination learning is commonly observed when children act in one way at home and differently at school. In this example, children have learned different rules regarding what is appropriate and inappropriate conduct in the two contexts. The signals for these rules are the complex stimuli that define for them "home" and "school."

Discrimination learning is, essentially, an association between a response and an environmental stimulus (or compound stimulus) that consistently identifies (signals) the consequence of the response. A signal stimulus, often called a discriminative stimulus, is informative as it reduces the uncertainty about the response outcome. In the presence of discriminative stimuli signalling positive response outcomes, for specific responses, the responses tend to become more probable or frequent. In the presence of discriminative stimuli signalling negative response outcomes for specific responses, these responses tend to be inhibited or suppressed. Responding thus becomes more selective and attuned to contextual circumstances.

With respect to a specific response, discriminative stimuli indicate when that response is appropriate and when it is inappropriate. They provide further information concerning the consequences of producing or inhibiting that response. From a different perspective, discriminative stimuli can be used to identify those specific responses among the myriad possible responses appropriate to a particular circumstance.

Rote Learning: Rote learning refers to learning products derived primarily from arbitrarily related events. A more traditional label for this is verbal learning. This label is somewhat restricting, however, since this form of learning does not involve words alone. In most cases, individuals are instructed to memorize events that occur together in space or time. These relationships are frequently temporary. However, they can become more permanently associated if the relationships subsequently become useful.

Learning the alphabetical sequence of letters, in which the position of each letter is arbitrary and based on social convention, is a good example of rote learning. Initially, learning this sequence of letters would be guided by the implicit or explicit consequences of *attempting* to learn it correctly. Once mastered, the value of this arbitrary sequence as a tool for filing, indexing, locating dictionary definitions, etc., would make this association meaningful. (Of course, if the meaningfulness of the exercise in rote learning could be made clear in some way from the outset, such learning would proceed more efficiently.)

Two types of rote learning have been distinguished: serial learning and paired-associate learning. In *serial learning,* the ordinal position or sequence of events is learned. Since we learn those letters that consistently precede or follow other letters, alphabetical order is a specific serial learning product. In *paired-associate learning,* events are consistently paired as if to convey an impression they somehow are related. This form of learning occurs whenever labels are given for objects, activities, or experiences, and definitions are provided for terms or symbols. The consequence of these arbitrary pairings is the tendency to seek meaningful relationships between the events to "justify" their pairing. This may take the form of a transfer of meaning where a novel event (such as the word "dog") becomes associated with what the individual already knows about a familiar event with which it is paired (a dog). If the events paired are each meaningful, their pairing may result in identifying some dimension on which these meanings can be related.

When children learn to interpret words as labels of objects, activities, or other events, they can begin to use language to represent their experiences and direct their behavior. This profoundly affects subsequent learning by making it more efficient. Words function as mediators of associations, which, as will be seen in Chapter 7, is extremely important for long-term retention of learning products.

Mediators, which link an external stimulus and an overt response to that stimulus, are usually both unobservable and verbal. As verbal associations with the external stimulus that help the child identify the appropriate response, they can then be used to identify relevant courses of action associated with these verbal associates.

In a more general sense, mediators free the child from dependence upon concrete experience. By representing their experience in words, they can more readily recognize mentally those events that share common associations. Their actions are then guided more by these representations then by overt trial-and-error experimentation.

Concept Learning: Concepts are unobservable cognitive structures abstracted from experience and form the basis for classifying new experiences, communicating with others, and solving problems. Cognitively, concepts are stable, organized patterns of identifying, interpreting, and responding to experience—the means by which we represent our knowledge of our experiences to ourselves and to others.

Concepts are formed from the associations or properties shared by otherwise diverse aspects of experience. The set of objects or other events contained within a concept identifies its denotational meaning. When labels such as words or symbols are associated with concepts, these labels denote similar meanings.

Concepts themselves are defined in terms of the common associations or properties of events included within the concept and the nature of their relationship. These relationships implicitly determine the rules for identifying those new experiences included in a concept. Johnson (1972) has identified four types of concepts: class, singular, dimensional, and explanatory.

Class concepts separate experiences into discrete categories, based on the presence or absence of some defining property (as in the classes of "red squares" or "mentally retarded children") or on some relationship between properties (as in the classes of "isosceles triangles" or "children whose IQs are lower than their parents' "). Whenever children distinguish between dogs and cats or animals and plants, they are applying class concepts.

Singular concepts are special cases of class concepts. They refer to specific objects or events, such as those indicated by proper names ("New York" or a specific child's mother). Self-concept is one of the most significant of singular concepts. Singular concepts organize many different associations and properties of a specific object or event around a common association with a single label.

Dimensional concepts abstract and generalize the continuous properties of objects or experiences that can be used as a basis for comparison between and evaluation of experiences (class concepts represent events in discrete, qualitatively different categories). Dimensional concepts (these include size, shape, color, height, weight, speed, intensity, etc.), because they are less directly related to direct experience, are more difficult to learn.

Explanatory concepts (principles) describe relationships between class concepts or dimensional concepts and are therefore more complex than the others and acquired more slowly. As Johnson (1972) notes, "principles are more important than concepts in the long run. Whereas concepts help us to refer to events, principles help us to understand and predict events (p. 36)." The major contribution of explanatory concepts is to the solution of problems and explanations of experience. We indicate our awareness of the principles relating our experiences through the propositions we use to describe and explain experience.

Learning as an Associative Process

Rather than viewing learning merely as a product, it might also be informative to think of it as a process. Learning could thus be defined as *discovering the relationships among our experiences*. If we disregard the specific content of learned associations, we can note that these relationships are of two basic forms: contiguity and contingency. Our process definition of learning might then be further refined to a statement like: "Learning is the process of discovering experiences that are contiguously or contingently related."

The contiguity relationship between experiences can be described as a correlation: when one experience occurs, the other experience is also likely to occur.

Contiguous relationships are observed whenever two or more experiences repeatedly appear at about the same time and or in about the same place. Rain may appear following the appearance of dark clouds in the sky. From this we learn that dark clouds and rain are somehow associated.

There is a limit on what can be learned when experiences are contiguously related. In the example above, for instance, if contiguity between rain and dark clouds were all that we ever experienced, we would never be able to learn that the dark clouds produced the rain. We must observe that rain occurs only in the presence of dark clouds. This is the nature of the contingency relationship between events, and this relationship is an important extension of the contiguity relationship. It is a more informative relationship, and hence more meaningful. Events to be associated in a contingency relationship must be contiguous, but a contingency relationship involves more than the repetition of events in close temporal or spatial proximity. A contingency is observed whenever one (or more) event consistently occurs *only* in the presence of another contiguously-related event. Stated in other words, event B occurs if and only if event A has occurred. Event B is thus contingent (or dependent) upon event A. We speak in terms of contingent relationships when we describe experiences as predictable or controllable, or as causing or affecting other experiences.

We may be tempted at this point to assume that whenever two experiences occur, either contiguously or contingently, an association will be formed. Recent research (Hinde & Stevenson-Hinde, 1973), however, suggests that contiguity and contingency are necessary, but not sufficient, conditions for associations to be learned. Some associations cannot be made, an inability perhaps due to immaturity or lack of experience, but often the result of biological and psychological limitations. Other associations, conversely, are easily made, suggesting we are predisposed to learn relationships between some experiences. This avenue of research, little explored with humans, has great practical importance.

Current knowledge of the biological and psychological limits placed on learning can be summarized briefly. We know that learning frequently requires repeated exposure to the relationships between events before a linkage of these relationships occurs. It is difficult to predict the amount of repeated exposure to any particular relationship that is necessary for learning. However, Seligman (1970) has proposed a dimension of *preparedness* that may prove useful for categorizing learning experiences. At one extreme of the dimension, associations may be considered *prepared;* they are very rapidly formed and are of major adaptive consequence. For example, we very readily learn to avoid dangerous or painful situations; we become particularly sensitive to the cues or signals that warn us of this danger or pain. Our level of cognitive sophistication also prepares us to learn certain associations quite easily. Infants as young as three months are prepared to learn that their responses have some consequences (Watson & Ramey, 1966). They learn to discriminate, within some limits, events that they can control and events that are uncontrollable. They are also uniquely prepared to learn human language, as they are quite sensitive and responsive to human speech sounds and speechlike sounds, and acquire the grammatical rules of language very early in life.

At the other extreme of the dimension of preparedness, associations may be considered *contraprepared*. These are impossible to make at any given point in development. The educational concept of readiness implicitly assumes some associations are contraprepared. Until children's muscles and brain are sufficiently developed, it is impossible for them to learn to coordinate the movements necessary for walking. For similar reasons, infants and young children may be contraprepared to learn the meanings of subtle emotions or how to display them. As we shall see later, the stage of cognitive development may actually prevent the child from making certain associations. Fundamental changes occur in the way that children think about their world. Until a more sophisticated cognitive stage is reached, a four-year-old child will be unable to recognize that an object can be a ball and a thing to play with at the same time. This same child may also be unable to recognize that a tall, thin glass can contain just as much lemonade as a short, fat glass. Experience has prepared them to identify the height of a column of liquid with the amount of liquid. They are contraprepared to realize that diameter of a glass compensates for difference in height.

Between the extremes of prepared and contraprepared associations is a range of associations that are *unprepared*. Unprepared associations can be learned, but require more time than prepared associations. Many of the arbitrary rules of social conduct and conventions of word usage that we learn are unprepared associations. There is no natural tendency to associate a plus sign with a mathematical operation involved in addition, yet we learn this symbolic relationship. Most formal and informal instruction involves unprepared associations.

Even though unprepared associations can be learned, some are more difficult to learn than others, since more experience is required to make difficult associations. Ideally, then, we should find ways of making difficult unprepared associations easier. In practice this could be accomplished by tackling easier associations before moving on to the more difficult ones. Often, the easier associations are prerequisite to successful formation of more difficult ones. This is what educators intend to do when they use task analysis and developmental lattices. The use of individualized educational plans in special education derives in part from the advantage gained by emphasizing more-prepared responses before less-prepared ones.

Since experiences will be associated only when their relationship provides new information about the environment, a second limitation is placed on what can be learned. Contiguouslyor contingently-related experiences are informative whenever they modify pre-existing associations to permit more effective adaptation to the environment. Since new events, therefore, are evaluated within the context of what we already know about our environment, new associations will not be learned (1) when events are redundant with prior experiences (they will provide no new information) or (2) when no context exists to indicate the significance of the events for effective adaptation. In this case, events are neither perceived as important at the time nor are they meaningful. Learning therefore is a selective cognitive process.

This limitation may be illustrated in avoidance learning. For health and safety, we must learn to avoid hazards. Suppose that as we are exploring an interesting object, we happen to touch something very hot. By reflex, we quickly withdraw our hand. This reflex action is a pre-wired association between very hot events and our behavior—something we do not have to learn. Since it would be better if we could learn to avoid contacting hot objects like the burner of a stove, we therefore look for environmental cues that help us avoid the painful burns that even this reflex cannot totally prevent. We may notice an unusual sound during our exploration of the stove. But if, in the absence of this sound, we still burn ourselves, this sound will not be associated with the painful burn from the hot stove. It does not provide the information necessary to avoid the burn, since it is not contingently related. But, we can learn to associate the red circle of light and the slight heat we feel emanating from the burner with this painful experience. Touching a hot stove will still be painful and elicit the withdrawing reflex, but now we have added to that prewired association information that enables us to avoid that contact in the first place.

Developmental Changes in Learning

The basic ability to learn associations between signals and important environmental events or responses and their consequences is present very early in infancy. Simple response chains directed at external environmental events probably are not learned much before 6-8 months. After this, the complexity of response chains that children can master increases rapidly—an apparent consequence of the emergence of language and representational abilities between 6-8 and 24 months.

Words are not effectively used to mediate associations until after 4-6 years of age. Once children begin to gain language proficiency and independence from the characteristics of immediate experience, verbal learning progresses rapidly and generalizes to new experiences. Since concept learning requires these prerequisite abilities, only very concrete class and dimensional concepts are likely to be learned before about 7 years of age. Explanatory concepts or principles are probably not well learned before early adolescence.

Stevenson (1972) has described further developmental changes in learning. First, he suggests that children of all ages are motivated to learn. However, this does not mean that children are always motivated to learn what a teacher or parent would like them to learn. By early childhood, children seem eager to please teachers or parent, thus providing a strong incentive for learning. Later, children seem more interested in pleasing themselves, motivated by a desire to succeed more than by a desire to obtain specific rewards.

Second, the effect of extrinsic reinforcement for learning appears to differ at different ages. We are likely to see young children repeat a response that earned them some sort of reinforcement. Older children, however, more prone to try out a new response as a result of reinforcement, will not simply repeat the reinforced response. Stevenson (1972) suggests that "older children are able to detach themselves from the immediate consequences of responses; having found one response to be correct does not necessarily mean that all others would be wrong." (p. 348)

Third, young children do not appear to benefit from verbal instructions and attend more to their immediate experience. It is probably not until about five to seven years of age that children are able to direct their responses based on further instructions.

Fourth, young children are not very flexible in their approach to learning. They tend to have strong response biases and preferences which persist even when inappropriate.

Fifth, young children who have difficulty focusing attention on relevant features of their experience are easily distracted. Older children are more likely to attend to the task demands. They tend aalso to respond more to "what is important rather than to what is momentarily interesting." (Stevenson, 1972, p. 349).

COGNITION VIEWED AS A PROCESS: Cognitive-Development Approaches

Jean Piaget

The extensive writings of the Swiss psychologist and philosopher, Jean Piaget, present the most comprehensive and systematically researched information on cognitive development in children. Piaget's observations stem from an attempt to identify the principles underlying the development of reasoning. Reasoning is a form of rational thought that conforms ultimately to logical principles, and Piaget distinguishes four major stages in this cognitive development. In each, children differ significantly in the ways they interpret, understand, and represent their experiences. Before considering these differences, it is important to realize the consistent properties of cognition at all stages of development. These identify the constancies that account for the continuity of cognitive development.

Piaget views cognitive activity as an attempt to adapt to experience. He argues that we do not merely adjust passively to the demands of experience, but instead actively impose a structure on our responses. This enables us to interpret our experience and is modified by feedback from the environment when cognitive structure inadequately represents significant aspects of experience. According to this interpretation, our knowledge of the world derives from modification and refinement of existing knowledge (prior cognition). Consequently, no knowledge is totally new; it always has a referent in prior knowledge. As a corollary statement: knowledge is organized and meaningful at all times, structured by the child's ways of knowing experience. Because these ways of knowing may not always be completely efficient, we are forced to refine them.

The structures that represent children's ways of knowing experience include both schemes and operations. *Schemes* are defined generally as organized patterns of responding that are repeatable and generalizable. New experiences are identified and interpreted with reference to the schemes applied to them. In Piaget's technical terminology, schemes thereby *assimilate* new experiences. One of the schemes of young infants is sucking. Various objects are assimilated to the sucking scheme whenever they contact an infant's mouth. From the differing degrees of satisfaction gained from sucking these objects, the infant comes to know some objects as suckable and others as not suckable. This dichotomy partitions the infant's experience into two distinct categories, at least with respect to this one scheme. In this manner knowledge begins to accumulate.

Some forms of experience do not lend themselves to the infant's crude schemes, i.e., some objects provide less satisfaction for sucking than others, and thus are not as readily assimilated to the sucking scheme. When this occurs, the infant begins to refine these crude schemes. Such refinements, as in the sucking example, illustrate the process of accommodation. *Accommodation* is the means by which schemes are changed to conform to the properties of experience. In this manner, but gradually, the schemes that represent the child's knowledge of experience come to reflect objective reality.

Operations are similar to explanatory concepts or principles. They describe integrated systems for mentally representing actions possessed by older children. Operations identify the rules governing the relationships between schemes or concepts and their application. "A useful rule of thumb," Flavell (1963, p. 166) suggests, "is to say that all the actions implied in common mathematical symbols like $+$, $-$, $\div$, $>$, $<$, etc., belong to, but do not exhaust the domain of what [Piaget] terms *intellectual operations*."

Infant Cognitive Development: The Sensorimotor Period

From birth to about two years of age, Piaget identifies a period in cognitive development where intelligence is primarily practical or action-based. Cognitive development during the sensorimotor period is sufficiently full and complex to require six descriptive stages for a complete explanation, and the sequence of these stages is invariant since the competencies that emerge during each stage are prerequisites for transition to the next.

Despite its crude beginnings, cognitive development during the sensorimotor period is marked by many significant advances. Through refinement and coordination of schemes which organize their experiences, infants, by the end of the sensorimotor period, demonstrate an emerging ability to use mental symbols, solve problems mentally, remember and imitate past events, and intentionally direct their own behavior. They further acquire an objective sense of causality and of space and time as properties of things. Infants also extract an invariant feature of experience represented in the concept of object permanence. This recognition that objects have substance and continue to exist in some form even when not immediately apprehended contributes to the definition of self-concept.

The First Stage: The Use of Reflexes (Birth–about 1 Month)

At birth, infants possess many reflex activities like sucking, swallowing, crying, and movements of the body and eyes that have the defining properties of schemes. Throughout the first month of life these schemes become more organized through exercise. Their use is not intelligent, however, since they primarily assimilate experience without making the accommodations required for adaptation. The first sensorimotor stage is significant insofar as it sets the foundation for subsequent cognitive development. The reflex-based schemes provide the initial structure by which experience can become known.

The Second Stage: The First Acquired Adaptations and the Primary Circular Reaction (about 1–4 Months)

Attempts to adapt to experience are first observed at stage two; in fact, these first adaptations are the defining property of this stage. These first-acquired adaptations retain something from experience that is external to the scheme itself. Infant responding is thenceforth a product of experience. What does this mean? In a sense, reflex-schemes during the first month are like the unconditional responses of signal learning, possessing a prewired association with an unconditional stimulus. All that is required to exercise the scheme is an object possessing the stimulus properties necessary to elicit the response. Acquired adaptations add something to this association as a result of experience. This would be analogous to introducing a conditional stimulus as a signal predicting the unconditional stimulus. The new association between the stimuli and the anticipatory conditional response thus adds something from experience to the prewired association.

Among the more significant Stage 2 adaptations is the coordination and integration of previously independent schemes. This enables infants, for the first time, to control their actions so that they can look at what they hear, suck what they grasp in their hands, and ultimately reach for what they see. This coordination of schemes occurs as a result of what Piaget calls *circular reactions*. In Stage 2, these are designated *primary circular reactions*. Other circular reactions designated secondary and tertiary appear at later stages. The basic concept of a circular reaction is the same at all stages; what is indicated by their primary, secondary, or tertiary nature is the focus of the circular reactions and the contexts in which they are produced.

Circular reactions are forms of assimilation that are precipitated by the nonintentional occurrence of interesting events, as when infants happen to brush their hands against their lips. Infants attempt to reproduce these events by reinstating the responses that preceded them. Largely through trial and error, infants gradually coordinate these responses into a new scheme. Thus, circular reactions are limited to reproducing experiences. New responses are not invented but are discovered as a consequence of some chance occurrence.

Primary circular reactions are centered around the infant's body. Chance coordinations of reflex-based schemes evoke attempts at reproduction. External environmental events are not likely to trigger circular reactions at Stage 2. Infants may notice interesting events in the environment, but they cannot successfully reproduce them since they lack the necessary response skills (coordinated schemes like visually directed reaching).

The Third Stage: The Secondary Circular Reactions and the Procedures for Making Interesting Sights Last (about 4–8 Months)

The accomplishment of eye-hand coordination during Stage 2 contributes to a major cognitive breakthrough: infants are able to shift their focus to the effects of their responses on the external environment. The onset of Stage 3 is thus marked by the first attempts to consolidate and coordinate responses that produce interesting effects on the environment. These effects occur initially by chance, but evoke *secondary circular reactions* (away from the body). Infant attention in secondary circular reactions is focused on responses that produce interesting consequences. The schemes produced in the context of secondary circular reactions represent the habitual patterns of responding that infants direct to particular events. They are not schemes used creatively to adapt to new experiences. Infants at Stage 3 seem to engage more in the repetition of responses producing predictable effects than in the application of responses to new experiences.

At Stage 3, infant responses are somewhat intentional, as their responses are object-oriented and directed to some external goal. This places them in a position to explore and notice more readily important features of their external environments. But the goals to which infants direct their actions are not decided in advance and actively sought. Rather, they are discovered in the course of their activities. What goals exist are identified *post hoc*. Truly intentional behavior further involves efforts deliberately to adapt responses to the goal sought. In Piaget's terms, responses must be subordinated to the goal, meaning that responses need to be regarded as the resources or means that can be applied to attaining a variety of goals. Responses can then be identified in advance, according to how well they adapt to the circumstances determining access to the goal. The simple and direct applications of habitual responses to reproduce interesting events observed in Stage 3 infants would consequently not be truly intentional.

*The Fourth Stage: The Coordination of the Secondary Schemes and Their
Application to New Situations (about 8–12 Months)*

Stage 4 marks the first point at which the goal-directed behavior can be
described as truly intentional. In addition, infants at this stage can begin to
anticipate external events that occur independent of their own behavior. They also
adapt more effectively to new and unfamiliar experiences.

These accomplishments result from the Stage 4 infant's ability to coordinate the
secondary schemes of Stage 3 in new combinations that are dissociated from their
habitual associations with specific events. Responses consequently become meaningful as resources for attaining goals, solving problems and adapting to new
experiences. They do not merely reproduce interesting familiar events.

The major coordination of schemes at this stage takes the form of a means-end
relationship. Sequences of schemes are systematically produced as the *means* to
reach a previously identified *end* (or goal). In order to solve a problem such as
retrieving a toy (end or goal) when direct access is blocked by a pillow, infants
must discover some scheme other than a habitual response to the pillow that
eliminates it as an obstacle. A scheme like pounding to flatten the pillow could be
integrated as a means to permit use of the scheme of reaching an accessible goal
object (end). A significant limitation is imposed on means-end coordination during
Stage 4. Only known responses can serve as means and ends. The only thing new
about means-end coordination at this point is the *coordination* of schemes itself.

Objects are also integrated as tools for attaining goals during Stage 4. This
indicates that the habitual associations of objects with responses can also be
disregarded by these infants. An additional consequence of the ability to disregard
these habitual associations is an increased interest in exploring novel objects as
novelties during Stage 4. Piaget notes that infants during Stage 3 are also interested
in novel objects. However, "the new object does not interest the child at all as a
novelty. Its novelty only arrests his curiosity fleetingly and the object immediately
serves as aliment to habitual schemata. Interest is consequently not centered on the
object as such but on its utilization" (Piaget, 1952, p. 258). In contrast, at Stage 4,
"the unfamiliar obviously represents to the child an external reality, to which he
must adapt himself and no longer a substance which is pliable at will or a simple
aliment for the activity itself . . . . [T]he child at this stage gives more the
impression of making an experiment than of generalizing his behavior patterns: He
tries to 'understand' " (Piaget, 1952, p. 259).

*The Fifth Stage: The Tertiary Circular Reaction and the Discovery of New Means
through Active Experimentation (about 12–18 Months)*

Tertiary circular reactions are evoked whenever familiar responses produce
unexpected effects when applied to new objects. The unexpected effects stimulate
infants to explore the properties of this new object. With their attention focused on

the effects produced in the object, infants repeatedly contact the object, each time varying the form of response. They adopt what Flavell (1977) calls a "let's-see-what-would-happen-if" attitude, applying a flexible and varied means-end sequence of behaviors. The flexibility of means-end relationships in goal-directed behavior at Stage 5 contrasts sharply with the fixed and stereotyped nature of goal-directed behavior during Stage 4.

One of the consequences of tertiary circular reactions is the discovery of new means through active experimentation. At Stage 5, infants are keenly attuned to the properties of objects and accommodate their responses to them readily. While exploring novel objects, some properties of these objects may resist infants' attempts to assimilate them to known schemes. Through systematic manipulation of their responses—a form of trial-and-error experimentation—infants may recognize new means for adapting to these objects. These new means could then be generalized to other new experiences.

The Sixth Stage: The Invention of New Means through Mental Combinations (about 18–24 Months)

The progressive refinements in cognitive abilities during the first five stages of the Sensorimotor Period coalesce at Stage Six, introducing a revolutionary change in cognitive perspective. For the first time, infants begin to use *symbols* to represent experience and structure their actions. Stage Six marks the beginning of an awareness of relationships among experiences and actions that transcends direct and overt trial-and-error manipulation of external events.

To appreciate the nature of this change, consider the following simple experiment that Piaget conducted with his daughter, Lucienne. Piaget makes a game of hiding a watch chain in an empty matchbox. As long as the opening in the matchbox was large enough for Lucienne to poke her finger inside, she had no trouble extracting the chain. All that was required was the application of familiar response schemes like turning over the box to shake the chain out or sliding her finger into the opening. However, making the matchbox opening only 3mm. introduced a problem for Lucienne that could not be solved by applying familiar response schemes. Lucienne's response was quite sophisticated, even though she had never seen how matchboxes open and close. Following her initial attempt to poke her finger into the matchbox opening,

> a pause follows during which Lucienne manifests a very curious reaction . . . She looks at the slit with great attention; then several times in succession, she opens and shuts her mouth, at first slightly, then wider and wider! . . . Apparently Lucienne understands the existence of a cavity subjacent to the slit and wishes to enlarge that cavity . . . . [D]ue to inability to think out the situation in words or clear visual images she uses a simple motor indicator as "signifier" or symbol . . . . [T]he motor reaction which pre-

sents itself for filling this role is none other than imitation . . . . This scheme of imitation, with which she is familiar, constitutes for her the means of thinking out the situation . . . . Soon after this phase of plastic reflection, Lucienne unhesitatingly puts her fingers in the slit and, instead of trying as before to reach the chain, she pulls so as to enlarge the opening. She succeeds and grasps the chain. (Piaget, 1952, pp. 337-338)

Lucienne may well have been able to solve this same problem earlier through the trial-and-error experimentation characteristic of Stage Five. The most compelling feature of her reaction, which clearly indicates her advance to Stage Six, is the dramatic reduction of overt manipulation before an appropriate response was "discovered." Instead, she manipulated her representation of the properties of the matchbox to identify a potentially appropriate response *before* that response was applied.

It may appear that this newly emerging use of symbols has no precedent in earlier sensorimotor development. However, there is a compelling sense of continuity between the cognitive accomplishments of Stage Six and their precursors in the preceding stages. In one respect, this continuity is expressed in the cycle of changes observed in the Sensorimotor Period. From Stage 3 onward, we can identify periods of *apprenticeship,* during which new responses (schemes) are discovered and reproduced, alternating with periods of *consolidation* when now familiar response schemes are applied to new circumstances. The apprenticeship of Stage 3 enabled infants to identify specific responses that had an effect on external events. Using these responses as tools, infants during Stage 4 were able to identify new contexts for applying these same tools in their attemps to solve problems. This consolidation and coordination of response schemes in new ways prepared them for a new period of apprenticeship at Stage 5. During Stage 5, infants experimented more flexibly with their response schemes to gain some practical understanding of external events. While making sense of unexpected reactions to their responses (tertiary circular reactions), they discovered new means of responding to external events.

In keeping with this cycle, Stage Six is a period of consolidation and application—accomplished in a new way, though, through mental combination of schemes. The new responses elaborated in Stage 5 are consolidated by mental application to new situations in Stage 6.

There is, however, an element of apprenticeship maintained in Stage 6 cognitive activity,* implied by the term "invention" in the title given this stage. This suggests no real break in the cycle; rather, we must recognize that infants during Stage 6 are successively able to consolidate, reorganize, and apply schemes and

---

*It should also be noted that there is some consolidation and application of new means discovered in the context of tertiary circular reaction during Stage 5.

invent creatively new schemes. The cycle is thus maintained within Stage 6, for as Piaget notes, "all invention presupposes a mental combination of already elaborated schemes (p. 333)."

To gain a more complete understanding of the continuities in the relationship between the accomplishments of Stage 6 of the Sensorimotor Period and those of the preceding stages, it is necessary to consider the defining properties of Stage 6 cognition—invention of new means and representation.

Invention of new means differs from discovery in two fundamental respects: (1) it is accomplished more rapidly, and (2) it has few overt manifestations in infant behavior. As was seen with Piaget's daughter Lucienne, once she detected that the problem of extracting the chain from the matchbox could not be solved by applying a familiar response scheme, she paused, attended to the matchbox, and shortly thereafter poked her finger in the slit, drew open the box and retrieved the chain. Most significant is that the only intervening overt response was an imitation with her mouth of one of the properties of the matchbox. During Stage 5, her response to this problem would have been different. She would have overtly experimented with the matchbox, identifying its properties by applying her familiar response schemes. In the course of these trial-and-error manipulations, she may or may not have been able to discove the new response that would provide her with the means (the response to open the box) to attain the end (retrieval of the chain). Even if successful, this arduous step-by-step approach to solving the problem is noticeably less efficient and more time-consuming than the invention of the new response that Lucienne exhibited in this example.

Except for the fact that the invention of new schemes operates at the mental level rather than at the level of overt behavior, invention is essentially no different from discovery in its operation. When Piaget uses the term "discovery" he indicates that new schemes are acquired in the context of overt manipulations of external events. As a consequence of some fortuitous contact with interesting events, familiar schemes are coordinated and integrated in new ways that distinguish them as new schemes. The novelty of these schemes is then recognized after their appearance, in the course of covert application to external events. New schemes invented through mental combinations in Stage 6 are similarly "discovered" in the course of manipulating familiar schemes. But, these manipulations occur covertly (mentally) before any application is made of the new schemes. Awareness of the novelty (and hypothesized appropriateness) of these new schemes therefore precedes their use.

The invention of new schemes through mental combinations is dependent on infants' ability to represent experience. Mental representation thus liberates infants from the limitations of immediate practical experience and enables them to relate knowledge gained from prior experience in the absence of its direct external referent. Representation takes the form of internalized symbolic images. The evolution of these images begins in Stage Two, where infants first detect environmental signals that are incorporated within their schemes of action. By Stage Four, these signals become sufficiently detached from infants' own immediate actions that they become "signs" of impending events to which infants respond. At this point, we find infants particularly attuned to the signs contained in their mothers' behavior that they have discovered to be associated with her departure. In anticipation of this event, they may begin to cry.

Signs, however, are not truly representational. Even though infants can anticipate events on the basis of the signs inherent in experience, this anticipation is possible only when immediate experience presents the signs. Stage Four infants apparently cannot fully sustain or recreate an image of an object or event in its absence. This is well illustrated by the tendency for 8-12-month-old infants to protest vigorously when their mothers prepare to leave them but to show few signs of seeking her in her absence.

The advent of symbolic images is made possible by infants' increased ability to distinguish more readily between signs contained in immediate experience and their own actions. As a direct consequence, during Stage Five, infants show a greater interest in accommodating to the properties of objects and events as they exist rather than in simply deriving enough information from experience to permit them to apply a familiar response scheme. By attending to objects and events directly, infants acquire stable perceptual schemes for representing experience. At Stage Six, these perceptual schemes or images can be evoked in the absence of the objects or events represented. Most significantly, these images can be responded to, manipulated, and transformed as cognitive contents in their own right. Consequently, infants are freed from the limitations of direct perception and can more flexibly relate knowledge gained from prior experience to the present (and ultimately plan for the future).

Piaget parallels the evolution of representational competence with the development of *imitation* and *play*. (See Table 6-1 for an outline of this development). At the same time that he identifies the contribution of representation to imitation and play, he derives some unique insights on the nature or representation by analyzing imitation and play as the observable manifestations of primarily accommodative (imitation) and assimilative (play) functions.

The role of representation is implicit in infants' ability to engage in deferred imitation and symbolic play during Stage Six. In general, imitation refers to the acquisition and repetition of new responses as a result of observing the same responses in the behavior of a model. Piaget calls imitation pure accommodation, as infants' primary focus is on accurate reproduction of the response observed. *Deferred imitation* reflects the ability to reproduce a novel response observed in one context at a later time, and perhaps in a different context. Representation is essential to deferred imitation, otherwise, how could infants retain the memory of what they observed over such a period of delay in the absence of continuing direct experience?

Not only do infants imitate the actions of other people. By Stage Five, they also imitate the actions of objects and imitate the properties of objects in their actions. Piaget was so intrigued by this observation that he suggested that representation at Stage Six is, in a sense, internalized imitation. We saw that this means of representation provided the basis for Lucienne's "thought" about how to solve the matchbox problem.

Piaget defines play as assimilation without accommodation. By this, he means that infants (and older children as well) frequently pursue activities for the sheer pleasure of exercising their response schemes without engaging in the serious business of attempting to adapt to environmental demands. Rather than a frivolous waste of time, however, Piaget regards play as the child's "work." Through play, infants and children perfect their competencies and gain knowledge of how responses can be coordinated. Play thus contributes an organization to schemes, and, as we shall see later, this relates directly to children's ability to structure experience conceptually.

The *symbolic play* of the Stage Six infant could also be called make-believe or pretense play. In symbolic play, infants tend to respond to one object or event *as if* it were something else. One object thus is used as a symbol to represent or refer to another absent object. At the same time, infants engaging in symbolic play recognize that the object used as a symbol is in fact *not* the same as the object it represents. Piaget's daughter Jacqueline frequently played a game of "going to sleep" that illustrates symbolic play. Various objects, including a fringed cloth, the collar of her mother's coat, her stuffed animals, and the tail of a rubber donkey appeared to remind her of her pillow. To each she responded similarly, as if it were her pillow: "She seized it, held a fold of it in her right hand, sucked the thumb of the same hand and lay down on her side, laughing hard. She kept her eyes open, but blinked from time to time as if she were alluding to closed eyes" (Piaget, 1951, p. 96).

In symbolic play, we can observe the essence of all symbolic relationships. Two elements are involved, one of which — a *signifier* in Piaget's terms — is a word, symbol, or object (as in the example above). These signifiers "call to mind" or refer to perceptually absent objects, events, or other experiences that Piaget calls *significates*. Signifiers must be differentiated from their significates, indicating simply that symbols must not be confused with what they represent.

Piaget rarely speaks of the acquisition of specific cognitive products, as his interest is primarily directed at describing the general development of cognitive processes. Yet he does devote considerable attention to four fundamental concepts that emerge during the Sensorimotor Period: *object permanence, causality, space,* and *time* as objective properties of objects and events. Each is significant as it provides a framework for objectively making sense of experience. Some details regarding development of the concepts of object permanence and causality are provided in Table 6-1. (While studying this table, note that the concepts are interdependent. Just as there are parallels in the development of representation, imitation and play, so too are there parallels within these concepts. The developmental stages indicated are highly correlated with the general stages of cognitive development during the Sensorimotor Period.)

The concept of *object permanence* is something we accept almost intuitively. Until Piaget, researchers assumed that infants recognized as well as adults that objects have substance and continue to exist even when not directly perceived. However, Piaget's observations of infants' reactions to disappearing objects indicates the inaccuracy of this assumption. Before about eight months, "out of sight" is literally "out of mind." Not until that time will infants actively search for hidden objects.

Even at Stages 4 and 5 there are limitations to infants' concepts of object permanence. To illustrate these limitations, consider Piaget's classic experiment for researching object permanence. An interesting toy is placed before infants and, while they are watching, it is completely covered by a blanket. Infants at Stage 4 of sensorimotor development and beyond readily remove the blanket and retrieve the toy. (Can you see why the general cognitive accomplishments of Stage Four are prerequisite to this? Hint: recall what was meant by "means-end coordination.") However, if after hiding the toy, we move it in full view of the child and place it in a second hiding place (visible displacement), Stage 4 infants will persist in looking for the toy where it was first hidden. Their search ends when they discover that the toy is not there. Only at Stage 5 are infants capable of following these visible replacements of the toy. They will look for the toy where it was last hidden.

The limitations of the concept of object permanence at Stage 5 are observed whenever the toys or other objects are hidden through a series of invisible displacements. Invisible displacements are like a game of "Button, Button, Who Has the Button?" If Stage 5 infants see a toy hidden in one place and the toy is then moved in such a way that they cannot see that it has been moved, their search for the missing toy will not proceed beyond the place where they actually saw it hidden. Only at Stage 6, when infants are able to represent the toy mentally in its absence, do they continue to search for the toy despite its invisible displacement. It is as if they recognize it exists somewhere and so it should be possible to find it. Only from Stage 6 onward can we assume that children possess a mature concept of object permanence. Of more general significance, as a consequence of object permanence, infants for the first time perceive themselves as one object in a world of objects. This differentiation is necessary to any subsequent development of a *self* concept.

At the end of the Sensorimotor Period, infants' knowledge of causality, space, and time does not reflect a fully mature *understanding* of these concepts. They have only become aware of some of the objective characteristics of their experiences. The concept of *causality* exists as knowledge that they can be causal agents, effecting changes in their environment. At the same time, they know that there are

Table 6-1 Selected Sensorimotor Accomplishments

	Imitation	Play	Object Permanence	Causality
Stage 1. (birth to about 1 month)	No imitation of new responses. May be stimulated to respond by external events (e.g., may start crying when hears other infants crying).	No evidence of play.	No object permanence (No sense that objects exist when not immediately perceived). "Out of sight, out of mind" (Objects are fleeting sensations).	No sense of causality.
Stage 2. (about 1-4 months)	No imitation of new responses. When *others* imitate infants' responses, infants may repeat or intensify own responses.	Infants will repeat primary circular reactions for the pleasure of repetition (called *functional assimilation*).	Infants may make aborted attempts to preserve/reproduce interesting events (primary circular reactions) by looking, listening, etc.	No sense of causality.
Stage 3. (about 4-8 months)	No imitation of new responses *but* infants will "imitate" model's response if that response is familiar to them *but* they can "imitate" in this way *only* responses that they can see or hear themselves perform.	Relaxed repetition of responses can be distinguished from the serious business of attempting to adapt to new experiences. Infants enjoy activity for its own sake without need for external reinforcement.	Anticipate movements of objects. Engage in brief search for objects that escape their grasp. Deferred circular reaction: infants may abandon activity with an object for a while and then rediscover it soon afterward.	By seeing themselves act, infants begin to distinguish between their actions and the consequences of these actions. Infants possess a magical, omnipotent sense of their actions as causes of interesting effects.

Table 6-1 *Continued*

	Imitation	Play	Object Permanence	Causality
			Reach for partially hidden object (recognize object based on only a small part of it).	(Subjective notion of causality) This is observed in their attempts to cause recurrence of effects directly (even when effects occur independent of their own actions).
Stage 4. (about 8-12 months)	Infants overcome the limitations of Stage 3. *Can* imitate simple new responses, even those they cannot see or hear themselves perform.	Infants can abandon goal-directed behavior in favor of playing with actions directed at obstacle. Engage in ritualized play (e.g. infants may act out ritual of going to sleep when they come upon their pillows).	Infants actively search for hidden objects. (Initially only if they are in the process of reaching when it disappears.) (Later, will remove obstacles to find hidden objects).	Beginnings of an objective sense of causality. Infants recognize that they are not the immediate causes of some effects. They act as though they are the ultimate cause of these effects, however, by attempting to induce the immediate causal agent to produce the effect. (e.g., may push an adult's hand to cause it to shake a rattle).

Stage				
Stage 5. (about 12-18 months)	Imitate more precisely the behaviors of a model, including more subtle or complex responses. Experiment with different ways of imitating different models.	Rapidly convert newly acquired responses to play rituals.	Search for hidden objects where they were last seen even though the objects were moved through a series of displacements to different hiding places before the infants can initiate their search. This is possible only when these displacements are in full view.	Infants begin to perceive themselves as influenced by other causal agents. They recognize correctly the external causes of effects that occur at a distance, but do not know how to influence these external causal agents.
Stage 6.	Readily imitate complex new behaviors. Imitate actions of objects as well as people.	Engage in symbolic play (pretense or make-believe).	Infants persist in search for hidden objects that have been displaced invisibly. (Do not have to know where objects were hidden to sustain their search.) Possess the full notion of object permanence since they recognize that objects exist somewhere even if they have not seen where they disappeared.	Infants can reconstruct the probable cause of an effect from the nature of the effect. Can anticipate an effect that would be the consequence of a particular caused action.

185

other effects caused independently of their own actions. Infants' concepts of *space* include the recognition that space is an objective, abstract, property of things. Objects take up space, move through space, and can be located in space. To an infant, *time* is the knowledge that actions have duration and that they occur in sequence. Of course, they are unable to represent time objectively or use it as a standard reference for organizing experience at this point in their development.

The discovery of causality, space, and time is made possible by the fact that infants' responses do produce effects (just as do other causal agents), that their actions produce displacements of objects in space, and that their actions are sequentially organized and have duration. The task for infants is to recognize these properties inherent in their own actions and abstract from their experiences the more general concepts. As we said before, however, infants only come to recognize these objective properties of their own actions, without really understanding or being able to describe or measure them. These latter accomplishments require many more years of experience.

From Sensorimotor to Symbolic-Representational Intelligence

By age two, infants have gained considerable knowledge of the characteristics of their experiences. They have discovered what they can do to their environment and how it responds to their reactions. They possess a practical sense of the properties of objects and events independent of their own actions. What they lack, however, is a conceptual framework for understanding how experience is organized and a system of principles for reasoning why this is so. As a consequence, infants are unable to plan, direct, and control their own actions. Instead of being able to hypothesize the possible outcomes of their actions (what would happen if . . . ?), they are restricted to discovering, on a piecemeal basis, what happens when they do something.

In contrast with the purely practical, action-based intelligence of the Sensorimotor Period, the newly emerging use of symbols to represent experience allows children to move to a new level of understanding. The many advantages of intelligent action based on symbolic representation are contrasted with sensorimotor intelligence below.

Sensorimotor Intelligence	Symbolic-Representational Intelligence
slow, step by step, one action at a time	faster, more flexible
oriented toward actions and concrete, practical results	interested in knowledge *per se*, concerned with information and truth

concrete and earthbound; present-oriented	potentially abstract, "free to soar" can begin to think about own thoughts
private, idiosyncratic, uncommunicable	can make use of socially-shared symbol system and can communicate with and become socialized by others

(adapted from Flavell, 1977)

This transition from sensorimotor to symbolic-representational intelligence poses many problems for young children. Indeed, it is not until early adolescence that children effectively master the process of conceptualizing and coordinating thought based on symbolic representation. Piaget distinguishes three major periods in this interval during which children construct stable concepts from their perceptions of experience (Preoperational Period), integrate their mental actions for manipulating, transforming, and coordinating these concepts into operational systems of interrelated actions (Period of Concrete Operations), and coordinate systems of operations to reason logically, hypothesizing and then testing out possible concrete and abstract relationships among experiences and concepts (Period of Formal Operations). With each succeeding period, children become increasingly aware of their own thoughts and are able to communicate them to others.

The Preoperational Period (from about 2—7 years)

Young children, particularly between the ages of two and four, which Piaget labels the Preconceptual Subperiod of the Preoperational Period, are faced with an immediate task of coming to grips with their new representational skills. Before symbols can be mentally manipulated usefully, children must translate their sensorimotor knowledge into equivalent symbolic representations and schemes of mental actions. The products of this translation process are concepts. Concepts provide an important structure from which children derive an understanding of experience. Efficiency in mental actions is promoted, since concepts permit children to respond to the common meaning shared by all elements contained within the concept. Therefore, knowledge abstracted in the context of experience with specific objects or events can be generalized at a conceptual level to similar objects or events.

Young children's concepts are usually unstable and inconsistent. One instance of this inconsistency is that young children seem unable to remember a consistent rule for classifying objects or events. When confronted with a task requiring sorting various objects of different shapes, sizes, and colors into appropriate groups (e.g., all squares, all circles, all triangles), they may fail totally, creating, instead, pictures with the shapes. Or, they may attempt to apply a rule but forget to apply the same rule throughout the sorting process.

This conceptual instability is reflected also in children's inability to recognize that some properties of objects remain unchanged despite changes in appearance. They possess no sense of themselves as the same person from the time they were babies until they reach adulthood. For example, some children may think that if they dress and act like boys, they *are* boys, but become girls if they dress and act like girls. Likewise, horses become something other than horses if a different arbitrary label like "dog" is applied to them. In general, young children fail to recognize *identity* as an inherent property of things that remains unchanged by perceivable transformations.

This instability renders children's understanding of experience very chaotic and unstructured. Interestingly enough, this apparently does not trouble them. Children's reasoning style (Piaget calls it *transductive reasoning*) reflects this. Inability to abstract general from particular experiences or to anticipate particular experiences based on general principles makes children's reasoning neither inductive nor deductive. Instead, they sense a need for general statements for interpreting experience but derive these statements from some perceived similarity between particular experiences. Their logical error comes in assuming that if two experiences are alike in one way, they must be alike in all ways, as the following example taken from the magazine section of a New Orleans newspaper illustrates:

Sole music

My young grandchildren, dressed in their best, were walking on the beach at Destin, Fla., for the first time. The sand there is extra white and fine.

Beth, intrigued, asked why the sand squeaked under their feet.

"Silly!" responded David, 5, disdainfully. "Don't you know why? It's because the sand is made out of Sunday School shoes."

(*Times-Picayune,* May 29, 1977.)

Young children are continually preoccupied with gaining information about experience, which accounts for their seemingly endless string of "who," "what," "where," "when," and "why" questions. Such questions make sense when you consider they are unable to understand and explain things on their own. They cannot derive the answers themselves from mental manipulation of their symbolic representation of experience; they must acquire this information from others more competent. From these answers, young children assimilate information that is comprehensible to them and thereby gradually accommodate their mental schemes to the way things are.

The most colorful examples of how young children conceptualize the world are contained in their attempts to explain how and why things happen (physical and social causality). For one, they tend to reason backward from effects to causes (finalism). When asked what causes night, they may say "night comes so we may go to sleep" (Laurendeau and Pinard, 1962). Young children also attribute life-like properties to inanimate objects (*animism*): understanding a little about their own motives, desires, and feelings, they infer that objects have similar characteristics that account for their actions. Piaget overheard one child describe the moon animistically.

> "There's the moon, it's round . . . . It goes on when we go on."
> [The moon disappears behind a cloud] "Look now it's been killed."
> [Later, attempting to explain the moon's disappearance] "Every now and then the moon disappears; perhaps it goes to see the rain in the clouds, or perhaps it's cold." (Piaget, 1960, p. 210)
>
> Other examples of animism in older children (from Piaget, 1960, p. 220):
>
> "The sun sometimes watches us," . . . . "when we're looking nice he looks at us.—Do you look nice?—Yes, on Sundays when I'm dressed like a man."
> The sun moves "to hear what we're saying."
> "The moon looks at us and watches over us," . . . . "when I walk, it walks; when I stand still it stands still. It copies like a parrot."—Why?—"It wants to do whatever I do."—Why?—"Because it's inquisitive."

Artificialism is an additional basis from which young children explain their experience. Children tend to regard things as products of human creation and apply their knowledge of themselves and others as causal agents to account for the origins of things. Some illustrations follow:

> "How are ladies made?" [Why do you ask?] Because there is meat on ladies . . . . I think it's a meatmaker who makes them, don't you?" (Piaget, 1960, p. 364)
>
> [Where did your little sister come from?] "Mummy still had some flesh [left] over from when I was born. To make my little sister, she modeled it with her fingers and kept it hidden for a long while." (Piaget, 1960, p. 364)
>
> [How does a baby get in mother's tummy?] "Just make it first."—How—"Well, you first make it. You put some eyes on it . . . . Put the head on, and hair, some hair all curls" . . . . "You make it with head stuff" . . . . "You find it at a store that makes it." (Bernstein & Cowan, 1975)

An overarching characteristic of thought during the entire Preoperational Period is its *egocentrism*. Frequently misinterpreted as selfishness, egocentrism is a cognitive limitation among two-to-seven-year-old children deriving from inability to recognize that other people have differing points of views, wishes, needs, desires, thoughts, and feelings. Children, little aware of their own thoughts, are certainly unlikely to have awareness of the thoughts of others, thus projecting an insensitivity to the need to adjust their own actions to those of others.

The most overt manifestations of egocentrism are in the use of language and in responsiveness to socialization attempts during the Preoperational Period. Young children do not communicate in the conventional sense; their utterances are frequently idiosyncratic with private, not socially shared, meanings. This may provoke frustration in parents who try to understand what their egocentric children are saying. Ultimately, of course, children become more conversant in language and acquire conventional meanings of experiences that other people describe to them in words.

It should not be surprising, in light of children's egocentric ''communication,'' to find that communications to them through language have little effect on their behavior. Until about seven, children cannot readily direct and control behavior through language. Rules represented by language alone may not be complied with, not because of resistance, but because they cannot always extract the meaning of the rules.

Piaget designates the later part of the Preoperational Period, from four-to-seven years, as the Intuitive Subperiod, from his observation that these children feel so certain in their knowledge of the world that they draw general conclusions from their experience, even though unaware of how they know what they know. Furthermore, with an egocentric perspective, they recognize no need to justify their conclusions to themselves and others. When pressed for justification, they fail to consider relevant information, relying instead on an assumption that the way things appear is in reality the way things are. A common response to a why question would tend to be ''because, just because.''

Children at the level of intuitive thought are quite sophisticated in their use of concepts. Stable mental schemes with consistent defining properties are applied to their representations of experience. Their classification abilities are more flexible; objects or events can be classified consecutively as examples of many different concepts.

Even with these advances in conceptualization, intuitive thought is limited. The key limitation stems from difficulty in resolving conflicts between immediate perceptions and their understanding of experience. Because their mental actions for coordinating representations and concepts are not systematically interrelated, they are more attentive to their perceptions, which very likely distort reality in such a way that relevant information is not noticed.

Intuitive thought is amply documented in the four-to-seven-year-old child's performance on Piagetian conservation tasks. *Conservation,* similar to the concept of identity, refers to the recognition that certain properties of objects (e.g., quantity, length, weight, number, area, and volume) frequently remain unchanged despite transformations in their outward appearance. Thus, a lump of clay would still have the same mass even though it could be shaped as a ball or a sausage, or broken down into five smaller balls *as long as* none of the clay has been removed in the course of these transformations. Similarly eight ounces of lemonade retain the same volume, regardless of the shape of the container.

At no time during the Intuitive Subperiod do children appear to understand the concept of conservation. This can be determined by observing the four-to-seven-year-old's response to a task like one assessing the conservation of number. Two rows of candy are laid out in one-to-one correspondence, as below. One row represents "my candy" and the other "your candy."

MY CANDY ⌒ ⌒ ⌒ ⌒ ⌒

YOUR CANDY ⌒ ⌒ ⌒ ⌒ ⌒

When asked if we both have the same number of candies, intuitive children will agree that we do. This is not sufficient evidence to conclude that these children recognize number conservation, for, if one row of candy is transformed thus,

MY CANDY ⌒ ⌒ ⌒ ⌒ ⌒

YOUR CANDY ⌒   ⌒   ⌒   ⌒   ⌒

they no longer agree that we each have the same number of candies. If they say they have more candy, they may explain this by pointing out that their row of candy is longer. If they suggest that I have more candy than they, they may justify this in terms of the greater density of candies in my row.

In both cases, their attention is focused on perceived appearance, apparently disregarding their earlier assertion that the number of candies in each row was initially the same, as well as any information contained in the way the rows were transformed. Since no candies were added or removed, their number should remain the same. Objectively, number is conserved; the transformation merely introduced a superficial change with no effect on this basic property of the candies.

The children's conclusions were based on intuition and transductive reasoning. In their experience, things that are longer, wider, or denser frequently do contain greater numbers or amounts. Since one row of candy is longer, wider, or denser than the other, it therefore must contain more candy.

191

The most surprising limitations of intuitive thought are indicated by the failure of children in this conservation task to consider that the rows of candy simultaneously differed in both length and density. If they recognized these two-dimensional differences, they may have been able to coordinate their perceptions more systematically. However, attention during the Intuitive Subperiod tends to be *centered:* children focus on one prominent perceptual feature (such as the fact that one row extends beyond the other) to the exclusion of other potentially relevant features.

The mental actions necessary to encompass these two dimensions of difference are also limited. During the Intuitive Subperiod, children cannot coordinate their mental actions to note that the perceived differences in the length of the two rows of candy are *compensated* by corresponding differences in the density of each row. Only with an understanding of a relationship like compensation could they reason that the perceived differences are irrelevant and produce no changes in the number of candies in each row.

The mental actions involved in compensation are one of two means by which thought can be identified as *operational.* Operations are mental actions integrated into systems for manipulating concepts. Within these systems, some operations can always be introduced to reverse or cancel the effects of other operations, returning thought to its point of origin. Compensation therefore represents one form of *reversibility* of operations. The other form can be identified in the following example. The operation of addition in mathematics or logic is part of a system of other mathematical or logical operations that include the reverse operation of subtraction. When five is added to two to produce seven, we can also recognize that we can return to our point of origin (two) by subtracting five from seven. This reversibility of operations is accomplished by *negation* or *inversion.* One mental action is introduced to negate or invert directly another mental action.

Children during the Intuitive Subperiod of the Preoperational Period are unable to reverse mental actions by negation or inversion, just as they are unable to reverse mental actions by compensation. The title of this period of cognitive development implies this inability: they are *pre*-operational in thought. Reversibility by negation or inversion, which does not appear until the Period of Concrete Operations, could be applied to the conservation of numbers task described above. Negation would take the form of mentally representing the actions required to restore the transformed row of candy to its original position to verify that the number of candies in each row really changed.

Before progressing to a brief consideration of cognitive development during the Period of Concrete and Formal Operations, a summary of the fundamental characteristics of Intuitive Thought is in order.

1. Intuitive thought is grounded in the perceived appearance of immediate experience. Children assume their perceptions provide a more reliable representation of reality than their inferred conceptualizations of reality. In truth,

however, these perceptions distort reality and provide only fleeting and unstructured impressions of experience.

2. During the Intuitive Subperiod, children draw conclusions and attempt to solve problems on the basis of information derived from immediate experience. They thus tend to concentrate on static end-states produced by a dynamic sequence of changes or transformations, paying little heed to the nature of the changes leading to the end-state. They also fail to apply their knowledge of the initial state of experience that existed prior to any transformations.

3. The attention of children during the Intuitive Subperiod is centered on salient features of a problem, which may be irrelevant to solution of the problem. Nevertheless, they are not flexible in their deployment of attention.

4. Mental actions applied in intuitive thought are isolated, uncoordinated, and above all irreversible.

5. Intuitive thought is egocentric and not subject to reflection. This implies that children are not aware of their own thoughts as possible objects of thought and consequently cannot understand how or why they think the way they do. Nor can they justify their conclusions and interpretations of experience to themselves or to others.

The Periods of Concrete Operations (about 7-11 years) and Formal Operations (from about 11-12 Years Onward)

Because the primary focus of this book is on the early childhood years, our discussion of cognitive development beyond seven years of age will be cursory. However, the information may provide a useful context for formulating reasonable expectancies regarding the cognitive abilities and limitations of preschool children and for identifying attainable goals in developmentally-based educational programs.

Operational thought, whether concrete or formal, leads children to execute mental actions in a playful manner. With respect to each particular problem situation, they can identify in advance the group of operations needed for solution. More attuned, therefore, to task demands they adjust their thinking accordingly, and no longer are consistently fooled by the appearance of things; they can recognize that circumstances are not always as simple as they appear. Apparent discrepancies in momentary experiences can be accounted for and resolved by understanding how overt and mental actions can change experience.

Operational thought is rule-based. As children become aware of these rules, they can generalize them to new circumstances and direct their mental actions accordingly. The simplest rules define the operation of isolated mental actions. Objects and events and their more abstract dimensional properties are assigned to conceptual categories according to these rules. Higher level rules indicate how concepts can be manipulated to construct more general or more specific concepts. These manipulations produce a hierarchy of conceptual relationships that makes thought more stable and integrated. Through these rules, children are able to reason that the class of "women teachers" represents a special class of people who jointly share the defining properties of the classes of "women" and "teachers." They are thus able to identify systematically the meaning of the concept of "women teachers" by abstracting this information from their understanding of the concepts of "people," "women," and "teachers" without having to construct the concept of "women teachers" from direct experience. Recognition of the hierarchical relationships among concepts can also lead to the recognition that "teachers," whether men or women, are also "people." Thus, perhaps contrary to their intuition about teachers, they may realize that teachers have a life of their own beyond the classroom and share many of the same needs, desires, and frustrations of other "people."

As a general statement, concrete and formal operational thought are alike in that neither is limited in any of the same ways as preoperational thought. Mental actions in operational thought are reversible and their application is less constrained by the perceived appearance of immediate experience. Attention is not centered and consequently is shifted more flexibly to consider relevant information and exclude irrelevant information. Egocentrism is less pronounced in operational thought.

Concrete and formal operational thought differ in a number of ways. These differences are most noticeable in the following contrasts:

1. Concrete thought is grounded in reality, whereas formal thought deals not just with what is real but also with what is possible.

2. Reasoning about problem situations during the Period of Concrete Operations begins with empirically derived information that is coordinated inductively to produce a general conclusion. During the Period of Formal Operations, reasoning can also originate with a hypothesis proposed to account for the problematic nature of experience from which children deduce a likely solution that is then tested against reality.

3. The mental actions of concrete operational thought are limited to manipulation of relationships between concepts or objects and events in immediate experience. The mental actions of Formal Operational thought can be used to coordinate relationships between operations as well. This ability unique to the Period of Formal Operations can be described as "operations on operations."

4. The conclusions and interpretations that children derive during the Period of Concrete Operations are justified in terms of their factual relationships with

reality. They state their conclusions in terms of concrete explanatory concepts or propositions that are then verified by empirical test. The explanatory concepts or propositions proposed by children in the Period of Formal Operations are analyzed for their logical consistency with other propositions to verify their truth or untruth. The *"formal"* nature of formal operational thought thus implies that children reason about the formal (or logical) relationship that holds between propositions and not just the relationship between a proposition and its referent in reality.

Implications of Piaget's Theory for Early Childhood Education

Much information can be derived from Piaget's descriptions of children's cognitive development that is relevant to the education of all young children. Of particular significance is evidence, such as that presented in Table 6-2, that developmentally disabled children progress through the same sequence of cognitive stages as their nondisabled peers. For developmentally disabled children, this progress differs only in that cognitive development is delayed. Their cognitive accomplishments consequently are slow in coming and tend to be less stable at any point in time.

All children actively construct their knowledge and understanding of reality through the dual functions of assimilation and accommodation. Assimilative functions imply that children's interpretations of new experiences, and hence their acquisition of new knowledge, are based on what they already know. They shape their perceptions and interpretations to fit meaningfully within the framework of past experience. Didactic approaches that emphasize drill and repetition to teach children facts fail to consider this important characteristic of cognitive development. From such approaches, children may learn to recite facts without understanding.

The assimilation of new information proceeds best from a discovery approach. The teacher's role in a discovery approach is threefold. First, the teacher can create a learning environment structured so that it stimulates children's interest in exploring objects. Exploration (and play) contributes the fundamental impetus for acquiring representational competence and the classification skills necessary for a conceptual understanding of the relationships between objects and events (and later operational intelligence). When creating learning environments, it is equally important to provide experiences that are surprising or moderately challenging to promote children's accommodation of their cognitive schemes. From these experiences, they can gain a new level of understanding.

Second, in discovery learning, the teacher can also foster children's intrinsic interest in cognitive activities. This is done by encouraging active attempts to solve problems rather than emphasizing correctness of solutions or answers, and by showing an interest in their exploration of objects and in make-believe play.

Table 6-2 Some Representative Comparisons of Performance on Piagetian Tasks by Normal and Exceptional Children

Author(s)	Exceptionality	Results
Brekke, Johnson & Williams, 1975	Physical Disability	Motorically-handicapped children reached conservation at a later age than did normals
Chabat, 1977	Learning Disability	Learning-disabled children differed significantly from normals on concrete operations' tasks which involved ordering symmetrical and asymmetrical relations, recognizing similarities and differences, and reorganizing and relating newly-acquired information
Delany & Fitzpatrick, 1976	Emotional Disorder	Severely disturbed 8-to-13-year olds passed through Piagetian stages more slowly than age or IQ would predict
Fraiberg, Smith & Adelson, 1969	Sensory Disability	Blind infants were incapable of coordinating actions of sound and grasping until about 10-11 months of age—a 6-month delay
Hatwell, 1966; Gromer, 1973	Sensory Disability	The blind showed the same cognitive-developmental sequencing as normals but at a slower rate; congenitally-blind subjects showed greater retardation of reasoning than did sighted
Inhelder, 1968	Mental Retardation	The mentally retarded passed through the same reasoning stages as normals, only progressively more slowly and progression through stages was arrested earlier
Miller, 1969; Tobin, 1972	Sensory Disability	Degree of visual impairment is related to performance on conservation tasks

Author(s)	Exceptionality	Results
Stephens, 1972	Mental Retardation	The mentally retarded did not show the ability to achieve flexibility of thought (classification, grouping, reversibility abilities) as easily or as thoroughly as did normals
Stephens, 1977	Sensory Disability	Blind children and adolescents, of average intelligence, did not achieve concrete operational thought as easily or as thoroughly as would seem likely on the basis of IQ test performance; particular problems were evidenced on spatial and imagery tasks
Swallow & Poulson, 1973	Sensory Disability	Low-vision and partially-sighted adolescents were unable to use spatial reasoning abilities to solve a coordination of perspectives task

Teachers' questions and comments should encourage children to justify their conclusions and stimulate them to see things in new ways.

Third, the teacher must also act as an observer in discovery, learning to gain understanding of each child's cognitive perspective and the developmental significance of a child's activities. Observation is particularly important in teaching young developmentally-disabled children, since their chronological age provides little information for anticipating what experiences are appropriate to their level of cognitive development.

Many excellent teacher guides are available in applying Piagetian theory. Foremost are the following references: Carew, Chan, & Halfar (1976), Forman & Kuschner (1977), Kamii (1972), Lavatelli (1973), and White and Watts (1973).

Teachers must not overlook accommodative aspects of intelligence. Children's attempts to shape cognitive schemes (their ways of knowing and understanding experience) to conform more precisely with reality often depend on direct teaching. Words as labels of objects and events, as well as rules of social conduct, are typically arbitrary and conventional. Children cannot discover these in the course of self-directed interactions with the environment. Of course, learning words and rules is facilitated by providing parallel experiences that teach children the concepts and meanings underlying these arbitrary experiences.

REFERENCES AND SUGGESTED READINGS

Bernstein, A. C. & Cowan, P. A. Children's concepts of how people get babies. *Child Development,* 1975, *46*, 77-91.

Brainerd, C. J. *Piaget's theory of intelligence.* Englewood Cliffs: Prentice-Hall, 1978.

Brekke, B., Johnson, C. L., & Williams, J. Conservation of weight with the motorically handicapped. *Journal of Special Education,* 1975, *9*, 389-393.

Carew, J. V., Chan, I., & Halfar, C. *Observing intelligence in young children.* Englewood Cliffs: Prentice-Hall, 1976.

Chabot, F. B. A comparison between learning disabled and normal second- and third-grade boys on four Piagetian tasks: Seriation, transitivity, equivalence, and conservation of number. In J. F. Magary, M. K. Poulson, P. J. Levinson, & P. A. Taylor (Eds.), *Piagetian theory for the helping professions.* Los Angeles: University of Southern California Press, 1977.

Cowan, P. A. *Piaget: with feeling.* New York: Holt, Rinehart, and Winston, 1978.

Cromer, R. Conservation by the congenitally blind. *British Journal of Psychology,* 1973, *64*, 241-250.

Delaney, F. I., & FitzPatrick, M. M. The use of conservation tasks with seriously disturbed children. In G. I. Lubin, J. F. Magary, & M. K. Poulson, (Eds.), *Piagetian theory and the helping professions.* Los Angeles: University of Southern California Press, 1975.

Flavell, J. H. *Cognitive development.* Englewood Cliffs: Prentice-Hall, 1977.

_____. *The developmental psychology of Jean Piaget.* New York: D. Van Nostrand, 1963.

Forman, G. E., & Kuschner, D. S. *The child's construction of knowledge: Piaget for teaching children.* Monterey, Calif.: Brooks/Cole, 1977.

Fraiberg, S., Smith, M., & Adelson, E. An educational program for blind infants. *Journal of Special Education,* 1969, *3*, 121-140.

Harter, S. Effectance motivation reconsidered: Toward a developmental model. *Human Development,* 1978, *21*, 34-64.

Hatwell, Y. *Privation sensorielle et intelligence.* Paris: Presses Universitaires de France, 1966.

Hinde, R. A., & Stevenson-Hinde, J. (Eds.), *Constraints on learning: Limitations and predispositions.* London: Academic Press, 1973.

Inhelder, B. *The diagnosis of reasoning in the mentally retarded* (W. B. Stevens, transl.). New York: John Day, 1968.

Inhelder, B., & Piaget, J. *The early growth of logic in the child.* New York: Norton, 1964.

Johnson, D. M. *A systematic introduction to the psychology of thinking.* New York: Harper and Row, 1972.

Kamii, C. An application of Piaget's theory to the conceptualization of a preschool curriculum. In R. F. Parker (Ed.), *The preschool in action: Exploring early childhood programs.* Boston: Allyn and Bacon, 1972.

Laurendeau, M., & Pinard, A. *Causal thinking in the child.* New York: International Universities Press, 1962.

Lavatelli, C. S. *Piaget's theory applied to an early childhood curriculum.* Boston: Center for Media Development, 1973.

Magary, J. F., Poulson, M. K., Levinson, P. J., & Taylor, P. A. (Eds.), *Piagetian theory for the helping professions.* Los Angeles: University of Southern California Press, 1977.

Mercer, C. D., & Snell, M. E. *Learning theory research in mental retardation: Implications for teaching.* Columbus, Ohio: Charles E. Merrill, 1977.

Miller, C. K. Conservation in blind children. *Education of the visually handicapped,* 1969, *12*, 101-105.

Neisser, U. *Cognitive psychology.* New York: Appleton-Century-Crofts, 1967.

Piaget, J. *The child's conception of the world.* Totowa, N.J.: Littlefield, Adams, 1960

_____. *The construction of reality in the child.* New York: Basic Books, 1954.

_____. *The origins of intelligence in children.* New York: Norton, 1952.

_____. *Play, dreams, and imitation in childhood.* New York: Norton, 1951.

Premack, D. D. Reinforcement theory. In D. Levine (Ed.), *Nebraska Symposium on Motivation.* Lincoln: University of Nebraska Press, 1965.

Reese, H. W. *Basic learning processes in children.* New York: Holt, Rinehart and Winston, 1976.

Seligman, M. E. P. On the generality of the laws of learning. *Psychological Review,* 1970, *77,* 406-418.

Singer, D. G., & Revenson, T. A. *A Piaget primer: How a child thinks.* New York: Plume, 1978.

Skinner, B. F. *Science and human behavior.* New York: Macmillan, 1953.

Stephens, B. *The development of reasoning, moral judgment, and moral conduct in retardates and normals, Phase II.* (Final report project 15-P-55121/3-OZ). Philadelphia Social Rehabilitation Services, Temple University, 1972.

_____. Piagetian theory—applications for the mentally retarded and the visually handicapped. In J. F. Magary, M. K. Poulson, P. J. Levinson, & P. A. Taylor, (Eds.), *Piagetian theory for the helping professions.* Los Angeles: University of Southern California Press, 1977.

Stevenson, H. W. *Children's learning.* New York: Appleton-Century-Crofts, 1972.

Tobin, M. S. Conservation of substance in the blind and partially sighted. *British Journal of Educational Psychology,* 1972, *42,* 192-197.

Wabash Center for the Mentally Retarded, *Guide to early developmental training.* Boston: Allyn and Bacon, 1977.

White, B. L., & Watts, J. C. *Experience and environment: Major influences on the development of the young child.* Englewood Cliffs: Prentice-Hall, 1973.

White, R. Motivation reconsidered: The concept of competence. *Psychological Review,* 1959, *66,* 297-333.

Chapter 7

Cognitive Processes and Intelligence

Thomas L. Kodera and S. Gray Garwood

COMPONENTS OF COGNITIVE ACTIVITY

As adults, we have reached a cognitive level that permits us to recognize that our experiences are, generally, patterned and meaningful. We have discovered that certain events are repeatable and often under our control. We recognize a complex set of rules that describe the conditions under which these events occur and the likely consequences of their occurrence. We note features of our experiences that are relevant to a given purpose and can ignore those that are irrelevant.

In the previous chapter, we discussed two theoretical interpretations of the acquisition of such cognitive competencies: the learning perspective and the cognitive-developmental perspective of Jean Piaget. This chapter deals more intensively with the specific cognitive processes involved in human information processing. Particular emphasis will be given to those processes that: (1) enable us to attend to sensory stimulation and to transform this stimulation into particular mental symbols associated with cognition; (2) store this information in memory; (3) alter, combine and recombine, synthesize, integrate and otherwise manipulate this information in tandem with other pieces of stored information; and (4) ultimately act on this experience in some way (to "think," express an "idea," show a preference, move a part of our body, etc.).

Figure 7-1 provides a basic outline for this discussion. Bear in mind throughout that the cognitive activities described in this figure represent the most effective application of cognitive competencies. While we might expect such effectiveness of mature adults, children, because of cognitive-developmental limitations, rarely exhibit mature competence in these areas.

Figure 7-1 A Scheme For Making Sense of Experience

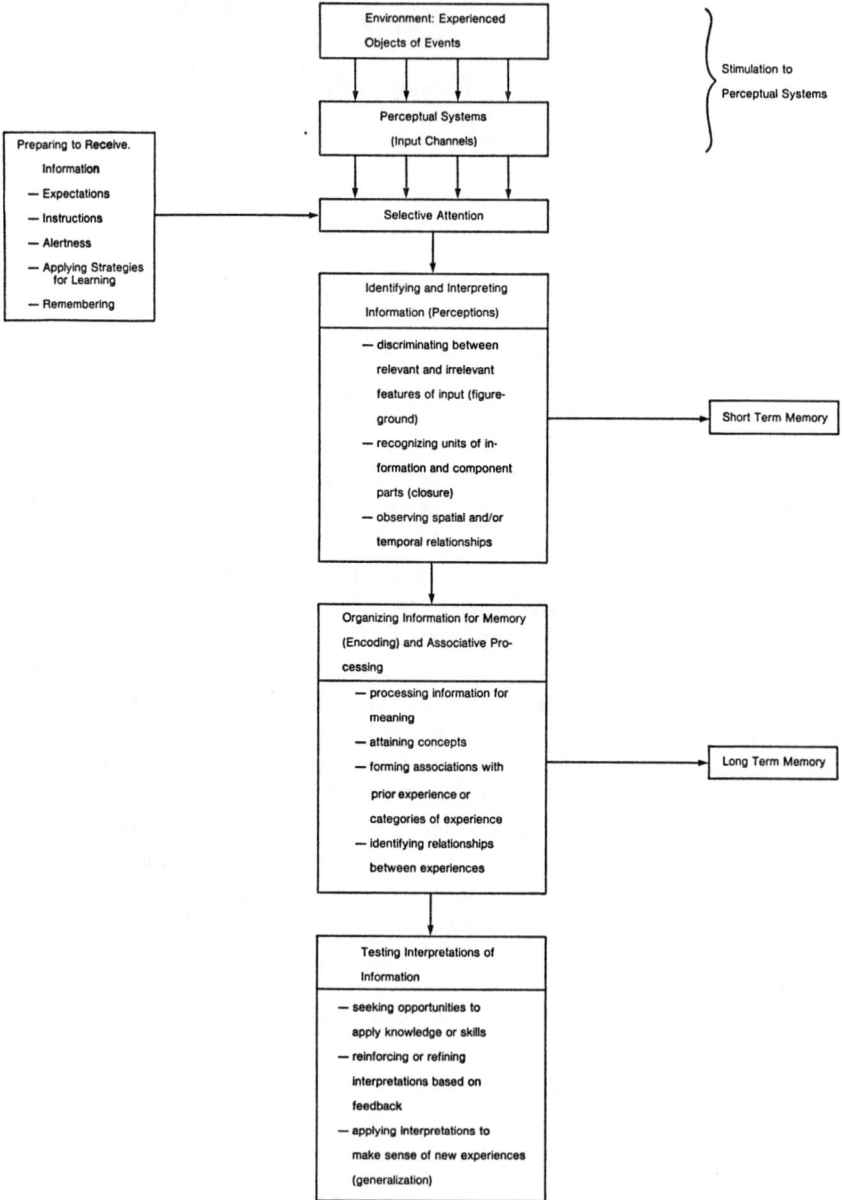

```
                                    ┌─────────────────────────┐
                                    │ Environment: Experienced│        ⎫
                                    │ Objects of Events       │        ⎬  Stimulation to
                                    └─────────────────────────┘        ⎭  Perceptual Systems
                                         │ │ │ │ │ │
                                    ┌─────────────────────────┐
                                    │ Perceptual Systems      │
                                    │ (Input Channels)        │
                                    └─────────────────────────┘
                                         │ │ │ │ │ │
┌─────────────────────────┐         ┌─────────────────────────┐
│ Preparing to Receive.    │         │ Selective Attention     │
│   Information            │ ──────► └─────────────────────────┘
│  — Expectations          │                   │
│  — Instructions          │         ┌─────────────────────────┐
│  — Alertness             │         │ Identifying and         │
│  — Applying Strategies   │         │ Interpreting            │
│     for Learning         │         │ Information (Perceptions)│
│  — Remembering           │         │                         │
└─────────────────────────┘         │  — discriminating between│
                                     │    relevant and irrelevant│
                                     │    features of input     │
                                     │    (figure-ground)       │         ┌──────────────────┐
                                     │  — recognizing units of  │ ───────► │ Short Term Memory│
                                     │    information and       │         └──────────────────┘
                                     │    component parts       │
                                     │    (closure)             │
                                     │  — observing spatial     │
                                     │    and/or temporal       │
                                     │    relationships         │
                                     └─────────────────────────┘
                                                   │
                                     ┌─────────────────────────┐
                                     │ Organizing Information   │
                                     │ for Memory (Encoding)    │
                                     │ and Associative          │
                                     │ Processing               │
                                     │  — processing information│
                                     │    for meaning           │
                                     │  — attaining concepts    │         ┌──────────────────┐
                                     │  — forming associations  │ ───────► │ Long Term Memory │
                                     │    with prior experience │         └──────────────────┘
                                     │    or categories of      │
                                     │    experience            │
                                     │  — identifying           │
                                     │    relationships between │
                                     │    experiences           │
                                     └─────────────────────────┘
                                                   │
                                     ┌─────────────────────────┐
                                     │ Testing Interpretations  │
                                     │ of Information           │
                                     │  — seeking opportunities │
                                     │    to apply knowledge    │
                                     │    or skills             │
                                     │  — reinforcing or        │
                                     │    refining              │
                                     │    interpretations based │
                                     │    on feedback           │
                                     │  — applying              │
                                     │    interpretations to    │
                                     │    make sense of new     │
                                     │    experiences           │
                                     │    (generalization)      │
                                     └─────────────────────────┘
```

EXPERIENCING THE ENVIRONMENT: The Perceptual-Input Systems

The information used in cognition is derived from our experience of the environment, but is not a direct copy of that experience. To illustrate this point, consider this illustration:

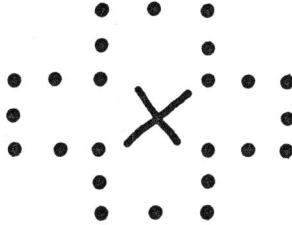

What you are probably seeing is a hollow cross composed of dots with an "X" in the center, with the figure superimposed on a white background. The organization and even the labels we apply to this visual experience are cognitive interpretations of the patterns of visual stimulation received by the eyes.

Our most direct contact with the outside world is through the perceptual systems. We see, hear, feel (or touch), taste, or smell as a result of some form of stimulation from the external environment. We also gain much information from the kinesthetic and vestibular perceptual systems which provide vital feedback about our body movements and our own actions. Thus, we may refer to each of these perceptual systems as an *input channel* for information, through which are relayed the raw materials for identifying and interpreting units of information.

Our perceptual systems translate stimulation from the environment into a code compatible with the brain's functioning. All environmental stimulation affects the brain by producing electrochemical messages transmitted by a series of neural pathways to regions of the brain where cognitive activities are performed (see Chapter 2). Science is as yet unable to describe the entire sequence of brain operations for "reading" such coded stimulation and performing cognitive activities, but, for our immediate purposes, here are some important points to consider:

1. Stimulation of all perceptual systems is basically coded the same way—as increases or decreases in the activity of nerves.
2. Stimulation received by each perceptual system is relayed to the brain along separate nerve pathways. For example, stimulation of the eyes (visual perceptual system) is kept distinct from stimulation of any other perceptual system, at

least until it reaches the brain, allowing the brain to identify the source of stimulation.

3. For each perceptual system, separate regions of the brain are specialized to interpret and coordinate or integrate the stimulation received.

Most of the information gained from experience is derived from vision, hearing, touch, and kinesthesis, but rarely do we benefit from information gained just from any one perceptual system in isolation. Cognitive tasks frequently require coordination or integration of information from two or more perceptual systems. To illustrate, consider what is involved in learning to read a word. Suppose the word is the name of a common object. We must coordinate the appearance of the object (visual perceptual system) with the appearance of the object's name spelled out (visual perceptual system). To demonstrate our ability to read a word correctly, we must also integrate the sound of the word spoken to us (auditory perceptual system) with the appearance of the word (visual perceptual system). If asked to write this same word, we must integrate the sound of the word (auditory perceptual system) with the appearance of the word (visual perceptual system) to coordinate the movements necessary for spelling out the word (kinesthetic perceptual system).

Units of Information

Ultimately, the patterns of stimulation received by our perceptual systems are organized into units of information that can be cognitively processed. One useful system for classifying these units of information was proposed by Guilford (1967), and is based on the environmental contexts from which units of information are derived: figural, symbolic, semantic, or behavioral. These are outlined below:

1. *Figural information* most directly represents the input to the perceptual systems, emphasizing the superficial physical characteristics of experience; i.e., the way things appear, sound, feel, taste, smell, etc. We use figural information, for example, whenever we try to distinguish between letters, numbers, and words (spoken or written) or to identify the shapes, sizes, colors, or other properties of objects and pictures.

2. *Symbolic information* operates in situations requiring the interpretation of the conventional (or socially agreed upon) significance of letters, numbers, mathematical signs, line drawings, gestures, etc. Central to symbolic information is the recognition that symbols are meaningful yet arbitrary means for representing important aspects of experience. The key to symbolic information does not necessarily reside in understanding the meaning associated with a symbol (this would be semantic information), but rather in

realizing that letters, numbers, etc., have meanings totally independent of the figural properties of the information.

3. *Semantic information* is produced whenever we attempt to interpret the meanings associated with figural or symbolic information. To define a word or concept like "animal," for example, we must recognize the characteristics shared in common by such diverse animals as dogs, chickens, whales, and skunks that distinguish them from such nonanimals as roses, pumpkins, bicycles, and rocks. These common characteristics constitute the meaning of the word or concept, and consequently form units of semantic information.

4. *Behavioral information* is derived from experiences where behaviors and their consequences are interpreted. Behavior is complex and dynamic, but within the behavioral changes that occur in social interactions there is some underlying consistency. We note and make use of behavioral information to comprehend what is happening to us and to others.

COGNITIVE PROCESSES FOR MAKING SENSE OF EXPERIENCE

Many cognitive processes are engaged in constructing the units of information that represent our experiences and manipulating these units to establish a sense of organization. As Figure 7-1 indicates, these processes include (in order of operation):

- attending to selected features of the stimulation channeled via the perceptual input systems *(attention)*
- identifying and interpreting information *(perception)*
- organizing information for *memory*
- testing and refining interpretations of information *(hypothesis testing and evaluation)*

Attention

Attentional processes serve many control functions necessary for effective execution of subsequent cognitive activities. These functions fall into two categories encompassing (1) *attention-sustaining functions,* which generally orient and direct cognitive activities to a given task and (2) *selective functions,* which focus on relevant input relayed by the perceptual systems and disregard irrelevant input.

Sustained Attention

Attention-sustaining activities establish optimal conditions for cognitive processing. Foremost of these conditions is a period of time free from interfering distractions that can be devoted to task-related activities. Imagine, for example, that you are shown a photograph of a complex machine. With a single brief glance at the photograph you would not likely derive sufficient information to identify the machine, its significant components, or its function. Repeated exposure may be needed. Further time is required to apply other cognitive processes for detecting relationships between the component parts of the machine, comparing the machine with others designed for similar purposes, or evaluating its novelty and utility.

Viewed in this way, attention-sustaining activities are defined in terms of the *time* an individual devotes to task-related cognitive processing. With no distractions, the duration of sustained attention, called *attention span,* gives a rough index of task complexity and the intensity of cognitive-processing activities devoted to a task. A frequent assumption has been that the more time someone spends "on-task," the more relevant information is acquired. If this task requires some immediate response, sustained attention is presumed to produce more correct answers.

We must, however, be very cautious about interpreting the significance of any individual's apparent sustained attention to a task. Individuals apparently show individual differences (labeled *cognitive styles*) in the ways they approach new experiences and problem-situations. Some people may be *reflective* in their approach, devoting longer periods of attention to a task before responding than do others who are *impulsive* in their approach, responding rapidly to task demands. There is some evidence that a reflective cognitive style typically produces greater problem-solving accuracy than does an impulsive cognitive style. However, reflectivity does not inevitably lead to greater response accuracy; many "impulsive" individuals are quick and accurate, while many "reflective" individuals are slow, methodical, and inaccurate. What appears to be important for accuracy is the match between cognitive style and cognitive abilities. In addition, individuals must adapt flexibly to the complexities of a task. Simple problems may be effectively solved impulsively, while complex tasks may compel us to respond more reflectively. For a complete discussion of cognitive styles in early childhood, see Kogan (1976).

Other individual differences exist in sensitivity to distractions that interfere with sustained "on-task" attention. These have been labeled persistence and distractability. *Persistence* is characterized by sustained attention to a task in the face of attempts by people or other events to shift attention elsewhere. In the extreme, persistent individuals continue to direct their attentions to a task even when it is inappropriate to do so. *Distractability* describes the individual's relative inability to remain "on-task" or to focus on task-related activities and ignore distraction. When judging distractability, it is important to distinguish between attention to competing experiences that distract a child from a task and attention to external, but task-relevant, features of experience. Useful, task-relevant information can be obtained from sources other than the primary task, giving the inappropriate impression of distractability.

Some properties of our experience promote sustained attention to tasks. For example, events and experiences that are moderately novel, complex, challenging, and/or surprising are attended to for longer durations than are familiar, simple, unchallenging, and/or completely predictable events or experiences. In addition to the likelihood that relatively novel, complex, challenging, and/or surprising events require greater cognitive effort before they can be understood, many researchers attribute this attentional preference to a human need for an optimal level of stimulation or arousal (Berlyne, 1967).

Selective Attention

Our perceptual systems are constantly bombarded by environmental stimulation, yet our capacity for processing this information at any one time is quite limited. Consequently, attention is focused selectively on those input channels most likely to yield task-relevant information. One aspect of selective attention is orienting or directing the appropriate perceptual systems to the source of stimulation. Thus, we look in order to see, listen in order to hear, touch in order to feel, etc. Appropriate regions of the brain are also activated to receive and process the specific input relayed by the perceptual systems.

How is this selectivity in attention accomplished? Some insight is provided by researchers investigating the orienting reaction and the process of habituation. The *orienting reaction,* which might be described as a general "What is it?" reaction (Sokolov, 1963), occurs whenever changes are detected in the environment. Components of the orienting reaction evoked by such environmental changes include momentary interruptions of ongoing activities, heightened arousal of the brain, and a localization of the source by, for example, turning the head or body toward the stimulus and concentrating on what was seen or heard, etc. The orienting reaction establishes the optimal conditions for intensive concentration on the source of stimulation. Prolonged or repeated exposure to the same stimuli, particularly if they provide no new information, leads to *habituation,* which is the gradual decrease in the intensity of the orienting reaction. Habituation is often described as the simplest form of learning, specifically involving learning *not* to respond to a meaningless or uninformative stimulus. The ability to "tune out" or ignore uninformative stimulation in this way promotes selective attention to meaningful or potentially meaningful information.

What is occurring during orienting that its end product should be habituation of responding to the stimulus? Some form of model or scheme (organized mental representation of the stimulus) is presumed to be under construction during orienting (McCall & Kagan, 1967; Sokolov, 1963). Since the mental model is usually incomplete following initial exposures to this stimulus, repeated or prolonged exposure to the stimulus evokes additional (or prolonged) orienting to provide further details to complete the mental model. Once completed, little attention needs to be devoted to the stimulus as it is adequately represented by the mental model. Habituation of the orienting response is the observable consequence of completion of the model-building process.

Habituation also contributes to another extremely significant ability: the flexible and rapid shifting of attention to other features of the environment, permitting detection of complex relationships that might otherwise be ignored.

Selectivity in attention is observed also in the use of *attentional strategies* for organizing input information. Based on prior experience, these represent consistent patterns of focusing the perceptual systems on environmental stimuli to extract information systematically.

One attentional strategy, used primarily with visual information, is *scanning,* a strategy observed whenever an individual reads a word, sentence, paragraph, or table of numbers. To extract meaningful information the individual must consistently move the eyes (scan) from left to right (in Western cultures) along the same horizontal line and then return to the extreme left, shift to the next horizontal line, and continue thus until the end. Scanning strategies are therefore *systematically inclusive* of all information, since, guided by conventional patterns of organization, they incorporate all meaningful features of the information in succession.

Similar scanning strategies are applied when attending to objects or pictures. Rather than darting around haphazardly, the eyes follow some consistent pattern of movement, as along the boundaries of figures.

Another attentional strategy, *searching,* is *systematically selective,* and is essentially "looking for" specific information. The direction for searching operations is provided by prior experience: stimuli are sought that match a mental model previously constructed or that fit a particular concept or rule.

Preparing to Receive and Process Information

Sustained and selective attention are necessary antecedents of cognitive processing. If not attended, information cannot be identified, interpreted, processed for meaning, remembered, or applied. What is attended was partially accounted for in the preceding section. Yet, there are other factors that affect attention by preparing the individual to receive, select, and process information. Their impact is twofold, affecting: (1) motivation to engage in cognitive activities, and (2) identification of the specific cognitive activities necessary for a given purpose. These factors include specific instructions or questions an individual receives regarding a task, expectancies specific to a task (which loosely might be thought of as self-generated instructions and preconceived notions about the task), generalized expectancies derived from prior experiences, and planfulness.

Instructions or questions, when appropriately understood, channel attention explicitly towards task-relevant information. They specify the conditions the information must satisfy to be considered "correct," which in turn guides the attentional search process. Instructions or questions further identify the units of information, the form of cognitive processing, and the nature of the response required by a task.

Specific expectancies are based on information gained from experience with similar cognitive tasks. We can remember how we approached similar tasks previously and whether the approach led to success or failure and if we were rewarded or punished. What we learned from our previous approaches (successful and unsuccessful) may be adapted to the present task by translating our memory of what we did previously to a set of self-initiated instructions that serve the same functions as externally presented instructions. In addition, the motivation to attempt the task is influenced by perceptions of our likelihood of succeeding and our interpretations of the value, challenge, and general interest level associated with the task. We tend to try harder if the task appears important, moderately difficult, and interesting as long as we can anticipate a modicum of success.

Generalized expectancies operate principally when we encounter novel situations. By definition, these novel situations have little precedent in our experience and consequently no specific expectancies are applicable. Nevertheless, prior experience affects the way we approach these experiences. Our curiosity and interest in exploring and understanding these experiences derive in part from a generalized expectancy for competence or effectance (Harter, 1978). Children learn very early that their actions cause many interesting things to happen; they are productive in most of their interactions (and can competently cope) with the outside environment. They may succeed or fail at specific tasks, but in general they learn that success is attainable, that most questions have answers, and most problems have solutions. Answers and solutions are discoverable, as long as cognitive competencies are actively applied. Girded by this generalized expectancy, children can better handle failure. Indeed, failure frequently challenges them to try harder, as they strive for success.

There are those who experience a disproportionate amount of failure in adapting to environmental demands. Not surprisingly, they exhibit low generalized expectancies of competence or effectance. In fact, they tend to show little motivation to attempt challenging tasks, exhibit an orientation to avoid failure rather than achieve success, rely little on their own capabilities, and look to external sources for answers or solutions. This condition has been labelled *outerdirectedness*.

Planfulness is a sophisticated form of preparing to receive and process information that is not well-developed in young children. Planfulness represents self-conscious planning and executing of cognitive processes in a manner that appropriately meets task demands. The key to planfulness is recognizing the potential and the limitations of the cognitive tools available to produce a desired end-product. If a task called for memorizing a list of terms, planfulness would require the recognition that memorizing a list of terms calls for special strategies for remembering, which then must be identified and spontaneously applied to the list of terms. This awareness would then be used to guide attention systematically through the list of terms and direct the sequence of cognitive operations performed on the terms as they are successively encountered.

Perception: Identifying and Organizing Figural Information

Perception is a term applied to the cognitive processes used primarily for constructing figural information. We saw previously how the nature of the perceptual-input systems and the attentional processes reduce some of the complexities of our experience. The messages relayed by the perceptual-input systems are structured somewhat by the pattern and order of stimulation received. But the input must be organized and translated into meaningful units of information. This is accomplished by perceptual processes that further reduce the complexities of the environment.

The product of perception, figural information, could be loosely described as a mental representation of the stimulus input. To construct units of figural information, we must make inferences about what we see, hear, feel, etc. Thus, perception has been described by Bruner (1957) as "going beyond the information given." To illustrate, input information selectively attended is like a partial set of puzzle pieces from which we must guess (infer) how the puzzle would look with all pieces present and properly arranged. We begin by assuming that what we sense is organized or structured and then attempt to impose a subjective organization upon the input information that adequately represents the world around us.

The perceptual inferences we make typically are guided by at least two organizing principles (Koffka, 1935). One is the *environmental probability principle,* which states that what we perceive is a mental representation of what *probably* exists in the environment. What is probable depends in turn upon what we have previously learned. Our inferences therefore about how the puzzle pieces fit together in the example above are based on the likelihood of occurrence of such an object or an event. In addition, we tend to make the simplest inferences about what we are seeing, hearing, feeling, smelling, or tasting. Input information, organized economically, includes as many details as possible. Thus, perceptual influences are also guided by a second organizing principle, the *parsimony principle.*

All of the raw materials for our perceptual inferences are contained in the pattern of stimulation relayed by the perceptual-input system. Therefore, if we fail to attend selectively to important aspects of our surroundings, our inferences may be faulty. To adapt effectively to our environments, our perceptual inferences must match what we are truly experiencing. Much of perceptual development therefore becomes a matter of seeking out relevant and ignoring irrelevant information. The following sections detail the kinds of information we seek for making appropriate perceptual inferences and how this information is organized in our mental representations of the world around us. Since most of the research on perceptual-inference processes is focused on visual information, the material to follow will necessarily underemphasize the nonvisual perceptual-input systems and processing of nonvisual information.

Figural Isolation and Figure-Ground Perception

As early as the first few months of life, infant attention is attracted to many environmental aspects that become extremely important for later perceptual inference-making. Infants appear to focus consistently on the contours of objects, looking at borders, straight lines, dots, or edges and corners, and seem to disregard areas of homogeneous color. Their attention is directed toward those areas of their environment that show great contrast between darkness and light and which provide most information about what exists around them.

This selectivity in infant visual attention suggests a rudimentary ability to isolate simple figures: they can distinguish a discrete pattern of stimulation that we might label a line or a dot from the relatively unpatterned stimulation that forms the figure's background. This has been termed *figure-ground perception.* There is an analogous process in hearing called *signal-noise perception,* in which certain patterns of sound (signals) are isolated from other more random, unpatterned sounds (noise). Thus, figures or signals are more prominent, standing out from their backgrounds of relatively unpatterned and uniform stimulation.

To illustrate figural isolation, consider the classic figure-ground illusion presented in Figure 7-2. Two wavy black lines, extending across a white field, seem to mark the contours of two possible images: two faces staring at each other or a vase. This determination is made by the individual by alternating central focus from white to the dark areas. Illusions such as this are rare in the real world, but they do suggest that the way in which figures are isolated influences the organization of figural information. Because isolated figures are complete units of information and stand out from background stimulation, they are easier to remember and to recognize when they reappear. Isolated figures repeated frequently in our experience also tend to be identified, labeled, and given meaning.

Form Perception and Figural Organization

Simple features like lines or dots or corners can be detected in most objects. With experience, patterns can be recognized that are interpreted as organized forms or more complex figures. Form perception and figural organization are perceptual inferences derived from the relationships of these simple features.

Figure 7-2 Figure-Ground Perception

Some of the relationships (proximity, closedness, similarity, orientation, continuity, and "common fate") that lead us to perceive specific figures or forms were described many years ago by Gestalt psychologists (Koffka, 1946; Wertheimer, 1945). Figure 7-3 illustrates several of these relationships.

Proximity refers to the nearness in spacing or timing of simple features. The simplest and most probable interpretation of this information is that it belongs together as a unit. Thus, in Figure 7-3, we might report seeing vertical pairs of horizontal lines since the lines are near each other (a). However, this interpretation of the same information changes dramatically if we add horizontal lines connecting some of the vertical lines (b). Our perception would now be of a row of boxes, a series of forms. The two unconnected vertical lines would probably be interpreted as sides of two more boxes only partially visible. Figures are readily perceived whenever open areas are completely surrounded by borders *(closedness),* and we perceive figures even more strongly when the area of the enclosed region is small. When gaps occur in the borders we tend to fill in the gaps to complete the figure—a process termed *closure.* Despite this tendency to provide closure, the information provided is often ambiguous. We may be wrong in our perception of what we are seeing.

Input information is often redundant, and much of it can be recognized as similar. Figure 7-3 (b) shows a set of similarly appearing forms; the tendency is to perceive these similar parts (or figures) as belonging together, especially if their arrangement is such that they form a higher-order pattern. The incoherent organization of Figure 7-3 (e) presents a randomly-arranged set of black and white dots (lines), despite our tendency to look for patterns. Contrast this with Figure 7-3 (d).

Figure 7-3 Gestalt Laws of Organization

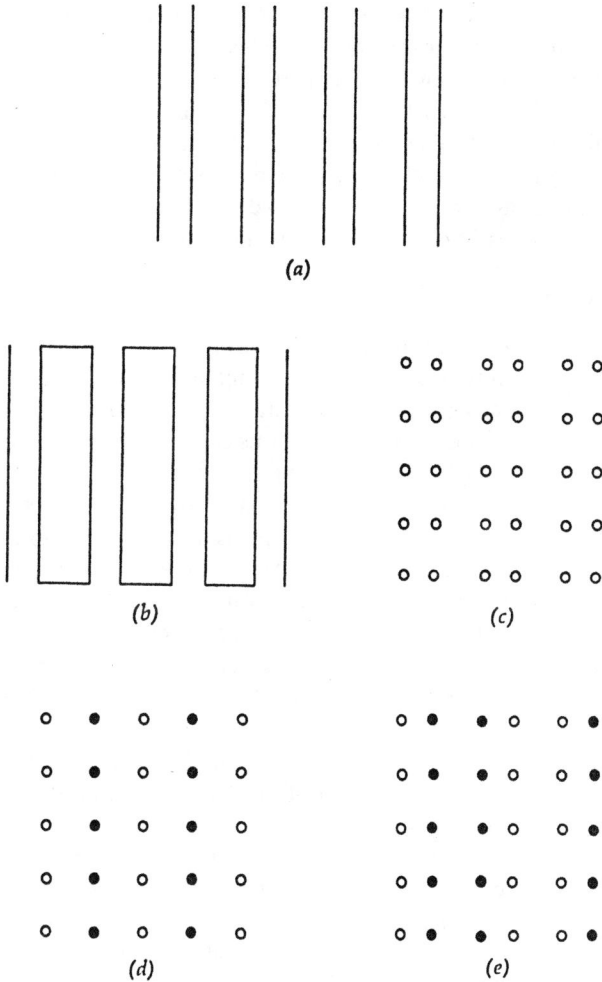

(a)

(b)

(c)

(d)

(e)

(a) Proximity: There appear to be four pairs of two lines, not eight separate lines. (b) Closure: The four proximity columns were destroyed by the addition of the horizontal lines. (c) Proximity: Circles become organized into three columns. (d) Similarity: We see vertical rather than horizontal lines. (e) Proximity and similarity in opposition.

Orientation contributes to the identification of higher units of figural information by arranging figures along common planes of reference. *Continuity* demonstrates the tendency to see lines or patterns as following the simplest, most unbroken course. *"Common fate"* identifies those simple features that make up an organized form through movement. Those features that move together in the same direction tend to be perceived as part of the same form, thus sharing a "common fate." At a tennis tournament, for example, the audience can be perceived or distinguished as separate from the players because the orientation of their movements differs. Even the form of stationary objects can be perceived in this manner because, as our eyes, our ears, and our bodies move, we are able to recognize those features of objects that share a common fate.

Perceptual Discrimination

Once the perception of a form has become stable, (i.e., the perceptual-input information is consistently interpreted as the same form), it is possible to make perceptual discriminations in which the characteristics of one form are distinguished from those of another form. Thus, forms can be responded to differently and can be given different labels or different meanings.

Perceptual discriminations require extraction of two invariant properties of forms: their distinctive features, and the dimensions on which forms can be related. *Distinctive features* are properties that distinguish one group of forms from all other forms. The distinctive features of a form we label a square could be described in words as four lines of equal length that join each other at right angles. Distinctive features are also illustrated in the perception and discrimination of letters. Consider the lower case letters, "b," "d," "p," and "q." These are all similar, composed of a straight vertical line and a circle. It would be easier to distinguish the letter "z," for example, from any of these other letters because it possesses none of these same features. But the distinctive features that become important in distinguishing between "b," "d," "p," and "q" are the relationships between the vertical lines and the circular shapes. The critical difference between a "b" and a "d" is the left or the right placement of the vertical line with respect to the circle. With "p" and "b," where the vertical line is to the left on both, the distinctive features are whether the vertical line extends above or below. Distinctive features can also be identified for spoken letters. Vowel sounds are uniquely different from consonant sounds, for example, because they are produced differently. Vowel sounds are made with open throat without the use of the lips or the tongue to modify the sounds. Consonants, however, use the throat, soft palate, and the lips.

Discriminations are not always based upon single distinctive features. Depending on the nature and complexity of the discrimination, it may be necessary to look at a pattern of features, which alone will be distinctive. A red square and a blue square may differ simply in color. However, to distinguish between the letters "b," "d," "p," and "q," we must notice the basic circle and vertical line features, as well as the relationship of the circle and vertical line. Forms may have many features that could prove distinctive. In general, since we seek the simplest distinctive feature in making perceptual discriminations, each perceptual discrimination may require use of different distinctive features.

Many forms are very similar. They share many features in common that might be distinctive for other perceptual discriminations, yet each form is different from the others. These common features identify these forms as the same in some dimensions and different in other dimensions. A *dimension* is a way of systematically classifying all the variations possible within a single feature of a form. Size, or color, or shape, or number of sides to a form, are all dimensions that represent similarities among most forms. Forms may differ on some dimensions, but at the same time they are the same on other dimensions. The forms below are the same in the dimensions of size and color and differ only in shape.

(a)

Unlike the forms in (a), the forms in (b) are all of the same shape and color but differ along the size dimension.

(b)
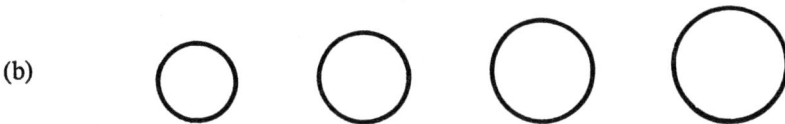

Dimensions can be of great advantage in making perceptual discriminations. If we observe the dimensions of similarity and of difference in forms, we can more efficiently search for the distinctive features. Our search can focus on those dimensions for which there is variation. Dimensions in which there is no variation between forms can provide no information about the distinctive features. Therefore they can be safely disregarded.

Many situations we encounter require us to discriminate more than the simple differences in appearance of forms. We must note some relationship that is independent of appearance. In (c) we see a small black square and a large white circle.

(c)

If this discrimination is important, we may soon learn that the large white circle is "correct." We are now presented with another pair of forms (d): the same large white circle and a larger black square.

(d)

Relying on what we learned before, we select the large white circle and find that it is incorrect. Why would our choice be incorrect now where it was correct before? Because the discrimination that was required by this task involved a relationship within the dimension of size, not a discrimination of forms. It might not take long before we learned to select the larger black circle as correct, but our correctness in subsequent trials of this same kind of problem requires us to make use of the size dimension and the size relationship demanded by this problem. Otherwise we would be forced to guess from trial to trial.

Perceptual Concepts

Perceptual concepts are additional ways in which we take into account similarities and differences between forms. These concepts classify the number of forms that share a particular pattern of distinctive features into a single group or unit. When, for example, all forms presented might be classified under the concept of "squares," there may be many differences among the particular items constituting the concept—differences that are irrelevant, however, to the basic concept. Many perceptual concepts are more specific than the concept of square. Thus, we may attain a concept of the appearance of the human face; here oval-shaped patterns, even though they share some features in common with the human face, would not be classified within this concept, since they do not share all the characteristics necessary for the concept. Still, a great variety of human faces might be included within this concept—male or female, black or white, sunburned or pale.

Perceptual concepts, which contribute significantly to making sense of our experiences, provide a framework for identifying new experiences. When observed forms are different, a new concept may emerge, particularly if the differences appear important. As a consequence, we can devote a greater share of our attention to the new perceptual information received.

Perceptual concepts may also define new dimensions for describing forms. Using the concept of the human face, we may characterize forms as appearing more or less face-like.

Because perceptual concepts are based on a limited number of distinctive features in a group of forms, they are remembered better than the discrete forms we might see. In addition, it is possible to label perceptual concepts, and this becomes important for communicating with others about our perceptual experiences. Unfortunately, there is no guarantee that the perceptual concept one person labels a square will match entirely the perceptual concept that someone else has labeled a square.

The searching strategies in attention which were mentioned earlier are possible only when an individual possesses specific perceptual concepts. With a well-established concept, we are able to visualize and anticipate the appearance of a particular form. Then we simply must scan our environments to find a similar form that matches closely our concept of how this stimulus would appear. Our figural concepts are removed from direct contact with the outside environment. Since they do not take into account all the details of the forms we see, they tend to be generalized, and some forms that should be kept distinct may be lumped together. Our perceptual concepts must be continually refined if they are to represent accurately what exists around us. By remaining actively involved with the environment, we are able to discover the information necessary to refine these concepts.

Trends in Perceptual Development

Gibson (1969) has described three major trends in the development of perceptual abilities. The first is an increased specificity in perceptual discriminations. Thus, with experience, fewer stimuli evoke the same response; children generalize less, as they become able to make finer discriminations between forms, and the variability of their responses to the same forms diminishes with development. As the interpretations of forms become more stable, so do responses become more consistent.

With age, children are able to make discriminations in less time. Thus, the second trend in perceptual development is toward increasing economy in acquiring information and greater efficiency in using distinctive features. In addition, since they make greater use of dimensions in making these distinctions, higher-order organization of forms is easier to recognize. By observing how smaller units of information can be reorganized to form more complex forms, children become increasingly able to deal with many forms simultaneously, and are thus more likely to recognize complex relationships within and between forms.

The third major trend in perceptual development relates to the use of attention for obtaining perceptual information. Attention, which was captured by contours and areas of great contrast during infancy, in older children becomes more exploratory, selective, and exclusive, and more under their control. In their search for perceptual information, attention also becomes more systematic, demonstrated by greater emphasis on attentional strategies.

A fourth trend that might be added to Gibson's is the increased tendency to form perceptual concepts, resulting from the increasing ability of children to focus selectively on relevant information and patterns of stimulation, and to ignore the irrelevant.

Finding Meaning in Experience

Figural information is identifiable, organized, and *potentially* meaningful. Even perceptual concepts, the most cognitively advanced units of figural information, are meaningless. Meaning is imparted to figural information only when it is related or associated predictably and consistently with significant environmental events. A red circular form would become meaningful, for example, if always associated with pain or with fear: it would become something to be avoided. A red circle of light in a traffic signal is meaningful because we are told that it means "stop." The meaning becomes clearer if we were to disregard the form, drive through the intersection, be stopped by an officer, and receive a fine. This might even broaden the definition and meaning of this form.

The meaning of a form or unit of figural information is also determined by its context. In the presence of the other forms detectable in a traffic signal, the bright red circle of light means something entirely different from a similar bright red circle of light emitted by the burner of an electric range.

Memory and Retention Processes

To profit from experience, new information gained must be retained in some form. Our discussion of how information is retained or remembered will focus primarily on the cognitive processes that promote the storage of information for longer or shorter periods of time. In addition, we will consider how information is retrieved from memory for use and then consider the general problem of forgetting.

Three levels of memory are traditionally distinguished: immediate, short-term, and long-term. *Immediate memory* is a relatively passive form derived from direct experience of stimulation, implying that the individual needs to engage in little more than attention for information storage. For a very brief period of time, on the order of two milliseconds, a very rich complete trace of what was seen, heard, etc. is retained. This trace is probably a product of the way the central nervous system functions. During its brief life, immediate memory provides sufficient information to direct attention more selectively to interesting or important aspects of the display contained in immediate memory. It may also permit detecting changes or constancies in experience from moment to moment. (Note that, because of immediate memory, we see the individual frames of a motion picture as representing a continuing sequence of actions rather than a series of discrete pictures.)

A more permanent residue of immediate experience can be retained in short-term memory. Features that are selectively attended are entered into short-term memory as a product of an individual's attempt to make sense of what is being perceived. The information retained in short-term memory is typically figural, representing the physical characteristics of what is experienced. Both the capacity and the duration of short-term memory are limited, however. Most adults are able to remember accurately between 5 and 9 distinct units of information about their experience for up to 18 seconds. These limitations would pose no problem if it were always possible to identify and interpret experience based on that limited information in that brief time. To operate efficiently within the limitations of short-term memory, it is often necessary to apply two active cognitive processes: chunking, and rehearsal.

Chunking is a means to expand the capacity limitations of short-term memory. The capacity of short-term memory is defined in terms of units of information. Chunking essentially refers to a redefinition of what constitutes a unit of information.

To illustrate this redefinition simplistically, look at this string of letters for a few seconds: X T P Q L M A F T O B. Now close the book and attempt to write the sequence of letters from memory 15 seconds later. How correct are you? Now repeat the same exercise with these letters: I N F O R M A T I O N. The differences in your ability to remember these two strings of letters derive from your ability to chunk the 11 letters of the second string into a single unit, the word "information." Your short-term memory was taxed by an equal number of letters in the first string. Because they could not be grouped in any larger units, you were forced to remember the letters as 11 different units of information.

The ways in which information can be chunked depend upon prior experience.

Chunking is therefore an application of prior knowledge to make retention of new information more effective. In general, chunking requires the detection of regularities, recurrent patterns, or previously learned associations of stimuli that can be organized into more complex units of information.

You may have "cheated" a bit in the exercise in short-term memory, thus illustrating the process of *rehearsal*. If, while your book was closed, you found yourself repeating the string of letters to yourself or practicing in some fashion what you saw, you were rehearsing. *Rehearsal* reduces the time limitation on the duration of short-term memory. By repeating the letters you were simultaneously reexposing yourself to your representations of what you saw and strengthening the sequential associations of one letter with those that preceded and followed it. Rehearsal may also provide the opportunity for discovering subtle consistencies within the sequence that could lead to chunking.

Children may differ from adults in short-term memory abilities in three ways. First, there are developmental changes in the capacity of short-term memory. Young children may be limited to retaining as few as three or four units of information, which, of course, would prove to be no impediment *if* their chunking abilities were well developed. There is less information about developmental differences in the temporal limits of short-term memory, but it is likely that young children have a reduced span.

Second, there may be developmental as well as individual differences in children's abilities to learn to chunk and rehearse. These competencies can be observed in preschool children, including developmentally disabled children, but children often fail to recognize when to use their capacities for chunking and rehearsing (this is a third difference between children and adults). They often lack a self-conscious understanding of what is needed to retain information effectively in short-term memory.

Short-term memory is limited in its permanence and capacity, as we have seen, and also in its content. Because it operates in the context of immediate perceptual experience, its content is figural information. To be thorough, it should also be noted that the content of immediate mental experience is also retained in short-term memory. This implies that, in the course of thinking about something, we retain some information about the concepts we considered and the mental operations we used.

To reconcile these seemingly contradictory remarks, note that we are speaking about information retained from immediate experience. Most importantly, this information is not particularly meaningful in its own right; it simply provides a temporary checklist of what occurred. As a consequence, information retained in short-term memory is superficial, significant only for the present.

Rehearsal of the contents of short-term memory, however, provides the opportunity to process for meaning beyond the superficial significance of information.

As long as information is retained in short-term memory, cognitive processes can be applied to identify associations between the units of information. Rehearsal might well be viewed from this perspective as a form of sustained attention to the contents of one's private representations of experience. This then promotes processing of information for meaning.

One characteristic of meaningful information is its apparently "permanent" retention in long-term memory. *Long-term memory* is relatively unlimited in its capacity and in its duration. This does not imply that information retained in long-term memory is always retained in the same manner and always accessible, as we shall see later. Information enters long-term memory by encoding, a process that may take various forms. Common to all encoding, however, is an associative relationship between new information to be remembered and information already contained in long-term memory. This new information thus is an addition to or refinement of existing information.

Forms of encoding include associative transfer, imagery, verbal elaboration, and mnemonic systems. *Associative transfers* involve application of verbal mediators, concepts, or principles to link new events with previously learned information, thereby giving new events extensional significance. They become meaningful in direct proportion to the number of associations that can be formed; the richer the meaning given to events, the better will be the long-term memory of this information. Both for purposes of remembering and applying information or knowledge, the more ways we "know" something, the more likely we will be to remember and use it effectively.

Encoding by associative transfer can be observed when learning and remembering long lists of words for later use. Asked to recall freely these words later, we tend to cluster those words that are similar in meaning or concept, even if the initial list was not organized in the same way.

This associative clustering provides a clue to the organization of long-term memory. Information to be retained seems to be stored according to a sophisticated filing system, indexed by its associations with other information. Retrieving information from memory is then accomplished by drawing on these associations, which is itself a mediated process. Cues to the retrieval of specific information are provided in immediate experience. Components of a task, and even instructions for performing a task, provide information previously associated with task-relevant information retained in long-term memory. Once identified, these retrieval cues lead to recall of the remembered information.

As a form of encoding, *imagery* makes use of visual representations of concrete events or concepts. Mental pictures of two or more events can be superimposed upon each other, visually mediating an association between the events. For example, if you wished to remember the words "elephant" and "umbrella" as paired associates, you could imagine a picture of an elephant holding an umbrella in its trunk. When asked to recall what word went with "elephant," the word could be used as a cue to retrieve your mental picture and with it the word "umbrella."

Imagery works best when events to be remembered are integrated within the same picture as vividly as possible. If you successively pictured an elephant and an umbrella, when hearing the words, the idea that they are related is not conveyed in your image, and retrieval of the word "umbrella" would be difficult. ,

Unless your imagination is creative enough to evoke images of abstract concepts like "love," "freedom," "justice," or "maturity," imagery successfully encodes only concrete information. Imagery has facilitated children's learning and retention of relatively abstract concepts like loud and soft or fast and slow when the concepts were represented by loud and soft (noisy and quiet) or fast and slow animals.

Verbal elaboration is a form of encoding that associates concepts with word labels by linking the words in sentence form. By using the grammatical structure of a sentence like **"The elephant carried an umbrella in its trunk,"** we may be able to recreate the sentence associated with the word "elephant" and recover the word "umbrella" contained within it. The word "elephant" serves as a retrieval cue for a limited number of sentences containing the word "elephant." The correct sentence could then be retrieved by cues identified with the context in which the sentence was created. Identifying the word "umbrella" then becomes a matter of selecting among the words contained in the sentence.

Mnemonic systems encode experience according to a well-defined and easily recalled set of retrieval cues, especially valuable when the order of information is as important to remember as its specific content. A mnemonic code locates in memory a particular unit of information; retrieving information associated with each element of the code merely requires recalling the code.

Organizing long-term memory by mnemonic codes is analogous to alphabetizing files. To locate a "correspondence received" file, we simply recall the sequential order of letters in the alphabet. Of course, if we forget this sequence, locating this file would become difficult.

If we wish to deliver a speech or lecture from memory, a mnemonic system can assist in the presentation. We begin by outlining key points in the proper order. Each point then is associated through rote memorization with an element of our mnemonic code. One useful mnemonic code is composed of major landmarks on a trip from home to office. When delivering our speech, we can then retrieve our points in succession by mentally noting each landmark on our trip. (This mnemonic system may be even more effective if we also apply imagery.)

Unfortunately, such mnemonic systems are cumbersome and useful only if the code is remembered; otherwise, retrieval cues are lost.

The Problem of Forgetting

Research suggests that information retained in long-term memory is never really forgotten. Indeed, children retain encoded information as well as adults do. This is equally true of mentally retarded persons and others who are developmentally disabled, once the information reaches long-term memory. Apparent differences in long-term memory reflect more on differences in the abilities of individuals to encode information than on memory abilities *per se*.

Yet information appears to be forgotten. Obviously, if never encoded, information could not be remembered; it would simply fall prey to the time constraints of short-term memory. The most likely cause of "forgetting' is the inaccessibility of the information. Since, as we indicated above, retrieval of information is directed by a limited set of cues that index the location of the information, a lack of retrieval cues would render the information inaccessible. The information is still retained in memory; it just cannot be retrieved.

Typically, many cues are associated with any unit of information in memory. This redundancy makes possible many routes to access the contents of long-term memory. If, however, information is encoded too specifically with very few associations, the number of possible retrieval cues is limited. Hence, it would be more probable that a specific experience that requires remembering this information would lack appropriate retrieval cues.

"Forgetting" could also be due to interference. If many units of information share the same associations and consequently the same retrieval cues, access to a specific unit of information is impeded. However, there may be an advantage to multiple associations with retrieval cues. Thus, where circumstances require some flexibility, as when attempting to solve problems, these retrieval cues identify many possible courses of action. In discrimination or concept learning, interfering associations may lead to a recoding of information and an identification of new dimensions or relationships.

Making Use of Experience

Retrieval of information from long-term memory is the most direct application of information gained from experience. Through retrieval, we demonstrate our comprehension or knowledge of the world. But, since comprehension and knowledge merely reproduce the products of our cognitive processes, we must also consider the productive applications of cognition that permit generalizing the results of prior experience to adapt effectively to new experiences.

Thinking and Problem-Solving

To understand thinking, psychologists have defined thought as those cognitive processes that are applied to the solution of problems. Problem situations arise when an individual's initial attempts to attain a goal are unsuccessful. Problems, therefore, contain obstacles to be surmounted. Reasoning is a specific form of thinking that follows the formal principles of logic to derive solutions to problems. (See discussion of Piaget in the previous chapter.)

In discussing problem-solving, Gagne (1965) states:

> problem-solving involves the combining of previously learned principles into a new higher-order principle that "solves" the problem and generalizes to an entire class of stimulus situations embodying other problems of the same type. Problem-solving occurs when the instructions provided the learner do not include a verbally stated "solution," but require him to construct such a solution "on his own." When this happens, the individually constructed higher-order principle is effective in generalizing to many situations and is at the same time highly resistant to forgetting (pp. 165-166).

Merrifield, Guilford, Christensen and Frick (1962) identified five phases in problem-solving that proceed in a relatively fixed sequence: preparation for problem-solving; analysis of the problem; production of a possible solution; verification, evaluation, or judgment of the solution; and reapplication of problem-solving activities when a solution is judged to be unsuccessful.

Preparation for problem-solving can be identified both in the immediate context of the problem and in the more remote context of prior experience. Preparation for problem-solving is reflected in sensitivity to problems when they arise and in recognition that a particular experience constitutes a problem. If we have some familiarity with the materials to be manipulated in solving the problem and with solutions to similar problems, we are further prepared for problem-solving.

Most problems are efficiently solved only when the concepts and principles represented in the problems are adequately understood. By definition, however, problems would never arise if concepts and principles were adequate to deal with this new experience. Since prior experience could prepare us for problem-solving by providing tools needed to discover solutions, we need some fluency in understanding the concepts and principles that define the problem, even if we do not possess the specific information required to solve the problem. Problem-solving is more effective if prior experience permits some flexibility in responding to the problem's unique demands. If we lack a wide range of responses that are potential solutions to the problem, solution is less likely. Limitations develop when definitions of concepts are overly generalized or overly specific. Further limitations occur when specific information can be meaningfully related to only a very few conceptual categories. Adequate general preparation for problem-solving, therefore, requires a diversity of associations and a wide range of possible options.

Analysis of a problem requires identifying the specific information contained within the problem and determining what further information is needed for solution. The information is often provided by the accompany instructions, in which the key words, by introducing associations with the meanings of the words that may mediate identification of the appropriate response, have a semantic effect. The structure of the instructions may also have a syntactic effect, identifying the sequence of required operations and the specific information needed for each step.

During this analysis phase, strategies are needed in searching for additional information not contained within the problem. These must be adapted to the complexity of the problems, the most difficult of which demand very efficient use of memory.

Problem-solving proceeds best when strategies for seeking additional information tend to emphasize representation and mental manipulation of concepts and principles rather than trial-and-error experimentation. In addition, information about principles and the relationships between concepts are more useful than specific factual information.

At the *production phase,* actual solutions are attempted, requiring integration of the new information obtained about the problem to produce an appropriate response. This assumes the individual has hypothesized some principle explaining the obstacle, and identified a response consistent with that principle.

The *verification phase* validates or invalidates the hypothesized principle according to the success or failure of the response, about which judgments are actually made before the production phase. Following production, these judgments are then verified. Imposing judgments too early in the problem-solving sequence may interfere with problem-solving. Otherwise, extremely significant options may be eliminated prematurely. Furthermore, early intuitive judgments may be based on too little information that incompletely analyzed the problem situation.

The *reapplication phase* of problem-solving occurs primarily when attempts to solve problems are judged unsuccessful, and further analyses of response production are required until success is achieved. However, following successful solutions, reapplication may also occur in an attempt to identify other possible solutions that conform to the operating principle.

Creativity may introduce a new dimension to problem-solving. To be creative presupposes an underlying competence in representing experience through concepts and relating concepts through principles. Beyond this, creativity imparts an ability to recognize remote associations between experiences or concepts. From these unusual and often unconventional associations, novel approaches to resolving problems may be identified.

Cognitive Processes and Intelligence

Cognition and intelligence may be considered synonymous in many respects, yet there are peripheral meanings (and a few controversies) associated with "intelligence" that prompt special treatment of the term. "Intelligence" is an abstract construct, much as is "cognition." When theorists attempt to make distinctions between the two, intelligence is commonly regarded as a unifying characteristic of all cognitive activity, underlying perception, thinking, knowing, remembering, etc. In this view, intelligence is a general factor and not simply a limited cluster of different cognitive competencies.

Because this definition is intimately related to the psychometric instruments—the intelligence or IQ (intelligence quotient) test—for assessing intelligence, it is important to examine some of the assumptions made about intelligence and its measurement.

Assumptions About the Nature of Intelligence and Its Assessment

Standardized intelligence tests, in practice, focus directly on abilities to perform a limited number of cognitive tasks. The particular tasks (or items) presented are selected on the basis of their relationships (correlation) with each other. Thus, if one's performance is highly related on a number of tasks—such as defining common terms, recalling strings of numbers, or putting pictures together in a logical sequence to tell a story—such tasks are included. Other tasks, although perhaps equally cognitive in nature, are not represented on these tests since they show little relationship with the other test components. Construction of intelligence tests in this way forces the conclusion that intelligence underlies cognitive activity. Before accepting this conclusion, however, it must be noted that exclusion of many cognitive tasks because they do not meet psychometric standards for test construction strongly suggests that all cognitive competencies are not related by the same general factor. The belief that intelligence is a single capacity common to all cognitive activity must therefore be labeled as an assumption, perpetuated principally by present instruments for assessing "intelligence." This assumption is not universally shared.

Additional assumptions about the nature of intelligence are equally problematic. These include views that intelligence is:

1. a finite capacity that limits an individual's intellectual potential
2. determined by genetic factors (and other biological factors that influence the functioning of the nervous system)
3. a stable characteristic that remains the same qualitatively
4. unaffected by environmental influences

Most of these assumptions would be more plausible and less controversial were it not for a critical assumption that accompanies all the rest—that intelligence tests actually measure intelligence (or intellectual potential). If intelligence tests in fact measure intelligence* then many of the assumptions about the nature of intelligence outlined previously are difficult to support. Observations of children's performance on intelligence tests provide evidence for the following statements:

1. Intelligence, as measured on IQ tests, is not a particularly stable characteristic. When assessed repeatedly during infancy and early childhood, overall IQ scores may fluctuate dramatically between test administrations. It must be noted, however, that intelligence test scores obtained for children older than about two to two-and-a-half years generally tend to predict later IQ test performances as long as their experience is not drastically altered. (McCall, Appelbaum & Hogarty, 1973).

2. Major changes in home and educational environments, especially when introduced early in life, can produce major changes in intelligence test performance (Heber & Garber, 1975). While this and similar evidence suggests that intelligence is greatly influenced by experience, intelligence must not be considered a product of experience alone. Genetic and biological factors are also influential and are translated into measured intelligence only through a complex interaction with experience.

3. There are qualitative changes in intelligence. The strongest support for this conclusion is contained in the child development research of Jean Piaget (to be discussed later). While Piaget did not consider intelligence test performance, his observations may account for the discontinuities, instability, and unpredictability of intelligence measures in infancy and early childhood.

What can we conclude about the nature of intelligence from the evidence so far presented? As indexed by intelligence test performance, intelligence fluctuates, in part because of experience and of qualitative developmental changes in ways of interpreting this experience. It may well be a limited potential determined by genetic inheritance and biological factors that influence brain functioning. Realistically, however, the limits of this potential are never fully reached.

This interpretation of the nature of intelligence is extremely popular and has some important practical implications, foremost of which are (1) emphasis on early intervention to provide optimal environments for intellectual development (which accounts in part for our concern for early childhood education), and (2) reevaluation of the explosive sociopolitical situations that result when a purely genetic basis for intelligence is asserted.

---

*Little would be gained by pursuing the consequences of an argument that intelligence tests do not measure intelligence. All of the previous assumptions about the nature of intelligence would remain untested as no other test instruments are available for their evaluation. Intelligence would remain an illusive, abstract construct that defies observation.

How is intelligence defined within the constraints of this interpretation of the nature of intelligence? Two definitions have often been cited, neither of which is incompatible with the other, differing mainly in emphasis. The most straightforward definition emphasizes intelligence as the ability to perform specific behavioral skills like perceiving, remembering, reasoning, and problem-solving (cognitive competencies). The other, with a more cognitive emphasis, describes intelligence as the ability to respond effectively to the demands of the environment. This definition basically incorporates the former, since effective responding requires the ability to apply existing cognitive competencies. The cognitive emphasis of this latter definition also more clearly incorporates the notion that qualitative changes occur in intelligence. Effective responding to environmental demands typically requires the ability to refine current cognitive competencies to develop new competencies.

If these definitions of intelligence sound reminiscent of the definition of cognition presented earlier, it is not coincidental. The activities involved in both are basically the same, with one slight distinction: a useful convention to follow would be to use cognition when referring to the interrelated competencies used to make sense of experience, solve problems, and maintain executive control over these activities. The term intelligence could then be reserved to refer to individuals' specific cognitive abilities relative to the abilities of their same-aged peers.

What Is Measured by Intelligence Tests?

Intelligence test scores have had a wide variety of applications. The composite IQ score has been treated as a convenient shorthand index for making decisions regarding educational placement and formulation of educational objectives, clinical diagnosis, and appropriation of financial resources. Frequently these decisions are based upon implicit acceptance of those same assumptions about the nature of intelligence and intelligence tests that were demonstrated previously to be unsupportable. Appropriate application of intelligence tests scores requires more intensive investigation of the content and structure of intelligence tests.

It was noted earlier that intelligence tests assess abilities to perform a limited number of cognitive activities and that these activities are related to each other in some abstract way. Our discussion of the content and structure of intelligence tests will therefore focus on two questions: (1) What are the specific cognitive abilities tested? and (2) How could the relationship between these activities be described?

The most frequently used intelligence tests for children are the Stanford-Binet Intelligence Scale (Terman & Merrill, 1960) and Wechsler Intelligence Scales for Children, revised version or WISC-R (Wechsler, 1974). For infants, a commonly used test is the Bayley Scales of Infant Development (Bayley, 1969). Each of these tests is administered individually; individually administered tests of intelligence, (it is believed) provide better assessments of a child's abilities than do group tests, because the examiner is better able to:

1. control distractions that might interfere with a child's performance;
2. take into account characteristics of the child's relationship to the examiner and the test conditions when interpreting the test results;
3. identify the approaches the child applies to dealing with the test problems in addition to the correctness or incorrectness of the answer given;
4. evaluate other characteristics of the child's behavior that might be of significance, since the standardized test conditions provide a context for comparison with other children.

Items in intelligence tests are based on the assumption that all children at a given age have had equivalent exposure, through experiences at home or in school, to the types of information sought. This does not mean that all children comprehend or interpret this information equally well, but simply that they must have been exposed to opportunities to acquire and make use of this information.

The Stanford-Binet and WISC-R heavily emphasize verbal comprehension and expression. Units of information children are required to process are also frequently verbal, although sometimes this verbal information must be coordinated with visual information (like the information obtained from pictures or objects). The content of other tasks (called performance tasks) on these two tests emphasizes nonverbal cognitive information. In general, the performance tasks require manipulating objects or pictures to demonstrate perceptual or conceptual abilities and perceptual-motor coordination.

What must children be able to do to perform well on intelligence tests? First, they must possess conventional knowledge and the ability to remember and apply knowledge. Such knowledge includes (1) general information about the words associated with pictures, objects, and behavioral events, (2) definitions of words stressing the essential characteristics of their meanings, (3) practical knowledge about appropriate responses in common social situations, (4) knowledge about symbol systems and arithmetic operations, and (5) knowledge about the way objects appear or events typically occur.

Second, children must be able to recognize similarities and essential differences among the units of information or concepts presented. Third, they must demonstrate an ability to remember new information, whether in the form of numbers, symbols, words, sentences, or prose passages. Fourth, they must show the ability to work toward a goal and solve problems.

These are primary abilities, specifically assessed on intelligence tests. It is very important to consider a number of additional prerequisite skills (even though they are not specifically isolated and evaluated on intelligence tests), since their lack clouds the interpretation of the primary abilities. Is failure to describe the similarity between an apple and an orange, for example, due to a primary deficit in recognizing similarity or could it, in fact, be due to a failure to understand the instructions or the meaning of the word "alike" or "similar" or the lack of any other prerequisite skills?

Skills prerequisite to performing well on intelligence tests include the abilities to:

- focus attention on the task
- hear and understand questions and instructions
- imitate actions of the experimenter
- make use of input information
- effectively remember and use information derived from prior experience
- express ideas in words fluently and appropriately

The Bayley scales, in many respects markedly different in content from the Stanford-Binet and WISC-R, notably deemphasize verbal skills, since language skills are rudimentary in infancy. Tasks presented to infants focus on cognitively-relevant behavioral accomplishments, while performance on any given task represents an infant's attainment of a significant developmental milestone.

The Structure of Intelligence Tests

The abilities measured on intelligence tests share four characteristics that may account for their interrelationship:

1. All are continuously represented in some meaningful form at all ages. This means that, whereas the units of information to which these abilities can be applied may change, the basic ability remains essentially unchanged throughout development. This is not true of all cognitive abilities.
2. All are measured in terms of increments in the effectiveness of using these primary abilities.
3. All items assessing the same primary cognitive ability are organized in order of increasing difficulty.
4. Average age-appropriate proficiency standards for each primary cognitive ability tested are based on the most complex application of the ability normally performed by children at a given chronological age.

Whether or not these structural similarities completely account for their interrelationships, the relationships exist and are indexed by two related scores—Mental Age (MA) and Intelligence Quotient (IQ). Mental Age, which is directly (Stanford-Binet) or indirectly (the WISC-R) computed from the sum of the scores obtained on each task, is a construct representing the absolute level of cognitive performance, regardless of chronological age (CA). Sometimes this performance may not be commensurate with that of other individuals of the same chronological age, and this discrepancy (between mental age and chronological age) is reflected in the IQ score. IQ is related to MA and CA by the formula, IQ = MA/CA × 100. If a child's MA = CA, its IQ would be 100, the arbitrary designation for average or normal intelligence. The child with an IQ of 100 is therefore able to apply its cognitive abilities to deal with the complexity of tasks normal for the child's chronological age. An ability to deal with more-complex or less-complex tasks than would be typical of the child's same age peers (i.e., MA>CA or MA<CA, respectively) is indicated when IQ scores are higher or lower than the average score of 100.

The constructs of mental age and intelligence quotient must be kept in proper perspective. Often, the implications of the MA score are overlooked when IQ is emphasized. Particularly when the IQ score is below average, we tend to look for deficits or lags in cognitive abilities. By considering MA scores too, we can recognize the cognitive abilities a child currently demonstrates. These abilities are basically the same as those possessed by other children of the same MA, whether they be of normal, below normal, or above normal IQ. (Caution: this interpretation of the MA score can be applied only to the cognitive abilities specifically tested on intelligence tests. Realize, also, that individuals do not always perform all primary cognitive tasks equally well.)

REFERENCES AND SUGGESTED READINGS

Bayley, N. *Bayley scales of infant development.* New York: Psychological Corporation, 1969.

Berlyne, D. E. Arousal and reinforcement. In D. Levine (Ed.), *Nebraska Symposium on Motivation.* Lincoln: University of Nebraska Press, 1967.

Bruner, J. S. Going beyond the information given. In *Contemporary approaches to cognition.* Cambridge: Harvard University Press, 1957.

Fellows, B. J. *The discrimination process and development.* Oxford: Pergamon Press, 1968.

Gagne, R. M. *The conditions of learning.* New York: Holt, Rinehart and Winston, 1965.

Gibson, E. J. *Principles of perceptual learning and development.* New York: Appleton-Century-Crofts, 1969.

Guilford, J. P. *The nature of human intelligence.* New York: McGraw-Hill, 1967.

Harter, S. Effectance motivation reconsidered: Toward a developmental model. *Human Development,* 1978, *21,* 34-64.

Heber, R., & Garber, H. The Milwaukee Project: A study of the use of family intervention to prevent cultural-familial mental retardation. In B. Z. Friedlander, B. M. Sterritt, & G. E. Kirk (Eds.), *Exceptional infant* (Vol. 3: *Assessment and intervention*). New York: Brunner-Mazel, 1975.

Koffka, K. *The growth of the mind.* New York: Harcourt-Brace, 1946.

_____. *Principles of Gestalt psychology.* New York: Harcourt-Brace, 1935.

Kogan, N. *Cognitive styles in infancy and early childhood.* New York: Wiley, 1976.

McCall, R. B., Appelbaum, M. I., & Hogarty, P. S. Developmental changes in mental performance. *Monographs of the Society for Research in Child Development,* 1973, *38* (No. 3).

McCall, R. B., & Kagan, J. Stimulus-schema discrepancy and attention in the infant. *Journal of Experimental Child Psychology,* 1967, *5,* 381-390.

Merrifield, P. R., Guilford, J. P., Christensen, P. R., & Frick. J. W. The role of intellectual factors in problem solving. *Psychological Monographs,* 1962, *76* (No. 529).

Sokolov, E. N. *Perception and the conditioned reflex.* New York: Macmillan, 1963.

Terman, L. M., & Merrill, M. A. *Stanford-Binet Intelligence Scale.* Boston: Houghton-Mifflin, 1960.

Wechsler, D. *Wechsler Intelligence Scale for Children.* New York: Psychological Corporation, 1974.

Wertheimer, M. *Productive thinking.* New York: Harper and Row, 1945.

Chapter 8

Language and Language Disorders in Young Children

S. Gray Garwood

LANGUAGE AND COMMUNICATION

Learning about the world begins as soon as an infant is capable of interacting with objects and people. Thus, learning depends to a great extent on interactions, through which we learn about the physical and social worlds, and about ourselves in these worlds. Successful interactions require communication—an ability to exchange ideas and experiences with others. This is possible only when people who wish to communicate adopt a common set of rules or conventions relating these ideas and experiences to symbols. In other words, communication is possible only when people share a common system, usually based on symbols. Such an agreed-upon system is called a *language*. There are many such languages: FOR-TRAN, mathematics, music, art, body language, and signing, to name but a few. Of special research interest in child development is verbal language, which is word-based and includes spoken utterances (speech or oral language) and writing (graphic language).

Communication requires both encoding (connecting an idea into a verbal symbol, oral or graphic) and decoding by converting verbal symbols into ideas. How this works is illustrated by my writing this material which you are reading.

ENCODING ⟶ TRANSMISSION ⟶ DECODING

(author's ideas are encoded into a symbolic form; in this instance, the printed word)

(printed words are being read by you)

(you convert the graphic symbols into ideas)

This makes sense to you because I am following agreed-upon convention in reporting my ideas to you. Likewise, you know how to recognize words from patterns of letters. You can understand the meaning of these patterned arrangements of graphic symbols because I follow conventional rules in structuring sentences, i.e., subject-verb-object relationships. In addition, your understanding these sentences is determined by their context. Finally, all of this is made easy because you were taught to read around age 6 or so. Now consider the difference between interpreting written symbols after receiving instruction and learning to interpret oral symbols without any formal instruction. And to make it more complex, six-year-olds learning to read are much more cognitively sophisticated than are toddlers learning oral language. Yet somehow preschoolers learn a sophisticated system for arranging sounds into meaningful communication that includes complexities of structure as well as meaning. How this comes about is receiving much attention, not only because scientists are not yet sure, but also because of the relationship between language and cognitive development. In addition, as Table 1-1 in Chapter 1 indicated, communication disorders are the chief handicapping condition. Delayed, retarded, or no language is associated with almost all exceptionalities.

LANGUAGE AND COGNITION

Cognitive development in early life is hampered by reliance on behavioral actions for communication. The prelinguistic child cries, coos, crawls toward an object, but is unable to say "I'm thirsty!" or "What is that?" or "Hold me." With the onset of symbolic means to represent actions and ideas, however, flexible and more powerful information-processing tools become available and learning becomes more rapid and efficient.

Cognitive growth is thus functionally related to development of language skills. And since communication is a social act, language acquisition has functional significance for social aspects of behavior as well. For example, language enhances interpersonal communication by increasing the ability to interact with others; this, in turn, increases sociability, causing a decrease in egocentrism, and the child becomes more capable of objective thought. Acquiring language also permits internalization of ideas and experiences by representing them symbolically and then storing them in memory in groups or categories under common labels. Language is also critical to problem-solving, in this case internalizing actions and manipulative operations which are used to deal with the environment. By internalizing these, a child can run through a problem-solving strategy mentally and not have to run through it physically step-by-step.

The influence of language on cognition is more clearly seen in the acquisition of concepts. A concept is a rule for determining how incoming information will be categorized. For example, since the rule for "triangle" is that it must have three sides, we can represent any instance of a three-sided figure as a triangle. We need only one category instead of many different categories for each triangle we see; this symbol or concept makes information-processing efficient and manageable. Without conceptual categories for interpreting, storing, and retrieving information from the environment, we would be rendered immobile. As this example illustrates, language enables a child to:

- recognize similarities and differences among various events by common characteristics or functions; this is called abstraction
- organize classes of similar events (abstractions) into symbolic categories under common labels or words
- use the symbolic labels in interpreting and responding to new experiences

Categories of experience classified through abstraction are called concepts. Verbal concepts are those given a symbolic word label and are stored in memory for later retrieval upon recognition of the labeling word. Children also use nonverbal concepts, like fear. If a child learns that various events all make him upset and uncertain, the associated feelings become a nonverbal concept of frightening events. Thus, language acts as a kind of filing system for experiences which generate both verbal and nonverbal concepts.

The stages in verbal-concept development indicate that a child's earliest concepts are primitive and simplistic. Piaget believes young children tend to associate any and all elements experienced simultaneously as parts of the same concept; he calls this *verbal syncretism*. With emergence of concrete operations, however, the lumping-together tendency tapers off and concepts become more subtly differentiated. This change in cognitive complexity (from preoperational to concrete operational thought) brings changes in conservation ability, reversibility, and class inclusion. Conservation and reversibility enable the child to recognize constancy through transformations of location, position, or orientation. A book, for example, is still a book, regardless of the viewing angle. Class inclusion permits reasoning about part-whole relationships and this facilitates awareness that objects or events can be instances of a concept one time but not another; that a block can be a block or a toy or a bookend. With logical capacities, children's classification schemes become more elaborate.

Another aspect of the symbolic function of language is behavioral regulation through verbal mediation. For example, a child may learn through different experiences that different events (a hot stove, a lighted match, or a burning cigarette) have a common quality—they burn the fingers when they are touched. These isolated learning experiences may be represented as separate stimulus-response associations like this :

Hot stove	DON'T TOUCH
Lighted match	DON'T TOUCH
Cigarette	DON'T TOUCH

Verbal mediation introduces an intermediate response, a subvocal cue, "HOT," and this one cue controls behavior. The mediated stimulus-response association is represented like this:

Hot stove
Lighted match   HOT   DON'T TOUCH
Cigarette

This verbal cue, which the child may recall in a similar situation, recognize when spoken by others, or use to label similar situations, becomes a device for accelerating future learning experiences. Instead of experiencing repeatedly the consequence of touching hot objects, the child can remember that DON'T TOUCH! applies to any event labeled HOT. Thus, *verbal mediation* is learning to use words internally (thought) as a substitute for, and an abstraction of, behavioral action.

The ability to recognize common properties or functions within one's own experiences provides a basis for abstraction. Verbal mediation includes both mediated generalization (verbal labels represent similarities of new and old experiences) and mediated discrimination (verbal labels represent differences among new and old experiences). In this way, verbal mediation aids in learning to discriminate different kinds of situations and to generalize appropriately past experience when confronting new experiences. Both mediated discrimination and generalization link verbal mediation to concept formation specifically and to cognitive development generally.

LANGUAGE AND BEHAVIORAL REGULATION

Just as children, using language, learn to communicate with others and to organize experiences into cognition, they also learn to regulate experience and behavior. And since communication is social in nature, language usage establishes an important relationship between the child and his culture, acting as the primary vehicle for socializing children into adult society. The child, through language, assimilates a culture's beliefs, customs, and values, thus attaining cultural stability and continuity.

Luria (1961), describing the regulatory functions of language, suggested that verbal regulation of behavior is first external and later internalized within the child. Luria differentiates the truly meaningful use of language (semantic) from language that functions merely as sound stimulus (impulsive), and describes the developmental progression of verbal regulation of behavior as follows:

1. From about one-and-a-half to three a child's behavior is controlled mainly by language acting as physical stimulus without symbolic meaning. The sound stimulus (an impulse without symbolic meaning) originates outside the child from other people.

    Examples: "Night, night!"
             "No, No!"

236

2. During years three to about four-and-a-half, behavior is controlled mainly by language consisting mostly of familiar or recognizable physical sound. There is limited symbolic meaning, and the language sounds are responded to similarly regardless of their origin, i.e., the child or from others.

> Examples: "I finish, Mommie!"
> "I'm a good boy."
> "Tommy go outside."

3. Behavior becomes internally regulated through meaningful symbolic language beginning about age four-and-a-half; the child uses verbal symbols to organize and arrange behavior internally.

> Example (unspoken): "Before I go to gym I must remember to get my shorts from my locker."

Similarly, Vygotsky (1962) suggests that children learn how to deal with problem situations in a social context. First using egocentric speech (that is, talking to themselves out loud, beginning around age three—Luria's second phase), gradually, with age and experience they turn this egocentrism and external speech into inner speech:

> Our experimental results indicate that the function of egocentric speech is similar to that of inner speech: it does not merely accompany the child's activity; it serves mental orientation, conscious understanding; it helps in overcoming difficulties; it is speech for oneself, intimately and usefully connected with the child's thinking.
>
> . . . Between three and seven years . . . its vocalization becomes unnecessary . . . . In the end it separates itself entirely from speech for others . . . and thus appears to die out.
>
> But this is only an illusion . . . . [To say] that this kind of speech is dying out is like saying that the child stops counting when he ceases to use his fingers and starts adding in his head . . . . The decreasing vocalization of egocentric speech denotes a developing abstraction from sound, the child's new faculty to "think words" instead of pronouncing them. (Vygotsky, 1962, pp. 133-135)

Kohlberg, Yaeger, and Hjertholm (1968) verified Vygotsky's thesis by monitoring speech of 112 middle-class children between ages of four and ten. They found that use of egocentric speech was related to problem-solving ability and to Stanford-Binet IQ scores. Brighter children used more egocentric speech early, showing a decline beginning at age four; the decline for children of average intelligence did not begin until about age seven.

SPEECH ACQUISITION

In acquiring verbal language, all children pass through certain stages. The first sound an infant makes—the birth cry—a purely reflexive sound caused by air passing rapidly over the vocal cords, is, of course, not speech.

The first month of life is characterized by undifferentiated cries, the infant using the same crying sound for any number of reasons. When differentiated cries appear, about the second month, the infant has begun to make different sounds on the basis of different needs. Reflexive and random vocalizations appear next as the child begins to play with various sounds but these sounds as yet have no symbolic meaning.

Babbling occurs about the fifth month, a stage characterized by more syllabic combinations like "baba" and "dada" While some of these combinations sound like true speech to many parents, this is not so. At this time vowel-like sounds, like a-a-a-a-a-a-a and o-o-o-o-o, begin to decrease and consonant sounds like g-g-g-g-g-g and b-b-b-b-b-b begin to increase. Foreign sounds (sounds not used in the language environment of the child) also begin to disappear.

At six months or so, the infant enters the lallation stage. Lallation—the imitation of sounds purely for pleasure—marks a major stage in language and speech acquisition. When the infant makes these sounds, he or she activates and becomes aware of certain muscular movements associated with the sounds. The muscular and auditory stimuli become associated, the infant begins to reproduce the muscular movements which previously resulted in certain sounds, and imitation begins. Because the child will frequently make such imitative sounds in the absence of others is evidence that social reinforcement is not required for maintenance of this behavior.

The echolalia stage occurs about the ninth month and is marked by the infant's ability to imitate sounds produced by others—particularly his mother. These pre-language speech stages can be thus summarized:

Approximate Age	Stage	Characteristics
One Month	undifferentiated cries	makes the same cries to indicate comfort or distress
Two Months	differentiated cries	vocally distinguishes between cries associated with pleasure and cries associated with pain
Three-to-Four Months	reflexive and random vocalization	plays with his repertoire of sounds randomly
Five Months	babbling	begins to string together similar sounds

| Six Months | lallation | begins to repeat sounds he has heard himself make and this repetition is pleasurable |
| Nine Months | echolalia | begins to repeat sounds he's heard others make |

Up to this point the infant's verbal behavior cannot be classified as true language, but all this changes with the child's first word (about the end of the first year), marking the beginning of vocalization as a means of communication—a critical event in the social and intellectual development of the child.

Speech Production

Speech sounds are produced by interaction of air-streams and phonatory, resonatory, and articulatory processes. The phonatory process, the most elemental, enables one to control breathing so as to produce speech sounds which are intelligible, sequential, and rhythmatic—essential to interpretation or decoding of speech sounds into meaning.

Speech sounds are either voiced or voiceless. *Voiced sounds* are generated when sound waves pass through the larynx, which rapidly opens and closes in response to the stimulation provided by this airstream. *Voiceless sounds* are made by pulses of breath (rather than a continuous flow of air) passing through the pharynx and oral cavity. (See Figure 8-1.)

Figure 8-1 Location of Some of the Major Organs of Speech

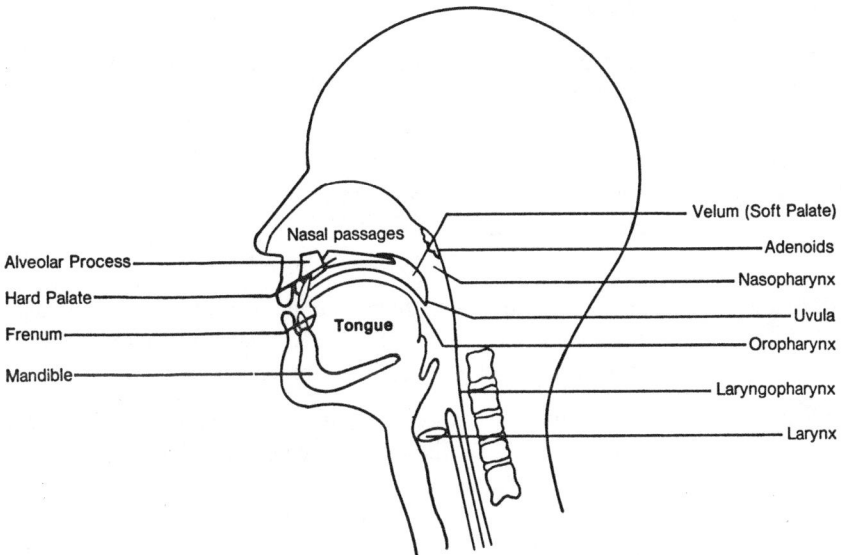

The sound waves which result from phonation are shaped by passage through the throat, mouth, and nose into speech sounds. *Articulation* refers to movements within the vocal tract area during speech-sound production, as in articulation of voiceless consonants like /t/ or /p/ or of voiced sounds like the vowels /i/ and /a/. Articulation enables one to determine the particular arrangement of oral symbols from which speech sounds may be extracted and comprehended. *Resonance* describes the quality of the speech sounds produced and depends on the size, shape, and texture of the vocal-tract organs.

The ability to reproduce specific speech sounds begins with learning to discriminate among different sounds—learning that certain sounds are made by the teeth and the tongue *(dentals),* others with the lips *(labials),* others by pressing the tongue against the roof of the mouth *(velars),* etc. At first the child learns to make only gross phoneme distinctions. A *phoneme* is the smallest unit of sound which serves to distinguish one sound from another. For example, in the words "tin" and "pin," the phonemes /t/ and /p/ distinguish between the two words. So, in language development, the child initially learns only to distinguish gross phoneme differences such as the differences between dentals like /d/ and /t/ and between labials like /p/ and /b/. Thus, children learn by experience that certain sounds are distinguishable by differences in (1) the amount of air required to produce them; (2) the amount of voiceness required (b, d, and g, are voiced whereas p, t, and k require less voice quality); and (3) the articulation procedures (differences in the movement of the speech organs) to produce sound.

LANGUAGE STRUCTURE

The psychological study of language and its use is called *psycholinguistics* and includes several specialized subfields:

Subfield	Purpose	Example
Phonology	studies basic language sounds	studying the onset, frequency, and changes in the child's ability to produce specific speech sounds (vowels and consonants)
Morphology	studies the use of sounds to form words	analyzing the child's ability to combine basic speech sounds (phonemes) into meaningful sounds (morphemes)
Syntax	studies how words are combined to form phrases and sentences	examining the orderliness of the child's ability to produce organized sentences

Semantics	studies how word meanings are learned	analyzing how children acquire a vocabulary of labels and how they learn the correct use of words

In pre-language speech (prior to the appearance of the first word), the infant does not use sounds symbolically to represent objects or events in his world. These early sounds are mostly random and only gradually, through learning, does phonological development take place. Phonemes, by themselves, are void of meaning; combined in various ways, they provide the base of a more meaningful unit of speech called the *morpheme*. The smallest unit of meaningful speech, a morpheme is a unit of speech that, if divided, would lose its meaning or be drastically altered in meaning. Thus, a morpheme is not the same thing as a syllable. For example, the word "novel" contains two syllables, but if divided in any way it would lose its original meaning. Thus "novel" consists of only one morpheme. The word "nothing" however, can be divided into "no" and "thing" and still retain much of its original meaning, so "nothing" has two morphemes.

Morphemes may be combined to create words and sentences. *Syntax* is the study of the rules which guide the morpheme-combining process, e.g., the proper placement of nouns, verbs, adjectives, etc. The study of *semantics,* on the other hand, concerns insight into the meaning of words and sentences.

LANGUAGE DEVELOPMENT

Language development in the young child appears to take place very rapidly, beginning early in the second year and is completed by about age five. But this view may be deceiving, for it ignores the prelinguistic development during the first years, prior to the production of adultlike speech. And although it is true that the child acquires much of his vocabulary between two and five, one should not underestimate the enormous contribution made to verbal development as the child, in growing older, learns to read, to manipulate mathematical and other symbols, and to use language in complex logical ways.

Children usually begin to "talk" around age one, though there is much individual variability in this age of onset. Very rapidly children develop a vocabulary of one-word utterances such as "milk," "car," "ball," "no," "more," and so forth, marking the beginning of syntax acquisition. Initially, children utter only these one-word sentences, *(holophrases),* which are believed to contain the meaning of a complete thought despite the fusion of noun and verb functions. Obviously the meaning of a holophrase is frequently difficult to detect. A child saying "bye-bye" may mean either goodbye, that he can't find something, or that some object (like a car) has passed out of sight.

Greenfield and Smith (1976) have suggested that holophrases have a stagelike quality. Early these single-word utterances represent a blend of language and action, such as saying "bye-bye" for coming and going. Next, holophrases become more cue-dependent, with children responding to objects or events with their label (i.e., seeing a ball and saying "ball"). The next stage in holophrastic development involves using single words to request or demand something, like "more" or "cookie." Finally during the child's second year, he uses holophrases to respond to more complex events, as when seeing father turn on a lamp and sitting down to read, and describing this sequence of events with the word "light." Bloom (1973), however, offers a different and more cautious interpretation, arguing that young children lack the intellectual ability to grasp (or to produce) the structures and meanings inherent in combinations of words. Since they still rely on sensorimotor capabilities, their one-word utterances are more than likely still under the control of their perceptions. If this is so, the suggested stagelike sequence suggested by Greenfield and Smith may require too much cognitive sophistication to attribute to young children.

Instead of developing in stage-like sequences, holophrases may be used differently by different children. McNeill (1970) describes four functional categories of language:

1. Expressive: to express feelings or moods

2. Conative: to express desires or needs

3. Referential: to indicate or designate specific objects or events

4. Predicative: to describe or comment about events or conditions

Nelson (1973), in regard to holophrastic complexity, suggests that some children use words for reference ("ball" refers to the round object before the child), but other children use words expressively ("more" means give me more coke and I'll be happy).

By the end of their second year, children begin to utter two- and three-word sentences. Some years ago Braine (1963), describing language development in terms of the child's use of open-class and pivot-class words, suggested that children learn a small number of highly flexible words (pivots), to which they begin to attach other (open-class) words. For example, "see dog," "see car," or "see house" all contain the pivot-word "see," with dog, house, car serving as open-class words. This conception of language development was supported by findings of others (Miller and Ervin, 1964; Slobin, 1969) so that pivot- and open-class structures became regarded as a universal feature of early language development. However, other investigators, Braine among them, have since discarded this notion (Bloom, 1970; Bowerman, 1973; Braine, 1976).

Roger Brown (1973) has investigated the meaning component of two-word phrases and has described 11 forms of sensorimotor knowledge which he finds evident in children's 2-word utterances. Gardiner (1978) has summarized these as follows:

Type	Sensorimotor Knowledge Implied	Example
Naming	there exists a world of objects, whose members bear names	it ball there doggie
Recurrence	a substance or activity can be prolonged made to reappear, added to, or otherwise enriched or lengthened	more ball
Nonexistence	an object can disappear from a situation	allgone ball no doggie
Agent-action	people do things	Johnny fall
Action-object	objects are acted upon	put truck change diaper
Agent-object	a person can perform actions on an object	Johnny stone me milk
Action-location	an action can occur in a specific place	sit chair fall floor
Object-location	an object occupies a specific place	book table
Possessor and possession	people possess objects	my ball Adam ball
Attribution	objects have characteristics	big ball little story
Demonstrative entity	one of a set of objects can be specified	that ball

Source: Derived by permission of the author and publishers from Roger Brown, *A First Language: The Early Stages* (Cambridge, Mass.: Harvard University Press, 1973). Copyright © 1973 by the President and Fellows of Harvard College. Adapted from H. Gardiner, Developmental Psychology, Little-Brown, 1978.

At about the same time that children begin to use two-word utterances, they begin also to acquire morphemes (the smallest units of meaning). Thus "ball," "toy," and "huh" are morphemes, as are endings, prefixes, plurals, etc. The addition of these morphemes enables the child to begin to use more complex language structures, and Brown (1973) describes 14 morphemes and their order of acquisition:

Morphemes and Usual Order of Acquisition

Morpheme	Meanings Expressed or Presupposed	Examples
Present progressive	temporary duration	I walk*ing*
in	containment	*in* basket
on	support	*on* floor
Plural	number	two balls
Past irregular [a]	earlierness [b]	it *broke*
Possessive inflection	possession	Adam's ball
Uncontractible copula [c]	number; earlierness	there it *is*
Articles	specific-nonspecific	that *a* book
		that *the* dog
Past regular	earlierness	Adam walk*ed*
Third person regular	number; earlierness	he walk*s*
Third person irregular	number; earlierness	he *does*
		she *has*
Uncontractible progressive auxiliary	temporary duration; number earlierness	this *is* going
Contractible copula [d]	number; earlierness	that'*s* book
Contractible progressive auxiliary	temporary duration; number; earlierness	I'*m* walk*ing*

[a] Formation of past tense by means other than *-ed*.
[b] Denotes understanding that an action or state may occur before the time of utterance.
[c] Use of the verb *to be* as a main verb without contraction.
[d] Use of the verb *to be* as a main verb with contractions.

Source: By permission of the author and publishers from Roger Brown, *A First Language: The Early Stages* (Cambridge, Mass.: Harvard University Press). Copyright © 1973 by the President and Fellows of Harvard College. Adapted from Gardiner, 1978.

Once children acquire this morpheme base, ever-more complex language is possible, since morphology rules—emphasizing use of inflections to form plural and past-tense constructions (see Table 8-1)—govern construction of words from morphemes. Prior to age four, children make consistent errors in forming plurals and past-tense forms but thereafter most children begin grasping the fundamental linguistic structures of their language including the mastering of such inflectional rules.

In addition, children begin to learn transformational rules which specify the relationship between the underlying structure of a sentence and its surface structure. These rules allow the child to generate more complex sentences (declarative, interrogative, negative, passive, etc.) from those he has learned to make with his newly acquired knowledge of phrase combination. How such transformations are learned by the child is still not clear though there is evidence that it is at least partly learned from parental expansion of the child's own sentences. In this process, the adult provides structural models that guide the child's learning of transformational rules.

The child's semantic development involves acquisition of semantic markers and development of a naming or labeling vocabulary. *Semantic markers* not only define or give meaning to a term but also indicate its appropriate usage within the sentence. For example, the words "puppy," "Fido," and "pooch" all have the semantic property of *dog* in common and this similarity influences the way the term is interpreted and used in sentence structure. Likewise, the word "run" can be used as a noun as well as a verb, but its placement in a sentence marks its meaning.

The child seems to accumulate a naming vocabulary through a differentiating process that moves from the general to the specific. Early in language development, the child might learn that most animals have four legs, some are large, and some small. For example, he might learn that cats are small and have four legs while dogs are large and have four legs. In this stage, the child might, upon seeing a toy poodle, call it a cat, or upon seeing a cow for the first time, call it a dog. Unlike the indirect learning in phonology and syntax acquisition, children receive direct tutoring from others in learning the names of things. Early errors are quickly corrected and the naming vocabulary increases rapidly. As Smith (1925) points out, the average vocabulary of a 1-year-old child is three words. At 2 years, 272 words; at 4 years, 1540 words, and by age 6, 2562 words. Nouns are learned first, followed by action verbs, adjectives, adverbs, and pronouns (McCarthy, 1954; Shirley, 1933). The last parts of speech to appear are prepositions and conjunctions, which are rarely heard in children below the age of two because such usage represents knowledge of relationships among ideas (Brown, 1965).

An understanding of language development encompasses both language production (speech) and language comprehension (listening and reading), as well as the characteristics of children's language and an examination of the functional

---

Table 8-1 Acquisition of Grammatical Inflections

Inflection	Meaning	Age of Acquisition in Two Typical Children	
		Girl	Boy
Verb + ing	to name an action	19½ mo.	
Noun + s	plural	24	33
Verb + ed	past tense	24½	39
Name + 's	possessive	25½	39½
Verb + s	third person	26	41

Source: Adapted from *The Acquisition of Language* by U. Bellugi and R. Brown (eds.) by permission of the Society for Research in Child Development, © 1964.

---

utility of language at different stages in the child's development: the variability of these elements in the course of the child's development makes describing language development a demanding task.

Dialects

From a sociological or anthropological point of view, language systems usually coincide with other boundaries of a common culture. Groups of people who interact regularly and extensively, or who are related politically and geographically, usually share a common language. Sometimes, however, miniature social systems (subcultures) develop within a larger culture and develop miniature-language systems that represent variations in the rules and conventions of the larger language system: these are called dialects. *Dialects* are much more than merely variations in pronunciation of spoken speech; they often involve variations of spelling and unique variations in the meaning of some words or symbols within the language. Moreover, dialects often have specialized variations in rules of grammar, syntax, and methods of assembling words into complex sentences.

Dialects usually grow out of group isolation from the larger society, an isolation produced either geographically (by mountains, rivers, or island boundaries), or by conditions of social, economic, and cultural insulation (ghettoes, ethnic groups). For example, the dialect learned by the American black in the inner city differs from middle-class English not only in pronunciations and inflections, but also in many special word meanings, unique spellings, and special rules of grammar and construction.

Table 8-2 Language Acquisition During The First Six Years

Age	Language Production	Language Comprehension
newborn	crying, predominantly in vowels rather than consonants	crude differential response to different pitches
1 month	differentiates cries for discomfort, pain, hunger	Distinguishes human voice from other sounds
2 months	vocalizes syllables, coos, babbles	attends and reacts to voices; may smile and vocalize when spoken to
4 months	vocalizes differently for pleasure or displeasure	orients head to sound of familiar voice
6 months	varies intonation of sounds; imitates intonations heard	differentiates familiar from unfamiliar, male from female voice
9 months	says "Mama" or "dada"; sounds begin to approximate those of the language spoken around him	understands gestures, familiar words or names, holophrases like "bye-bye"
12 months	one to three meaningful words; imitates and repeats words	responds to simple commands
18 months	vocabulary of 20 words or more	points to nose, eyes, hair; comprehends simple questions
24 months	names objects; combines words into phrases	points to pictures; names objects in response to simple questions; carries out instructions
3 years	repeats sentences; knows name; names objects in a picture	recognizes familiar signs and symbols; vocabulary of 800-1000 words
6 years	writes name; copies letters of alphabet; can recite alphabet, at least by rote; can describe pictures	vocabulary of 15,000 to 20,000 words; recognizes own name in print

Source: Adapted from McDavid & Garwood, Reprinted by permission of the publisher from *Understanding Children,* (Lexington, Mass.: D.C. Heath and Company, 1978).

The recent interest in viewing language as a communication tool for the child represents an approach to analyzing the functional utility of language, which, in turn, has renewed interest in dialects—now regarded not as a substandard language, but as legitimate alternatives to the dominant language. Typical is the work of William Labov (1972), among others, who treats Black English Vernacular (BEV) as a dialect version of English, with variant rules of spelling, pronunciation, grammar, inflection, and syntax. In this sense, the black inner-city child really uses not a deficient but a different language.

Theories of Language Acquisition

Current theories of language development are incomplete. Much work in this area is based on behavioristic stimulus-response learning theory, although, as yet, no theory has satisfactorily explained how children acquire so early and so quickly their complex linguistic abilities, much of which cannot be traced to a linguistic environment. Mowrer (1950) explains the first stage of language development, the reproduction of word sounds, on the basis of secondary-reinforcement principles. According to his theory, as the child is fed and/or fondled by the mother, she utters sounds which the child learns to associate with this pleasurable activity. As the child develops the ability to vocalize, he may accidentally utter sounds similar to those heard from the mother during the feeding-fondling activity. The extent to which these sounds remind the child of the pleasurable experiences of being fed and fondled may determine their value to the child and, ultimately, his motivation to practice imitating them. At first learning only empty words, the child with experience gradually learns to associate the word with the object, thus, also learning meaning. Mowrer contends that sentences are also learned in this way.

One reason why Mowrer's theory seems inadequate as an explanation of fully developed language abilities is that much of a child's linguistic ability does not appear in the structure of the sentences it hears, yet somehow the child still learns the structures inherent in sentences and the transformational rules necessary to relate the underlying structure to the surface structure of a sentence.

Another interesting approach is that of B. F. Skinner (1957), whose Functional Analysis Model is a purely descriptive scheme. Skinner ignores any possibility of intervening variables (inferred, but unobservable, internal influences) in language development. Instead, he analyzes verbal behavior simply by isolating the various conditions which control verbal behavior. Skinner focuses on *operant behavior*—behavior emitted by the individual without clear reference to stimuli causing the behavior. Operant behavior (which includes verbal behavior) may be either learned or not learned, according to the consequences which follow the behavior and whether these consequences are either rewarding or punishing.

Skinner has created a number of descriptive terms to explain verbal behavior. The *mand* describes verbal behavior which is under the control of the individual's various drive states, such as hunger or thirst; its function is to reduce or alleviate the particular drive state which is aroused. Mands (the term is chosen from the stem occurring in words like *demand* and *command*) specify either the listener's behavior (Pay Attention) or the ultimate reinforcement desired (Water!), or both (Pour the water.). Though a mand is under the control of a drive state, such states are not directly observable and therefore mands show no relationship directly with a prior stimulus.

A *tact*, a labeling response for physical objects or events, describes verbal behavior involved in making "contact" with the nonverbal world. Skinner also describes verbal behavior as (1) *echoic*, the repetition of previously heard speech; (2) *textual*, behavior controlled by nonauditory verbal stimuli like printed words; and (3) *intraverbal*, behavior controlled by verbal behavior of a different form like trite responses to cliches ("knock, knock . . . Who's there?") or word-association response patterns (day . . . night; boy . . . girl).

A number of other studies suggest that verbal conditioning does occur, yet what is learned in verbal-conditioning experiments is apparently only awareness of the relationship between emitting a certain response and the reinforcement that results from this response (response-reinforcement contingencies), not true verbal behavior. Furthermore, Skinner's approach ignores the meaning component of verbal behavior and Osgood (1958) has demonstrated that meaning is significantly related to behavior. Skinner's approach is a useful classificatory scheme but is unable fully to explain language behavior.

To overcome some of these difficulties, Osgood proposed a three-stage theory to account for the learning of both structure and meaning in language development. Each of his levels *(projection, integration,* and *representation)* contains three processes: *decoding, association,* and *encoding.*

1. The *projection* level is not directly concerned with language behavior; it serves primarily as a neural relay system for automatic and predictable stimulus-response patterns.
2. The *integrational* level accounts for behavior involving rapidly executed motor skills, as in speech—the nervous system groups or integrates repeatedly experienced stimulus-or-response events at this level.

   Integrations may occur as either predictive or evocative situations. *Predictive* situations are those allowing some prediction of the likely response; *evocative* situations are those where the occurrence of the event is sure to produce a certain response. At the integrational level, language behavior includes almost automatic awareness of grammatical rules, such as in the forming of plurals and verb tenses.
3. The *representational* level is concerned with awareness of meaning. Here stimulus events evoke interrelated physiological and psychological response chains resulting in awareness of the meaning of the stimulus event and

appropriate behavioral action. The decoding process (reception, projection, integration, and decoding of stimulus significance) begins with auditory (hearing) or visual (reading) reception of language stimuli and ends with internal responses to these stimuli. Encoding (intentional selection, integration, and expression of linguistic units) begins with awareness of meaning and ends with some behavior like speaking. The connections between decoding and encoding are made by the association process. Table 8-3 illustrates Osgood's model.

Table 8-3 Osgood's Three-Stage Mediational Theory

Stage	Definition	Example
Projection	This stage is not directly concerned with language behavior. Its main function is to receive, integrate, and evaluate (decoding) a stimulus event and associate it with a predetermined response pattern (encoding) which may include some form of language behavior.	You touch a hot stove and automatically withdraw your hand. Usually this action is accompanied by a cry, such as "ouch!"
Integration	The production of speech sounds and concern for rules of language is the function here. Stimulus events, when decoded, indicate either a predictable response or the event is such that it evokes a likely response as in word associations.	Creating plurals and altering verb tenses depending on the context of the situation; forming word associations like "boy . . . girl," "day . . . night," etc.
Representation	At this level the stimulus event brings into awareness the meaning associated with the event and the response pattern indicates appropriate behavioral action which includes consideration of this meaning component.	If you see ice cream as good and poison as bad, you are more likely to go for ice cream and to avoid poison.

The major problem with learning theories of communication and language, such as those described above, is that they are unable to explain how the child acquires linguistic knowledge which is seldom, if ever, explicitly taught him. For this reason, present learning theories are unable to provide a full explanation of language acquisition. The major alternatives to learning theories are views that explain language functions as innate and biologically derived, typified by Lenneberg's (1967) position, which maintains that language, like the upright walk of humans, is innate to the species. This argument rests on four important factors in language development: (1) all languages make use of a small number of phonemes and there is little variation within the species in this aspect; (2) language development depends on organic development that follows fixed biological timetables and is independent of sociocultural influences; (3) language knowledge develops in spite of physiological abnormalities, as in deaf children, indicating an innate capacity for language acquisition among humans; and (4) if language were a learned phenomenon it could be traceable to its origins, and since this has not been done it must not be a purely learned behavior but reflects instead man's innate capacity for language acquisition. While Lenneberg's arguments for biological bases for language acquisition may be considered dubious by many psychologists and biologists, the model he proposes nevertheless allows for description and explanation of some facets of language development which are inadequately handled by the learning-theory approaches.

Noam Chomsky (1966) advocates a genetic view of language development—language is derived from neurological structures that guide the course of language acquisition. This argument is based on Chomsky's differentiation between surface structures and deep structures. *Surface structures* are the apparent and visible arrangements of symbols into phrases. *Deep structures* are the underlying cognitive systems governing meaning or interpretation of phrases. The sentences, "John is eager to please," and "John is easy to please," have different meanings even though the superficial arrangement of words in the two is parallel. Likewise, "The boy threw the toy," and "The toy was thrown by the boy," contain essentially the same meaning but have different superficial structures. It is deep structure that provides the key to interpreting the meaning of these sentences. Children are not taught this when they learn language, at least not directly, but they learn to recognize the differences of meaning despite the superficial structural similarity of sentences. Thus Chomsky argues that linguistic structures are genetically determined, and proposes that the development of language is guided by a language-acquisition device (LAD) inherent within the child.

Inhelder and Piaget (1958) have described the intellectual development of the child with reference to his verbal and symbolic activity. They point out that in early stages of development, the child does not associate the verbal symbol with the object, person, or event it represents. They propose that during the first two years of life (the sensorimotor stage), the child displays minimal symbolic activity.

251

Between the ages of two and seven (the preoperational stage), the child learns to label objects and events, and its verbal concepts are concrete and based on the perceptual qualities of the thing itself. Between 7 and 11 (the stage of concrete operations), the child begins to display logical intellectual activity, but involving merely the application of logical rules to concrete objects. Only during adolescence (the stage of formal operations) does the individual become capable of truly abstract thinking, which involves the manipulation of abstract symbols in thought and the capacity for deductive reasoning and simultaneous manipulation of a number of related operations and ideas.

Piaget also describes children's language development as moving from the egocentric or self-centered to the more communicative; that is, the early stages of language development emphasize the representational qualities of language; the later the logical and communicative qualities. This progression might be described as follows:

Semiotic (symbol recognition)	learning letters and numbers; simple word recognition
Semantic (meaning)	learning vocabulary; becoming familiar with the consensus about meanings associated with symbols
Syntactic (sentence construction and grammar)	learning to use phrases to communicate ideas; becoming familiar with society's rules about assembling letters, words, punctuation, and sentences to exchange complex ideas completely
Logic (rational communication through language)	learning to distinguish symbols from their referents; learning to manipulate language symbols and ideas in problem solving and decision making

THE NEUROLOGY OF SPEECH AND LANGUAGE

The human brain contains three structures believed to control language-proficiency skills. *Language proficiency* includes both production and comprehension components. *Language production* refers to the ability effectively to communicate ideas to others, including the production of both oral language (speech) and graphic language (writing, signing, etc.) *Language comprehension* describes one's ability to comprehend others' meaning, and includes the understanding of oral and graphic forms of language.

The three neurological structures which determine language proficiency are the *angular gyrus* and *Wernicke's area,* located near the border of the temporal, parietal, and occipital lobes, and *Broca's area,* located in the brain's frontal lobe.

Structure	Function	Effects of Impairment
Broca's Area	controls speech musculature	interferes with speech production

Example:

"I am taking—ah—Sherriks—ah—Sherring's mixture (laugh). It's easier for me to—stalk—talk staccato and breaking up each word—into sentences—breaking up sentences into words provided they have ah—not many syllables."

Wernicke's Area	involved in understanding speech and speaking meaningfully	interferes with understanding others and speaking meaningfully

Example:

"Well, I thought thing I am going to tell is about my operation and it is not about all I can tell is about the preparation the had was already the time was when they had me to get ready . . . .

Angular gyrus	involved in visual-spatial aspects of speech	interferes with ability to read or write with comprehension

Example:

Spring Lake Heights
Jan. 10, 1969

Dear Jim an Syvlia

Dear Willam brought me down after some Day in him Jan 9 Yesterday.

I wonder if could send the interest of the year 1967. With the asthere Edith has to after every thing desmalted the house, etc. etc.

Eitheth it easy coull if inconsistent the ask you there send me the balance a this account, too would other low. The amount is $271.00 plus 1967 interest Totals $281.80

You affating & Loving Father

(I took out a hour to right this)

Note: The first example is from E. Lenneberg, *Biological Foundations of Language*. New York: Wiley, 1967. The second example is from W. Penfield and L. Roberts, *Speech and Brain Mechanisms*. Princeton: Princeton University Press, 1959. The final example is from S. Farnham-Diggory, *Cognitive Processes in Education*. New York: Harper & Row, 1972.

Language and Speech Disorders.

Language proficiency is critical to all aspects of child development. Therefore, any disorder in the development of proficiency in language usage can affect cognitive, social, and personal areas. Such disorders in speech and/or language are generally termed organic or functional, depending on the origin of the disorder.

Organic disorders result from neurological or structural abnormalities. Since all behavior depends on appropriate neurological functioning, the relationship between brain damage and speech or language disorder is easily understood. Examples of organic disorders affecting speech and language are aphasia, muscle control-speech production problems, and integration problems.

Aphasia is a language deficit resulting from brain damage. (Two examples of aphasia in adults were given above in describing Broca's and Wernicke's areas.) By this definition, aphasia occurs after language has been acquired, and accordingly, adults or children can become language-disabled through brain damage, which includes the language and speech structures described above.

Brain injury can interfere with other aspects of communication as well as language. Figure 8-2 shows that damage to parts of the motor area could interfere

---

Figure 8-2 The Brain

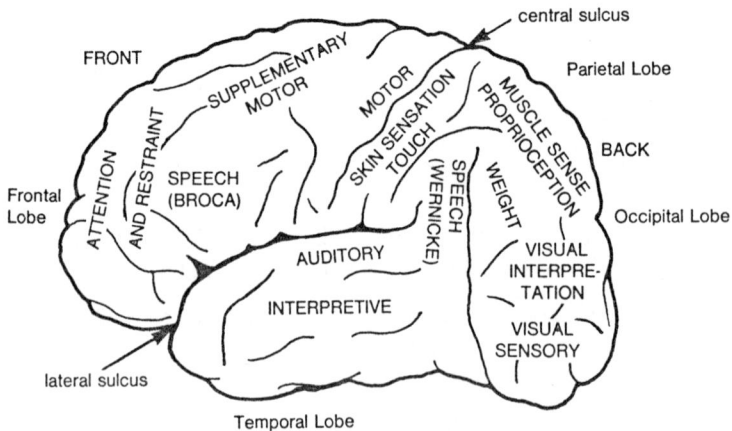

Figure 8-2 locates Broca's and Wernicke's area. In about 97 out of 100 people, these three structures are located in the left cerebral hemisphere (Geschwind, 1972).

---

with ability to produce speech sounds correctly, resulting in articulation problems. Perkins (1971) has described four types of articulation problems: additions, omissions, substitutions, and distortions, and these are illustrated below.

Type of Error	Characteristic	Example
Omissions	only portions of words pronounced	"_ake me _ith _ou."
Substitutions	substituting phonemes in words	wike" for "like" "woom" for "room" "thunday" for Sunday"
Additions	adding extra sounds to words	"aluminumnum" for "aluminum" "morer" for "more"
Distortions	alterations in sound	(none given)

All children make such errors at one time or another. Therefore, when determining whether a small child is displaying an articulation error, consider such variables as the child's age, how often the error occurs (type of error, consistency with which the child makes the error, and the child's language environment). A severe articulation problem is called *dysarthria,* a condition common to many cerebral-palsied children.

Brain damage can also affect communication by altering normal language production and comprehension-integration functions. For example, if brain damage destroys the neurological connections between Broca's area and Wernicke's area (while leaving the areas intact), the child could talk clearly and understand others but its speech would be meaningless and incomprehensible to others.

Structural defects affect communication usually by interfering with speech production directly, as in cases of cleft palate or cleft lip (see Chapters 3 and 4), or indirectly, as in cases where structural defects occur in the hearing mechanisms interfering with language and speech.

Functional disorders include all other non-organically-based communication disorders, including disorders resulting from psychological and from environmental factors. It should be obvious, then, that functional disorders include the majority of speech and language problems. The articulation problems listed earlier can just as easily be considered functional disorders, depending on etiology. That is, instead of being organically based many articulation problems may be the result of environmental conditions which fostered particular articulation disorders.

Stuttering is usually considered a functional disorder, involving an alteration in normal flow of speech, characterized by partial disruptions, usually taking the form of halting repetitions of speech sounds. In explaining origins of stuttering, some deemphasize organic factors but others stress the role of tension, anxiety, and fear. In fact, several kinds of stuttering exist, representing combinations of physiological and psychological factors.

Organic interpretations assume Broca's area is the site of coordinated speech functions, and that damage to this area can produce stuttering as well as aphasia. Johnson's (1955) work focuses on stress and anxiety as functional sources of stuttering (a position based on learning theory) and suggests that stuttering is the result of conflict among several kinds of learned behaviors. Thus, any kind of inconsistency or conflict during early experience and training could produce stuttering problems.

Stuttering does not occur randomly; it occurs with greater frequency on certain language elements, usually adjectives and nouns, with less on the short connecting words. Stuttering is also more likely to occur on consonants than on vowels, probably because they require more complex lingual and labial adjustments. Also, most stuttering occurs on initial words in a phrase or sentence, and rarely in rhythmic recitations such as singing or poetry.

Basically a childhood phenomenon, it begins usually around age two to four and occurs considerably more frequently in boys than in girls. Fortunately, nearly all stutterers (80 percent or so) eventually develop normal speech (Sheehan and Martyn, 1970).

Closely associated, and often confused, with stuttering is cluttering. *Cluttering* includes the difficulty in initiating speech sounds associated with stuttering, but also includes excessive speed of speaking, poor sentence structure, and articulation difficulties. This latter characteristic, in particular, makes communication a problem for clutterers, making it difficult to understand them.

Table 8-4 Characteristics of Language Disorders In Various Exceptionalities

Brain Injury—Aphasia

Normal to near-normal pure tone thresholds; differential responsivity to same stimuli is possible across presentations
Speech sounds evoke little interest or selective attention
Imitative efforts for speech sounds are lacking
Auditory comprehension is impaired
Phonological development is impaired
Telegraphic speech is characteristic
Dyslexia may be present
Memory abilities are impaired

Mental Retardation

Delay in language onset
May have hearing impairments
Meager vocabulary
Poor grammatical structures
Articulation difficulties
Thinking is limited to concrete relationships
There is a higher than normal incidence of abnormal voice quality
There is a higher than normal incidence of stuttering
The child is unable to generalize language rules once learned

Emotional Disturbance

Diminished vocabulary
Inappropriate and non-communicative language
Mutism
Neologisms or meaningless words are frequent
Articulation difficulties
Echolalia or repetitive speech
Pronoun reversals occur
Comprehension difficulties
Inappropriate pitch, intensity and rate

Social-Environmental Deprivation

Short, grammatically simple and often unfinished sentences, with poor syntactical form
Simple and repetitive use of conjunctions
Rigid and limited use of adjectives and adverbs
Inability to hold a formal subject through a speech sequence
Ability to follow directions but inability to recall what had been done
Inability to use simple tenses to describe past, present, and future actions

Hearing Loss

Speech development is retarded
Voice has a characteristic tonal quality
Gestures are used to communicate needs/wants
Uses simple sentences
Vocabulary contains a larger number of nouns than normally found in hearing children

Working With Language-Delayed Children

Since language and communication are vitally linked to all aspects of development, helping children develop normal language proficiency or overcome some or all of the disabling effects of speech and language disorders is important. To this end, parents, teachers, and speech and language specialists must work together towards amelioration or remediation. For parents and preschool teachers, this can be difficult (especially when the disability is mild), since in early childhood years normal language behaviors are being acquired and the child's language repertoire is necessarily error-prone, making it difficult to spot potential language problems early.

As a guide for deciding on mild problems, parents and teachers can follow the criteria listed for articulation problems. Specifically, observe the frequency, consistency, and the type of language errors and take into consideration the child's age and language environment. But, when in doubt, consult a specialist in language problems.

For more severe language problems, the evidence is usually at hand, making detection obvious. Children with structural defects may need corrective surgery and/or speech therapy. Children with organic disorders can often benefit from speech therapy or from being taught an alternative communication mode, such as signing. For the many children with moderate-to-severe functional disorders, such as stuttering, early speech therapy is dictated. In all such cases, a professional speech or language person should be consulted, both for diagnosis and for remediation techniques that can be used by teachers and parents.

REFERENCES AND SUGGESTED READINGS

Anastasiow, N.J., & Hanes, M.L. Cognitive development and the acquisition of language in three subcultural groups. *Developmental Psychology,* 1974, *10,* 703-709.

Bereiter, C., & Englemann, S.E. *Teaching disadvantaged children.* Englewood Cliffs: Prentice-Hall, 1966.

Berko, J. The child's learning of English morphology. *Word.,* 1958, *14,* 150-177.

Blank, M. Cognitive functions of language in the preschool years. *Developmental Psychology,* 1974, *10,* 229-245.

Bloom, L. *Language Development.* Cambridge: M.I.T. Press, 1970.

Bloom, L. One word at a time: The use of single word utterances before syntax. *The Hague Mouton,* 1973.

Bowerman, M. Early syntactic development: A cross-linguistic study with special reference to Finnish. London: Cambridge University Press, 1973.

Braine, M. The ontogeny of English prose structure: The first phrase. *Language,* 1963, *39,* 1-13.

_____. On learning the grammatical order of words. *Psychological Review,* 1963, *70,* 323-348.

_____. Children's first word combinations. *Monographs of the Society for Research in Child Development.* Chicago: University of Chicago Press, 1976, *41,* 1-104.

Brown, R. *Social psychology*. New York: Free Press, 1965.

_____. *A first language: The early stages*. Cambridge: Harvard University Press, 1973.

Brown, S. F. The influence of grammatical function on the incidence of stuttering. *Journal of Speech Disorders*, 1937, *2*, 207-215.

Cazden, C.B. Subcultural differences in child languages: An interdisciplinary review. *Merrill-Palmer Quarterly*, 1966, *12* (3), 185-219.

_____. *Child Language and Education*. New York: Holt, Rinehart and Winston, 1972.

Chomsky, N. *Topics in the theory of generative grammar*. The Hague: Mouton, 1966.

Clark, Eve. What's in a word? On the child's acquisition of semantics in his first language. In T.E. Moore (Ed.), *Cognitive development and the acquisition of language*. New York: Academic Press, 1973.

Gardiner, H. *Developmental psychology*. Boston: Little-Brown, 1978.

Geschwind, N. Language and the brain. *Scientific American,* 1972, *226,* 76-83.

Greenfield, P.M., & Smith, J. *The structure of communication in early language development*. New York: Academic Press, 1976.

Hess, R.D., & Shipman, V.C. Early experiences and the socialization of cognitive models in children. *Child Development,* 1965, *36,* 869-886.

Inhelder, B., & Piaget, J. The growth of logical thinking from childhood to adolescence (translated by A. Parsons and S. Pilgram). New York: Basic Books, 1958.

Johnson, W.J. *Stuttering in children and adults*. Minneapolis: University of Minnesota Press, 1955.

Jones, L.V. & Wepman, J.M. Dimensions of language performance in aphasia. *Journal of Speech and Hearing Research,* 1961, *4,* 220-232.

Kohlberg, L., Yaeger, J., and Hjertholm, E. Private speech: Four studies and a review of theories. *Child Development,* 1968, *39,* 691-736.

Labov, W. *Language in the inner city: Studies in Black English vernacular*. Philadelphia: University of Pennsylvania Press, 1972.

Lenneberg, E.H. *Biological foundations of language*. New York: Wiley, 1967.

Luria, A.R. *The role of speech in the regulation of normal and abnormal behavior*. London: Pergamon, 1961.

Macnamara, J. Cognitive basis of language in infants. *Psychological Review,* 1972, *1,* 1-13.

McCarthy, D. Language development in children. In L. Carmichael (Ed.), *Manual of child psychology* 2nd ed.). New York: Wiley, 1954.

McNeill, D. The development of language. In P. Mussen (Ed.), *Carmichael's manual of child psychology* (Vol. 1). New York: Wiley, 1970.

Miller, W., & Ervin, S. The development of grammar in child language. In U. Bellugi and R. Brown (Eds.), *The acquisition of language*. Monograph of the Society for Research in Child Development, 1964, *29,* 9-34.

Mowrer, O.H. *Learning theory and personality dynamics*. New York: Ronold, 1950.

Nelson, K. Structure and strategy in learning to talk. *Monograph of the Society for Research in Child Development,* 1973, *38,* (nos. 1-2).

Osgood, C.E. A question of sufficiency: Review of B.F. Skinner, *Verbal Behavior. Contemporary Psychology,* 1958, *3,* 209-212.

Perkins, W. H. *Speech Pathology: An Applied Behavioral Science*. St. Louis: Mosby, 1971.

Piaget, Jean. *The language and thought of the child*. New York: Harcourt, Brace & World, 1926.

_____. *The origins of intelligence in children*. New York: International Universities Press, 1952.

Pozner, J. & Saltz, E. Social class, conditional communication, and egocentric speech. *Developmental Psychology,* 1974, *10,* 764-771.

Sheehan, J.G., & Martyn, M.M. Stuttering and its disappearance. *Journal of Speech and Hearing Research,* 1970, *13,* 279-289.

Shirley, M.M. *The first two years: A study of twenty-five babies* (Vol. II): *Intellectual Development.* Minneapolis: University of Minnesota Press, 1933.

Shriner, T.H. & Miner, L. Morphological structures in the language of disadvantaged and advantaged children. *Journal of Speech and Hearing Research,* 1968, *11,* 605-610.

Skinner, B.F. *Verbal behavior.* New York: Appleton-Century-Crofts, 1957.

Slobin, D.I. Universals of grammatical development in children. Working Paper No. 22, Language Research Laboratory, University of California, Berkeley, 1969.

Smith, M.E. An investigation of the development of the sentence and the extent of vocabulary in young children. *University of Iowa Studies in Child Welfare,* 1925, *3* (5).

Taylor, I.K. The properties of stuttered words. *Journal of Verbal Learning and Verbal Behavior,* 1966, *5,* 112-118.

Vygotsky, L.S. *Thought and language.* Cambridge: M.I.T. Press, 1962.

Chapter 9

Learning Disabilities in Young Children

Betty A. Hare and James M. Hare

INTRODUCTION

During the last 15 years a new handicapping classification has emerged to designate children who are having unusual trouble learning school-related tasks. Termed *Specific Learning Disability,* (LD) it describes a diverse group who, while usually otherwise normal, experience difficulty in mastering many of the tasks associated with school learning, such as reading, spelling, and so forth. Despite this common focus, these children demonstrate a wide variety of problems, many of which appear to be motor-related. Indeed, one, hyperactivity (too much uncontrolled movement), has become a most overused and misused term in the schools today. Originally the word was used to describe the behavior of children who were so uncontrolled and uncontrollable they could not be managed within the context of a regular school system. Alfred Strauss, a neurologist who studied and described their behavior, attributed their difficulties to brain injury—inability to process the abundance of stimuli that impinge on their sense organs—and identified the cluster of problems resulting from damage to the central nervous system as the *Strauss Syndrome.* Strauss and Laura Lehtinen Rogen established the Cove School, designed to reduce stimulation by controlling classroom environment, the materials and methods used, even the dress and accessories of the teachers. For, in addition to uncontrolled activity, these children were easily distractible, had poor coordination of body parts, and acted (or overreacted) impulsively. Their book, *The Psychopathology and Education of the Brain Injured Child* (Strauss and Lehtinen, 1947) is still informative reading for teachers interested in LD.

Many LD children have perceptual problems. Gerald Getman, an optometrist who had training also in child development, recognized that successful "seeing" was as much a function of the brain as of the eye. Psychologists such as Marianne Frostig noted the inaccurate performance in visual and visual-motor tasks; Newell Kephart and William Cruickshank, following the lead of their mentor, Strauss, continued to work on perception and attention problems.

Specific learning disability was also assumed to be responsible for language problems. Helmer Myklebust, whose field was originally speech and hearing, became interested in children whose hearing was intact but who acted as if they were deaf. While understanding spoken language, some were unable to produce it themselves. Joseph Wepman, his colleague at Northwestern University, studied the problems of auditory perception, particularly since auditory discrimination ability was related to reading. Written language disorders, especially reading, were central to the interest of another neurologist, Samuel Orton, and his student, Anna Gillingham. Psychologist Grace Fernald developed a multisensory technique for learning to read at her laboratory school at UCLA. Her text, although published in 1943, is another landmark book for teachers of children with severe reading problems.

Some LD children have problems adjusting to and relating with other persons, tending to be emotionally explosive, overacting to frustration or other stresses. Often appearing to resent authority, they, nevertheless, need structure and limits. They tease and taunt peers, but wail that they have no friends; have little confidence in their abilities, but attribute failure always to someone else. These youngsters then, tend to have social and behavior problems, but are not considered as primarily emotionally disturbed.

As this brief introduction points out, *Learning Disability* is a category that includes a diversity of problems, and embraces diverse disciplines, with contributions from professionals whose interests, training, and points of view have varied. However, long before LD became a school-related phenomenon, the traits associated with this disability were identified in many preschool children. Strauss-Syndrome children were often diagnosed soon after birth by various behavioral patterns associated with (1) sleep (sleep-awake pattern was reversed; they slept about 4 hours and were wakeful about 20 hours); (2) motor activities ("klutzy" children late in walking and performing other gross-motor tasks); and (3) language acquisition (aphasic or language-disordered children who did not develop oral language when other children did).

Not until Samuel Kirk questioned the wholesale diagnosis and placement of children into classes for the educable mentally retarded were the problems of this group of children considered school-related, or the disability one of learning.

The issue contemporary educators must wrestle with is the high incidence of children having school-related learning problems. In some areas as many as 30 percent of children have been identified as having a learning disability. Despite the number of possible contributory factors, such as the inappropriateness of schooling for tomorrow's citizens, the effect of pollutants in our air, water and food, poor teaching, and the lack of good research in the field itself, it is clear that something must be done to reduce learning problems in children. A logical approach is prevention. If we can provide appropriate experiences for young children, perhaps we can preclude the development of some problems, and if a disability does exist,

---

BOX 9:1 ORIGINS OF LD

The term, "learning disabilities," was made legitimate in 1969, with passage of the "Children with Specific Learning Disabilities Act." But learning disabilities did not come into existence with this federal legislation; they existed under more than 90 different labels such as association deficit pathway, minimal brain dysfunction, hyperkinetic behavior syndrome, dyslexia, and problem reader. Table 9-1 contains a listing of these many labels.

This recognition of learning disabilities as a distinct category was the result of lobbying efforts by parents and professional educators. In *1963*, legislation made available federal funds for scholarships and research in the area of "handicaps" and established specific categories of handicapping conditions:

- mental retardation
- severe emotional disturbance
- speech, hearing, and visual deficits
- health related impairments

There was no provision for children who were having trouble learning but were otherwise apparently "normal."

In *1965* the Elementary and Secondary Act provided funds to state and local educational agencies for developing special educational programs for both the economically disadvantaged and the handicapped. But, since LD children were still not included, lobbying efforts resumed, and were aided by the development of national organizations like the Council for Exceptional Children and Association for Children with Learning Disabilities.

A necessary first task confronting groups lobbying for learning disabilities was to arrive at a consensus regarding the definition of a Learning Disability, to insure that Learning Disabilities became a recognized separate category of exceptionality and therefore would not syphon off funds set aside for other handicapping conditions (such would have been the case if Learning Disabilities were lumped in with the other categories). Thus, in *1969*, the Children with Specific Learning Disabilities Act was passed, dealing separately with this category of exceptionality. This independent status was lost but Learning Disabilities' categorical integrity was maintained when, in *1970*, the Elementary and Secondary Education Amendments Act integrated all handicapped categories into a unified program under the Bureau for the Education of the Handicapped. And, of course, the most recent legislation is PL 94-142: The Education of All Handicapped Children Act which requires that appropriate educational services be provided for all handicapped children between the ages of 3 and 21.

Table 9-1 Various Terms Used to Describe Learning-Disabled Children

Association deficit pathology	Choreiform syndrome
Organic brain damage	Minor brain damage
Organic brain disease	Minimal brain injury
Organic brain dysfunction	Minimal cerebral injury
Minimal brain damage	Minimal chronic brain syndrome
Diffuse brain damage	Minimal cerebral damage
Neurophrenia	Minimal cerebral palsy
Organic driveness	Cerebral dys-synchronization syndrome
Cerebral dysfunction	Problem learners
Brain injured	Problem readers
Minimal dysfunction	Psycholinguistic disabilities
Minimal cerebral dysfunction	Psychoneurological learning disorders
Brain damaged	Reading disability
Brain dysfunction	Remedial-education case
Minimal brain dysfunction	Special learning difficulties
Strauss syndrome	Special learning disorders
Hyperkinetic-behavior syndrome	Specific learning difficulties
Character-impulse disorder	Specific learning disorders
Hyperkinetic-impulse disorder	Underachiever
Aggressive-behavior disorder	Hyperkinetic disorder
Learning impotence	Catastrophic behavior
Hyperkinetic syndrome	Neurophysiological dysynchrony
Dyslexia	Central nervous system disorder
Specific dyslexia	Word blindness
Hyperexcitability syndrome	Learning block

Perceptual cripple
Perceptually handicapped
Neurologically handicapped
Primary-reading retardation
Specific reading disability
Clumsy-child syndrome
Hypokinetic syndrome
Aphasoid syndrome
Conceptual handicapped
Attention disorders
Interjacent child
Developmental imbalance
Maturational lag
Educationally handicapped
Language disorders
Learning disorder
Learning disability
Learning impaired
Performance deviation
Performance disability
Performance handicapped

Strephosymbolia
Congenital alexia
Congenital strephosymbolia
Bradylexia
Agraphia
Disgraphia
Acalculia
Dyscalculia
Tactual agnosia
Auditory agnosia
Visual agnosia
Sensory aphasia
Receptive aphasia
Expressive aphasia
Motor aphasia
Alexia
Specific language disability
Learning and language disability

Source: Medical Psychology and education literature, compiled by Faas, 1976.

early intervention during the preschool years could ameliorate or circumvent its effects.

A difficulty remains: we have few empirically validated assumptions on which to base further research. In addition, research is not a high priority in our society, and therefore funding to support such validation has been scarce. The future may be brighter, as the Bureau for the Education of the Handicapped has recently awarded to universities five grants specifically designated for research and curriculum development in *learning disabilities*. We must recognize, however, that our fund of knowledge is actually small while the demand for services is great. In the meantime, temptation to jump on remediation bandwagons is pervasive. In an effort to be innovative, or out of desperation, educators may be too easily tempted to spend time trying to train a skill that cannot be trained, using a device that cannot accomplish what it is intended to achieve, or developing an ability that cannot be transferred or generalized.

Definition

How a thing is defined determines diagnosis and treatment, which, in turn, also affect definition. This, of course, is circular definition. The definition for learning disabilities is no exception. Those who view LD as resulting from *neurological dysfunction* have attempted to identify *organic causes for learning disabilities*. Others, attending to the *uneven and inconsistent scatter of intelligence subtest scores,* have attributed LD to *"developmental lag."* Still others, concerned about the significant discrepancy between a learning-disability child's intellectual potential and actual level of performance, have labeled such children a "slow learner" group.

Out of this diversity, *Learning Disabilities* has been defined as follows:

> Children with learning disabilities exhibit a disorder in one or more of the basic psychological processes involved in understanding or using spoken or written languages. These may be manifested in disorders of listening, thinking, talking, reading, writing, spelling or arithmetic. They include conditions which have been referred to as perceptual handicaps, brain injury, minimal brain damage, dyslexia, developmental aphasia, etc. They do not include learning problems which are due primarily to visual, hearing, or motor handicaps, to mental retardation, severe emotional disturbance, or to environmental disadvantages."

Based on this definition, current estimates of the prevalence of LD in the general population indicate that from 1 to 30 percent of all children may be learning-disabled, but more conservative estimates hold with 1-3 percent to 7-8 percent. This lack of consensus reflects, to some extent, political concerns by professionals who recognize that if the incidence of LD is too high, it becomes a "regular education" problem and not a "special education" problem.

The above definition is still not satisfactory. To date, neither professionals in the field nor bureaucracy in the Office of Education have been able to suggest a really satisfactory working definition. There are some components, however, on which there is consensus: learning disability is manifest in a language-related problem (which includes the mental manipulation of symbols), and the *Principle of Disparity*. The latter merely means that the problem is unexpected; there is a significant difference between the child's estimated potential and the actual level of performance or achievement. Even this concept has its pitfalls when applied to children culturally different from the dominant social group or who come from economically-disadvantaged families. It should be noted here that learning disability and underachievement are not synonymous; remedial education and techniques to ameliorate learning disabilities are not the same.

CHARACTERISTICS OF LEARNING-DISABLED CHILDREN

As the above definition implies, and as mentioned earlier, LD is not a unitary phenomenon. The most frequently mentioned characteristics of learning-disabled children include the following:

- *Ability level:* near-average to average to above-average in ability
- *Activity level:*
  Hyperactive—constant motor activity; restless tapping of finger or foot; jumping out of seat; skipping from task to task, etc.
  Hypoactive—the opposite of hyperactivity; fail to react or seem to do everything in slow motion
- *Attention problems:* short attention span and easily distractible; unable to concentrate on any one task for very long; often perseverate; attention becomes fixed upon a single task which is repeated over and over: this may be motor or verbal activity
- *Motor problems:* generally clumsy or awkward, with poor, fine and gross motor coordination; poor tactile discrimination; excessive need to touch; poor writing and drawing performance
- *Visual Perceptual problems:* unable to distinguish between visual stimuli (visual discrimination), perceive a foreground figure against a background (visual figure-ground), fill in missing parts when only part of a word or object is seen (visual closure), or remember and revisualize images or sequences very well (visual memory)
- *Auditory Perceptual problems:* unable to distinguish between sounds (auditory discrimination), obtain meaning from the spoken word and/or environ-

mental sounds (auditory comprehension), attend to important auditory stimuli by pushing all other auditory stimuli into the background (auditory figure-ground), fill in missing sounds when only part of the word is heard (auditory closure), or remember auditory stimuli or sequences very well (auditory memory)

- *Language problems:* delayed or slow development of speech articulation; inability to organize words to form phrases, clauses, or sentences that follow standard English grammar
- *Social-Emotional Behavior problems:*
  impulsive: fail to think about consequences of behavior
  explosive: display rage reaction or throw tantrums when crossed
  lack social competence: often below average for age and ability
  unable to adjust to change: slower than others
  rapid mood variation, from hour to hour
- *Orientation problems:* poorly developed concepts of space, a distorted body image, trouble in judging distance and size, and difficulty in discriminating figures from ground, parts from the whole, and left from right (spatial organization); disoriented in time, experience trouble relating concepts like before and after, now and then, and today and tomorrow (temporal concepts).
- *Work Habits:* organize work poorly, work slowly, frequently confuse directions, or rush through work carelessly
- *Academic disabilities:* problems in reading, arithmetic, writing, spelling

No LD child, of course, is characterized by all these descriptors. A given child may have one or more such characteristics, but, unfortunately, there are enough of these to provide unique deficiencies for all learning-disabled children.

ORIGINS OF LEARNING DISABILITIES

It is uncertain what causes a learning disability; consequently, models have been constructed to attempt to explain the phenomenon. One such, the *physiological model,* holds that learning disabilities result from abnormalities in physical functioning, mostly due to neurological factors associated with pre- and post-natal development. The model is strongest in explaining "hyperactivity" because the data do indicate a relationship between hyperactive behavior and early birth/brain trauma.

Because this model assumes an organic basis for learning disability, it provides the rationale for chemotherapy: drugs (like Ritalin and Cylert) are used in treating learning-disabled children by adherents of the physiological model. Some chemotherapy advocates use mega-vitamin treatment, assuming that learning disabilities can result from dietary deficiencies and/or malnutrition: Adherents claim successful treatment of schizophrenia, childhood autism, the common cold, and learning disorders.

Another approach utilizes the *socioenvironmental model,* which focuses on the relatively worse academic and cognitive performance of lower-SES children. Research with humans and animals suggests a single (major) change in a child's early environment can result in severe deficits in

- visual-pattern discrimination
- visual acuity
- fine visual-motor coordination
- auditory-information processing
- impulse-activity control

Many children who have experienced such early environmental changes suffer from learning disabilities.

A secondary component of the *socioenvironmental model* is the *educational model,* which points, not to deficiencies in the child, but to variation or inadequacy in the school, such as poor teaching, poor curriculum, poor materials, or poor motivation. It is doubtful that this subcomponent is a legitimate explanation of learning disabilities.

The third, the *developmental model,* embraces the critical role of early experience and some aspects of the physiological model. As an example, consider Piaget's Cognitive-Developmental Theory, an exciting approach for psychologists and educators because it adds so much to the understanding of *how* children learn. To illustrate how this theory fits this last model, consider the reflex behaviors present at birth: grasp reflex, sucking reflex, rooting reflex, etc. Piaget contends these reflexes are primary mechanisms by which a child comes to "know" its world, serving as the basis for early child-environment interaction. Whatever physical/neurological flaws exist in the child will affect the quality of the learning that occurs through these interactions. Likewise, the quality of the child's environment will affect the quantity and quality of what is learned.

Further, according to Piagetian theory, intellectual development is viewed as an orderly progression through sequences of cognitive development, and inadequate or slow progress results in the child being at odds with his educational surroundings: expectations are inconsistent with the child's level of ability at that point in time. But when learning is viewed as a function of developmental level and not chronological age, then determination of levels becomes essential for the prescription of teaching approaches for all children.

These three models are generally used to explain the causes of learning disabilities. The most effective, in terms of remediation, appears to be the developmental model, because it facilitates development of strategies appropriate for educational settings.

CHILD DEVELOPMENT AND SYMPTOMS OF LEARNING DISABILITY

To find an operational commonality that differentiates the learning-disabled from other handicapped children, the *process approach* was developed. Advocates of this approach attempt to measure and train the child's information-processing or sensory-input systems, those that are assumed to scan, select, manipulate, and store information, and which control output or responding behavior. For several years many educators followed this process approach to remediate LD. Recent research now suggests this is a questionable approach, although the evidence may be reflecting more than the efficacy of process measurement and training. The measurement devices themselves may not be valid or precise enough to tap the purported abilities; the hypothesized abilities may not be discrete to the point that they can be isolated, assessed, and trained. Or human variability may be so great that measurement and training of process (or psycholinguistic) abilities are not predictable enough to be useful for diagnostic and programming purposes.

From a developmental viewpoint, there is evidence that children acquire skills in a fairly invariant order, and that many skills have hierarchical relationships to earlier-acquired abilities. However, there is a wide range among children both as far as age at which a given skill is achieved and the degree to which the skill is accomplished—a variability that confounds the diagnostic accuracies of assessment. There is also evidence that, on an individual basis, poorly developed skills can be enhanced through appropriate training. That is, a child's motor skills, attention, memory, speech, visual-auditory association and discrimination can be improved with opportunities to learn and time to practice. The question then remains whether a learning disability existed or merely a lack of opportunity to learn under appropriate conditions at a critical time. A teacher of young children must be knowledgeable about normal and abnormal growth patterns (physical and psychological) to make judgments about such issues and to develop appropriate programs.

Educators unfortunately tend to overgeneralize and to make decisions on inadequate evidence. A tendency exists, also, to treat as identical several concepts related to problems in learning: *developmental lag, difference, deficit,* and *defect.* The developmental mileposts (e.g. walking, speaking, "conserving," sharing) are not at the same distances in the growth pattern of all children. In addition, there can be intraindividual differences, where acquisition of a specific skill is inordinately delayed, frequently observed in the speech habits of little boys. Delay can also occur in the behaviors comprising psychological constructs or traits; these are much more difficult to identify and assess. An example of such a *developmental lag* would be the unexpected inability to relate sounds to a visual symbol despite the child's ability to understand spoken language and to discriminate among speech sounds in isolation.

Difference is most obvious in cultural attributes, including habits such as native language. An eight-year-old's inability to learn to read English is not a learning disability if he has just arrived from the Middle East (or Puerto Rico or Japan or Hungary) and has not yet learned to speak English. Differences occur also in learning style or modality preferences; these are problems only when opportunities to learn are so rigid or so method-specific they do not allow for individual differences (a term acknowledged but not incorporated into the curriculum of many public school systems).

A *deficit* is a shortage of a trait or ability—the child does not have enough to learn something dependent upon it. Again, an obvious example would be the visually-impaired (but not the blind) child, where sight exists, but not enough to learn to read print material without low-vision aids. With magnification, lighting devices, or large print materials (depending on the nature of the visual disability), the child can learn to read. Auditory discrimination may be a psychological condition analogous to sensory deficit. The child is not hard of hearing, but cannot differentiate among sounds that resemble each other. The child had no trouble learning to understand spoken language, because clues from context and the environment aided him, but when learning to read, there were arbitrary and absolute relationships between visual and auditory symbols. When these are presented in isolation, the child cannot tell the difference between /i/ and /e/, between /p/ and /b/; when provided with earphones and linguistic devices allowing the child to attend to the sounds without extraneous noise and practice discriminating between them and among others, the skills can be developed. Two assumptions must exist; first, his developmental level (readiness) is appropriate for acquisition of the skill, and second, a basic ability exists to a degree, however limited.

A *defect* is a fault or imperfection, such that the ability does not exist or cannot exist at all. If a child is deaf (no hearing), all the amplification possible will not allow him to hear; if a child is blind (totally, not legally), all the magnification aids invented will not help him to see. A learning disability resulting from an injury to a critical area of the central nervous system is a defect. If a child cannot control leg movements because of a lesion or damaged neural tissue in brain motor areas (cerebral palsy), that control cannot be restored by training. Current knowledge and techniques still do not include rejuvenating neural tissue in human beings. Provision of leg braces and crutches, and instruction in walking with these supports are the available methods. The same is true for *Specific Learning Disability,* an irremediable condition, if due to some organic damage. Learning disabilities cannot be cured, but many alternative strategies (e.g., for learning to read or to express thoughts in writing) to help the child achieve established goals are available. The brain is remarkably adaptive, and the child with severe problems can use compensatory skills to acquire objectives. These tend, however, to take much longer to learn, and the child rarely achieves the facility in the skill that a normally-learning child does.

Differences among the four types of problems are much easier to identify in physiological than in psychological problems. In fact, it is rarely possible to identify the brain damage to which a learning disability is attributable. The evolution of the term *Minimal Cerebral Dysfunction* (which has no educational implications) is a direct result of this phenomenon. In those few instances when a causal relationship between brain injury has been established, it has not been helpful in establishing the most advantageous educational intervention. Human variability is so great that a program successful with one child can be totally ineffective with another with identical symptoms and with comparable characteristics. With younger children, the dilemma is compounded: growth and development changes are rapid during the early years, and available measurement devices are often least reliable with preschoolers, since they rely heavily on the perceptual and motor systems, and at times inappropriate generalizations to other systems are made. In addition, since the existence or nonexistence of psychological traits must be inferred from the young child's behavior (which is not always consistent), it cannot be certain that what is observed represents the child's true *capability* or just chance performance. Internal activity, which results in conceptualization, thinking and knowing, and which probably is influenced by affective features, is always inferred from the child's overt behavior. If the child's response or behavior is affected by a lack of understanding of what is expected, performance may not be a true measure of capability.

Among misconceptions held by earlier proponents of programs for learning-disabled children was the notion that cognitive development was somehow rooted in motor learning, and that perceptual systems and higher intellectual performance both grew out of motor experiences. It followed, then, that if a child was not organized motorically and neurologically, it could not develop cognitively to optimum levels. Research has not conclusively demonstrated that even fine motor, much less cognitive, skills are dependent on gross motor activity. If this were true, congenital paraplegics would not be able to develop symbolic thinking. The authors accept Cratty's position that movement "is not the imperative base from which all cognitive, perceptual, auditory, emotional and social attributes must necessarily spring (1969, p. 9)." If there is a relationship among these abilities, it is most certainly not a causal one. Young children, however, should be encouraged, for their own sakes, to participate in exploratory play, to help them become more coordinated, integrated, and efficient human beings.

Motor activities are quite observable; perceptual abilities are not. Perception occurs in the brain, so once again we must rely on overt behavior to make judgments about internal activity. While in most children, the perceptual systems appear to be completely developed by ages 7½ to 8, there is again variability among children; the systems apparently paralleling mental age. Young children (under age five) are less sensitive to perceptual features; if such skills are not developed by the time they are expected to learn to read, activities such as tracing must be provided to help them learn. Preschool opportunities to manipulate objects and to develop perceptual abilities will probably reduce the number of children with these problems in the primary grades. (There is evidence that for most children perceptual training after age eight is not productive.) Contributions of linguists and cognitive psychologists now facilitate evaluation of the *quality* of a young child's language; only a few years ago we were limited to essentially quantitative measures combined with speech skills. Many difficulties persist, however, in distinguishing between language delay and language disability. For the teacher, the provision of many opportunities to practice receptive and expressive language is the most important consideration.

Research in learning disabilities in young children yields contradictory evidence concerning occurrence of change. Despite the proliferation of such programs as those intended to enhance visual-perception skills in kindergarten children, most of them provided too little training using unvalidated materials and unreliable criterion measures. Single-subject research such as some recent studies reported in the *Journal for Applied Behavior Analysis* are more encouraging.

IDENTIFICATION, ASSESSMENT, AND EVALUATION

A primary argument for early identification of learning disorders is the possibility for intervention during optimal periods, before the disability permanently affects performance and self-image. Unfortunately, most of the more subtle handicaps remain undiagnosed until the child is of school age.

Early diagnosis itself involves some risk of making two types of errors: false positives and false negatives. Measurement devices are not yet refined to the point where we can have total confidence in the results of assessing an individual child. Thus, learning problems are identified when none exists, and often existing disabilities are not discovered.

The inadequacies of tests are most striking in those designed to tap traits during the sensorimotor and preoperational periods. The failure of measurement devices to identify psychological or learning disorders during infancy was demonstrated by Werner (1971), who examined the records of 1,000 children: of 21 children with less overt congenital defects, only 5 were recorded at birth. Physicians generally are effective in identifying severely handicapped children and those with physical defects, but do not (nor should they be expected to) recognize developmental and cognitive disorders as a rule. A growing body of evidence supports the concern that conventional methods of identification are ineffective for discovering learning disabilities.

There are dangers, too, in the screening practices of programs such as *Child Find,* in which there is always the possibility of stigmatizing as handicapped those youngsters whose problems are in fact remediable. Worse, these screening practices miss the subtle but developmentally important handicaps. Screening is most successful when applied to *all* children in a community, not only to those suspected of having learning disorders.

If screening, then, is potentially insidious and often ineffective, the responsibility for early identification of the more covert psychological disorders must be the teacher's. Fortunately, the authors of PL 94-142 recognized the need to provide services for children aged three to five years; unfortunately, the age limits for this priority group were not extended downward even further. If children are observed continuously, patterns of behavior emerge and unusual evidence or warning signals are much more easily discerned. Even more important, experiences that satisfy the developmental needs of the child can be programmed, which, in turn, may prevent some problems and reduce the diagnosis of deviance.

Even under ideal conditions, however, teachers must be trained to differentiate among developmental lag, mental retardation, and specific learning disability. They must learn the skills of astute observation combined with knowledge of normal and abnormal development rather than trying merely to become experts in administering batteries of tests. However, appropriate assessment devices are available to help the teacher determine the child's strengths and weaknesses and, when an unexpected deviancy occurs, alert us to the possibility of a learning disability. Teacher assessment may serve also to corroborate or refute the results of formal tests administered by other professional persons, and can reduce redundancy of other batteries of tests. Time is important, for young children change rapidly; if months (or even weeks) elapse while waiting for evaluations by others, programming specifically for the child tends to cease. The child cannot afford such wasted time.

The hazards of standardized tests have been alluded to earlier. Those given during early childhood years are not good predictors of later performance. When discussing the use of the Scales she designed, Bayley (1971) wrote, ". . . the observed fluctuations in the scores of individual children indicate the need for utmost caution in the predictive use of a single test score, or even two such scores." In addition, there are *too many tests,* many of them unacceptable for individual programming. Except when knowledgeable in interpreting reliability and validity data (which sometimes are not provided by the test publisher or author), the teacher may not be able to evaluate critically a test nor distinguish between poor tests and good tests (there are fewer of the latter). Teachers must learn everything possible about a test—its validity (does it measure what it purports to measure and is it valid for the particular child?). There must be reliability coefficients that satisfy requirements for decision making. If there are subtests, each must be consistent so that it can be assumed to reflect a true score for *that* child. There are surprising fluctuations in test reliability across age groups, so the coefficients must be checked to warrant confidence in diagnostic usefulness. In addition, test results must be checked against daily performance: If a child has no problems in remembering auditory information (days of the week, alphabet song) yet scored low on the ITPA digit-span subtest, chances are better that he does *not* have an auditory memory disability—the ITPA Auditory Sequential Memory subtest was merely *not* a true reflection of this child's ability. A great danger in using formal tests is overgeneralizing from scores while not attending to contrary evidence in the child's daily behavior.

Many books and references can assist in determining what tests to use. The appendices in this book are one. Chapter 2 of Hare and Hare, *Teaching young handicapped children* (1977), contains annotations to many of the diagnostic and assessment tests. Other sources include Buros' *Seventh mental measurements yearbook* (1972), Hoepfner, et al. (Eds.) CSE-ERC *Preschool/Kindergarten test evaluations* (1971), and Walker's *Socioemotional measures for preschool and kindergarten children* (1973).

A good teacher makes use of informal evaluation. Prescriptive or clinical teaching employs various kinds of informal assessment (check lists, inventories, criterion-referenced tests, other teacher-made devices). Combined with data from daily observations (how the child manages his body on the jungle gym, how he attends to verbal directions, his preference for using one hand rather than the other) this information can provide specific programming guidelines.

BOX 9-2: STEPS IN IDENTIFYING AND ASSESSING LD

The Interview

The interview or case history is important because it provides birth, health, and developmental information pertinent to diagnosis. Interviews may be conducted by educators, psychologists, or medical personnel, using a standard format which insures that all relevant information is collected. (See the appendix for samples.) Interviews may be conducted in a variety of settings such as the child's home, school, or doctor's office.

Observation

Careful and systematic observation of the child often provides helpful diagnostic clues. For example, how does the child deal with unfamiliar words? Is the child's behavior specific to one situation or does it cut across all areas of classroom activity? How does the child react to change? Who are his friends? How well does the child follow directions?

Testing

Testing can be both informal and formal:
Informal tests provide easily obtained data useful in supporting requests for

---

diagnostic help. These may include prepackaged materials providing information on social behavior, reading, etc., or designed by the teacher for assessment of a child's functioning level.

Formal testing is usually conducted by school psychologists, clinical psychologists, or trained psychometricians, and consists of:

- *intelligence testing,* using an individually-administered test such as the Stanford-Binet or the WISC (this provides a measure of general intellectual functioning)
- *achievement testing,* which enables assessment of the child's cognitive performance in relation to his or her peers
- *specific tests for learning disabilities* (since there are many types of learning disabilities, tests for specific types of learning disabilities can be misleading unless the individual doing the testing interpretation considers the diversity of learning disabilities and the possibility that strong points can mask weak points)

The Wechsler Preschool and Primary Scale of Intelligence (WPPSI) and the Wechsler Intelligence Scale for Children (WISC-R) are individually administered tests consisting of verbal and performance measures.

Verbal tests measure:

1. General Information: determined by
   a. knowledge gained from experience and education
   b. alertness to surrounding world
   c. social awareness
   d. associative thinking
2. General Comprehension: determined by
   a. common sense
   b. social judgment
   c. cultural background
   d. practical knowledge
   e. reasoning
3. Arithmetic: requires
   a. mental alertness
   b. arithmetic reasoning
   c. concentration of attention
   d. visualization
   e. auditory memory
4. Knowledge of Similarities: requires
   a. logical thinking

    b. abstract thinking

    c. concepts

5. Vocabulary: determined by

    a. word knowledge gained from experience and schooling

    b. fund of information

6. Digit Span: requires

    a. attention and concentration

    b. memory

    c. auditory perception

Performance tests include:

1. Picture Completion: requires

    a. visual alertness

    b. visual memory

    c. recognition of details

    d. conceptual abilities

    e. perceptual abilities

2. Picture Arrangement: assesses

    a. interpretation and social situation

    b. social intelligence

    c. attention to details

3. Block Design: measures

    a. ability to perceive patterns

    b. ability to analyze whole parts

    c. ability to synthesize the parts

    d. visual-motor coordination

    e. abstract thinking

    f. ability to plan and organize

4. Object Assembly: requires

    a. putting together simple puzzles

    b. perception of the whole and relation of the parts

    c. visual-motor coordination

    d. spatial relationships

5. Coding: measures

    a. visual perception

    b. speed of learning and writing symbols

    c. manual of dexterity

6. Mazes: assess

    a. ability to work mazes

    b. eye-hand coordination

Many learning-disabled children show a great deal of scatter in performance across the different subtests. This scatter is important to analyze because looking at only final verbal and performance scores can be misleading if strong points in one area successfully mask or compensate for weak points in others.

There are three general patterns of atypical WISC Performance:

(1) a. scatter in either or both verbal and performance scales
   b. low scores (relative to others) in Arithmetic, Block Design, Object Assembly, Digit Span, Coding and Mazes
   c. final verbal and performance IQs are nearly equal
(2) verbal IQ is from 15-40 points higher than performance IQ, and the difference can be even more pronounced if arithmetic score is dropped
(3) performance IQ is 10-30 points higher than verbal IQ, probably indicating a dyslexic condition

While these characteristic patterns exist for some learning-disabled children, they do not exist for others, probably because of the diversity of the phenomena and the variety of their manifestations.

Other frequently used intelligence tests are:

Stanford-Binet
Slosson Intelligence Test for Children and Adults
Peabody Picture Vocabulary Test

Specific intellectual, perceptual, and cognitive factors can be analyzed by a variety of tests:

• Illinois Test of Psycholinguistic Abilities — attempts to measure certain perceptual and cognitive aspects related to intellectual development
• Detroit Test of Learning Aptitude — provides scores in 19 areas of mental functioning
• The Bender Visual-Motor Gestalt Test
• The Developmental Test of Visual-Motor Integration
• The Frostig Developmental Test of Visual Perception
• The Wepman Test of Auditory Discrimination

Some suggested reading tests:

• Gates-McKillop Reading Diagnostic Tests
• Durrell Analysis of Reading Difficulty
• Woodcock Reading Mastery Scales

Achievement is frequently assessed by:

• Iowa Test for Basic Skills
• California Achievement Tests

- Metropolitan Achievement Tests
- Standard Achievement Tests
- Wide Range Achievement Tests

Motor tests include:

- Heath Railwalking Test
- Purdue Perceptual Motor Survey
- Southern California Perceptual-Motor Tests

And other specific assessment areas include:

- receptive and expressive speech
- social maturity
- visual and auditory acuity

Since learning disabilities are manifested in so many ways, it is not possible to recommend a specific battery of tests. Generally, assessment should include the three components of formal testing mentioned earlier: an individualized intelligence test, a measure of achievement or cognitive functioning, and specific tests. These specific tests will be determined by the child's presenting behavior and refined by the testing process.

Such information lessens the need to label the child according to a non-educationally-relevant classification. If programming is based on experiential needs (e.g., manipulative puzzles, toys to enhance visual-motor integration, grasp techniques), a label describing them as perceptually impaired or having fine motor disabilities is not necessary. A label denoting categorical disability for funding purposes may continue to be necessary; however, dependence upon such descriptors for programming purposes is often unwarranted. In many states, funding for LD children is compounded by other factors. Some agencies do not recognize learning disability as a handicapping condition; the children must be diagnosed as brain-injured or MCD by a neurologist. Therefore, assessment and classification may be influenced by political or organizational realities that are local-specific. Generally, if classifying or labeling a child is not going to lead to positive results *for the child* it should be avoided.

A common truism supports prevention rather than remediation. The degree to which SLD can be prevented is questionable, unless central nervous system injury during the pre-, and peri- and postnatal periods can be eliminated. However, these cases probably represent a very small percentage of the causes of learning disorders in children. Those that are environmental in nature, including inappropriate and inadequate early experiences, surely can be reduced or ameliorated by stimulation and good nutritional and medical care. Meier reported that upon analyzing existing intervention systems for developmentally learning-disabled children, several shortcomings became evident:

1. a preventive approach is rarely taken; when it is, it is at an age too late to be most effective
2. treatment is initiated after the handicap has severely disabled the child, and secondary complications have arisen
3. treatment focuses on only one aspect of the multiple problems presented, and the attempts to alleviate one symptom before others are attacked often result in incomplete or unsatisfactory results (1976, p. 154)

Primary prevention impinges on issues that lead into moral and political debate. An example is the furor over the establishment of day-care centers in economically-depressed areas, intended to free welfare mothers so they could hold jobs. Despite the obvious inability of some mothers to provide adequate nutrition and experiences for their children, the right of parents to rear their offspring according to their own value systems was a very powerful argument used to delay and reduce subsidies for such programs.

Two assumptions formerly accepted have been discredited, pointing the way to encouraging early intervention to prevent later problems. The first assumption — "fixed intelligence" — was that deprivation of experience can cause marked retardation in intellectual development. Head Start findings support the notion that IQs can and do change when children are offered opportunity to learn. The second assumption was that of predetermined development, originally proposed by G. Stanley Hall. Evidence now exists that development is a function of intra- and extraindividual factors; that is, the level of functioning is determined by the interaction of genetic inheritance and the environment and experiences the individual encounters. It follows, then, that problems resulting from deprivation, whether experiential, nutritional, or medical, may be reduced by providing optimal experiences, good food, and medical care.

PROBLEMS IN COGNITIVE DEVELOPMENT

In their review of research on cognition, Gray and Miller (1967) suggested that early experience has four dimensions: its nature, its time within the developmental period, duration, and intensity. Further, each dimension may differentially affect cognitive development, and intervention should consider these dimensions in terms of the child's present levels of functioning.

If one accepts a model based on Piaget's theory, sensorimotor behaviors provide information about the young child's intelligence level. The pre-operational period, too, suggests connotations that will influence the nature, timing, and intensity of activities for preschoolers. Apart from these general levels of intellectual development, teachers of learning-disabled children should consider that LD children, in addition to other specific weaknesses, appear to have *organizational* problems. This difficulty in classifying and categorizing objects may in turn explain problems in memory, and suggests that preschoolers must have experiences that will develop storage, maintenance, and retrieval skills. Multisensory techniques coupled with use of language to support sensory inputs are most effective, and the teacher must plan sorting and concept-learning activities to assist the child to learn.

Mentally-retarded children often demonstrate similar problems in organization, but their behavior is characterized by generalized delayed functioning. What signals a possible learning disorder is the unexpected disability. The retarded child tends to accomplish motor (sitting, walking), perceptual (hand-eye coordination, auditory discrimination), language and social skills later than would be expected. The learning-disabled child, on the other hand, demonstrates an unexpected problem while other indicators of development appear to be normal. A developmental lag results in postponement of acquisition of a single trait, or related clusters of skills; however, given minimal stimulation, the child does acquire it as he matures. If a child does not outgrow a problem (and many do not), he may have a learning disability (timing is of the utmost importance). The child who fails to learn for lack of opportunity will respond to appropriate intervention, that is, problems are remediable if motivation and cultural factors are considered. The learning-disabled child cannot learn despite optimal conditions unless the program is adjusted to account for intraindividual differences.

Intelligence, regardless of how conceptualized or defined, is probably a multi-trait phenomenon. All experiences, then, conceivably contribute to intellectual functioning, which responds to the child's interactions with the social and physical environment. Indeed, the *people* in the child's world and personal interactions may be the most critical aspect of early experiences (Carew, 1976).

Optimal cognitive development requires a wide range of experiences. Thus, learning-disabled children require adjustments to the curriculum and specifically designed activities in order to learn. These activities, in addition to inculcating concepts and skills of reasoning (classification, categorization and seriation), should lead to critical thinking skills, and even at the preschool level can include recognizing absurdities, seeing relationships, making inferences, and predicting outcomes. Learning-disabled children can learn such skills, but they usually need a highly structured environment in which to do so.

PROBLEMS IN MOTOR AND PERCEPTUAL DEVELOPMENT

Sensory systems provide information from the environment. If this information is misinterpreted by the brain, we assume something wrong with the way we *perceive* objects. Perception, a developmental phenomenon, is dependent on learning, acquired during a fairly short period (mostly before the child enters school), and based on opportunities to interact with the environment, both with objects and persons.

Recent research emphasizes the importance of the *integration* of information from all the senses — particularly relevant for learning-disabled children. Constantly bombarded by stimulation of the sense organs, we learn through scanning, selecting, and manipulating these inputs. Experience in manipulating objects and interacting with others does not appear sufficient to help LD children organize received information. As a result, they often cannot remember some things children need to know to succeed even in the primary grades: names of colors, letters of the alphabet, numbers up to ten. Often, they have difficulty attending long enough to develop consistent patterns of learning behavior; it seems as if each sensory system is sending *conflicting* information, and the child's mind jumps from one set of signals to another. Attempting to absorb everything, the child receives a jumble of unintegrated, incoherent information.

It is hypothesized that when information about the world is not integrated, concepts of spatial relationships (including those of the body and its position in space) are affected. Making judgments of distance, speed, and movement are dependent on accurate perceptions of the environment. Equally important is understanding concepts such as *under, above, next to,* and *behind.* Therefore, basic perceptual-motor competency is necessary for the development of many skills. While other children learn these concepts merely through interacting with objects and events, a learning-disabled child often must be taught concepts deliberately for his own sake, not for some assumed relationship to symbolic language skills.

Organicity, often used when referring to learning-disabled children, refers to impairment of the central nervous system, primarily the brain. When demonstrable, as in some cases of cerebral palsy, the effects on the child are clear. It is assumed that brain injury is responsible for some instances of poor coordination of gross or fine muscle movement, for poor ability to plan and execute a motor task (kicking a ball that is rolled toward the child), inability to inhibit movement, impaired sensory discrimination ability, poor understanding of language, inability to track objects with the eyes. and inability to recall familiar objects or events. Even with expert neurological examination, clear evidence of a causal relationship between damage to the brain and such symptoms is rarely possible. As a result, the speculation of organic involvement and the search for causes "within the child" are generally of limited benefit. Even if such damage could be documented, it does not help very much simply to know what is wrong and why. Ultimately, the child's teachers and parents must find ways to help the child learn, and a neurologist cannot be expected to contribute very much to this challenge.

Measurement of perception, since it is a function of the brain, is always confounded by possible problems in the response mechanisms. That is, since perception is not directly observable, we must infer perceptual abilities from behavioral responses to sensory stimulation. Since the skills are developmental, interindividual differences may vary both as a function of the child's maturation patterns and experiences. Further, most tests of perception, in addition to being contaminated by motor factors, assume they are testing discrete and autonomous abilities (despite evidence that the *integration* of inputs is most likely of great importance). While visual perception would appear to be critical for learning to read, it does not correlate highly with successful reading achievement beyond the first-grade levels; auditory skills are at least as important for acquiring initial code-breaking skills. But neither is as necessary as the ability to *associate* visual and auditory symbols. Many of the tests that purport to measure readiness for school place unusual demands on young children. For example, the ability to draw a diagonal line is often not achieved until age seven. Yet we often expect preschoolers to learn to print a capital letter A. In fact, many paper-and-pencil tests are very difficult physiologically and perceptually for preschool children. If the child has a problem which delays such learning, expectations of performance may compound his difficulties.

PROBLEMS IN LANGUAGE DEVELOPMENT

A specific learning disability invariably affects one or more aspects of language. The disorder very likely is manifest in the child's ability to interpret or understand spoken words, to express verbally with fluency and correct articulation, to interpret or understand written language (reading, for example), or to spell or to express thoughts in writing. Since language skills are generally considered hierarchical, problems in listening and talking are usually followed by difficulties in learning to read and write. Therefore, it is particularly important to help the child learn auditory-verbal language skills during the preschool years.

Language development is a complicated process, thought to be related to cognitive development itself. Psychologists often rely on the vocabulary and general language behavior as an indicator of IQ. Since the child is an information processor at birth, it suggests that thought processes occur before speech. Most children, within a very short time and without deliberate teaching, learn to use language purposefully, to express thought, and to communicate.

Despite their interrelationships, verbal language can be conceptualized as involving three processes: inner, receptive, and expressive. *Inner language,* what we refer to as *thinking,* involves processing information during the prespeech period. A learning-disabled child may have a disorder at this level, but it is difficult to diagnose; we are dependent upon the child's responses to language he hears and upon the verbal language he initiates. If the child does not respond to spoken words, but seems to depend on visual clues or gestures before acting, he may have a disability in *receptive* language. First, we must determine the status of auditory acuity—can the child hear? If the sense organ is intact and there is no hearing loss, specifically designed training in receptive language skills is in order.

Some children have difficulty with *expressive* or *spoken language:* even if reception is adequate, language delay is not uncommon. However, there are children whose spoken language disorder does not develop even after maturational factors are accounted for. In addition to modeled language and appropriate learning experiences, these youngsters may need further highly structured training. Language acquisition is systematic and the stages appear to be invariant; therefore, careful assessment of language skills should determine the direction for programming. An interdisciplinary approach is most beneficial, with input from audiologists and language therapists usually critical.

Children sometimes exhibit behaviors that signal a problem—possibly a learning disability or language delay. Among the clues are (1) not responding to questions unless gestural cues accompany verbalizations, (2) verbal responses are not "on target" (answers "just don't make sense"), (3) a need to search for words so utterances are arhythmical or syntax is inappropriate. At times the child seems slow in comprehending verbal language, yet all other indicators suggest normal cognitive ability.

An important first step for all children who appear to have problems in language, whether learning disability, language delay, or mental retardation is suspected, is a complete audiometric examination. Deafness and hearing losses actually account for a larger number of learning disorders than are identified, and if not diagnosed during the critical years for language acquisition, the skills usually acquired during this period are achieved only with much difficulty, if at all.

A serious language problem is *aphasia*. Originally meaning *loss of language,* the term was applied to adults who had learned language skills but lost them because of some traumatic event, such as stroke or accident. Aphasia received special attention when American soldiers in World War I returned after "shell shock" and exhibited language losses. Physicians, noting similar behaviors in children who never acquired speech, began to refer to "childhood aphasia." Quite frequently used (or misused) to describe receptive and expressive language problems, the term (like minimal cerebral dysfunction) has no intrinsic educational significance, and teachers should have little need to use it. A child with aphasia soon becomes *aphasic,* and decisions made for the child then become biased. It is preferable to suggest the child has a problem in verbal expression, and, with appropriate intervention, expect it to be ameliorated.

Various scales and tests to measure language abilities have been introduced. In the past, items for young children have been those intended to evaluate labeling ability, spontaneous language in a structured situation, and *quantity* of words in utterances. During the past decade, other devices have been introduced, directed to the child's use of syntax and his knowledge of language structure. Most tests present limited (or no) data on their validity or reliability.

Several tests for specific skills, such as Carrow's *Test for Auditory Comprehension of Language,* are available. Some scales designed to measure early development include an assessment of language as *The Portage Guide to Early*

Education. If such devices are used, acceptance of the scores should be weighed against standardization data, the correspondence between test results and everyday performance, and consideration of the reason the test was used for the specific child in question. Unless the results have direct implication for programming or for the delivery of services not otherwise obtainable, sole reliance on test scores is not recommended.

The clinical judgment of persons trained to use formal tests, who use such information to arrive at recommendations, and who offer them within the context of a Child Development or Interdisciplinary Team can be very useful. Decisions affecting the lives of young children must be based on judgments reflecting many factors—not on test scores alone. This applies particularly to language-related abilities, where our knowledge is still sparse. Since much research is now directed to linguistics and language acquisition, we can be more optimistic about the future.

LEARNING DISORDERS AND BEHAVIOR PROBLEMS

Most classroom teachers have at least two continua for tolerance: one for deviance in achievement, and one for deviance in behavior, the latter having a much shorter range. In fact, the child with a learning problem is often not referred for help until there is a wide discrepancy between performance and expectation, unless behavior in a group becomes unmanageable. Brain-injured children were excluded from school not for academic reasons, but because hyperactivity and distractibleness disrupted a regular classroom. Such behavior has excluded normal children from kindergarten unless given tranquilizers—a black mark on education's record indeed!

Children with learning problems frequently develop behavior problems as well, and the cyclical dilemma worsens: is the child's learning difficulty causing an emotional problem, or is the child disturbed because he can't learn? "Mildly" handicapped children often do not manifest these conditions until they are in school; children with a specific learning disability usually reveal them during preschool years.

A problem with an organic base frequently is manifest in driven, out-of-control *hyperactivity*—not because all hyperactive children are brain-injured, but because there is wide variation among individuals. *Degree* of over-activity itself, and to which it affects other behaviors (including developmental status) is important. Five-year-old children are active organisms, and a key to when their activity becomes "too much" is the child's ability to control movement. The driven child, who cannot "put on the brakes" is often the child who demonstrates other symptoms of learning disability (unpredictable behavior, unresponsiveness to correction and discipline, high distractibility, inability to concentrate on a single toy or activity for more than a few seconds, and destructiveness).

There are researchers who feel that even these negative behaviors are a function of environment, and not inherent or disease-induced. Battle and Lacey attribute many behaviors, including hyperactivity, to reinforcement history. "The reactions and reinforcement he receives from peers, parents, and other adults may result in the kind of negative behaviors (aggression, defiance, discipline problems) which have been observed in clinical samples (1972, p. 758)."

Despite the recognized difficulties in managing hyperactive children, the most significant thing for the teacher to know is that hyperactivity is not a symptom of learning disability. While LD children are often described as hyperactive (many hyperactive children do indeed have learning problems in school), there is no unequivocal evidence that hyperactivity results in learning disability or that learning disabilities make a child hyperactive. "It is likely that true learning disabilities . . . are only related to hyperactivity by virtue of the fact that the learning disabled child who is also hyperactive is more likely to be referred for study than will be the child who, though learning disabled, sits quietly in his seat (Ross, 1976, p. 95)."

Children react to frustration differently from adults. The latter learn to express it in socially acceptable ways, including physical symptoms. Young children tend to be more direct, and display frustration by screaming, kicking, or throwing objects or themselves to the ground. When this behavior is reinforced, it persists. Obviously, tantrums are hard to ignore. When the young child exhibits such behavior in a classroom, he endangers other children. When the habits are not extinguished, and the child continues to attack others and to display aggressive and hostile behaviors, he is frequently seen as disturbed, as well as a behavior problem. Therefore, teachers of preschoolers must reduce opportunities for tantrums, ignoring (only to the degree possible without harmful effects on the child or others present) such aggressive behavior when it does occur, and reinforcing acceptable and desired behaviors. Useful techniques include careful planning of activities, eliminating those that tend to lead to frustration or conflict until the child learns to control his own behavior, and providing modes of expression. Since learning-disabled children often have difficulty learning social codes, deliberate teaching of such behavior is often necessary and fruitful.

Helping the child to learn *self control* is an important, even critical, part of the teacher's role. Here, behavioral approach is far preferable to dependence on other agents, such as drugs, for several reasons. Of reported research on use of drugs to control hyperactive behavior, none demonstrates unequivocally the effectiveness of amphetamines or tranquilizers. On the contrary, even after observing the paradoxical inverse effect of the amphetamines on the immature organism, most of the studies report that the drugs help some children, have no effect on others, and show deleterious results on a third group. Despite serious methodological problems in such studies (e.g., identification of a population based on reliable criteria), it is difficult to nourish the idea that acceptable research can be done.

Clearly, potent and dangerous drugs are given to young children to control their behavior. Dexedrine, which has been administered in great quantities to 5-year-olds, when taken as a pep pill by a 15-year-old, is illegal. Evidence shows these drugs are harmful to young children, suppressing growth and weight (Safer, Allen and Barr, 1972), and causing listlessness, loss of appetite, stomach cramps, and psychotic episodes (Greenspoon and Singer, 1973). The positive effect on learning by these drugs is dubious; at best they appear to enhance ability to stay on task and to perform rote-type learning, with no evidence they actually increase intelligence. Our concern, in addition to the dangerous side effects and the potential for addiction, is that the child is denied the opportunity to learn to control his behavior. Applied behavior analysis techniques have been successfully used on individual and classroom management bases, and are certainly recommended to the teacher. The responsibility for learning is that of education; educators should not and need not rely on drugs to bring about desired learning, including skills of behavior and self-control.

APPROACHES TO AMELIORATION AND REMEDIATION

Reviewing her work as a researcher and a teacher of learning-disabled children, Douglas wrote, "I have become convinced that the fundamental cause of their maladaptive behavior lies in their inability to focus, sustain, and organize attention, and to inhibit impulsive responding (1972)." With this as a guide, teachers of preschool learning-disabled children, should provide opportunities to learn the skills necessary to focus attention, stay on task, and to develop impulse control. Of course, these must be acquired in a way and to a degree consistent with developmental level.

While it may not be possible to "cure" specific learning disabilities, techniques to circumvent their effects have been developed. Basing their notion on Luria's hypothesis that a child learns to develop behavioral control through internalized verbal commands, Meichenbaum and Goodman (1971) trained impulsive children to develop self-control by talking to themselves. The researchers maintain that in the earliest years, the speech of caretakers is primarily responsible for directing the child's behavior. Gradually, the child's own inner language assumes a regulatory role. If impulsive children fail to develop this covert self-control, they must learn by recapitulating its development, deliberately and overtly (and later covertly) verbalizing directions.

Increasing attending behavior is unquestionably a goal for many learning-disordered children, whether the problem is specific learning disability or any other type of learning problem. O'Leary and O'Leary (1972) furnish examples of successful use of behavioral principles. As the child learns to attend to critical stimuli and receives reinforcement for desired behavior, the incidence of maladaptive behavior (which is inconsistent) also decreases.

During preschool years, when evidence of learning disabilities is generally clouded by unclear criteria and less-than-satisfactory measurement devices, a positive approach to preventing school failure is recommended. High priority probably should be given to curricula that include opportunities to learn to attend to critical aspects of the environment, organize information, develop systems to monitor and control one's behavior, and acquire the concepts and language necessary for school success.

Programs designed to enhance skills in these areas have been successful and warrant replication. Recent preschool programs were primarily designed as compensatory programs (they emphasized skills to permit economically disadvantaged preschoolers to "catch up" to their middle class peers at school entrance). The advantage of these programs (e.g., the Bereiter-Engelmann Program and its successor, the Oregon Direct Instruction Model of Engelmann and Becker) for *some* learning-disabled children was their tendency to be highly structured.

The High/Scope Cognitively Oriented Preschool Curriculum, based on Piagetian concepts of development, grew out of the Perry Preschool Project at Ypsilanti, Michigan. The Perry School attendance area had a history of low academic achievement. Selecting a population of three-year-olds from the neighborhood's low SES group, Weikart operated a preschool from 1962 to 1967, and followed successive groups of the children who attended through high school. The children attended the preschool for two years, and experienced activities specifically designed to enhance cognitive development. The curriculum is described in *A Cognitively Oriented Curriculum* by Weikart, Rogers, Adcock, and McClelland (1971). Longitudinal data, reported in the research report (1977), suggest the program had lasting effects on the reading, language, and arithmetic achievement of disadvantaged children as measured by standardized tests. The program has been adapted for use with an integrated (handicapped and non-handicapped children) classroom and has been effective with motor- and language-impaired children. Demonstration preschool teachers plan specifically for each handicapped child and support the child to maximize the degree to which he can profit from both the regular classroom experiences and individualized activities.

The above programs, each based on different theoretical frameworks, present activities that emphasize the learning of preschoolers with cognitive development problems. They are representative of a large number of programs, some of which are funded by the Bureau for the Education of the Handicapped. Although demonstration projects such as these have shown that educational stimulation of three- and four-year-olds appears to enhance intellectual development, there has been no systematic external evaluation to determine the most successful approaches for children with specific problems. Probably this is impossible to ascertain; however, we assume that specific learning disability and developmental retardation can be prevented in children at risk for socioeconomic, cultural, or organic reasons. To validate this premise, there must be systematic evaluation of early intervention programs to develop activities and materials with demonstrated efficiency. To date these do not exist.

To accommodate children with perceptual and motor problems, it is important to adapt the preschool classroom so as to encourage appropriate activities. Since the physical space provides the environment for the learning that is to take place, it must facilitate and support both structural and exploratory movement. Equipment must be accessible and "childproofed" for activities such as sand and water play, wheel toys, and movement exercises. The outdoor playground is an extension of the classroom and should be considered as such. For children who have not developed skills of balance, coordination, and agility, the playground is of primary importance.

The classroom can serve as a stimulating environment for remediating language-acquisition problems. Some problems in reception are related to attending difficulties. Although there is evidence that understanding familiar language is not impeded by noise interference, unfamiliar sounds are not distinguished by young children in the same setting. Language therapists, who work with language-delayed and learning-disabled children, usually have only limited time they can spend with individual children. The preschool teacher, working with the therapist and providing specific, language-rich experiences to support the therapy, will invariably accelerate children's progress.

In addition to its physical surroundings, the manner in which the classroom is managed is critical. Of all professionals, the teacher is the specialist and the decision-maker in classroom management. Learning-disabled children in particular need structure—a framework providing security and predictable consequences. The teacher must be consistent in reinforcing and delivering consequences. To know the boundaries of acceptable behavior, children need rules, and these rules should be few, and fairly and consistently adhered to.

To implement programs with individualized components, some one-to-one training may be necessary. Parents and paraprofessionals can be the instructors as long as they are trained, are given explicit instructions, and can report the child's behavior in a clear and specific manner. The teacher often becomes responsible for instructing aides and other assistants. If this responsibility is not assumed by other school district personnel, it is critical that the teacher do so to avoid role conflict and confusion about programmatic concerns.

Regardless of the apparent severity of a learning disorder, a child can learn. Despite a lack of consensus among educators and a paucity of empirical data on early childhood intervention, there is ample evidence of the progress children make when developmental abilities and preschool activities are synchronized. One has only to visit a preschool for handicapped children—or better, one where they are integrated with non-learning disordered children—to become aware that all children, regardless of degree of impairment, can indeed learn. The assurance of this opportunity is central to the relevant legislation and litigation that has been a hallmark of the 1970s. Critical to the success of programs is the teacher, who, in the long run, is the one who makes learning happen.

SPECIFIC LEARNING DISABILITY TEST REFERENCES

Ayres, A. J. *The Ayres Space Test*. Western Psychological Services, Los Angeles, 1962.

_____. *The Southern California Motor Accuracy Test*. Western Psychological Services, Los Angeles, 1964.

_____. *The Southern California Figure-Ground Perception Test*. Western Psychological Services, Los Angeles, 1966.

_____. *The Southern California Kinesthesia and Tactile Perception Tests*. Western Psychological Services, Los Angeles, 1966.

_____. *The Southern California Perceptual-Motor Tests*. Western Psychological Services, Los Angeles, 1968.

Baker, H. J. and B. Leland. *The Detroit Test of Learning Aptitude*. Bobbs-Merrill, Inc., Indianapolis, 1967.

Beery, K. E. and N. A. Buktenica. *The Development Test of Visual-Motor Integration*. Follett, Chicago, 1967.

Dunn, L. M. and F. C. Markwardt. *The Peabody Individual Achievement Tests*. American Guidance Service, Circle Pines, Minnesota, 1970.

Frostig, M. and D. Horne. *The Frostig Program for Development of Visual Perception*. Follett, Chicago, 1964.

Frostig, M., P. Maslow, D. W. Lefener, and J. R. B. Whittlesey. *The Frostig Developmental Test of Visual Perception*, 1963 Standardization. Consulting Psychologists Press, Palo Alto, California, 1964.

Getman, G. N., E. R. Kane, M. R. Halgren, and G. W. McKee. *Developing Learning Readiness: A Visual-Motor-Tactile Skills Program*. McGraw-Hill, New York, 1968.

Goldman, R., M. Fristoe, and R. W. Woodcock. *The Goodman-Fristoe-Woodcock Test of Auditory Discrimination*. American Guidance Services, Circle Pines, Minnesota, 1970.

Goldman, R. and M. E. Lynch. *Goldman-Lynch Sounds and Symbols Development Kit*. American Guidance Services, Circle Pines, Minnesota, 1971.

Kirk, S. A., J. J. McCarthy, and W. D. Kirk. *The Illinois Test of Psycholinguistic Abilities*. University of Illinois Press, Urbana, 1968.

Kirk, W. D. A tentative screening procedure for selecting bright and slow children in kindergarten. *Exceptional Children*, 1966, (No. 33), 235-241.

Myklebust, H. R. *Picture Story Language Test. Development and disorders of written language* (Vol. 1). Grune and Stratton, New York, 1966.

Myklebust, H. R. *The Pupil Rating Scale*. Grune and Stratton, New York, 1971.

Peterson, W. *A Program for Early Identification of Learning Disabilities*. Special Child Publications, Seattle, 1970.

Roach, E. G. and N. C. Kephart. *The Purdue Perceptual-Motor Survey*. Charles E. Merrill, Columbus, Ohio, 1966.

Terman, L. M. and M. A. Merrill. *The Stanford-Binet Intelligence Scale, Form L-M*. Houghton-Mifflin Company, Boston, 1960.

Wechsler, D. *The Wechsler Intelligence Scale for Children*. Psychological Corporation, New York, 1949.

Wechsler, D. *The Wechsler Adult Intelligence Scale for Children*. Psychological Corporation, New York, 1955.

Wechsler, D. *The Wechsler Intelligence Scale for Children-R*. Psychological Corporation, New York, 1974.

Wepman, J. *Auditory Discrimination Test*. Language Research Associates, Chicago, 1958.

REFERENCES

Battle, E. S., & Lacey, B. A. A contest for hyperactivity in children over time. *Child Development,* 1972, *43,* 757-773.

Bayley, N. The stability of mental test performance between two and eighteen years. In Jones, et al. (Eds.), *The course of human development: Selected papers from the University of California, Berkeley, longitudinal studies*. New York: Wiley, 1971.

Buros, O. K. (Ed.). *The seventh mental measurements yearbook* (Vols. 1 & 2). Highland Park, N.J.: Gryphon Press, 1972.

Carew, J. V. *Environmental stimulation: A longitudinal observational study of how people influence the young child's intellectual development in his everyday environment*. Paper presented at the Annual Meeting, AERA, San Francisco, April 22, 1976.

Carrow, E. *Test for auditory comprehension of language*. Austin, Tex.: Learning Concepts, 1973.

Chalfant, J., & Scheffelin, M.A. *Central processing dysfunction in children: A review of research*. Washington, D.C.: U.S. Printing Office, 1969.

Coles, G. S. The learning disabilities test battery: Empirical and social issues. *Harvard Educational Review,* 1978, *48,* 313-340.

Cratty, B. J., & Martin, M. *Perceptual-motor efficiency in children: The measurement and improvement of movement attributes*. Philadelphia: Lea & Febiger, 1969.

Douglas, V. I. Stop, look, and listen: The problem of sustained attention and impulse control in hyperactive and normal children. *Canadian Journal of Behavior Science,* 1972, *4,* 259-281.

Fernald, G. M. *Remedial techniques in basic school subjects*. New York: McGraw-Hill, 1943.

Gearhart, B. R. *Learning disabilities: educational strategies*. St. Louis, Mo.: Mosby, 1973.

Gray, S., & Miller, J. O. Early experience in relation to cognitive development. *Review of Educational Research,* 1967, *37,* 5, 48-112.

Greenspoon, L., & Singer, S. B. Amphetamines in the treatment of hyperkinetic children. *Harvard Educational Review,* 1973. *43,* 4, 515-555.

Hare, B. A., & Hare, J. M. *Teaching young handicapped children: A guide for preschool and the primary grades*. New York: Grune and Stratton, 1977.

Haring, N. G. (Ed.). *Behavior of exceptional children*. Columbus, Ohio: Charles E. Merrill, 1974.

Hoepfner, R., Stern, C., & Nummedal, S. G. (Eds.). *CSE-ERC preschool kindergarten test evaluations*. Los Angeles: Center for the Study of Evaluation and Early Childhood Research Center, UCLA, 1971.

Johnson, D., & Myklebust, H. *Learning disabilities: educational principles and practices*. New York: Grune and Stratton, 1967.

Kaluger, G., & Kolson, C. J. *Reading and learning disabilities*. Columbus, Ohio: Charles E. Merrill, 1969.

Kephart, N. C. *The slow learner in the classroom (2nd ed)*. Columbus, Ohio: Charles E. Merrill, 1971.

Kirk, S. A. *Educating exceptional children* (2nd ed). Boston: Houghton-Mifflin, 1972.

Kirk, S. A., & Kirk, W. D. *Phycholinguistic learning disabilities: diagnosis and remediation*. Urbana, Ill.: University of Illinois Press, 1971.

291

Lane, P. Educational therapy for adolescent nonreaders. *Academic Therapy,* 1970-71, *8,* 155-159.

Lerner, J. *Children with learning disabilities:* Boston: Houghton-Mifflin, 1976.

Mainprize, D., & Mann, P. Educating adolescents with emotional and delinquency problems. *The Clearing House,* 1977, *50,* 403-405.

Meichenbaum, D. H., Goodman J. Training impulsive children to talk to themselves: A means of developing self-control. *Journal of Abnormal Psychology, 77,* No. 2, 115-126.

Meier, John H. *Developmental and learning disabilities.* Baltimore: University Park Press, 1976.

Miller, W. H., & Windhauser, E. Reading disability tendency toward delinquency? *The Clearing House, 171, 36,* 183-187.

Myklebust, H. R. (Ed.). *Progress in learning disabilities* (Vol. 1). New York: Grune and Stratton, 1968.

Myklebust, H. R. (Ed.). *Progress in learning disabilities* (Vol. 2). New York: Grune and Stratton, 1971.

Myklebust, H. R. (Ed.). *Progress in learning disabilities* (Vol. 3). New York: Grune and Stratton, 1975.

O'Leary, K. O. & O'Leary, S. G. *Classroom management: The successful use of behavior modifications.* Elmsford, N.Y.: Pergamon, 1972.

Portage Guide to Early Education. Portage, Wis.: Portage Preschool Project, 1969.

Raygor, B. R. Mental ability, school achievement, and language arts achievement in the prediction of delinquency. *The Journal of Educational Research,* 1970, *64,* 68-72.

Research report. Can preschool education make a lasting difference? *Bulletin of the High/Scope Foundation* (No. 4). Ypsilanti, Mich.: High/Scope Foundation, 1977.

Ross, A. O. *Psychological aspects of learning disabilities and reading disorders.* New York: McGraw-Hill, 1976.

Safer, D., Allen, R., & Barr, E. Depression of growth in hyperactive children on stimulant drugs. *New England Journal of Medicine,* 1972, *287,* 217-219.

Strauss, A. A., & Lehtinen, L. *The psychopathology and education of the brain-injured child.* New York: Grune and Stratton, 1947.

Tarnpol, L. Delinquency and minimal brain dysfunction. *Journal of Learning Disabilities,* 1970, *3,* 201-206.

Valett, R. *A psychoeducational evaluation of basic learning abilities.* Belmont, Calif.: Fearon Publishers, 1967.

Valett, R. *The remediation of learning disabilities: a handbook of psychoeducational resource programs.* Belmont, Calif.: Fearon Publishers, 1967.

Valett, R. *Programming learning disabilities.* Belmont, Calif.: Fearon Publishers, 1969.

Walker, D. K. *Sociometric measures for preschool and kindergarten children.* San Francisco: Jossey-Bass, 1973.

Wallace, G., and Kauffman, J. *Teaching children with learning problems.* Columbus, Ohio: Charles E. Merrill, 1973.

Waugh, K. W., and Bush, W. F. *Diagnosing learning disabilities.* Columbus, Ohio: Charles E. Merrill, 1971.

Weikart *et al. A cognitively oriented curriculum: A framework for preschool teachers,* Washington, D.C.: National Association for Education of Young Children, 1971.

Werner, E. E., Bierman, J. M., & French, F. E. *The children of Kauai.* Honolulu: University of Hawaii Press, 1971.

Chapter 10

The Young Mildly Retarded Child

Paul A. Alberto

NATURE OF MENTAL RETARDATION

John is six years old. He can play in the street with the kids and understand the rules of games and of friendship, but has an absolute fit when he loses. He can communicate his wants and needs, find his way around the neighborhood, do errands for his mother and if you give him a dime and a nickle he can buy a Milky Way at the corner candy store. In school he has problems pronouncing his words, cannot do take-away problems, and is still trying to memorize the alphabet. The school psychologist says he has an IQ of 62. Is John mentally retarded?

Definition

Recognition of the mentally retarded as an identifiable population subgroup dates back hundreds of years. Various ways of labeling and educating the retarded have been used. Attempts at definition have gone through numerous revisions dating as far back as the middle of the 13th century, when it was the prerogative of the king to identify "idiots"—those who had not understanding of their "nativity." Around 1500, Sir Anthony Fitzherbert defined a retarded person as one who "cannot account or number, nor can tell who was his father or mother, nor how old he is, so as it may appear he has not understanding of reason what shall be his profit or his loss."

Since 1959, the accepted definition is that published in the *Manual on Terminology and Classification in Mental Retardation* by the American Association on Mental Deficiency (AAMD). The current definition (1973/7) is as follows:

MENTAL RETARDATION REFERS TO SIGNIFICANTLY SUB-AVERAGE GENERAL INTELLECTUAL FUNCTIONING EXIST-ING CONCURRENTLY WITH DEFICITS IN ADAPTIVE BE-HAVIOR, AND MANIFESTED DURING THE DEVELOPMENTAL PERIOD.

Criteria for Classification

Contained within this definition are the three criteria for classifying a child as mentally retarded: (1) significantly subaverage intellectual functioning, (2) existing concurrently with deficits in adaptive behavior, and (3) manifested during the developmental period.

1. *Significantly subaverage intellectual functioning:* the indicator is the child's intelligence quotient or IQ score, determined by an individually administered test of intelligence, most commonly the Wechsler Intelligence Scale for Children-Revised (WISC-R). Other tests used with young children include The Stanford-Binet Intelligence Scale, The Bayley Scales of Infant Development, The Cattell Infant Intelligence Scale, and the Wechsler Preschool and Primary Scale of Intelligence. The subtests making up the WISC-R are divided into verbal and performance scales:

Verbal	Performance
Information	Picture Completion
Similarities	Picture Arrangement
Arithmetic	Block Design
Vocabulary	Object Assembly
Comprehension	Coding
(Digit Span)	(Mazes)

If the WISC-R were administered to the general school population, the childrens' scores would result in a "normal distribution," yielding a proportional spread of scores as shown in Figure 10-1.

Figure 10-1 The Normal Curve

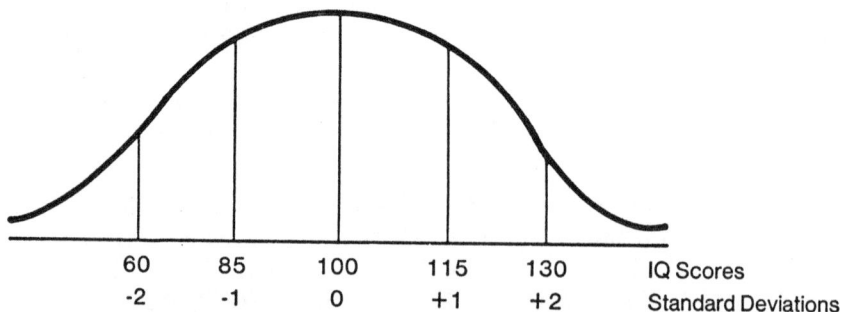

60	85	100	115	130	IQ Scores
-2	-1	0	+1	+2	Standard Deviations

The average IQ score for children in the population would fall between 90 and 110, with a mean score of 100. Scores are grouped in 15-point intervals, because we say that members of the population are statistically, significantly different from one another at a point where their scores vary in 15-point increments from the mean of 100. Each of these 15 points is referred to as a standard deviation. Operationally, we are saying that a child with an IQ of 85 (-1 standard deviation below the mean) is significantly below average in current abilities and potential school performance from a child with an IQ of 100; a child with an IQ of 70 (-2 standard deviations below the mean) is still further below average in current abilities and potential school performance from the child with an IQ of 85.

To meet this first criterion of mental retardation, a child must have a measured IQ equal to or greater than -2 standard deviations below the mean, or an IQ score equal to or less than 70.

2. *Existing concurrently with deficits in adaptive behavior:* Several class-action suits have contested the content of intelligence tests on the basis of cultural bias, especially in reference to children of minority groups. Because of cases such as Larry P. vs. Riles (1971) and Diana vs. Board of Education (1970), now written into federal (P.L. 94-142) and various state laws, IQ scores may not be the sole determinant of a mentally-retarded classification for school placement. Additionally, tests must be administered in the child's primary language. This second criterion, which is in accordance with these rulings, is the demonstration of deficits in adaptive behavior. Adaptive behavior is defined as: "The effectiveness or degree with which an individual meets the standards of personal independence and social responsibility expected for age and cultural group." This definition requires assessment of the child's ability to perform those tasks necessary for functioning within the community, and the child's ability to make and be responsible for its own decisions.

Commonly used testing instruments developed to measure adaptive behavior include the AAMD Adaptive Behavior Scales, The TMR Performance Profile, The Vineland Social Maturity Scale, and The Balthazar Scales of Adaptive Behavior. A recently developed instrument which attempts to take directly into account cultural differences is the System of Multicultural Pluralistic Assessment (SOMPA). Typical of the subtests found in these instruments are those of the AAMD Adaptive Behavior Scales:

PART I	PART II
Independent Functioning	Destructive Behavior
Physical Development	Antisocial Behavior
Economic Activity	Nonconforming Behavior
Language Development	Untrustworthiness
Number and Time Concepts	Withdrawn Behavior

Vocational Activity
Self-Direction
Responsibility
Socialization

Odd Mannerisms
Interpersonal Manners
Vocal Habits
Eccentric Habits
Hyperactive Tendencies
Psychological Disturbances
Use of Medication

In establishing deficits in adaptive behavior, the two critical variables that must be considered are the expectations of age and cultural group. For this purpose three age groupings are delineated: Infancy and Early Childhood, Childhood and Early Adolescence, and Late Adolescence and Adult Life. When considering adaptive behavior in the first group, sensory-motor development, speech and language, self-help and socialization skills are assessed to determine delays in the sequential-acquisition patterns of maturation. Indicators of adaptive behavior deficits commonly found among young children are delays in standing, walking, and fine motor tasks; delayed language expansion; poor understanding of safety and money, and problems in number and word recognition. In the second group, the application of basic academic skills, reasoning and judgment in mastery of the environment and social skills are assessed to determine the child's ability to learn as a function of experience. During late adolescence and adult life, vocational performance and social responsibility are assessed to determine the potential for independence, maintaining employment, and conformity to community standards.

3. *Manifested during the developmental period:* For a classification as mentally retarded, the diagnosis must be made between ages 0 and 18 years (the developmental period).

In summary, classification as mentally retarded requires an IQ score of 70 or below, concurrent with an identified deficit(s) in adaptive behavior, diagnosed between ages 0 and 18 years.

Levels of Retardation

Individuals classified as mentally retarded fall within a wide range of ability, requiring vastly different services. To manage these needs, retardation is divided into four classification schemes of potential ability. Two of these are those used by the AAMD and the public school system. As seen in Figure 10-2, though the different labels are used, the demarcation criteria among levels are essentially the same. It should be noted that within the educational system exact IQ limits are set by departments of education or public instruction in each of the states. Therefore, you will find minor variation from state to state as to which children fall within each category.

The highest level— or the "least retarded"—are the mildly retarded or *Educable Mentally Retarded (EMR)*. These children will display delays of only one to

three years in school performance and so are capable of learning fundamental academics and personal responsibility. As adults they should be self-sufficient and live independently as productive members of the community. Until the 1970s these children were automatically placed in self-contained special education classes. However, legal (LeBanks vs. Spears, 1973) and legislative (P.L. 94-142) rulings have insisted upon placement in the "least restrictive educational alternative" *appropriate* to meeting the educational needs of each child. In schools this has meant implementation of mainstreaming. *Mainstreaming* has revised the traditional system of service delivery so that most mildly retarded children are placed within regular classes, with provision of special education assistance in maintaining reasonable academic and social progress.
This type of assistance has been provided through resource rooms and itinerant teachers.

The second level of retardation includes the moderately retarded or *Trainable Mentally Retarded* (TMR). These children, with a functioning ability approximately one-half to one-third that expected of their chronological age, are expected to master self-care skills, basic language, and cognitive concepts. As adults, with minimal supervision, they will be able to live in community homes and work within supervised workshop facilities. Traditionally, these children have been educated within segregated schools, training centers, or private facilities. Recently more and more classes for the trainable retarded are being integrated into regular public schools. Attempts at increased socialization opportunities with normal children, especially during the younger years, are being explored.

The educational emphasis for the *Severely Mentally Retarded* (SMR) is on acquisition of self-care, motor and language skills. As adults they will require continuous supervision, though community placement is becoming widespread. Traditionally, this is one of the retarded populations housed within institutions. Along with increasing awareness of the debilitating effects of institutional life and with the advent of the social philosophy of normalization, these individuals are being moved from institutions into community group homes to provide them with the routines and experiences of daily living representative of normal living. As of the 1978 school year, compliance with P.L. 94-142 requires that classes for the severely retarded be set up within the public school systems.

The most involved individuals are those classified as *Profoundly Mentally Retarded* (PMR), who are housed, like the severely retarded, within institutions. There is growing controversy as to the discrimination ability of testing in making differential diagnoses between these two lower levels of retardation, and whether there is any merit in such differentiation. It is becoming more apparent that the distinction between the severely and the profoundly retarded may not rest upon IQ scores, but upon factors of responsivity to environmental stimulation, the potential for a means of communicating wants and needs, and the necessity of continuous medical monitoring.

Figure 10-2 Two Systems for Classification of the Mentally Retarded.

American Association on Mental Deficiency (adaptive behavior not accounted)			Public Schools	
	IQ*	Sd		IQ
Mentally Retarded	≤70	≥−2	Mentally Handicapped (MR)	≤70
Mildly Retarded	69-55	−2 to −3	Educable Retarded (EMR)	70-50
Moderately Retarded	54-40	÷3 to −4	Trainable Retarded (TMR)	50-25
Severely Retarded	39-25	−4 to −5	Severely Retarded (SMR)	
				less than
Profoundly Retarded	<24	≥−5	Custodial (CMR, PMR)	25

*WISC-R values

Etiology

In general, children classified as mildly retarded show some aspect of environmental deprivation as the cause (etiology) of their retardation. For approximately 85 percent of the EMR population (referred to as the Cultural/Familial Retarded [Zigler, 1967]) no known organic cause is known; cause is attributed to a lack of "cultural" experiences, malnutrition, or some form of social isolation. The implication of such etiology is that provision of extensive exposure to life experiences, a variety of stimulation activities and problem solving opportunities will ameliorate the behaviors inducing retardation. For the lower three levels of retardation, the indicated cause is one directly attributable to some organic syndrome (e.g. Down's Syndrome, Wilson's Disease, Hydrocephalus, Turner's Syndrome) with a manifestation of retardation. Because of their physical involvement, most of these children are multihandicapped, with pronounced secondary sensory, physical, or emotional handicaps.

Prevalence

Prevalence is a demographic statistic referring to the percentage of a population that falls within a given category, classification, or subgroup. The prevalence figure of mental retardation is 3 percent of the population, which yields an estimated 6.4 million Americans, in a population of 214 millions, classified as mentally retarded (this equals the populations of Colorado, Delaware, Kansas, New Hampshire and South Dakota.) It is estimated that approximately 2,100 mentally retarded infants are born each week. As seen in Figure 10-3, the greatest proportion of this 3 percent are individuals within the range of mild retardation.

Figure 10-3 Prevalence of Mental Retardation

Level of Retardation	Estimated % of Total Population	% of MR Population	MR in Total Population	MR in School-age Population
EMR	2.6	85.0	5,564,000	1,391,000
TMR	0.3	12.0	642,000	160,500
SMR/PMR	0.1	3.0	214,000	53,500
Total	3.0	100.0	6,420,000	1,605,000

In recent years, numerous objections to using 3 percent as the prevalence figure for the retarded have come from researchers such as Mercer (1973) and Tarjan (1973), mostly concerning the assumptions regarding the mildly retarded segment of the population. If the following objections were taken into account, it is felt that the actual prevalence of retardation would be closer to 1 percent.

1. To date, diagnosis is still made primarily on the basis of IQ scores. If cultural differences were taken into account, the number of EMR children would be significantly reduced.
2. The concept of prevalence assumes a retarded individual can be identified at birth. Such an early diagnosis cannot be made for potentially mildly retarded individuals where later environmental conditions play a critical role.
3. This figure assumes a diagnosis of retardation does not change. Classification decisions at any given time should be made in relation to behavioral standards and norms in comparison to age and cultural group. An individual labeled as mentally retarded at one time of life may not be at another, depending on an alteration in intellectual functioning, adaptive behavior, and changes in societal expectations. A diagnosis of retardation does not necessarily imply prognosis; the latter must be related to such factors as the presence of secondary handicapping conditions, and the effects of training and treatment.
4. Studies (Farber, 1959, 1968; Levinson, 1962; Heber & Dever, 1970) have shown that while the incidence of the more severe levels of retardation remains stable across populations, there is great variability in incidence at the mild level. Higher figures for mild retardation have been found among racial and ethnic minorities, low socioeconomic communities, and people in rural, isolated and inner-city ghettos. Most noticeably, there are higher figures during the school years than in later life.

5. A 3 percent figure assumes that the mortality rate of the retarded is similar to that of the general population. While life expectancy of the mildly retarded is similar, the mortality rate among the more severe levels of retardation is higher. Recent advances in medical technology are making some progress in reducing the mortality rate among the more severely retarded.

NATURE OF THE CHILD

A child is most often first recognized and labeled as mildly retarded when entering a formal learning setting. The developmental delays the child displays before being confronted with the demands of a structured school environment are usually so minor they are overlooked. Once in school, these delays appear in patterns of low achievement and inappropriate classroom performance. No single list of characteristics is found in all mildly retarded children, but there is a matrix of potential characteristics, various possible combinations of which a given child may display. Mental retardation is described as an overall developmental disability; that is, in varying degrees, delays will be present in each of the learning domains. It would be an error in the understanding and identification of the mildly retarded for the teacher to look for a single learning or behavioral deficit, such as in reading or parallel play, to target for remediation. The teacher should expect a pattern of development characterized by delays from one to three years across the various curriculum domains of cognitive, motor, social, self-help, and language learning. It is a difference in the degree, not in the kind, of delay that characterizes the mildly retarded child in school.

Certain overriding characteristics (deficiency in memory function or language development) may be attributed to most retarded children. However, each child will demonstrate a unique degree and/or pattern of domain-specific development, dependent upon previous experiences at home and in school where strengths and weaknesses, likes and dislikes have been shaped. Differences in characteristics are referred to as *interindividual* differences. Therefore, most of the assumptions we bring to the learning situation concerning the child are probably a stereotype and not a reality in the child's behavior.

A phenomenon traditionally ascribed to the learning experience of retarded children is that of a *cumulative failure effect*. Because of depressed mental age (MA) (performance on an intelligence test has yielded a below-average IQ score), retarded children are not ready to begin the traditional school curriculum at the same chronological age (CA) as are normal children. The MA (MA $= \frac{CA \ (IQ)}{100}$) will indicate a functioning ability equal to one-half to one-third that expected of a normal child of the same chronological age. This can be interpreted to mean that a child with an IQ of 80 will have an MA of 6.5 at the age of 8 years; a child with an IQ of 50 will have an MA of 6.5 at the age of 13 years. Therefore, these children begin school behind their normal peers in age-appropriate ability. Faced with repeated failure and frustration in the classroom, they fall further and further behind academically. Parallel to the cumulative effect of academic failure is a cumulative effect of frustration caused by inappropriate expectations and tasks, and continuous failure, resulting in a child with repeated behavior problems in class.

The teacher of the young mildly retarded must place major emphasis on prevention. Through extended periods of readiness activities, individualized instruction, opportunities for overlearning, the teacher may prevent onset of cumulative failure. Teachers should provide a foundation of varied experiences in situations that approximate real life. The earlier the schools and the teacher can intervene to prevent the onset of, or interrupt, this failure cycle the greater the possibility of negating its effects.

Intelligence develops rapidly during the first few years of life, after which it slows and stabilizes. Environmental intervention has the greatest impact during the preschool years. Variations in environment probably have reduced impact after the age of eight years. Although a diagnosis of mild retardation does not imply a stable condition, a number of early intervention projects have been undertaken, notably Heber's Milwaukee Project, Karnes' PEECH Project at the University of Illinois Child Development Center, and Bricker's Intervention for Young Developmentally Delayed Children at Miami's Mailman Center (Tjossem, 1976). Each has dramatically demonstrated the benefits of early intervention for delayed or potentially delayed children.

Learning-Readiness Skills

Certain basic skills are a necessary foundation upon which instruction and the ability to receive information are built.

Discrimination

The basis of instruction is ability to distinguish between instances and non-instances of a given stimulus or object. This is exemplified by the ability to say that a given stimulus is an instance of the letter A and another is not an instance of the letter A; this is an instance of green and this is not an instance of green; this is an instance of a boy and this is not an instance of a boy. This instruction brings the child to the understanding that objects vary along dimensions and therefore can be distinguished from each other or grouped into sets (classified). This decision of similarity or difference is based upon the presence or absence of relevant dimensions across objects.

One format for such instruction is the oddity problem. The child is presented with an array of objects from which it selects the one that is different. The array would consist of three objects which have all dimensions in common, while a fourth varies along one dimension, e.g., three blue one-inch cubes and a red one-inch cube, or three seven-inch silver spoons and one seven-inch silver fork.

Relativity

In the early stages of cognitive development a child lives in a world he has divided into extremes. This dichotomous division soon proves inadequate for making judgments concerning relativity in even the simplest choice decisions such as selecting the biggest of three balloons. The ability to make relative comparisons along dimensions of size, distance, time, and ordinality (first, second, third, etc.) is the basis for more complex tasks involving measurement, sequencing of events, memory, and the further structuring of the environment into abstract hierarchical classifications.

Cause-and-Effect Relationships

An understanding that certain events cause others to occur will enable the child to predict events and anticipate consequences. With this understanding, the child can be expected to take increasing responsibility for actions. The teacher has thereby set the foundation for reinforcement and corrective feedback as a part of instructional procedure.

A child's progression through such early cognitive growth is a result of maturation and opportunity for interaction with the environment and is facilitated by appropriate instructional activities arranged by the teacher.

Mediation

A consistent finding in the learning difference between the retarded child and his normal peers is difficulty in retaining information the teacher has just presented. This deficit in short-term memory is attributed to inability to use mediation processes. In remembering numbers, words, and days of the week, normal children will rehearse by repeating information to themselves or aloud. Retarded children do not rehearse new information without being instructed to do so (Ellis, 1970). Two strategies effective in overcoming this deficit are clustering and small group instruction. *Clustering* is the teacher's grouping of new information input into recognizable categories, such as man, lady, boy; red, green, blue; dog, cat, horse; or presenting a string of numbers such as 695742 as 695, 742. Rehearsal is facilitated by presenting new information in *small learning groups*. As each group member takes a turn repeating the new information aloud, the other children are afforded repeated opportunities to rehearse the information at the same time. Once the information has been memorized, the retarded child is equally efficient as his peers in retaining that information.

Imitation

Generally, the teacher will be saying to the child "watch me do this . . . now you do it." When requesting a child to replicate a skill or behavior just demonstrated, we are asking him to imitate. Imitation is a skill normal children develop naturally through play and learning at home and with peers. Retarded children do not develop this vital learning skill in the same manner (Striefel, 1974). Many require specific instruction and practice, involving teaching to imitate gross motor movement (Simon Says) and fine motor movements (manipulation of materials). It is important to remember that in such instruction the teacher's objective is not the child's learning the specific motor movement being imitated, but the concept "Do this" — "Do as I am doing."

Speech and Language

Moderate delays in speech and language development are prevalent among the mildly retarded. Seldom, however, are these delays sufficient by themselves to predict retardation in the preschool years.

The teacher must remember that speech and language are distinct processes and should therefore be instructed differently. Speech is the motor process involved in the production of sound; language is the cognitive process of making object-label associations.

Speech

Speech defects range from 8-37 percent among retarded children (Keane, 1972)—higher than that found in the general population. Certain defects (most commonly articulation errors and voice disorders) are found more often than others, though no single pattern can be identified with the mildly retarded.

There are four basic types of articulation errors that the teacher may expect to encounter:

1. *Omissions* are errors in which only parts of words are pronounced: A particular letter may be consistently omitted as in "__his is my __eddy," or may be consistently omitted except when it appears as an ending sound as in "I __ove my __ittle __o__ __ipop."

2. *Substitutions* are errors in which the sound of one letter is pronounced in place of another. Examples of common letter sound substitutions are:
   (w) for (r) as in "wed" for red
   (w) for (l) as in "wike" for like
   (b) for (v) as in "bery" for very
   (f) for (θ) as in "baf" for bath
   (t) for (k) as in "tite" for kite

3. *Additions* are the inclusion of an extra sound (phoneme) in words as in "sumber" for summer and "sawr" for saw.

4. *Distortions* are improper production or pronunciation of a sound. Completely accurate articulation should not be expected until the child is between the ages of six and eight, and the teacher should therefore realize the presence of these errors may be "age appropriate." A two-year-old is expected to say the word "baf" — but this may be an articulation error for a seven-year-old. The teacher should also realize that dialectal differences are not considered articulation errors.

Voice disorders concern the child's use and modulation of three components of his voice. Disorders of *pitch* are recognizable by monotone or sing-song production. Disorders of *voice quality* are recognizable by words that are nasal, hoarse, thin, or rough. *Loudness* is demonstrated by continuous yelling or whispering.

These disorders and the more severe speech problems are the specialty of the Speech Therapist. This professional is trained in remediation techniques and should be consulted when planning intervention.

Language

The language proficiency of the mildly retarded child is below the level of his normal peers and below that expected of his mental age. Most common characteristics are the limited pool of vocabulary, shorter sentence length, and the use of fewer abstract words (McLean, Yoder, & Schiefelbush, 1971, Miller & Yoder, 1972). Rules of grammar are acquired by most of these children, but at a slower rate. Many educators relate these characteristics to the child's limited exposure and demand for practice which restricts his proficiency in expressive and receptive language.

The retarded child's language development is *quantitatively,* not qualitatively, different from that of his normal peers. That is, their stages of language development are the same and in the same order as those of normal children. Their lower IQ does not result in bizarre language but in longer periods at primitive stages—where they will remain without appropriate intervention. This developmental similarity is important because it implies that the basic approaches to language instruction of normal children are applicable to the mildly retarded given extended readiness, exposure, and practice.

Readiness activities emphasizing oral-language stimulation appear effective with the mildly retarded. At the preschool and early primary levels, oral-language instruction can be considered more important than instruction in reading and writing. Language instruction should not be thought of as an isolated curriculum component; opportunities for verbal expression should be provided during various activities throughout the day. Suggested readiness activities for language development include:

- auditory discrimination

- increased opportunity for describing objects and their functional use, activities that take place in class, and events they have experienced outside the classroom
- use of imaginary play
- choice situations where more than a yes or no answer is required
- group activities that require peer communication
- stories read by the teacher, records, dramas, and puppetry

Social/Emotional development

The teacher's goal in social/emotional development is to prevent frustration due to inappropriate interactions with peers and adults. Though no particular behaviors are definable, the slow maturation of the retarded child results in poor social judgment and immaturity around his peers and in the classroom. The child's social maturity is more directly associated with MA than CA. This developmental discrepancy becomes more noticeable with time: intellectual limitations inhibit development and evaluation of alternative problem resolutions, thus bringing on many situations in which an appropriate or socially acceptable manner of behaving cannot be determined.

While the findings are mixed, it appears that children placed in segregated special classes tend to become over-confident and unrealistic about their abilities as their self-concepts (success experiences) improve. Children placed in regular classes tend to be more fearful of failure. There is some evidence that in a partially integrated setting, the retarded show greater improvements in self-concept over the year than those in a totally segregated class. Former special-class children returned to a regular class program had more favorable attitudes towards themselves and school, and considered themselves to be viewed as less deviant by the other students than children in a special class (Meyerowitz, 1962, 1967; Carroll, 1967; Cegelka & Tyler, 1970; Göttlieb & Budoff, 1972; Kaufman & Alberto, 1976).

Studies of EMRs who have been mainstreamed suggest a correlation between lower intelligence and lower social status in the classroom (Dentler & Mackler, 1962). Retarded children in the regular classes tend to be ignored or rejected, but this has been attributed by their classmates to negative behaviors such as belligerence and aggressiveness, not solely to intellectual status. These behaviors may be a result of the retardate's social immaturity in cooperative work and play situations. This social isolation is also apparent in neighborhood play groups where lack of acceptance is seen independently of class placement. The main thrust in overcoming this low social status has met mixed results. When mildly retarded children were paired with popular students for academic work, were seated close together, or put on joint projects, the immediate result was a gain in peer acceptance; but this acceptance diminished over time.

Suggested readiness activities in the area of social development include:

- role playing of problem situations (simulation activities)
- assignment of high-status responsibilities in the classroom
- committee assignments
- team sports
- joint responsibility for class activities such as planning field trips
- class plays and other presentations for outside audiences

Motor Development

The mildly retarded differ least from their normal peers in motor development. Retardation in 85 percent of these children is related to cultural/familial factors rather than to a clinical cause as found in the more severely retarded populations. Most mildly retarded children do not present significant physical and motor impairments, and approach CA expectancy in height, weight, and skeletal maturity. However, they lag behind their peers on measures of gross motor proficiency and physical fitness, showing a marked difference in body coordination generally described as "clumsiness." This deficiency is evident in activities which involve:

- complex responses requiring coordination of both sides of the body
- sequential patterns of movement
- eye-hand coordination
- eye-foot coordination
- fine motor activities which are timed
- balance

A number of programs have reported that the mildly retarded have increased their efficiency in these areas after structured training programs were consistently scheduled as part of the school day. Classroom teachers can include similar activities outside of formal physical education periods such as the following:

Gross motor
- movement exploration to music
- directionality exercises
- ball throwing, bean bag toss (aiming)
- running, relay races, team sports
- balance beam, obstacle courses

Fine motor
- tracing, cutting, pasting
- coloring within lines
- manipulative puzzles, pegboards, geoboards
- clay modeling, sand writing

Self-Help Skills

As in any discussion of early education, a major concern of programming for the young retarded child is the acquisition of self-help skills that provide independence in personal care. Inability to perform these skills may have two possible sources: (1) overly helpful parents and siblings creating a home environment that inhibits independent performance, (2) a correlated deficiency in a prerequisite skill, such as an inability to imitate or a deficiency in his fine motor capabilities. In most instances of self-help instruction, the teacher will demonstrate for the child how to push a button through a hole or zip a zipper and then ask him to do the same (ability to imitate cannot be assumed). Along with an assessment of self-help skills, the teacher should determine the child's fine motor abilities such as grasping and releasing, pulling and pushing materials, and picking up small objects. These are necessary prerequisites for pulling clothing on and off, zipping, buttoning, and fastening, and for manipulating items such as shoe laces and toothpaste caps.

Four primary self-help skills are feeding, toileting, grooming, and dressing. When planning instruction for any of these, the intent must be for the child to see how individual behaviors are related within an entire matrix. The teacher should plan for repertoires of behaviors, not for acquisition of isolated skills. Feeding is not just getting a bit of food off a fork and into the mouth, but rather a matrix of many related abilities. Figure 10-4 is an example of viewing toilet training as a repertoire of related individual skills.

When planning individual instruction remember that there are various approaches for acquiring most self-help skills. For example, a coat may be put on in various ways: (1) one arm at a time from the back, (2) arms placed in the sleeves of a coat layed out on a table in front of the child and lifted over his head, (3) a coat layed out behind the child into which he places both arms and then is lifted onto his shoulders. If one approach is not successful, try another.

Academics

Generally, the mildly retarded will fail to begin reading, writing, and arithmetic in the first grade. The average child is expected to begin reading at about a CA of six years. The retarded child at that age may have an MA of three to four years, and will not be ready to read until MA approaches the CA at which the average child begins to read. The retarded are usually eight to ten years old before they are ready for traditional reading instruction. Their rate of mastering new skills is slower, so that without appropriate intervention they fall increasingly behind.

Reading

The mildly retarded do not perform in this area up to what may be expected at their mental age. Generally, they will make two-thirds of a year's progress for each

Figure 10-4 Components of a Total Toileting Repertoire.

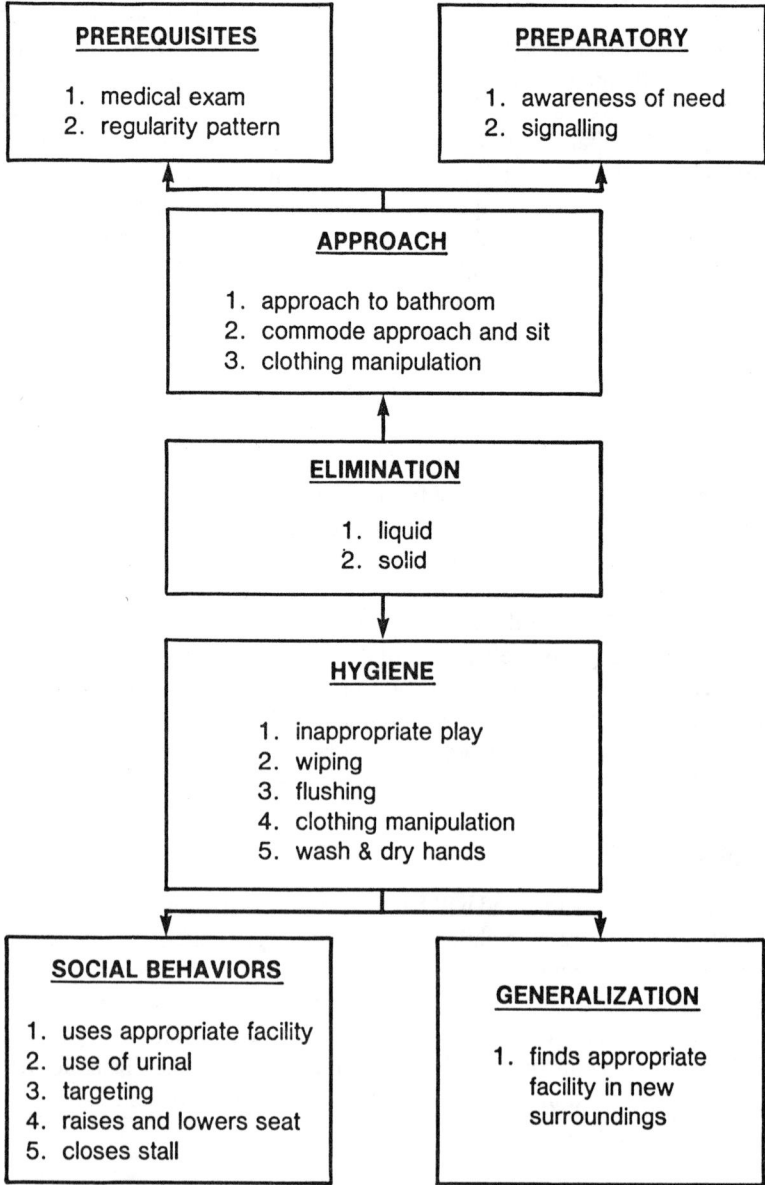

```
┌─────────────────────────┐      ┌─────────────────────────┐
│      PREREQUISITES       │      │       PREPARATORY        │
│                          │      │                          │
│   1. medical exam        │      │   1. awareness of need   │
│   2. regularity pattern  │      │   2. signalling          │
└─────────────────────────┘      └─────────────────────────┘

        ┌────────────────────────────────────────┐
        │                 APPROACH                │
        │                                         │
        │   1. approach to bathroom               │
        │   2. commode approach and sit           │
        │   3. clothing manipulation              │
        └────────────────────────────────────────┘

        ┌────────────────────────────────────────┐
        │               ELIMINATION               │
        │                                         │
        │              1. liquid                  │
        │              2. solid                   │
        └────────────────────────────────────────┘

        ┌────────────────────────────────────────┐
        │                 HYGIENE                 │
        │                                         │
        │   1. inappropriate play                 │
        │   2. wiping                             │
        │   3. flushing                           │
        │   4. clothing manipulation              │
        │   5. wash & dry hands                   │
        └────────────────────────────────────────┘

┌─────────────────────────┐      ┌─────────────────────────┐
│    SOCIAL BEHAVIORS      │      │                          │
│                          │      │     GENERALIZATION       │
│  1. uses appropriate     │      │                          │
│     facility             │      │   1. finds appropriate   │
│  2. use of urinal        │      │      facility in new     │
│  3. targeting            │      │      surroundings        │
│  4. raises and lowers    │      │                          │
│     seat                 │      │                          │
│  5. closes stall         │      │                          │
└─────────────────────────┘      └─────────────────────────┘
```

year spent when routine attention is given to reading. In classes where reading is stressed throughout the school day, they are often brought to MA expectancy.

In oral reading (recognition), the mildly retarded are inferior in word-attack skills—significantly more vowel sound errors and omissions, and require more words to be pronounced. This relates to their difficulties in oral-speech development. Additionally, context clues as a source for word meaning have not been successful; skill in these relies upon inferential or incidental learning, which is a deficient source of input in all domains.

The mildly retarded tend to be more deficient in reading comprehension than in oral reading. They are noticeably inferior in locating relevant facts, main ideas, and in drawing inferences and conclusions (Cegelka & Cegelka, 1970).

Research in the variety of approaches to reading instruction has not demonstrated that any single method of teaching reading to EMRs is consistently superior to another. The teacher's choice among phonics, linguistics, kinesthetic, etc., should be related not to the fact that the child has been labeled as retarded, but to the deficiency characteristics he displays. A phonic reading program for a retarded child with pronounced articulation difficulties is probably unwise (Cegelka & Cegelka, 1970; Gillespie & Johnson, 1974; Kirk, Kliebhan, & Lerner, 1978).

Evidence is also very mixed on the effectiveness of teaching machines and programmed instruction. Each of these has produced reading gains but apparently the value of these technologies (e.g. rebus, i/t/a, etc.) depends on the teacher's proficiency and commitment. A teacher needs to know and use a variety of methods adequately to serve children of different backgrounds and characteristics who may be assigned to his or her class.

Arithmetic

The mildly retarded are inferior to normal peers in all aspects of arithmetic ability, apparently lacking ability to grasp advanced concepts and having difficulty in making generalizations without specific instruction.

Their strongest performance is in the computational and functional areas of arithmetic where they perform up to MA expectancy. These areas lend themselves to concrete instruction and practice, and mild retardates can master the basic mechanics of addition and subtraction, although showing limited understanding of the process and, therefore, little transfer of their ability across situations. In computation they become and remain more dependent upon crutches such as counting on their fingers, using chips or numberlines. Their accuracy is hindered by weaknesses in work habits typified by careless errors, fast pacing, and impulsivity. Some educators are adapting Michenbaum's (1977) steps of self-instruction (process practice) to reduce these weaknesses. Self-instruction has five basic steps:

1. teacher performs the task while guiding herself aloud
2. child performs the task while teacher provides verbal guidance

3. child performs the task while guiding itself aloud
4. child performs the task while guiding itself in a whisper
5. child performs the task while guiding itself with "private" or silent speech

The mildly retardeds' weakest performance is in arithmetic reasoning involving reading and problem-solving (Peterson, 1973). Their low arithmetic vocabulary and poor ability to deal with concepts of sequence and temporal relationships add to the difficulty of following directions and organizing material. Poor skills in verbal mediation and inability to separate irrelevant from important information in a word problem contributes to poor performance.

These children develop quantitative concepts in the same order and stages as normal children do, but at a later period. This acquisition is achieved through a combination of teaching and maturation. Even when drilled in the performance of more advanced Piagetian quantitative tasks they will appear to have the skills but will not have understanding of the concept. Some suggested readiness activities in arithmetic include:

- concrete experience in object permanence and conservation of number
- seriation, classification, and equivalence experience
- combinations and identification of sets of various objects
- functional use of objects leading to one-to-one correspondence
- rational counting leading to rote counting
- number recognition, matching numerals and quantities, and ordination

NATURE OF INSTRUCTION

Principles of good teaching are applicable to all children in a class. Instructional techniques highlighted for use with the mildly retarded are those required of any child having difficulty learning a particular skill. Certain practices and characteristics of learning are known to be of particular importance to remember when instructing the mildly retarded.

1. Direct instruction of a skill or concept is absolutely necessary. The teacher cannot assume that the child will acquire important information through inferential or incidental learning while engaged in another learning experience.

2. Complex skills should be presented in small sequential steps to assure mastery.

3. Opportunities for overlearning or repeated practice must be provided if information is to be retained. Practice of a skill in small increments distributed over time will be more effective in assuring continuing ability of a learned skill than will concentrated or massed practice within one or two lessons.

4. Presentation of new concepts or skills should use concrete examples or

representations of the learning to take place. These children require realistic experience with new learning tasks in order to understand the relationships or process being taught.

5. External sources of motivation provided by the teacher will increase the rate at which new learning is acquired. There is no doubt among educators that reinforcement through praise, attention, and/or stars and classroom privileges will increase the probability that the skill or behavior will repeat. Immediate and continuous feedback provides important guidance to the mildly retarded child.

6. Once a skill or behavior has been taught and learned, the teacher should make followup checks during the year of the child's maintenance of that ability.

7. The mildly retarded child is highly susceptible to distractors in the learning environment and in instructional materials. The teacher should keep to a minimum excess noise and movement, and the number of irrelevancies found in instructional materials, and keep verbal instructions clear and unencumbered by extraneous words and movement.

8. When planning work activities, the teacher should build in success opportunity, since the retarded child has experienced the frustration of failure, which causes him to give up. Begin work sessions with problems the child can successfully solve, and end sessions before long periods occur when he cannot provide any correct answers.

Task Programming

The bridge between assessment, planning, and instruction is the process of *task programming*—a compound process that combines three elements of instructional technology: stating behavioral objectives, task analysis, and behavioral programming.

The *behavioral objectives* which are listed in individual education programs (IEP) target the need for particular skill instruction based upon assessment information. These should be written for each new learning experience. *Task analysis* is the process in which the teacher outlines plans for instruction of complex skills, in a sequence of constituent components of complex skills. *Behavioral programming* is the preparation of a full instructional blueprint for those skills which are proving to be of particular difficulty for the child.

Behavioral Objectives

A staffing committee and the teacher must gather specific information concerning a child's functioning level and skill deficiencies in order to select appropriate learning targets for inclusion in the IEP. Sources of this information are numerous:

- standardized assessment instruments
- criterion referent examinations

- curriculum guides
- developmental checklists
- parents
- environmental demands
- functional analysis of behavior
- resource personnel
- last year's teacher

All learning targets cannot be dealt with simultaneously. To manage properly the child's learning and the classroom schedule, the teacher must set priorities, taking these factors into consideration:

1. Are there inappropriate behaviors that must be brought under control before formal instruction can begin?
2. What are the immediate concerns of the parent or primary caretaker(s)?
3. What are the skills the child is lacking for current appropriate functioning in his home and school environments?
4. How functional an activity is it for the child—what skills may be built upon this one?
5. Consider the prerequisites of the skill and how it fits into a lattice of skills across content areas.
6. What is the child's history of skill acquisition?
7. What is the amount of instructional time available for the child—within the school day and within the total school experience?
8. What resource personnel are needed and available, e.g., speech therapist, remedial reading teacher, physical therapist.

A *behavioral objective* is a statement of intent of an individualized instructional target, describing a proposed change in behavior. A properly written objective will guide the teacher in using a curriculum and planning instructional sequences, and provide criteria for determining when a target has been achieved. In addition, behavioral objectives permit the teacher to transmit to parents and administrators information concerning goals for the child, as well as how and when they are expected to be accomplished.

There are four basic components to a properly written and easily communicated behavioral objective:

1. *Identify the learner*. This individualizes the focus of learning and instruction to the specific child.

2. *Identify the desired performance*. What will the child be doing when demonstrating achievement of the objective. For precise interpretation, the desired performance should be written in observable, measurable, and repeatable terms. To aid

in clarity, the verb used within the description of the desired performance should meet these three requirements. A child's ability can be verified only when the teacher is able to see or hear the behavior or a direct product of the behavior. This insures identifying the behavior in teaching sessions that follow, accurate data, and instruction or confirmation by a third party. The following are examples of verbs which are actions that cannot be directly observed and therefore must be inferred from other behaviors, making consistent agreement on their presence or absence difficult:

- to appreciate
- to discover
- to know
- to feel
- to become competent

- to distinguish
- to understand
- to learn
- to recognize
- to analyze

The following are examples of verbs which are precise statements of directly observable behavior:

- to circle
- to point to
- to underline
- to fill in

- to remove

- to say
- to name
- to write
- to read (count, repeat) orally
- to place

3. *Identify the conditions under which the child will perform:* If the learning experience is to be repeated accurately in later teaching sessions, and if the child's ability to perform the task across a variety of materials, settings, and cues is to be generalized at a later date, the objective should contain the conditions the teacher has set for this learning to take place.

- when the sign for "drink" is given . . .
- without the aid of . . .
- given an array of materials containing . . .
- when presented with . . .
- with the use of . . .
- when given a pullover sweater . . .

4. *Identify the criteria.* The teacher should include criteria for acceptable performance, that is, to what extent the child will be able to perform the desired behavior, given the conditions specified. The nature of the criterion will vary depending upon the specific behavior, the level of learning (e.g. acquisition,

fluency, generalization), the method of instruction, and the form of data collection. Examples of the variety of criteria include the following:

- 25 out of 40 correct responses, in five minutes for three consecutive days.
- label all 10 objects within 40 seconds for two consecutive days
- with 85 percent accuracy for three consecutive math sessions
- 5 consecutive successful trials on four consecutive days
- on 4 out of 5 trials for three consecutive sessions
- complete all steps in the handwashing program independently for 5 consecutive days
- will return within 10 minutes on three consecutive trips to the bathroom

To assure inclusion of all the elements of a behavioral objective, it is suggested that a standard format be devised for writing objectives. One such format is:

condition   –   learner   –   behavior   –   criteria

Given a tube sock with the toe color cued red/John/will pull on the sock appropriately without assistance while in a sitting position/ on three out of four trials for five consecutive days.

Given the words GO, STOP, MEN, WOMEN, EXIT, written in block letters/ Kelly/ will orally identify the words/ with 100 percent accuracy within three minutes on three consecutive training sessions.

Task Analysis

The key to programming from a curriculum guide or developmental sequence is task analysis—it provides a format in which to plan for bringing the child from his current level of functioning to the behavior described in the behavioral objective. Task analysis is the identification of the component abilities or intermediate steps which, when merged, will result in a complex task. In other words, task analysis is the breaking down of a complex task into its simpler component tasks. Each step is listed in serial order and is prerequisite for the one that follows.

The format for a task analysis has three basic elements:

1. Terminal objective
2. Task components
3. Prerequisite skills

1. *Terminal objective* is a restatement of the behavioral objective already discussed. It includes the four basic elements: learner, behavior, conditions, and criteria.

2. *Task components* is a listing, in serial order, of the skills that lead to acquisition of the complex task. This breakdown of the task continues until all component skills or steps have been identified. It may take a child from picking up a sock to putting it on his foot, or from identifying a blue block in isolation to identifying it within an array of blocks of different colors.

Components or steps may be identified by (a) doing the task yourself and noting each time you make a change in body position, (b) watching someone else do the task, (c) listing a new step each time you change an action verb while describing the task, e.g., pick up, place, say, push, turn, repeat.

Some complex tasks may involve phases in addition to the listing of steps. For instance, teaching a child to put on his pants may be viewed as having four phases: 1) pulling his pants on to his waist, 2) snapping, 3) zipping, and 4) buckling his belt. Each phase will have its own steps listed.

3. *Prerequisite skills* means thinking through and listing those skills you are assuming the child is already capable of when beginning to teach this new task. One way to do this is to review the first three or four steps in your list of components. If in listing your prerequisite skills you identify a particular skill the child cannot perform then that should be taught first.

Terminal objective: Given a tube sock with the toe color cued red John will pull on the sock appropriately without assistance while in a sitting position on three out of four trials for five consecutive days.

Task components:
1. The student will pick up his sock with either hand.
2. The student will bend his leg up and bend from the waist.
3. The student will grasp the sock with both hands, turning the opening up.
4. The student will place both thumbs inside the opening of the sock.
5. The student will pull his hands apart to open sock.
6. The student will put his toes into the opening of the sock.
7. The student will pull his arms toward his body, pulling the sock to his heel.
8. The student will pull the sock over the heel and up to the ankle.

Prerequisite skills:
1. The student can follow one-step directions.
2. The student can balance in a chair.
3. The student has appropriate grasp.
4. The student can recognize a sock.

The task analysis you have written out is referred to as a *logical task analysis*. You have worked out logically each step making up the behavior, but it is untested.

Once you verify the accuracy of your analysis by using it with a child and have made any necessary alterations, you then have an *empirical task analysis.* In trying out your task analysis you may find you left out a step, placed steps in improper order, or overlooked a prerequisite skill.

Whereas a behavioral objective is focused on the individual child, task analysis focuses on the components of a particular skill. A well-written task analysis may be used with any child. After probing current ability, a child may be started on the next step of the task analysis.

Behavioral Programming

Behavioral programming, a further expansion of task analysis, returns the focus to the individual child. While task analysis divides complex instructional objectives into a sequence of less complex components or steps, it is not a statement of how to teach. With behavioral programming we bring this total process to that point. To the existing format of a task analysis we add steps specific to the instruction that is to occur.

The written format of behavioral programming begins with the three elements of task analysis and includes five additional ones:

1. Terminal objective
2. Task components
3. Prerequisite skills
4. Method
5. Materials
6. Constraints
7. Procedure: Phase-
        Step:
            cue:
            response:
            criterion:
8. Data collection

Method

Indicated here is the overall method selected for instructing the particular task. Selection of a method should consider the child's characteristics and the nature of the task. A wide variety of methods are available:

- shaping
- chaining (forward and backward)
- fading
- novelty

- paired-associate
- match-to-sample
- visual-visual match
- visual-verbal match

- oddity
- imitation

- auditory-visual match
- verbal-motor match

Materials: For consistency in instruction from session to session and/or from teacher to aide, it is important to list the materials selected, e.g., objects included in an array, type of number line, specific Peabody pictures, items that have particular adaptations. Also listed here is the reinforcer(s) being used.

Constraints: This is a notation of child-specific characteristics to which one must be alert, e.g., type of child response (verbal, gestural, mechanical), physical limitations of the child, limitations of receptive and/or expressive vocabulary.

Procedure: This is where the teacher specifies the instruction within each step. Listed are the cues to be used, i.e., the exact verbal instruction and material presentation, the exact response the child is to make to the verbal cue, and the criterion for success of the particular step. The steps are listed in the sequence in which they are to be taught. A step is taught only after the child has reached the specified criterion of the previous step.

Data Collection: To delineate success and failures, the teacher must record ongoing child performance during each training session so that adjustments can be made where necessary programming adjustments are feasible, and to validate performance to criterion.

If the data you are collecting on the child's performance indicate the child is not acquiring the skill, or is doing so at an unacceptable rate, the teacher should examine the following points regarding the task program:

1. Is the reinforcer still effective or has satiation set in?
2. When setting the criteria for each step have you provided sufficient opportunity for overlearning or repeated practice?
3. Are the steps too large, or have you left out a step?
4. Would another methodological approach be more efficient?
5. Is your definition of the behavior specific enough so that you are looking for the same behavior during each trial or session?
6. Are the materials you are using confusing or distracting to the child?

Interaction between Teacher and Child

When teaching a specific skill involving one-to-one interaction between teacher and child, such as imitation, self-help, or motor skills, the teacher's approach must be consistent and systematic. The child should be given the opportunity to perform the requested response, without teacher interaction overpowering or interfering with the child's attempt at complying with a request. Figure 10-5 a five-step sequence of interaction systematically increasing the degree of instructional interaction between teacher and child for the facilitation of a response.

317

Figure 10-5 Model of Instructional Interaction Pattern

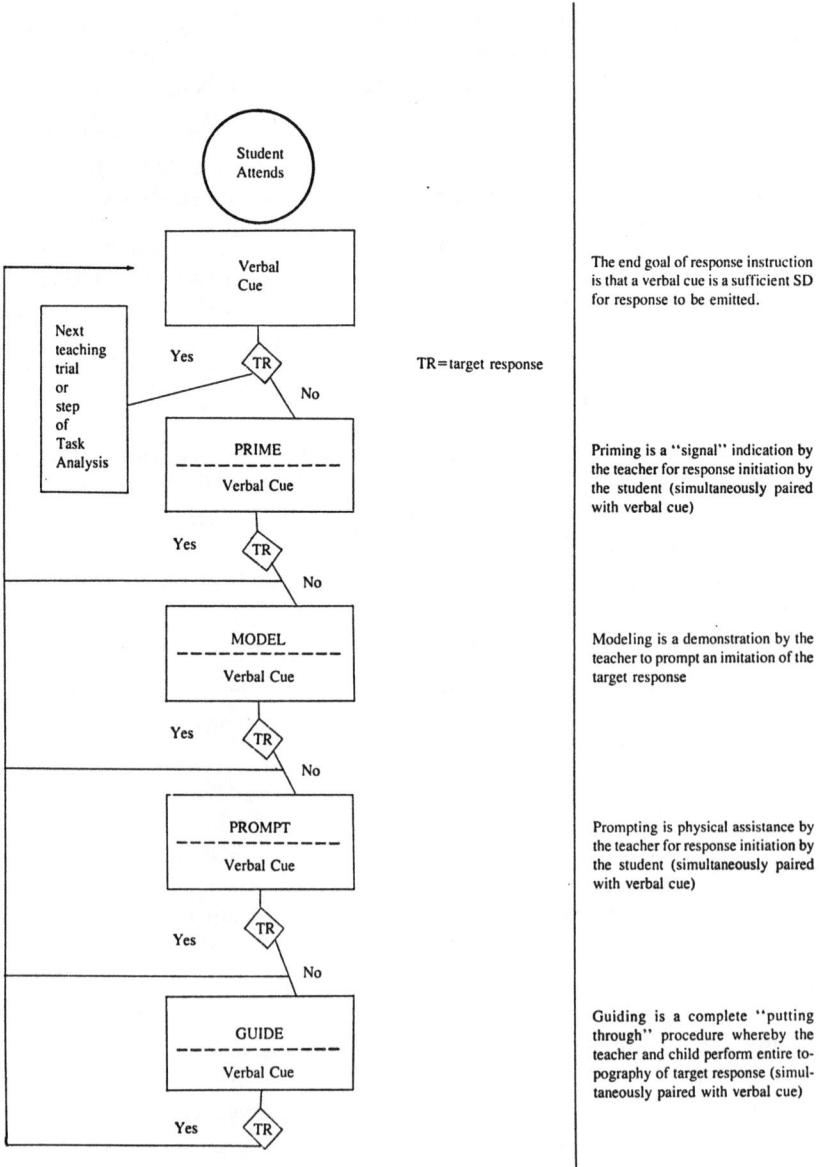

Student
Attends

Verbal
Cue

The end goal of response instruction is that a verbal cue is a sufficient SD for response to be emitted.

Next teaching trial or step of Task Analysis

Yes   TR   No

TR=target response

PRIME
- - - - - -
Verbal Cue

Priming is a "signal" indication by the teacher for response initiation by the student (simultaneously paired with verbal cue)

Yes   TR   No

MODEL
- - - - - -
Verbal Cue

Modeling is a demonstration by the teacher to prompt an imitation of the target response

Yes   TR   No

PROMPT
- - - - - -
Verbal Cue

Prompting is physical assistance by the teacher for response initiation by the student (simultaneously paired with verbal cue)

Yes   TR   No

GUIDE
- - - - - -
Verbal Cue

Guiding is a complete "putting through" procedure whereby the teacher and child perform entire topography of target response (simultaneously paired with verbal cue)

Yes   TR

Within *a given teaching trial* the teacher, as necessary, would progress sequentially through each of the five steps, (Verbal Cue, Prime, Model, Prompt, and Guide) until the child has produced the desired target response.

The desired goal of most instruction is that a verbal cue or direction be a sufficient interaction for the response to be performed by the child. Thus, the first step in the sequence of instruction is the presentation by the teacher of only the *verbal cue*. If this is not sufficient to facilitate the response, the teacher repeats the verbal cue simultaneously with the use of a prime. A *Prime* is a signal or gesture indication by the teacher for the child to initiate the response. If this is still not sufficient interaction, the teacher should pair the verbal cue with the use of a model. *Modeling* is a demonstration by the teacher so that the child may imitate the target response. This step may be bypassed in cases such as compliance commands "come" and "stop." The next degree of interaction would be the use of a prompt paired with the verbal cue. A *Prompt* is physical assistance by the teacher which initiates the response by the child. The greatest amount of teacher interaction occurs in the final alternative—use of a guide. *Guiding* is where the teacher and child perform the entire target response together. The teacher is in fact putting the child through the entire response after having presented the verbal cue. In instances where the child has never been called upon or had the opportunity to perform a similar response before, the use of a guide in the first two or three trials may be necessary before following the normal sequence of steps of this interaction pattern.

REFERENCES

Adams, A., Coble, C., & Hounshell, P. *Mainstreaming language arts and social studies*. Santa Monica, Calif.: Goodyear Publishing Company, 1977.

Balthazar, E. E. *Balthazar scales of adaptive behavior*. Palo Alto, Calif.: Consulting Psychologists Press, Inc., 1971-1973.

Bayley, N. *Bayley scales of infant development*. New York: The Psychological Corporation, 1969.

Bellamy, G., & Bellamy, T. Descriptive concepts for preschool retarded children. *Education and Training of the Mentally Retarded*, 1974, *9*, 115-122.

Bloom, B. *Stability and change in human characteristics*. New York: Wiley, 1964.

Carroll, A. The effects of segregated and partially integrated school programs on self-concept and academic achievement of educable mental retardates. *Exceptional Children*, 1967, *34*, 93-99.

Cattell, P. *Cattell infant intelligence scale*. New York: The Psychological Corporation, 1969.

Cegelka, J., & Cegelka, W. A review of research: Reading and the educable mentally retarded. *Exceptional Children*, 1970, *37*, 187-200.

Cegelka, W., & Tyler, J. The efficacy of special class placement for the mentally retarded in proper perspective. *Training School Bulletin*, 1970, *67*, 33-68.

Chenault, J. Improving the social acceptance of unpopular educable mentally retarded pupils in special classes. *American Journal of Mental Deficiency*, 1967, *72*, 455-458.

Coble, C., Hounshell, P. & Adams, A. *Mainstreaming science and mathematics*. Santa Monica, Calif.: Goodyear Publishing Company, 1977.

Connor, F., Williamson, G., & Siepp, J. *Program guide for infants and toddlers with neuromotor and other developmental disabilities*. New York: Teachers College Press, 1978.

Corder, W., & Pridmore, H. Effects of physical education on the psychomotor development of educable mentally retarded boys. *Education and Training of the Mentally Retarded*, 1966, *1*, 163-167.

Cratty, B. *Motor activity and the education of the retarded*. Philadelphia: Lea & Febiger, 1969.

Dentler, R., & Mackler, R. Ability and sociometric status among normal and retarded children: A review of the literature. *Psychometric Bulletin*, 1962, *59*, 273-283.

DiNola, A. J., Kaminsky, B. P., & Sternfield, A. E. *T.M.R. performance profile for the severely and moderately retarded*. Ridgefield, N.J.: Reporting Service for Children, 1968.

Doll, E. A. *Vineland social maturity scale*. Circle Pines, Minn.: American Guidance Service, Inc., 1965.

Ellis, N. R. Memory processes in retardates and normals. In N. R. Ellis (Ed.), *International review of research in mental retardation, Vol 4*. New York: Academic Press, 1970.

Farber, B. Effects of a severely mentally retarded child on family integration. *Monographs of the Society for Research on Child Development*, 1959, 24 (2, Series No. 71).

Farber, B. *Mental retardation: Its social context and social consequences*. Boston: Houghton Mifflin, 1968.

Gardner, W. Personality characteristics of the mentally retarded: Review and critique. In H. J. Prehm, L. A. Hamerlynck, & J. E. Crossen (Eds.), *Behavior research in mental retardation*. Eugene, Ore.: University of Oregon Press, 1968.

Gardner, W. *Behavior modification in mental retardation*. Chicago: Aldine-Atherton, 1971.

Gillespie, P., & Johnson, L. *Teaching reading to the mildly retarded child*. Columbus, Ohio: Charles Merrill, 1974.

Gottlieb, J., & Budoff, M. Attitudes toward school by segregated and integrated retarded children. *Studies in Learning Potential*. Cambridge: Research Institute for Exceptional Problems, 1972, *2*, 1-10.

Grossman, H. *Manual on terminology and classification in mental retardation*. Washington, D.C.: American Association on Mental Deficiency, 1977.

Hammill, D., & Bartel, N. *Teaching children with learning and behavior problems*. Boston: Allyn & Bacon, 1978.

Heber, R., & Dever, R. Research on education and habilitation of the mentally retarded. In H. C. Haywood (Ed.), *Social-cultural aspects of mental retardation*. New York: Appleton-Century-Crofts, 1970.

Heber, R., & Garber, H. The Milwaukee Project: A study of the use of family intervention to prevent cultural-familial mental retardation. In B. Friedlander, G. Sterritt & G. Kirk (Eds.), *Exceptional infant: assessment and intervention* (Vol 3). New York: Brunner-Mazel, 1975.

Hunt, J. McV. *Intelligence and experience*. New York: Ronald Press Company, 1961.

Ingalls, R. *Mental retardation: The changing outlook*. New York: Wiley, 1978.

Johnson, V., & Werner, R. *A step-by-step guide for retarded infants and children*. Syracuse, N.Y.: Syracuse University Press, 1975.

Jordan, J., Hayden, A., Karnes, M., & Wood, M. (Eds.). *Early childhood education for exceptional children*. Reston, Va.: Council for Exceptional Children, 1977.

Kaufman, M., & Alberto, P. Research on efficacy of special education for the mentally retarded. In N. Ellis (Ed.), *International review of research in mental retardation* (Vol 8). New York: Academic Press, 1976.

Kaufman, M., & Alberto, P. Research on efficacy of special education for the mentally retarded. In N.R. Ellis (Ed.), *International review of research in mental retardation*. New York: Academic Press, 1976.

Keane, V. E. The incidence of speech and language problems in the mentally retarded. *Mental Retardation*, 1972, *10*, 3-8.

Kirk, S., Kliebhan, J., & Lerner, J. *Teaching reading to slow and disabled learners*. Boston: Houghton-Mifflin, 1978.

Lambert, N., Windmiller, M., Cole, L., & Figueroa, R. *American association on mental deficiency adaptive behavior scale, public school version*. Washington, D.C.: American Association on Mental Deficiency, 1975.

Levinson, E. J. *Retarded children in Maine: A survey and analysis*. Orono, Me.: University of Maine Press, 1962.

Lilly, M. Improving social acceptance of low sociometric status, low achieving students. *Exceptional Children*, 1971, *37*, 341-347.

Linde, T., & Kopp, T. *Training retarded babies and pre-schoolers*. Springfield, Ill.: Charles C. Thomas, 1973.

MacMillan, D. Special education for the mildly retarded: Servant or savant. *Focus on Exceptional Children*, 1971, *2*, 1-11.

MacMillan, D. The problems of motivation in the education of the mentally retarded. *Exceptional Children*, 1971, *37*, 579-586.

MacMillan, D. *Mental retardation in school and society*. Boston: Little-Brown, 1977.

McLean, J., & McLean, L. S. *A transactional approach to early language training*. Columbus, Ohio: Charles E. Merrill, 1978.

McLean, J., Yoder, D., & Schiefelbusch, R. (Eds.), *Language intervention with the retarded: Developing strategies*. Baltimore: University Park Press, 1972.

Meichenbaum, D. *Cognitive behavior modification*. New York: Plenum Press, 1977.

Mercer, C., & Snell, M. *Learning theory research in mental retardation: Implication for teaching*. Columbus, Ohio: Charles E. Merrill, 1977.

Mercer, J. *Labeling the mentally retarded*. Berkeley, Calif.: University of California Press, 1973.

Mercer, J. R., & Lewis, J. F. *System of multicultural pluralistic assessment*. New York: The Psychological Corporation, 1977-1978.

Meyerowitz, J. Self-derogation in young retardates and special class placement. *Child Development*, 1962, *33*, 443-451.

Meyerowitz, J. Peer groups and special classes. *Mental Retardation*, 1967, *5*, 23-26.

Miller, J., & Yoder, D. On developing the content for a language teaching program. *Mental Retardation*, 1972, *10*, 9-11.

Mittler, P. *Research to practice in mental retardation: Care and intervention (Vol. 1)*. Baltimore: University Park Press, 1977.

Morrison, D., & Potheir, A. Two different remedial motor training programs and the development of the mentally retarded preschooler. *American Journal of Mental Deficiency*, 1972, *77*, 251-258.

Otto, W., McMenemy, R. & Smith, R. *Corrective and remedial teaching*. Boston: Houghton-Mifflin, 1973.

Park, A., & Fairchild, T. *Mainstreaming the mentally retarded child*. Austin: Learning Concepts, 1976.

Paul, J., Stedman, D., & Neufeld, G. (Eds.). *Deinstitutionalization: Program and policy development.* Syracuse, New York: Syracuse University Press, 1977.

Payne, J., Polloway, E., Smith, J., & Payne, R. *Strategies for teaching the mentally retarded.* Columbus, Ohio: Charles E. Merrill, 1977.

Peterson, D. *Functional mathematics for the mentally retarded.* Columbus, Ohio: Charles E. Merrill, 1973.

Reynolds, M. A framework for considering some issues in special education. *Exceptional Children,* 1962, *28,* 368.

Robinson, H., & Robinson, N. *The mentally retarded child: A psychological approach.* New York: McGraw-Hill, 1965.

Schurr, K., Joiner, L., & Towne, R. C. Self-concept research in the mentally retarded: A review of empirical studies. *Mental Retardation,* 1970, *5,* 39-43.

Simeonsson, R., & Weigerink, R. Early language intervention: A contingent stimulation model. *Mental Retardation,* 1974, *12,* 7-11.

Soloman, A., & Pangle, R. The effects of a structured physical education program on physical, intellectual and self-concept development of educabally retarded boys. *Exceptional Children,* 1967, *33,* 177-181.

Stephens, W. B. (Ed.). *Training the developmentally young.* New York: John Day, 1971.

Striefel, S. *Managing behavior: Teaching a child to imitate.* Lawrence, Kans.: H&H Enterprises, 1974.

Tarjan, G., Wright, S., Eyman, R., & Keeran, C. Natural history of mental retardation: Some aspects of epidemiology. *American Journal of Mental Deficiency,* 1973, *77,* 369-379.

Terman, L. M., & Merrill, M. A. *Stanford-Binet intelligence scale, third revision.* Boston: Houghton-Mifflin, 1960.

Tjossem T. (Ed.). *Intervention strategies for high risk infants and young children.* Baltimore: University Park Press, 1976.

Uzgiris, I., & Hunt, J. McV. *Assessment in infancy.* Urbana: University of Illinois Press, 1975.

Wallace, G., & Kauffman, J. *Teaching children with learning problems.* Columbus, Ohio: Charles E. Merrill, 1973.

Wechsler, D. *Wechsler preschool and primary scale of intelligence.* New York: The Psychological Corporation, 1967.

Wechsler, D. *Wechsler intelligence scale for children, revised edition.* New York: The Psychological Corporation, 1974.

Weintraub, F. Recent influences of law regarding the identification and educational placement of children. *Focus on Exceptional Children,* 1972, *4,* 1-11.

Wolfensberger, W. Normalization: *The principle of normalization in human services.* Toronto: National Institute on Mental Retardation (Canada), 1972.

Zeaman, D., & House, B. The role of attention in retardate discrimination learning. In N. Ellis (Ed.), *Handbook of mental deficiency.* New York: McGraw-Hill, 1963.

Zigler, E. F. Familial mental retardation: A continuing dilemma. *Science,* 1967, *155,* 292-98.

Chapter 11

Working with Sensorily Impaired Children Part I: Visual Impairments

Rebecca F. DuBose

the need is obvious that education of blind children according to their needs be provided in their parental home and in the school of their community, and that education of the blind be whenever possible incorporated into the regular institutions for the people's education, the public schools (Klein, 1845, p. 26 as translated in Lowenfeld, 1973, p. 14).

Although many of the founding fathers of educational services for blind children were associated with the establishment of institutions for the blind (Huay in France, Howe in the United States, and Klein in Austria), they advocated keeping visually handicapped children in home environments, if at all possible. Today 60 percent of registered visually impaired children attend public schools; the remaining 40 percent are in residential schools. The percentage of such preschool children living with their families and attending local educational settings is ever greater. With renewed concern that visually handicapped children be educated in community schools, parents and educators should be informed about the effects of visual impairments on early childhood development, the special needs generated by impaired vision, and techniques effective in teaching appropriate skills to young visually-impaired children.

DEFINITION AND INCIDENCE

There are no consistent procedures for defining certain handicapped populations or for determining criteria for inclusion in a particular category. Definitions and criteria are usually worded to reflect the units of measurement or particular services an agency provides to permit easy classification.

Measurement

Units of measurement are expressed in reference to Snellen Chart notations of visual acuity. The Snellen Chart consists of lines of numbers, letters, or symbols that decrease in size and are read at a distance of 20 feet. The symbol size corresponds to the standard distance at which a person with normal vision can recognize the symbol. An acuity of 20/20 means that a person can read the 20-foot-size symbol at a distance of 20 feet, a ratio considered representative of normal vision. If, at this distance, a person can read only the 200-foot-size letter (2½ inches), vision would be considered 20/200. Functionally, this means that an object a person with normal vision (20/20) can see at 200 feet, must be brought to 20 feet away for the person with 20/200 acuity to read it. When visual acuity is more significantly impaired (20/400 or worse), or when very young or handicapped persons are tested, it is frequently necessary to test vision at distances of less than 20 feet. In these cases, the numerator will be less than 20, usually 10 or 5. A reading of 10/200 means that an object that can be distinguished by persons with normal acuity at 200 feet must be brought as close as 10 feet for recognition.

Definition

The definition of blindness was first stated in terms that would render legal and economic decisions. The definition currently used was written into the Social Security Act of 1935, primarily to identify aged persons in need of increased benefits:

> visual acuity for distant vision of 20/200 or less in the better eye, with best correction; or visual acuity of more than 20/200 if the widest diameter of field of vision subtends an angle no greater than 20 degrees (National Society for the Prevention of Blindness, 1966, p. 10).

Since a need existed to identify persons whose vision was sufficiently limited to require special education services (*partially seeing* children), Hathaway (1959) provided this classification:

1. Children having a visual acuity of 20/70 or less in the better eye after all necessary medical or surgical treatment has been given and compensating lenses provided when the need for them is indicated. Such children must, however, have a residue of sight that makes it possible to use this as the chief avenue of approach to the brain.
2. Children with a visual deviation from the normal who, in the opinion of the eye specialist, can benefit from the special educational facilities provided for the partially seeing (p. 16).

In recent years, educators have indicated that the most important visual consideration is *functional visual efficiency,* or how well the child uses his vision rather than the particular measure of visual acuity. Visual efficiency (American

Table 11-1 Central Visual Acuity for Distance and Corresponding Percentage of Visual Efficiency

Snellen measure of central visual acuity	Percent of visual efficiency
20/20	100
20/40	85
20/50	75
20/80	60
20/100	50
20/200	20

Source: A.M.A. Committee Report, *Estimation of loss of visual efficiency.* A.M.A. Archives of Industrial Health, October 1955.

Medical Association Committee Report, 1955) includes visual acuity at a distance and near vision, as well as visual fields, ocular motility, binocular vision, adaptations to light and dark, color vision, and accommodation (Lowenfeld, 1973). It should be noted that experimental programs for children with severely limited vision have demonstrated that visual training can achieve significant gains in visual efficiency (Ashcroft, Halliday, & Barraga, 1965; Barraga, 1964). Table 11-1 presents the relationship between Snellen measurements of distance acuity and the percentage of visual efficiency.

Functional vision is either central or peripheral. *Central vision* is concerned with receptor cells (cones), which provide color discrimination and permit sharp seeing tasks such as spotting an M & M on the floor or a picture in a book. *Peripheral vision* involves the receptor cells (rods), which provide awareness of movement and permit recognition under decreased illumination. With peripheral vision, the infant can locate a bottle on one side of him and track it 180 degrees. A child with damage in the peripheral areas can see things only right in front: "gun barrel" or "tunnel vision." For the teacher, functional vision is a determinant of where materials are placed, their size, the colors chosen, and the light selected (Langley & DuBose, 1976).

Incidence

Visual defects requiring eye care occur in about 20 percent of the general population, but most are corrected through prescriptive lenses. It is highly significant that noncorrectable visual impairments are found in only about 1 student per 1,000, and only 3 out of 10 such children are considered blind for educational purposes (Reynolds & Birch, 1978). Of the 83.8 million youth aged 0-21 in the United States in 1970, there were approximately 21 million who required eye care;

180,000 were partially sighted whose measurable acuity in the better eye was 20/70 or less with correction (of whom 32,000 were legally, but not totally blind), and about 13,000 were totally blind (Rand Report, 1974).

ASSESSING PRESCHOOL CHILDREN WITH VISUAL IMPAIRMENTS

Visual Screening

Routine examinations in day-care centers and preschool settings is a frequent source for discovery of children with severe visual problems. Tests useful in vision screening of young children are:

- *A Flash-Card Vision Test for Children*. (1966). This test was designed for preschool children and has proven successful with children 27 months of age. Three symbols (apple, house, umbrella) are presented in Snellen-acuity notation. The children can verbally or manually label or match symbols at ten feet or less to determine visual acuity.

- *The Home Eye Test*. (Boyce, 1973). This test has been successfully used with children as early as the age of three. It is easy to administer and is reliable and inexpensive. The kit consists of an "E" chart, with instructions for training and administration. It is given at a distance of ten feet.

- *The Snellen Symbol Chart*. (National Society for Prevention of Blindness). The Snellen Chart is a chart of symbols that are read at a distance of 20 feet. The basic unit of measurement is a visual angle of 1 minute of arc, a visual distance clearly distinguishable by the normal eye at 200 feet.

- *Stycar Vision Tests (Screening Tests for Young Children and Retardates)*. (Sheridan, 1973). One test of the Stycar Test battery is the miniature toy test, designed for children with limited verbal and coordination skills. The child is shown a set of ten familiar toys or objects and is asked to name them from a distance of three meters or ten feet. If he cannot name the toys, he matches them to a duplicate set.

Assessment of Behavior

Formal tests of children with visual impairments should examine the same behavioral domains assessed in sighted children. Without formal measures designed for visually-impaired children, many tests must be adapted or administered in part (DuBose, 1978; DuBose, Langley, Bourgeault, & Harley, 1977; DuBose, Langley, & Stagg, 1977). Table 11-2 lists instruments that can be used or adapted for use with this population. These tests were selected because of the information they provide about the child's use of his vision and because they do not penalize him for his poor vision.

Table 11-2 Tests for Use with Preschool Visually Impaired Children

Test	Age Range	Domain	Skills Assessed
Developmental Activities Screening Inventory (DASI) Teaching Resources 100 Boylston Avenue Boston, MA 02116	6-60 months	Screening of Cognitive Development	A teacher-administered screening instrument to determine general cognitive-adaptive functioning levels, accompanied by developmental activities suggestions. This instrument includes specific instructions on how to adapt materials for use with visually impaired children.
Maxfield-Buchholz Scale of Social Maturity for Preschool Blind Children American Foundation for the Blind, Inc. 15 West 16th Street New York, NY 10011	0-72 months	Screening of Social Maturity	Adaptation of the Vineland Social Maturity Scale for Blind Children. This scale of social development evaluates children in areas of general motor development, dressing, eating, locomotion, socialization, communication, and occupation.
Callier Azusa Callier Center for Communication Disorders 1966 Inwood Road Callas, TX 75235	84 months	Screening of General Development	Provides for assessment of socialization, daily living skills, motor development, perceptual abilities and language development. An observation model is used.

Table 11-2 *Continued*

Test	Age Range	Domain	Skills Assessed
Ordinal Scales of Psychological Development Uzgiris, I.C., & Hunt, J. McV. Assessment in infancy: Ordinal scales of psychological development. Urbana, IL: University of Illinois Press, 1975.	0-24 months	Cognitive Development	Series of 6 ordinal scales, based on Piagetian observations of sensory-motor schemas. Concerned with the hierarchical interrelationship of achievements at different levels. Six scales include visual pursuit and permanence of objects, development of means for obtaining desired environmental events.
Bayley Scales of Infant Development Psychological Corp. 757 3rd Avenue New York, NY 10017	0-30 months	Cognitive Development	Similar to Cattell. It includes separate motor and social scales in addition to a mental scale.
Infant Intelligence Scale (Cattell) Psychological Corp. 757 3rd Avenue New York, NY 10017	0-30 months	Cognitive Development	Contains manipulative tasks for determining sensory motor development, including imitation, problem solving, and a few language items.

Merrill-Palmer Scales of Mental Development Stoelting Co. 1350 S. Kostner Ave. Chicago, IL 60623	18-71 months	Cognitive Development	The scales assess not only the child's cognitive abilities, but expressive and receptive language and fine and gross motor skills. Comprised largely of performance items, some of which are timed. Provision is made for a child's refusal of an item.
McCarthy Scales of Children's Abilities Psychological Corp. 757 3rd Avenue New York, NY 10017	30-102 months	Cognitive Development	An instrument to measure general cognitive functioning, as well as child's strengths and weaknesses in verbal and perceptual performances. Quantitative, memory, motor development, and lateral skills also are examined.
Wechsler Preschool and Primary Scale of Intelligence (WPPSI) Psychological Corporation 757 3rd Avenue New York, NY 10017	48-78 months	Cognitive Development	The verbal subtests usually given to blind children include: Information, Comprehension, Similarities, Arithmetic and Vocabulary. The supplementary subtest of sentences is also useful with this population.
Sequenced Inventory of Communication Development University of Washington Press Seattle, WA 98105	4-48 months	Language Development	Receptive and Expressive scales permit examiner to assess the child in an informal play atmosphere.

Table 11-2 *Continued*

Test	Age Range	Domain	Skills Assessed
Receptive Expressive Language Assessment for the Visually Impaired S. Raynor Ingham Intermediate School Dist. Mason, MI	0-72 months	Language Development	An adaptation of the REEL for preschool blind children.
Inner Language Scale Rebecca F. DuBose Peabody College Box 328 Nashville, TN 37203	0-24 months	Language Development	The way in which a child responds to objects and environmental stimuli is assessed on this scale, based on Piagetian theory.
Developmental Sentence Analysis Lee, L.L. Developmental sentence analysis. Evanston, IL: Northwestern University Press, 1974.	24-96 months	Language Development	Analyzes children's spontaneous speech samples into eight major syntactic categories to derive a sentence score comparable to normal language development.

Laura Lee's Developmental Sentence Types (see above)	Pre-syntactic formations	Language Development	Analyzes children's spontaneous speech into the early developing pre-syntactic structures based on single- and two-word combinations, and elaborated constructions.
Environmental Prelanguage Battery Charles E. Merrill Publishing Co. 1300 Alum Creek Drive Box 508 Columbus, OH 43216	Early communication stages	Language Development	A series of diagnostic procedures for the nonverbal client. Assesses semantic and cognitive requirements for language through attention, gestures, imitation, play, comprehension and single words.
Environmental Language Inventory (see above)	One and two word utterance level	Language Development	A diagnostic and treatment model that assesses early semantic-based grammar through imitation, conversation, and play. Provides extensive data on early experimental parent-based programs using the ELI design and adaptations to total communication, later language and classroom use.

Table 11-2 *Continued*

Test	Age Range	Domain	Skills Assessed
Peabody Developmental Motor Scales Monograph #25 IMRID Publications Box 154 Peabody College Nashville, TN 37203	0-84 months	Motor Development	An instrument for use in assessing gross and fine motor development. The scoring section allows the child credit for minimum success rather than a pass or failure. The scales are accompanied by developmental activities for each area assessed.
Peabody Mobility Scale c/o Randall K. Harley Box 36 Peabody College Nashville, TN 37203	48-167 months	Motor Development	Scales and intervention materials for multiply handicapped blind children in the areas of basic motor, sensory, conceptual and mobility skills.

THE EYES AS SENSORY RECEPTORS

How Our Eyes Work

Much of what we learn comes to us through combined efforts of eyes and brain. For our eyes to receive information, light must fall on the image. As light rays are reflected from the image to the eyes, they pass through the *cornea,* or clear front window surrounding the eye, the *aqueous,* or watery liquid behind the cornea, the *pupil,* or opening in the colored *iris,* and the *lens.* The lens bends the light rays, inverting the image and focusing it on the *retina,* the rear inner lining of the eye. After hitting the retina, which contains rods (black and white receptors) and cones (color receptors), light rays are converted to electrical impulses that are relayed via the optic nerve to the brain. The brain adds meaning to the sensation, and we experience the image in a form compatible with what we know about the image or what it means to us in that given moment.

Common Causes of Visual Dysfunction

Refractive errors are the most common of eye problems, with one out of every two persons having a refractive error. Such an error means that the light rays entering the eye do not fall exactly on the retina. When the eyeball is too long, the image falls in front of the retina and *myopia (nearsightedness)* results. Nearsighted persons can see things close up, but they cannot distinguish images at a distance. When the eyeball is too short, the image falls in back of the retina and *hyperopia (farsightedness)* occurs. Farsighted persons see things better at a distance than when images are near to them. However, to view things clearly at various distances requires excessive accommodation of the lens curvature and can cause fatigue and restlessness.

If the cornea of the eye has an imperfect curvature, light rays focus separately rather than at a single point—*astigmatism (distorted and blurred vision).* The same person can have astigmatism along with nearsightedness or farsightedness.

Many young children have *amblyopia* or "lazy eye," a dimness of vision in one eye which causes the child to suppress the weaker eye and use only the stronger one. The condition may be due to eye-muscle imbalance, refractive error, or other defects present when the infant is learning to use his vision.

When the eyes do not focus together properly, *heterotropia* exists. One eye usually focuses on an object while the other eye is directed elsewhere. Other terms for this abnormality are *squint* and *strabismus.*

A *cataract*—the leading cause of blindness in the United States—is a cloudy condition or opacity in the lens of the eye, which interferes with vision. Opacity begins gradually as the light rays are partially blocked and are distorted by the time they fall on the retina. Cataract surgery, which involves the removal of the lens, is successful in 95 percent of cases. In young children, cataracts occur most frequent-

Figure 11-1 Horizontal Section of a Right Eyeball

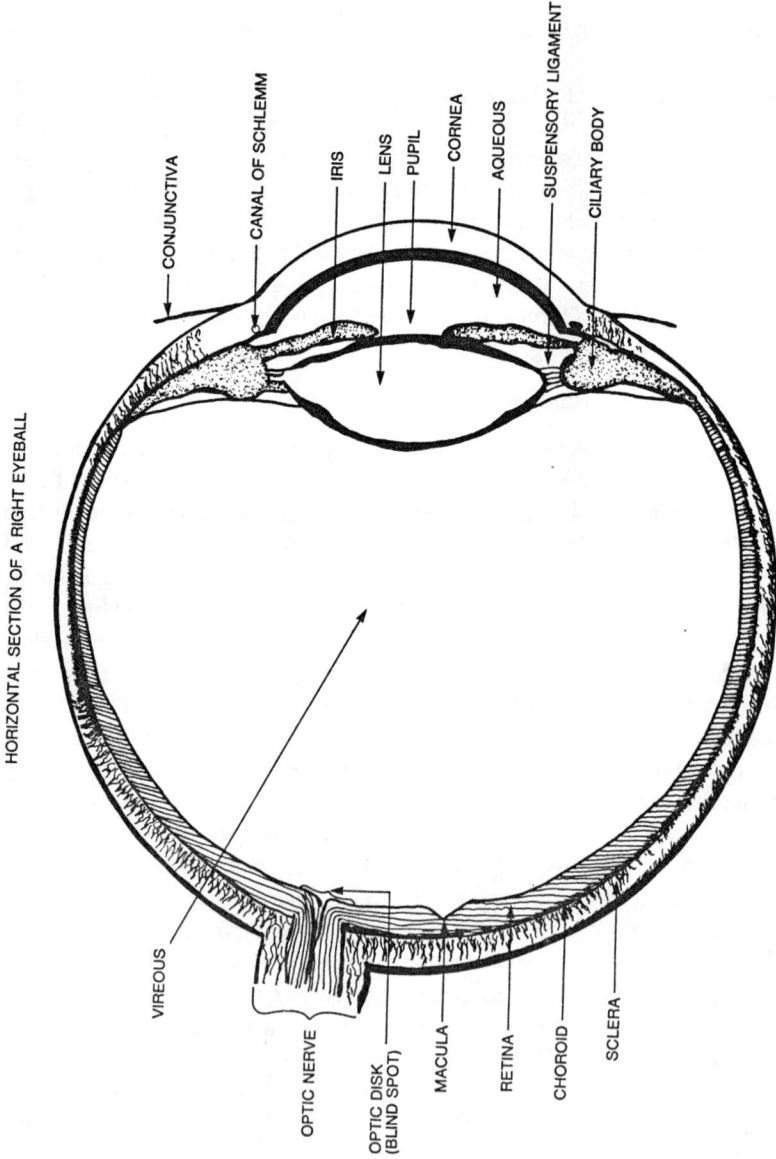

HORIZONTAL SECTION OF A RIGHT EYEBALL

CONJUNCTIVA

CANAL OF SCHLEMM

IRIS

LENS

PUPIL

CORNEA

AQUEOUS

SUSPENSORY LIGAMENT

CILIARY BODY

VIREOUS

OPTIC NERVE

OPTIC DISK (BLIND SPOT)

MACULA

RETINA

CHOROID

SCLERA

Source: Publication 169, by National Society to Prevent Blindness, Reprinted with permission.

ly because of damage to the fetus during the early months of pregnancy. Surgery is usually performed when the ophthalmologist considers the cataract "ripe."

Vision loss produced from increased pressure within the globe of the eye is called *glaucoma*. In glaucoma, the watery fluid in the eye fails to drain out properly and pressure builds up, damaging the nerve fibers of the optic nerve and causing impaired vision. Early symptoms develop slowly and are very difficult to detect. If diagnosed early, proper treatment can prevent damage. Researchers have found that primary glaucoma is inherited and offspring of glaucoma patients may be carriers, passing the disorder to their children without manifestations themselves.

Retinitis pigmentosa is an inherited disease caused by changes in the retina. The disease gradually destroys the rods and cones and decreases ability to see at night, resulting in *night blindness*, frequently a first symptom of the disease. Later, retinitis pigmentosa decreases peripheral or side vision even in daytime or when light is present, and results in *tunnel vision*.

When the inner layer of the retina separates from its outer layer, a condition known as *retinal detachment* results. This condition occurs most frequently when a tear or hole develops in the retina and vitreous fluid located in the interior chamber of the eye seeps between the retinal layers and causes the separation. Vision is usually affected by a darkening of one portion of the visual field; other signs are sootlike spots or light flashes. If diagnosed early, surgery can restore vision in 85 percent of cases.

In some cases, a degeneration is limited to a very small but important area of the retina, called the *macula*. The macula, located in the central retina, is responsible for perception of fine details. Reading is very dependent on a properly functioning macula, and *macular degeneration* results in a gradual loss of central vision.

Signs of Visual Difficulty

There are observable signs of visual problems that can be noted by teachers or other care providers. Some of these are listed in Table 11-3.

Visual Aids and Treatments

Corrective lenses (eyeglasses or contacts) are the aids most often used to improve impaired vision. Many preschool children, however, are not being fitted with contact lenses when large refractive errors are found.

Amblyopia is treated by patching the stronger eye, forcing use of the amblyopic eye.

Cataracts are treated by surgical removal of the damaged lens, and implantation of a substitute lens, special eyeglasses or contact lenses may be prescribed. Surgery is also possible to correct *retinal detachment*.

Glaucoma is treated by drugs, or, if necessary, surgery to create another outlet

---

Table 11-3 Observable Signs of Visual Problems

1. Eyes turn in or out at any time.
2. Red or watery eyes.
3. Encrusted eyelids.
4. Frequent styes.
5. Swollen eyes.
6. Frequent head adjustment when looking at distant objects.
7. Focusing difficulties.
8. Tracking difficulties.
9. Rubs eyes frequently.
10. Complains of itchy, scratchy, or stinging eyes.
11. Avoids close work.
12. Frequent blinking, frowning, or scowling.
13. Tilts or turns head to focus on objects.
14. Tires after visual tasks.
15. Moves head rather than eyes while looking at a page.
16. Frequent confusion of similarly shaped letters, numbers, and words.
17. Covers one eye to sight with other eye.
18. Unusually clumsy or awkward.
19. Poor eye-hand coordination.
20. Headaches or nausea after close visual tasks.

---

for the fluid. *Heterotropia* is treated with lenses, prisms, occlusion, visual training, drugs, or surgery (Harley & Lawrence, 1977).

In many cases of eye disease, early detection and treatment can mean usable vision for a longer period.

THE EFFECTS OF VISUAL IMPAIRMENT ON DEVELOPMENT

Motor Development

Mary Stewart (1974) views the secret of coordination as performing the right action at the right time: the present, the past, or the future. The present is a comparison of current sensory perceptions with goal definitions; the past consists of (a) knowledge of results following completion of an act, and (b) "fresh traces" representing comparison of what is now happening with what happened a microsecond earlier. The future is concerned with the image of an act yet to be, and involves the ability to anticipate. If Stewart's analysis is correct, it helps explain why visually-impaired children have difficulties in motor coordination. In the present, they do not receive accurate reflections; past experiences may have given them inconsistent data; and they lack complete visual images for anticipating what will occur.

Children whose visual impairments are so severe they are considered blind or have light perception only, experience their world differently, resulting in selective lags in developing certain motor and locomotor behaviors. On early development of blind infants, information is limited to tabular data provided by Norris, Spaulding, and Brodie (1957) and Selma Fraiberg and her associates. Table 11-4 compares developmental milestones of sighted and blind children, using data from Fraiberg (1977).

The table shows that items falling within the normal range were rolling, independent sitting, and independent standing behaviors, as well as taking stepping movements when hands were held. These motor performances required a low and relatively stable center of gravity and could be performed by blind children with little risk or danger, since they did not require leaving the immediate base of support.

Lags were reported in behaviors requiring the infant to project his body into space (elevating upper torso by arm support, raising self to sitting, pulling to stand, crawling, or walking). In an older preschool population, Folio (1974) found more

---

Table 11-4 Gross Motor Items and Age Achieved by Blind (Child Development Project) and Sighted (Bayley)

ITEM	Age Range		Median Age		Difference in Median Ages
	Sighted	Blind	Sighted	Blind	
Elevates self by arms, prone	.07-5.0	4.5-9.5	2.1	8.75	6.65
Sits alone momentarily	4.0-8.0	5.0-8.5	5.3	6.75	1.45
Rolls from back to stomach	4.0-10.0	4.5-9.5	6.4	7.25	.85
Sits alone steadily	5.0-10.0	6.5-9.5	6.6	8.00	1.40
Raises self to sitting position	6.0-11.0	9.5-15.5	8.3	11.00	2.70
Stands up by furniture (pulls up to stand)	6.0-12.0	9.5-15.0	8.6	13.00	4.40
Stepping movements (walks hands held)	6.0-12.0	8.0-11.5	8.8	10.175	1.95
Stands alone	9.0-16.0	9.0-15.5	11.0	13.00	2.00
Walks alone, 3 steps	9.0-17.0	11.5-19.0	11.7	15.25	3.55
Walks alone, across room	11.3-14.3	12.0-20.5	21.1	10.25	7.15

NOTE: *All ages given in months.*

Source: Table 5 from *INSIGHTS FROM THE BLIND: Comparative Studies of Blind and Sighted Infants,* by Selma Fraiberg, p. 204, © 1977 by Selma Fraiberg, Basic Books, Inc., Publishers, New York.

advanced projectile skills of running, hopping, jumping, and skipping also delayed.

Prehension Skills

Fraiberg (1977) has poignantly portrayed the dramatic effects of loss of sight on development of prehension in early infancy.

> In the biological program it is 'intended' that vision and prehension evolve in synchrony. The story of prehension is not the story of the maturational and adaptive functions of the hand alone, but the story of hand and eye, eye and hand. . . . The hand unites the infant with a world 'out there,' in which the purposeful reach gives intentionality to action and a sense of voluntariness in the formative period of the ego. . . . In cruelest irony, these hands quite literally groping in the near void of the blind child's world derailed in their progress by a deficit in the biological plan, must come to serve the blind child as primary perceptual organs—something not 'intended,' either, in human biology (pp. 147-148).

The most obvious difference in young sightless infants relative to prehension is the position of the hands when seated. At five months, when the sighted infant is developing proficiency in intentional reaching, the blind infant maintains his hands at shoulder height in a neonatal posture. If a rattle is placed in his hand, he will grasp it firmly and retain it; if a second toy is introduced, the first is dropped; if a favorite toy drops, the hands do not search for it.

Grasping in the blind infant, while apparently emerging within the range for sighted infants, is clumsy and unpracticed. When interest wanes, or the hands are empty, they return to the shoulder position. A major difference is the lack of engagement of the hands at midline: the head has found its midline orientation, but the hands have not. The mutual fingering seen in sighted infants is apparently sustained through the visual spectacle, which is not possible for the sightless infant; thus, hand reciprocity and coordination of hand and eye in intentional reaching remain static in nascent form.

The various forms of grasps, while basically in the blind infant's repertoire, are not always functional. For example, the sighted infant at nine months may choose to use a neat pincer grasp to secure a piece of dry cereal from his tray. The blind child reverts to a raking movement, since it is more adaptive and efficient in helping him locate and secure the small morsel.

Behaviors dependent on prehension, such as holding two objects simultaneously, one in each hand, and the transfer of objects were delayed in the blind infants.

The ability to reach for and attain an object occurs in sighted infants around 4.6 months, while, even with intervention, blind babies who had substituted hearing for vision were at the 8.27 months range (6:18-11:01) when they demonstrated this behavior.

The developmental differences in gross motor skills and in prehension are more significant than they may appear. The infant's tendency to resort to more primitive responses or to clumsily executed behaviors affects coordination experimentation with variations, acquisition of problem solving skills, and other behaviors more obvious in the delays experienced in the cognitive development of sensorimotor schemata.

Language Development

Unfortunately, language development in blind children has been investigated by only a few researchers. Warren (1977) concludes after thorough review that blind children develop the expected language although some intervening differences are noted before four and five years of age.

In the first year of life, very few differences in early vocalizations and imitation are observed, since these depend on neurophysiological maturation and performance, and are not deterred by blindness. Interestingly, blind babies in Fraiberg's study (1977) imitated words above the mean for sighted babies.

During the early part of the second year, sighted infants begin to utter single words. By 14 months, sighted babies say two words under test conditions, but blind babies achieve it by 18.5 months. Fraiberg suggests that representational behavior is involved and, without visual experiences, the blind child must rely solely on experiences with things touched or heard and thus has a deprived experiential base. Another possible factor is mobility: the sighted infant has been creeping for seven months and is now walking; the blind child's mobility is significantly delayed and thus experiences with objects in the surrounding world and the opportunity to learn names to associate with those objects are hampered.

When the Bayley Scale item, "uses words to make wants known," was assessed, blind infants' responses were approximately on the same level as sighted infants. The wants expressed by babies apparently derive from internal-need states, and blindness, therefore, does not impede verbal expression of those needs.

A lag of six months was noted when assessing "sentences of two words." Putting two words together is a function of concept development and, like the delay in initial single words, the linking of two words is delayed because of lack of exposure to attributes, actions, and qualities that are readily visible to the sighted youngster.

An interesting aspect of language, so deeply embedded in self-concept, social, and cognitive behavior that it cannot clearly be distinguished as language development, is the use of "me" and "I." Sighted children begin to represent themselves in their world of play around two-and-a-half years of age. For blind children, these interactions occurred between three and four-and-a-half years. The use of these pronouns is closely related to the symbolic representation of the self and the delay is a factor of this play behavior.

In summary, language development in blind children follows different milestones in the early years of language acquisition, but these differences are overcome by five years of age.

Cognitive Development

Jean Piaget, the Swiss psychologist, traced the origins of cognitive development to the sensorimotor period, during which the infant progresses from reflexive responses to representational behavior. Table 11-5 presents the major stages of the sensorimotor period and the effects of blindness at the various stages.

Earliest indications of divergence in acquisition of sensorimotor schemata occur in the third stage when blind infants fail to reach for objects. Lack of sensory stimulation hinders integration of the blind child's sensorimotor experiences. Toward the end of the first year, auditory senses begin to be used actively as visual substitutes, and evidence of organization of the world begins to emerge.

Perhaps the most obvious delay experienced by blind infants is in object concept, considered by Fraiberg (1968) to emerge between ages three and five years, in contrast to two years for the sighted child. Delayed object concept stems from the child's failure to engage in sustained search behavior and the closely related delay in attainment of object permanence. The delay in object concept further inhibits acquisition of spatial concepts and causality.

Delays reduce the information about the surrounding world reaching the blind child and therefore diminish understanding of the relatedness of objects to other objects, events, persons, and experiences. These deficiencies, in turn, affect acquisition of higher-level cognitive skills such as classification and conservation. Piaget and Inhelder (1969) noted:

> The sensory disturbance peculiar to those born blind has, from the outset, hampered the development of sensory-motor schemes and slowed down general coordination . . . action learning is still necessary before these children develop the capacity for operations on a level with that of the normal child . . . (pp. 88-89).

Fortunately, there is evidence (Brekke, Williams, & Tait, 1974) of conditions in which certain kinds of delays (weight conservation) do not exist for blind children, thus reinforcing the importance of intervention.

Social and Emotional Development

Socialization is the process by which skills are acquired to live in harmony with those around one and to care for one's physical, mental, and emotional needs. It is a continuous process, starting at birth and continuing throughout life, as one adapts to new situations and changing needs. The loss of vision will alter the child's

Table 11-5 Effects of Blindness on Sensorimotor Development

Period	Expectations	Blindness
I. Reflexes (0-1 month)	The infant's behavior is characterized primarily by reflexive responses to his own body and to some aspects of the external world. Some refinement of reflexive behavior occurs as the infant discovers, for example, that some objects are "suckable" and some are not.	1. no pupillary restrictions to light in some cases.
II. Primary Circular Reactions (1-4 months)	The infant begins to repeat selectively those actions that produce effects that are interesting or satisfying to him. These actions are primarily directed to his own body rather than to external objects.	1. no visual tracking. 2. no examination of feet and hands. 3. no intentional grasping of objects.
III. Secondary Circular Reactions (4-9 months)	The infant reproduces behaviors that produce effects in the external world that are satisfying or interesting to him. This stage marks the beginning of the infant's effective orientation to the external world.	1. continues bodily centered sensations. 2. fails to follow rapid movements of persons and objects. 3. fails to understand the cause or source of object activation. 4. no search for lost objects.
IV. Coordination of Secondary Circular Reactions (9-12 months)	The beginnings of intentionality are seen in the fourth stage, in that the infant begins to coordinate	1. fails to visually attend to objects or persons or imitate movements.

Table 11-5 *Continued*

Period	Expectations	Blindness
	his behavior with respect to the external world in more complex ways. His use of specific ends demonstrates his increasing organization of the world. He begins to anticipate the effects of his own actions and those of other people.	2. fails to realize similarity in objects; thus, does not generalize old schema to new objects. 3. cannot see a distant goal to attain it.
IV. Coordination of Secondary Circular Reactions (con't.) (9-12 months)		4. fails to perceive of self in relation to environment. 5. less likely to initiate interaction with adult to repeat an action.
V. Tertiary Circular Reactions (12-18 months)	In this stage, the infant's behavior clearly involves active trial and error experimentation on the world. His behavior becomes more flexible in that he can systematically vary his actions to obtain a specific goal. He seems to seek novelty for the sake of learning more about the world.	1. fails to see relationships between action and solution that can be accomplished to produce activity. 2. less problem solving in environment. 3. fails to attack barriers to secure toys. 4. fails to see the usefulness of tools to assist in securing goals.
VI. Invention of New Means through Mental Combination	This stage marks the beginning of internalized thought. The child need no longer engage in overt trial-and-error behavior, but rather	1. delayed in internalization of action schema. 2. cannot categorize objects by

(18-24 months)	can think about possible behaviors and the effects that they would have. According to Piaget, this stage is a landmark in that it frees the child from his own perceptions and behaviors. He begins to imagine behaviors and their consequences.	salient dimensions. 3. does not pretend by imitating adult behavior previously observed.

acquisition of social targets because the child cannot read the context or situation to be noted, and, as importantly, the person interacting with the child, may respond differently.

Hallenbeck (1954) found that a significant factor associated with absence of emotional disturbance in a group of residential school blind children was whether a child had established a good relationship with some person before entering school. Lowenfeld (1964) pinpointed the attitude of parents as more critical to the child's development than the particular child-rearing techniques employed. The role of the blind child's family, and more importantly, the mother, in fostering a positive self-concept and establishing an appropriate base from which to develop acceptable interaction and self-care skills cannot be underestimated. "They hold the string of his independence, and they must slowly let it go, giving him all the freedom he can handle at a given time, so that he can develop self-reliance and the ability to function quite apart from them" (DuBose, 1976).

From birth through the first few months of life, the blind child is quiet and passive, and will likely remain so if outside stimulation does not evoke pleasurable experiences. It is critical that the blind child be cuddled, enjoyed, and placed at the center of family activities. The emotional message that must be conveyed is that the child brings pleasure to those around him and that others can provide pleasure for him.

An early sign of appropriate social behavior is smiling. Blind babies smile less frequently and less dramatically. "During the second year, open displays of affection remain induced responses and the child behaves as if he cannot himself be the initiator of a relationship" (Lairy & Harrison-Corello, 1973, p.5). This is seen in the failure to develop independence from the mother; hence, separation anxiety intensifies and continues beyond the second year. When separation does occur, the child reacts with helplessness and regression.

Tait (1972) has suggested that play and exploratory behavior are related to the degree of social attachment experienced by the blind child. These behaviors move the infant away from himself and toward the external world where both social independence and adequate social reciprocity with others than parents can develop.

Development of a positive view of one's self is also critical to social competency. Scott (1968) maintains that self-concept is acquired in large part through interactions and expectations of others, particularly the parents. These perceptions, transmitted from significant caregivers to the child, will make him the *blind man* Scott has referred to or will make him a man who happens to have a visual impairment.

Self-Care Development

Development of independence in caring for his own physical needs (these are very similar to those of sighted children) is critical for the blind child. Strategies for teaching independence will need to be adapted to each child's learning style.

Eating

It is important that blind babies get verbal input during feeding that will prepare them for what is to come; without sight, they cannot anticipate what is coming. With a hand on the adult's mouth, the child can begin to associate opening the mouth with food intake. The child will also need to be provided time to smell food. Finger feeding is very important and should be introduced around the end of the first year. Spoon training should likewise be encouraged once finger feeding has been mastered.

Movement from strained to solid foods is sometimes very difficult for blind babies, and there is a tendency for the baby to rebel. Frequently parents back off and fail to move the child from strained foods. The same resistance is seen when chewing is introduced. Again, allowing the child to feel the adult's mouth imitating chewing and possibly manually exercising the child's jaw can facilitate the process. Chewing can be introduced by placing foods, such as peanut butter, on the roof of the mouth or between the back teeth and cheek in order to have the child begin manipulating the mouth.

Introduction of a piece of bread as a "pusher" is usually necessary to insure that the blind child locates food on the plate. Since this skill requires some degree of hand coordination, it is usually not introduced until the third year. The eating process should follow the same order, and the verbal input should alert the child to expectations. These inputs are essential for appropriate development.

Toileting

Parents of blind children report greater difficulties in toilet training blind children than sighted children. Physiologically, there is no reason for this, and the problems could well be a factor of the environment. A main difference in toilet training revolves around the need to explain to the child what the toilet is and how it is used, since the child cannot observe others using it. The general milestones and procedures for training vary little from those of sighted children.

Dressing

Ability to dress independently is related to development of gross and fine motor skills and of concepts. Delays in these areas are predictive of delays in dressing.

Again, sequencing and consistency are critical in training the blind child to acquire dressing skills. Proper orientation of clothing is a necessity in finding, for example, the various holes in shirts and pants.

Slight delays can be expected in attainment of self-care objectives: the sequence of learning is simply longer, frequently because the caregivers do it *for* the child rather than taking the time to train the blind child to perform a task. Instruction in new tasks should follow an orderly progression that builds on skills already possessed. Instruction should be: (1) *concrete,* using objects or events being experienced; (2) *individual,* adapted to meet particular needs; (3) *unified,* using prior knowledge or experience; (4) *structured,* introducing concepts or ideas in a logical manner; and (5) *motivational,* requiring the child to initiate ways to care for needs and act independently in as many situations as possible.

In summary, this section has presented an overview of the early development of blind children. Attention has focused on the sameness and the differences one can expect in the early learning experiences of blind children when compared to sighted peers. The environment's role in fostering development has been stressed as central in hastening or restraining acquisition of behaviors the child is ready to learn. Particular delays, observed in young blind children, have been stressed to point out where intervention will be needed.

INSTRUCTING INFANTS AND TODDLERS

The frequently heard adage that we should "teach/treat a handicapped child like we do any other child" has been taken out of context and misused by parents and teachers. The content of instruction for the visually impaired is usually the same as it is for sighted children; however, materials and procedures may be the same or be quite varied. In many respects, caregivers' responses to the handicapped should be the same as the responses to their nonimpaired peers; however, a handicap signifies the need for special instructions to lessen the effects of the impairment on the child's developing behavior.

Home-Visitor Programs

When an infant's vision is severely limited, it is critical that caregivers be aware of the effects this limitation has on the developing child and begin special instruction in the early weeks of life. The first professional educator is usually a home or parent visitor. The home visitor's responsibilities can be:

1. To provide information regarding
   a. availability and options for other services
   b. effects the lack of vision is having on all areas of development
   c. instructional procedures for minimizing effects of visual loss on developing schemas
   d. parents who have experienced similar events
2. To work with the parent in setting periodic objectives
3. To provide access to materials needed to facilitate instruction
4. To demonstrate teaching strategies
5. To observe and record the child's progress
6. To provide the parent with feedback on the child's progress and on their own progress
7. To serve as a resource and support to the parent as needed
8. To engage in parent counseling

Infant and Preschool Programs

Once major medical problems have been addressed and the child's immediate physical condition is stable to the point that exposure to other young children does not present problems, ongoing programs for young handicapped children may be undertaken.

In infant programs, the training of the caregivers remains paramount; however, the infant does receive more attention and instruction than provided in the home-visitor model. The programs provide support frequently from other parents with similar children, and direct access to ancillary services and to lending libraries that provide books, toys, and materials. The programs are likely to provide also a more precise data system for measuring child progress and program effectiveness; thus, caregivers are more likely to have a clearer understanding of a child's current abilities and potential.

Several infant, toddler, and preschool programs include visually-impaired youngsters following a mainstreaming model. Other programs have been designed specifically for visually-impaired children. The very comprehensive manual *Alive . . . Aware . . . A Person* describes in detail the program for visually-impaired preschool children in the Montgomery County (Maryland) Public Schools.

CURRICULAR CONCERNS FOR PRESCHOOL VISUALLY-IMPAIRED CHILDREN

Sensory Development

Development and refinement of the remaining senses is critical to the young blind child's knowledge of the surrounding world. Instruction should include goal-directed use of the nonimpaired sensory channels and of the visual channel if any vision remains.

1. Kinesthetic Modality. The seeing child learns about body expression by mimicking what he sees. The blind child must learn the body movements, and be told that they convey feelings and messages and that these are being received by others.

a. Physically and orally, prompt appropriate body responses such as "yes," "no" head turns, waving, happy faces, sad faces, winking, directing head movements at persons communicating to them.
b. Relate body actions to language; teach all prepositions by physically directing the child in the movements of under, over, into, beside, etc.
c. Permit the child to experience as many physical movements as possible: crawling, pivoting, tiptoeing, galloping, jumping, stretching, running, throwing and catching are all important skills for the blind child.

2. Tactual. The tactual sense (sense of touch) will play a major role in the child's development. Through the fingertips, the child will explore, label, classify, compare, and eventually read. The refinement of the tactual sense is critical to the child's exploratory behavior and eventual learning about the world.

a. Physically prompt the child to touch surfaces that differ, stress labeling and comparisons. Some examples are: coarse, damp, furry, dry, rough, soft, smooth, wet, sharp, hard, oily, etc.
b. Encourage the child to experience different surfaces with many parts of the body; have the child walk, run, jump, etc., on grass, gravel, concrete, dirt, etc. Have the child roll on mats, hardwood, grass, up hills and down hills, etc.
c. Blind children are frequently exposed to only parts of large objects, yet learn the label for the large object. It is essential that the trainer present the whole concept to the child. Let the child feel the entire object, move the various parts, then feel miniature replicas of the whole object for a global understanding of how the parts fit together. Check the child's understanding of whole concepts by having him describe the total concept.

3. Auditory. The auditory modality is the major channel for the blind child's learning. The modality will not be keener of its own accord, it must be trained.

a. Help the child learn to identify sounds that are high, low, loud, soft, close by, far away, slow, fast, rhythmic, moving, stationary, etc.
b. Lengthen auditory attention span through games, sequenced instructions, citations of important information such as name, address, telephone number, etc.

c. Use music, television, radio, citizens' radio, etc., to help the child develop listening and attention skills; ask the child questions to check for comprehension and organization of auditory memory, e.g., "Today is Wednesday, what programs can we listen to tonight?"

4. Olfactory. The sense of smell will alert the blind child to danger or pleasure. Encourage him to develop the olfactory sense and learn to label experience and the meaning carried by the labels.

a. Let the child associate smells with different family members.
b. Help the child identify foods, places, and events by smell; e.g., let the child tell you when you are at the gas station, bakery, shoe store, fish market, hospital, etc.
c. Encourage the child to smell many more things than one would introduce to the sighted child through smell: clothes, furniture, foods, kitchen cleansers, seasonings, paper products, bathroom creams, etc.

5. Gustatory. The sense of taste will also serve the blind child as a receptive channel. Encourage the child to sample a broad array of foods and other edibles.

a. Emphasize the differences between hot (temperature) and hot (spicy).
b. Expose the child to foods that are: sweet, sour, salty, mild, rich, bland, cold, lukewarm, acidic, starchy, raw, cooked, etc. Label each, then subsequently have the child label the food.
c. Do not try to confuse the child through foods. It is important that the child have all the cues available to know what is being tasted and to develop preferences. It is important that the child be encouraged to eat a very broad selection of foods. Explain what the various foods do for the body.

6. Vision. If any light perception remains, it should be trained to be as efficient as possible; using it will not harm the remaining vision, but failure to use it will make it even less functional; it will not improve the acuity, but it will improve its functional efficiency.

a. Introduce high contrast items; e.g., yellow on black.
b. Exphasize heavy outlines of objects, pictures, letters, etc.
c. Use the overhead projector to teach identification of objects by shape.
d. Gradually decrease size and intensity of objects as the child becomes more proficient in identification.

Gross Motor Development

1. Reaching. Not knowing that an interesting spectacle is before him, the blind child is not likely to reach for objects. To facilitate reaching, let the blind child touch a noisy object; gradually withdraw the object, but sound the object as the child searches. Let the child again grasp the object when arms are outstretched in an exploratory manner. Make it known that if the child wishes an object, he must explore to find that object.

2. Transferring. The blind child perseverates in unilateral handling of objects. To encourage transference from hand to hand, let the child play with a small car on a table, rolling from hand to hand. After the child has one object in his hand, present another to the same hand. Present a bottle or favorite toy to the nonpreferred hand.

3. Midline Skills. The blind child needs to operate the hands together on an object with each hand performing a different task. Present the child with a toy drum that must be held with one hand while being hit with the other hand. Present a pot into which the child can drop kitchen utensils such as measuring spoon, jar lids, small cups, etc. Present toys that must be activated by turning handles, etc., while holding the toy.

4. Throwing. Without visual judgment of distance, the blind child does not develop propulsion skills. Have the child drop balls through a suspended hoop. Tie a yarn ball on a string to the child's wrist and physically guide a release through the hoop or just in the space. Use auditory balls and have him throw against walls or to another person.

5. Head Control. When child is in prone position with arms elevated on adult's thigh, dangle sound toys above the child's head.

6. Crawling and Creeping. Use human voices and sounds of favorite toys to encourage the child to move out in space. Use a crawl-a-gaitor or make a diaper sling and lift the child's abdomen off the floor in a physically-prompted crawl.

7. Walking. Support the child around the waist in walking exercises. Walk the child on top of the adult's feet. Walk the child through a ladder on the floor so that the feet must be lifted.

Fine-Motor Development

1. Grasping. Without sight to identify objects in space, the blind child uses the hands to locate things. Because more space can be covered in sweeping, palmar motions, the child resorts to these to accommodate searching behavior. To facilitate higher forms of grasps, provide cradle gyms that must be achieved; small toys to squeak; formboards with holes to finger. The child can also benefit from squeezing small pieces of dough between hand and fingers. A rubber band can be placed over the four fingers and thumb; then the child can flex the hand, thus developing grasping action.

2. Locating Objects. Provide a play table with raised edges so toys will not be out of reach. Place assorted objects at various places for child to find and explore. Turn on a radio or phonograph at various positions in the room and have the child locate; this can also be done with a rattle, squeeze toy, or other sound source. Drop an object that creates a sound, such as keys, rattle, etc., and have the child locate. Child can also drop or throw object and retrieve it. In this procedure, the child is building in an awareness that objects lost can be found by the sound they emit.

3. Body Sensitivity to Objects. Use objects of various shapes, textures, and temperatures, then play games with the child by rolling them across various body parts. Have the child identify the object and the body part; for example, the child might respond, "You drove my truck up my back and it stopped on my neck." After brushing the object over the child, have the child pick it up from a group of objects nearby. Using a paint brush, brush parts of body and have child say when he is being touched and where.

4. Handcrafts. Encourage activities with play dough, clay, finger paints, paper and cloth weaving, painting on an easel, making mosaics, using glue and various materials, stringing activities, etc.

5. Spatial Orientation. Provide experiences in block building, peg and peg-boards, Lego blocks, nesting cups and blocks, puzzles, model building, Tinker Toys, construction sets, etc.

6. Cutting. Begin with scissors with four-finger holes so that the adult can guide the activity. Progress from straight lines heavily marked to curved lines, then zig-zag lines, to encourage eye-hand coordination. If vision is very limited, glue string or yarn to paper in various designs and have child cut around yarn or string. Raised-line designs can be made on paper with seamstress tracing wheel. Place pressure on the wheel on one side of heavy manila or construction paper, and the design will be inverted on the other side.

7. Touch Identification. Begin with common objects that must be briefly touched, then identified. Move to raised outlines of the pictures of the objects.

8. Marking and Drawing. Teach the child to follow lines between edges of hard liquid glue. Use templates of various shapes and let the child experience the continuity of movement and shape.

9. Tracing. With tracing paper over first flat objects, then raised picture outlines, let child locate and then trace shapes. Move to more abstract designs, letters, numbers, etc.

10. Reproduction. Use pairs of peg boards and rubber band-nail boards. Have the child reproduce on his board the design he feels on another board. Provide two pegboards and have child create his own identical designs. Present child with a design made from toothpicks and let child create an identical design. Do the same with parquetry designs.

11. Sequencing. Begin with simple discriminations on one dimension with two sizes. Move to more items that must be arranged in a continuum of large to small, left to right. Increase difficulty by adding dimensions, such as shape, color, texture, and have child reproduce a model of the sequence. Bead-stringing using various shapes is a good way to apply this concept. Move to raised outlines of shapes and vary depending on child's vision and ability.

12. Pre-Braille. For totally blind children, begin teaching the shape of the basic braille cell and expose child to numbers and name in braille after teaching scanning skills. Have him match braille letters and numbers to like braille and numbers, and then match whole words from two to three letter words to more complex ones.

Receptive Language Development

An understanding of the meaning of sounds will come from listening and experiencing; therefore, provide opportunities for these to coincide.

1. Attending to Sound. Call attention to sounds; physically prompt child to stop and listen.

2. Localization of Sound. Prompt child to turn ear, then nose, in the direction of the sound source. Turn on a radio, phonograph, or shake a sound toy momentarily and ask the child from where the sound was being emitted.

3. Discrimination of Sounds. This follows child's ability to attend, localize, and identify. Encourage child in noting sameness, differences along several dimensions and at several distances. Shake, roll, or squeeze toys, ask child what object emits the sound heard. Later ask child to identify the names with the noises of others in his immediate environment or sounds that animals or other situations (weather, door opening) make. These sounds may be reproduced from records. Move from object sounds to oral sounds.

4. Sound-Symbol Association. As child develops sound-symbol association, say object words and have him locate the object, then later perform acts with the object such as "Put the spoon in the bowl."

5. Vocabulary Comprehension. Have child respond in different ways such as raise left or right hand, hit drum or table different number of times when you name objects that are classified differently; e.g., people vs. actions; places vs. descriptive words; physical attributes vs. location (prepositions).

6. Laterality. Emphasize identity of left and right parts of body and of objects. Some examples are: place your left hand on the table, lift your right foot, or place your left hand on your right shoulder.

7. Directionality. Have child place things according to directions, permit child to move in space according to simply stated commands. Emphasize number of steps, etc., as skills develop. Playing "Simon Says" is an example of how this can be incorporated into a game. Move from simple one-stage commands to more complex stages. Some examples are: "pick up the ball, then pick up the ball and place it on the table."

8. Listening for Sequences. Provide child with proper sequences that have omissions and errors, and let him spot the error.

9. Auditory Overload. Blind children can be oversaturated with radio input. Encourage selectivity in radio and phonograph input, and do not let this take the place of human contact. Encourage the child to seek out peers for information and socialization.

Expressive Language Development

1. Expressions of Feeling. Identify cries and sounds with the appropriate emotions, saying to the child, "Oh, you are sad" or "You are happy." Repeat the sound as child realizes the meaning conveyed.

2. Babbling. Repeat sounds as one would with any child. Let child feel the sound through your mouth, nose, and throat.

3. Vocabulary Building. As words emerge, be sure to attach as much meaning as possible to words, so that concept relations develop along with labeling. Keep examples as concrete as possible; e.g., if teaching the word "ball," give the child a ball to tactually explore. Give as many different examples as possible until the child really understands what the object is. Expand the meaning of "ball" with examples that vary on dimensions such as size and texture.

4. Self-Image. Encourage self-awareness by early identification of body parts and properties on self and others. Stress use of "I," "me," "mine" and other personal pronouns applied correctly to others.

5. Concept Statements. Provide experiences that are meaningful, then cautiously expand the abstract statements that can be applied so that language maintains its symbolic representation purpose for the child. Provide many different experiences, objects, and events that will provide transfer between statements.

Cognitive Development

1. Causality. Provide experiences that enable the child to understand that a motor act causes something to happen. This can be experienced through toys that vibrate or continue moving after the child pushes or hits them to initiate movement such as a roly-poly toy, a toy secured by suction on a tray, or a pound-around. Make sure that the child feels the effects.

Encourage the child to move about freely in a safe environment in which many objects have been placed to provide causality relationships. This will allow the child the opportunity to experience the causality of objects and events as they will occur naturally as his mobility develops and will negate some of his fears as the child travels into more unfamiliar environments.

2. Means-End. Provide experiences similar to number one; however, the effects should be auditory or tactile. For example, he shakes a toy and it continues to make noise; he activates a music box that plays a tune; he turns a handle and feels the water run.

3. Object Permanence. The blind child is unable to solve simple problems such as finding a toy that might be slightly out of reach, or hidden under another object. Play hide and seek games, telling the child that the toy is hiding and he must search for it. Model and physically prompt the searching behavior.

4. Problem-Solving. The blind child is slow to realize that objects in the environment can be used in multiple ways, particularly to solve problems that might exist separately from the object itself. Encourage multiple use of objects, and association of the object with other things. For example, let the child see that by climbing first on a footstool, he can get to the sofa without help; or beating up detergent in a pan of water produces bubbles.

5. Classification. The ability to classify is very important in the developing blind child. Stress qualities that make objects the same or different. Let the child feel and verbally repeat these characteristics. Play games in which the child must classify objects according to a specified dimension, then reverse the situation and give him a series of objects, having him tell you why they are alike or different. Some examples are: sorting different size beads, blocks, or other objects into separate containers. Stress shape, size, texture, and weight; do not stress one without the others.

6. Environmental Structure. The ability to order one's environment or to understand the order others have imposed is a most important skill. Always maintain furniture and objects in their same and appropriate place. Help the child to identify the objects and tell where they belong. Provide opportunities for the child to manipulate the environment as with moving an object (such as a chair) closer to the open window so that he will feel cooler on a hot day. This will facilitate grasping the idea that the child can manipulate its needs or personal comfort.

7. Reasoning. Play simple games that lead to reasoning, then check them out to see if they are true. For example, say "If we open the refrigerator door, we will _____ _____ _____ (feel cold air)." If we turn on the left hand faucet in the sink, we will _____ _____ _____ (get hot water)." Provide the child with concrete examples that will lead to proper reasoning of events. While asking the questions or having the child fill in the blanks, allow him to actually experience what will occur and later repeat the questions to see if he has grasped what occurred.

8. Concept Development. Distortions of real objects are quite common in blind children, because their tactual experiences have been with small replications. Provide comparisons and let the child tactually experience real dimensions when possible. Check verbal understanding by having the child describe size, shape, etc. Whenever possible, provide concrete examples in their real context. Removing examples from their context may distort the child's grasp of what the object is and what function it serves.

9. Generalization. It is common for blind children to center on one object or behavior, thus stereotyping play results. Provide experiences that broaden the child's interest in people, events, and objects. For example, if the child develops an attachment for an object such as keys, provide many sets of keys, then move to other objects on a chain or string.

10. Conservation. Provide opportunities for the child to handle the same materials under different circumstances, as a prerequisite to an understanding of conservation. For example, let the child roll the same mass of play dough into various shapes, pour the same can of water into containers of varying sizes, feel two cups of dried corn that are the same, then feel them when they are in two very different-sized containers.

Social Development

1. Emotional Responses. Blind babies should be reinforced for showing appropriate emotional responses. It is important that their faces express feelings; therefore, they should make happy or smiling faces, sad faces, etc. and feel others with appropriate faces. Say, "Oh, your face says you are happy when you hear Daddy's voice."

2. Separation. Separation anxiety can be extended for a longer period when a child cannot sense that the adult is still present at a distance or that other sources of comfort are still nearby. While working from various distances in the child's proximity, say that you are still present although not directly in front of the child.

3. Fear of Strangers. Fear of strangers evokes negative reactions to strangers. Carefully prepare the child for a new person; let the child be touched by the new person while a familiar person is present, then gradually release the child to the new person.

4. Parental Influence. Social problems in young blind children are frequently created by parents who are having a very difficult time adjusting to a handicapped child. Parent counseling is critical; it is particularly valuable to introduce the parents to other parents who have been through similar experiences. Try to understand the parent-child relationship, and foster the positive aspects of both the parent's responses to the child and the child's responses to the parents.

A major factor in appropriate social development seems to be in the child's development of a close emotional bond with a significant other. Stress this aspect to the parents, and help the child realize he is important to his parents.

5. Development of Independence. Foster all the independence possible for a child at a given time. Remove all extremely dangerous obstacles, but do not hinder the child by overfondling or overprotection from coming into contact with situations that will teach lessons about objects or events to be contacted in later life. Example: if the child comes into contact with a footstool and falls, he will learn, as a consequence, to be aware that one can trip over objects. Be very careful, however, that the first experiences in exploring the child's environment are manipulated so as to provide excitement and joy when traveling. Do not provide an environment that frightens the child and stops further exploration. The child must be allowed and encouraged to act for himself even if performances are not always correct. The child must take independent steps—dressing, fixing a glass of soda pop, etc.

Self-Care Development

1. General Principles
   a. Before beginning a new activity with a blind child, simply say what is going to happen. "I am going to help you put on your shirt"; "It's time to have a drink of milk." This prepares the child for slight changes that otherwise cannot be anticipated.
   b. Establish a place for everything and make sure objects are always in the same place; the spoon is always on the right hand side of the plate, the hairbrush on the dresser at the same place.
   c. Mark objects difficult to distinguish. The child's toothbrush, comb, brush, bath towels, etc. should bear tactile identification so the child can quickly determine whether it is a personal object.
   d. In teaching new behaviors, work from behind the child if possible. Slowly provide less and less help, requiring the child to perform the task independently.

e. Call attention to the sounds associated with self-care events. "I can hear Daddy shaving with his electric razor"; "We can hear Mom stirring the iced tea."

2. Eating

a. Emphasize the identification of foods by smell. While holding a spoon of peas before the child's mouth, say, "Now you are ready for your peas; can you smell them?"

b. Use bowls or plates with raised edges when teaching the beginning stages of self-feeding.

c. It is quite proper to encourage the blind child to use bread as a pusher when securing food.

d. Before beginning the self-feeding task, tell the child where certain foods are on the plate. For children who have a sense of time, using a clock is a good reference—food by time. "Your meat is at six o'clock, your peas are at three o'clock," etc.

e. When learning to fill glasses, train the child to use the finger of the hand holding the glass to measure the amount of fluid in the glass. The child pours until the finger is wet, signifying the glass is full.

f. Encourage the child, as soon as possible, to ask, receive, and serve himself from the containers being passed. The child should also be encouraged to pass the containers to others.

g. The proper manners children observe and imitate are not available to the blind child. It will be important to tell the child, "We chew with our mouths closed"; "We do not eat with our elbows on the table"; etc.

3. Dressing

a. Be sure there are identification marks that permit the child to distinguish the fronts of garments from the backs.

b. Have shoes, gloves, etc., carefully marked to distinguish left from right.

c. Be extremely consistent in how the child is to wear garments: always to wear certain shirt tails tucked in, for example. This permits him to know when he is properly dressed.

d. Teach buttoning, zipping, buckling, snapping, etc., using the child's own garments when dressing so that hand and tactile impressions are as they are likely to be. If garments cause difficulties, adaptations may sometimes prove rewarding, such as a piece of string attached to the zipper which can later be removed as the task proves easier.

e. It is encouraging to have the child attempt to dress himself in the context of the situation. Do not dress a child in the morning and later during the day have him attempt to dress alone. The child should be encouraged to dress independently when awakening and, if need be, some steps remediated at this time.

Also, if the child is to go outside during the day, encourage his seeking out and putting on his own outside garments. Teach the child what type of clothing should be worn in different types of weather situations, such as rain, snow, etc.

4. Toileting
   a. The sequence, the verbal commands, and timing should remain very consistent in teaching toileting skills. Instructions should be short and to the point. "Sit on the toilet"; "Flush the toilet"; "Wash your hands."
   b. Stress tactile awareness as a key to needs. Frequently ask "Are you dry?" If he answers, "yes" and he is dry, reinforce with "Good, you have dry pants!" If pants are wet say, "No, your pants are wet." Change pants in the bathroom (have child remove them alone, if possible), and do not talk to the child during the process.
   c. Let the blind child accompany other family members to the bathroom so there will be more experiences to imitate.
   d. Tie down a toy to the toilet seat or chair for the child to play with while sitting on the toilet.
   e. Limit time on the toilet to 8-10 minutes. A cue to prerequisite toilet behavior is the ability to remain dry for two hours.

5. Grooming
   a. Bathing skills should be taught as to any other child. Have faucets marked hot and cold.
   b. Teach child as many ways as possible to check appearance: feeling hair, buttons, zippers, checking shoes for paper or trash stuck on the bottom.
   c. Find short cuts and alternative ways to accomplish grooming tasks. Squirt toothpaste on teeth rather than on brush bristles; teach frequent use of napkins and handkerchiefs.
   d. Discuss with the child the necessity of grooming and when grooming occurs during the day, such as when awakening, after meals, after playtime, before retiring, etc.
   e. Have blind child initiate feedback from others rather than wait to be told something is not right. For example, he might say "Is my hat on straight?"
   f. Stress appropriate dress. It is important that the blind child be dressed comfortably, in manageable clothes that are clean, and in keeping with those of sighted peers.

6. Peer Interaction
   a. Encourage appropriate peer interaction. The blind child cannot see the toy the other is enjoying and thus misses out on modeling behavior. Circumvent this through verbal comment, close parallel play, cuing in to sound-play identification.

7. Understanding the Body

    a. Encourage as much appropriate bodily exploratory behavior as is acceptable. The child needs to feel physical body differences in parents, sameness in one's self to siblings, etc.,and to understand why one cannot always explore the entire bodies of everyone contacted. Ask relatives always to wear a certain watch, ring, or bracelet around the blind child and teach the child to associate those objects with the voice, etc.

8. Self-Concept

    a. Self-concept is a critical factor in any child's development, but even more important in the development of a handicapped child. Stress human differences, but particularly emphasize strengths that signify attributes in the handicapped child. It is important for the professional to state the traits he/she values in the blind child in the presence of the child and parents.

9. Helping Others

    a. The ability to do things for others instead of just having others do for you is important, particularly for handicapped children, since many people feel sorry for them and want to "help" them. Provide opportunities for the blind child to assist others, to serve others, to be on the receiving end of "thank you."

REFERENCES

A Flash-Card Vision Test for Children. New York: The New York Association for the Blind, 1966.

American Medical Association committee report. *Estimation of loss of visual efficiency.* A.M.A. Archives of Industrial Health, October 1955.

Ashcroft, S. C., Halliday, C., & Barraga, N. *Study II: Effects of experimental teaching on the visual behavior of children educated as though they had no vision.* Nashville: George Peabody College (Grant No. 32-52, 0120-1034), 1965.

Barraga, N. *Increased visual behavior in low-vision children.* New York: American Foundation for the Blind, 1964.

Boyce, V. S. The home eye test program. *Sight Saving Review,* 1973, *43.*

Brekke, B., Williams, J. E., & Tait, P. The acquisition of conservation of weight by visually impaired children. *Journal of Genetic Psychology,* 1974, *125,* 89-97.

DuBose, R. F. Assessment of behavioral repertoires of severely impaired persons. In A. H. Find (Ed.), *International perspectives on future special education.* Reston, Va.: Council for Exceptional Children, 1979.

DuBose, R. F., Langley, M. B., Bourgeault, S.E., Harley, R.H., & Stagg, V. Assessment and programming for blind children with severely handicapped conditions. *Visual Impairment and Blindness,* 1977, *2,* 49-53.

DuBose, R. F., Langley, B., & Stagg, V. Assessing severely handicapped children. *Focus on Exceptional Children,* 1977, *9,* (7), 1-13.

DuBose, R. F. *Assessment of visually impaired infants*. Paper presented at the Westar/Model Preschool Center for Handicapped Children Topical Conference on Infant Assessment and Intervention. Seattle, June, 1978.

DuBose, R. F. Developmental needs in blind infants. *The New Outlook for the Blind*, 1976, *2*, 49-52.

Folio, M. R. *Assessing motor development in multiply handicapped children*. Paper presented at annual meeting of Council on Exceptional Children, New York, April, 1974.

Fraiberg, S. *Insights from the Blind*. New York: Basic Books, 1977.

Fraiberg, S. Parallel and divergent patterns in blind and sighted infants. *Psychoanalytic Study of the Child*, 1968, *23*, 264-300.

Hallenback, J. Two essential factors in the development of young blind children. *New Outlook for the Blind*, 1954, *48*, 308-315.

Harley, R. D., & Lawrence, G.A. *Visual impairment in the schools*. Springfield, Ill: Charles C. Thomas, 1977.

Hathaway, W. *Education and health of the partially seeing child* (4th ed.). New York: Columbia University Press, 1959.

Lairy, G. C., & Harrison-Covello, A. The blind child and his parents: Congenital visual defect and the repercussion of family attitudes on the early development of the blind. *Research Bulletin, American Foundation for the Blind*, 1973, *25*, 1-24.

Langley, B., & DuBose, R. Functional vision screening for severely handicapped children. *The New Outlook for the Blind*, 1976, *70* (8), 346-350.

Lowenfeld, B. *Our blind children: Growing and living with them* (2nd ed.). Springfield, Ill.: Charles C. Thomas, 1964.

Lowenfeld, B. *The visually handicapped child in school*. New York: John Day, 1973.

National Society for the Prevention of Blindness. *N.S.P.B. fact book: Estimated statistics on blindness and visual problems*. New York: The Society, 1966.

Norris, M., Spaulding, P. J., & Brodie, F. H. *Blindness in children*. Chicago: University of Chicago Press, 1957.

Piaget, J., & Inhelder, B. *The psychology of the child*. New York: Basic Books, 1969.

Rand Report: Improving services to handicapped children. R-1420-DHEW, May, 1974.

Reynolds, M. C., & Birch, J. W. *Teaching exceptional children in all American schools*. Reston, Va.: Council for Exceptional Children, 1977.

Scott, R. *The making of a blindman*. New York: Russell Sage Foundation, 1968.

Sheridan, M. D. *Manual for the Stycar Vision Tests*. Windsor, Ontario: JFER Publishing Co., Ltd., 1973.

Stewart, M. L. *The process of motor coordination in the human infant*. Monograph Series College of Education, Western Michigan University, Kalamazoo, 1974.

Tait, P. Play and intellectual development of blind children. *New Outlook for the Blind*, 1972, *66*, 361-369.

Warren, D., *Blindness and early childhood development*. New York: American Foundation for the Blind, Inc., 1977.

Chapter 12

Working with Sensorily Impaired Children Part II: Hearing Impairments

Rebecca F. DuBose

INTRODUCTION

To advocates of care for children with hearing impairments must go credit for being the first caregivers to push for intervention services during the preschool years. They were quick to note the negative effects of hearing impairment on acquisition of basic skills, particularly language development, and were aware that sounds in the environment attracted the infant to attend, to associate with people and objects, to discriminate, to imitate, to internalize, and later to formulate sounds into words. With words, the infant began communicating, using the system others were using, signifying his entry into a purely human experience.

Definition

The Conference of Executives of American Schools for the Deaf, at its June 22, 1975 meeting, adopted definitions that classify persons as to ability to process auditory input and restated the definition of hearing impairment for the field:

> A *deaf* person is one whose hearing disability precludes successful processing of linguistic information through audition, with or without a hearing aid.

> A *hard of hearing* person is one who, generally with the use of a hearing aid, has residual hearing sufficient to enable successful processing of linguistic information through audition.

> *Hearing Impairment:* A generic term indicating a hearing disability which may range in severity from mild to profound; it includes the subset of deaf and hard of hearing.

Incidence

It has been difficult precisely to measure the number of hearing-impaired persons, since degree of loss is a critical factor. An estimate prepared by the

Deafness Research and Training Center at New York University reports 2,000,000 Americans lack sufficient hearing to understand speech. The Rand Report (1974) estimates 390,000 youth aged 0 to 21 years to have losses of 41 dB or more; it cautions the reader to be aware that children with other handicaps and a loss of <41 dB might be functionally more handicapped and in need of services. Silverman and Lane (1970) reported about 39,000 school-aged deaf children (loss >55 dB) enrolled in educational programs. Children under six years of age were less likely to be adequately accounted for or receiving support services. During the 1967-68 academic year, Silverman and Lane identified 5127 preschool deaf children receiving educational support services. The actual number of hearing-impaired preschool children is likely to be much much higher because of delay in early detection.

HOW WE HEAR

The ability to communicate orally is a distinctly human trait. The combined efforts of ears and brain allow us to acquire and use a language system. Sound waves are collected by the *outer ear* or *pinna* and channeled into the *ear canal* where they strike the *eardrum* or *tympanic membrane*. The eardrum is a clear window that allows one to see into the *middle ear* where three small bones, the *hammer* (malleus), *anvil* (incus), and *stirrup* (stapes) transmit the sound waves to the *oval window* at the far end of the middle ear. Opening into the middle ear from the pharynx is an air passage regulator, the *eustachian tube*. Sound waves exit the middle into the *inner ear* or *labyrinth* that contains the *cochlea,* which is the organ of hearing, and the *semi-circular canals,* which are central to balance. Fluid activated by the movements of the *oval window* circulates through the labyrinth and stimulates the *auditory nerve,* which mediates sensations of sound. The brain perceives the sound in the *temporal lobe,* adds meaning to the vibrations, and the individual understands the meaning of the sound.

SCREENING FOR HEARING IMPAIRMENTS IN CHILDREN

Since no system exists for mass detection of hearing deficits in infants, professional organizations, including the American Academy of Ophthalmology and Otolaryngology (AAOO), the American Academy of Pediatrics (AAP), and the American Speech and Hearing Association (ASHA), issued a joint statement recommending using case histories and physical deficits. One or more of the following characteristics will cause a neonate to be considered at risk:

1. history of hereditary childhood hearing impairment
2. rubella or other nonbacterial intrauterine fetal infection (e.g., cytomega-lovirus infection, herpes infection)

3. defects of ear, nose, throat; malformed, low-set or absent pinnae; cleft lip or palate (including submucous cleft); any residual abnormality of the otorhino-laryngeal system
4. bilirubin less than 1500 grams (approximately 3.3 pounds)
5. bilirubin level greater than 20 mg.; 100 ml serum (A neonate at risk according to these factors should be given a complete audiologic evaluation during the first two months of life.)

The most commonly used hearing-screening procedure for the neonate is behavior-observation audiometry (BOA), which is accomplished by presenting sound and observing the neonate's response to the stimulus. Although a very gross measure, it provides sufficient audiologic information to permit a tentative hypothesis and to initiate habilitative procedures (Cox & Lloyd, 1976).

With use of the history, physical examination and BOA procedures have produced a large number of false positives; thus, researchers have attempted to

---

Figure 12-1 Cross Section of the Hearing Mechanism

Cross Section of the Hearing Mechanism

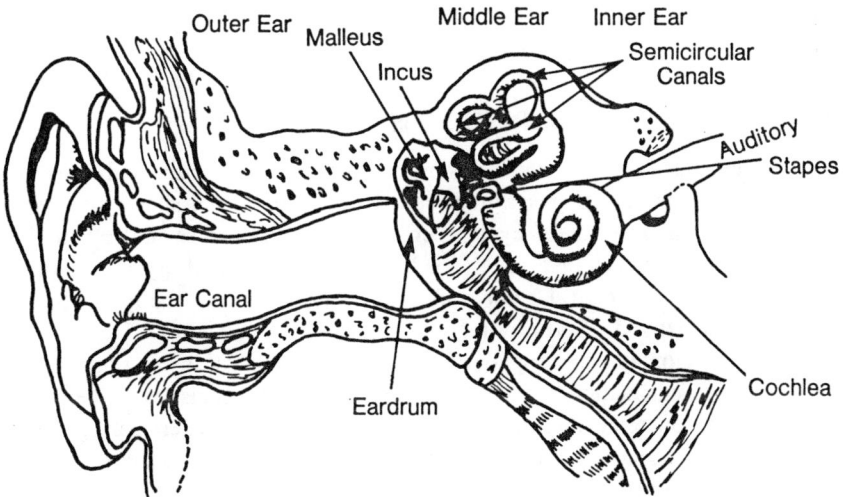

Source: Reprinted with permission from C. R. Reynolds and J. W. Birch; *Teaching Exceptional Children in All American Schools.*

---

identify other procedures that will more precisely identify hearing-impaired between 3 and 12 months of age. By 3 months of age, the developing infant is a more reliable testee, responding less reflexively and more purposely to sound stimuli.

Watrous, McConnell, Sitton and Fleet (1975) developed a procedure to determine a predictable developmental pattern as a function of age in the first year of life. Subjects for the study were 40 normally developing infants from the Rubella Follow-up Project at Vanderbilt University. Children under 6 months exhibited greater percentages of responses in reflexive and early-attending response (body, startle, eye blind, eye widening, eye movement, brow movement, and head movement). Attending responses (brief cessation of activity, initiation of momentary increase in activity, prolonged facial grimace, listening behavior, and searching behavior) were also more common among the younger subjects. Localizing responses were far more prevalent in older infants, particularly after the age of 6 months. Inspection of responses revealed that localization on a horizontal plane with the head was the predominant response for 6-8-month-olds, while localizing on a vertical plane did not occur at all in the younger group and quite infrequently in the 6-8 month group, yet was the preferred response for the 9-12-month-old infants.

Children 18-36 months of age are better able to signify possible hearing problems; thus, testing becomes more widespread and useful. Parental questionnaires supplement information from pure-tone audiometric procedures usually measured through some form of play audiometry, such as putting a block in a can, or a peg in a pegboard. Children above 3 years of age generally are able to respond to pure-tone audiometry and should be tested annually to detect possible middle-ear pathology, a major cause of hearing deficits at that age.

MEASUREMENT OF HEARING LOSS

An audiometer is an electronic device that measures sharpness and range of hearing. Results are recorded on a graph called audiogram, which shows *frequency* in Hertz (Hz), a measure of cycles per second, noted across the top of the audiogram. *Intensity* is a measure of loudness and is expressed in decibels (dB) along the side of the graph. Decibels are scaled by standards of the International Standard Organization (ISO) or American Standard Association (ASA).

Pure-tone audiometry uses signals of known frequencies within the communication range of human audibility (e.g., 250-8000Hz). These signals are delivered by the air-conduction route through earphones, sound-field speakers, or by bone conduction. Bone conduction is accomplished through a small oscillator placed on the child's mastoid bone behind the ear or on the forehead.

The degree of handicap is usually classified by the descriptors noted on the audiogram in Figure 12-2. The effects of the degrees of impairment are noted in Table 12-1.

Figure 12-2 Frequency in Hz

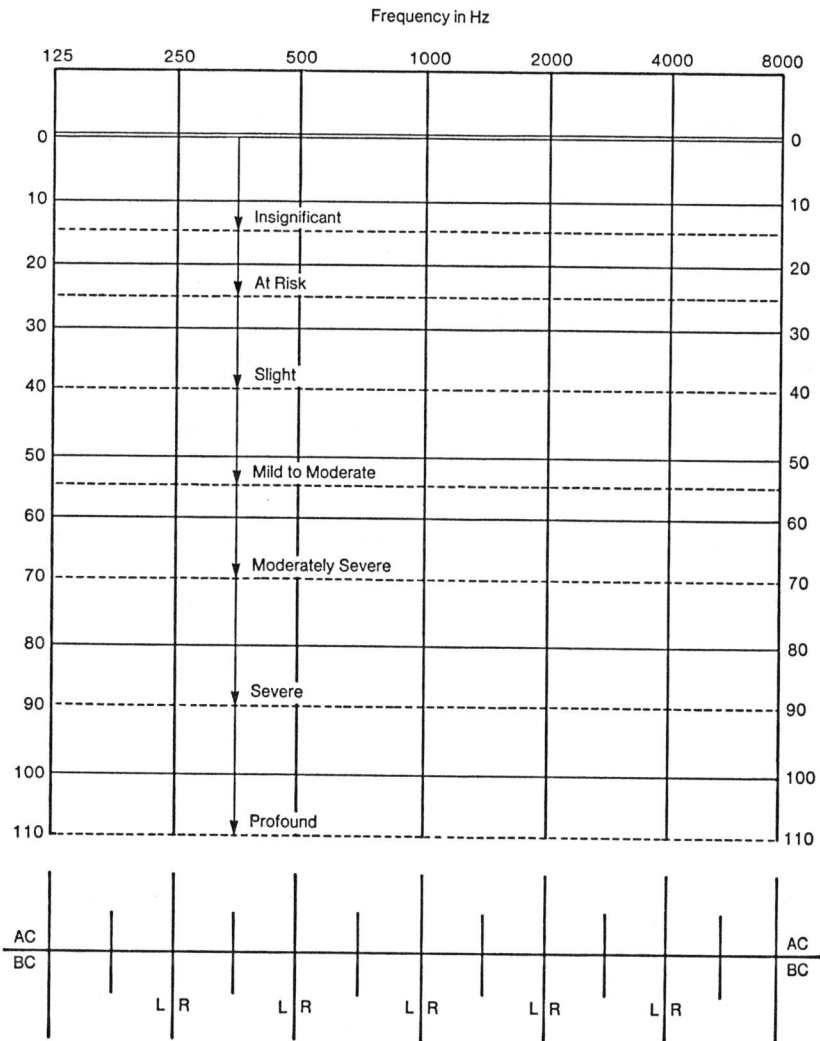

Frequency in Hz

Table 12-1 Relationship of Amount of Hearing Loss To Communicative Efficiency

Decibel Loss in Speech Range (I.S.O.)	Degree of Impairment	Effects
0-15	Insignificant	Only difficulty will be with faint or distant sounds.
15-25	At Risk	Without awareness of hearing needs, problems in language and speech may emerge.
26-40	Slight	Has difficulty with whispers and faint speech; understands conversational speech at 3 to 5 feet. Will need auditory training, language training, and hearing aid.
41-55	Mild to Moderate	Has frequent difficulties with normal speech; with sufficient training and no other impairments will function in regular classroom with minimum support.
56-70	Moderately Severe	Conversational speech must be loud; will experience difficulties with classroom discussions and telephone conversations; will need considerable support in acquiring speech; many will use total communication systems.
71-90	Severe	May hear voice a foot away; difficulty with consonants; some understand strongly amplified speech; many will use total communication systems.
91-	Profound	Maximally amplified speech is not understood; most will use total communication systems.

Audiogram Configuration

The configuration of the responses recorded on the audiogram is important in identifying the kind of hearing loss and determining potential for amplification. If responses are recorded across the frequency spectrum or on a flat configuration, it is likely that much help can be obtained from amplification; and if hearing is within the speech range (500-2000Hz), amplification probably will also benefit the person. If responses are noted outside the speech range, chances of assistance through amplification are much less (Larson & Miller, 1978).

TYPES OF HEARING LOSS

Conductive Hearing Loss

A conductive loss results from malformations or problems associated with the outer or middle ear, preventing a clear transmission of sound waves to the inner ear. Sources of such problems are impounded wax, foreign objects such as beans or candies, or excess fluid in the eustachian tube. A conductive loss will be identified by loss of air-conducted sounds. Thus, the sounds transmitted through bone conduction and going directly to the inner ear are heard normally. Most conductive impairments are amenable to medical intervention or amplification.

Sensorineural Loss

Defects in the inner ear or dysfunction caused by the auditory nerve result in a sensorineural loss. The outer and middle ear are likely to be normal, air- and bone-conduction thresholds are likely to be nearly the same, and sensorineural losses are not likely to be corrected surgically or medically. With training, some children respond well to amplification; however, with more sensorineural losses, children do not respond well to amplification, the amplified sound remaining distorted and unclear. Common sensorineural impairments include inherited deafness, maternal rubella, or other syndromes associated with deafness.

Mixed Hearing Loss

When both a conductive loss and a sensorineural loss are present, the loss is classified as a mixed loss. A significant air/bone gap may exist, but, if the conductive loss is corrected, the air-conduction component will be resolved. Many persons with mixed losses can benefit from amplification although some will have problems similar to those of persons with sensorineural losses.

AGE OF ONSET

The age at which an individual becomes hearing impaired affects the degree of the language handicap. If the impairment is present at birth, it is a *congenital loss,* and is far more likely to impact severely on language acquisition. An impairment acquired some time after birth is an *adventitious loss;* the later it occurs, the less impact on acquisition of language. Among the skills that are advantageous to the adventitiously deaf child are: (1) knowledge of one's native language, (2) clear oral speech, (3) understanding of the oral speech of others, (4) ability to read with speed and comprehension, and (5) understanding of abstract concepts (Reynolds & Birch, 1977).

CAUSES OF HEARING IMPAIRMENT IN CHILDREN

Deafness results from two major sources: genetic or chromosomal abnormalities, and disease or trauma.

Genetic Conditions

Genetic factors—conditions that cause deafness to be transmitted from parents to child—account for 40-60 percent of all causes of deafness. When compared to other deaf children, the genetically deaf are least likely of all major etiologic groups to be multiply handicapped. The major ancillary handicap among these children is a visual problem. Of the 57 identified forms of genetic deafness, 10 involve both hearing and vision (Larson & Miller, 1978).

When deafness appears in parents and grandparents or brothers and sisters, it is likely that a dominant gene is involved. When marriages between deaf and hearing people produce deaf children, dominant genes are present; that is, most individuals who have the gene are deaf. Recessive deafness occurs when deaf parents produce deaf children and there is no deafness in the grandparental generation. For recessive deafness to occur, both parents must pass the same kind of recessive gene to their offspring (Jones, 1976).

Disease and Trauma

External agents that result in deafness fall into three major categories:

Disease

The most prevalent diseases that result in deafness are viral infections, such as maternal rubella. Mothers contracting the rubella virus during their first three months of pregnancy may give birth a child with deafness. Deafness can be the only handicap or the child might have a visual impairment, mental retardation, heart or kidney problems.

Meningitis is the cause of deafness for about 10 percent of all occurrences. High fever associated with the illness results in a sensorineural loss.

In young children, serous otitis media is the most common ear disorder, generally caused by blockage of the eustachian tube that forces the middle ear to become partially closed and the gases in it partially absorbed, resulting in a collection of fluid in the middle ear. Treatment is usually aspiration of the middle-ear fluid by myringotomy (incision of the eardrum) followed by placement of a hollow plastic tube to enable the ear to remain open.

Toxicity

Drugs taken either by the mother or the child may produce hearing impairments; however, these impairments are often recoverable after the drug is discontinued.

Physical injuries, malformations, and trauma

Blows to the head can cause serious hearing losses. Injury to bones in the ossicular chain or other internal ear parts are likely to affect hearing. Damage can occur in any part of the sound-reception and -processing system. The middle ear is particularly vulnerable to infections from the throat and nasal passages via the eustachian tube. Frequent infections can cause scar tissue to form or produce other changes that prevent the concatenate functioning of the bones to operate. The inner ear can be damaged through the lymph and additionally through prolonged exposure to high-intensity sounds.

Blood incompatibility accounts for 3-4 percent of all deafness. In almost all residential schools, one can find children whose deafness can be traced to this factor. Birth complications, such as fetal stress, prolonged labor, or prematurity, are other sources of deafness.

HEARING AIDS

In the 1940s, hearing aids weighing about two pounds, with batteries kept in a pocket or strapped to a leg, were developed in packs that could be worn by small children. By the middle 1950s, space-technology advances produced a transistor battery and miniaturized circuitry and components leading to more power and greater fidelity in aids. Yet it is important to realize that no aid has been able to substitute for the normal human ear.

Simply put, hearing aids are tiny amplifiers. They make all sounds louder, including extraneous noises to which most of us selectively fail to attend. The deaf child is bombarded with all environmental sounds and must be carefully and laboriously trained to distinguish speech sounds from environmental noises.

Because young children are fitted with aids as early as possible, it is not unlikely that hearing-impaired children will be found in increasing numbers in preschool settings.

Although only about 10 percent of all hearing aids are body-worn, young children are more likely to use body aids. The young child requires an instrument that is sturdy, can deliver high quality sound, uses a battery with longer life, and is acoustically more flexible (Ross, 1975).

The body aid contains microphone and amplifier in the same chassis, with wires connecting the amplifier to the receiver (or earphones) at the ear (Ross, 1976). A cord can go to a single ear, or a Y-cord, with the output split into two channels, can connect with both ears. For a more thorough explanation of Y-cord versus single-cord reception, see Northern and Downs (1974).

A disadvantage of body aids is the production of clothing noise caused by the microphone rubbing against clothing.

Care and Maintenance

Keeping a hearing aid in proper working condition is quite difficult. Ross (1976) states it bluntly, "there are perhaps more hearing aids and auditory trainers gathering dust in school storerooms than serving the purpose for which they were designed" (p. 317). Without a properly functioning instrument, all the theoretical benefits of early intervention are minimized. A few explanations of functions of the major parts of hearing aids can serve as guidelines to proper functioning.

1. The batteries should be tested for power before the child leaves home each morning. A spare should always be available at both home and school.
2. Small controls regulate the amount of amplification much like the knob on the radio. Since the small child does not have the manual dexterity to manipulate these controls, parents and other caregivers must know how to set these.
3. The sound is received by the small power unit serving the same function as a person's external ear, and transmitted through a cord or cords attached to an earmold molded to fit the child's ear or ears. Cords can be defective and should be checked regularly to insure proper transmission.
4. The earmold must be cleaned to remove ear wax that collects at the mold openings. Small brushes, such as those used by artists or a typist's eraser brush, are very useful in cleaning molds. When the mold is not inserted properly, or slips from the snug fitting, a squealing can be detected by others. It should be gently reinserted.
5. The mold should be checked periodically for proper fit as a child develops; a new fitting is needed if bleeding develops.
6. An inexpensive battery tester and stethoscope are valuable tools in testing aid functioning.

ASSESSMENT OF YOUNG HEARING-IMPAIRED CHILDREN

The formal assessment of hearing, using audiometric procedures has been discussed previously. It is important that teachers and day-care workers be aware of possible signs of a hearing loss. Table 12-2 gives a list of observable behaviors that could be associated with a hearing impairment.

Table 12-2 Behaviors Indicating Possible Hearing Difficulty

Physical Signs	**Behavioral Signs**
A. Frequent earaches	A. Cocks head to one side
B. Ear discharges	B. Shows preference for high or low-pitched sounds
C. Mouth breather	C. Extreme shyness in speaking
D. Complains of buzzing or ringing in ear	D. Delayed or abnormal speech
E. Hears noises in head	E. Frequent unresponsiveness when addressed
F. Frequent problems with tonsils	F. Abnormalities of articulation
	G. Abnormalities in voice
	H. Attention difficulties

The formal assessment of development of young hearing-impaired children is possible through a number of formal measures, some of which can be administered as noted in the test manual; others must be adapted so that the deaf child's hearing impairment does not handicap him unduly. Table 12-3 gives a list of tests to be used or adapted for hearing-impaired preschool children.

Table 12-3 lists a number of language measures that have not been adapted for deaf children, and one must be therefore extremely cautious in using these instruments. Language measures, such as the ones noted, are frequently employed to measure change in the language of young deaf children and, for that reason, have been included.

EFFECTS OF HEARING IMPAIRMENT ON DEVELOPMENT

Motor Development

Schlesinger and Meadow (1972) offer convincing documentation supporting their conviction that a hearing impairment alone will not result in concomitant delays in motor development. Table 12-4 shows the relationship among chronological age, motor development, and language development in one deaf child, Ann.

Children with hearing impairments resulting from inner-ear damage may have gross motor problems related to balance and equilibrium. These skills should be carefully checked to see if weaknesses do exist. If such problems are noted, then they can be expected to be manifested in all motor skills requiring static or dynamic balance.

Table 12-3 Tests for Use with Preschool Hearing-Impaired Children

Test	Age Range	Domain	Skills Assessed
Peabody Developmental Motor Scales, Rhonda Folio and Rebecca F. DuBose, IMRID Publications, George Peabody College for Teachers, Nashville, TN 37203	0-6 years	Motor Development	Gross and fine motor skills are assessed using both a developmental and a criterion-referenced measurement system. The skills are programmed for training in the accompanying activities section.
Lakeland Village Adaptive Behavior Grid, Lakeland Village Medical City, WA	0-16 years	Social and Self-Care Development	This scale covers all self-care domains and a variety of social behavior domains.
California Preschool Social Competency Scale, Levine, Elzey and Lewis, 1969, Consulting Psychologists, 577 College Ave., Palo Alto, CA 94306	2½-5½ years	Social Development	Measure the adequacy of the child's interpersonal behavior and the degree to which he assumes social responsibility.
McCarthy Scales of Children's Abilities, The Psychological Corporation, 757 Third Avenue, New York, NY 10017	2½-8½ years	Cognitive Development	Among the cognitive skills tapped are memory, object concept, problem solving, means-end relationships. There are some subtests that will definitely be difficult for deaf children, thus one must adapt this test to fit the child's communication means.

Test	Age	Area	Description
Merrill-Palmer Scale of Mental Tests, Rachel Stutsman, Stoelting Company, 1350 S. Kostner Avenue, Chicago, IL 60623	1½-6 years	Cognitive Development	This test has a large number of manipulative items, thus does not penalize the deaf child as much as some other cognitive measures. It taps object concept, visual discrimination, spatial relationships, motor planning, means-end relationships.
Brigance Diagnostic Inventory of Early Development, Albert Brigance, Curriculum Associates, Inc., Woburn, MA 61801	0-7 years	All areas of development	Psychomotor, self-help, speech and language, general knowledge and comprehension, and early academic skills are assessed in a criterion-referenced and normative-referenced test.
Columbia Mental Maturity Scale, The Psychological Corporation, 757 Third Avenue, New York, NY 10017	3-9 years	Cognitive Development	The test is nonverbal and requires only a pointing response. The concepts of visual discrimination, association, spatial relations are tapped.
Uzgiris-Hunt Ordinal Scales of Psychological Development, I.C. Uzgiris and J. M. Hunt, University of Illinois Press, Urbana, IL	0-2 years	Sensorimotor Development	Assessment of object permanence, causality displacement, imitation, means-end relationships, object concepts.
Test for Preschool Deaf Children Dr. Altahena Smith, California School for the Deaf, Riverside, CA	2-4 years	Cognitive Development	This test is not commercially available. Most materials are in the offices of psychologists.

Table 12-3 *Continued*

Test	Age Range	Domain	Skills Assessed
Sequenced Inventory of Communication Development, University of Washington Press, Box 5569, Seattle, WA 98105	4 months- 4 years	Language Development	Assesses both receptive and expressive language using both parent report and the child's play with objects.
Motor-Free Vision Perception Test, R. P. Colarasso and D. D. Hammill, Academic Therapy Publication 1539 - 4th Street, San Rafael, CA 94901	4-8 years	Visual Perception	Assesses spatial relationships, visual discrimination, figure ground, visual closure and visual memory.
Bayley Scales of Infant Development, Nancy Bayley, The Psychological Corporation, 757 Third Avenue, New York, NY 10017	0-2½ years	Cognitive Development Motor Development Social Development	Three separate scales assess aspects of early child development. A well standardized infant scale.
Developmental Potential of Preschool Children, Else Haeussermann, 1968, Grune & Stratton, Inc., 757 Third Avenue, New York, NY 10017	2-6 years	Cognitive Development	This test is particularly good for children with language problems. It covers physical development, sensory skills, mentation, and general social development.

Test	Category	Age	Description
Hiskey Nebraska Test of Learning Aptitude, Marshall Hiskey, 5640 Baldwin, Lincoln, NE 68508	Cognitive Development	2½-17½ years	This is the only test for deaf-blind children. Among the skills assessed are imitation, sequencing, memory, picture identification, association, manipulation, visual attention span, discrimination.
Leiter International Performance Scale, Russell Leiter, Stoelting Company, 1350 S. Kostner Avenue, Chicago, IL 60623	Cognitive Development	2-18 years	This nonverbal test assesses association, sequencing, discrimination, and other non-verbal learning processes.
Learning Accomplishment Profile, M. Griffin, A. R. Sanford, D.C. Wilson, Kaplan School Supply Corp, 600 Jamestown Rd., Winston-Salem, NC 27103	Screening all areas	1-6 years	A general screening test that assesses gross motor, fine motor, self-help and cognitive development.
Developmental Activities Screening Inventory, Rebecca F. DuBose and Beth Langley, Teaching Resources, 100 Boylston Street, Boston, MA	Screening of Cognitive Development	½-5 years	General cognitive skills, fine motor, sequencing, association.
Preschool Inventory Revised Ed., Bettye M. Caldwell, Cooperative Tests and Services, Educational Testing Services, Princeton, NJ	General Development	3-6 years	Assesses personal-social responsiveness, associative vocabulary, concept activation-numerical and concept activation-sensory.

Table 12-3 *Continued*

Test	Age Range	Domain	Skills Assessed
The Test of Syntactic Abilities, S.P. Quigley, M.W. Steinkamp, D.J. Power & B.W. Jones, Doemac, Inc., P.O. Box 752, Beaverton, OR 97005		Language Development	Specifically designed for deaf children.
Environmental Pre-language Battery, James D. MacDonald, D. S. Horstmeier, Charles E. Merrill, 1300 Alum Creek Drive, Box 508, Columbus, OH 43216	½-2 years	Language Development	This can be used with nonverbal children and assesses semantic and cognitive requirements for language through attention, gestures, imitation, play comprehension, and single words.
Environmental Language Inventory, James D. MacDonald, D. S. Horstmeier, Charles E. Merrill, 1300 Alum Creek Drive, Box 508, Columbus, OH 43216	1½-4 years	Language Development	Assesses child's application of semantic-based grammar through imitating conversation and play.
Basic Concepts Inventory, S. E. Engelmann, Follett Educational Corporation, Department DM, P.O. Box 5705, 1011 West Washington Boulevard, Chicago, IL 60607	4-10 years	Concept Development Language Development	The BCS consists of three parts: 1) basic concepts, 2) statement repetition and comprehension, and 3) pattern awareness.

BOEHM Test of Basic Concepts, Ann Boehm, Psychological Corporation, 757 Third Avenue, New York, NY 10017	5-8 years	Concept Development Language Development	Assesses the child's knowledge of concepts considered necessary in the first years of school.
Porch Index of Communicative Ability in Children, Bruce E. Porch, Consulting Psychologist Press, Inc., 577 College Avenue, Palo Alto, CA 94306	3-5 years	Language Development	Assesses general communication ability in terms of certain verbal, gestural, and graphic skills.

Table 12-4 Interrelated Patterns in Ann's Motoric and Linguistic Development

Age	Motor Development	Language Development
8 months/1 day	Stands holding on; thumb opposition when grasping plastic beads	Blinking in response to sound with hearing aid. "Vocalization and gestures convey emphasis and emotions."
9 months	Playing "peek-a-boo"	
10 months/5 days	Claps hands; pulls to standing position; creeps efficiently (S10)	"Beginning to differentiate words by making differential adjustment"; waves "bye-bye." Hits side of head with heel of open hand (like *father*). Hits side of head with fist (like *stupid*). (S10)
10½ months		Hands in loose fist to mouth (like *eat*).
11 months	Secures toy from under cup (C10) Four teeth	Vocalizes negatively after mother gives a mock scolding with "*no*."
12 months	Hits cup with spoon (C10) Marks with pencil (C12) Squeezes doll (C11) Stands alone	Covers face with both hands to avoid mother. Turns to see who is recipient of sign language. SIGNS: *pretty; wrong*. Understands "come here." (S12)
13 months	Takes first steps alone	

14 months

SIGNS: *cat, sleep, bye, sleep.*

14½ months

Unwraps toy (C14)
Inserts peg (C14)
Holds three cubes (C14)

SIGNS: *hat, eat, no;* imitates mother.

15 months

Drinks from straw

SIGNS: letter *r, smell, dirty, no smart, mommy, daddy, kitty, dog, pretty, wrong, sleep, eat, milk, bye-bye, good, car, no,* Ann (with letter *a*).
SIGN VOCABULARY TOTAL 19
SAYS: "mama" and "hi"
Points to nose and ear upon oral request. (S12)

16 months

Drinks from cup and glass

SIGN: *cow.*

17 months

Sits in regular chair

Joins two words (C22; G21): *Bird wait bird*
water milk
good finished
eat cracker
cookies more
home car
girl funny
sleep up
dirty dog

18 months/ 10 days

Throws ball with both hands, gait semi-still (S18)

SIGN VOCABULARY TOTAL: 106
LETTER TOTAL: 3

Table 12-4 *Continued*

Age	Motor Development	Language Development
19 months	Scribbles spontaneously (C18) Builds tower 5 blocks (C20 with 3) Walks upstairs with help (B20.3) Walks downstairs with help (B20.5) Twelve teeth	Points to 3 parts of doll (C20). Attempts to follow directions (C20). Pulls person to show (G21). Echoes by gestures or words (G21). Identifies 2 pictures from name (C22). SIGN VOCABULARY TOTAL: 117 LETTER TOTAL: 5 (fingerspelling)
L(¼ months)		SIGN VOCABULARY TOTAL: 142 LETTER TOTAL: 14 (fingerspelling)
22 months/ 10 days	Runs (S24) Alternates between sitting up and standing (S24)	*Boy girl play* *Me girl* *Hello, thank you food* Language creation and interest (S24)

KEY: C = Cattell Score (in months)   G = Gesell Score (in months)
       B = Bayley Score (in months)   S = Slobin Score (in months) from
                                                 Lenneberg, 1967

Source: Schlesinger, H. S., & Meadow, K. P. *Sound and sign: Childhood deafness and mental health.* University of California Press, 1972, pp. 57-59. Reprinted with permission.

Language Development

The language system a child acquires depends entirely on the system used by caregivers. They shape the child's language through modeling and reinforcement, for both hearing and hearing-impaired persons. Deaf children, raised by parents who communicate manually, quickly acquire the manual-language system (Schlesinger & Meadow, 1972).

Throughout life, the language element will be given the highest priority in the deaf child's education. It is through language that the child expresses feelings, understands what others are feeling, and shares experiences with others. Language training is the responsibility of every person in the deaf child's world; the parents, the siblings, the school teacher, the swimming instructor, the neighbor, etc. The mutual sharing of language-training responsibility is based on particular understanding of what language is and how it is acquired. Clark (1974) stated "language does not develop 'in vacuo'; it develops with the functions of representing thoughts, precepts, and feelings (p. 105)." DuBose (1978) maintains "physical attachment and interaction were as necessary for survival before birth as social attachment and interaction are for survival after birth (p. 38)." Language is the key to interaction; with it, more expressions of thoughts, precepts, and feelings occur.

A first language is learned, it cannot be taught, from active participation in the world around one. The young child actively participates in bottle feeding: he comes to associate hunger, bottle, smell, sounds, caregiver, satisfaction, etc., with his bottle. Gradually, he visually associates his needs with the object and later adds phonemes to what already has a semantic meaning. "Ba-ba" then "bottle" gradually take on signal, then symbolic representation and enter into the child's language repertoire.

Perhaps the most poignant writing on how language is acquired, both in hearing and deaf children, can be found in the writings of Miss Sullivan, the teacher of Helen Keller:

> We visited a little school for the deaf. Two of the teachers knew the manual alphabet, and talked to her without an interpreter. They were astonished at her command of language. Not a child in the school, they said, had anything like Helen's facility of expression, and some of them had been under instruction for two or three years. I was incredulous at first; but after I had watched the children at work for a couple of hours, I knew that what I had been told was true, and I wasn't surprised. In one room some little tots were standing before the blackboard, painfully consructing 'simple sentences.' A little girl had written: 'I have a new dress. It is a pretty dress. My mamma made my pretty new dress. I love mamma!' A curly-headed little boy was writing: 'I have a large ball. I like to kick my large ball.' When we entered the room, the children's

attention was riveted on Helen. One of them pulled me by the sleeve and said, 'Girl is blind.' The teacher was writing on the blackboard: 'The girl's name is Helen. She is deaf. She cannot see. We are very sorry.' I said: 'Why do you write those sentences on the board? Wouldn't the children understand if you talked to them about Helen?' The teacher said something about getting the correct construction, and continued to construct an exercise out of Helen. I asked her if the little girl who had written about the new dress was particularly pleased with her dress. 'No,' she replied, 'I think not; but children learn better if they write about things that concern them personally.'

There was the same difficulty throughout the school. In every classroom I saw sentences on the blackboard, which evidently had been written to illustrate some grammatical rule, or for the purpose of using words that had previously been taught in the same, or in some other connection. This sort of thing may be necessary in some stages of education; but it isn't the way to acquire language. Nothing, I think, crushes the child's impulse to talk naturally more effectually than these blackboard exercises. The schoolroom is not the place to teach any young child language, least of all the deaf child. He must be kept as unconscious as the hearing child of the fact that he is learning words, and he should be allowed to prattle in monosyllables if he chooses, until such time as his growing intelligence demands the sentence. Language should not be associated in his mind with endless hours in school, with puzzling questions in grammar, or with anything that is an enemy to joy. (As cited in Pollack, 1970, p. 108)

A hearing impairment's greatest effect on the developing child is in the language system—affecting the receptive and the expressive systems. During the first year of life, the normal child hears thousands of words and soon begins to attach meaning to some of them.

Northern and Downs (1974) concluded that children with hearing impairments are identical in their vocalizations to children without impaired hearing until the age of five or six months. Babbling is thus a reflexive, preadaptive behavior. The hearing-impaired infant fails to progress past this stage or is characterized by marked delay in any further progression of speech development. If language potential is to be maximized then intervention must be timed to coincide with critical periods of experience essential to language and speech development. Because the stages through which the hearing-impaired infant progresses will be longer in duration, it is important that efforts be made to maximize critical input during the stage and encourage movement to the next stage (Simmons, 1972).

The impact of deafness becomes more critical in the second year of life when there is a large increase in naming things and in putting together agents and actions.

The normal-hearing child knows about 25 words at age two years, about 600 words at three years, 1500 words at four years, and 2000 at age five. Simmons (1966) found preschool hearing-impaired children failed to achieve language at this rate. Some idea of the language skills of hearing-impaired children trained in preschool settings can be seen in Table 12-5, which compares children from two programs.

According to Schlesinger and Meadow (1972), there is a paucity of literature on the language achievement of deaf children between the ages of nine months and six to seven years. The authors reported results of Mecham scores of the deaf and hearing subjects in their preschool program, which can be seen in Table 12-6.

In reports of older children, performance on word-meaning and paragraph-meaning subtests are significantly below results in normal children. Furth (1966) reports only 12 percent of deaf adults achieve true linguistic competencies and only 4 percent are proficient speech readers and speakers.

Cognitive Development

Lenneberg (1972) wrote that the development of cognition is relatively unimpaired (at least up to a certain age level) if only one sensory avenue is blocked. In the measurement of mentation, linguistic competence plays a major role in determining one's performance—an importance that increases with age, and this has caused a number of deaf persons to be erroneously labeled retarded. Psychologists must be extremely cautious in selecting instruments for assessment of the deaf.

During their younger years, deaf children are less likely to be penalized by intelligence testing. Measures of sensorimotor intelligence include a high percentage of visual and fine motor-manipulating tasks. Macnamara (1972) and Bloom (1970, 1971) suggest that thought development precedes and is essential for linguistic development. According to Macnamara (1972), infants learn their language by first determining, independently of language, the meaning a speaker intends to convey, then working out the relationship between meaning and language. "The infant uses meaning as a clue to language, rather than language as a clue to meaning" (p. 1).

Furth and Youniss (1976) investigated the presence of formal operations in deaf and hearing adolescents (mean age for both groups was 16-17 years). Subjects were tested in symbolic logic, probability, and combinations, with results demonstrating rather large differences among subject groups on symbol logic, but only small differences on probability and combinations. The researchers concluded that the data "support a view that sees in a special environment, including its verbal aspect, a powerful factor in motivating individuals toward selective formal operatory functioning without, however, making language the determining cause underlying these operations" (p. 407). The study indicated that language facilitated certain formal operations that were expressed in a symbolic medium, but not on other formal operations.

Table 12-5 Results of a 5-Year Comparative Study of Language Development

	Denver Program	Cleveland Program
Mean age (in months)	60.3	67.6
Range	59-63 months	58-74 months
Mean hearing level (better ear)	69 dB	71 dB
Range	58-95 dB	43-95 dB
Mean hearing level (poorer ear)	77 dB	72 dB
Range	62-95 dB	57-100 dB
Mean Length of Time Using the Aid	19.7 months	35.1 months
Range	11-44 months	16-55 months
Number Agreed Words	869	172
Mean	74.4	10.8
Range	0-170	0-75
Mean Length of Responses	1.8 words	.76 words
Range	0-15	0-2.1
Mean Structural Complexity	4.8	.25
Range	0-15	0-1
Parts of Speech		
N. Adjectives—Range	0-16	0-1
N. Pronouns—Range	0-59	0-5
N. Prepositions—Range	0-14	0-1

Source: Stewart, J. *The effectiveness of educational audiology on the language development of hearing handicapped children.* University of Denver, 1965.

Table 12-6 Mecham Scores of Deaf and Hearing Children

Language Age in Months (quartiles)	Deaf %	Deaf (N)	Hearing %	Hearing (N)
5-16	35	(14)	—	(0)
17-28	40	(16)	—	(0)
29-52	23	(9)	25	(5)
53-69	3	(1)	75	(15)
Totals	101	(40)	100	(20)
Average Age	43.8		43.7	

Source: Schlesinger, H. S., & Meadow, K.P. *Sound and sign: Childhood deafness and mental health.* University of California Press, 1972, p. 57-59. Reprinted with permission.

One must conclude from the findings reported that cognition as an entity separate from language is not impaired in the young deaf child. However, when one looks at functional mentation and the expectations of school aged and adult persons, hearing-impaired individuals fall considerably behind their hearing peers. In the Babbidge Report (1965) of an 11-member advisory committee appointed by HEW to study the educational opportunities for the deaf, the following statements clearly demonstrate the effects deafness has on achievement. "The average graduate of a public residential school for the deaf—the closest we have to generally available 'high school' for the deaf—has an eighth grade education . . . Five-sixths of our deaf adults work in manual jobs, as contrasted to only one-half of our hearing population" (p. xv).

Social Development

Levine (1960) stated that the deaf tend to lag behind the hearing in social maturity and its related behavior and adjustments. In reporting the followup results of children who had attended the Infant Program at the Rochester School for the Deaf, Castle and Warchol (1974) noted that the children enrolled in private nursery schools made a good adjustment except in the social-interaction area. For the most part, they played alone, chose their own activities, and seemed disinterested in teacher-initiated activities.

Rainer and Altshuler (1966) describe a cluster of symptoms found in adult deaf patients as a lack of understanding and regard for the feelings of others; limited awareness of the impact of their behavior on others, i.e., an egocentric view of the world; coercive demands to have their needs and wishes satisfied; immature reaction to frustrations; few self-imposed controls and constraints.

One of the more illuminating analyses of the effects of deafness on social development was offered by Schlesinger and Meadow (1972) as they traced the development of the deaf individual in an Eriksonian epigenetic scheme. Erikson (1968) viewed each successive step a potential crisis ''. . . a crucial period of increased vulnerability and heightened potential; and therefore, the onto-genetic source of generational strength and maladjustment'' (p.96). A synopsis of the periods that occur during the preschool years follows:

Basic Trust Versus Mistrust

This period spans the 12-to-18-month period during which the infant finds that the physical environment and the caregivers are trustworthy and that they respond to needs in positive and predictable ways. New parents of a deaf child are frequently disappointed by the experts that serve them because they fail to provide the needed support. These parents suffer from the infant's auditory deficit, making it more difficult to assess accurately the impact of the deficit on the infant.

Autonomy Versus Shame and Doubt

Between 18 months and 3 years, the child develops autonomy, a feeling of being a separate human entity with control over his body and influence over the environment. Deaf youngsters show delayed resolutions of the crisis of autonomy in many areas, delayed toilet training, feeding problems, failure to adhere to safety measures, and delayed verbal-skill learning.

Initiative Versus Guilt

From three to six years, the child's task is to develop a sense of initiative with a feeling of purposefulness of life and of one's self. The normal child is both motorically and verbally very active; the deaf child is verbally very inactive, yet motorically, possibly more active. However, in actuality, the child is inhibited by the innumerable safeguards parents place on him to limit his explorations of the outside world. Preschools also stress immobility by requiring the child to sit for long periods observing the teacher.

Another critical impact on the child at this stage is a developing self-esteem—a sense of how the family views the child as a person. The child begins to act like the person he thinks others expect. Another influence on self-esteem is the child's view of the surrounding adults. If the child has known only deaf adults, he may develop distorted expectations of what happens to deaf children when they grow up.

INSTRUCTIONAL PROGRAMS FOR INFANTS AND TODDLERS

The importance of early intervention with hearing-impaired infants cannot be underestimated. Horton (1976) points out that failure to stimulate an organism with sound during the first months of life causes irreversible hearing damage. Despite excellent neonatal screening and service, a recent study of 100 profoundly deaf children showed that most of the children have a 26-month lag between first suspicion and something actually done (Pollack, 1976).

The failure of the deaf child to enter into the period of curiosity and bombard others with a myriad of questions, or to absorb much of what is said around him, leaves the child with an impoverished understanding of the environment. If language potential is to be maximized, then intervention must coincide with periods of experience essential to language and speech development. Because the stages through which the hearing-impaired infant progresses will be longer in duration, it is important to maximize critical input and encourage movement to the next stage (Simmons, 1972).

PARENT TRAINING

In reviewing the role of parent training as a major service model for intervention with handicapped children, we can again point to programs for preschool deaf children as a pacesetter. During the 1960's, the John Tracy Clinic in Los Angeles began a program of parent training with the home as the focal point. Soon the Central Institute for the Deaf in St. Louis, the University of Kansas Medical School, and the Bill Wilkerson Hearing and Speech Center in Nashville adopted similar programs.

In describing the program at the Bill Wilkerson Center, Horton (1974) reported measured success in language growth and auditory development in the child participants. Eighteen of the early participants entered regular first and second grades and were performing successfully, a major accomplishment for a deaf child. Horton cites the use of parents as change agents as the key to the children's success. The program objectives fall into five general categories: (1) to teach parents to optimize the auditory environment; (2) to teach parents how to talk to their child; (3) to familiarize parents with the principles, stages and sequence of normal language development and how to apply the frame of reference in stimulating their child; (4) to teach parents strategies of behavior management; and (5) to supply affective support to aid the family in coping with their feelings about their child and the stresses that a handicapped child places on family integrity.

Baldwin (1977) reviewed programs for hearing-impaired children and reported six common characteristics of quality programs: (1) leadership; (2) esprit de corps; (3) curriculum centralization; (4) systematic use of amplification; (5) speech and language instruction; and (6) high level of expectation.

CURRICULA INSTRUCTION FOR PRESCHOOL DEAF CHILDREN
Language Instruction

Programs for deaf children adopt a philosophy of language acquisition, then follow the general guidelines of instruction for that particular philosophy or program. Rather than detail the specifics of language development, it seems more appropriate to present an overview of the major approaches used in preschool programs.

Auditory-Training Instruction

After a child has been fitted with appropriate amplification, a training program must be initiated to make maximal use of residual hearing. Audiologists and programs differ in how they train the child to use hearing. Programs that emphasize the auditory input only are referred to as unisensory or aural methods (Pollack, 1970). Programs emphasizing auditory input but including visual and contextual cues are referred to as oral-aural methods or natural-language methods (Groht, 1958).

Many of the programs emphasizing auditory input have developed guidelines for parents. The guidelines for the Bill Wilkerson Hearing and Speech Center are presented in Table 12-7.

Total-Communication Instruction

A recent study by Jordan, Gustafson, and Rosen (1976) revealed that the number of classes reporting use of total communication as a primary mode is far greater than the number of classes using all other modes combined, evidencing a clear trend toward total communication in education of the deaf. Garretson (1976) states that total communication is neither a method nor a prescribed system of instruction, but an approach that encourages a climate of communication flexibility, free of ambiguity, guesswork, and stress. It acknowledges the need for visual support. Research by Chasen and Zuckerman (1976) and White and Stevenson (1975) offered convincing evidence that children using the total-communication approach improved significantly more in academics than did children in oral classes. There are some disadvantages to this approach: lack of a nationally agreed-upon sign system and difficulty in mainstreaming.

Total communication can be divided into several subcategories as noted in Table 12-8.

Verbotonal Instruction

This program, developed from a rhythm-based technique for teaching foreign language, uses body movements to establish speech patterns and auditory perception of these patterns. Since emphasis is on acoustic memory for these patterns, games and play activities are used to teach language, speech, use of residual hearing, and, later, academic skills.

Table 12-7 Rules of Talking

CREATING THE CLIMATE FOR COMMUNICATION

Because children must want to communicate before they will learn language, we must provide a maximum of opportunities which encourage children to use language—to listen to and send language messages . . .

Get down on your child's level.
Tune into your child's interests.
Let your child participate. Language is best learned while doing.
Let your face and voice tell your child you're interested.

LISTENING FOR A CHILD'S MESSAGE

Because children must develop confidence in their ability to use language, we must develop our capability to fully understand their messages . . .

Show your child you want to understand.
Listen to your child's tone of voice. Voices reflect feelings.
Watch the face, the body, the hands. They help you understand your child's message.

MAKING YOUR TALK RELEVANT

Because children learn language from hearing language, and because children listen to language that is obvious, meaningful, and interesting to them . . .

Talk about the here and now.
Talk about the obvious—what your child is doing, hearing, seeing, smelling, or tasting.
At times talk for your child.
Put your child's feelings into words.

ENCOURAGING A CHILD TO USE VOICE TO MAKE SOUNDS

Because sounds are the building blocks of speech and language, children must be encouraged to vocalize—to play with, practice, and use the sounds of speech . . .

Reward your child for using his or her voice.
Chant and sing simple rhymes and songs.
Add voiced sounds to accompany the child's repeated movement.
Vary the sounds you make to your child. Make yourself interesting to listen to.
Encourage your child to use voiced sounds to get your attention.
Imitate the sounds your child makes and add new sounds.

HELPING A CHILD UNDERSTAND WORDS

Because children learn words from hearing them hundreds and thousands of times in different ways, and because words comprise the cornerstone of language . . .

Everything has a name. Use the name.
Use short simple sentences. Avoid using single words.
Use natural gestures when you talk.
Tell, then show your child what you want him or her to do.
Use repetition. Say it again and again. Give your child a chance to show he or she understands.

TALKING WHEN A CHILD BEGINS TO USE WORDS

Because the process of children's language learning depends on their hearing adult feedback, correct and expand their words, their phrases, and their sentences . . .

Reward your child when he or she attempts to say a word.
When your child uses a single word, repeat it and put it back into a sentence.
When your child uses incomplete or incorrect language or speech, repeat the message correctly.
Expand your child's vocabulary by adding new words.
Let your child hear new and more difficult sentence forms.
When your child expresses an idea, repeat it and then expand his or her thoughts by adding new information.

Source: Produced by Language Development Programs, Bill Wilkerson Hearing and Speech Center, Nashville, Tennessee. Copyright 1976 by the Bill Wilkerson Hearing and Speech Center; reprinted by permission. Special acknowledgment is accorded Sue M. Lillie and the teaching staff of the Mama Lere Home. Funded by the Bureau of Education for the Handicapped.

Motor Development

There are no widely recognized motor programs specifically designed for hearing-impaired preschool children. Many schools for the deaf have designed their own programs and a number of teachers of self-contained deaf children have adapted traditional motor programs. The motor area is one of the easier areas in which to integrate deaf children with non-hearing-impaired children. For the most part they can follow the motor cues of peers and have few delays that are directly related to their hearing loss.

What will be presented are some particular areas that may prove difficult for the deaf child and some suggestions for instruction.

Table 12-8 Elements of Total Communication

American Sign Language (Ameslan or ASL)		
	Standard signs	Unique grammar
	Non-English language	Unique syntax
	Some fingerspelling	
	one sign = one concept	
Aural/Oral		
	Amplification	Oral gesture
	Lipreading	Speech
	Cued Speech (eight hand configurations, four facial positions)	
	One lipsign = one or more phonemes	
Fingerspelling		
	Finger rather than hand signs	
	Letters run together as in oral or written production	
	Rochester method (fingerspelling combined with speech)	
	one hand configuration = one letter	

Table 12-8 *Continued*

Gestemic	Childrenese Esoteric (localisms) International sign one gesture = one concept	Natural gestures Pantomime
Manual English	Seeing essential English Signed English Signing Exact English Linguistics of Visual English one sign = one word or affix	Fingerspelling Standard sign often used as root Creation of new signs for inflections endings, tense, affixes, articles
Siglish (Sign English)	Pidgin Sign English Fingerspelling Syntax heavily English-oriented one sign = one concept	Standard sign modified on continuum toward English Gear-shifting between English and ASL idiom

Source: Reprinted from Chapter 13, Total Communication, M.D. Garretson, p. 92, *The Volta Review,* A Bicentennial Monograph on Hearing Impairment: Trends in the USA, 78, No. 4, Robert Frisina, Ed. © The Alexander Graham Bell Association for the Deaf, 3417 Volta Place, NW, Washington, DC 20007, publisher.

Visual-Perceptual Coordination

Without dependable cues from auditory stimuli in the environment, hearing-impaired children can profit from refined visual-perceptual skills. The child can sense the stimuli and respond immediately, thus coordinating his motor responses in synchrony with the patterns followed by those responding to auditory cues.

To facilitate visual-motor coordination, let the child learn dance sequences where cues can be taken from the steps of others, then perform the sequences with proper timing.

Engage in ball activities where child must adjust body after following the trajectory of a ball.

On a card or chalkboard, place a pattern, which can be in colors or shapes to mean forward, backward, or side movements. Let the child then follow these movements according to the visual cue.

Static Balance

It is likely that many hearing-impaired children will have balance problems. The motor curriculum should, therefore, stress balance, with static balance activities including supine positions in which the child imitates movements of the head and shoulders, shoulders and arms, body and trunk, legs, knees, ankles and feet, and combined movements. The same movements should likewise be stressed from a prone position.

Further emphasis on static balance can be placed by having the child crawl in place on his stomach with a homolateral or a cross pattern.

Dynamic Balance

Movement of the body in space requires an internal perception of body movement in order to make the adjustments necessary for equilibrium. Maintaining balance is facilitated by crawling activities using both a homolateral and a cross pattern, creeping with the homolateral and cross patterns, imitating various animals, and following obstacle courses. Also important are dynamic balance in a seated position involving trunk movements, rotations and body extensions; arm movements; and leg and knee exercises. In an upright position, the child can engage in stretching movements, exercises, running, marching, jumping in place, etc. Trunk rotation and bends are directed toward dynamic balance. Walking, running, hopping, trotting, galloping, marching, and combinations are more advanced dynamic motor procedures.

Social Development

Like motor instruction, there is little in social-competency instruction designed specifically for deaf children. Instruction in this area is less structured and seldom programmed but should be taught in context with the situation at hand. That is, the teacher, parents, and others involved with the child should intervene in the situation and instruct or model for the child the proper behavior in the situation present. Teachers report social maturity based on their observations of a child's interactions with others around him and note lags that may be apparent.

Trust

Trust must be learned from another, then internalized and expressed to others. The deaf child, like all other children, needs to feel that caregivers and the world (in predictable ways) can be trusted. The child must be provided chances for mutual trust. In addition, perhaps through family animals and peers or siblings, the child must experience itself in a different trusting role, where others are trusting and dependent on the child for specific responses.

Self-Concept

Because the deaf child cannot communicate with surrounding ones, the child is likely to be more passive, to initiate fewer interactions, to see himself as a person others must help and whom others pity. If these feelings persist, the child will take on actions to justify the way others are responding. It is critical to build independence, to stress the child's strengths, to stress progression in overcoming problems relating to his worthiness.

Independence

It is a natural reaction of humans to want to help those who cannot perform as well as they would like. The young deaf child is far more often on the receiving end than on the doing-for-others end and should be provided planned opportunities to do things for others. Showing a friend how to perform a task that has been mastered, playing the mother or father role in child-play activities, pretending to be professional persons such as dentists, doctors, teachers, and sportsmen are ways in which the child can play at an independent and responsible role.

Cognitive Development

In innate mental ability, the young deaf child is not different from the hearing child; however, in expressing understanding in measurable ways, the deaf child's facility decreases with increasing language requirements. In addition to specific instruction in language, there are other areas, particularly in the preoperational stage, where specific instructions can facilitate mental development of the child with a hearing loss.

1. Labels, Symbols, or Signs for Objects or Events Not Present

It is important to stress representation of things not visually present. This can be done through hide-and-seek games, activities requiring imitation or reasoning.

The child can be given objects and told to use them in different ways to convey different meanings:

    A. Ask the child about current situations and surroundings; encourage a reply.
    B. Involve the child in many different activities in the home, school, and away; encourage communication by asking questions.
    C. Use appropriate facial expressions and body gestures to express joy, anger, fear, love, etc.

2. Classification Skills

    A. Have child sort objects or pictures using a model.
    B. Have child sort objects or pictures without a model.
    C. Have child associate pictures or objects that have a direct relationship to one another, such as lamp and light switch.

3. Time Sequences

    A. Have child arrange pictures in the order of naturally occurring events.
    B. Have child tell or draw what happened yesterday and what will happen tomorrow.
    C. Have child explain the sequence of events that will occur in the classroom (example: What will come first, a class subject or lunch and where will recess fit in?).
    D. Have child explain the sequence of dressing in the morning (what articles first) and the sequence of events up to school time.
    E. Have child sequence what he did while playing outdoors or explain sequences to certain tasks that must be accomplished in the classroom.

4. Distance Sequences

    A. On a game board or similar map, lay out places for movement to and from places. Have child follow a long way, a short way, etc.
    B. Have child actually follow different routes to various destinations indoors and out and ask him which was shorter, longer, or the same.
    C. Create mazes and have child follow the shortest or longest route, with finger or pencil, and find the goal.
    D. Create mazes using desks, chairs, or other objects present and have the child crawl or walk the shortest or longest route to the door, window, etc.

5. Size Sequence

    A. Give child objects that must be sequenced according to size (examples: beads, block or cubes, balls).
    B. Have child sequence the chairs or desks in the classroom according to size.

C. Have child sequence the other persons or their body parts, such as legs and arms, according to size.

D. While looking from a window, have child sequence the cars in the parking lot or pedestrians passing by according to size.

6. Patterned Sequences

A. Present a bead pattern with one variable, and have child replicate. Build a more complicated pattern and have child copy by color and shape. After child can do this, use pattern as a memory task with brief exposure to the model.

B. Line up children in the room, have the child study their positions, one child changes positions while observer turns away; then must explain or physically move child back into original position.

7. Number Conservation

A. Use comparisons to see if child can identify more, less, same.

B. Use direct correspondence tasks in which child must match a number to the grouped objects.

C. Present a set of objects and have child arrange an equivalent set.

8. Missing Elements

A. Remove one item from a group and have child identify the missing element. This can also be done with children in a same-like situation.

B. Show child pictures that have missing elements and identify where something is missing and describe what it is. This task can also be done with children: one child removes part of clothing such as shoe, socks, hat, glove, coat, etc., and observer must state what is missing.

C. Plan sequences with something missing. Show child possible missing parts; then child selects correct part.

REFERENCES

Babbidge, H. *Education of the deaf in the United States*. The Report of the Advisory Committee on Education of the Deaf, Washington, D.C.: U.S. Government Printing Office, 1965.

Baldwin, R. L. Characteristics of quality programs for hearing impaired children. *Volta Review*, 1977, *77*, 436-439.

Bloom, L. *Language development: Form and function in emerging grammars*. Boston: M.I.T. Press, 1970.

Bloom, L. Why not pivot grammer? *Journal of Speech and Hearing Disorders*, 1971, *36*, 40-51.

Castle, D. L., & Warchol, B. Rochester's demonstration home program: A comprehensive parent-infant project. *Peabody Journal of Education*, 1974, *51*, (3), 186-191.

Chasen, B., & Zuckerman, W. The effects of total communication and oralism on deaf third grade "rubella" students. *American Annals of the Deaf,* 1976, *121,* 394-401.

Clark, E. V. Some aspects of the conceptual basis for first language acquisition. In R. L. Shiefelbusch & L. L. Lloyd (Eds.), *Language perspectives: Acquisition, retardation, and intervention.* Baltimore: University Park Press, 1974.

Cox, & Lloyd, L. L. Audiologic considerations. In L. L. Lloyd (Ed.), *Communication assessment and intervention strategies.* Baltimore: University Park Press, 1976, 123-193.

DuBose, R. F. Development of communication in nonverbal children. *Education and Training of the Mentally Retarded,* 1978, *13* (1), 37-41.

Erikson, E. H. *Identity, youth and crisis.* New York: Norton, 1968.

Furth, H. G. *Thinking without language: Psychological implications of deafness.* New York: Free Press, 1966.

Furth. H. G., & Youniss, J. Formal operations and language: A comparison of deaf and hearing adolescents. In D. M. Morehead & A. E. Morehead (Eds.), *Normal and deficient child language.* Baltimore: University Park Press, 1976, 387-410.

Garretson, M. D. Total communication. *Volta Review,* 1976, *78,* 88-95.

Groht, M. *Natural language for deaf children.* Washington, D. C., Volta Bureau, 1958.

Horton, K. B. Infant intervention and language learning. In R. L. Schiefilbusch & L. L. Lloyd, *Language perspectives–Acquisition, retardation, and intervention.* Baltimore: University Park Press, 1974, 469-491.

Horton, K. B. Why early intervention? In Watrous, B. S. (Ed.), *Developing home training programs for hearing impaired children.* Albuquerque: The Indian Health Service, Southwest Hearing Speech and Language Associates, Inc., 1976.

Jones, P. A. Causative factors and prevention of childhood deafness. *Volta Review,* 1976, *78,* 268-274.

Jordan, I. K., Gustafson, G., & Rosen, R. Current communication trends at programs for the deaf. *American Annals of the Deaf,* 1976, *121,* 527-532.

Larson, A. D., & Miller, J. B. The hearing impaired. In E. L. Meyen (Ed.), *Exceptional children and youth: An introduction.* Denver: Love Publishing Company, 1978, 430-369.

Lenneberg, E. H. Prerequisites for language acquisition by the deaf. In T. J. O'Rourke (Ed.), *Psycholinguistics and total communication: The state of the art.* Washington, D. C.: American Annals of the Deaf, 1972.

Levine, E. S. *Psychology of deafness.* New York: Columbia University Press, 1960.

Macnamara, J. Cognitive basis of language learning in infants. *Psychological Review, 1972, 79,* 1-13.

Northern, J. L., & Downs, M. P. *Hearing in children.* Baltimore: The Williams & Wilkins Company, 1974.

Pollack, D. *Educational audiology for the limited hearing infant.* Springfield: Charles C. Thomas, 1970.

Pollack, D. The auditory approach: Can a hearing impaired child *really* hear? In B. S. Watrous, (Ed.), *Developing home training programs for hearing impaired children.* Albuquerque: The Indian Health Service, Southwest Hearing Speech and Language Associates, Inc., 1976.

Rainer, J. D., & Altshuler, K. Z. *Comprehensive mental health services for the deaf.* New York State Psychiatric Institute, Columbia University, 1966.

Rand Report: Improving services to handicapped children. R-1420-DHEW, May, 1974.

Reynolds, M. C., & Birch, J. W. *Teaching exceptional children in all America's schools.* Reston, Va: Council for Exceptional Children, 1977.

Ross, M. Hearing aid selection for preverbal hearing-impaired children. In M. Pollack (Ed.), *Amplification for the hearing impaired*. New York: Grune & Stratton, 1975, 207-242.

Ross, M. Amplification systems. In L. L. Lloyd (Ed.), *Communication assessment and intervention strategies*. Baltimore: University Park Press, 1976, 295-324.

Schlesinger, H. S., & Meadow, K. P. *Sound and sign childhood deafness and mental health*. Berkeley: University of California Press, 1972.

Silverman, S. R., & Lane, H. S. Deaf children. In H. Davis & S. E. Silverman (Eds.), *Hearing and deafness* (3rd ed.). New York: Holt, Rinehart and Winston, 1970, 384-425.

Simmons, A. A. The language growth for the pre-nursery deaf child. *Volta Review,* 1966, *68* (3), 201.

Simmons, A. A. The critical stages of language development. Presented at the Council for Exceptional Children Convention, March 21, 1972, Washington, D. C.

Stewart, J. The effectiveness of educational audiology on the language development of hearing handicapped children. Denver: University of Denver Press, 1965.

Watrous, B. S., McConnell, F., Sitton, A., & Fleet, W. Auditory responses of infants. *Journal of Speech and Hearing Disorders,* 1975, *40* (3), 357-366.

White, A. H., & Stevenson, V. M. The effects of total communication, oral communication, and reading on the learning of factual information in residential school deaf children. *American Annals of the Deaf,* 1975, *120*, 48-87.

Part IV
Social Development

Chapter 13

Theoretical Issues in Social Development

David Page and S. Gray Garwood

SOCIAL DEVELOPMENT AND SOCIALIZATION

Our lives are complexly interwoven with the lives of others, so it is hard to imagine human growth and development apart from social interaction. Young children would hardly survive were it not for interactions with others, beginning at the very moment of birth. Infants must acquire necessary life-sustaining skills through a gradual learning process. This chapter discusses the processes by which newborns develop into socially competent individuals. Social development is multifaceted and includes events that are developmental achievements in their own right, such as the infant's relationship with the mother and how this is the basis for development of relationships with other people; how children learn to see themselves as boys or girls (sex-role identity); and how the child internalizes social standards and develops a conscience. In most cases, normal development will be emphasized; that is, how development usually proceeds, given optimal conditions. Discussion of atypical development will be reserved for those events usually leading to inadequate social development, e.g., institutionalization, poor parent-child relationships, and father absence.

Social development describes the process by which we acquire the interests and skills necessary to form and sustain interactions and interrelationships. Society controls the behavior of its members through established rules (socialization), an intricate process which inculcates in children behaviors that are rewarding and help them accomplish their goals. The child must learn a complex network of clues to determine which actions are appropriate in which situations. For example, a child must learn to behave differently not only in different classrooms, but also on the playground, or at club meetings; likewise, the child must learn to react differently to the same people seen in different situations. A student may learn it is OK to kid a teacher on the playground, but once in class, such behavior is not alright. In other ways, we learn general rules to guide behavior in almost all situations. For example, children usually learn that lying, cheating, being too active or too aggressive, or being overly dependent are behaviors that in most situations will result in disapproval from others. On the other hand, being polite, honest, and relatively independent are examples of behaviors almost always resulting in approval.

A variety of social agents (individuals or institutions that present the culture to the child) help insure that the socialization process will be carried out effectively; that is, will lead to the child's acquiring those skills necessary for effective social interaction. Socialization is initially controlled by significant individual agents such as parents, teacher, or other caretaking agents. In some cases, however, collective groups, like peer groups or other social groups, guide socialization. Sometimes superstition, rituals, and the supernatural also influence socialization; many of you may still recall from childhood the threat of the bogey man or the promise that Santa would record your good behavior. In many homes, religious beliefs and practices are interwoven with socialization, and God and the Devil are utilized as socialization agents.

Socialization, however, is not totally controlled by these external forces; the child also is an active participant. For example, the infant's relationship with the mother is, in part, due to efforts to seek and sustain contact with the mother; thus maximizing the possibility of a healthy and stable relationship. The child continues to be an active agent of his own socialization, gradually incorporating the standards held by important external socialization agents. The child acquires a conscience and learns to experience pride and guilt, and in doing so, guides the continuing socialization process.

Another important issue pertaining to socialization centers around that means by which children acquire the skills and behaviors for effective social functioning. The significant persons in a child's life and the child himself are the ones primarily responsible for social development. Several mechanisms have been postulated to account for this process, the most important depending on which theoretical perspective is followed. Both the postulated mechanisms and the theoretical perspectives will be discussed in detail later in the chapter.

Social development varies with the child's culture or social system. For example, Indian children are socialized to be respectful and obedient, Japanese children to be submissive and dependent, American children to be autonomous and individualistic (Gaudill and Wenistem, 1966). These differences seem to result from culturally dependent parental beliefs as to the basic nature of children and how they are to be molded into the ideal adult. It is assumed, however, that the means by which these varying traits and skills are acquired are not culturally dependent—the process of social development is thought to be similar across social systems.

THEORETICAL PERSPECTIVES ON SOCIAL DEVELOPMENT

Theories provide conceptual frameworks used to organize and explain natural phenomena. Since theories usually include notions as to which factors are determinants or causes of specific events, they can be classified into general types of causes thought to be most important. Some emphasize factors external to the individual as being the primary causes of behavior (i.e., traditional learning theory); others see factors within the individual, such as drives or instincts, as being the primary determinants of social development (Freud's psychosexual theory; ethological theories). Still other theories emphasize interaction of internal and external factors (social-cognitive theories: Erikson's psychosocial theory, social learning theory). Each approach will be discussed individually.

The Hereditary Perspective

Ethology is the study of the organism in its natural habitat. Until recently used almost exclusively to study non-human animals, it has lately been applied to human research (Eibl-Eibesfeldt, 1970). Extensive work has now been done on such human behavioral patterns as mother-infant relationships (Bowlby, 1969) and children's interactions with peers in nursery schools.

Typically, ethologists are concerned with *species-specific behaviors* (behaviors potentially shown in all members of a species). In order to understand how these specific behavior patterns developed, ethologists work from an evolutionary perspective and examine the functions of behaviors. Their concern is with how certain behavior patterns help to insure survival of a species by maximizing the possibility that a member of the species will be able to reproduce. In this respect, species-specific behaviors are said to be adaptive, or have *functional significance*. Ethologists emphasize the genetic component of behaviors. Insofar as a behavioral pattern has functional significance, the genes responsible for the particular behavior have been, and will be, passed on by members of the species from generation to generation. If a behavior no longer has functional significance, because of changing environmental demands, then it is likely that the genetic basis for this behavior will change, be reduced in frequency, and will slowly drop out of the behavioral repertoire of the species.

When the functional significance of a species-specific behavior can be determined (that is, when scientists can determine *how* the behavior maximizes the possibility of survival of an individual), ethologists will usually consider individual members of a species as predisposed to exhibit the particular behavior; hence, organisms are sometimes said to have an instinct to behave in a certain manner. Ethologists also consider the environment in the analysis of behavior, maintaining that the overt manifestation (phenotype) of an instinctually based behavior (genotype) will not occur unless the environment is appropriate. Certain types of environmental stimulation (termed *sign stimuli,* or *releasers*) are thought to *elicit* or *trigger* the phenotypic expression of the genotype. Consequently, it is possible for an organism to have an instinct to behave in a certain manner, yet, in actuality, not behave accordingly.

The type of analysis described above is applied by ethologists in analyzing human social development on the assumption that the human species is fundamentally social. Social behaviors have functional significance since they increase the chances that a child will be accepted within the social system, survive, and pass on his genes. Consequently, the process of social development can be understood in terms of genetically preprogrammed social behaviors being evoked by appropriate environmental stimulation. Intrinsic to this evolutionary perspective is the notion that the child is an active force in his socialization. Since social behaviors are possibly instinctive, it is the child himself who largely determines social development.

The Psychodynamic Perspective

The *psychodynamic* viewpoint, conceptualizing human behavior and development in terms of unconscious motivational sources, has had much influence on the study of social development. It assumes that human beings are born with a fixed amount of psychic energy providing the impetus for behavior. (This is conceptually similar to the ethological assertion that inborn instincts influence our behavior.) In this view, social development consists of acquisition of skills and abilities needed to control these motivations in socially acceptable manners. The originator of this viewpoint is Sigmund Freud, who, at the turn of the century, formulated a theory of psychosexual development, viewing sexual drives as the primary motivations in development. Freud's originality in conceptualizing human development brought him a number of followers who supplemented and extended his theory, developing fairly new and distinctive ideas. The new thinkers—among them, Carl Jung, Alfred Adler, Karen Horney, and Erik Erikson—have traditionally been called *Neo-Freudians* (literally ''new''-Freudians) since they nevertheless retain many of Freud's ideas. For our purposes we will discuss only those theories which have had a profound impact on thinking concerning social development: Freud's original theory, and the neo-Freudian psychosocial theory of Erik Erikson.

According to Freud, human beings are born with a fixed amount of psychic energy *(libido)* that manifests itself primarily through sexual (Eros) and aggressive (Thanatos) drives. Implicit in this assumption is the hydraulic notion which asserts that, if these drives are not discharged, they will gradually build up within the organism leading to a state of discomfort. In the course of development, drives are discharged through various parts of the body. This discharge is thought to be gratifying and consequently is a pleasurable experience for an organism. The body part which serves as locus for drive discharge is determined by the child's current developmental status. Freud postulated five stages of development as outlined in Table 13-1.

Of greater import to social development is the *structural* aspect of Freud's theory. According to Freud, the mature adult personality is composed of three

---

Table 13-1 Freudian Theory of Psychosexual Development Applied to Early Childhood

ORAL

Duration

0 - 1 year

Associated Behaviors

Dependency and independence;
Feeding & weaning;
Sucking & chewing.

Duration

Maintaining comfort;
Seeking food when awake and
  active;
Learning that parents are
  dependable;
Exploring the world by
  placing objects in the mouth.

Associated Behaviors

Care and nurturance of child;
Adjustment of eating and
  sleeping schedule to fit
  convenience of family
Demonstration of affection for
  the child.

ANAL

Duration

1 - 2½ years

Associated Behaviors

Sphincter reflex control; Fecal
  retention and expulsion;
  Obstinacy, stubbornness, neatness,
  aggression and hostility.

Interests & Activities of Child

Keeping the body clean and
  comfortable;
Limits of physical self and
  "what is mine"—first sense
  of self.
"Territorial rights" on property
  and personal freedom;
Assertion of the self.

Concerns & Attentions of Parents

Adjustment of toilet (bowel) habits
  to fit convenience of the family
  and specific situations or times;
Cleanliness and personal hygiene;

Establishment of limits to child's
  personal rights.

Table 13-1 *Continued*

PHALLIC

Duration	Associated Behaviors
2½ - 5 years	Discovery of biological and cultural differences.

Interests & Activities of Child	Concerns & Attentions of Parents
Discovery that boys have a penis, while girls do not; Discovery that men have social power, while women do not; Boys fear its loss: *castration anxiety;* Girls wish they had it: *penis envy.*	Sex-role training: sons should do boyish things, and daughters should do girlish things; Monitoring of toy preferences, play activities; Restriction of early sex-exploration.
Oedipal (not, strictly speaking, a stage) (coincident with phallic phase)	Parental identification with same-sexed parent; Resolution of identity conflicts; Adoption of sex-appropriate behavior; Internalization of superego standards for experience of guilt and anxiety.
Identification with same-sexed parent; Achievement (by imitation) of adult-like behavior; Independent sense of self as a complete being.	Training for adult masculinity and femininity; Arousal of child's pride and guilt in connection with right and wrong behavior; Training in social standards for desirable behavior.

interdependent components: *Id, Ego,* and *Superego.* The *Id* is thought to be present at birth and is the home or source of psychic energy. The Id seeks continuous and immediate gratification of its inborn impulses, operating via the *pleasure principle.* Consequently, at birth the human infant is viewed as being relatively asocial and hedonistic. However, during the oral stage the Ego develops and, in turn, regulates the discharge of Id impulses. The process of Ego development is largely a function of the child's experience with reality. At birth, the child does not make any distinctions between self and world since the constant and immediate gratification of urges provided by most parents leads the child to view the world as no more than an extension of self. But as a result of delays in gratification plus punishments, which predictively occur as the child attempts to satisfy drives, the child no longer conceives of the world as simply an extension of self, since delays in drive gratification are inconsistent with this belief. The outcome of this process is development of the Ego: a source of self distinct from reality. The Ego in turn takes control over the expression of the Id's impulses while operating via the reality principle. Consequently, the drives are discharged in accordance with realistic considerations imposed by the outside world. According to the psychodynamic viewpoint, Ego development is the first event in the child's becoming a mature social being.

Although a necessary component of social development, the Ego is not sufficient for mature social functioning. Whereas the Ego does take into account considerations reflecting reality while controlling drive gratification, it is rather immune to social standards and morals, which, according to society, should also bear on one's behavior. The internalization of social norms as standards for drive discharge and behavior does not occur until the phallic stage, when the child is confronted with either the Oedipus Complex (if male) or the Electra Complex (if female)—intense love for the opposite sex parent and intense dislike for the same-sex parent. (These processes will be considered in detail later under sex-typing). The resolution of either of these complexes occurs when the child identifies with the same-sex parent and internalizes arbitrary social standards, morals, and values represented by the parent. Identification results in formation of the Superego (conscience and internalized standards) which in turn assumes further control over expression of Id impulses. In a sense, the child is thought to become a parent, regulating expression of drives in much the same way as mature adults. Superego development is thought to be the hallmark of social development in childhood since the child is now truly on the path to becoming a mature social being.

As a Neo-Freudian, Erikson's (1963) theory of psychosocial development operates basically within a psychodynamic framework but differs from Freud's theory on three basic points. First, as do all the Neo-Freudians, Erikson rejected the fundamentally sexual nature of human motivation that Freud hypothesized. According to Erikson, development is marked by more than an increasing sophistication of expression of sexual and aggressive urges; development also involves the creative, adaptive, and reality-oriented aspects of personality. Basically, the functioning of the Ego is elaborated; while the Ego is responsible for the control of psychic energies, it is also thought to be responsible for the overall social competency of the individual: language, thinking, acquired motivation (e.g., achievement), etc. Second, while Freud viewed social development as terminating with the genital stage in adolescence, Erikson conceived of development as a process extending from birth through old age with new social abilities and competencies continuously being developed. Third, and most important, is the *psychosocial* aspect of Erikson's theory. While Freud did take into account social influences on human development, he treated them with far less importance than Erikson. According to Erikson, social environment is of utmost importance in determining development, exerting various influences and demands that shape human development. Moreover, Erikson felt that environmental demands change as the child matures, the satisfaction of the varying societal demands leading to acquisition of corresponding new social abilities.

The last difference between Freudian and Eriksonian theorizing forms the nucleus of Erikson's theory. To reiterate: when new adjustment demands are placed on an individual, new Ego capacities must be gained to meet differing environmental demands. According to Erikson, environmental demand on an individual takes the form of an emotional crisis. Development consists of attempts to resolve this emotional crisis by acquiring appropriate capabilities to meet the challenge. If the challenge is met and the abilities are developed, development proceeds in a healthy manner. Each newly acquired ability is considered part of the developing ego.

Erikson postulated eight stages of development (Table 13-2 includes stages 1-3), each of which is differentiated in terms of the nature of environmental demands and the types of conflicts evoked by the varying demands. Successful resolution of an emotional conflict leads to a new Ego capability, which in turn facilitates coping with emotional crises in subsequent stages. For example, in Stage 1, Trust vs. Mistrust, the newborn child finds himself in a new stimulating environment (the world) which is in marked contrast to the child's prior environment (the womb). The child is literally bombarded by sensory stimulation which in turn must be coped with, evoking emotional crisis (trust-mistrust). If the stimulation is perceived as good and benign, the child will acquire a sense of basic trust and be able to cope effectively with the new environment. If the stimulation is experienced as aversive and threatening, the child will develop a sense of mistrust which will in turn inhibit interacting in the world. Only an appropriate resolution to the conflict will lead to basic trust which subsequently will facilitate coping with the emotional crisis of Stage 2: Autonomy vs. Shame and Doubt. During this stage, society demands that the child learn complete muscular control (autonomy), and this will be facilitated by a sense of basic trust in others.

Erikson also viewed each of these stages as a critical period for development of

Ego capabilities. Inherent in Erikson's theorizing is a maturational notion (the epigenetic principle), which states that ". . . anything that grows has a ground plan, and out of this ground plan the parts arise, each having its time of special ascendancy, until all parts have arisen to form a functioning whole" (Erikson, 1959, p. 52). Thus, in addition to social factors, Erikson offers a principle of development primarily maturational and postulating a timetable of ego development. Not all Ego capabilities are present at birth; each part has a time or stage in which to develop. During a particular stage, the focus of development is on a particular ability and when the next stage of development comes about, the focus of development is switched to it. This timetable moves on even though an Ego capability may not be developed. Thus, to become a fully functioning social individual, it is important to develop capabilities inherent in particular stages *during that stage of development,* for there will be no other change.

Table 13-2 Erikson's Stages of Psychosocial Development Applied to Early Childhood

Stage	Age Range	Characteristic Concerns
Basic Trust vs Mistrust	infancy	Parents respond to the needs of the defenseless newborn, gaining her trust and creating in her a sense of confidence in the reliability of the world.
Autonomy vs Shame & Doubt	1½-3 yrs.	Child increases repertoire of physical skills needed to explore/manipulate the world; gains independence, but remains under the control of external reward and punishment (shame) from others.
Initiative vs Guilt	3-5½ yrs.	Awareness of sex differences increases, with respect to both parents and peers; the child becomes more evaluative of her competence, ability, ideals, and standards.

Source: Adapted and reprinted by permission of the publisher, from McDavid, J. W., & Garwood, S. G. *Understanding children,* Lexington, Mass.: D. C. Heath, 1978.

In summary, Erikson describes eight stages of psychosocial development. Each of these stages is differentiated in terms of varying environmental demands and particular Ego components that have to be developed to resolve emotional crises evoked by environmental demands. Social development is the acquisition of a multitude of Ego capabilities enabling the individual to cope effectively with society.

The Learning Perspective

The learning-theory approach to social development differs dramatically from hereditary and psychodynamic perspectives. These differences are especially striking when one compares the latter two with the traditional behavioristic approach. While the hereditary and psychodynamic approaches have emphasized internal factors (instincts, drives, ego capacities) as primary influences on social development, behavioristic notions reflect exclusively external factors. However, new conceptions of learning (social learning theory) have recognized the impact of internal factors (attention, cognition) on social development. Because of these differences, each type of learning, behavioristic and social, will be discussed separately.

The traditional behavioristic view of behavior virtually negates cognition and other organism factors as possible influences on social development, and asserts that behavior change and development are due solely to external environmental factors, such as stimulation and reinforcement. The child is a passive recipient of these external causal factors. The behavioristic system is quite simple and does provide parsimonious and intuitively logical explanations of social development. It is largely because of this simplicity that the behavioristic account of social development maintained the unquestionable status of being the best portrayal of social development.

Social development, according to behaviorism, is largely dependent on factors that are both antecedent and consequent to a particular response made by an individual. Antecedent factors are customarily considered to be stimulus variables; consequent factors are conceptualized in terms of reinforcement variables. Specific consequent variables are reinforcement, punishment, and non-reward. *Reinforcement* is any event that rewards a child for performing a specific behavior and consequently increasing the probability that the child will repeat that behavior in the future. Two types of reward are considered important in social development: positive reinforcement and negative reinforcement. Positive reinforcement involves the presentation of a pleasant event, such as praise, candy, or affection, after an appropriate behavior. Negative reinforcement refers to the removal of an aversive event, again after the child behaves correctly; e.g., letting a child get out of his room only after he stops crying. Reward consolidates productive behavior that leads to satisfaction or facilitates goal achievement. It increases the chances that a particular action will occur again in similar situations. Furthermore, reward induces positive attitudes on the part of the learner, which tend to spread to the entire related learning situation, including the people, objects, or events present. Thus, reward not only influences accumulation of specific behavioral habits in children, but also affects many attitudes about learning to enjoy particular activities or situations.

Punishment deters behavior that leads to stressful or painful conditions. It presents an aversive event (e.g., a spanking) or the removal of a pleasurable event (e.g., not permitting the child to watch television), and by direct suppression or inhibition, decreases the likelihood that a particular action will occur again. Sometimes the effects of punishment spill over to make the child apprehensive about similar situations in the future. Such learned fear is called *anxiety*. Often a residue of apprehension and anxiety remains behind the experience of punishment, even when the child has forgotten the specific episode itself. When it results from punishment in an otherwise harmless situation, this kind of anxiety can in some cases be strong enough that a child may go to considerable trouble to avoid risking a repetition of the punishment. For reinforcement and punishment to be effective in controlling and teaching appropriate social behaviors, they must be *contingent* on a particular behavior. That is, in nonbehavioristic terminology, the child must perceive a connection between behavior and consequent events for behavior to be changed as a result of reward and punishment.

A third type of consequent event (or more appropriately "non-event") is nonreward. *Nonreward* is the absence of punishment or reward following a given action; the child is left in a status quo condition with respect to goal-directed efforts. Being neither nearer nor farther from the goal, the learner merely continues to try, usually seeking behavioral alternatives that may be more productive. This continued goal-seeking along alternate lines leads to abandonment of nonproductive activities (extinction).

In summary, behavioristic theorists conceptualize social development as basically a learning process. New skills and abilities are acquired chiefly because performance of these behaviors is rewarded by significant people in the child's environment. Similarly, those behaviors not valued by a particular social system, because they are inappropriate, are either punished or go nonrewarded. The consequence is that nonvalued behaviors slowly drop out of the child's behavioral repertoire.

Also, according to behavioristic notions, antecedent factors bearing on social development are usually conceptualized in terms of discriminative stimuli, which indicate whether or not a particular social behavior should be performed. Adequate socialization involves more than teaching a child required social behaviors; the child must also know the conditions under which such behaviors should be emitted. In behavioristic terminology, the behavior then comes under stimulus control, largely as a result of association, that is, reinforcement and punishments do not exist in isolation. A particular punishment, for example, becomes associated with other stimulus characteristics in the environment. Consequently, these stimulus characteristics acquire aversive properties as a result of being paired with the punishment. The outcome of this association is that the presence of aversive stimuli on future occasions may be sufficient to prohibit the child from behaving in a fashion similar to when he actually received punishment.

The association process described above also applies to rewarded behavior. In this case, associated stimuli acquire reinforcing properties and may be sufficient to evoke the child's behavior which had been reinforced in the past. In summary, by association, the child learns the appropriate time and place to perform previously learned behaviors and consequently becomes a more capable functioning member of society.

A relatively new theoretical framework falling within the learning perspective is *Social Learning Theory*. The social aspect stems from the assumption that culture is a source of secondary or learned motivation, and behavior was therefore viewed as resulting from a combination of psychological principles and social conditions. This original theoretical position has changed over the years, the most recent change being delineated in Bandura's Social Learning Theory (1977).

Presently, social-learning theory is remarkably different from its behavioristic orientation both in assumptions and conceptualization of the learning process, most notable in its rejection of the behavioristic assumption that cognition (thinking) is irrelevant to learning. Cognitive processes are now viewed as important in the "new" social learning theory which focuses on mental activities and stresses the active means used by humans to process stimulus material and generate meaning. Social-learning theory also assumes that much of what we learn results from observation of others' behavior and subsequent imitation. Thus, modelling and imitation are considered important to social development, and serve to define observational learning as the acquisition of new forms of behavior by observing the actions of a model.

Social-learning theory distinguishes between learning and performance. Traditional behaviorists made no such distinction; performance was simply equal to learning. Social learning views learning as an *unobservable* process by which the individual selects and makes sense out of information. Performance, as distinct from learning, refers to the overt manifestation of a learned behavior, which then serves as an index of learning—a distinction similar to the difference between "knowing" and "doing." There are many things children and adults know, but for a variety of reasons may not perform, so that we cannot conclude that the absence of performance reflects a lack of knowledge. For example, let us assume a child scores low on an intelligence test. The resulting IQ score is an index of the child's performance but it does not necessarily reflect inferior intellectual functioning. The child may indeed be bright but other factors (e.g., cultural bias of the test or a lack of motivation) may prevent demonstration of everything the child knew.

Another distinction between social and traditional learning theory is the belief held by social-learning theorists that reinforcement is not necessary for learning. Both reinforcement and punishment may have an important effect on whether a child actually performs a particular behavior, although they may not have as crucial an effect on learning. For example, a child may observe an older sibling performing a particular behavior (like putting a finger in an electrical wall outlet) and thus may learn to avoid this behavior without being reinforced for observing the sibling or performing the actual behavior.

Basic to observational learning is the assumption that modelling influences will produce learning primarily through their information function. That is, as a result of observing a model, children acquire information in the form of symbolic representations of the modeled activities. This is learning and it, in turn, can be translated into overt behavior (performance). Basic to observational learning are three distinct elements: *attention, retention,* and *motoric reproduction.* First, for observational learning to occur, the child must pay attention to the actions of a model. A number of factors influence the attentional process, among which is the value of the model to the child, and this is determined by the status, attractiveness, and social power of the model. Children are more likely to attend to "important" as opposed to "unimportant" models (Bandura, 1977). Other influences on the attentional process are those which directly affect the observer. For example, the child's sensory capacities are obviously crucial. A child who can see and hear is more likely to engage in efficient observational learning than one whose sensory capacities are not functioning normally. The child's construction of an accurate symbolic representation of the observed behavior depends on attention, and this aspect is largely influenced by the child's coding capabiliites (both imagined and verbal) as well as by rehearsal capabilities.

Motoric reproduction, the third component, involves translation of the symbolic representation of a behavior into overt activity (performance). Motoric reproduction is not necessary for observational learning, but it can help, as is reflected in the fact that children can learn via self-observation of their reproductions of other's behaviors ("practice makes perfect"). As a result of observing themselves reproduce their behaviors, children can assess the accuracy of, then modify, what has been learned.

What is learned through observation is not necessarily identical with the information supplied by the model; observational learning acknowledges the possibility of originality in the learning process. Thus, social-learning theorists assert that through observation, children can learn not only specific behaviors, but also general abstract rules for behavior. "The evidence accumulated to date suggests that, depending on their complexity and diversity, modelling influences can produce, in addition to mimicry of specific responses, behavior that is generative and innovative in character." (Bandura, 1971, p. 38). In Bandura's view, children do not merely mimic specific responses, they also abstract productive rules from their diverse observations even when not reinforced for matching a model or performing overtly the model's behaviors. Support for this creative component of observational learning can be found in research on language development, demonstrating that children can abstract grammatical rules exemplified in the language of models (Bandura and Harris, 1966).

Motivational processes are also important to observational learning. While reinforcement is not necessary for observational learning, social-learning theorists acknowledge that, if available, it may enhance learning. The motivational component in observational learning is thus viewed in terms of reinforcement and punishment. Direct external reinforcement (or punishment) and vicarious reinforcement (or punishment) may have an influence on observational learning. Direct reinforcement and punishment can serve as incentive conditions to influence the attentional component of observational learning. For example, if a child is told he will receive a reward for observing a particular model, he is likely to pay more attention to the model. Through this increased attention, the child may be able to retain more precisely the information provided by the model and construct a more accurate symbolic representation. Conceivably, the opposite would occur if a child is told he will be punished for observing a model.

Vicarious reinforcement (or punishment) refers to reinforcements or punishments received by a model for some behavior. Observing this can influence the likelihood of the child's performing the model's behavior. Bandura (1977) has hypothesized that vicarious reinforcement may influence learning insofar as it affects the attentional component of observational learning. If a child on one occasion sees a model being rewarded (punished) for a behavior, the child may show increased (decreased) attention to the model's behavior on future occasions since the child may perceive the model as more (or less) important. This in turn will have a direct influence on the accuracy of the information encoded and learning.

In summary, social-learning theory conceptualizes social development in terms of observational learning. Children acquire social skills largely through observing the social behaviors of parents, peers, teachers, and even televised models. The accuracy of such learning is largely influenced by the attentional and retentional (cognitive) capacities of children. Further, observational learning may be enhanced by rewarding children for observing certain models or rewarding the models observed by the children. In this way, children can learn abstract norms governing behavior. Whether or not children actually perform social skills learned by observing others is determined by the accuracy of their learning as well as by rewards and punishments resulting from their behaviors. Overall, the quality of a child's social development is a function of the appropriateness of the social behaviors emitted by the significant others in a child's environment.

The Cognitive Perspective

At this time cognitive theory does not represent a well-organized theoretical approach to understanding social development. In simply asserts that a child's level of cognitive development is an important determinant of social development, a factor not thoroughly considered by any of the previously discussed approaches to social development. Hence, the cognitive perspective does not yet provide a clear alternative to describing social development, but gives instead a supple-mentary view that may facilitate understanding of the child's acquisition of social skills.

Within developmental psychology investigations of cognitive development and social development have traditionally followed independent courses—for these reasons: (1) lack of knowledge concerning social and cognitive development as separate entities which hindered research on how they interrelate and (2) domina-tion by traditional learning theory of the field of social development. Because of this domination, cognition was not considered a variable that might influence social development. However, recent advances in cognitive development, particu-larly research stimulated by Piaget's contributions, plus the inclusion of cognition as a variable within learning theory, have helped break down the barriers separat-ing the two areas. Developmental psychologists and educators are becoming increasingly more aware of how social and cognitive development influence each other. Contemporary research on such processes as attachment, sex-typing, and moral development has clearly delineated this relationship between social and cognitive development and has indicated that level of cognitive development is a variable predictive of a child's social development. Thus, any attempt at under-standing social development must also include cognition as an explanatory con-struct.

A new area has resulted from this interface between cognition and social development: *social cognition*—cognition which takes humans and human social affairs as objects of thought. Social cognition deals strictly with the social world, not with the world of physical knowledge (the latter is in the domain of cognitive development). The scope of social cognition, however, is very wide and conceptu-ally includes any object of thought that can be considered social: intentions, attitudes, emotions, ideas, personalities, and thoughts, which lie in other people or in the self, are all the result of social cognition. Social cognition thus includes thinking about others as well as about one's self; development of self-concept is a social-cognitive achievement. Moreover, social cognition includes thinking about dimensions underlying relationships among people; for example, love, power, cooperation, competition, influence, aggression. Because effective execution of these social behaviors requires competent and efficient thinking about the self and others, the acquisition of social skills is determined in part by one's level of cognitive development.

While social cognition can be distinguished from the traditional concept of cognitive development in terms of the objects of thoughts, it cannot be distin-guished in terms of the cognitive abilities that permit development in both areas. John Flavell's assertion that ''. . . the head that thinks about the social world is the selfsame head that thinks about the non-social world" points out the basis for parallels in the development of social and nonsocial cognition (Flavell, 1977, p. 122). Flavell views quantitative attitudes, invariant formations, and abstract and hypothetical thinking as developmental trends common to both social and physical cognition.

Social cognition can be further characterized in terms of the processes necessarily contributing to a successful act of social cognition. Flavell (1977) has delineated three preconditions for such an act: existence, need, and inference. *Existence* refers to a person's basic knowledge of the existence of social phenomena in others. Logically, to think about an event, one must know that it exists. For example, a child must be aware that others may have their own thoughts in order to try to infer the other's thoughts. *Need* refers to a disposition (or sensed need) to make an act of social cognition. Let us assume that a young child is aware that others may possess distinctive feelings or motives. While necessary, this perception of the existence of social phenomena is not sufficient for making a social-cognitive act; the child must also want to do so. He must perceive the *need* or necessity to make the act happen in order for the act actually to occur. The act will not be carried out if the child does not want to, does not see it is necessary, or does not think to do it.

The third precondition, *inference,* refers to the child's skill or capacity in carrying out a given act of social cognition successfully. The perception of existence and need may guarantee the child will attempt to make a social-cognitive act, but the correctness and consequent utility of the act are determined by the child's skill or capacity to integrate and interpret information provided by various cues relevant to the act. Thus, the above preconditions, *existence, need,* and *inference,* impinge on the nature of development in social cognition—development of awareness of distinctive events in others, perception of the need to think about these events, and ability to think about them.

In summary, the cognitive perspective maintains that social and cognitive development are closely related and any attempt to comprehend the nature of social development must include an examination of the child's cognitive capacities. This interplay is exemplified by social cognition, a new field of study encompassing thinking about events in the social world both in respect to others and to one's self. This new field is important for a complete understanding of both social and cognitive development.

THE ORIGINS OF SOCIABILITY

Infancy includes development from birth up to two years of age, and is a period of rapid development in all aspects of growth: personal, social, physical, and cognitive. The newborn is thrust from the protective environment of the mother's womb into a new world of objects, events, and people. This change poses many challenges for the infant, including how to become acquainted with the social world and to acquire skills in dealing with people in that world. Most of us now take our social-interaction skills for granted and no longer think of them as special skills. It is easy to forget how awkward and ineffective we once were until we gradually learned to handle ourselves in social situations. But we did learn these skills—sometimes by painful trial and error and almost always under the influence of examples and models we saw in others, our parents and other adults, as well as our playmates and peers.

Attachment

Sociability and general social outgoingness begin very early. Even in the crib, newborns show special interest in people, learning very early to discriminate the human form and voice from other sights and sounds. Given this cognitive ability which is required to discriminate, the child quickly learns to recognize the existence of other people. Most particularly, he learns to recognize his primary caretaker, usually the mother, thus creating a special attachment. *Attachment* designates the infant's earliest significant social relationships, which may be anyone who becomes familiar and meaningful to the young child, but especially the mother, who may be predisposed to be particularly sensitive and responsive to her infant's needs (Bowlby, 1969; Ainsworth, 1964, 1969; and Shantz, 1975).

The formation of an attachment between the infant and the primary caretaker is the most notable aspect of social development in infancy. Research by Bowlby, Ainsworth, and others indicates that the attachment bond may be crucial for normal social development. This concept includes two basic components: behavior and affect. The behavioral component is reflected in the child's tendency to approach particular people, receptiveness to being cared for by these people, and being most comfortable when in the presence of these people. The affective component is illustrated in the pleasure of child and primary caretaker in being with each other. The infant develops positive feelings toward those who are warm, supportive, and nurturant, and, although unable to express these feelings elaborately, these feelings can be easily inferred from the systematic attention, interest, and orientation the child directs toward those with whom attachments have been formed, as well as by the primary caretaker's showing these same behaviors toward the infant.

Before examining the development of attachment, two important distinctions are in order. First, while attachment is conceived of as a bond with behavioral and affective components, it is not equivalent to them. The behaviors and affect may be present or absent in certain times or situations, but the bond itself binds time and distance and is not conceived of as being present or absent. The second distinction is that attachment and dependency are not equivalent. *Dependency* includes all kinds of attention-seeking and help-seeking behavior on the child's part and suggests those activities stemming from a genuine need for help where the child is incapable of independent success, rather than those activities or situations in which the child is merely seeking attention or affection as an end in itself. *Instrumental* dependency is characterized by help-seeking activity growing out of need for assistance in meeting other needs or goals. In contrast, *emotional* dependency includes those activities whose purpose is to gain attention or affection simply as a goal in itself. The nurturant social contact thus gained is a luxury rather than a necessity for the child.

Attachment is not the same as instrumental and emotional dependency. Dependency, as a construct, revolves around gratification of the child's needs by others. Attachment implies more than that; it is an active affect-laden process. Research indicates that dependency, as an explanatory construct, is more appropriate to explain behavior during early childhood (2-5 years) than during infancy. The following findings support this notion: (1) strongly attached infants may become dependent or independent later on in life, (2) children may be dependent on others to satisfy needs (e.g., an older sibling) but yet not be attached to that person, and (3) older infants whose needs are taken care of by others (e.g., aunts and uncles) may still be strongly attached to their mothers (Bowlby, 1969). These findings indicate the importance of making the conceptual distinction between attachment and dependency.

Traditionally, the theoretical interpretation of the close mother-infant bond in the first year of life has been stated in terms of learning theory, which assumes this relationship was due to a conditioning of positive reward value to the mother. That is, the mother was associated with the gratification of the child's needs (primarily hunger and thirst) and as a result the mother acquired reward value. The infant thus learned that to approach this source of pleasure would lead to immediate gratification of needs. Also, according to the principle of stimulus generalization the child would learn to approach the mother when other needs are aroused (such as discomfort due to temperature or injury) since these stimuli are similar to the original one (hunger). Moreover, the child's approach response, when in need, to other humans besides the mother could also be accounted for by learning principles. That is, since the mother is similar to other humans, the approach response would generalize to others because of stimulus generalization. This formulation of the attachment process enables one to predict that if the child's initial feeding is not rewarding, because the mother may have been tense or may have force-fed him, then the mother would acquire aversive characteristics (especially if this experience occurred frequently) and not be perceived as rewarding; consequently, the attachment would not be formed.

Several important experimental findings with rhesus monkeys have important implications for human attachment and have fostered a new theoretical approach to mother-infant relationships. Originally, Harry Harlow of the University of Wisconsin was interested in the cognitive abilities of rhesus monkeys. To minimize the possibility of disease in the monkey colony, Harlow separated infant monkeys from their mothers and raised them separately in their own cages. He observed that, while the infant monkeys became physically mature, they seemed to be socially handicapped. In contrast to those infants raised with their mothers, the isolated infants were withdrawn and socially inactive, and spent a lot of time clinging to their cheese-cloth diapers. Harlow also noticed striking parallels between the isolated infant monkeys and human infants raised apart from their mothers in minimal-care institutions. The human infants would not respond to environmental stimulation and were, most of the time, pathetically huddled in the corners of their cribs. These observations led Harlow to believe that, possibly, mother-infant interaction was crucial to normal social development of infants. Subsequently, Harlow initiated a research program (Harlow, 1966) to explore the apparent necessity for mother-infant interaction and to delineate the aspects of the interaction contributing to social development.

To specify the particulars of mother-infant interaction that might bear on normal social development, Harlow raised infant monkeys with artificial surrogate mothers: one made with stiff wire, and the other covered with soft terrycloth. The importance of the feeding response in the mother-infant relationship was tested by inserting a milk bottle into the wire mother, but not the terrycloth mother. The results were astounding. While the infant monkeys did feed on the wire mother, they spent most of their time on the terrycloth mother. When frightened, infant monkeys would run to the terrycloth mother for comfort, but not to the wire mother. Those infants raised with only terrycloth mothers huddled to them for safety in much the same way a human infant does when frightened. The behaviors of those monkeys raised with only wire mothers were much less encouraging; they simply withdrew and showed self-stimulatory behaviors: responses very similar to infant monkeys raised in isolation. Harlow also found that infant monkeys formed relatively strong attachments to the terrycloth surrogate mothers; when separated from them for a period of time, infants quickly returned to them when they were reintroduced to the cage. These results demonstrate the importance of mother-infant attachment; moreover, they question the traditional learning-theory interpretation of attachment which emphasizes passive conditioning around the feeding response. The behavior of Harlow's subjects indicates that infant monkeys imitate and actively influence the formation of an attachment, suggesting, therefore, that infant monkeys may be predisposed (i.e., are particularly influenced) to form this type of bond.

However, motherhood is more than just providing a soft body to which the infant can cling. The long-term effects of having been raised by a terrycloth mother did not include mature social behavior. Harlow found that, in adulthood, these monkeys were abusive with peers and sexually incompetent (although not to the same extent as those infants raised in isolation). Harlow's research also indicates that the first year of life may be critical for development of attachment. He found that if infant monkeys were raised in isolation for six months or less they would respond to "therapy" (interaction with mother and peers) and become social. However, if the isolation experience lasted a year or longer, monkeys rarely became social even with the help of peers.

What of the human infant? Is the development of attachment in our species similar to that of rhesus monkeys? To answer this question, one has to turn to the work of Bowlby. In 1949, Bowlby was commissioned by the World Health Organization to examine the effects of separation from mothers on human infants. After researching the published literature, interviewing adults who had been separated from their parents at an early age, and observing infants raised in minimal-care institutions, Bowlby concluded that the child's experience of a warm, loving, continuous, and enjoyable relationship with the mother was essential to mental health. He found that people who did not have such experiences were, for the most part, unable to relate to others effectively and were afraid to venture forth to discover the world.

Bowlby was criticized for not stating the reasons for such effects and for making wide extrapolations from his data. To answer this criticism Bowlby attempted to derive a theoretical framework to organize his position. Bowlby turned to ethology, the study of organisms in their natural habitat, to understand the development and functional significance of attachment behaviors. His ethological analysis can be described as follows. At birth, the human infant is totally dependent on other humans for survival, since unlike other species (e.g., fish) the human newborn cannot satisfy its own needs. Moreover, within the human species, the period from birth up to the point where the child could be self-sustaining is quite long (varying with the complexity of various cultures, but usually a number of years). For the infant to survive during this caretaking period, it may be adaptive to form a strong relationship with the primary caretaker. This would maximize the possibility that the infant would be taken care of and survive and be able to reproduce to further the existence of the species.

Viewed from this point of view, human attachment can be seen as an analogue to the imprinting response found in many species of waterfowl. Konrad Lorenz has demonstrated that most ducklings will imprint on the mother duck and follow her around: an adaptive response, since this may insure the survival of the young duckling in a hostile, predator-filled environment. Lorenz also found that, if the imprinting response is to occur, the duckling must observe a moving object within three days after hatching (the critical period for the response to develop). Moreover, ethological research has indicated that the duckling will imprint any moving stimulus and not necessarily its mother. For example, ducklings have been found to imprint on nonliving objects such as balls, models of adult ducks, and living members of other species (Lorenz himself). If one is to apply this type of analysis to the human organism, it would be necessary to identify those genetically determined behavioral responses of young infants that are analogous to the duckling's following response, and those environmental stimuli (analogous to the moving stimulus for the duckling) that trigger the responses infants may be predisposed to perform. Bowlby has undertaken this task with respect to human infants.

In his analysis of human attachment from an evolutionary perspective, Bowlby (1969) has outlined various infant behaviors he regards as precursors to attachment: rooting and sucking, postural adjustment, looking, listening, smiling, vocalizing, crying, grasping, and climbing. Each of these behaviors can be elicited by appropriate environmental stimulation; for example, the young infant is most likely to vocalize in response to a female voice, smile in response to the perception of high-contrast stimuli (especially the eyes of another onlooker) and again a female voice, and adjust posture (cuddle) for maximum comfort when held by an adult. Basically, such behaviors are thought to fulfill two different functions: they convey to the caregiver that the infant is receptive and "happy" when receiving such care, and these behaviors evoke care-giving responses on the part of the mother. The formation of an attachment is largely a dyadic function in which the child responds in a fixed manner to stimulation provided by the caregiver and in turn actively evokes from the caregiver "mothering" behaviors.

Investigations of mother-child interaction have consistently emphasized that her warmth, reinforcement, and nurturance directly enhance the formation of social attachments and dependent relationships. Thus, the mother who facilitates infant attachment is both sensitive to the needs of her child and alert and responsive in answering those needs. There is considerable evidence suggesting that the mothering behaviors of cats and rats (Rosenblatt, Turkewirtz, and Schnerla, 1961; Rosenblatt, 1969) are largely controlled by internal biological factors, especially hormonal changes accompanying the birth process and lactation. There has been only minimal research on the biological basis of mothering behavior in humans, but the fact that a mother's predisposition for maternal behaviors does fit neatly into an evolutionary approach to attachment has led theorists (Bowlby, 1969; Ainsworth, 1973) to assert that hormonal changes accompanying birth tend to make the mother especially attuned and responsive to her infant's behaviors.

The infant's predisposition for various behaviors and the mother's responsiveness to those behaviors together maximize mother-infant interaction. The question remains, however, as to how the attachment bond actually develops. Research indicates that the mature bond is not an instant accomplishment occurring shortly after birth. Instead, the attachment bond appears to develop only after a fairly long process covering the first six to eight months of the child's life. Ainsworth (1964, 1969) has catalogued early maternal-attachment behaviors in infants. During the first two months, the infant responds indiscriminately to others. But by the eighth week, the infant begins to respond differentially with his mother, and by the middle of the first year this unique response to the mother is clearly observable. Finally, toward the end of the first year and later, the infant gradually begins to expand his interest in other people. Some of the important milestones in the development of social attachments are summarized in Table 13-3. By the end of the first year of life the infant shows a clear recognition of the primary caretaker and unique styles of interaction with this particular person, and the attachment is said to be formed.

The fact that it takes so long for attachments to crystallize suggests that genetic predisposition, while necessary, is not sufficient for the mature bond to develop. The lengthy course of its development implicates experimental factors and associated developments in formation of the attachment bond; new research suggests level of cognitive development is an important determinant. The infant's earliest social relationships with others are limited and defined by the primitive state of his information-processing skills. Since the infant must first learn to recognize and attend to others (Piaget and Inhelder, 1969; Shantz, 1975; and Flavell, 1977), recognition obviously is important in forming social attachments. This had been demonstrated by research tracing the development of the infant's smiling response to familiar faces and the ability to recognize faimliar people.

Evidence that memory development is critical to formation of early social attachments is found in Piaget's analysis of cognitive development, showing the child's recognition of familiar objects or people may not occur until late in the second year, at which time the infant becomes capable of "response to the absent object" or object permanence. Thus, the infant who lacks memory of the absent object can respond only to those people and things immediately present, and attachments must necessarily be short-lived and limited to momentary interest or attention—"out of sight, out of mind." This suggests that a mature attachment can be formed only when the infant can recall his mother and recognize her in memory.

Once the bond is formed, the child reacts negatively when the bond is threatened. This is illustrated in the phenomenon of *separation anxiety* which begins to occur about ten months of age. Separation anxiety is an anxiety response (crying and associated trauma) occurring when the infant is apart from the primary caretaker. There is considerable controversy as to why separation anxiety begins to occur only at about 10 months of age. One hypothesis is that it is only at this age that the infant's scheme (or representation) of the mother is well formed and that this scheme also includes the representation of the mother in a variety of places. It is also assumed that the infant's trauma in the absence of the mother is due to a perception of a discrepancy between the event and the scheme (mother absent when usually present). Consequently, if a child experiences the departure of the mother in a variety of places and situations, it will take a long time to develop a scheme. Until the scheme is fully developed, the perception of a discrepancy is not possible and separation anxiety will not occur. If the infant is with the mother most of the day and does not experience many absences from her, then the infant's scheme of the mother will form at an earlier age. Consequently, the infant is likely to perceive a discrepancy when the mother departs and to experience separation anxiety at an earlier age.

Table 13-3 Steps in the Development of Attachment

Attachment Pattern	Infant's Behavioral Activity
Differential crying	Cries when held by someone other than mother.
Differential smiling	Smiles more often and more readily in interaction with the mother than with others.
Differential vocalizing	Vocalizes more often and more readily in interaction with the mother than with others.
Visual-motor orientation	Maintains a continuous orientation toward the mother when not directly at her side.
Crying when mother leaves	Cries when mother breaks her visual contact with him.
Following	When able to crawl, attempts to follow mother when she leaves.
Scrambling	Climbs over, explores, and plays with mother.
Burying the face	Buries his face in her lap following exploration away from mother or while scrambling over mother.
Exploration from mother as a base	Takes brief excursions away from mother.
Clinging	Displays excessive holding and grasping, particularly when strangers are present.
Lifting arms in greeting	Raises arms, smiles, and vocalizes toward mother after a period of absense.
Clapping hands in greeting	Claps hands when mother appears.
Approach through locomotion	When able to crawl, moves toward mother as quickly as possible and thus terminates greeting responses.

Source: Adapted and reprinted by permission of the publisher, from McDavid, J.W., & Garwood, S.G., *Understanding children.* Lexington, Mass.: D.C. Heath, 1978.

Another controversy about separation anxiety is whether or not it can serve as an indicator of the strength of the attachment bond. If a year-old infant shows severe anxiety upon the mother's departure, does this mean a strong attachment to the mother? On the surface the answer would seem to be "yes," but, a finer analysis reveals this may not be so. First, separation anxiety is influenced by such factors as differences in infants' temperament and whether or not the infant is able to make a response in the mother's absence. Such factors prevent us from inferring a direct link between strength of attachment and separation anxiety. For a recent review of this controversy, see Weinraub and Lewis (1978).

Another behavior related to attachment is a response termed *stranger anxiety*. Between 6 and 12 months of age, many infants show an acute fear of unfamiliar persons. This phenomenon occurs shortly after an attachment is well formed and the child's response to a stranger is typically to seek out the person to whom he is attached. Also, the infant is less likely to show a distress response to a strange person when the attachment figure is present. The explanation provided for stranger anxiety is similar to that provided for separation anxiety and again illustrates the relationship between social and cognitive development. Basically, it is only toward the end of the infant's first year of life that his scheme for the mother and other familiar figures is complete, and the child reacts negatively when perceiving a person whose appearance is discrepant from the schemes formed for familiar people. There is also considerable controversy concerning this phenomenon. Rheingold and Eckerman (1973) found that infants do not always show fear of strangers and will even accept and make friendly overtures to a stranger provided that the stranger was friendly and gave the child an opportunity to make a response (e.g., play with a toy). Consequently, stranger anxiety may not be as universal a phenomenon as previously thought.

In summary, the ethological view of attachment conceptualizes the mother-infant relationship as an adaptive set of behaviors with functional significance. Both mother and child are considered predisposed to be responsive to each other in a way that will lead to an emotional bond. Such bond develops gradually in the infant's first year and also seems to depend on experiential factors and development of cognitive capacities. Stranger fear and separation anxiety may be related to formation of the attachment bond as well as to the relationship between social and cognitive development.

A common theme underlying theoretical approaches to attachment is the importance of quality mothering behaviors. Bowlby (1958), Ainsworth (1967), and Erikson (1963) all stress quality caregiver-child interaction and maintain that those relationships characterized by mutual delight (as opposed to routine care) are more likely to result in an effective attachment bond. This assertion has had a certain amount of controversy. Specifically, while quantity of interaction is easily measurable and amendable to scientific investigation, quality interaction is not. There is a debate as to how quality should be measured as well as to what specific mothering behaviors constitute quality mothering. More research is needed to specify those mothering behaviors contributing to a mature attachment and those inhibiting mature development of the bond. Once the behaviors have been identified, careful experimentation will be necessary to examine *how* the behaviors influence attachment. Research is already beginning to isolate types of behaviors associated with effective and ineffective mothering (Ellison, Clarke-Stewart, 1975; White, 1975). Looking at and talking to the child, responding to infants' distress and social expressions, playing with objects, expressing positive feelings and suppressing negative feelings have all been identified as behaviors typical of effective mothering and, in turn, yielding competent infants.

Institutionalization

The importance of quality mothering is highlighted when one examines the effects on infants of institutionalization in a minimal-care facility, where, generally both quality and quantity of caretaker-infant interaction are lacking. Typically monkeys reared in isolation became withdrawn, socially immature, abusive, and sexually incompetent. It is, of course, rare that human infants are raised in environments similar to that of isolated rhesus monkeys, but a few bizarre cases have been documented. (The reader is reminded that information concerning these children is necessarily *post hoc*).

Information about the isolation condition must come from the not-so-normal person or persons responsible for isolating the child. A classic case was reported by David (1940). Anna was the five-year-old illegitimate child of a rural woman who did not want to assume responsibility for raising the child. Anna was kept for the first five years of her life in a small "attic-like" room containing a dirty bed and a chair, with no attention beyond the minimum to maintain life. During this time her diet consisted primarily of cow's milk in a baby bottle. When discovered, Anna appeared to be blind and deaf, and totally unresponsive to people and sights and sounds around her. She would not walk or talk, and showed no signs of intelligent behavior.

Efforts to rehabilitate Anna led to limited success similar to that experienced with Victor, the Wild Boy described in Chapter 1. Two years after her discovery she was able to walk, understand simple commands, and feed herself. She would not talk, and overall behaved like an infant between one and two years of age. By ten years of age she had developed rudimentary language skills equivalent to a three-year-old; she could walk well and run and appeared to have a pleasant disposition. However, Anna died of hemorrhagic jaundice at ten-and-one half years of age. Given the slowness of her development, it is unlikely that she would ever have experienced complete recovery. The case of Anna is a tragic portrayal of the effects of severe environmental deprivation on normal development.

Examination of infants reared in minimal-care institutions provides additional evidence of the effects of environmental deprivation on social development.

Institutionalized infants do not differ from infants raised in traditional nuclear families until about three to four months of age, at which time, institutionalized infants typically vocalize very little, cry very little, and do not adjust their posture when picked up by an adult. By eight months of age, these infants are less interested in grasping and playing with toys, begin to lose interest in their external environment, and tend to show self-stimulatory behaviors such as body-rocking (Provence and Lipton, 1962).

It is difficult to pinpoint the precise factors that contributed to Anna's atypical development and to the retarded development of institutionalized children. In both cases, not only is the mother absent, but there is also a lack of stimulation in general. Minimal-care facilities, by definition, are understaffed—one attendant may be in charge of many infants. In addition, infants placed in minimal-care institutions may be different in some manner or other from those not institutionalized. Consequently, it is difficult to say if the distinctive behavior of institutionalized infants is due to the lack of stimulation in general, the absence of a primary caretaker, or to some other characteristics possessed by such infants. Jerome Kagan's (Kagan & Klein, 1973) observations of Indian villages in Guatemala where infants are kept continuously with their mothers reveals the same kind of listless and apathetic behavior shown by institutionalized infants, suggesting that the absence of a single consistent caretaker is not critical. However, both the Guatemalan children and institutionalized infants experienced little variety of cognitive and affective stimulation, had little opportunity to explore the environment, and experienced little interaction with adult caretakers. Hence, the critical factor producing nonalertness and general aloofness may be the absence of *distinctive stimulation,* stimulation intended for the infant and that attracts its attention. There is some research support for this notion. If children are raised in enriched environments within institutions with an abundance of stimulation, they usually show the typical sequence of normal social development (Dennis, 1960). In fact, infants raised in good institutions, where care may be better than that obtained in the nuclear family, may show advanced social development (Brackbill, 1962).

In summary, it appears that minimal care of an infant in the first year of life does adversely affect social development, and the critical factor may be the lack of distinctive stimulation. However, research on enriched institutional environments indicates that, when distinctive stimulation is provided by substitute caretakers, adequate social development is likely to follow.

One final point should be made. Infants seem to possess a remarkable capacity for recovery. Research has indicated that, with age, the effects of a deprived environment diminish provided the environment improves (Kagan, 1972). Retarded development in the first year of life is a poor predictor of future functioning, because, even though infants may not be able to actualize genetic potential, their social adaptability is not lost and can emerge at a later point provided appropriate stimulation is obtained. Lack of a primary caretaker and distinctive stimulation need not doom the child to permanent incompetence.

REFERENCES AND SUGGESTED READINGS

Ainsworth, M. Object relations, dependency, and attachment: A theoretical review of the infant-mother relationship. *Child Development,* 1969, *40,* 965-1025.

Ainsworth, M. Patterns of attachment behavior shown by an infant in interaction with his mother. *Merrill-Palmer Quarterly,* 1964, *10,* 51-58.

Ainsworth, M.D.S. *Infancy in Uganda.* Baltimore: Johns Hopkins Press, 1967.

Bandura, A. *Social Learning Theory.* Englewood Cliffs: Prentice-Hall, 1977.

Bandura, A. *Social Learning Theory.* Morristown, N.J.: General Learning Press, 1971.

Bandura, A., & Harris, M.B. Modification of syntactic style. *Journal of Experimental Child Psychology,* 1966, *4,* 341-351.

Bowlby, J. *Attachment and loss* (Vol. 1, Attachment). New York: Basic Books, 1969.

Bowlby, J. Psychoanalysis and child care. In J.D. Sutherland (Ed.), *Psychoanalysis and contemporary theory.* London: Hogarth, 1958.

Brackbill, Y. *Research and clinical work with children.* Washington, D.C. American Psychological Association, 1962.

Caudill, W., & Weinstein, H. Maternal care and infant behavior in Japanese and American urban and middle class families. In R. Konig & R. Hill (Eds.), *Yearbook of the International Sociological Association, 1966.*

Clarke-Stewart, A. *Dealing with the complexity of mother-child interaction.* Paper presented at the Society for Research in Child Development. Denver, April, 1975.

Davis, K. Extreme social isolation of a child. *American Journal of Sociology,* 1940, *45,* 554-565.

Dennis, W. Causes of retardation among institutional children: Iran. *Journal of Genetic Psychology,* 1960, *96,* 47-59.

Eibl-Eibesfeldt. *Ethology: The Biology of Behavior.* New York: Holt, Reinhart and Winston, 1970.

Erikson, E. H. *Childhood and Society* (2nd ed.). New York: Norton, 1963.

Erikson, E. H. Identity and the life cycle. *Psychological Issues.* 1959, *1,* 18-164.

Flavell, J. *Cognitive development.* New York: Prentice-Hall, 1977.

Harlow, H., & Harlow, M. H. Learning to love. *American Scientist,* 1966, *54*(3), 244-272.

Kagan, J. *The plasticity of early intellectual development.* Paper presented at the meeting of the Association for the Advancement of Science, Washington, D.C., 1972.

Kagan, J., & Klein, R. E. Cross-cultural perspectives on early development. *American Psychologist,* 1973, *28,* 947-961.

Provence, S., & Lipton, R. C. *Infants in institutions.* New York: International Universities Press, 1962.

Rheingold, H. C., & Eckerman, C. O. Fear of strangers: A critical examination. In H. W. Reese (Ed.), *Advances in child development and behavior* (Vol. 8). New York: Academic Press, 1973.

Rosenblatt, J. S. The basis of synchrony in the behavioral interaction between the mother and her offspring in the laboratory rat. In B. M. Foss (Ed.), *Determinants of infant behavior III.* New York: Basic Books, 1969.

Shantz, C. U. The development of social cognition. In E. M. Heatherington (Ed.), *Review of child development research* (Vol. 5). Chicago: University of Chicago Press, 1975.

Weinraub, M., & Lewis, M. The determinants of children's responses to separation. *Monographs of the Society for Research in Child Development,* 1978, *42* (No. 4).

White, B. *The first three years of life.* Englewood Cliffs: Prentice-Hall, 1975.

Chapter 14

Acquiring Social Skills
in Early Childhood

S. Gray Garwood and David Page

SOCIAL DEVELOPMENTAL ACHIEVEMENTS IN PRESCHOOLERS

A child's preschool years are marked by major changes in ability to become more social. The strong attachment bond (See Chapter 13), which provides the foundation for social interaction with others, begins to weaken in early childhood, allowing for increased sociability. As a child passes the second birthday, the attachment behaviors shown toward parents change. While the young infant usually requires actual physical contact with parents, with increasing age the child may not require actual physical contact to feel secure; perceptual contact may be sufficient. Older preschoolers may require only symbolic contact to parents (as represented by aunts, uncles, and grandparents). Beyond the third year, children will accept temporary parent absences without much protest, as well as substitute attachment figures such as relatives, teachers, and peers. This slackening of ties seems to be natural, since the preschooler's needs for a close relationship are not as great. The preschooler can now walk and talk and engage in active exploration of the environment and can learn to satisfy his own needs, which will be done as long as situations arousing alarm or anxiety are infrequent. The preschooler who experienced a strong attachment in infancy is now secure in the knowledge that maternal support is available when needed.

Paralleling these changes in attachment behavior are other changes. Increased physical abilities enable the child to interact with others. Changes in intellectual capabilities, including efficient cognitive mechanisms for symbolically processing information from the child's expanding social world, appear and give rise to a number of other important social achievements in early childhood: conscience formation, sex-role development, and self-concept.

Conscience Development

One of the most significant achievements during early childhood is the development of *conscience,* the internalized set of social standards that serves as a personal code for behavior, which permits the young child to evaluate his behavior and decide on appropriate, and reject inappropriate, courses of action. Conscience development in early childhood is largely a function of the child's interaction with external agents of socialization, and this is most important in the young child's relationship with parents and the parents' disciplinary tactics. The significance of these events is illustrated in Freud's notions concerning Superego development and Justin Aronfreed's (1968) work on development of the capacity for self-criticism.

According to Freud, events occurring during the early childhood years are instrumental in conscience formation. Freud believed the child now experiences some form of adult sexual desires, and maintained that children direct these sexual urges to the opposite sex parent, a phenomenon labeled by the *Oedipus complex* (boys) or the *Electra complex* (girls). Children also experience an intense but unconscious conflict between the desire to express sexual urges and guilt at the thought of expressing them. Resolution of the conflict involves repression of the sexual urges and identification with the same-sex parent. As one aspect of identifying with parents, children take on the values, attitudes, and beliefs of their preschool society as represented in the parents: this results in formation of the Superego—the representation of internalized values and the conscience.

While the Freudian formulation of conscience development is colorful, it lacks empirical validation (largely because notions concerning complicated unconscious emotional events do not lend themselves to scientific scrutiny). Despite this, it appears that the child's relationships with parents is of utmost importance to the successful development of conscience.

Unlike Freudian formulations, Aronfreed's notions on self-criticism (stemming from a social-learning viewpoint as opposed to psychoanalytic) can be validated, since they are based on empirical research, and are probably a more valid representation of conscience development during early childhood. According to Aronfreed, the key to conscience development is the capacity to engage in *self-criticism* (defined as the process by which the child comes to label his acceptable behaviors as "good" and his inappropriate behaviors as "bad"), which is very similar to our definition of conscience. Aronfreed (1968) sees development of self-criticism as fairly complex, involving social learning and affective and cognitive components. Children are thought to develop self-criticism only when an association has been formed between a feeling of anxiety and a cognition (knowledge) of the particular situation (timing of the various components is considered crucial).

Aronfreed tested his conceptualization in a series of laboratory studies examining children's responses to transgression to see if children learned to label their behaviors as "bad." Transgression was defined as "any form of behavior . . . when it has become discriminantly associated with punishment that is sufficiently aversive to produce some degree of behavioral suppression" (Aronfreed, 1968,

p. 169). The types of transgression used in his studies typically involved choosing an attractive toy over an unattractive one or pulling an incorrect lever. Aronfreed's research has illuminated conscience development and demonstrated that, to develop self-criticism, the child's behavior must be labeled "bad" by socialization agents *after* the child is punished for the particular behavior. This finding is explained in terms of learning theory; that is, the use of the label "bad" at the end of a punishment sequence terminates (negatively reinforces) the anxiety that the child builds up while experiencing the punishment, and, the child learns to label his behavior; this external reaction (self-criticism) is a learned way of relieving anxiety associated with a transgression. If the label is used at the onset of the punishment, sufficient anxiety has not been aroused and the label does not acquire tension-reducing properties. Once children have learned to label particular behaviors as "good" or "bad," they will be able to predict the consequences of their behavior: an important achievement since the child can become increasingly internal and self-directing.

Aronfreed's conception of the development of conscience has not gone unchallenged. Cognitive and learning theorists have questioned the importance of the affective component (as described by Aronfreed), since children have been shown to imitate adults towards whom they feel no emotion (Kohlberg, 1969; Bandura, 1974). Moreover, Kuhn (1973) has questioned the validity of Aronfreed's generalizing to the real world findings obtained in artificial laboratory situations. Further research is needed, but Aronfreed has pointed out the importance of parents' rationally explaining to the child reasons for punishments, thus making the child probably more likely to benefit from the demands of external socialization agents by developing an internalized set of personal standards.

Aronfreed has also clarified the connection between parental discipline and development of conscience (Aronfreed, 1968), demonstrating that punishment and reward by themselves may not be sufficient to develop the child's capacity for self-criticism. Appropriate development requires that parents label the child's particular behaviors and explain why a reward or punishment was given. By using firm, but rational, control over children, and directing children toward autonomous action, parents are more likely to foster conscience development in children.

Aronfreed has also outlined two general techniques of socialization that further illustrate the effect of varying styles of parenting on conscience development: induction and sensitization. *Inductive socialization* relies strongly on reward for desirable behavior, with nonreward or indifference for undesirable behavior. Clear models demonstrating the desirable behavior are provided, and the occurrence of punishment is minimized. Socialization by induction fosters a close relationship, with positive feelings (affect) occurring between child and agents of socialization. Such techniques also reinforce feelings of security and facilitate the child's internalization of the agents' values.

In contrast to this, sensitizing socialization is based heavily on punishment for undesirable behavior, with desired behavior treated as the expected minimal standard, deserving no special attention. Models for defining and demonstrating desirable behavior may be ambiguous or possibly absent. Socialization by sensitization threatens the relationship between child and socialization agents, because negative affect, fear, and anxiety, associated with punishing agents, tend to become associated with all (and their values and beliefs) and may come to be feared and avoided. Thus, the child's internalization of the values of socialization agents is hindered and discouraged.

In summary, conscience development in early childhood is a fairly complex process influenced by a number of factors. Of primary importance are the child's relationship with parents and parental disciplinary tactics. Optimal conditions for development seem to be warm, yet firm parents who foster good relationships with their children, and who are clear in specifying why certain rewards and/or punishments are being given. Under these conditions, the young child is more likely to identify with parents, develop warm feelings toward them, and internalize their values. As a result, children learn to evaluate their own behavior and be guided by an internalized code of conduct.

Sex-Typing

Sex-typing is the process by which children come to know their biological sex, acquire values and adopt behaviors appropriate to their sex—in the following sequence. About age three, children begin to know the labels ''boy'' and ''girl'' and can usually apply the terms to themselves, but do not understand that their sex is constant; that is, they think they may change sex by wearing clothes appropriate to the opposite sex or simply by wanting to be different. It seems as though young children do not understand the relationship between genital structures and sex, and categorize themselves and others as being male or female on the bases of clothing and other external characteristics (such as hairstyle). At age 4, children still do not have a complete understanding of sex constancy; they are consistent in categorizing others and can use appropriate pronouns, but the tendency remains to categorize others simply on the basis of external sex-appropriate characteristics. It is only between ages 5 and 6 that children understand they cannot change into the opposite sex and they know the relationship between sex and genital differences; and now, children begin to show consistent imitation of same-sex parents and other adults.

The classic interpretation of sex-typing is psychoanalytic, based on Freud's view of development during the early childhood years. Freudian theory names *identification* as the process a child goes through to copy or identify with the same-sex model, usually the father for the boy, the mother for the girl. Freud further distinguished two types of identification: *anaclitic* and *defensive*. Both male and female children are initially very dependent on the mother for need satisfaction and attention: she is the love object. Girls have no particular problem here, for identification is with the same-sex model. But boys, dealing with a cross-sex model, must make the change from identification with the love object (*anaclitic identification*) to more socially acceptable identification with a male model.

When the male child is about age three or four, the mother begins to try to reduce his dependency on her. The child, disturbed by this visible loss of attention-giving, seeks to recapture her attentions and, according to Freud, does this by imitating and reproducing her in actions and fantasy. The child resents this possession of the mother by the father, and envy begets anxiety and fear. This negative emotional state is called *castration anxiety* because the father is big and powerful and therefore could castrate this youthful contender for mother's attention (at least figuratively). Because this anxiety is unpleasant, the child resolves this Oedipal Complex* by *defensive identification,* identifying with the aggressor (the father) and trying to become more like him. In this way, boys adopt male characteristics or sex-typed behaviors. In summary, according to psychoanalytic notions, children learn what it is to be male or female by identifying with the same-sex parent and imitating their behaviors.

In contrast to Freud's purely descriptive and somewhat romantic position, other theorists have proposed that sex-typing occurs through social learning (observation and imitation). They view identification as a process whereby the child (male or female) observes same- and opposite-sex models, imitates their behaviors, is selectively reinforced for certain of these behaviors, and adopts those sex-typed behaviors that are most rewarded and rewarding.

The social-learning position includes these aspects:

- Parents are the most available models for young children; they are nurturant and powerful and therefore most likely to be copied, particularly in the preschool years when children spend most of their time with them.
- Children are more frequently with their mothers, and early in development will tend to acquire feminine behavior. Boys will later spend more time with male models and will begin to assume more masculine behaviors.
- Children will tend to imitate same-sex models more than cross-sex models, because of perceived similarity to their own sex.

The social-learning position accounts for sex-typing in terms of learning principles. Children gradually learn to discriminate sex-typed behavior patterns and discover their own sex as a result of parents' use of appropriate pronouns (he, she) in reference to the child and approval (reinforcement) of the child's correct labeling of self. Also, parents reinforce children for sex-appropriate behaviors and for imitating the same sex parent.

---

*Freud never fully treated female identification mechanisms. He did describe a similar process, the Electra Complex, but it received only cursory attention.

Social-learning theory and (especially) psychoanalytic theory do not completely account for sex-typing: both ignore the developmental sequences mentioned earlier. A relatively recent formulation (Kohlberg, 1966) emphasizes the cognitive aspects of the developmental sequence and the child's role as a processor of information. The child, actively involved in discovering his or her own gender and sex-appropriate behaviors, is not conceived of as a passive agent who learns about his or her sexuality simply by imitating same-sex adults. Since individuals learn about their environment and behaviors of others through cognitive processes, it makes sense that they also learn about sex-typed behaviors and gender in this same manner.

Basically, children learn to use the labels *boy* and *girl* by actively forming appropriate cognitive concepts. By associating various cues with the labels (first, external characteristics such as clothing and hairstyle, and later genital differences), children construct increasingly mature concepts about sex and apply them to themselves and others. Using this growing conceptual ability and discrimination skills, children learn sex-appropriate and sex-inappropriate behaviors. With the same cognitive processes used in learning the constancy of physical objects, children (between five and six years of age) are able to form an increasingly stable concept of boy or girl identity (association of genital differences with sex differences). This achievement coincides with attainment of conservation, or realization of constancies in the physical world (e.g., the amount of water remains the same despite the shape of the container, and the amount of clay is constant whether or not in the shape of a ball or a sausage). Research (Slaby and Frey, 1975) supports this cognitive theory of sex-typing—the occurrence of decision-making whereby the child adopts certain behaviors as sex-appropriate.

Self-Concept

The self-concept is important to an understanding of social development because it is integrative in nature. It cuts across all areas of experience, organizes and unifies habits, abilities, attitudes, beliefs, and values; it is one of the general factors determining social behavior. Most people behave according to what they think they are and aspire for what they feel they can reach. The developed self-concept provides a standard for understanding our behavior.

Various factors contribute to development of self-concept; the most important is cognitive in nature—the concept of an identity. Identity formation implies the child's cognitive isolation or differentiation of a permanent quality of an object. Basic to self-concept is acquisition of a rudimentary physical self-concept: some sense that he or she is that object called his or her body. Research suggests this comes about during the early part of the second year of life. One technique used to determine this involved putting a spot of rouge on an infant's nose and placing a mirror in front of the child. Observers then examine how the infant interacts with the mirror image. Findings indicate that 6- to 12-month-old infants react toward the image as a sociable playmate, making few attempts to investigate the spot of rouge on the nose that can only be seen in their mirror image. At about 14 or 15 months of age, children begin to show avoidance of the mirror image and at the same time tend to show some self-admiring behavior suggesting self-recognition. By the end of the second year most infants know they are seeing themselves in a mirror—the nucleus of the self-concept. In subsequent years, the self-concept becomes broader, more defined, integrated, and more complex. The quality and sophistication inherent in one's self-concept are directly related to the range and depth of one's experience.

Verbal labels help organize experience into an integrated self-concept. The child's earliest words concern self and physical body: me, toe, mouth, and so on. Gradually children learn to label the objects and people most significant to their existence: Mama, Daddy, toy, and so on. Eventually, they learn to label thoughts and actions with evaluative descriptive labels: good, bad, smart, naughty, ugly, and the like. All these labels are important, classifying and organizing our experience with ourselves. Those which evaluate behavior as good or bad are especially important in establishing how we feel about ourselves and judge ourselves.

Another important determinant of the self-concept is social feedback. G. H. Mead, in his theory of symbolic interactionism, has asserted that we react to and evaluate ourselves in much the same way as others respond to us. This rests upon role-taking ability—a cognitive skill. To fully appreciate others' reaction to us, we first must learn what it is like to be in the other person's position. As this quality develops, children become increasingly better able to view themselves as others do (feedback), and this is incorporated into the self-concept.

A final contributor to self-concept development is the feeling we have after experiencing successes and failures (or pain and distress). Such feelings are associated with all the activities and experiences that accompanied the original situation. Self-perception and evaluation in the given context are thus enhanced by positive feelings (success) or damaged by negative feelings (failure). A similar process is at work when we are praised or criticized by others. Praise and positive reactions are usually pleasurable and rewarding, causing us to feel good about ourselves. Criticism can be painful and unpleasant, especially if offered before we are certain we have failed in our own efforts. Thus, praise and criticism from other people comprise an especially important kind of evaluative feedback that helps shape the self-concept.

Children who successfully meet the expectations of others are usually rewarded in some way, making them feel good about themselves and experiencing personal pleasure and satisfaction on meeting the expectations of others. Clear and consistent recognition for success is important, providing the major ingredient for building a healthy self-concept. Likewise, children who experienne failure, who are unable to meet the expectations of others, begin to associate those unpleasant personal feelings (anxiety) with the whole context.

Thus, the self-concept acts as an integrating force behind individual performance. If children learn to view themselves as competent, this self-attitude guides their behavior towards increasing (or at least maintaining) this competence. But the reverse is also true. Children who consider themselves incompetent usually hold a self-defeating, negative attitude toward themselves. Pessimistic about success, such children tend to avoid situations requiring cognitive or social achievement and continue to miss opportunities that might change this negative self-image. The self-concept indeed is a central clearing house for directing social behavior.

FACTORS INFLUENCING SOCIAL DEVELOPMENT

In addition to typical early social environment, there are other influences on children's continuing social development: type of parenting, socioeconomic background of the child's family, absence of a parent (either mother or father), level of cognitive development, and school environment. Each of these will be discussed along with their typical contribution to social development.

Types of Parenting

Not all children show increased social maturity during the preschool years. In fact, most show some form of dependency (either emotional, instrumental, or both) on either parents or other people. A principal influence on these types of behaviors is the style of parenting shown by the primary caretakers.

Various means have been used to categorize parental styles. One approach is to classify parents as authoritarian, authoritative, or permissive (Baumrind, 1966). The behaviors characteristic of each of these parenting styles are outlined below:

Authoritarian parents:
- exert a high degree of control
- stress obedience to absolute standards
- tend to use punitive disciplinary measures
- strongly emphasize respect of authority, tradition, and order
- interact very little verbally with children

Authoritative parents:
- use firm, but rational control
- show respect for a child's interests
- direct the child toward autonomous action but encourage disciplined conformity
- value the child and encourage his efforts
- use reason and power in combination to discipline the child

- interact freely and verbally with the child
- avoid overrestrictiveness
- may promote nonconformity

Permissive parents:

- try to behave nonpunitively with the child
- positively accept the child's impulses, desires, and actions
- consult with the child about family policy
- make few demands for order and household responsibility
- act as a resource for the child
- encourage the child's self-regard
- exert little control over the child

Authoritative parents provide a learning setting conducive to acquisition of independent behavior. The child's social skills are enhanced since those parents typically engage in a lot of "teaching behaviors," impart a great deal of information and reasoning, encourage independent decision-making, and stress mature ways of thinking and reasoning. Since they are warm and nurturant, these parents are probably effective reinforcers of mature independent behavior. Authoritarian parents typically have children who show varying amounts of dependency, since these parents are highly controlling, use their power freely, and do not encourage the child to express himself when disagreeing. Children who are the least self-reliant, most dependent, and least self-controlled are those whose parents demonstrate the permissive style of parenting. These parents may be warm, but are not well-organized or effective in running their households. They are lax both in disciplining and rewarding the child, and pay little attention to training for independence and self-reliance.

In general, dependent children have parents who tend to be overprotective. Such parents prevent the child from learning how to deal with environmental crises, thus causing a sense of helplessness (Kagan and Moss, 1962). Dependency (especially emotional dependency) derives also from "withdrawal of love": giving of love and affection when the child behaves in accordance with the parents' wishes, and withdrawing it when the child behaves in a disapproved way. A related phenomenon is inconsistency: Inconsistent parents deprive the child of normal social and psychological development, making it difficult to locate and establish boundaries. Results may be disorientation and, in extreme cases, even difficulty defining reality. Such a child has difficulty establishing self-conception and relationships to others and, under stress, this unstable sense of self may collapse. Some clinical psychologists have even labeled extremely inconsistent parents schizophrenogenic—schizophrenia producing. They place the child in a position where he is "damned if he does" and "damned if he doesn't"—a double-bind situation. Double-bind parenting tends to lead to inconsistent handling of the child's dependency, thus increasing the child's anxiety and eliciting immature dependency behaviors such as reassurance-seeking (Ferguson, 1970).

Until recently most parent-child research has been interpreted unidirectionally, that is, the focus has been on the characteristics of parents that affect the behaviors of children. It is obvious, however, that children also affect parents' behavior: the loudly crying child, the very active little girl, the child who barely responds to anything—these behaviors affect parental interaction with their children. Most of the research in this area has been correlational: that is, researchers have merely examined those behaviors of children and parents that seem to be associated and few attempts have been made to discover specific cause-and-effect variables. Consequently, it is conceivable that parental styles may be the effect of temperamental and behavioral differences in their children, while children's behaviors may be the cause. In either case, the outcome is the same, but the reinterpretation does reflect not only the parents' effect on the child, but also the child's effect on the parents.

Social Class

A major influence on social development, both at home and in the school, is the child's social class. *Social class* refers to behaviors, attitudes, values, beliefs, etc., associated with a particular group of people. Differences in these behaviors usually result from differences in education, income, occupation, neighborhood, or religion. The study of social-class differences is made difficult by the fact that social-class membership is simultaneously related to a number of confounded factors. Ethnic and social-class differences are hard to differentiate in our culture. Members of minority groups have typically suffered from reduced or restricted employment opportunities (and to some extent limited educational opportunities), and thus are more likely to fall into the lower socioeconomic classes. It is true, particularly in terms of social development, that there are differences in the skills and competencies valued and considered as necessary for optimal coping by individuals in different social-class groupings. Hence, one would expect to find consistent differences in terms of the nature, as well as the rate, of social development, depending on the socioeconomic level or social class to which a child belongs.

Basic values of the American lower or working class and the middle class differ in several important ways: the middle class is dominant in our society, representing the core culture, with values shared by the greatest numbers, and determining general standards of social desirability. These values tend to be imposed on virtually all children through schools and other social institutions. Within individual homes and families, however, there is much variation according to social-class differences, some of which are illustrated by research on childrearing practices and maternal attitudes:

1. Middle-class mothers talk more with their children when training them; lower-class mothers are more likely simply to reward or punish the child's behavior according to its appropriateness.
2. Middle-class mothers are more likely to use verbal praise for good behavior to achieve discipline; lower-class mothers are more likely to use physical punishment.
3. Middle-class mothers are more easygoing regarding toilet-training; lower-class mothers are likely to be more demanding and strict in toilet-training.
4. Middle-class mothers are likely to accept more dependency in their children; lower-cless mothers are likely to become more irritated by dependency needs.
5. Middle-class mothers are more relaxed in sexual training; lower-class mothers are usually more anxious and strict about the child's sexuality.
6. Middle-class mothers are likely to tolerate more the child's aggression against adults (talking back or fighting back); lower-class parents are stricter about such aggression.

Development differences between children from middle-class and lower-class homes have also been observed in other areas. Some of these, critically related to success in educational settings, follows:

1. Middle-class children are usually superior to lower-class children in performance on standard measures of intelligence, achievement, and mental abilities.
2. Middle-class children are more likely to be work-oriented and achievement-motivated.
3. Middle-class children tend to show more rapid development of verbal abilities (reading, writing, grammar, and vocabulary) than lower-class children.

Class differences in values and parent-child interactions contribute heavily to performance at school, particularly for lower-class children, who are expected to function within the culture-bound middle-class educational system.

Parent Absence

Another factor with important implications for social development is parent absence. When one parent is not present for some reason, it is usually the mother who raises the children. Consequently, parent absence usually is equivalent to father absence. There is little research on children raised by fathers in the absence of mothers, but there is a considerable amount on children of working mothers. While these mothers are not in reality absent, they spend less time with their children as opposed to non-working mothers.

The effects of father absence depend on a number of factors such as length of separation, the child's age at the onset of separation, and the child's sex. Since for boys, the father is the chief model for appropriate sex-typing, the effect of father absence on identification is of concern. Freudian theory would predict that father absence would result in the male child's identifying with the mother and becoming a latent or overt homosexual, a view that does not consider the presence of other adult and peer male models in the child's world. In general, studies of the effects of father absence on young males indicate that less appropriate sex-typing does occur, although an increased incidence of homosexuality has not been confirmed. The effects of father absence on girls is not clear, but there does appear a tendency for father-absent girls to have difficulty in adolescence and adult relations with males. Father-absent girls may experience difficulty in adjusting to marriage, because of lack of early experience in relating to males.

Effects of father absence are even greater if separation occurs early in the child's life. Father absence, when male children are pre-school age, is often associated with problems in masculinity development. Pre-schoolers whose fathers are absent are usually less aggressive than other males, possess fewer masculine sex-role stereotypes, and show less involvement with physical-contact games. They are more likely to engage in nonphysical activities, such as reading, constructing puzzles, and collecting things, and are also more likely to have lower I.Q.'s, lower academic aptitudes, and lower academic achievement. Delinquency rates are also higher for boys raised by their mothers. In general, the greater the length of father absence and the earlier the onset, the greater the effects.

Identification with the father appears necessary for internalization of many social standards and behavioral consistency with these norms later in life. However, it is possible that the effects of father absence are mediated by changes in the mother's behavior toward her children after the father leaves the home. It has been shown that mothers in father-absent homes become more indulgent and over-protective toward children. Mothers are also more likely to be isolated from social contacts and more concerned with child obedience as opposed to the child's happiness and self-realization. That mother's behavior may be important is illustrated in the effects of father absence on female children, who show higher dependency on mothers, and are more likely to have emotional problems and school maladjustment, and to engage in antisocial "acting-out" behaviors.

Mothers now are more likely to work when their children enter school, and many researchers have tried to find out how outside employment affects her children. Although, in general, no consistent differences have been found between children of employed and non-employed mothers (Howell, 1973), some research has indicated a few interesting effects: Working mothers of school age children provide different role models and their children are more open in their sex role views and have higher educational and career aspirations. Daughters of employed mothers are more likely to select careers in traditionally male fields (Miller, 1975).

Indeed, there seem to be few if any negative effects of maternal employment if the children are of school age. On the other hand, if the children are very young (below one year), in theory maternal employment may have severe effects, since, during this period, formation of an attachment bond is of great importance and repeated mother absences may be detrimental.

Parent absence does not always have adverse effects. Other models are available in addition to, or instead of, male and female parent models. For example, older brothers and sisters may function as substitute identification figures as may aunts and uncles. Organizations such as the Big Brother Program can offer substitute models for children with absent parents, as can mass-communication media (television and movies). Unfortunately, these models generally tend to be highly stereotyped and probably promote adoption of somewhat unrealistic sex-typed behavior patterns.

Birth Order

Along with parental styles and parent absence, birth order may affect social functioning. In general, first-born and only children tend to be more affiliative under stressful situations, more dependent, more conforming, more responsible, less aggressive, more achievement-oriented, and more cooperative. Later borns are likely to be more outgoing and independent, less conforming, less responsible, and more likely not to achieve in non-traditional manners. However, these findings are not clear-cut and seem to depend on such factors as spacing between siblings as well as their sex (Koch, 1956). Some of the factors considered responsible for the psychological differences between first-borns and later-borns revolve around the different social-learning situations experienced by the first-born.

Cognitive Development

In Jean Piaget's conception of cognitive development, the pre-school child is in the preoperational stage of cognitive development. The major cognitive achievement of this period is the ability to engage in symbolic representational thought. The rapid advances in language development during these years (2-6) further enable the child to deal with the world symbolically, no longer bound by concrete reality and confined to obtaining knowledge by strictly sensory and motor actions. This has important implications for social development. For example, the preoperational child is able to en--gage in symbolic play, such as "Playing House" or "Cowboys and Indians." The pretending games typical of this age represent exercises in practicing the representation of objects or events symbolically (naming, pretending, role playing, talking to one's self).

Symbolic thought contributes to enhanced social functioning by enabling the child to engage in a wider variety of social interactions that further the acquisition of social skills. For example, communication has a great deal to do with developing social skills. Until the child is physically and intellectually ready for language and speech, social interactions are very limited. Without language, ideas cannot be exchanged; with true communicative language, when the child approaches the third year of age, new doors open to enrich the quality of these developing social skills. Also, as already mentioned, imitation and identification are important to development of a conscience and the child's understanding of his or her sex. Restricted cognitive skills keep the infant from imitating models in their absence, symbolically representing the model's behavior, and engaging in deferred imitation (imitation in the absence of a model). However, since the preoperational child possesses the ability to symbolize events, which enhances memory capabilities, he or she is able to show deferred imitation: an event that certainly has an important bearing on continued social development.

Egocentrism, an aspect of cognitive functioning during the preoperational stage, can hamper acquisition of new social skills. The preoperational child is highly self-centered and cannot interpret or assimilate information from any frame of reference other than his own. For example, a young girl who says to her father on the telephone, "See my pretty dress!" is unable, in her egocentrism, to comprehend that while she can see the dress, the person on the other end of the telephone cannot. This affects social development insofar as the egocentric child may not be able to take the point of view of another person. Many social behaviors (for example, cooperation and friendship) require sensitivity to the behavior and needs of others. Cooperation requires ability to coordinate behavior with that of another person. An egocentric child unable to sense the position of another person is consequently handicapped in acquiring social skills.

The effects of egocentrism and its waning are clearly evidenced in types of play engaged in by children. Some years ago, Mildred Parten (1932) noted that very young children are more or less wrapped up in themselves; even when others are present, they are engaged in *solitary play.* It is nevertheless productive play, for the children are exercising cognitive information-processing operations. As they grow older, children increasingly take notice of others—at first passively, in *parallel play* and later more actively, in *associative play.* As they grow older, they engage in more direct social interaction, but not until school age does this interaction become very rich or complex in *interactive play.*

This progression moves from the self-centered or egocentric to the socially centered or sociometric, with the child's developing maturity. As children mature cognitively, they become increasingly able to shift focus while interpreting information and can take alternative frames of reference, thus escaping the tendency to be bound totally by their own point of view. As the child's cognitive skills gradually enable him to decenter, development of social-interaction skills is enhanced by increasing ability to see things from others' points of view (role-taking or perspective-taking). New information is now available to the child, and a new source of reinforcement comes from anticipation of the responses to his own actions (Flavell et al., 1968; Flavell, 1977). Recent research indicates that children begin to show this ability to take the perspective of others as early as three years of age (Zahn-Waxler, Radke-Yarrow, and Brady-Smith, 1977).

Shedding egocentrism and development of role-taking skills, which occur during the later phases of the preoperational period, are prerequisite to such prosocial behaviors as sharing, mature helping behaviors, and empathy. Enhanced prosocial behavior facilitates the child's intellectual and cognitive skills, and sensorimotor development. Taking the perspective of others is preliminary to recognizing and meeting the needs of others. This ability has been observed in even very young children; Zahn-Waxler, Brady-Smith, and Radke-Yarrow (1977) found that sharing, helping, and comforting in three-year-old children are directly related to ability to take the perspective of others. Specifically, preschool age children are able to engage in empathic inference; that is, they are able to infer a particular emotion another person is experiencing and may themselves experience a related feeling. Moreover, preschoolers are also able to engage in non-empathic inference—inferring another person's feelings without expressing it themselves. These abilities do not exist among infants whose role-taking skills are not developed, again reaffirming the interconnection between social and cognitive development.

PROSOCIAL AND ANTISOCIAL BEHAVIORS

Mature social development involves many complex adjustments. Children must learn to deal with other people individually and in groups, to respond appropriately to their expectations and standards, requiring a delicate balance between dependency and autonomy or independence. Too much of either is generally unwarranted, and the amount varies with age and situational condition. Children also must learn to handle positive and negative emotions toward others, and in socially acceptable ways. Acquisition of these skills is slow and gradual, paralleling physical and cognitive capabilities. Those children who do develop effective social interaction skills apparently have an advantage over those who do not. Research (Waldrop and Halverson, 1975) shows that children socially effective at two-and-a-half were likely to also be socially effective at seven-and-a-half. At two-and-a-half they were described as friendly, socially involved, and able to cope with other children. Five years later, these children were described as socially at ease with others, more involved in peer activity, and actively participating in peer decision-making. Unfortunately, socially isolated or unsociable children are more likely to develop problem behaviors, including delinquency and mental-health problems. And as adults, unpopular children are more likely to be treated for behavioral pathologies and to attempt suicide.

Social behaviors can be prosocial and antisocial. *Prosocial behaviors,* based in positive attraction to others, tend to draw people closer together and conversely to diminish social distance; they include the following:

- Dependency   help-seeking or attention-seeking behaviors which draw people closer

- Nurturance   care-giving behaviors

- Altruism   behaviors intended to help others without reward to the person being altruistic; unselfishness

- Cooperation   coodinating individuals' behaviors to reach a common goal

These prosocial behaviors, generally learned (though some claim a biological-survival base, arguing that their presence facilitates survival of the species), appear to rely on early experiences which encourage children to associate reward, satisfaction, and pleasure with the presence of other people. Thus, children who have a variety of positive early experiences with others will be more likely to develop prosocially in early childhood.

Antisocial behaviors have the opposite effect: they increase social distance because they disrupt interpersonal relationships. Generally, they are viewed as learned, and include the following:

- Aggression   the intent to harm or destroy; results usually in young children when frustration is experienced

- Hostility (anger)   feelings which usually accompany aggressive behavior

- Acting-out   unrestrained or uninhibited behavior

- Competition   in social situations, achieving mastery over others

Most antisocial behaviors (except competition) are not encouraged in our culture. However, since much antisocial behavior results from frustration of individual desires, we will always have antisocial behavior. These behaviors can be managed and reduced in early childhood by careful analysis of the (frustrating) situation to identify the causes and by redirecting the child's behavior into more prosocial situations or by eliminating the source of frustration when possible. Eliminating frustration is not always possible, nor always totally desirable, since coping appropriately with frustration is an effective social skill. However, it is wise not to expose children to too much frustration; those who experience much frustration, and who have to cope with it by aggression, will, more than likely, learn that aggression is rewarding and can attract attention from others, with consequent growth of antisocial skills.

Effective social interaction is pleasurable, vital, and important. Since it is impossible for humans to live alone, we are compelled to depend on others for satisfaction and welfare. Truly, "no man is an island."

THE YOUNG CHILD IN SCHOOL

The young child's entry into a formal educational setting is a significant event for the child and for the family. Experiencing sudden expansion of the psychological world, the child encounters new people, new places, new expectations, new experiences, greater independence, and freedom from supervisory control—as well as greater demands and expectations of responsibility for the consequences of actions.

A child's entry into the school setting also represents, to the maximum, society's role in the socialization of its children. This is important for several reasons. The school is the most highly institutionalized formal structure society has evolved to facilitate child development beyond the home, lasting until the child is virtually ready to assume an adult role in society. Thus, the school monopolizes the greater portion of the child's total waking hours during the most formative years of development. It is an institution committed to integrating the child's personal development—an arena in which the child may learn and practice development of physical, cognitive, social, and personal competencies.

Various factors influence whether or not a child's adjustment to school and concomitant acquisitions of new social skills is satisfactory. Among them are parental attitudes toward education, parents' relationships with their children, the nature of the school, and how teachers relate to their students. Generally, the more positive the family's attitudes toward the school setting, the more favorably inclined will be the child. The more positive the family's attitudes toward the child, including respect for his limited but developing capability for self-care, the more optimistic will be the child about his ability to cope.

The nature of the school also exerts a great influence. Traditional schools place primary emphasis on acquisition of knowledge and view academic competence as the primary goal. However, recent changes are placing more emphasis on total development: intellectual, social, and psychological. Whether or not children profit more from one system or another is determined in part by their level of anxiety. Those low in anxiety function better in the traditional format, while those who are minimally anxious perform optimally in more open settings (Dowalby & Schummer, 1976). Other research indicates children seem to mature socially at a faster rate in an open system (Minuchin, Biber, Shapiro, Zimiles, 1969); however, very bright children seem to founder in the open school. These studies show that no one educational system will contribute optimally to the development of *all* children; it would seem to be up to the teacher and her effectiveness and sensitivity to maximize each child's performance within the school.

The teacher is likely to be the first adult, outside of the immediate family, who plays a major role in the child's life. In fact, for many children the teacher becomes a substitute mother; many children have been known to transfer to the teacher feelings and attitudes held toward their mothers (Franco, 1964). Teacher behavior can therefore have a profound influence on child behavior. For example, since elementary school teachers usually are women, many children, especially boys, are likely to perceive school activities as being ''feminine'' and consequently more appropriate for girls. This attitude may bolster girls' interest and greater ability in mastering reading and spelling. But it also may account for many boys' underachievement in these areas, especially if teachers hold traditional stereotypes and expect females to do well in these areas.

There is also evidence that teachers are more likely to single out boys for negative sanctions. This is not surprising when you consider those behaviors which are valued and reinforced by teachers in schools. Desired behaviors are most often feminine in character: neatness, quietness, attentiveness, and inhibition of aggressive behaviors. Sloppiness and mischievous behavior are most often expected of boys and boys are more likely to be punished for them. Hence, boys are more likely than girls to have a difficult time making a good adjustment to the ''feminine'' school situation.

Also of concern are those factors that influence the child's educational aspirations in the school. Many events (parental influences, peer influences, and the child's socio-economic status) have been implicated as contributors to the child's aspirations. School achievement refers to the extent to which a person is effective and productive in school. Just as children vary in their degree of adjustment to different situations, children also differ widely in achievement levels.

A major influence in school achievement is parental expectations and attitudes. These expectations vary with parents' socioeconomic status and ethnic origin. Students' expectations are shaped primarily by their parents—some intentionally, by warnings and advice about how to handle the situation and others unintentionally, by implicit values reflected in casual conversation and remarks. Most middle-class parents (especially if well-educated) hold very positive attitudes toward the public school system and impart these to their children both explicitly and implicitly. With such expectations, a child is likely to profit maximally from school experience. On the other hand, many children (especially those from ethnic and socioeconomic minorities) hold very different expectations about school. Their parents may doubt the worth of formal education; they may believe that teachers' true motives are something other than interest in the welfare of their children; and they may fear that the school experience will be painful and unhappy. These attitudes are easily communicated to children. In some cases, parents may even directly warn children to be prepared for such malicious intent on the part of teachers and schoolmates. A child who distrusts the system will most certainly not accept the values represented by the system.

In addition, the socioeconomically disadvantaged student is likely to be poorly prepared to progress in the educational system. As a result of social learning experiences, which vary markedly from those of the middle and upperclass child, the lower-class student may be handicapped on approaching academic tasks requiring specific types of cognitive abilities. The middle-class child is not likely to suffer this disadvantage, since the school system most likely simply represents an extension of the values and attitudes shared by the home-life situation. In particular, a socioeconomically disadvantaged child's language skills will not prepare him as well as those of a middle-class child for the educational system. Once inside the school system the disadvantaged child may be further hampered by feelings of inadequacy and depressed self-concept resulting from the marked differences between his customary social environment and that of the school.

REFERENCES AND SUGGESTED READINGS

Aronfreed, J. *Conduct and conscience: The socialization of internalized control over behavior.* New York: Academic Press, 1968.

Bandura, A. (Ed.), *Psychological modeling: Conflicting theories.* New York: Lieber-Atheatin, 1974.

Baumrind, D. Current patterns of parental authority. *Developmental Psychology Monographs,* 1971, *4,* 1-103.

Baumrind, D. Effects of authoritative parental control on child behavior. *Child Development,* 1966, *37,* 887-907.

Dowaliby, F. J., & Schumer, H. Teacher centered versus student centered mode college classroom instruction as related to manifest anxiety. *Proceedings 79th Annual Convention of the American Psychological Association,* 1971, *6,* 541-542.

Ferguson, L. R. *Personality development.* Monterey, Calif.: Brooks/Cole, 1970.

Flavell, J. *Cognitive development.* Englewood Cliffs: Prentice-Hall, 1977.

Flavell, J. H., Bothin, P. T., Fry, C. L., Wright, J. W., & Jarvis, P. E. *The development of role taking and communicative skills in children.* New York: Wiley, 1968.

Franco, D. The child's perception of "the teacher" as compared to his perception of "the mother." *Dissertation Abstracts,* 1964, *24,* 3413-3415.

Howell, M. C. Employed mothers and their families. *Pediatrics,* 1973, *52*(2), 252-263.

Kagan, J. & Moss, H. A. *Birth to maturity: A study in psychological development.* New York: Wiley, 1962.

Koch, H. C. Some emotional attitudes of the young child in relation to characteristics of his siblings. *Child Development,* 1956, *27,* 393-426.

Kohlberg, L. A cognitive-developmental analysis of children's sex-role concepts and attitudes. In E. M. Maccoby (Ed.), *The development of sex differences.* Stanford: Stanford University Press, 1966.

Kohlberg, L. Stage & sequence: The cognitive developmental approach to socialization. In D. A. Goslin (Ed.), *Handbook of socialization theory and research.* New York: Rand McNally, 1969.

Kuhn, D. Imitation theory and research from a cognitive perspective. *Human Development*, 1973, *16*, 157-180.

Miller, S. M. Effects of maternal employment on sex role perception, interest, and self esteem in kindergarten girls. *Developmental Psychology*, 1975, *11*(3), 405-406.

Minuchin, P., Biber, B., Shapiro, E., & Zimiles, H. *The psychological impact of school experience.* New York: Basic Books, 1969.

Parten, M. B. Social participation among pre-school children. *Journal of Abnormal and Social Psychology*, 27 (1932-1933), 243-269.

Waldrop, M., & Halverson, C. Intensive and extensive peer behavior. Longitudinal and cross-sectional analysis. *Child Development*, 1975, *46*, 19-26.

Zahn-Waxler, C., Radke-Yarrow, M., & Brady-Smith, J. Perspective taking and prosocial behavior. *Developmental Psychology*, 1977, *13*, 87-88.

Chapter 15

Emotional Disorders in
Young Children

James Kauffman

There is a persistent myth among students considering careers in special education that emotionally disturbed children, especially young ones, are simply victims of parental mismanagement or social cruelties. The myth includes the idea that if disturbed children are treated kindly, permissively, and with insight into the meaning of their behavior, the latter will improve quickly and dramatically. These oversimplified notions of causes and cures of disturbed behavior are fostered by popular books, magazine articles, movies, and TV programs, many of which portray dramatic incidents in play therapy or special classrooms. In contrast to popularized accounts of what disturbed children are like and how they can be helped, current research reveals they are typically victimizers as well as victims in social relationships, that such children usually respond better to firm direction and control than to permissiveness, and that helping them change their behavior for the better is an arduous task at which even the most experienced and competent can fail.

DEFINITION AND CLASSIFICATION

Definition

Disturbed children make people uncomfortable—psychologically, and often physically as well. They are not pleasant to be around, and often they themselves are miserable. Their behavior simply does not fit expectations, and so they become disappointments to adults and other children. In fact, disturbed children are such serious and constant disappointments to others that adults around them begin to say to themselves, "This can't go on. Something has to be done to protect other people from this child and/or to protect this child from himself. If we don't intervene, someone will suffer too much." Thus Rhodes and Paul (1978) have defined the disturbed or deviant child in terms of concern for the stability or continuation of the social environment:

> Handicapped children are those children who either conflict with or fail to contribute to the perpetuation needs of the environment over a sufficiently long period of time and with sufficient intensity as to cause the environment alarm over its own welfare or that of the individual or both (p. 135).

In short, the definition of emotional disturbance in children relies very heavily on the subjective judgment of adults that a child is too threatening or burdensome to others and/or too negative toward himself to be tolerated. There simply is no sufficiently valid and reliable standard or test to separate the disturbed from the nondisturbed.

When considering children of school age, one can point to several characteristics that define emotional disturbance. Bower (1969) has said that a child may be considered disturbed if he exhibits one or more of the following *to a marked extent and over a period of time:*

1. Inability to learn that cannot be explained by intellectual, sensory, or health factors.
2. Inability to build or maintain satisfactory interpersonal relationships with peers and teachers.
3. Inappropriate types of behavior or feelings under normal conditions.
4. A general, pervasive mood of unhappiness or depression.
5. A tendency to develop physical symptoms, pains, or fears associated with personal or school problems (pp. 22-23).

Bower's definition comes close to being an "official" definition for educators because it is used in federal rules and regulations governing provision of special education services to disturbed children. It is the definition used, for example, in Public Law 94-142.

When considering very young children, particularly those not in a formal educational setting, where Bower's definition is most appropriately applied, one needs to be sensitive to developmental norms and parental expectations. Often the first signs of serious emotional disturbance are seen in difficulties experienced with basic biological functions or early social responses (e.g., the infant's mastery of eating, eliminating, sleeping, responding positively to a parent's attempts to comfort, "molding" to the parent's body when being held). At the toddler stage, failure to begin talking is potentially a sign of emotional difficulty. In short, failure to pass ordinary developmental milestones is a danger signal in the case of emotional development, just as it is in cognitive development. In fact, cognitive and emotional development are closely related, and one cannot often consider either aspect of a young child's life in isolation from the other.

One final and crucial point about definition is that normal children do, at some time during their development, just about everything emotionally disturbed children do. Having temper tantrums, being fearful of strangers, being preoccupied with objects, refusing to obey reasonable requests, fighting, stealing, masturbating . . . these are things almost every normal child does, although they characterize disturbed children as well. What sets disturbed children apart from the normal is that they do such things much more frequently, persistently, and at an age when normal children have "outgrown" them. Disturbed children's behavior upsets others and handicaps the children themselves because it is *developmentally inappropriate and persistent.*

Classification

Psychiatrists and clinical psychologists have attempted to devise systems for classifying disturbed children, but what they have come up with is not very helpful to people in their own professions or to other child-care professionals (see Hobbs, 1975). In their classifications there is so much subjectivity, ambiguity, and unreliability in predicting how to work successfully with the child that it is hardly worth discussing the schemes at all. However, it is recognized by many professionals working with disturbed children that *behaviors* can be fairly reliably and usefully classified. That is, types of behaviors can be seen to go together in clusters statistically, so it can be said that a child who exhibits one behavior in a cluster is likely to exhibit others in that cluster (or "factor" in statistical terminology) as well. Quay (1972), for example, has found three major factors or clusters of behavior:

1. Behaviors grouped under the term *conduct disorder:* disobedience, disruptiveness, fighting, destructiveness, temper tantrums, irresponsibility, impertinence, jealousy, anger, bossiness, profanity, attention seeking, and boisterousness. These are often displayed by the child who assaults others, defies authority, is irritable and quarrelsome, and strikes out with hostile aggression.

2. Behaviors forming a cluster called *personality disorder:* feelings of inferiority, self-consciousness, social withdrawal, anxiety, crying, hypersensitivity, chewing fingernails, seldom smiling, depression, chronic sadness, and shyness. The picture is one of a child who is timid, shy, seclusive, sensitive, and a worrier.

3. A factor or cluster of behaviors called *immaturity:* short attention span, preoccupation, clumsiness, passivity, daydreaming, sluggishness, drowsiness, masturbation, giggling, preference for younger playmates, chewing objects, being "picked on" by others, and so on. These are traits of children not competent to deal with complex situations and demands for age-appropriate behavior.

451

Characteristic Behaviors of Disturbed Children

In some studies, the distinction between *personality problem* and *immaturity* has not been clear, and we are left with two major ways children tend to cause consternation among their caretakers: by striking out against others (aggression in its many forms) or interacting too little with others (withdrawal in all its varieties). *Aggression* is often accompanied by hyperactivity (high rates of socially inappropriate behaviors), distractibility (not being able to focus attention on the appropriate thing), and impulsivity (acting quickly without considering alternatives). *Withdrawal* is often accompanied by immaturity (behavior that is "babyish" or inappropriate for the child's age) and inadequacy (inability to meet the day-to-day demands of social situations).

A few moments of reflection on these behavioral characteristics will probably bring to mind several children you have known. At the least, a little reflection will make it obvious that children who show these characteristics for very long will be unlikely to endear themselves to adults or other children. Furthermore, they will not be likely to see themselves in a very positive light. It is easy to see why our society does not treasure these characteristics of children, and why such behaviors should be changed.

Degrees of Severity

It is a truism that everyone is a little bit emotionally disturbed, more so at certain times of stress than at others. Emotional health and emotional illness are not clear-cut psychological states or diagnostic categories into which adults or children can be placed. Problems in living, troublesome behavior, undesirable psychological states—these are things that *all* of us experience. There is a range of problems all the way from insignificant difficulties commonly experienced by almost everyone to difficulties so profound that one is almost totally incapacitated. When it comes to emotional disturbances of young children, professionals tend to distinguish between mild/moderate disorders, in which the child is typically more like than unlike his normal peers, and severe/profound disorders, in which the child is grossly deviant in his behavior and seems to lack an understanding of reality. Mild and moderate disorders are often referred to as "neurosis" or "psychoneurosis," while severe and profound disorders are often called "childhood psychosis" or "autism." The milder disorders typically involve differences from normal behavior that are primarily quantitative. That is, the mildly or moderately disturbed child is defined as such primarily because he or she does much more of the abrasive, undesirable things normal children do only occasionally (e.g., crying, whining, throwing tantrums, running away, refusing to obey adults). Severely or profoundly disturbed children, however, often show qualitative as well as quantitative differences from normal behavior. Some of the extreme differences from normal shown by severely disturbed children may include the following:

1. Extreme aggression toward other people or animals, in which they are calculatedly cruel.
2. Self-injurious behavior, including biting, scratching, poking, bumping, or otherwise hurting themselves so that unless they are stopped they will eventually mutilate or kill themselves.
3. Self-stimulation, which consists of any stereotyped, repetitive behavior that is not useful in any way except to provide sensory feedback (e.g., rocking, twirling objects, staring, flapping hands).
4. Language and speech deviations, including delayed language, misuse of pronouns (e.g., "he" for "I"), meaningless jargon, strange voice quality, or echolalia (repeating parrot-like whatever is heard).
5. Unrelatedness to other people to such an extent that others are totally ignored or treated like inanimate objects.
6. Cognitive deficits that render the child functionally retarded even though he may have some remarkable but useless special abilities (e.g., being able to do amazing calculations or feats of memory without being able to use skills to solve everyday problems).
7. Perceptual deviations that make the child seem to be auditorally or visually impaired or make him unable to understand auditory or visual stimuli.
8. Lack of daily living skills such as dressing, feeding, or toileting oneself.

While there is no way of distinguishing precisely between mildly and severely disturbed children, there are some general rules or guidelines for judging severity. First, the *rate* at which children exhibit maladaptive behavior is a key consideration. Severely disturbed children differ more than mildly disturbed children do from the rate that is normal. Second, the more disturbed the child, the more *chronic* is the behavioral problem. Third, the problems of severely disturbed children often appear at an early age, and *early age of onset* is therefore sometimes an indication of how severe the difficulty may prove to be. Finally, the *prognosis* for severely disturbed children is much gloomier than for the mildly disturbed. A sizeable proportion of psychotic children will be institutionalized or be viewed as disturbed or retarded when they reach adulthood, whereas a very high proportion of mildly disturbed children will be considered normal as adults.

Special Considerations for Young Children

Definition and classification of emotional disturbance are necessarily quite different for children than for adults. With children, one must keep in mind the developmental changes in behavior normally seen from year to year. Furthermore, children do not refer themselves for psychiatric treatment (like adults) or special education but are selected by adults to receive services. With children of school age, it is possible to compare their behavior with that of a substantial number of peers, and their behavior is easily scrutinized by quite a few different adults. But the infant or preschool child is typically seen by fewer adults and in smaller groups of children the same age, making it a little more difficult to judge the adequacy of behavior patterns. In addition, there are other factors that complicate the picture for very young children: (1) the developmental tasks for young children are fewer and simpler, which means there is a restricted range of normal behaviors to sample; (b) there is great variability in child-rearing practices of parents and parental expectations for their young children's behavior, which means that one must guard against inappropriate comparisons; (c) in this period of life normal development is rapid and often uneven, which means it is difficult to judge the prospects for "spontaneous" improvement and that deviations from the norm must be extreme in order to justify viewing them as abnormal; and (d) it is generally in the early months of life that the most profound emotional disorders make their appearance, making it difficult many times to distinguish such an emotional disturbance from mental retardation or deafness. If a child begins to show extreme social withdrawal (e.g., unrelatedness to people, preoccupation with objects, extreme self-stimulation) or other extremely deviant behavior before the age of 30 months, he is often classified as "autistic," whereas if the onset of the disorder comes after 30 months of age he is usually labeled "childhood schizophrenic" or something else. Autism is not a well-defined or well-understood condition and is often confused with mental retardation, deafness, brain damage, or other problems.

Behavioral Characteristics and IQ

Intelligence and emotional health are not the same thing by any means, but there is a positive relationship between the two. Numerous studies have shown that mentally bright children tend to have fewer emotional difficulties compared with children of dull intellect. Certainly it is absurd to believe that being mentally retarded somehow means that one cannot be emotionally disturbed. In fact, it is clear that being mentally retarded *increases* chances of being disturbed. (This does *not* imply a *causal* relationship between intelligence and emotional disturbance—a child is not necessarily disturbed *because* he is retarded or retarded *because* he is disturbed.) Some emotionally disturbed children are extremely bright—the vast majority are not. Most disturbed children are somewhat below average in IQ, and the more severely disturbed tend to have lower IQs. As a group, severely disturbed (i.e., "psychotic" or "autistic") children have IQs in the mildly to severely retarded range (30 to 70).

Behavioral Characteristics and Socioeconomic Status

Most children from poor homes are not considered emotionally disturbed. However, it is clear that being poor increases a child's chance of being disturbed. Spivack and Shure (1974) have reviewed research showing that children reared in poverty are less likely than middle-class children to see alternative ways of behaving in situations involving interpersonal problems. Poor children tend to see fewer options in dealing with others and are prone to seek aggressive solutions (e.g., If you want a toy another child has, hit him and grab it.) than are middle class children.

Behavioral Characteristics and Sex

More boys than girls are considered emotionally disturbed, and this is true by a wide margin (4 or 5 to 1) across age groups and levels of severity. Boys are more often considered hyperaggressive and disruptive or destructive. Many more boys than girls are considered autistic.

Behavioral Characteristics and Prognosis

It has already been stated that the prognosis for severely disturbed children is much poorer than for mildly disturbed children. Many severely disturbed children exhibit profound social withdrawal, which has led to the misconception that the outlook for withdrawn children is generally poorer than for the acting-out aggressive type. However, among the mildly disturbed it is the antisocial, aggressive youngster who is least likely to overcome his difficulty and be considered well adjusted in later years. When aggression, low IQ, and school failure occur together, the child is most likely to have a long history of difficulty getting along and to be institutionalized or incarcerated as an adult. Hostile aggression carries more social penalties in our culture than any other single behavioral characteristic.

ASSESSMENT

The assessment of children has several major purposes. First, it is necessary to find out just what the child's problems and points of strength are. Second, one must use the information obtained to plan a program of help for the child. Third, assessment is necessary to evaluate the child's progress toward therapeutic goals. Fourth, assessment should allow one to make a reasonable statement about the future, i.e., to arrive at a prognosis. Classification of the child, which has been a major purpose of traditional psychiatric and psychological "diagnosis," is important or useful only insofar as it contributes to one or more of the four stated purposes of assessment.

Adequate assessment of emotionally disturbed children requires more than a single strategy. In addition to standardized tests, interviews and behavioral observations are necessary (see Evans & Nelson, 1977).

Standardized Instruments

Standardized tests have the advantage of comparison of the child's performance under specified conditions with that of a large normative population. Thus one can see how the child compares with others, not just in overall performance but (on

455

some tests) on specific subtests or items as well. In some cases, standardized instruments may point to the child's relative areas of strength or weakness aside from comparison with the normative population.

Screening Tests

Screening means administering an assessment procedure to each member of a group for selecting out those who *may* be disturbed, retarded, or handicapped in some other way. The individuals selected are not automatically identified as needing help but, rather, are studied in more detail to see if they do need special educational or psychological services. For children in kindergarten or first grade, screening for emotional disturbance might involve use of the *First Grade Screening Test* (Pate & Webe, 1967), *A Process for In-School Screening of Children with Emotional Handicaps* (Bower & Lambert, 1962), or other tests. However, it is usually the case, especially with children younger than kindergarteners, that teachers or parents simply observe what they perceive to be problem behavior and refer the child to a specialist for assessment.

A screening test usually samples several different abilities considered crucial for the child's success in school (see Wallace & Kauffman, 1978, for brief descriptions of several other screening tests and lists of potential problem behaviors). For example, the child might be asked to identify pictures when named (a picture-vocabulary task included in some IQ tests), draw objects (to sample perceptual-motor skills), or judge emotions expressed by drawings of faces. The instrument constructed by Bower and Lambert (1962) asks children to judge whether or not they themselves or their classmates often act like children shown in various pictures.

Intelligence Tests

The social-emotional development of young children is so inseparably tied up with cognitive and physical development that any competent assessment of a young emotionally disturbed child will include an IQ test. (It should be noted here that competent assessment will include attention to all aspects of the child's development, including a thorough physical examination, tests for sensory deficits, and an appraisal of speech and language abilities.) One can hardly know what to expect behaviorally from a child without knowing how well the child responds to tasks requiring conceptual (reasoning, thinking) skills. It is true there are dangers in using IQ test results inappropriately. (For example, one must beware of the pitfall of concluding that a child cannot or will not learn because he scores low on an IQ test.) But because children's performance on IQ tests is correlated substantially with how they perform in many important areas of development and because IQ scores are moderately good predictors of how fast and successfully children will develop, they often provide useful information to guide professionals in deciding whether or not a child needs special help. An IQ score is merely a comparison of a child's performance on selected tasks with the performance of many other children of the same chronological age—it does not *cause* the child to behave in any particular way, nor does it reveal what the child's *potential* is.

Achievement Tests

For children who have been in school for several years, tests of academic achievement are useful. One of the most important indications of emotional problems of school-age children is failure to learn basic academic skills. Does school failure cause emotional disturbance or does a child fail at school because he is disturbed? The answer is that one can seldom say which is the first cause and that school failure and emotional disturbance seem to feed each other, as will be discussed further. The point to be made here is that academic achievement is an important aspect of child development from the first school years onward, and standardized achievement tests will reveal to what extent the child is keeping up with expectations for someone his age.

Special Considerations

Very few standardized tests are available for very young (prekindergarten) children. Many severely disturbed children are untestable with standard procedures. Furthermore, it can be argued that because of their deviant response patterns, it is unreasonable to compare disturbed children with normals on standardized tests—the disturbed children are at an unfair disadvantage and cannot show their true potential on IQ and achievement tests because of their maladaptive behavior in the testing situation. It is true that tests must often be adapted especially for severely disturbed children and that adequate testing of any disturbed child requires particular sensitivity and skill on the part of the examiner. Regarding the disadvantage of disturbed children, though, it is important to remember that IQ and achievement tests *do not tap potential*—their purpose is to find out what the child can do now, the way he *is,* in order to make a reasonable guess about what he will be able to do in the future, the way he *will be,* unless something special is done to change his progress. The fact that disturbed children do poorly on standardized tests and show interfering social behavior should be interpreted to mean that intervention is necessary, not that they have no potential for improvement.

Rating Scales and Checklists

One way of assessing children is to provide adults (e.g., teachers, parents, social workers) with a list of descriptive statements (e.g., "throws temper tantrums," "seldom smiles," "fights," "cries easily") and have them check the ones they believe are true of the child or have them rate on a scale (e.g., 1 = not true at all, never; to 5 = very true, almost always) the extent to which they believe each statement applies. While checklists and rating scales are relatively efficient ways of gathering information and can be very useful, it is important to note their limitations. First, there is the possibility that the items selected for the list or scale are not the most important ones or are poorly stated so that the results are of questionable validity. Second, the items may call for a great deal of opinion or subjective judgment so that the results are of questionable reliability.

Interviews

It is inconceivable that an adequate assessment of a disturbed child could be made without interviewing the adults responsible for him. If the child has language skills, it is highly likely that the assessment should include an interview with the child as well. It is sometimes desirable to interview the child's siblings or peers, who may contribute to the problem and/or its solution. The purpose of the interview, whether with an adult or a child, is to get as clear a picture as possible of the interviewed person's perception of the problem, its history, and what solutions have been attempted. Parents, teachers, and children are not always accurate, reliable, unbiased reporters, and one must not have unquestioning faith in what they say. However, getting their views of the situation is always useful, and in some cases their reports may lead to a swift, straightforward solution to a seemingly complex behavioral problem. For example, a child who cried loudly and almost incessantly in the classroom stopped crying almost immediately when his teacher, through discussing the problem with him and his classmates, found that one of his greatest desires was to be called "Sam" instead of "Sammy." Sam and his classmates agreed that when he cried he would be called "Sammy" but that when he was not crying he would be addressed as "Sam" (Kaufhold & Kauffman, 1974).

Interviewing sounds simpler than it really is. Getting adults (particularly parents) and children (especially disturbed children) to talk openly and sincerely about the problem requires more than good intentions; it requires a great deal of sensitivity and interviewing skill. By the time a disturbed child comes to the attention of child-care specialists, his behavior has become such an irritant to others and such a negative mark of distinction for the child himself that everyone connected with the case is on the defensive. It is not easy to win the confidence of the interviewees, put them at ease, and get the straight scoop.

Behavioral Observation

The assessment strategies discussed so far—testing, ratings and checklists, and interviews—are useful but are poor substitutes for the strategy of actually watching what happens in the problem situation. Granted it may sometimes be impossible to observe in the home or to avoid influencing behavior just by the presence of observers, but the most helpful assessment data can usually be obtained by direct observation and measurement of behavior. It is what the child does or does not do under particular circumstances that is the problem, and it is therefore crucial to

458

determine objectively and reliably how often the child behaves in certain ways. There are many different observation and recording techniques useful in measuring behavior meaningfully but they will not be discussed here. The point is simply that in addition to opinions, feelings, subjective reports, and test results it is of crucial importance to assess objectively the extent to which the problem behavior is happening. Furthermore, it is necessary to assess the behavior as it is embedded in other events, i.e., its antecedents and consequences.

ABC Analysis

When a child exhibits a problem behavior (e.g., cries) it is helpful to consider its relation to a sequence of other events, usually its relation to what typically happens just before (its antecedents) and to what typically happens just afterward (its consequences). The reason antecedents and consequences are important is that they usually have a lot of control over the behavior in question; and if they are the controlling variables, then they can be changed to modify the behavior. Thus, analysis of the behavior (B), its antecedents (A), and its consequences (C) represents an assessment strategy that should lead directly to an effective intervention. For example, direct observation might indicate that when a child cries (B) it is usually in response to having been teased by another child (A) and that he then receives attention from an adult (C) in the form of comforting, distraction (encouraging him to engage in another activity), or mild reprimand. Two sensible intervention strategies, then, would be: (a) to reduce or prevent teasing and (b) to shift adult attention from crying to noncrying behavior. Either strategy alone or the two in combination may quickly break up the tease-cry-get attention sequence that is troublesome.

Naturalistic Observation

If it is possible for observers to enter the typical environment in which the child is having difficulty, then there is no need to make guesses about exactly what goes on in those situations. Obviously, this is usually the ideal, even if it requires extra time, effort, and training on the part of the observers. Naturalistic observation is almost always best when the object is service to the child and the adult caretakers; it serves well for many research projects as well.

Laboratory Observation

There are circumstances in which laboratory observation is preferable to observation in the natural environment: (a) when the presence of observers or equipment has too many unwanted effects on the targets of observation, (b) when it is not feasible to move experimental equipment into the natural environment, (c) when adequate experimental control over the natural environment is not feasible, or (d) when the data of interest can be best obtained from a contrived or somewhat standardized laboratory setting, such as having an adult present a child with a particular task or setting up a particular play situation for the child. Note here that observation of the young child at play may be an extremely helpful means of assessment, not because of what the child's play may reveal about his unconscious motivations or hidden feelings but because learning to play is a crucial developmental task. One can learn a great deal about a child's cognitive and social competence by watching how he uses toys and play materials (e.g., how appropriate, imaginative, and spontaneous he is) and how he responds to other children or adults.

CAUSAL FACTORS

The reasoning of professionals who seek the causes of children's emotional disturbances is this: If we can find the cause, then we will know how to devise a cure and prevent the trouble from occurring in the first place. At first thought this seems to be a very rational proposition. However, the reasoning often does not apply to children's behavior problems because it is derived from (i.e., analogous to) reasoning about physical diseases. The first professionals to deal coherently with disorders of behavior were physicians, and they tended to see problems in thinking, feelings, and socializing as *diseases of the mind*. It is now apparent that the vast majority of difficulties emotionally disturbed people have are not diseases in any usual sense of the word, yet it remains common to speak of "mental illness" and "mental health." And, in addition, it is still a common belief that the discovery of the cause is possible and necessary for the cure of most emotional difficulties. Nevertheless, it is true even in medicine that cure is sometimes found before cause and that finding the cause of a disease does not mean its cure is just around the corner. Furthermore, in the realm of behavior it is extremely seldom that the cause of the problem can be pinpointed and verified, yet effective help can be provided without verification of the cause. One final point regarding the relationship of cause and cure is important to remember: Do not be misled into thinking that because a cure has been found (i.e., that a behavior problem has been successfully resolved) the cause has been identified. For example, it would be a mistake to assume that because a disturbed child began behaving appropriately when his parents changed the consequences for his behavior, the cause of his misbehavior in the first place was the consequences his parents had provided.

An important concept in thinking about the causes of emotional disturbance is the idea of *contributing factors*. A lot of different events or conditions may work together to cause the problem and it is the combination of factors, not any one in isolation, that is the cause. For example, it may be a combination of genetic factors, physical disease, parental mismanagement, and school failure that results in a child's maladaptive behavior. Some contributing factors, perhaps genetics, increase a child's susceptibility to disorders and are said to give the child a *predisposition* to develop problems. Other contributing factors may trigger or *precipitate* a behavior problem. Precipitating factors may be events such as a divorce, being teased by peers, failing an exam, or something else that provides the occasion for the child's undesirable behavior. Remember that stressful situations can be expected to result in temporary behavior problems in many normal children. The disturbed child does not rebound from situational stress—his behavioral difficulties are chronic, not transient.

Interactional-Transactional Model of Influence

Until recent years the usual pattern of thinking about causal factors was unidirectional; that is, the disturbed child was seen as being acted upon by others, as being the victim of others' behaviors. Now social scientists are recognizing that children affect their parents and other adults as much as children are affected by adults (see Bell & Harper, 1977; Sameroff & Chandler, 1975). Children, by their appearance and behavior, contribute to their own treatment and can make adults their victims. It is the *interactions* and *transactions* among disturbed children and other individuals in their environment that are problems. For example, an irritable, whiney infant should not be viewed just as a product of parental caretaking that produces irritable, whiney behavior but also as a source of concern to the parents, an infant likely to elicit less than optimum caretaking responses from most adults. Children and adults appear to influence each other reciprocally. A mother's responsiveness to and stimulation of her young child may increase the child's cognitive development, while the child's positive social and emotional responses to the mother reciprocally increase her responsiveness and sensitivity to the child's needs (see Clarke-Stewart, 1973).

An interactional model of influence does not apply only to parent-child relations. Interactive effects are obvious among siblings, schoolmates, playmates, and teacher-child relations. Even the child's physical and emotional status reciprocally affect each other (being ill increases the probability that the child will exhibit undesirable behavior, and depression or anxiety increases the child's chances of becoming ill).

Biological Factors

Hypotheses about biological causes of behavior disorders include these:

- they are a result of neurological defects
- they are a result of biochemical defects
- they are a result of genetic defects
- they are a combination of one or more of the above

The biological and behavioral sciences are not yet advanced enough to demonstrate that any one of these hypotheses is true for the majority of cases. True, there are cases in which injury, disease, chemical factors, or genetic inheritance are known to result in aberrant behavior, but these represent a very small percentage of cases. Most of the time there is simply no convincing scientific evidence that there is anything biologically wrong with a disturbed child. Biological causes are more likely to be found for severe and profound disturbances than for mild or moderate behaviors, but specific biological causes for autism and childhood schizophrenia are yet to be confirmed by research.

One type of contributing biological factor that has been suggested is *temperament* (see Thomas, Chess, & Birch, 1968). From birth, children may show a characteristic behavioral style or temperament (apparently a pattern determined by genetic and neurochemical factors). *Temperament* may be defined by things like general level of activity, rhythm or regularity in biological functions, approach to or withdrawal from new stimuli, adaptability to new situations, intensity of reactions, level of responsiveness to stimuli, distractibility or persistence in activities, and so on. A "difficult" temperament (characterized by irregularity, irritability, high intensity of response, negative responses to new stimuli, etc.) does not necessarily mean a child will be emotionally disturbed, nor does an "easy" temperament mean that a child will be immune to disturbance. But in interaction with the way adults respond to him, a child's temperament may be a significant contributing factor.

Parental Factors

There is never any argument from rational people about the fact that parents influence their children's behavior. The arguments concern how and to what extent parents contribute to making children disturbed. Traditional psychoanalytic thought gives supreme importance to the mother-child relationship, but modern social-learning theory leads to a broader view. As reviews of research by Becker (1964) and Martin (1975) have shown, the outcome of parental-management techniques depends on the *consistency* of the parents and the interaction between the child's temperamental characteristics and the parents' behavior. Sensitivity to children's needs, love-oriented disciplinary techniques, reinforcement (e.g., attention and praise) for appropriate behavior, and consistency will facilitate emotional development. Conversely, general laxness in discipline combined with hostile, cruel, rejecting responses to misbehavior will foster behavioral problems. Beyond these simple generalizations, however, it is clear there are many ways to be a good parent and one cannot write a detailed prescription for parental management that will fit every case.

Other Psychosocial Factors

Home and Community Environment

Besides parents, siblings, peers, and community standards affect a child's behavior. Broken, disorganized homes and poverty-stricken neighborhoods in which the predominant models of behavior observed by children are gang members or delinquents certainly can be expected to have a negative influence on a young child's behavior. However, many children do survive deplorable home and community conditions without exhibiting behavior that results in their being labeled emotionally disturbed. Part of the reason they are not considered disturbed is that their behavior is adaptive for the situation in which they find themselves. Were they to exhibit the same behavior in a different setting or under a different set of circumstances, they might well be considered disturbed.

Television

A lot of emotional words have been spoken and written regarding the influence of television on young children. Aside from any cognitive influences it may exert, there is concern for how it may affect children's social behavior, particularly their aggression and prosocial acts. There is agreement among most researchers that young children watch a lot of TV and that watching prosocial programs (e.g., Mister Rogers' Neighborhood, Captain Kangaroo) does not lead to undesirable behavior and may increase prosocial responses like helping, cooperating, and sharing. However, there is hot disagreement regarding the influence of watching violent programs. Lesser (1977) reviewed the research and concluded that there is little or no good research data showing that watching violence causes children to become more aggressive. Stein and Friedrich (1975) reviewed much the same research and concluded that watching TV violence does indeed tend to raise children's level of aggression. Certainly there is no sound evidence indicating that viewing TV violence makes young children less aggressive or more prosocial.

School

It is possible that the young child's experiences at school contribute to emotional disturbance, even though the school is supposed to be a major socializing institution. When the child comes to school, he encounters many new demands and stresses. Parents' and teachers' expectations for performance may be far too high or far too low, making the child feel either inadequate or undesirable. There are schools in which discipline is too lax or too rigid for the child's previous experience and temperament. Too, it is possible the child might be ignored as long as he is not causing any trouble but gets a lot of attention for misbehavior, a situation almost certain to teach that the way to "be somebody" is to be disruptive.

Causal Factors and Risk

Part of the reason for wanting to find the causes of emotional disturbance is the desire to prevent disorders from developing. Specific causal factors that operate in isolation have not been found for the vast majority of disturbed children but a variety of possible contributing causes have been noted. When children are exposed to these contributing factors, they are said to be "at risk" for developing emotional disorders. Currently, there are "risk studies" underway to identify the factors that do give rise to disturbance, assessing their relative contribution and interaction with other factors, and devising means of prevention. Mosher and Gunderson (1974) have noted that in schizophrenia research

> By following vulnerable individuals from their earliest years through the period of risk, . . investigators hope to identify pre-existing biochemical, physiological, psychological, or life-history characteristics which consistently differentiate those who ultimately develop schizophrenia from those who do not (p. 13).

At this time we know that poverty, malnutrition, neglect or abuse by parents, failure at school, and other factors give a child an increased chance of having behavioral difficulties. It is these children at risk who should be the focus of prevention programs.

INTERVENTION

Ask a group of professionals (psychiatrists, psychologists, special educators, social workers) how to help disturbed children and you will probably get a grab-bag of answers. Why? Partly because different members of any one of these professions are likely to be guided by different conceptual models. A conceptual model is a way of viewing the nature of the problem and, based on that theoretical view, designing techniques of dealing with the problem. There are several different conceptual models that today's professionals may choose from. Five of them are outlined in Table 15-1. Although it is very likely that a competent professional will be guided *primarily* by the basic assumptions and strategies of a single conceptual model, few people are so dogmatic as to reject completely *everything* about other, competing points of view. That is, most individuals recognize that there are *some* useful insights, *some* valuable practices associated with each of the conceptual models presented in Table 15-1 (and perhaps other points of view as well; see Hallahan & Kauffman, 1978; Kauffman, 1977; Kauffman & Lewis, 1974; Reeve & Kauffman, 1978; Rhodes & Paul, 1978; Wolman, 1978, for elaboration).

All conceptual models do not enjoy the same amount of support from empirical research. Probably there is much more scientific support for the behavioral approach or model than for any competing view. That is why a few basic behavioral strategies and techniques for dealing with disturbed behavior are discussed here.

Behavioral Intervention

A great deal has been written during the past ten years about behavior modification, its philosophy, techniques, successes, and problems (see Leitenberg, 1976).

Table 15-1 Approaches to Educating Disturbed Children

	PSYCHOANALYTIC APPROACH	*PSYCHO-EDUCATIONAL APPROACH*	*HUMANISTIC APPROACH*	*ECOLOGICAL APPROACH*	*BEHAVIORAL APPROACH*
THE PROBLEM	A pathological imbalance among the dynamic parts of the mind (id, superego, ego).	Involves both underlying psychiatric disorders and the readily observable misbehavior and underachievement of the child.	The disturbed child is out of touch with his own feelings and can't find self-fulfillment in traditional educational settings.	The child interacts poorly with his environment; child and environment affect each other reciprocally and negatively.	The child has learned inappropriate responses and failed to learn appropriate ones.
PURPOSE OF EDUCATIONAL PRACTICES	Use of psychoanalytic principles to help uncover underlying mental pathology.	Concern for unconscious motivation/underlying conflicts *and* academic achievement/positive surface behavior.	Emphasis on enhancing child's self-direction, self-evaluation, and emotional involvement in learning.	Attempt to alter entire social system so that it will support desirable behavior in child when it is withdrawn.	Manipulation of child's immediate environment and the consequences of his behavior.
CHARACTERISTICS OF TEACHING METHODS	Reliance on individual psychotherapy for child and parents; little emphasis on academic achievement; highly permissive atmosphere.	Emphasis on meeting individual needs of the child; reliance on projects and creative arts.	Use of nontraditional educational settings in which teacher serves as resource and catalyst rather than as director of activities; nonauthoritarian, open, affective, personal atmosphere.	Involves all aspects of a child's life, including classroom, family, neighborhood, and community, in teaching the child useful life and educational skills.	Involves measurement of responses and subsequent analyses of behaviors in order to change them; emphasis on reward for appropriate behavior.

Source: Daniel P. Hallahan and James M. Kauffman, *EXCEPTIONAL CHILDREN: Introduction to Special Education,* © 1978, p. 209. Reprinted by permission of Prentice-Hall, Inc., Englewood Cliffs, New Jersey.

No attempt is made here to provide anything beyond a brief discussion and illustration of a few strategies with young children. Do not assume that the behavioral approach consists of only these few methods or that behavioral techniques can often be successfully applied without appropriate training and clinical skill.

First, it should be noted that the behavioral approach involves direct observation and measurement of behavior as an assessment strategy. The child's problem behavior is defined in measurable terms so that a reliable, objective, daily record of its occurrence can be kept. The direct daily measurement of behavior is useful both in assessing the extent of the problem to begin with and in judging the success of the methods used to modify it.

Second, the fundamental assumption underlying the behavioral approach is that the most important factor controlling behavior is its consequences—what happens immediately after the behavior occurs. Therefore, the majority of intervention techniques have to do with changing the consequences a child experiences when he behaves in a certain way. Consequences may be changed not just to decrease the occurrence of inappropriate behavior but to increase appropriate behavior as well. The idea is to use consequences to *teach* new behavior patterns to the disturbed child.

Three basic techniques for changing behavior are extinction, time out, and reinforcement. Extinction and time out are ways of decreasing inappropriate behavior. Reinforcement can be used to increase desirable behavior and to decrease undesirable behavior as well (when an alternative behavior to the undesirable one is reinforced). Examples are given here of how each technique has been used to decrease problem behavior of a young disturbed child.

Extinction

A behaviorist assumes that a person keeps on doing what he does because reinforcing consequences follow his acts. Therefore, if the reinforcing consequences can be kept from occurring, the behavior will stop too. The idea behind extinction is to find the reinforcers for a behavior and put an end to them. A case described by Williams (1959) illustrates the idea. The parents of a 21-month-old boy were seriously troubled by their son's tyrannical behavior at bedtime. At night and at his afternoon nap, he would insist that an adult sit vigilantly by his bed until he fell asleep. This required an hour and a half or two of an adult's time each time he was put to bed. If his parent tried to read or do something else rather than give complete attention to him or if his parent tried to sneak out of the room when he appeared to be asleep, he would throw a temper fit. Williams worked from the assumption that the parents' acquiescence to the child's demands were reinforcers for his tantrums and that if his tantrums were no longer reinforced by the parents' compliance with his bratty ultimatums, then his tantrums would end. Therefore, the parents were instructed to put their son to bed in a pleasant, relaxed manner (making sure before putting him to bed that he was not hungry, wet, or without a nightlight), leave the room, close the door, and not return regardless of how he might rage and scream. After a 45-minute tantrum the first time he was put to bed, the child quickly learned to go to bed without demanding unreasonable attention; i.e., extinction worked.

Time Out

Imagine a situation in which you cannot identify a single reinforcer for a problem behavior or you simply have no way of keeping the reinforcing consequence from happening unless you completely remove the child from the situation. Under such circumstances time out might be a good technique to use. Time out means that as a consequence for a specific undesirable behavior the individual is confronted with a situation in which he cannot be reinforced—it is *time out from reinforcement for a while.* (Time out is a very useful technique but is open to abuses; see Gast & Nelson, 1977, for guidelines.) Often, this means removing the child from ongoing activities for a short while; in effect, isolating him briefly from the situation in which his misbehavior occurs. Such was the case reported by Wolf, Risley, and Mees (1964), in which they were called upon to deal with the behavior of Dicky, a 3½-year-old boy diagnosed as a childhood schizophrenic. Dicky had severe tantrums, frequently injured himself, and during his tantrums threw his glasses. It was extremely important for him to wear his glasses because he had cataracts, and without his glasses his vision would deteriorate. So Dicky was placed in his room—isolated from social contact, given a time out—immediately whenever he started a tantrum. He was kept in time out for ten minutes or until he was quiet (if his tantrum continued during time out). The time-out consequence successfully rid Dicky of his undesirable, dangerous behavior.

Reinforcement

Wolf et al. did not stop with halting Dicky's tantrums, important as that task was. They realized that Dicky had to be taught some appropriate behaviors, that extinction and time out for inappropriate behaviors are "dead end" techniques unless accompanied by positive teaching procedures. Reinforcement means finding a behavior you want to occur and making sure that it is followed immediately and consistently by consequences the child sees as desirable. You have to start with what the child already does, some step he takes in the right direction, and then gradually increase what you expect before giving the reward. Wolf and his fellow behavior therapists wanted Dicky to wear his glasses. But since he wouldn't tolerate having them on his face, they began by rewarding him with little bits of food and praise for just holding empty glass frames. After he got used to that, they reinforced him for putting empty frames up to his eyes, then for holding plain lenses up to his eyes, next for looking through prescription lenses, and so on until step-by-step they taught him to wear prescription lenses.

Sometimes reinforcing desirable behavior reduces problem behavior, especially when the behavior you reinforce is the opposite of the one that is a problem. Kauffman and Hallahan (1973) worked with a 6-year-old boy who was extremely hyperactive and aggressive. This budding Hun would pummel anyone who got in his way (child or adult) and had habits of throwing, banging, stomping, or otherwise abusing play materials. Since extinction and time out were not reasonable alternatives in the preschool classroom the boy was attending, the teacher was cued to reinforce the boy with praise and a small extrinsic reward if he had been nonviolent for a little while (as short a time as 20 seconds in the beginning). In this case, the problem (rough physical behavior) was greatly reduced by offering reinforcement for gradually longer periods during which the opposite type of behavior was exhibited.

Behavioral Strategies for Aggression and Withdrawal

As discussed earlier, the two major types of maladaptive behavior shown by children are aggression and withdrawal, and much behavioral research has gone into developing methods for dealing effectively with them. More effective intervention strategies are still needed, but at present the available research supports the following:

Aggression

Show the child models (adults or other children, live or filmed, human or cartoon characters) of how to respond nonaggressively to frustrating or aggression-provoking situations. Use role-playing and rehearsal to give the child practice in being nonaggressive in hypothetical situations. Give rewards for specific nonaggressive behaviors (e.g., playing without hitting) and withhold rewards for aggression (e.g., do not give in to tantrums). If punishment for aggression is necessary, emphasize withdrawal of rewards or restriction of activity (e.g., time out) rather than physical punishment.

Withdrawal

Show the child models of children who have fun playing with others or overcoming their fear of an object, place, activity, or situation. Give children practice, through role-playing and rehearsal, in using specific social skills. Arrange play conditions and materials conducive to social interaction. Offer rewards for approximations of appropriate social behavior. Allow fearful children to approach feared situations gradually while experiencing pleasurable activities. Prompt the child's peers to approach the child and initiate desirable social interaction.

These are not revolutionary new techniques. They are commonsensical methods supported by empirical research. Perhaps it should not be surprising that behavioral science is confirming many "old fashioned" ideas about child management.

Current Trends in Intervention

Two recent developments in the behavioral approach are worthy of note: the experimental comparison of drugs and behavior modification in treating hyperactivity and developing cognitive-behavior modification techniques with disturbed children. Both developments represent an attempt to extend and elaborate on the techniques already discussed. (For a detailed discussion of these trends, see Kauffman & Hallahan, 1979.)

Drugs vs. Behavior Modification

Drugs, especially central nervous system stimulants, and behavior modification have become popular for managing children who are hyperactive. Both approaches have advantages and disadvantages, and both have frightened people who either do not understand them or understand them and are concerned about their possible misuse. Researchers are now beginning to compare the two approaches rationally, attempting to determine the circumstances under which each method works best. So far, the comparative research has not been extensive, and therefore not many conclusions can be reached. However, it is clear that drugs affect children in very different, unpredictable ways, that they do have a calming effect on some children, and that they do not help most children learn unless a good teaching program is also provided. Behavior modification has the distinct advantage of being designed to teach appropriate behavior. It appears that each child's responses to each type of treatment must be assessed individually, through direct daily measurement of behavior.

Cognitive Behavior Modification

Many behavior-modification proponents have begun to realize that manipulating consequences is somewhat of an oversimplification of successful behavior-change strategies. They are now looking for ways to get individuals more involved cognitively—to think more about what is happening to them and why—in the behavior-change process. Even young children are being taught to talk to themselves about what they are doing so that they can exercise more self-control. An example of self-instructional techniques was provided by Bornstein and Quevillon (1976), working with three 4-year-old boys in a Head Start classroom—serious behavior problems who seldom paid attention, and were hyperactive and aggressive. In fact, direct daily measurement of class behavior during baseline assessment showed they were paying attention and doing their assigned work less than 20 percent of the time. Each boy was given an individual two-hour session with an adult who first demonstrated self-instruction, then had the child practice the self-instruction aloud, and then practice silently. Self-instruction consisted of questions like: "What does the teacher want me to do?", then rehearsing the answer, such as, "Oh, that's right, I'm supposed to copy the picture"; then giving instructions about how to perform, for example, "OK, first I draw a line here," and finally reinforcing oneself, perhaps by saying, "How about that; I really did that one well!" After receiving instruction in how to use these self-instructional techniques, each boy's behavior in class improved very dramatically.

Behavioral intervention is being refined and elaborated so that it is more efficient, more effective, and more in the hands of the person whose behavior needs changing. New developments should move us closer to the ultimate goal of intervention—teaching emotionally disturbed children to control themselves.

Making Behavioral Change More Worthwhile

When working with a disturbed child one always hopes the child's behavior will improve in various ways and in various settings, and that the change will last—that generalization and maintenance will come about. If generalized and lasting changes in behavior do not occur, it is easy to get the feeling that intervention was not really worthwhile. One of the most frustrating things that can happen (aside from being unable to get the child to change at all) is to see the child make a lot of progress in your class but not at home or anywhere else, or to see the child learn each new task as if it had no logical relationship to any of the other tasks learned. And one of the biggest disappointments in dealing with a disturbed child is to see improvement as a result (you believe) of your intervention, followed by reverting to old habits.

Researchers have not been able to find any quick and easy answers to generalization and maintenance problems. There are ways one can apparently increase the chances that generalization and maintenance will occur, but these strategies are not, for the most part, supported by a lot of research data with disturbed children (see Stokes and Baer, 1977). One strategy is to try to teach the child self-control techniques, as discussed previously, under the assumption that behavioral change will be more general and last longer if the child is not dependent on external control. A second strategy is to teach behavior-control techniques to a variety of people the child comes into contact with, particularly his parents and family. The assumption is that the child's behavior will be responsive to environmental conditions, and if more of the people who care for the child are trained to manage him skillfully then his behavior will change in more settings and be more permanent. Furthermore, the training of the child should take place in a number of different settings if behavior change is to generalize. A third strategy is gradually to change the contingencies of reinforcement, making them closer to "natural" conditions under the assumption that the child can be weaned away from artificial or highly contrived consequences. For example, the child might gradually receive reinforcement less and less frequently and gradually begin receiving praise instead of food as a reward.

It is perhaps a mistake to believe that children can be immunized against behavioral problems. The behavior of all children appears responsive, eventually, to environmental conditions, and it may be unreasonable to expect any child to stand up for very long against a set of conditions known to be misbehavior-producing. An ethical, morally defensible approach to disturbed children must include careful scrutiny of the child's environment and remediation of any serious environmental deficits. To focus on what is wrong with the child alone is not just irrational but places an unfair burden of responsibility on the child.

SUMMARY

Disturbed children chronically exhibit behavior that causes discomfort to others and/or to themselves. Identifying a child as disturbed requires subjective appraisal of the child's behavior; there are no objective standards or tests to go by. Some of the most noticeable characteristics of disturbed children are: inability to learn not explained by intellectual, sensory, or health factors; inability to establish and maintain adequate interpersonal relationships; inappropriate behavior and feelings; pervasive unhappiness or depression; and physical complaints or fears associated with personal problems. The yardstick to use in deciding whether a child is disturbed is whether his behavior is developmentally inappropriate to a marked extent and persistent.

Traditional psychiatric classifications for disturbed children have not been of much use. However, the behaviors disturbed children exhibit have been statistically clustered into three major groups: conduct disorder, personality disorder, and immaturity. The two major dimensions of disturbed behavior are aggression (conduct disorder) and withdrawal (personality disorder and immaturity).

Two levels of severity of emotional disturbance can be described: mild/moderate (neurotic) and severe/profound (psychotic). Generally, more severely disturbed children are distinguished by higher rates of deviant behavior, problems that are more chronic, an earlier age of onset of problems, and poorer prognosis. Many severely/profoundly disturbed children are characterized by one or more of the following: extreme aggression, self-injurious behavior, self-stimulation, language and speech deviations, unrelatedness to people, cognitive deficits, perceptual deviations, and lack of daily living skills.

Disturbed children, on the average, are lower in IQ, academic achievement, and socioeconomic status than normals. More boys than girls are considered disturbed. The behavioral characteristic associated most clearly with poor prognosis for mildly/moderately disturbed children is hostile aggression.

Assessment is necessary to define the problems, plan intervention, evaluate progress, and arrive at a prognosis. Adequate assessment includes standardized testing (usually screening, IQ, and achievement tests), behavior rating scales or checklists, interviews, and, most importantly, behavioral observation. Direct observation and measurement include an ABC analysis, i.e., analysis of antecedents and consequences in addition to the behavior. Observations of behavior may be made in the natural environment of the child or in laboratory settings.

The causes of most behavior problems of children are unknown. Biological, parental, and other psychosocial factors (home and community environment, television, school) may contribute to emotional problems. Some contributing factors may predispose a child to develop a problem, whereas other factors may precipitate problems. An interactional transactional model of influence recognizes that a child influences adults as much as adults influence him, i.e., that effects are reciprocal. Preventive efforts should focus on children who are at risk for developing behavior problems.

Intervention approaches differ widely, partly because of the different conceptual models they are based on. More empirical research supports the behavioral conceptual model than any other. Direct daily measurement is a primary feature of behavioral intervention. Three basic behavioral techniques for dealing with problems are extinction, time out, and reinforcement. Behavioral research supports specific strategies for dealing with aggression and withdrawal. New developments in the behavioral approach include comparison of drugs and behavior modification in dealing with hyperactivity and the use of cognitive-behavior modifications techniques. Behavioral change can be made more worthwhile if strategies can be found to promote generalization and maintanence.

REFERENCES

Becker, W. C. Consequences of different kinds of parental discipline. In M. L. Hoffman & L. W. Hoffman (Eds.), *Review of child development research* (Vol. 1). New York: Russell Sage Foundation, 1964.

Bell, R. Q., & Harper, L. V. *Child effects on adults.* Hillsdale, N. J.: Lawrence Erlbaum, 1977.

Bornstein, P. H., & Quevillon, R. P. The effects of a self-instructional package on overactive preschool boys. *Journal of Applied Behavior Analysis,* 1976, *9,* 179-188.

Bower, E. M. *Early identification of emotionally handicapped children in school* (2nd ed.). Springfield, Ill.: Charles C. Thomas, 1969.

Bower, E. M., & Lambert, N. M. *A process for in-school screening of children with emotional handicaps.* Princeton, N. J.: Educational Testing Service, 1962.

Clarke-Stewart, A. K. Interactions between mothers and their young children: Characteristics and consequences. *Monographs of the Society for Research in Child Development,* 1973, *38* (6-7, Serial No. 153).

Evans, I. M., & Nelson, R. O. Assessment of child behavior problems. In A. R. Ciminero, K. S. Calhoun, & H. E. Adams (Eds.), *Handbook of behavioral assessment.* New York: Wiley, 1977.

Gast, D. L., & Nelson, C. M. Legal and ethical considerations for the use of timeout in special education settings. *Journal of Special Education,* 1977, *11,* 457-467.

Hallahan, D. P., & Kauffman, J. M. *Exceptional children: Introduction to special education.* Englewood Cliffs: Prentice-Hall, 1978.

Hobbs, N. (Ed.). *Issues in the classification of children* (Vols. 1 & 2). San Francisco: Jossey-Bass, 1975.

Kauffman, J. M. *Characteristics of children's behavior disorders.* Columbus, Ohio: Charles E. Merrill, 1977.

Kauffman, J. M., & Hallahan, D. P. Control of rough physical behavior using novel contingencies and directive teaching. *Perceptual and Motor Skills,* 1973, *36,* 1225-1226.

Kauffman, J. M., & Hallahan, D. P. Learning disability and hyperactivity (with comments on minimal brain dysfunction). In B. B. Lahey & A. E. Kazdin (Eds.), *Advances in child clinical psychology.* New York: Plenum, 1979.

Kauffman, J. M., & Lewis, C. D. (Eds.), *Teaching children with behavior disorders: Personal perspectives.* Columbus, Ohio: Charles E. Merrill, 1974.

Kaufhold, S., & Kauffman, J. M. Sammy: Frequent crying spells. In J. Worell & C. M. Nelson (Eds), *Managing instructional problems.* New York: McGraw-Hill, 1974.

Leitenberg, H. (Ed.). *Handbook of behavior modification and behavior therapy.* Englewood Cliffs: Prentice-Hall, 1976.

Lesser, H. *Television and the preschool child.* New York: Academic Press, 1977.

Martin, B. Parent-child relations. In F. D. Horowitz (Ed.), *Review of child development research* (Vol. 4). Chicago: University of Chicago Press, 1975.

Mosher, L. R., & Gunderson, J. G. The study of children at risk—A research strategy whose time has come. *Schizophrenia Bulletin,* No. 8, Spring, 1974.

Pate, J. E., & Webb, W. W. *First grade screening test manual.* Circle Pines, Minn.: American Guidance Service, 1967.

Quay, H. C. Patterns of aggression, withdrawal, and immaturity. In H. C. Quay & J. S. Werry (Eds.), *Psychopathological disorders of childhood.* New York: Wiley, 1972.

Reeve, R., & Kauffman, J. M. The behavior disordered. In N. G. Haring (Ed.), *Behavior of exceptional children* (2nd ed.). Columbus, Ohio: Charles E. Merrill, 1978.

Rhodes, W. C., & Paul, J. L. *Emotionally disturbed and deviant children: New views and approaches.* Englewood Cliffs: Prentice-Hall, 1978.

Sameroff, A. J., & Chandler, M. J. Reproductive risk and the continuum of caretaking causalty. In F. D. Horowitz (Ed.), *Review of child development research* (Vol. 4). Chicago: University of Chicago Press, 1975.

Spivack, G., & Shure, M. B. *Social adjustment of young children.* San Francisco: Jossey-Bass, 1974.

Stein, A. H., & Friedrich, L. K. Impact of television on children and youth. In E. M. Hetherington (Ed.), *Review of child development research* (Vol. 5). Chicago: University of Chicago Press, 1975.

Stokes, T. F., and Baer, D. M. An implicit technology of generalization. *Journal of Applied Behavior Analysis,* 1977, *10,* 349-367.

Thomas, A., Chess, S., & Birch, H. G. *Temperament and behavior disorders in children.* New York: New York University Press, 1968.

Wallace, G., & Kauffman, J. M. *Teaching children with learning problems* (2nd ed.). Columbus, Ohio: Charles E. Merrill, 1978.

Williams, C. D. The elimination of tantrums by extinction procedures. *Journal of Abnormal and Social Psychology,* 1959, *59,* 269.

Wolf, M. M., Risley, T. R., & Mees, H. Application of operant conditioning procedures to the behavior problems of an autistic child. *Behavior Research and Therapy,* 1964, *1,* 305-312.

Wolman, B. B. (Ed.). *Handbook of treatment of mental disorders in childhood and adolescence.* Englewood Cliffs: Prentice-Hall, 1978.

473

Appendixes

An Annotated Guide to Selected Assessment Measures for Use in Early Childhood[*]

GENERAL COGNITIVE MEASURES

Bayley Scales of Infant Development
Columbia Mental Maturity Scale
Culture Fair Intelligence Tests
Detroit Tests of Learning Aptitudes
Gates-Macginitie Readiness Skills Test
Hiskey-Nebraska Test of Learning Aptitudes
Leiter International Performance Scale
McCarthy Scales of Children's Abilities
Merrill-Palmer Scale of Mental Tests
Peabody Picture Vocabulary Test
Slosson Intelligence Test
Stanford-Binet Intelligence Scale
Wechsler Intelligence Scale for Children
Wechsler Preschool and Primary Scale of Intelligence

---

[*]These instruments have been selected because they are in general use. Prospective users of any of these measures will want to assure themselves of the effectiveness of a particular instrument for their needs. Therefore, you will want to examine carefully the administration and technical manuals for information regarding a test's reliability and validity, sampling procedures, basis for deriving norms, physical and other limitations that may alter a child's performance, etc. The *Mental Measurements Yearbook*[**] contains review information that will be helpful in determining if a test will fit your particular needs.

The publisher and the authors do not intend this presentation to be an endorsement of these particular instruments.

[**]Buros, O. K. (Ed.) *Seventh Mental Measurements Yearbook,* Highland Park, N.J.: Gryphon Press, 1971.

VISUAL-MOTOR AND VISUAL PERCEPTION

Bender Gestalt Test for Young Children
Beery Developmental Test of Visual-Motor Integration
Frostig Developmental Test of Visual Perception
Motor-Free Visual Perception Test

SENSORY INTEGRATION

Southern California Sensory Integration Test

LANGUAGE, SPEECH AND HEARING

Arizona Articulation Proficiency Scale
Assessment of Children's Language Comprehension
Auditory Discrimination Test
Houston Test of Language Development
Illinois Test of Psycholinguistic Abilities
Northwestern Syntax Screening Test
Preschool Language Scale
Test for Auditory Comprehension of Language
Utah Test of Language Development

BEHAVIOR RATING SCALES

Adaptive Behavior Scale
California Preschool Social Competency Scale
Child Behavior Rating Scale
Cooperative Preschool Inventory
Denver Developmental Screening Test
Gesell Developmental Schedules
Lexington Developmental Scale
Preschool Attainment Record
Vineland Social Maturity Scale

GENERAL COGNITIVE MEASURES

Bayley Scales of Infant Development

Author: Nancy Bayley

Publisher: The Psychological Corporation

Scores: Mental Scale Score; Motor Scale Score; Infant Behavior Record

Ages: Birth to 2-6 years

Administration: This test should be administered by a trained examiner in an individual setting; approximately one hour.

Child Performance: The ability to hear, see, vocalize, verbalize, and perform motorically is needed.

Test Description: Mental Scale: measures sensory-perceptual acuities and discriminations, early acquisition of object constancy and memory, learning and problem-solving ability, the beginning of verbal communication, and early indications of the ability to generalize and form classifications.

Motor Scale: measures the degree of control of the body and coordination of large and small muscles such as balance and manual dexterity.

Infant Behavior Record: deals with social orientation, emotional variables, how the child relates to objects, motivation for specific actions, activity level and reactivity to stimuli, and areas of sensory interest.

Columbia Mental Maturity Scale

Authors: B. Burgemeister, L. H. Blum, I. Lorge

Publisher: Harcourt, Brace, Jovanovich

Scores: Age Deviation Score (equivalent to I.Q. score), Percentile Rank, Stanine, and Maturity Index.

Ages: 3-0 years to 10-0 years

Administration: Individually administered by an examiner familiar with its use; no time limit, but usually takes from 15 to 30 minutes.

Child Performance: Hear and understand verbal directions, but verbal responses are not required. The child points to the response of his choice. Adequate vision is required.

Test Description: Three to five pictures appear on a 6-by-19-inch card and the child is required to indicate which one of the items on the card does not belong with the other items. Adequate vision and good visual perception are needed.

Culture Fair Intelligence Tests (Scale 1)

Authors: R. Cattell and A. Cattell

Publisher: Institute for Personality and Ability Testing

Scores: Mental Age and I.Q.

Administration: Trained examiner required to give and score. Scale 1 requires about 22 minutes to give, and some individual testing is required.

Child Performance: Requires visual and auditory ability.

Test Description: Eight subtests are contained in Scale 1, four of these must be given individually.

Detroit Tests of Learning Aptitude

Authors: H. J. Baker and B. Leland

Publisher: Bobbs-Merrill

Scores: Picture and Verbal Absurdities, Pictorial and Verbal Opposites, Motor Speech and Precision, Auditory Attention Span for Unrelated Words, Oral Commissions, Social Adjustment A and B, Visual Attention Span for Objects and for Letters, Orientation (conceptual relationships), Free Associations, Memory for Design, Number Ability, Disarranged Pictures, Oral Directions, and Likenesses and Differences.

Ages: 3 through adult

Administration: Trained individuals give usually 9 to 13 of the subtests, depending on age and handicap; time varies (usually 30 to 90 minutes).

Child Performance: Verbal, auditory, visual, and fine motor behavior is required.

Gates-Macginitie Readiness Skills Test

Authors: A. I. Gates and W. H. MacGinitie

Publisher: Teachers College Press

Scores: Eight: Listening, Comprehension, Auditory Discrimination, Visual Discrimination, Following Directions, Letter Recognition, Visual-Motor Coordination, Auditory Blending, and Word Recognition (optional). A total score is also possible.

Ages: 5 and 6 years

Administration: Can be given by teacher or paraprofessional; is untimed and takes about two hours.

Child Performance: Child is required to use auditory, visual, and motor abilities.

Test Description: A standardized readiness test which can be used to determine child's strengths and weaknesses regarding school-related academic abilities.

Hiskey-Nebraska Test of Learning Aptitude (for deaf children)

Author: M. S. Hiskey

Publisher: Union College Press, Lincoln, Nebraska

Scores: Learning Age and Learning Quotient for Deaf Children; Mental Age and Deviation I.Q. score for hearing children.

Ages: 3-0 to 17-0 years

Administration: Requires individual administration by a trained examiner; approximately one hour.

Child Performance: See fine detail in pictures and manipulate two-and three-dimensional materials.

Test Description: Tasks include matching bead and block patterns from direct examples, pictures, and then from memory. Folding paper into specific patterns, and visual-memory tasks (i.e., remembering a series of pictures or a series of printed digits) is required. Concrete and abstract-visual association tasks are presented.

Leiter International Performance Scale

Author: R. G. Leiter

Publisher: Western Psychological Services

Scores: Mental Age: Ratio I.Q. score

Ages: 2-0 to 18-0 years

Administration: A trained examiner in an individual setting is needed; approximately one hour.

Child Performance: The child manipulates small blocks that have a visual stimulus on one side into a series of square slots designed to hold the blocks. No verbal directions or responses are necessary. Good visual acuity is needed. A motor-impaired child is not penalized as none of the items in the preschool range are timed.

Test Description: The following conceptual areas are purportedly measured by subtests:

Figure Ground Discrimination	Object Recognition
Spatial Relations	Visual Discrimination
Visual Closure	Perceptual Constancy
Perception of Position	Perception of Spatial Relationships
Classification	Number Concepts
Sequencing	Similarities
Visual Association	Visual Sequential Memory

McCarthy Scales of Children's Abilities

Author: D. McCarthy

Publisher: The Psychological Corporation

Scores: Verbal Score; Perceptual-Performance Score; Quantitative Scale Score; General Cognitive Index (composed of the Verbal, Perceptual-Performance, and Quantitative Scores); a Memory Score; and a Motor Score.

Ages: 2½ to 8½ years

Administration: Requires individual examination by a trained examiner; approximately one hour.

Child Performance: Verbal scale: children respond using words, phrases, or sentences. Performance scale: children are not required to respond verbally, just to manipulate objects (but must be able to understand oral directions). Requires adequate vision.

Test Description: Verbal Scale: measures ability to express one's self verbally and the maturity of verbal concepts. Perceptual-Performance: measures motor skills plus ability to perceive pictures and three-dimensional objects accurately. Quantitative Scale: measures aptitude for numbers and understanding of quantitative words. Motor Scale: assesses fine and gross motor tasks, and eye-and-hand dominance.

Merrill-Palmer Scale of Mental Tests

Author: R. Stutsman

Publisher: Eastern Psychological Services

Scores: Mental Age; Deviation scores from the mean

Ages: 18 months to 6 years

Administration: Requires individual administration by a trained examiner; time is about ½ to 1 hour.

Child Performance: Manipulates buttons, blocks, paper and pencil, and puzzles, and vision should be adequate for these tasks. Children are also required to understand oral directions. Verbal responses required are: repetition of single words, repetition of phrases; single-word responses to questions.

Test Description: A series of tasks which are mostly performance in nature, and many are highly speeded.

Peabody Picture Vocabulary Test

Author: L. M. Dunn

Publisher: American Guidance Service

Scores: I.Q. Score; Mental Age; Percentile Rank

Ages: 2-6 to 18 years

Administration: Requires individual administration but the examiner does not have to be highly trained; time is about 10 to 15 minutes.

Child Performance: Children listen to a cue word and then point to a picture representing the cue word; requires adequate hearing and auditory perception plus adequate vision. Some motor coordination is also needed.

Test Description: Consists of four pictures to a page; the child must determine which picture corresponds best to a cue word. Items range from simple nouns to highly abstract verbs and concepts.

Slossen Intelligence Test

Author: R. Slossen

Publisher: Slossen Educational Publications

Score: I.Q. score

Ages: Infant to adult

Administration: The Slossen is individually administered, and can be used by teachers. It is a short test and easy to give.

Child Performance: Varied

Test Description: Based on Gesell Scale and Stanford-Binet Scale items. Many verbal responses required.

Stanford-Binet Intelligence Scale (Form L-M)

Authors: L. Terman and M. Merrill

Publisher: Houghton-Mifflin

Scores: I.Q. Score; Mental Age

Ages: 2-0 to 22-0 years

Administration: An individual setting and a trained examiner are needed; approximately one hour.

Child Performance: Understand oral directions; some language is required to respond to many of the items. Fine-motor responses are required for items such as bead stringing, pointing, and paper/pencil manipulation, etc. Adequate vision is required for small, detailed pictures.

Test Description: The Stanford-Binet consists of six subtests which vary greatly in what is required at each testing level. The tasks are usually interesting for young children. It may not be possible to obtain a score on a child who has problems that could interfere with performance, i.e., poor vision, lack of receptive or expressive language, or impaired motor skills.

Wechsler Intelligence Scale for Children – Revised (WISC-R)
Wechsler Preschool and Primary Scale of Intelligence (WPPSI)

Author: David Wechsler

Publisher: The Psychological Corporation

Scores: Verbal I.Q.; Performance I.Q.; full Scale I.Q.

Ages: WPPSI—3-11 years to 6-6 years WISC-R—6-0 years to 16-11 years

Administration: Requires a trained examiner and individual testing; approximately one hour.

Child Performance: The verbal section requires the child to respond verbally to various questions. The performance section does not require verbal responses but does require the ability to understand oral directions. On non-verbal tasks, adequate vision, fine-motor manipulative skills and paper/pencil skills are needed.

Test Description: There are six verbal and six non-verbal subtests, but only five of each type are used to determine I.Q. These subtests include:

Verbal Scale

Information: (WISC-R & WPPSI) Reflects alertness and interest; influenced by cultural background.

Similarities: (WISC-R & WPPSI) Ability to generalize and reason abstractly.

Arithmetic: (WISC-R & WPPSI) Ability to reason numerically; requires concentration and attention.

Vocabulary: (WISC-R & WPPSI) Word knowledge acquired from experience and education; expressive language skills.

Comprehension: (WISC-R & WPPSI) Ability to use practical judgment in everyday social situations.

Digit Span: (WISC-R only) Attention and immediate auditory memory; ability to sequence verbally.

Sentences: (WPPSI only) Attention and immediate auditory memory.

Performance Scale

Picture Completion: (WISC-R & WPPSI) Reflects reality perception and observation in identifying missing parts from a whole.

Animal House: (WPPSI only) Sign/symbol association; reflects memory and goal awareness.

Picture Arrangement: (WISC-R only) Ability to comprehend and evaluate social situations; sequential planning.

Mazes: (WISC-R & WPPSI) Visual planning and foresight and visual-motor coordination.

Block Design: (WISC-R & WPPSI) Ability to analyze and form abstract designs; involves visual-motor coordination.

Geometric Design: (WPPSI only) Reflects visual perception and visual-motor functioning.

Coding: (WISC-R only) Measures visual memory; speed and accuracy in copying symbols.

Object Assembly: (WISC-R only) Visual-motor task involving perception and organization of concrete forms.

VISUAL-MOTOR AND VISUAL-PERCEPTION

Bender-Gestalt Test for Young Children

Author: E. Koppitz

Publisher: Grune & Stratton

Score: A composite visual-motor performance score

Ages: 5 to 10 years

Administration: An individually administered and untimed test, given by a psychologist.

Child Performance: Copy nine geometric patterns.

Test Description: A projective test which assesses the child's emotional adjustment and developmental level, and is based on L. Bender's original test.

Beery Developmental Test of Visual-Motor Integration

Authors: K. Beery and N. Buktenica

Publisher: Follett Educational Corporation

Scores: Raw Score; Age Equivalent Score

Ages: 2-0 years to 15-0 years

Administration: While the test may be administered in either a group or individual setting, individual administration is usual at the preschool level. Can be administered by trained paraprofessionals, but interpretation of the results takes training and experience.

Child Performance: Reproduces geometric figures with paper and pencil; must be able to understand the oral or pantomimed directions; verbal responses not required.

Test Description: Consists of a series of geometric shapes to be reproduced by the child. The test is not timed.

Frostig Developmental Test of Visual Perception

Author: Marianne Frostig

Publisher: Consulting Psychologists Press

Scores: Raw Scores; Scale Scores; Age Equivalents for each of the subtests; and an overall Perceptual Quotient.

Ages: 4-0 to 8-11 years

Administration: The test is administered in either an individual or group setting. The examiner should be experienced in the administration and evaluation of the test, and time is approximately 30 to 45 minutes in an individual setting.

Child Performance: Adequate hearing, vision and fine-motor coordination are required to interpret instructions, perceive the correct answer, and make an appropriate graphic response; verbal responses required.

Test Description: The test contains five subtests: *Eye-Motor Coordination* measures the child's ability to draw a continuous straight, curved, or angled line between boundaries of various widths.

Figure-Ground Discrimination assesses the child's shift in perception of figures against increasingly complex backgrounds.

Constancy of Shape assesses the child's ability to recognize circles and squares in a variety of sizes, shadings, and positions in space.

Position in Space assesses the child's ability to discriminate reversals and rotations in figures presented in a series.

Spatial Relations assesses the child's ability to analyze and copy forms and patterns from the very simple to the very complex.

Motor-Free Visual-Perception Test

Authors: R. P. Colarusso, D. D. Hammill

Publisher: Academic Therapy Publications

Scores: Raw Scores; Perceptual Ages; and Perceptual Quotient in visual perception.

Ages: 4-0 to 8-11 years

Administration: The test is administered in an individual setting by teachers, psychologists, educational specialists, therapists, and others who have minimal training with it.

Child Performance: Pointing is the child's response mode. The concept of "same and different" must be understood, and the child must comprehend the oral directions to take the test.

Test Description: Consists of 36 items presented in multiple-choice fashion, measuring the following areas of visual perception: spatial relationships, visual discrimination, figure-ground, visual closure, and visual memory.

SENSORY INTEGRATION

Southern California Sensory Integration Test

Author: A. Jean Ayres

Publisher: Western Psychological Services

Scores: Raw Scores and Standard Deviations from the mean. Also left- and right-side scores can be determined and used to compare the performance abilities between the two sides of the body.

Ages: 4-0 to 10-0 years

Administration: The test is individually administered by a skilled examiner; time is two to three hours.

Child Performance: Varies with the subtest being administered; a great deal of paper/pencil work is required. Adequate vision, hearing, and the ability to listen and follow directions are needed.

Test Description: A variety of subtests designed to detect and determine the nature of sensory integrative dysfunction make up the battery. These include:

Form and Space Perception: ability to perceive the constancy of a form regardless of factors that may appear to change it (i.e., different size, texture, angle, etc.) and to perceive the position of one object in relation to another. This area includes the following subtests:

Position in Space: perception of the same form in different orientations.

Space Visualization: perception of stimuli composed largely of spatial elements including mental manipulation of space.

Design Copying: the capacity of the brain to perceive visually a geometric design and to duplicate that design.

Kinesthesia: the capacity to perceive joint position and movement in the body and extremities.

Manual Form Perception: tests stereognosis (identifying the visual counterpart of a geometric form held in the hand with the child's vision of his hand occluded).

Figure-Ground Perception: assists in determining deficits in visual perception that require selection of a foreground figure from a rival background.

Graphesthesia: tactile perception.

Postural and Bilateral Integration: ability of the brain to integrate the two cerebral hemispheres so that the two body sides work in a smooth, coordinated manner. Integration of the two body sides involves the ability to use the two body sides together (bilaterally), to use them independently at the same time (reciprocally—contrasting activities), and to maintain good postural adaptations (as in sitting and standing balance). Subtests include:

Standing Balance—Eyes Open and Eyes Closed: measures the ability to balance one's self while standing on one foot with and without benefit of vision.

Crossing Midline of the Body: requires the child to imitate the examiner as the examiner uses either his right or left hand to point to either his right or left ear. Example: right hand/left ear; left hand/right ear, etc.

Right-Left Discrimination: requires discrimination "right from left" on self, another person, and location of an object in the room.

Bilateral Motor Coordination: requires smoothly executed movements of an interaction between both upper extremities (arms).

Kinesthesia: measures the capacity to perceive joint position and movement in the body and extremities.

Developmental Apraxia: inability or reduced ability to perform non-habitual, skilled movements. Subtests include:

Imitation of Postures: assesses ability of the child to assume a series of non-habitual positions or postures as demonstrated by the examiner.

Motor Accuracy Left and Right (Hand): assesses ability to trace a line with a pencil first with the dominant hand, then with the non-dominant hand.

Bilateral Motor Coordination: assesses ability to smoothly execute movements of an interaction between both upper extremities.

Design Copying: measures the capacity of the brain to perceive visually a geometric design and to duplicate that design.

Tests of Tactile Perception:

Manual Form Perception: measures stereognosis (identifying the visual counterpart of a geometric form held in the hand occluded).

Graphesthesia: measures tactile perception as the child attempts to reproduce a simple design on the back of his hand as was previously drawn there by the examiner.

Localization of Tactile Stimuli: measures tactile perception. Child is expected to place his finger on a spot on his own hand or arm previously touched by the examiner.

Double Tactile Stimuli Perception: two tactile stimuli are applied simultaneously to either or both cheek and hand of the child, who then identifies where he was touched.

LANGUAGE, SPEECH AND HEARING

Arizona Articulation Proficiency Scale

Author: J. B. Fudala

Publisher: Western Psychological Services

Scores: Consonant Score; Vowel Score; Total Score; Severity Rating; and Intelligibility Rating.

Ages: Can be used with any age.

Administration: A trained examiner and individual testing are required; approximately 10 to 20 minutes.

Child Performance: Adequate vision and vocabulary for naming medium-sized black-and-white pictures; child must be able to imitate a verbal model.

Assessment of Children's Language Comprehension

Authors: R. Foster, J. Giddan, J. Stark

Publisher: Consulting Psychologists Press

Scores: Vocabulary Score, the ability of the child to understand utterances containing two, three, and four critical elements.

Ages: 3-0 to 6-6 years

Administration: The test is administered in an individual setting by a trained examiner; time is 20 to 35 minutes.

Child Performance: Adequate vision, hearing, and pointing skills are needed. Verbal responses are not required.

Test Description: There are four sections: single words, utterances with two critical elements, utterances with three critical elements, and utterances with four critical elements. Critical elements should not be confused with the number of words in the utterance.

Auditory Discrimination Test

Author: J. Wepman

Publisher: Western Psychological Services

Score: Auditory discrimination score (adequate or inadequate)

Ages: 5 to 8 years

Administration: This is an individually administered test which measures the child's ability to discriminate English language phonemes.

Child Performance: Listens and responds to examiner.

Test Description: Examiner calls out a number of word pairs and asks child to respond "same" or "different" to the word pair sounds.

Houston Test of Language Development

Author: M. Crabtree

Publisher: The Houston Test Company

Score: Language Age Equivalent

Ages: 6 months to 6-0 years

Administration: This test is administered in an individual setting by a trained examiner; approximately 15 to 30 minutes.

Child Performance: At the younger ages, this is mostly an observation scale. Older children are required to name pictures, draw with crayons, and manipulate objects. Motor performance or visual difficulties can lower scores.

Illinois Test of Psycholinguistic Abilities

Authors: S. A. Kirk, J. J. McCarthy, W. D. Kirk

Publisher: University of Illinois Press

Scores: Individual Subtest Scale Scores; Composite Psycholinguistic Age Score; Mean Scale Score.

Ages: 3-0 to 10-3 years

Administration: This test is administered in an individual setting by a trained examiner; approximately one to one-and-a-half hours.

Child Performance: Verbal response ability, adequate vision and hearing are required.

Test Description: The subtests include:

Auditory Reception: Ability to derive meaning from verbally presented material.

Visual Reception: Ability to gain meaning from visual symbols.

Auditory Association: Measures the ability to relate concepts presented orally.

Visual Association: Ability to relate, organize, and manipulate visual symbols in a meaningful way.

Verbal Expression: Ability to express one's own concepts orally.

Manual Expression: Ability to express ideas manually.

Auditory Memory: Short-term sequential memory for digits.

Visual Memory: Ability to reproduce sequences of nonmeaningful figures from memory.

Grammatic Closure: Ability to handle syntax and grammatic inflections.

Visual Closure: Ability to find several known, partially concealed objects in a detailed field; figure-ground discrimination.

Auditory Closure: (Supplementary test) Ability to fill in missing sounds and syllables to produce a complete word.

Sound Blending: Ability to synthesize the separate parts of words into a whole.

Northwestern Syntax Screening Test

Author: L. Lee

Available from: Dr. Laura Lee, Northwestern University, Evanston, Illinois, 60201.

Scores: Receptive Score and Percentile Rank; Expressive Score and Percentile Rank.

Ages: 1-6 to 6-0 years

Administration: This instrument is administered in an individual setting by a trained examiner; approximately 30 to 40 minutes.

Child Performance: Good visual discrimination and verbal abilities are needed. The child must be able to point to pictures on the receptive section of the test and to verbalize on the expressive section of the test.

Preschool Language Scale

Authors: I. L. Zimmerman, U. G. Steiner, R. L. Evatt

Publisher: Charles E. Merrill Publishing Co.

Scores: Auditory Comprehension Age score; Verbal Expression Age score; Language Age score (the Language Age score can be converted to a Language Quotient).

Ages: 1-5 years to 8-0 years.

Administration: The test is administered in an individual setting by a trained examiner; approximately 20 minutes to 1 hour.

Child Performance: Both pointing and verbal responses are required; therefore, adequate vision, hearing, and some vocalization skills are needed; some fine-motor manipulative skills are also required.

Description of the Test: Consists of two main parts—Auditory Comprehension and Verbal Ability. Developmental ages are given for items; age scores can be derived from the child's scores.

Test for Auditory Comprehension of Language

Author: E. Carrow

Publisher: Learning Concepts

Scores: Age Equivalence; Percentile Rank of comprehensive abilities.

Ages: 3-0 to 6-11 years

Administration: The test is administered in an individual setting by a trained examiner; 25 to 45 minutes needed.

Child Performance: Only non-verbal pointing responses are required; adequate vision and hearing skills are needed.

Test Description: Norms are available for Anglo, Mexican-American, and Black populations at the kindergarten and first-grade levels. The instrument assesses the child's understanding of the meaning of vocabulary and his understanding of various speech and language structures.

Utah Test of Language Development

Authors: M. Mecham, J. L. Jex, J. D. Jones

Publisher: Communication Research Associates Inc.

Scores: Language Age Equivalent Score

Ages: 1-6 to 14-6 years

Administration: The test is administered in an individual setting by an experienced trainer; time is approximately 30 to 45 minutes.

Child Performance: Adequate vision, hearing, and fine-motor skills are required. Both non-verbal and verbal responses are required.

Test Description: Measures expressive and receptive language skills. A language age is derived from correct and incorrect responses.

BEHAVIOR RATING SCALES

Adaptive Behavior Scale

Authors: A. Madow, H. Leland, B. Libby, and K. Nihira.

Publisher: American Association on Mental Deficiency

Ages: 3 to 6-9 years

Administration: Can be administered by paraprofessionals; can be completed by third-party assessment or interview; requires about 20 minutes.

Child Performance: None required.

Test Description: Measure of daily living skills (independent functioning, physical development, self-direction, responsibility, socialization, etc.) and of personality and behavior (antisocial and destructive behavior, nonconformity, lack of trust, withdrawal, vocal habits, hyperactivity, etc.). Norms for age 3 upward are available.

California Preschool Social Competency Scale

Authors: S. Levine, F. Elzey, and M. Lewis

Publisher: Consulting Psychologists Press

Score: A total reflecting overall performance.

Ages: 2 to 6 years

Administration: Teachers or parents rate child on 30 items, using a 4-point scale.

Test Description: A teacher-rating scale that taps preschool children's interpersonal behavior and social responsibility. Items measure how well the child responds to instruction, shares, helps others, starts activities, deals with frustration, etc. Each item reflects four degrees of competency.

Child Behavior Rating Scale

Author: R. Cassel

Publisher: Western Psychological Services

Score: Six: self, home, school, social, physical, and total.

Ages: 5 to 8 years

Administration: Nonprofessional rating of child's behavior on 78 items. Ratings use a 6-point scale.

Cooperative Preschool Inventory

Author: B. Caldwell

Publisher: Addison-Wesley Testing Service

Scores: Four: personal-social relationships, associative vocabulary, concepts— numerical, and concepts—sensory.

Ages: 3 to 6-6 years

Administration: Individually administered by teachers; directions are verbal (English or Spanish available); requires about 15 minutes.

Child Performance: Requires verbal and motor responses.

Test Description: Used to determine school-entry readiness levels. There are 64 items; norms are based on 1500 Head Start children.

Denver Developmental Screening Test

Authors: W. Frankenberg, J. Dodds, and A. Fandel

Publisher: Ladoca Project and Publishing Foundation

Scores: Personal-Social, Fine Motor-Adaptive, Language and Gross Motor

Ages: Birth to 6 years

Administration: Paraprofessionals can give the test to the child. Time is variable. Items scored as pass, failure, refused, and no opportunity.

Child Performance: Uses large and small muscles, demonstrates language skills, sociability, and cognitive ability.

Test Description: A series of 105 items that require the child to carry out a number of tasks, i.e., name a pictured object, walk backwards, pick up raisins, etc.

Gesell Developmental Schedules

Authors: H. Knobloch and B. Passamanick (eds.)

Publisher: Harper and Row

Scores: Developmental age and developmental quotient

Ages: 4 weeks to 5 years

Administration: Administered only by professionals for individual developmental assessment of infants and preschool children, normal and handicapped.

Child Performance: Varied.

Lexington Developmental Scale

Authors: J. Irwin, M. Ward, C. Deen, and A. Greis

Publisher: United Cerebral Palsy of the Bluegrass (Lexington, Ky.)

Scores: Five: Motor, Language, Personal-Social, Cognitive, and Emotional

Ages: Birth to 6 years

Administration: May be completed by teachers.

Child Performance: Varied.

Test Description: Consists of items measuring the five areas listed above.

Preschool Attainment Record

Author: E. Doll

Publisher: American Guidance Service

Scores: Three main areas and subareas: physical—ambulation, manipulation; intelligence—information, ideation, creativity; and social—rapport, communication, responsibility.

Ages: 6 months to 7 years

Administration: An interview format; anyone familiar with the child can provide the data.

Child Performance: None required.

Test Description: This is a 96-item scale covering the areas listed above.

Vineland Social Maturity Scale

Author: E. Doll

Publisher: American Guidance Service

Scores: Four: Self-help, locomotion, communication, and socialization

Ages: Birth through 25 years

Administration: Anyone familiar with the child can provide information required by interview

Child Performance: None required.

Test Description: The Vineland contains 117 items and measures the social adaptation of the mentally retarded.

A List of Selected Diagnostic Curriculum and Screening Materials for Use in Early Childhood[*]

GENERAL COGNITION

Brigance Diagnostic Inventory of Basic Skills (1978)
Childcraft Activity Cards
Developmental Activities Screening Inventory (DASI)
Fairbanks-Robinson Program. Levels I and II
First Grade Screening Test (1969)
Peabody Individual Achievement Test (1970)
Color Discovery Cards
Color, Object, Number Grouping Cards
Figure-Ground Activity Cards
Halves to Wholes Cards
Orientation Views
Same or Different Color Cards
Same or Different Design Cards
Same or Different Proportion Cards
Same or Different Size Cards
Shapes Dominoes
Symmetrical Match-Up
Visual Discrimination Matching Cards
Visual Matching, Memory, and Sequencing Exercises
Visual Sequential Memory Exercises

LANGUAGE, SPEECH, AND HEARING

Childcraft Activity Cards (1977-78)
Del Rio Language Screening Test

NOTE: These materials are selected from many such materials on the market today. Their inclusion here is not to be considered an endorsement by the publisher or the authors.

Developmental Language Lessons
Fokes Sentence Builder
Gem Early Languages Activities Kit (1977-78)
Goldman-Fristoe Test of Articulation (1972)
Goldman-Fristoe-Woodcock Test of Auditory Discrimination (1970)
Lindamood Auditory Conceptualization Test
Parts of Speech
Peabody Articulation Decks (1975)
Perceptual Skills Curriculum
Verbal Language Development Scale (1971)
Vocabulary Comprehension Scale (1977)
Yellow Brick Road (1977)
Sentence-Building Sequential Cards

SOCIAL DEVELOPMENT

Childcraft Activity Cards (1977-78)
First Grade Screening Test (1969)
Preschool Attainment Record (Research Edition) (1966)
Primary Self-Concept Inventory (1977)
Vineland Social Maturity Scale (1965)

MOTOR SKILLS

Childcraft Activity Cards (1977-78)
Erie Program (1978)
First Grade Screening Test (1969)
Perceptual Skills Curriculum (1978)
Preschool Attainment Record (Research Edition) (1966)
Vanguard School Program (1978)
Yellow Brick Road (1977)

VISUAL

Developmental Activities Screening Inventory (1977)
Erie Program (1978): Four Sets of Games
Look and Learn (1978)
Perceptual Skills Curriculum (1978)
Vanguard School Program (1978)
Yellow Brick Road (1977)

Action Symbols (1978-79)
Figure-Ground Activity Cards (1978-79)
Halves to Wholes Cards (1978-79)
Orientation Views (1978-79)
See It!—Do It (1978-79)
Shapes Dominoes (1978-79)
Training for Independence (1978-79)
Visual Matching, Memory, and Sequencing Exercises (1978-79)
Visual Memory Cards (1978-79): Sets I, II, III, and IV
Visual Sequential Memory Exercises (1978-79)

GENERAL SCREENING

Alike Because: Level 1 (1978)
Developmental Activities Screening Inventory (1978)
Fairbanks-Robinson Program Revised Edition: Levels I and II (1978)
Pupil Record of Educational Behavior (1978)
Search & Teach (1978)
Vanguard School Program: Motor and Perceptual Training (1978)
What's Missing? Level 1 (1978)
What's Wrong Here? Level 1 (1978)
Woodcock-Johnson Psycho-Educational Battery (1978)
Action Symbols (1978-79)
Before-And-After Sequential Cards (1978-79)
Color Association Picture Cards (1978-79)
Color, Object, Number Grouping Cards (1978-79)
Figure-Ground Activity Cards (1978-79)
Halves to Wholes Cards (1978-79)
Same or Different Color Cards (1978-79)
Same or Different Design Cards (1978-79)
Same or Different Proportion Cards (1978-79)
Same or Different Size Cards (1978-79)
Shapes-Dominoes (1978-79)
Symmetrical Match-Up (1978-79)
Visual Matching, Memory, and Sequencing Exercises (1978-79)
Visual Sequential Memory Exercises (1978-79)

SELF-CARE

TFI—Training for Independence (1978-79)
When A Child Misbehaves
Self-Care Sequential Cards (1978-79)

GENERAL COGNITION

Brigance Diagnostic Inventory of Basic Skills (1978). For use with students whose achievement is between kindergarten and 6th-grade level. Designed to be used as a resource by different curriculum personnel in different ways to meet different program needs. For assessing and recording achievement and progress of students; developing curriculum in performance tests; communicating instructional objectives to all concerned; and designing individualized instruction. Results may be utilized to devise individualized programs to meet specific needs of the learner. An early childhood version, the BRIGANCE INVENTORY OF EARLY DEVELOPMENT (1978), is just now coming on the market. (Curriculum Associates, Inc.*)

Childcraft Activity Cards. Set of 5″ × 8″ activity cards for the following skill areas: Gross Motor, Developmental Language; Social-Emotional and Adaptive Living Skills; Perceptual-Fine-Motor and Cognitive. (Childcraft)

Developmental Activities Screening Inventory (DASI). Screens children 6-60 months. Non-verbal DASI measures the abilities of children functioning at 6-60 month level to provide early detection of developmental disabilities. Informal, individualized, adaptable. Provides remedial direction. Skills assessed include fine-motor manipulation, cause-effect relationships, associations, number concepts, size discriminations, and sequencing. (Teaching Resources)

Fairbanks-Robinson Program. Levels I and II (Revised Edition). For use in basic curriculum in special-education classroom. Comprehensive, in-depth program to develop the following pre-academic skills: line reproduction; shape and size perception; coloring; cutting; spatial relationships; figure-ground discrimination; sequencing; parts-to-whole relationships. Also suitable for reinforcement and remedial work in kindergarten and first-grade and selective use with older students deficient in specific skill areas. Available in two levels. For individualized use. (Teaching Resources)

First Grade Screening Test (1969). A group-administered test to identify potential learning difficulties (kindergarten and beginning first grade). FGST was designed to identify children who are likely to experience significant difficulty during their first year of school. Provides early identification of children who need individual assessment, so appropriate compensatory or remedial attention can be given. Seeks to identify three major kinds of handicaps: intellectual deficiency; central nervous system dysfunction; emotional disturbances. (American Guidance Service)

---

*Addresses are contained at the end of this section.

Peabody Individual Achievement Test (1970). A wide-range individual screening test of achievement. The PIAT is an instrument designed to survey a subject's level of educational attainment in basic skills and knowledge. It is intended for individual assessment in schools, and the five subjects cover: Mathematics; Reading Recognition; Reading Comprehension; Spelling; General Information. In addition to Subtest Scores, Total Score gives a picture of subject's overall level of achievement. Kindergarten through adult. (American Guidance Service)

Peabody Picture Vocabulary Test (1965). An individual screening test of verbal intelligence, for age ranges 2-6 to adult. It is especially appropriate for speech-impaired, cerebral-palsied, withdrawn, distractible, mentally retarded, and remedial-reading cases. (American Guidance Service)

Color Discovery Cards. Designed for multilevel use in color naming, matching, and patterning, the 67-card sets come in 11 colors. One card of each color group bears the color name in large letters printed in Spanish or English. (Developmental Learning Materials)

Color, Object, Number Grouping Cards. Forty-five cards to be used in categorization exercises based upon object identity, color, number of objects, or any combinaton thereof. Valuable aid at elementary school level as well as sophisticated cross-categorization level. Randomly placed objects insure that number values of groups will be reached by counting rather than pattern recognition. (Developmental Learning Materials)

Figure-Ground Activity Cards. Offers practice in improving visual-perception skills. Eighteen pictures printed on both sides of 9 cards. (Coated, 11″ × 7½″; can be wiped clean after use.) Each picture has 2 or 3 objects, keyed in upper right hand corner and also appearing in pictures themselves. Language development is encouraged as students locate keyed objects and circle them with overlay marking pencil and the objects are named. (Developmental Learning Materials)

Halves to Wholes Cards. This matching game can be used in visual-discrimination exercises and can be beneficial in teaching categorization and in stimulating language development. Students must discern relationships between upper and lower halves as well as recognize inappropriate matches. Can be played individually or as a group. (Six examples in each of 5 categories.) (Developmental Learning Materials)

Orientation Views. Forty-five cards, which present 3 views each of 15 familiar objects. (Above, below, and from the side.) Helps students relate each part to the 3-dimensional whole and integrate different views into a coherent whole. (Developmental Learning Materials)

Same or Different Color Cards. Thirty cards featuring pairs of 15 different items which stress color differences and likenesses. An effective readiness activity for math and other academic activities, the cards are designed to aid students in color discrimination. (Developmental Learning Materials)

Same or Different Design Cards. Slight differences in design make this set suitable for more able or perceptually advanced students. Trying to locate slight differences offers students excellent readiness activity for reading, writing, and math. (Developmental Learning Materials)

Same or Different Proportion Cards. Helps students observe differences in proportion and develop a vocabulary of comparative terms such as taller/shorter, etc. (Developmental Learning Materials)

Same or Different Size Cards. Thirty colorful cards; 15 have items with identical sizes; other 15 different sizes. Students practice visual-perception skills. (Developmental Learning Materials)

Shapes Dominoes. Offers an excellent way to stimulate visual discrimination and organization. Set of 36 cards printed with 8 mathematical shapes. (Developmental Learning Materials)

Symmetrical Match-Up. Stresses visual-discrimination skills, recognition of symmetry, and the math concept of halves to wholes. (Developmental Learning Materials)

Visual Discrimination Matching Cards: Sets I, II, III. Each series contains 3 sets of cards; each set 3 groups; each group contains 4 pairs of pictures. This series of cards gives students practice in learning to discern subtle variations in visual presentations; aids in developing problem-solving aspects of learning. (Developmental Learning Materials)

Visual Matching, Memory, and Sequencing Exercises. Provides developmental exercises to train students to match colors, figures, shapes, designs, and letters visually and from memory. (Developmental Learning Materials)

Visual Sequential Memory Exercises. Thirty visual memory exercises to help develop skills of perception, memorization, and reproduction of visual sequences and transfer these skills to academic work. Exercises progress from geometric shapes through letters to words. (Developmental Learning Materials)

LANGUAGE, SPEECH, AND HEARING

Childcraft Activity Cards (1977-78). Set of 5″ × 8″ cards covers the following skills areas: Gross Motor; Developmental Language; Social-Emotional and Adaptive Living Skills; Perceptual-Fine Motor and Cognitive. (Childcraft)

Del Rio Language Screening Test. For use in special education programs and bilingual classrooms. Provides means of rapidly identifying both English- and Spanish-dominant young children with deviant language skills. Also provides normative developmental data for Spanish-speaking children. (Special Learning Corp.)

Developmental Language Lessons. Designed to teach children basic grammatical structure in a conversational setting, primarily for the language-delayed child, but can also be used with hearing-impaired, learning-disabled, and mentally retarded by classroom teachers, and speech and language clinicians. Intended to be used alone in classroom setting or as an adjunct to language therapy. Provides formal and informal diagnostic procedures; allows for spontaneous use of language; provides remediation for syntactic structures in 8 grammatical categories. (Teaching Resources)

Fokes Sentence Builder. Comprehensive, structured oral-language program that helps develop skills of verbal expression, comprehension, and sentence construction through structured approach to teaching grammar. Color-coded boxes of cards represent five categories of words: WHO; WHAT; IS DOING; WHICH; and WHERE. Two or more boxes are placed on a Sentence Line at one time. Students choose cards from each category to create their own grammatically correct sentences. Instruction may be given individually or in small groups by classroom teachers or language therapists. Specific suggestions for use with children with severe language delays, mild language delays, and those whose language is not delayed. (Teaching Resources)

Gem Early Languages Activities Kit (1977-78). Fosters basic communication skills, builds receptive and expressive vocabulary, and develops memory skills. Arranged under 4 broad categories: motor; visual; auditory; verbal. For professional and paraprofessional classroom personnel and for home-based programs. For children functioning between 1½-3 years; for parents of handicapped children. Division into 4 skill areas aids teacher of children with specific learning disabilities to select those activities most appropriate to a given child's needs. (Childcraft)

Goldman-Fristoe Test of Articulation (1972). A systematic assessment of articulatory skills. Ages 2 years and above, with norms available for ages 6 to 16+. Three subtests provide a wide-range sample of an individual's articulatory skills. Especially appropriate for distractible, mentally retarded, and young children. (American Guidance Service)

Goldman-Fristoe-Woodcock Test of Auditory Discrimination (1970). An individual screening test of ability to discriminate speech sounds in quiet and in noise. For 4 years and above. The G-F-W evaluates speech-sound discrimination under both quiet and distracting noise conditions. Requires little preparation and training for examiner. (American Guidance Service)

Lindamood Auditory Conceptualization Test. Preschool through adult levels. No prior knowledge of the alphabet or sound-symbol association is required. Permits early identification of students with auditory-perceptual deficiencies. Given individually. No special training required to administer or score. Normative data and guidelines for educational planning and remediation included in manual. Alternate forms permit test and retest. (Teaching Resources)

Parts of Speech (1978). Five units of picture cards organized on basis of parts of speech to help children develop basic language skills. One part of speech to each unit: nouns; verbs; adjectives; adverbs; prepositions. Units may be used independently or combined. Many supportive activities included in accompanying guides. (Learning Resources)

Peabody Articulation Decks (1975). Ten decks of small full-color picture cards for speech development and remediation in children and adults. Strong remedial focus on the 18 most commonly misarticulated consonant sounds of the English language. (American Guidance Service)

Perceptual Skills Curriculum. Used developmentally, Pre-K, K, and grade 1, and in special education, grades 1 through 8. Builds foundation for all basic skills in reading and arithmetic; provides a complete structure of sequenced tests and learning activities; a system designed to detect and correct children's perceptual shortcomings before they cause school failure. Four Programs: Visual-motor skills; Auditory-motor skills; General-motor skills; and Introducing Letters and Numerals. (Special Learning Corp.)

Verbal Language Development Scale (1971). For ages 1 month to 16 years. VLDS yields language age equivalent based on characteristics of communication; valuable for use with those difficult to assess by other methods. (American Guidance Service)

Vocabulary Comprehension Scale (1977). Ages 2-6. Provides clinicians and teachers of language/learning-disabled children with baseline information about comprehension of pronouns and words of position, quality, quantity, and size. (Learning Concepts)

Yellow Brick Road (1977). Screening instrument to identify functional strengths and weaknesses in preschool children. Each of the four batteries (Motor; Visual; Auditory; Language) contains 6 subtests. Can be administered individually or in groups. Aides, volunteers, and parents can assist the examiners with administration. Results identify children for immediate referral or therapy. (Learning Concepts)

Sentence-Building Sequential Cards. Thirty cards, with 10 sequences of 3 cards each depict simple, practical situations familiar to students. Subject on 1st card;

verb on 2nd, object on 3rd. Promotes both verbal and written expression. Some sequences also encourage prepositional phrases. (Developmental Learning Materials)

SOCIAL DEVELOPMENT

Childcraft Activity Cards (1977-78). Set of 5″ × 8″ cards covers the following skill areas: Gross Motor; Developmental Language; Social-Emotional and Adaptive Living Skills; Perceptual-Fine Motor and Cognitive. (Childcraft)

First Grade Screening Test (1969). A Group-Administered Test to Identify Potential Learning Difficulties (kindergarten and beginning first grade). FGST was designed to identify children who are likely to experience significant difficulty during their first year of school. Provides early identification of children who need individual assessment, so appropriate compensatory or remedial attention can be given. FGST seeks to identify 3 major kinds of handicaps: intellectual deficiency; central nervous system dysfunction; emotional disturbance. (American Guidance Service)

Preschool Attainment Record (Research Edition) (1966). A Preschool Scale of Attainment. Ages 6 months through 7 years. PAR provides global assessment of physical, social, and intellectual functions of young children. Items arranged in order of increasing difficulty within: Ambulation; Manipulation; Rapport; Communication; Responsibility; Information; Ideation; Creativity. Especially useful in cases of sensory impairment; speech and language difficulty; emotional disturbance; neuro-muscular impairment; resistance to other testing; and cultural difference. The child need not be present. (American Guidance Service)

Primary Self-Concept Inventory (1977). Grades K-6. The inventory identifies children with low self-concept. Instrument can be used as a preand post-test for program evaluation and as a screening instrument to identify children with potentially low self-concepts. Measures: Social-Self; Personal-Self; Intellectual-Self. (Learning Concepts)

Vineland Social Maturity Scale (1965). A checklist to measure successive stages of social competence from infancy to adulthood, for teachers, counselors, etc. interested in assessing child development. Lists performances which indicate progressive capacity for looking after one's self and participating in activities leading toward adult independence and civic usefulness. Six categories with items in order of increasing average difficulty: Self-Help; Locomotion; Occupation; Communication; Self-Direction; Socialization. (American Guidance Service)

MOTOR SKILLS

Childcraft Activity Cards (1977-78). Set of 5'' × 8'' cards covers each of the following skill areas: Gross Motor; Developmental Language; Social-Emotional and Adaptive Living Skills; Perceptual-Fine-Motor and Cognitive. (Childcraft)

Erie Program (1978): Four Sets of Games. Visual-Perceptual; Perceptual Bingo; Visual-Motor Template Forms; Perceptual Card and Dominoes Games. Can be used individually or as a complete program at preschool and kindergarten levels or with primary-grade children with visual-perceptual problems. Carefully controlled progression of difficulty within each set of games. Six basic geometric shapes emphasized: circle; square; triangle; rectangle; ellipse; diamond. (Teaching Resources)

First Grade Screening Test (1969). A Group-Administered Test to Identify Potential Learning Difficulties. Ages kindergarten and beginning first grade. FGST was designed to identify children who are likely to experience significant difficulty during their first year of school. Provides early identification of children who need individual assessment, so appropriate compensatory or remedial attention can be given. FGST seeks to identify 3 major kinds of handicaps: intellectual deficiency; central nervous system dysfunction; emotional disturbance. (American Guidance Service)

Perceptual Skills Curriculum (1978). Used developmentally Pre-K, K, and grade 1, and in special education, grades 1 through 8. Builds foundation for all basic skills in reading and arithmetic; provides a complete structure of sequenced tests and learning activities; a system designed to detect and correct children's perceptual shortcomings before they cause school failure. Four Programs: Visual-motor skills; Auditory-motor skills; General-motor skills; and Introducing Letters and Numerals. (Special Learning Corp.)

Preschool Attainment Record (Research Edition) (1966). A Preschool Scale of Attainment. Ages 6 months through 7 years. PAR provides global assessment of physical, social, and intellectual functions of young children. Items arranged in order of increasing difficulty within: Ambulation; Manipulation; Rapport; Communication; Responsibility; Information; Ideation; Creativity. Especially useful in cases of sensory impairment; speech and language difficulty; emotional disturbance; neuro-muscular impairment; resistance to other testing; and cultural difference. The child need not be present. (American Guidance Service)

Vanguard School Program (1978). Motor and Perceptual Training: Four independent parts: Body Awareness; Visual-Motor Integration; Discrimination and Classification; Spatial Relationships. May be used independently or as a continuing program of skills development. Designed for small groups of students, followed by individual work in workbooks. Program includes developmental and remedial activities for slow learners, perceptually handicapped, and older students. (Teaching Resources)

Yellow Brick Road (1977). Ages 5-6. Screening instrument to identify functional strengths and weaknesses in preschool children. Each of the four batteries (Motor; Visual; Auditory; Language) contains 6 subtests. Can be administered individually or in groups. Aides, volunteers, and parents can assist the examiners with administration. Results identify children for immediate referral or therapy. (Learning Concepts)

VISUAL

Developmental Activities Screening Inventory (1977). Screens children 6-60 months. Non-verbal DASI measures the abilities of children functioning at 6-60 month level to provide early detection of developmental disabilities. Informal, individualized, adaptable. Provides remedial direction. Skills assessed include fine-motor manipulation, cause-effect relationships, associations, number concepts, size discriminations, and sequencing. (Teaching Resources)

Erie Program (1978): Four Sets of Games. Visual-Perceptual; Perceptual Bingo; Visual-Motor Template Forms; Perceptual Card and Dominoes Games. Can be used individually or as a complete program at preschool and kindergarten levels or with primary-grade children with visual-perceptual problems. Carefully controlled progression of difficulty within each set of games. Six basic geometric shapes emphasized: circle; square; triangle; rectangle; ellipse; diamond. (Teaching Resources)

Look and Learn (1978): Designed to develop visual memory and sequencing skills. Involves showing children stimulus for a short period, removing it, having child mark workbook pages to show which item they saw as the stimulus. Program in two parts: Part 1 develops and reinforces visual memory for individual items. Part 2 develops and reinforces visual memory for sequences of items. Kindergarten through third grade and with children at higher levels who have special learning needs. Stimulus Book 1: pictures; geometric shapes; numerals; lower case letters of alphabet. Stimulus Book 2: words grouped into six categories on basis of element to which child must attend; initial letter change; final letter change; transposition of initial and final letters; medial letter change; word endings; internal order. (Teaching Resources)

Perceptual Skills Curriculum (1978). Used developmentally Pre-K, K, and grade 1, and in special education, grades 1 through 8. Builds foundation for all basic skills in reading and arithmetic; provides a complete structure of sequenced tests and learning activities; an easily managed system that detects and corrects children's perceptual shortcomings before they cause school failure. Four Programs: Visual-motor skills; Auditory-motor skills; General-motor skills; and Introducing Letters and Numerals. (Special Learning Corp.)

Vanguard School Program (1978). Motor and Perceptual Training: Four independent parts: Body Awareness; Visual-Motor Integration; Discrimination and Classification; Spatial Relationships. May be used independently or as a continuing program of skills development. Designed for small groups of students, followed by individual work in workbooks. Program includes developmental and remedial activities for slow learners, perceptually handicapped, and older students. Used successfully with students from 5-14. (Teaching Resources)

Yellow Brick Road (1977). Ages 5-6. Screening instrument to identify functional strengths and weaknesses in preschool children. Each of the four batteries (Motor; Visual; Auditory; Language) contains 6 subtests. Can be administered individually or in groups. Aides, volunteers, and parents can assist the examiners with administration. Results identify children for immediate referral or therapy. (Learning Concepts)

Action Symbols (1978-79). Thirty-six cards—four cards picturing each of the nine actions: clapping, stamping, etc. Students read the meaning of the picture and perform the appropriate action. (Developmental Learning Materials)

Before-and-After Sequential Cards (1978-79). Twenty-four colorful cards. Ideal for beginning practice in visual sequencing. Two cards in each of the 12 before-and-after sequences. (Developmental Learning Materials)

Figure-Ground Activity Cards (1978-79). Offers students practice in improving visual-perception skills. Eighteen pictures printed on both sides of 9 cards. (Coated; 11″ × 7½″; can be wiped clean after use.) Each picture has 2 or 3 objects, keyed in upper right hand corner and also appearing in pictures themselves. Language development is encouraged as students locate keyed objects and circle them with overlay marking pencil and the objects are named. (Developmental Learning Materials)

Halves to Wholes Cards (1978-79). This matching game can be used in visual-discrimination exercises and can be beneficial in teaching categorization and in stimulating language development. Students must discern relationships between upper and lower halves as well as recognize inappropriate matches. Can be played individually or as a group. (Six examples in each of 5 categories.) (Developmental Learning Materials)

Orientation Views (1978-79). Forty-five cards, which present 3 views each of 15 familiar objects (above, below, and from the side). Helps students relate each part to the 3-dimensional whole and integrate different views into a coherent whole. (Developmental Learning Materials)

See It—Do It (1978-79). Diagnostic and corrective materials contained in this program offer teachers guidance and specific help they need to aid students experiencing problems with visual perception. Developed in England and modified by DIM for regular as well as remedial classes in the United States. Illustrated workbooks designed to structure student's learning to promote perceptual readiness and to aid in the diagnosis of specific perceptual difficulties. (Developmental Learning Materials)

Shapes Dominoes (1978-79). Offers an excellent way to stimulate visual discrimination and organization. Set of 36 cards printed with 8 mathematical shapes. Makes discriminating between and matching basic shapes fun. (Developmental Learning Materials)

Training for Independence (1978-79). Spatial-Relation Picture Cards 1. Thirty full-color picture cards depict spatial relationships of 5 different objects. Each group depicts 6 different spatial relationships of the object. (Developmental Learning Materials)

Symmetrical Match-Up (1978-79). Stresses visual-discrimination skills, recognition of symmetry, and the math concept of halves to wholes. (Developmental Learning Materials)

Visual Matching, Memory, and Sequencing Exercises (1978-79). Six-book series provides developmental exercises that train students to match colors, figures, shapes, designs, and letters visually and from memory. Each book has from 3 to 6 parts in which the exercises follow the steps of perceptual development. Especially vital for reading and spelling skills. (Developmental Learning Materials)

Visual Memory Cards (1978-79): Sets I, II, III, and IV. I—Colors; II—Objects; III—Shapes; IV—Letters. Flash cards designed to provide training in visual discrimination, sequencing, and memory. The smaller cards can be arranged in sequence to match the larger cards. Sequencing pattern involves from 1 to 5 items. (Developmental Learning Materials)

Visual Sequential Memory Exercises (1978-79). Thirty visual-memory exercises help children develop cognitive skills of perception, memorization, and reproduction of visual sequences and transfer these skills to academic work. Exercises progress from geometric shapes through letters to words. (Developmental Learning Materials)

GENERAL SCREENING

Alike Because:Level 1 (1978). Flip books to develop association and generalization skills by comparing pictures of common objects. Any picture on the left can be compared with any picture on the right for likenesses and differences. Has guide describing activities that encourage verbal expression. (Teaching Resources)

Developmental Activities Screening Inventory (1978). Screens children 6-60 months. Non-verbal DASI measures the abilities of children functioning at 6-60 month level to provide early detection of developmental disabilities. Informal, individualized, adaptable. Provides remedial direction. Skills assessed include fine-motor manipulation, cause-effect relationships, associations, number concepts, size discriminations, and sequencing. (Teaching Resources)

Fairbanks-Robinson Program Revised Edition: Levels I and II (1978). For use as basic curriculum in special education classroom. Comprehensive, in-depth program to develop following pre-academic skills: line reproduction; shape and size perception; coloring; cutting; spatial relationships; figure-ground discrimination; sequencing; parts-to-whole relationships. Also suitable for reinforcement and remedial work in kindergarten and first grade and selective use with older students deficient in specific skill areas. Available in two levels. For individualized use. (Teaching Resources)

Pupil Record of Educational Behavior (1978). Diagnostic Inventory for use at preschool to upper-primary functional levels. Evaluates child's level and pattern of functioning and provides descriptive information about child's individual pattern of strengths and weaknesses in certain skill areas. Wide range of skills; easily administered; available in Spanish. (Teaching Resources)

Search & Teach (1978). Program to detect learning difficulties in 5- and 6-year-olds and help prevent later school failure. SEARCH, A Scanning Instrument for the Identification of Potential Learning Disability. TEACH—a resource book of instructional tasks designed to mesh with SEARCH. SEARCH is an individual test, designed to be given to all children in a class during the kindergarten year or in the early months of first grade. (Special Learning Corp.)

Vanguard School Program: Motor and Perceptual Training (1978). Four independent parts: Body Awareness; Visual-Motor Integration; Discrimination and Classification; Spatial Relationships. May be used independently or as a continuing program of skills development. Designed for small groups of students, followed by individual work in workbooks. Program includes developmental and remedial activities for slow learners, perceptually handicapped, and older students. Used successfully with students from 5-14. (Teaching Resources)

What's Missing? Level 1 (1978). Some details are purposely left out of the drawings on these sets of picture cards so that children can attempt to identify what is missing. Level 1: 32 cards present simple line drawings of common objects, animals, and people. Each drawing has one or more details missing. Plastic laminated cards; child can fill in the missing part with crayon; markings may be wiped off with soft cloth. (Teaching Resources)

What's Wrong Here? Level 1 (1978). Picture cards depict a variety of familiar scenes with incorrect details. Children are asked to identify. Small line drawing of picture is reproduced on back of each card for teacher reference, along with a variety of specific teaching suggestions, discussion questions, and related activities. (Teaching Resources)

Woodcock-Johnson Psycho-Educational Battery (1978). Preschool through adult levels. Provides comprehensive overview of learning aptitudes, scholastic achievement, cognitive ability, and interest level from which to proceed with specific diagnostic procedures and instructional planning. Primary application for student evaluation. Can also be used for vocational rehabilitation counseling, and as research instrument for use with preschool to adult populations. (Teaching Resources)

Action Symbols (1978-79). Thirty-six cards—four cards picturing each of the nine actions: clapping, stamping, etc. Students read the meaning of the picture and perform the appropriate action. (Developmental Learning Materials)

Before-and-After Sequential Cards (1978-79). Twenty-four colorful cards. Ideal for beginning practice in visual sequencing. Two cards in each of the 12 before-and-after sequences. (Developmental Learning Materials)

Color Association Picture Cards (1978-79). Contains 15 pairs of colorful identical cards for students to match. Teaches basic skills in recognizing and classifying attributes of form and color, important in readiness for math, reading, and writing. (Developmental Learning Materials)

Color, Object, Number Grouping Cards (1978-79). Forty-five cards to be used in categorization exercises based upon object identity, color, number of objects, or any combination thereof. Valuable aid at elementary level as well as sophisticated cross-categorization level. Randomly placed objects insure that number values of groups will be reached by counting rather than pattern recognition. (Developmental Learning Materials)

Figure-Ground Activity Cards (1978-79). Offers students practice in improving visual-perception skills. Eighteen pictures printed on both sides of 9 cards. (Coated; $11'' \times 7\frac{1}{2}''$; can be wiped clean after use.) Each picture has 2 or 3 objects, keyed in upper right hand corner and also appearing in pictures themselves. Language development is encouraged as students locate keyed objects and circle them with overlay marking pencil and the objects are named. (Developmental Learning Materials)

Halves to Wholes Cards (1978-79). This matching game can be used in visual-discrimination exercises and can be beneficial in teaching categorization and in stimulating language development. Students must discern relationships between upper and lower halves as well as recognize inappropriate matches. Can be played individually or as a group. (Developmental Learning Materials)

Same or Different Color Cards (1978-79). Thirty cards featuring pairs of 15 different items which stress color differences and likenesses. An effective readiness activity for math and other academic activities, the cards are designed to aid students in color discrimination. (Developmental Learning Materials)

Same or Different Design Cards (1978-79). Slight differences in design make this set suitable for more able or perceptually advanced students. Trying to locate slight differences offers students excellent readiness activity for reading, writing and math. (36 pairs of cards.) On one card of each pair designs differ slightly. (Developmental Learning Materials)

Same or Different Proportion Cards (1978-79). Thirty cards. Helps students observe differences in proportion and develop a vocabulary of comparative terms such as taller/shorter, etc. (Developmental Learning Materials)

Same or Different Size Cards (1978-79). Thirty colorful cards; 15 have items with identical sizes; 15 others, different sizes. Students practice visual-perception skills. (Developmental Learning Materials)

Shapes—Dominoes (1978-79). Offers an excellent way to stimulate visual discrimination and organization. Set of 36 cards printed with 8 mathematical shapes. (Developmental Learning Materials)

Symmetrical Match-Up (1978-79). Stresses visual-discrimination skills, recognition of symmetry, and the math concept of halves to wholes. Each object has only one possible match-up. (Developmental Learning Materials)

Visual Matching, Memory, and Sequencing Exercises (1978-79). Six-book series provides developmental exercises that train students to match colors, figures, shapes, designs, and letters visually and from memory. Each book has from 3 to 6 parts in which the exercises follow the steps of perceptual development. Especially vital for reading and spelling skills. (Developmental Learning Materials)

Visual Sequential Memory Exercises (1978-79). Thirty visual memory exercises help children develop cognitive skills of perception, memorization, and reproduction of visual sequences and transfer these skills to academic work. Exercises progress from geometric shapes through letters to words. (Developmental Learning Materials)

SELF-CARE

TFI—Training for Independence (1978-79). Developed by Outreach and Development Division of Exceptional Child Center, Utah State University. Fundamental self-care and functional training for daily living are the objectives. The programs are intended for use with trainable, low educable, preschool, and Head Start students. Can be administered effectively by teachers, paraprofessionals, and parents. (Developmental Learning Materials)

When a Child Misbehaves. Reference book with practical techniques for modifying and establishing appropriate behavior. The seven skill-development programs have been extensively field tested, with careful attention to recommendations from parents and teachers. These include: The Independent Use of Zippers, Buttons, Shoes, and Socks; Independent Dressing Skills; Counting of Objects; Identification of Coins; Recognition of Functional Words; Understanding of Functional Words and Phrases; and Retention of Important Oral Phrases and Numbers.

Self-Care Sequential Cards (1978-79). Twenty-four colorful, high-interest cards teach daily self-care. Four sequences of 6 cards each: brushing teeth; washing face, etc. Promote language development as well as grooming and hygiene. (Developmental Learning Materials)

RESOURCES

American Guidance Service
Publisher's Building
Circle Pines, Minn. 55014

Childcraft
20 Kilmer Road
Edison, N. J. 08817

Curriculum Associates, Inc.
6 Henshaw Street
Woburn, Mass. 01801

Developmental Learning Materials
7440 Natchez Avenue
Niles, Illinois 60648

Learning Concepts
2501 N. Lamar
Austin, Texas 78705

Special Learning Corporation
42 Boston Post Road
Guilford, Conn. 06437

Teaching Resources Corporation
100 Boylston Street
Boston, Mass. 02116

Suggested Guidelines for Forms for Use in Preparing Individualized Educational Programs

Exhibit A. Referral Form
Exhibit B. Screening Information
Exhibit C. Parent Information Form
Exhibit D. Medical Information Form
Exhibit E Community Services Record
Exhibit F. Sample IEP Form

Exhibit A
REFERRAL FORM

Year Mo. Day

Taken by: _____ Referred by: _____ Date: ____ ____ ____

Child's Name: _____ Sex: _____ DOB: ____ ____ ____
           Last   First   Middle

CA: ____ ____ ____

Type of disability and reason for referral: _____

_____

_____

Child's daytime location: _____

Parent/Guardian's Name:

                                    Relationship to
    Male: _____ Child: _____
                                    Relationship to
    Female: _____ Child: _____

    Home Address: _____ Phone: _____
                  Street   City   Zip

    Work Address: (FA) _____ Phone: _____

    Work Address: (MA) _____ Phone: _____

What is the major language spoken in the home? _____

In what language is the child most fluent? _____

What services (medical, S.T., O.T., P.T., educational) has the child previously received?

        What and Where   When   By Whom

    _____ _____ _____

    _____ _____ _____

    _____ _____ _____

    _____ _____ _____

Parent aware of referral: Yes: ___ No: ___ Registration packet sent:
                                            (date) _____

Date seen for screening: _____ Status: Accepted: _____ Rejected: _____

If rejected, why: _____

Parents notified: Yes: _____ No: _____ By Phone _____ Letter _____ In Person _____

General comments: _____

_____

_____

Exhibit B
SCREENING INFORMATION

Description of the child: _____

_____

_____

Comments by parents: (M or F)_____

_____

_____

Demonstrated Language Ability of the child: _____

_____

_____

Demonstrated Cognitive Ability of the child:_____

_____

_____

Demonstrated Motor Ability: _____

_____

_____

Social/Emotional behavior demonstrated:_____

_____

_____

Estimated teaching level: _____

Comments and status: _____

_____

_____

_____

_____

Exhibit C
PARENT INFORMATION FORM

PLEASE NOTE: The information requested below is considered to be essential for planning a program which will best meet the needs of your child. Care should be taken to ensure that all questions are answered as accurately as possible.

This information will be kept confidential and is subject to all laws concerning the privacy of the individual and the confidentiality of information. Only persons working directly with your child (i.e., teachers, administrators, appraisal personnel) will have access to this information.

Child's Name _____ Birthdate _____

Ethnic Background _____ Male _____ Female _____ Age _____

Mailing Address _____ Telephone_____
      (street)

    _____
    (city)   (county)   (state)   (zip)

Lives with (name) _____ Relationship_____

Address if different from above_____

Father's Occupation _____ Mother's Occupation _____

 Work Address _____ Work Address _____

 Work Phone _____ Work Phone _____

Who referred you? _____

Is the child adopted? _____ Yes _____ No   Adopted at what age? _____

List all those living in the home by name, including the parents:

Name	Age	Relationship	School	Grade	Occupation

THE CHILD'S PRESENTING PROBLEM

What is the child's problem or handicap as you understand it? _____

_____

_____

When did you first feel that something was different about your child?

_____

Who diagnosed the problem or handicap?   Date _____

   Name _____ Position or relationship _____

   Address_____ Telephone _____

What was the medical diagnosis? _____

Is the child on medication now? _____ Yes _____ No   If yes, what type? _____

_____ To be administered during school? _____ Yes _____ No

Has the child been on medication in the past? _____ Yes _____ No   If yes, what

type? _____

Have people outside the family noted the problem? _____

Is the child teased or ridiculed because of this problem?_____

Does the child have any food allergies? If so, please list food(s):_____

_____ AND describe reaction:_____

_____

Is there any reason whatsoever that your child's physical activity should be limited?

Yes _____ No _____   Please explain if yes: _____

_____

Please indicate any medical reasons or health reasons that may cause absences from
school or may interfere with your child's progress in class:

_____

_____

_____

_____

_____

DEVELOPMENTAL HISTORY

1. Pre-natal: What was the mother's condition during the time she carried the child?

    _____ If any difficulties

    occurred, please note: _____

    _____

    Length of Pregnancy: Full term _____ Premature _____

    Months _____

2. Delivery: Normal _____ Prolonged _____ Hold back delivery _____

    "Pop" delivery _____ Weight of child _____ Length _____

3. Post-delivery: Did the mother have any unusual post-delivery surgery? _____

    _____

    Did the child receive any unusual medical attention? _____

    _____

    Attending physician _____

    Hospital _____

4. Post-Natal: If you kept records or can recall, please put the age at which child
    developed. If not, circle normal, slow, fast compared with other
    children in family.

                    Age

Sat alone _____	Normal	Slow	Fast	compared with other children
Crawled_____	Normal	Slow	Fast	compared with other children
Walked alone _____	Normal	Slow	Fast	compared with other children
Said single words _____	Normal	Slow	Fast	compared with other children
Made sentences _____	Normal	Slow	Fast	compared with other children
or phrases _____	Normal	Slow	Fast	compared with other children
Got first tooth_____	Normal	Slow	Fast	compared with other children
Toilet trained _____	Normal	Slow	Fast	compared with other children
Bowel _____	Normal	Slow	Fast	compared with other children
Bladder_____	Normal	Slow	Fast	compared with other children
Night _____	Normal	Slow	Fast	compared with other children

How much does the child talk now? _____

How long is the child's usual sentence? _____

How much of this speech can mother understand?

        All _____ Most _____ Some _____ None _____

How much can other adults understand?

        All _____ Most _____ Some _____ None _____

How much does the child use gestures to help others understand?

_____

Has the child learned to say nursery rhymes? _____ Sing

songs? _____

Have the parents done anything to help the child with his/her speech?

_____ If so, what? _____

Did the child have any difficulty with sucking? _____

Swallowing? _____ Chewing? _____ Does the child drool? _____

Was the child very quiet as a baby (did not babble and coo as much as most

babies)? _____

Is he/she toilet trained?   Totally _____ Partially _____ Not at all _____

   Is he/she on a schedule? _____ If so, what:_____

Which (if any) of the following behaviors were or are frequent problems:

Column A	Past Concern	Present Concern	Column B	Past Concern	Present Concern
Whining			Shyness		
Fighting, hitting			Sensitiveness		
Excessive crying			Irritability		
Quarreling with siblings			Listlessness, inaction		
Hair pulling			Competitiveness		
Thumb sucking			Aggressiveness		
Undue demand for attention			Fearfulness		
Masturbation			Daydreaming		
Nose picking			Awkwardness		
Nail biting					
Head banging			Phobia (fear of		
Spitting			certain persons,		
			places, things)		
Bites self			Destructiveness		
Bites others			Excitable		
Screams			Nervousness		
			Other (explain details)		
Destroys or damages toys and household items					
Runs in the house					
Plays in the street					
Throws tantrums					
Rocks back and forth					
Other (give details)					

Which three problems in Column A concern you the most?

1. _____ Why? _____

2. _____ Why? _____

3. _____ Why? _____

Which three problems in Column B concern you the most?

1. _____ Why? _____

2. _____ Why? _____

3. _____ Why? _____

Family

Is any other language than English spoken in the home? _____ If so,
which? _____

Has anyone else in the family had a disability or handicap? (Physical, or mental
handicap, learning problem, hearing loss, heart murmur, psychological problem, etc.)

_____

_____

Has the child ever been separated for periods of time (long or short) from the
mother? _____ father? _____ Give details: _____

_____

_____

How did she/he adjust? Comments: _____

_____

_____

Do you feel that this child takes more time than most children? _____

When it is time to discipline him/her, who usually is responsible? _____

What methods do you use to correct the child? _____

_____

_____

In general, do mother and father agree on child-rearing process?

Yes _____ No _____ Please explain: _____

_____

Siblings and playmates

Does the child show any signs of jealousy of any siblings? Yes _____ No _____

Please explain: _____

_____

With whom does he/she prefer to play? Brother _____ Sister _____ Playmate _____

What age? _____

What activities, toys do they prefer when they are together? _____

_____

When your child is alone, what does he/she prefer to play with? _____

_____

_____

522

In what ways do your feel that this preschool placement may help your child? _____

_____

_____

_____

Is there anything else you feel we should know about the child? _____

_____

_____

_____

_____

_____

_____   _____
          Date   (Signature of parent or guardian)

                                  _____
                                  Interviewer's Signature

Exhibit D
MEDICAL INFORMATION FORM

NAME _____ SEX _____ BIRTHDATE _____

PARENT'S NAME _____ STUDENT'S SCHOOL _____

ADDRESS_____ PHONE _____

MEDICAL HISTORY (TO BE OBTAINED FROM PHYSICIAN)

I. PRENATAL AND BIRTH (Information supplied by attending physician, not from mother)

    A. Length of pregnancy _____

    B. Complications of pregnancy _____

    C. Length of labor _____

    D. Type of delivery _____

    E. Complications of delivery _____

    F. Condition at birth _____ Wt. _____ Length _____

    G. Other _____

II. DEVELOPMENTAL HISTORY (Approximate age at which each item was well established)

    A. Rolled over _____ D. Used single words _____

    B. Sat without support _____ E. Used full sentences _____

    C. Walked without support _____ F. Bowel and bladder control _____

III. HISTORY OF IMMUNIZATIONS AND TESTS (Enter dates received)

    A. Smallpox _____ Results _____

    B. DPT _____ Booster _____

    C. DT _____ Booster _____

    D. Polio Sabin _____ Booster _____

    E. Measles (Live) _____

    F. Mumps _____

    G. Tuberculosis Test _____ Results _____

    H. Other _____

IV. PAST MEDICAL HISTORY (Enter age and any complications)

A. Diphtheria _____   H. Convulsive Disorder _____

B. Whooping Cough _____   I. Operations _____

C. German Measles _____   J. Any high persistent fever _____

D. Measles _____   K. Congenital defects _____

E. Chickenpox _____   L. Asthma _____

F. Rheumatic fever _____   M. Other _____

G. Mumps _____   _____

V. PREVIOUS HOSPITAL ADMISSIONS? _____

_____

VI. PREVIOUS DIAGNOSTIC EVALUATION? _____

_____

VII. IS THE CHILD ON ANY MEDICATION AT THE PRESENT TIME?   Yes _____   No _____

If yes, please give name of drug and dosage _____

_____

PHYSICAL EXAMINATION

I. GENERAL

Height _____ Weight _____ Temperature _____ Pulse _____

Blood pressure _____

II. EYES

Visual acuity: Right _____ Left _____

Is an ophthalmological examination needed? _____

Please describe any condition of the eyes that would affect this child's

capacity to learn _____

_____

Other _____

III. MOUTH AND THROAT

Condition of teeth _____

Abnormality of tongue or palate? _____

Other _____

Please describe any anomaly of mouth, etc., which would affect his ability to

speak normally _____

IV. EAR

Evidence in middle ear of mastoid disease?_____

Please describe any condition of the ears which could affect his ability to

learn _____

Is an audiogram indicated? _____

V. ABDOMEN

Scars _____

Masses _____

VI. CIRCULATORY SYSTEM

Heart: Normal _____ Abnormal _____ Describe _____

_____

Limitations on activities? _____

VII. URINARY TRACT & BOWEL FUNCTION

Please describe any abnormality which would affect bladder and/or bowel

control.

_____

VIII. MUSCULOSKELETAL SYSTEM

Essentially normal _____ Abnormal _____ Please describe any

abnormalities _____

_____

IX. NERVOUS SYSTEM

Cranial Nerves _____

Motor Abnormalities:

    Gait _____

    Station _____

    Involuntary movement _____

    Tremor _____

    Spasticit   _____

    Rigidit _____

Muscle Tone or atrophy _____

Coordination _____

Articulation _____

Sensory _____

Reflexes: Right _____ Left _____

Aphasia _____

Apraxia _____

Brain Damage   ( ) <u>Definitely</u> present   ( ) <u>Possibly</u> present

                ( ) Not present   ( ) No physical evidence but
                                           psychometrics testing
                                           suggests brain damage.

X.   DIAGNOSIS _____

_____

XI. RECOMMENDATIONS:

Classes for Mentally Retarded: ( ) Educable   ( ) Trainable

Classes for Physically Handicapped: ( ) Vision   ( ) Orthopedic

                                     ( ) Hearing   ( ) Brain Inj.

( ) Classes for Emotionally Disturbed: _____

( ) Referred to following physicians: _____

XII. COMMENTS: _____

_____

XIII. IS OCCUPATIONAL THERAPY INDICATED FOR ANY ONE OR ALL OF THE FOLLOWING CATEGORIES?

( ) Self help   ( ) Fine motor coordination   ( ) Gross motor

development   ( ) Perceptual motor testing and remediation

                                           _____
                                           Physician's Signature

                                           _____
                                           Date

Please return to:

Exhibit E
COMMUNITY SERVICES RECORD

The Early Childhood Program needs detailed information on services you have obtained for your child. Please list names and addresses for <u>all</u> services your child has received in <u>each</u> of the categories below. Also list the name of a contact person in that agency.

A. General Pediatric Care
B. Care and Evaluation from medical
   specialists: (eye, ear, nose,
   throat, dental, neurologist,
   orthopedist)
C. Therapy (physical, speech,
   occupational)
D. Counseling and psychological
   evaluation

E. Educational or Day Care
   Programs
F. Financial Assistance
   (Commission for the Blind,
   Crippled Children, Medicaid,
   etc.)
G. Other:

Type of Service	Name/Address of Agency or Individual	Contact Person

Exhibit F
SAMPLE IEP FORM

```
                                    Initial Date: _____
                              Establish at 3 month intervals
                                        Re-eval. 1:_____
                                        Re-eval. 2:_____
                                        Re-eval. 3:_____
```

Student:_____ Birthdate:_____

Teacher:_____ School:_____

Planners:_____

        _____

        _____

Present Status/Description of Child: (Presenting problem, physical appearance, out-standing characteristics, and/or typical classroom behavior.)

Basic Instructional Level:

Estimated Rate of Learning:

Relative Strengths:

Relative Weaknesses:

Best Learning Modalities:

    Input:

    Output:

Educational Program Provided:

Services Rendered (Including any regular education):

		Dates		
Type	Purpose	Initial	Proj.	Comp.

Committee:

Name	Position	
	Administration	
	Instruction	
	Appraisal	
	Parent	
	Speech Therapy	
	Occupational Therapy	
	Physical Therapy	

Evaluation Key: Indicate dates for initiated, projected goals, and completed goals for each goal and objective listed.

A = Objective 100% completed -- spontaneously exhibited and generalized to other context

B = Objective 100% completed -- exhibited in structured situations only

C = Exhibits behavior 80% or more of the time

D = Exhibits behavior 50% or more of the time

E = Exhibits behavior 50% or less of the time; objectives not attempted (NA); objectives appear inappropriate (I); or objectives may be too advanced (please note which).

Language Goals and Intermediate Objectives

	Date			Rating				
	Init	Pro	Comp	A	B	C	D	E

1. Language Goal:_____

    Short-term Objectives:

    1. _____

    2. _____

    3. _____

    4. _____

2. Language Goal: _____

    Short-term Objectives:

    1. _____

    2. _____

    3. _____

    4. _____

COMMENTS:

Cognitive Goals and Intermediate Objectives

	Date			Rating				
	Init	Pro	Comp	A	B	C	D	E

1. Goal: _____

    _____

    Short-term Objectives:

    1. _____

    _____

    2. _____

    _____

    3. _____

    _____

    4. _____

    _____

2. Goal: _____

    _____

    Short-term Objectives:

    1. _____

    _____

    2. _____

    _____

    3. _____

    _____

    4. _____

    _____

COMMENTS:

Psychomotor-Perceptual Goals and Intermediate Objectives

	Date			Rating				
	Init	Pro	Comp	A	B	C	D	E

1. Goal: _____

_____

Short-term Objectives:

1. _____

_____

2. _____

_____

3. _____

_____

4. _____

_____

2. Goal: _____

_____

Short-term Objectives:

1. _____

_____

2. _____

_____

3. _____

_____

4. _____

_____

COMMENTS:

Social-Behavioral Goals and Intermediate Objectives

	Date			Rating				
	Init	Pro	Comp	A	B	C	D	E

1. Goal: _____

   _____

   Short-term Objectives:

   1. _____

      _____

   2. _____

      _____

   3. _____

      _____

   4. _____

      _____

2. Goal: _____

   _____

   Short-term Objectives:

   1. _____

      _____

   2. _____

      _____

   3. _____

      _____

   4. _____

      _____

COMMENTS:

General Guidelines for Developmental Assessment in Early Childhood

Section 1
GENERAL GUIDELINES FOR DEVELOPMENTAL ASSESSMENT
IN EARLY CHILDHOOD

I. <u>GENERAL PHYSICAL OBSERVATIONS</u>: Check any item that causes concern and/or should
be assessed by an appropriate professional.

Hearing _____	Dental _____
Vision _____	Motor Ability _____
General Health _____	Physical Size _____

II. <u>LANGUAGE EXPRESSION</u>: Check each item appropriately.

Expresses self: clearly _____

easily _____

readily _____

Verbal output is appropriate to

communicate needs, feelings, or

ideas to:

children _____

adults _____

III. <u>LANGUAGE ARTICULATION</u>: Check each item appropriately.

	NEVER	SOMETIMES	USUALLY	ALWAYS
A. Individually spoken words are unintelligible				
B. Some words within sentences are unintelligible				
C. Conversation is unintelligible				
D. Multiple, obvious articulation errors				
E. Drools				

IV. SOCIAL BEHAVIORAL SKILLS: Circle appropriate response.

1. Ability to work with adults on task: good   fair   poor

2. Ability to work with a child on task: good   fair   poor

3. Ability to work with two or more
    children on task: good   fair   poor

4. Task Completion: <u>MUST</u> complete all tasks no   NO   YES
    matter how difficult or time
    consuming (compulsive).

    <u>NEVER</u> completes a task no   NO   YES
    matter how short or easy.

5. Varies his/her selection of materials or   NO   YES
    activities when given a choice.

6. Plans tasks carefully or carries out planned   NO   YES
    tasks in an activity.

7. Can independently select materials   NO   YES
    or activities in the room.

8. Displays curiosity about new items   NO   YES
    or ideas.

9. Ability to communicate needs to peers: good   fair   poor

10. Ability to communicate needs to adults: good   fair   poor

11. Ability to initiate and/or engage in
     conversation with:

                          peers: good   fair   poor
                          adults: good   fair   poor

12. Ability to change from one activity to
     another upon teacher direction: good   fair   poor

13. Ability to follow teacher directions: good   fair   poor

14. Uses materials appropriately.   NO   YES

15. Explores alternate or creative means of
     using familiar materials.   NO   YES

16. Activities or materials that the child favors: _____

_____

17. Activities or materials that the child avoids or resists: _____

_____

18. Level of socialization skills: Check all levels appropriately.

	NEVER	SOMETIMES	USUALLY	ALWAYS
A. Isolate Play: plays alone or away from others.				
B. Parallel Play: plays beside other child -- usually with similar materials.				
C. Associative Play: wants to play with others; usually sharing and interacting; no basic goals other than manipulation of materials.				
D. Cooperative Play: coopera- tion and sharing is usual; dramatic play or a desire to complete a task such as build- ing a structure with blocks are examples.				

19. Attention span (approximate minutes of sustained, on-task behavior) in:

A. Large group (7 or more peers) _____

B. Small group (2 to 6 peers) _____

C. Independent teacher-assigned classroom work --
   (write the alphabet, etc.) _____

D. Unstructured teacher-chosen activity (i.e., go
   play with blocks) _____

E. Self-chosen activity _____

F. Individual work with the teacher or other adult _____

Section 2
GENERAL GUIDELINES FOR GROSS MOTOR BEHAVIOR

	YES	NO

0 to 12 months

Raises head to look around while lying face down ....

Head does not lag behind body when child is pulled into sitting

position ....

Sits with support with head erect but tires shortly or easily...........

Rolls over front to back and back to front by himself...................

Extends arms to catch self if falling...................................

Crawls on hands and knees but may be slow and hesitant..................

Sits steadily with support for indefinitely long periods of

time ....

Pulls self to standing position using a support ....

12 to 24 months

Creeps (crawls) in well-coordinated, rapid fashion (hands/feet or

knees ....

Walks independently--may be unsteady ....

Climbs into adult sized chair by himself ....

Goes up and down stairs on all fours or in sitting position ....

Walks into large ball sitting on the floor when trying to

kick it ....

24 to 30 months

Runs safely on whole foot, stopping and starting with ease ....

Pulls wheeled toy by cord ....

Bends at waist to pick up something from floor ....

Jumps from bottom step; usually straight down (may step off

slightly)..

Walks upstairs alone; may hold rail and place both feet on

each step..

Attempts to step on walking board......................................

Walks backward about 10 feet...

YES   NO

30 to 36 months

Pushes and pulls large toys skillfully; has difficulty

moving them around corners...................................... _____

Kicks large ball (12-inch ball that is at rest on the floor)............ _____

Balances on one foot for one second................................ _____

Walks upstairs alternating forward foot (downstairs holds

rail-2 feet/step)... _____

Keeps feet on line for 10 feet while walking forward.................... _____

Jumps over string held 2 inches high................................ _____

Makes broad jump 24 to 34 inches.................................... _____

36 to 48 months

Walks downstairs alternating forward foot (may hold

to rail)... _____

Turns wide corners on tricycle...................................... _____

Jumps from bottom step out 6 to 8 inches with both feet................ _____

Can swing self... _____

Can turn around obstacles and corners while running.................... _____

Can turn around obstacles while pushing and pulling large toys........... _____

Uses pedals while riding tricycle.................................... _____

Balances on one foot for 2 to 5 seconds............................... _____

48 to 60 months

Walks heel to toe forwards on a line on the floor alternating

feet... _____

Walks alone up and down stairs, one foot per step; does not

hold rail.. _____

Runs on tiptoe after demonstration by another.......................... _____

Rides tricycle expertly and with ease................................ _____

Throws ball overhead (9-inch ball--12 feet--direction only

fair).. _____

540

	YES	NO

Jumps from height of 12 inches (both feet, does not step off

with one foot).. _____

Hops on one foot in place.................................... _____

Balances on one foot for 10 seconds.......................... _____

Walks backward, heel-to-toe on a line on the floor alternating

feet... _____

60 to 72 months

Active and skillful in climbing (slides, ladders, trees,

etc.).. _____

Can hop 2 to 3 yards forward on each foot separately......... _____

Can jump rope swung by others slowly......................... _____

Can walk forward on a narrow plank alternating feet.......... _____

Runs with few falls while playing games at the same time..... _____

Section 3
GENERAL GUIDELINES FOR FINE MOTOR BEHAVIOR

	YES	NO

0 to 12 months

Fist clenches tightly when touched by object--does not grab object... _____

Holds small items placed in hands--puts them in mouth (rattle).. _____

Transfers items from one hand to the other................................. _____

Holds two items; one in each hand (blocks, sticks, etc.)................. _____

Is able to release objects on purpose (can drop objects intentionally).. _____

Picks up items with neat pincer grasp; tip of index finger and thumb... _____

12 to 24 months

Imitates scribble demonstrated by examiner (crayon and paper)... _____

Builds tower of 2 one-inch cubes... _____

Turns pages of a book--several pages at one time......................... _____

Opens simple containers (box with loose fitting lid like a shoe box).. _____

Can empty open bottles by dumping (this must be done on purpose).. _____

24 to 30 months

Removes paper wrapping from small sweet................................... _____

Makes spontaneous circular scribble and dots with paper and pencil.. _____

Imitates vertical line drawn by another using crayon and paper... _____

Imitates circle with crayon & paper when demonstrated by adult.. _____

	YES	NO

Turns pages one at a time in books...................................... _____

Rolls, pounds, squeezes, pulls clay or play dough...................... _____

Interested in painting process, not product

(may just smear paint)... _____

Builds towers of 6 cubes for play...................................... _____

Makes one single cut with scissors (may be a short cut)................ _____

Strings beads with large holes... _____

30 to 36 months

Moves to music while watching others do the same....................... _____

Experiments with vertical, horizontal lines, dots,

circles (pencil, crayon, paint).. _____

Imitates V and H strokes from demonstration by adult................... _____

Folds paper on demonstration leaving crease in paper................... _____

Builds tower of 7 one-inch cubes....................................... _____

Copies circle from picture when told "make one like this".............. _____

Imitates bridge built with 3 blocks after demonstration................ _____

Can be trusted to carry breakable objects.............................. _____

36 to 48 months

Makes a long "snake" or other object with play dough................... _____

Builds tower of 9 one-inch cubes....................................... _____

Copies square from model or picture without demonstration.............. _____

Copies V H T from model with no demonstration.......................... _____

Draws head of man and usually with one other part...................... _____

Drives nails and pegs with hammer into soft base....................... _____

Imitates cross on demonstration (+).................................... _____

Cuts with scissors (can be many single cuts that fringe

paper) -- more than one cut.. _____

Catches bounced ball (two hands; 12-inch ball or larger)............... _____

	YES	NO

Strings beads with small holes.. _____

Is able to complete 4-piece form board (also single piece

puzzles)... _____

48 to 60 months

Builds tower of 10 or more one-inch cubes............................. _____

Builds 3 steps with 6 cubes after demonstration...................... _____

Draws man with two or three parts.................................... _____

Adds three parts to incomplete man................................... _____

Draws very simple house.. _____

Holds paper with other hand in writing or drawing.................... _____

Copies star (*) from model with no demonstration..................... _____

Has appropriate pencil grasp... _____

Cuts construction paper in a straight direction with

scissors... _____

60 to 72 months

Draws man with head, trunk, legs, arms, and facial

features... _____

Writes a few letters spontaneously................................... _____

Prints numbers 1 through 5, uneven and medium sized.................. _____

Catches a ball 5 inches in diameter.................................. _____

Laces shoes.. _____

Draws house on command (house has door, windows, roof,

chimney)... _____

Uses stencils appropriately to make shapes with pencil

or crayon.. _____

Section 4
GENERAL GUIDELINES FOR SELF-HELP SKILLS

0 to 12 months | YES | NO |

Becomes excited and eager when sees bottle for feeding.............. _____

Eats baby food well--does not push out of mouth with

tongue unless full... _____

Holds baby bottle without assistance, retrieves dropped

bottle... _____

Feeds self cracker or cookie... _____

Will accept water, juice, or milk from cup held by adult............. _____

12 to 24 months   _____

Removes shoes and/or socks... _____

Cooperates in dressing (puts arm in sleeve; extends

leg for pants)... _____

Holds cup alone (may use two hands).................................. _____

Chews and swallows lumpy foods (cottage cheese,

peas, etc.).. _____

Partly feeds self with spoon but frequently spills.................. _____

24 to 30 months   _____

Lifts and drinks from cup and replaces on table..................... _____

Feeds self with spoon with only some spilling....................... _____

Chews competently.. _____

Dry during the day--does not wet pants except for

occasional accidents .... _____

Takes off shoes, mittens without help............................... _____

Pulls down pants at toilet but seldom able to pull up............... _____

Unzips zippers either on clothes or on zipper board................. _____

Removes coat or dress when buttons or zippers are open.............. _____

	YES	NO

30 to 36 months

Eats skillfully with spoon--spills only infrequently................ _____

Buttons one button on a button strip--is slow....................... _____

Helps put things away... _____

Has to be helped during whole process of dressing

(coat on at school)... _____

Feeds self for at least first half of meal (wants

independence)... _____

Dries own hands... _____

Buttons two large buttons (2-button strip).......................... _____

Avoids simple hazards (does not walk in front of swings,

bat, etc.)... _____

Puts on coat or dress unassisted.................................... _____

36 to 48 months   _____

Unbuttons accessible buttons (like those on the

front of a coat, shirt)... _____

Feeds self totally with little spilling, using a

fork and spoon well... _____

Pours well from pitcher or milk carton.............................. _____

Spreads **butter** on bread with knife (soft butter)................ _____

Can pull pants down and up but may need help with buttons........... _____

Buttons coat or dress... _____

Pulls on shoes, not always on correct foot.......................... _____

Washes hands unaided and does a good job; may get

clothes wet... _____

Cares for self at toilet totally (accidents due

to illness excluded).. _____

	YES	NO

48 to 60 months

Can brush teeth.. _____

Laces shoes but does not tie... _____

Distinguishes front and back of clothes............................. _____

Buttons 4 large buttons on a 4-button strip......................... _____

Can cut with knife.. _____

Dries face and hands and does a good job............................ _____

Washes face unassisted.. _____

Dresses self except for tying with only minimal

supervision........................ .... _____

60 to 72 months

Uses knife and fork very well....................................... _____

Washes and dries face and hands without getting

clothes wet.............. .... _____

Undresses and dresses alone except for tying shoes.................. _____

Puts toys away neatly in box.. _____

Brushes and combs hair successfully................................. _____

Uses bathroom by himself for all needs

toileting, washing, etc.).. _____

Section 5
GENERAL GUIDELINES FOR SOCIAL DEVELOPMENT

	YES	NO

0 to 12 months

Regards adult face or smiles when talked to and looked at...........

Watches as people move around.....................................

Vocalizes ("talks back") in nonsense when talked to
by adult..

Spontaneously smiles at adults to initiate social
interaction...

Waves bye-bye when demonstrated by adult..........................

Actively explores environment within limits of his
mobility..

12 to 24 months

Repeats performances laughed at by adults.........................

Shows item by extending it to another person--
may not release it..

Actively plays with doll or stuffed animal--
does not just carry...

Pulls person to show them a specific item.........................

Demonstrates food preference when given a choice..................

24 to 30 months

Attends to story or music for 5-10 minutes with an adult
present...

Has tantrums when frustrated but is easily distracted by
another activity introduced by adult..............................

Does not share willingly..

Plays near other children but not with them (parallel play).........

Calls attention to clothes--especially shoes, socks................

Labels objects as "mine"..

Plays some interactive games--usually with adults (tag).............

548

	YES	NO

30 to 36 months

Throws violent tantrums when thwarted or unable to
express needs...

Prolonged domestic make-believe with pots, pans--
wants adult near...

Watches other children at play, may join for a
few minutes..

Brings favorite toy to school but will not share....................

Separates from mother easily...

36 to 48 months

Can take turns with supervision--may not want to....................

Enjoys floor play with bricks, boxes, cars--alone or
with peers...

Usually shares play things and/or sweets--
may need some urging...

Plays interactive game like tag or housekeeping with
peers..

Helps put things away..

48 to 60 months

Usually expresses anger verbally rather than physically
(about 75% of the time)..

Plays competitive exercise games (foot races, tag, etc.).............

Needs other children to play (is alternately
cooperative and aggressive)..

Shows concern for playmates in distress
(calls adult attention to)...

Does simple errands out of room (takes note to
the office)..

Calls for attention to own performance (watch me)....................

Asks for adult or peer assistance when it's needed...................

Offers assistance to another child or will help another
child upon adult request...

	YES	NO

60 to 72 months

Continues domestic and dramatic play from day to
day at school.. _____

Plans and builds constructively (elaborate block
structures).. _____

Plays very complicated floor games (trains,
cars, block road, etc.)...................................... _____

Cooperates with companions -- waits for his turn or usually
accepts peer group decision on games to be played.................... _____

Understands need for rules and fair play............. .... _____

Actively comforts playmates in distress (puts
arm around, talks to).. _____

Enjoys dressing up in adult clothes (dresses by himself)............. _____

Will usually let another finish talking before responding............. _____

Section 6
GENERAL GUIDELINES FOR LANGUAGE DEVELOPMENT

	YES	NO

0 to 12 months

Vocalizes other than crying and/or noises--makes

comfort sounds... _____

Babbles (regularly repeats a series of same sounds:

ma ma ma ba ba)... _____

Turns head toward a sound or a voice............................. _____

Laughs out loud or smiles when played with by

another person.. _____

Responds to own name or "no-no" by looking and/or

stopping activity... _____

Imitates sounds modeled by adult (e-e-e; m-m-m;

car noises, etc.)... _____

12 to 24 months

Vocalizes nonsense or jabbers when playing alone.................... _____

Shows shoes or other clothing on adult command.................... _____

Waves bye-bye or claps hands on verbal command

(no demonstration).. _____

Points to desired objects (gestures to

communicate needs).. _____

Responds appropriately to "sit down," "stand up,"

"come here".. _____

Points to self on request: "Where's Johnny?"...................... _____

Echoes some words and phrases he hears or echoes

what he says himself.. _____

Uses common expressions learned as single words

(uh-oh, bye-bye, all gone, okay, hi, no, etc.)...................... _____

	YES	NO

Imitates environmental sounds in play (motors,

animal sounds, etc.)...................................... _____

Uses verbs without indicating tense (set, eat, go)................... _____

Uses single words to communicate wants or desires--

may say "want" and point to object (shoe, apple, car)............... _____

24 to 30 months

Talks to himself continually as he plays, using words............... _____

Sings phrases of songs, generally not on pitch...................... _____

Puts two or more words together to form simple

sentences (want milk, boy kick, kick ball, sit

chair, etc.).. _____

Asks for "another" or "more" (more milk, another cookie)............ _____

Repeats four single words on verbal commands

(birdie, ball, kitty, dinner).. _____

Responds to 2-part related commands (ex. Pick

up the paper and put it in the trash can)......................... _____

30 to 36 months

Identifies action in pictures--walking, sitting,

throwing, flying, etc. ("Show me eat/sleep/run" etc.)............... _____

Can state first and last name upon request........................... _____

Uses pronouns I, me, you, but not always correctly.................. _____

Names actions in pictures with verb or verb + ing.................. _____

Points to hair, mouth, feet, ears, hands, eyes on

picture when asked... _____

Uses plurals that end in "s" or "z" sound (balls,

cars, trees, etc.).. _____

...

	YES	NO

Vocally expresses desire to take turns (but may

not want to share himself).. _____

Can indicate where fingers and shoes are when asked................ _____

Can answer correctly "Are you a boy or a girl?"..................... _____

Uses some irregular past tenses of verbs (saw,

feel, gave, etc.)... _____

36 to 48 months

Recites poem or simple song from memory............................ _____

Identifies action vs. "not" action (Ex. Show me

the boy who is not sleeping)....................................... _____

Can follow 2-part unrelated commands (Ex. Get the

book and turn off the light)....................................... _____

Refers to himself by pronoun (I want, give me, etc.)............... _____

Relates experiences, describes activities (vague,

one-sentence descriptions) when asked (Ex. What did you

have for breakfast? Where did you put your picture, etc.?)........ _____

Asks many "wh" questions (when, what, where, why, etc.)............ _____

48 to 60 months

Follows 3-stage unrelated command made by an adult who

does not use gestures when giving commands. Pick up

car, put paper on table, close door)............................... _____

Can put self in positions of "beside, between, and move

forward and backward" when requested.............................. _____

Uses many "how," "why," and "what if" questions.................... _____

Can verbally list a number of things to eat....................... _____

	YES	NO

Answers simple who, what, where questions after listening to a story.. _____

Understands terms indicating past, present, future but may not use them when speaking (Ex. yesterday, today, tomorrow)... _____

Uses comparative forms of adjectives (big/bigger, small/smaller)... _____

60 to 72 months

Speaks fluently and correctly except for confusions of s/f/th.. _____

Understands "if, because, when" in sentences used by others.. _____

Gives age and usually birthday (not usually year of birth)... _____

Defines concrete nouns by use ("What is a ball?" "It bounces.").. _____

Answers "why" questions with an explanation......................... _____

Asks the meaning of abstract words.................................. _____

Answers "how" questions and understands causal relationships... _____

Uses future, present, and past tense of verbs (will jump, jumps, jumped).. _____

Section 7
GENERAL GUIDELINES FOR COGNITIVE DEVELOPMENT

0 to 12 months   YES   NO

Regards item held in own hand.. _____

Purposefully shakes noisemaker held in own hand..................... _____

Fingers objects in containers without removing

(a cube in a cup)... _____

Will look at pictures that are named and pointed to

by adult... _____

Removes objects from containers (one cube from

large cup or box).. _____

12 to 24 months

Attempts to stack cubes after adult demonstration

(may fail at attempt).. _____

Places object in container after demonstration

(block in box).. _____

Attempts to imitate crayon strokes of adult

(failure is permissible).. _____

Scribbles on paper with crayon when told to make

something... _____

Can place circle in 3-piece form board without

demonstration... _____

24 to 30 months

Points to picture and repeats words for hair, hands,

feet, nose, eyes... _____

Likes to talk about pictures.. _____

Names 3 of the following objects when shown (chair, car,

box, key, fork)... _____

	YES	NO

Identifies self in a mirror when asked............................. _____

Follows command to give pencil, paper, to examiner

(when choices are a pencil, paper, book)......................... _____

Attempts to fold paper upon demonstration by adult

(failure permissible).. _____

Draws object closer using string (uses both hands

alternately, first one hand, then the other)..................... _____

Nests 4 cubes.. _____

Answers correctly "What do you hear with?" (points or

states ears).. _____

30 to 36 months

Identifies action in pictures (walking, sitting,

throwing, etc.).. _____

Continually asks questions beginning with "what"

and "where".. _____

Enjoys looking at books alone.................................... _____

Labels own mud and clay products as pies, cakes, etc.............. _____

Matches colored blocks (primary colors) or identical

pictures... _____

Points to floor, window, door, on command....................... _____

Names block structure as bridge, bed, track

(whatever he wants it to be).................................... _____

36 to 48 months

Can complete 3-piece form board, all forms same color............ _____

Can immediately perform above item when board is

placed upside down.. _____

Can point to smaller of 2 squares............................... _____

Can tell which of 2 sticks is longer............................ _____

Can sort identical items by color (red and green

blocks, etc.).. _____

Can count 2 blocks with one-to-one correspondence................ _____

	YES	NO

<u>48 to 60 months</u>

Can select heavier weight when given two objects to hold............ _____

Matches and names 4 primary colors.................................... _____

Counts 4 objects and answers "how many"............................ _____

Draws man with two or three parts on command

"draw a man".. _____

<u>60 to 72 months</u>

Matches 10 or 12 colors.. _____

Demonstrates knowledge of left from right........................... _____

Can count 6 objects when asked "how many"........................... _____

Can tell how crayon and pencil are same and how they are

different.. _____

Can tell what number follows 8...................................... _____

Index

Page numbers in *italics* represent figures.
Page numbers followed by (t) represent tables.